# EXPLORER'S GUIDE

# VERMONT

3/19 Ingram 22.00

# EXPLORER'S GUIDE

# VERMONT

FIFTEENTH EDITION

CHRISTINA TREE, LISA HALVORSEN
& PAT GOUDEY O'BRIEN

THE COUNTRYMAN PRESS
A division of W. W. Norton & Company
*Independent Publishers Since 1923*

917.43
TRE
2018

For information about permission to reproduce selections from this book, write to
Permissions, The Countryman Press, 500 Fifth Avenue, New York, NY 10110

For information about special discounts for bulk purchases, please contact
W. W. Norton Special Sales at specialsales@wwnorton.com or 800-233-4830

Manufacturing by Versa Press
Series book design by Chris Welch
Production manager: Devon Zahn

The Countryman Press
www.countrymanpress.com

A division of W. W. Norton & Company, Inc.
500 Fifth Avenue, New York, NY 10110
www.wwnorton.com

978-1-68268-166-4 (pbk.)

10 9 8 7 6 5 4 3 2 1

To Bill Davis, my companion on and off the road. —C. T.

To Melanie, Riley, and David, for your continued support in the writing of this book. —L. H.

To my brothers and sisters, always up for adventures. —P. G. O.

# EXPLORE WITH US!

We have been fine-tuning *Explorer's Guide Vermont* with a new edition every two or three years since 1983, a period during which lodging, dining, and shopping opportunities have more than quadrupled in the state. As we have expanded our guide, we have also been increasingly selective, making recommendations based on conscientious research and personal experience. We describe the state by locally defined regions, giving you Vermont's communities, not simply its most popular destinations.

**WHAT'S WHERE** In the beginning of the book you'll find alphabetical listings of important information, special highlights, and things quintessentially Vermont. We include advice on everything from antiques to weather reports.

**LODGING** *Prices.* For the first time in this edition we have embraced the $ symbol instead of using precise rates for lodging. Bear in mind, too, that this simplification can be misleading, depending on what is included and the number of guests a high-end rate may accommodate. Also, be aware that Vermont adds a 9 percent state room and meals tax to published rates, and there may be a 1 percent local option tax in addition. Some lodging establishments may also add a gratuity, and others (admittedly few) include all taxes in their rates. It's best to check when booking.

*Lodging Prices:*

| | |
|---|---|
| $ | Inexpensive: less than $150 |
| $$ | Moderate: $150–$240 |
| $$$ | Expensive: more than $240–300 |
| $$$$ | Very expensive: $300+ |

## KEY TO SYMBOLS

✪ **Authors' favorites.** These are the places we think have the most to offer in each region, whether that means great food, outstanding rooms, beautiful scenery, or overall appeal.

♂ **Weddings.** The wedding-ring symbol appears beside establishments that frequently serve as venues for weddings and civil unions.

☜ **Special value.** The special-value symbol appears next to lodging and restaurants that combine high quality and moderate prices.

🐾 **Pets.** The dog-paw symbol appears next to lodgings that accept pets (usually with a reservation and deposit) as of press time.

✐ **Child-friendly.** The kids-alert symbol indicates lodging, restaurants, activities, and shops of special appeal to youngsters.

♿ **Handicapped access.** The wheelchair symbol appears next to lodgings, restaurants, and attractions that are partially or fully handicapped accessible.

((•)) **Wireless Internet.** Virtually all Vermont lodging places now offer Internet access. This symbols highlights cafés, restaurants, and public spaces with Wi-Fi.

*Smoking.* State law bans smoking in all places of public accommodation in Vermont, including restaurants and bars.

RESTAURANTS We describe upscale restaurants under *Dining Out* and use the $ symbol for dinner entrées:

| | |
|---|---|
| $ | Inexpensive: less than $15 |
| $$ | Moderate: $16–25 |
| $$$ | Expensive: $26–35 |
| $$$$ | Very expensive: $35+ |

*Eating Out.* Less expensive restaurants are described under *Eating Out.*
  *Note:* Most upscale restaurants offer inexpensive pub fare options, and many places that we group under *Eating Out* may have one or two more expensive entrée items.

We would appreciate any comments or corrections. Please write to:

Explorer's Guide Editor
The Countryman Press
500 Fifth Avenue
New York, NY 10110

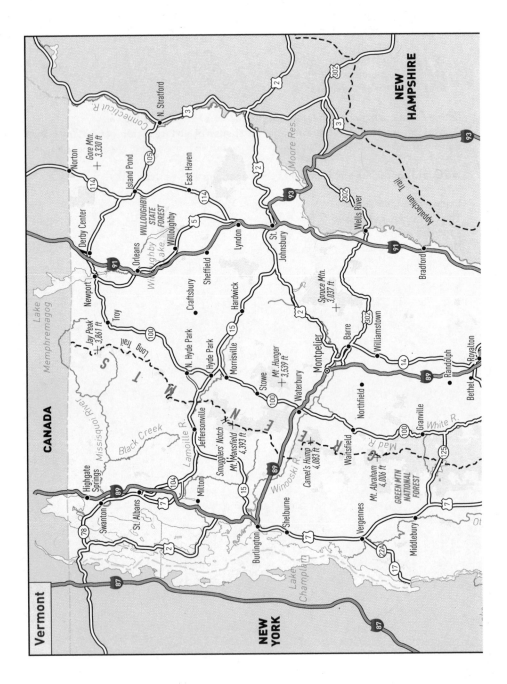

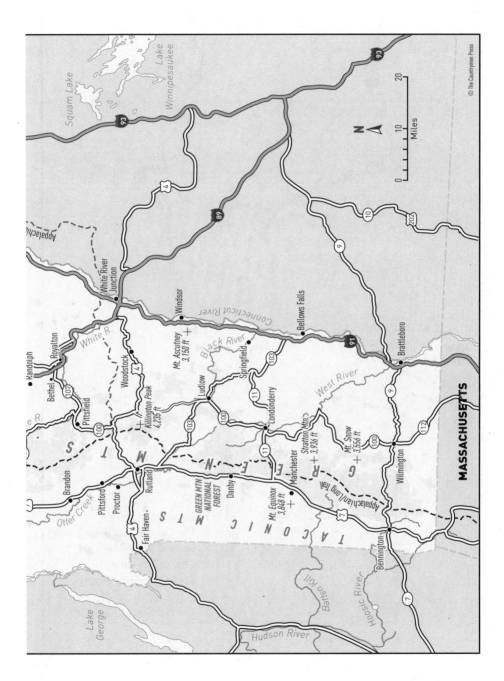

© The Countryman Press

**MASSACHUSETTS**

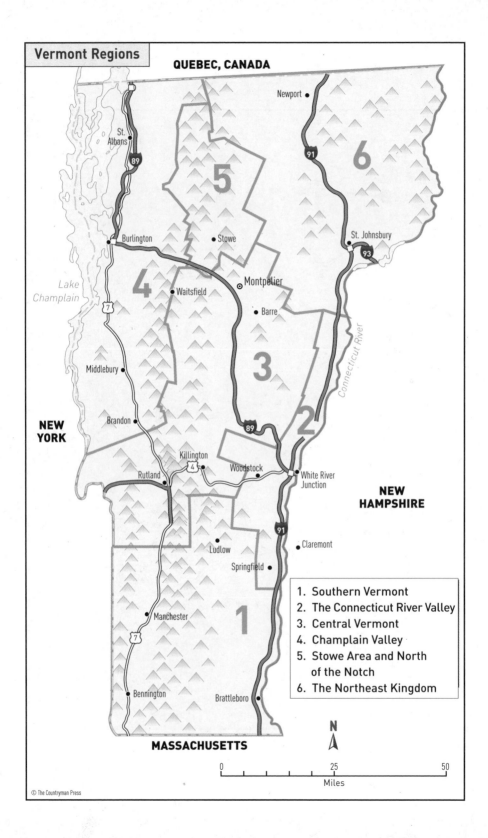

**Vermont Regions**

QUEBEC, CANADA

Newport

St. Albans

89

5

6

91

Burlington

Stowe

St. Johnsbury

93

Lake
Champlain

4

Waitsfield

⊙ Montpelier

Barre

7

Connecticut River

Middlebury

3

NEW
YORK

Brandon

2

89

Killington

4

Woodstock

White River
Junction

Rutland

91

Claremont

NEW
HAMPSHIRE

Ludlow

Springfield

1. Southern Vermont
2. The Connecticut River Valley
3. Central Vermont
4. Champlain Valley
5. Stowe Area and North
   of the Notch
6. The Northeast Kingdom

Manchester

1

7

Bennington

Brattleboro

MASSACHUSETTS

N

0          25          50

Miles

© The Countryman Press

# CONTENTS

# MAPS

# INTRODUCTION

**W**elcome to the Green Mountain State and to the most comprehensive guide to its distinctive landscape, character, things to do, and places to see and stay. No other portrait of Vermont gathers so much practical information between two covers—so much that even Vermonters find it useful. We are particularly proud of this 15th edition of the guide, the first in full color.

We have divided the guide into generally accepted regions. Each section begins with a verbal snapshot of the area against a historical background and includes descriptions of just about every legal form of recreation, from skiing and swimming to fat tire biking.

We describe roughly half of Vermont's places to stay: B&Bs, farmstays, and family-owned (but not chain) motels and hotels. We are candid about what we like and don't like. We revisit our choices with every new edition.

With this edition, we have to say, we are distressed by the ways in which Air-bnbs and online reservations are affecting Vermont's established B&Bs, which have invested big bucks in meeting safety and health codes. Of course, vacation rentals can make sense if you are looking to accommodate a family or group for a week or more. If you're looking for a shorter stay, though, we have to put in a plug for hosts dedicated to hospitality and adept at tuning guests in to their surroundings.

We critique upscale restaurants (*Dining Out*) and everyday options (*Eating Out*), plus good delis, bakeries, country stores, and coffeehouses. Local entertainment, interesting shops, and special events round out our coverage of virtually every city and town and just about every village of interest to visitors.

We assume that our readers are not "tourists." We figure that anyone who buys a Vermont guidebook in this online era is interested in going beyond the obvious attractions and places to stay. We don't attempt to program your "36 Hours" to get "the best" out of a destination. Readers tell us that this guide is like a well-thumbed family cookbook, filled with all the ingredients for days filled with discovery.

Vermont is not an in-your-face kind of place. Most of the things we like best about it are not obvious. Of course there are the ski resorts, country inns, and "attractions" like Ben & Jerry's, the Shelburne Museum, and the Rock of Ages granite quarries. Vermont is found, however, in its vast network of unpaved roads and hiking paths, in craft studios, visiting or staying at a farm, picnicking by a waterfall or covered bridge, eating at a community supper, or shopping at farmers' markets.

Ironically, Vermont's success as an autumn and winter destination has upstaged that of its original tourist season. Vermont's summer calendar is studded with events but the season is essentially soft, still, and deep. While traffic jams New England's coastal resorts, Vermont's roads and widely scattered lodgings remain relatively quiet. Wooded paths and swimming holes are never far but rarely obvious. In fall, traffic thickens on major tourist routes but not along many of our suggested "Scenic Drives." In winter, the focus shifts to the state's major ski resorts, each of which we profile as a destination in its own right.

Since the first publication of this guide in 1983, Vermont's rural character has changed, but not essentially. Farming and processing locally grown and produced products is a flourishing industry that continues to evolve. Growing and eating locally sourced food and drink has become almost a religion in diners and delis as well as in the most expensive restaurants and inns.

True, today's shopping-center culture has made inroads here. Still, for every acre of open land paved for a parking lot, currently at least 10 acres are added to the holdings of the Vermont Land Trust, thereby shielded from development. The administrators of Act 250, the state's pioneering land-use program, also still exercise sensible control over new commercial development, defeating sporadic efforts to dilute the act's provisions. Vermonters have been loath to tear down the past. Abandoned farmhouses have been restored, and in a score of towns, adaptive preservation techniques have been thoughtfully applied, frequently with the help of the Preservation Trust of Vermont, which works quietly—building by endangered building—to preserve the traditional look of the state.

Contrary to its image, Vermont's landscape varies substantially from north to south and even more from east to west. Rather than following the main tourist routes (east–west VT 9 and US 4 and north–south VT 100), we suggest that (weather permitting) you drive the dramatic but well-paved "gap" roads (see *Gaps, Gulfs, and Gorges* in "What's Where") east or west across the state's relatively narrow width, bundling very different landscapes—mountain valleys and the broad sweep of farmland along Lake Champlain—into a few hours' drive.

While focusing on all the state's regions through the same lens (our format), we fervently hope that this book conveys the full spectrum of Vermont's beauty: the river roads of the Upper Valley; the high rolling farmland around Tunbridge and Chelsea; the glacially carved, haunting hills of the Northeast Kingdom; and the limestone farmsteads of Isle La Motte. Villages range from elegant, gentrified resorts such as Stowe, Woodstock, and Manchester to the equally proud but far less traveled villages of Craftsbury Common, Grafton, and Newfane, and the Victorian brick streetscapes of Brattleboro, Bellows Falls, and Burlington.

Vermont has never been a "rich" state. Except for machine tools, the Industrial Revolution passed it by; as one political scientist noted, Vermonters leaped from "cow chips to microchips." Nevertheless, at least a few nineteenth-century families made their fortunes from lumber, wool, marble, and railroads. The 14 years that it existed as a sovereign nation (between 1777 and 1791) stamped Vermont with a certain contrariness. Many examples of its free spirit animate its subsequent history, from the years when Ethan Allen's rabelaisian Green Mountain Boys wrested independence from the grip of Hampshiremen, 'Yorkers, and "The Cruel Minestereal Tools of George ye 3d" to their quashing of British attempts to retake the Champlain Corridor. This autonomous spirit was later responsible for the abolitionist fervor that swept the state in the years before the Civil War and propelled Vermonters to enlist in record numbers when President Lincoln appealed for troops. Vermonters voted their consciences with much the same zeal when, in both world wars, the legislature declared war on Germany, in effect, before the United States did. More recently, Vermont was the first state to legalize civil unions between same-sex couples. It boasts one of the nation's highest percentages of women in the legislature and a strict environmental policy, and it is always prepared—if push comes to shove—to secede.

## The Authors

A flatland author, born in Hawaii, raised in New York City, and living near Boston, Chris Tree claims to be a professional Vermont visitor. Her infatuation with the state began more than 50 years ago in college. The college was in Massachusetts; a classmate was a native Vermonter whose father ran a general store and whose mother knew the name of every flower, bird, and mushroom. She jumped at invitations to come "home" or to "camp" in Jamaica, VT. As a travel writer for *The Boston Globe*, Chris spent more than 35 years writing newspaper stories about Vermont towns, inns, ski areas, and people. She interviewed John Kenneth Galbraith about Newfane and Pearl Buck about Danby, rode the Vermont Bicentennial Train, froze a toe on an inn-to-inn ski trek, camped on the Long Trail and in state parks, paddled a canoe down the Connecticut, slid over Lake Champlain on an iceboat as well as paddling it in a kayak, soared over the Mad River Valley in a glider, and hovered above the Upper Valley in a hot-air balloon. She has also tramped through the woods collecting sap, led a foliage tour, collided with a tractor, and broken down in a variety of places. Research for this edition represents the fifteenth time that Chris has combed regions around the Green Mountain State, traveling back roads to check out lodging, craftspeople, cheesemakers, and swimming holes. It all seems to take longer than it once did, perhaps because there's more to talk about along the way. Vermont is as much about people as about landscape, and both welcome both new and old friends.

Lisa Halvorsen's love of travel and the natural world has taken her on a lifelong journey in search of adventure around the globe. It's a wanderlust that was instilled at an early age when her engineer father's work took the family to several US states from New Jersey to California. As an adult, she settled in Australia and New Zealand where she worked as a journalist for agricultural and scientific research stations and spent her free time exploring the Pacific Rim countries. But her love of the Green Mountains, Lake Champlain, and the people and places of Vermont has always drawn her back home. She has explored the state by car, canoe, kayak, sailboat, cross-country skis, on foot, and even from the sky in a two-seater plane, searching out the lesser-known places—notebook in hand—always looking for the next great travel story. She has turned her travels in Vermont and throughout the world into thousands of articles for US and foreign publications, as well as travel/geography books for children, and most recently, *Explorer's Guide Vermont*.

A New Jersey native, Pat Goudey O'Brien would not change a thing about her adopted state. She cut her teeth writing for newspapers in towns near Boston and wrote several nonfiction books before moving to Vermont more than 20 years ago. Here her writing focuses on local culture and commerce, quirky people, and delicious food and on photographing and describing "one of the most delightful landscapes on the planet." She has also been helping to shepherd one of Vermont's oldest cultural organizations, the League of Vermont Writers, and enjoying life among her large family, many of whom—including her dad (a journalist), her mother (a writer), her sister (a writer), her brother (a sculptor), and her brother-in-law (a fine-art photographer)—have also relocated to the Green Mountain State. For this book, Pat has enjoyed scouring the far corners of the state, meeting new people, and experiencing the vitality and hospitality of this place she is proud to call home.

## Acknowledgments

Chris is deeply indebted to Peter Jennison, a sixth-generation Vermonter, who coauthored this book during its first eight editions, and many of the best words in it remain his. Peter was born on a dairy farm in Swanton, attended one-room schoolhouses, and graduated from Middlebury College. After 25 years in the publishing business in New

York City, he became a "born-again" Vermonter, returning to his native heath in 1972 and founding The Countryman Press.

She is also deeply grateful for the work of her two Vermont coauthors for this fifteenth edition.

For help with research during this edition, Chris owes special thanks to former coauthor Diane Foulds of Windsor, Jane Doerfer of Brookfield, Mary Howe of Jamaica, Darcie McMann of the Northeast Kingdom Chamber of Commerce, and Lynn Barrett of southern Vermont—as well as a big thank-you to Bill Davis, fellow explorer and proofreader.

Lisa Halvorsen owes a huge debt of gratitude to the many individuals she met while researching this book, who took the time to share their local knowledge of the area and its hidden gems—from historic covered bridges spanning slow-moving rivers to little known museums and favorite eateries. Without these chance encounters, as well as the assistance of the staff at many town visitor centers and chambers of commerce, she might not have ventured down many of Vermont's back country roads or stopped to explore state parks, historic sites, and other praiseworthy attractions.

Pat Goudey O'Brien is endlessly grateful to Christina Tree, who has been a marvelous and enormously generous mentor in this endeavor to make this state accessible to more people who will appreciate what it has to offer. Thanks also to Diane Foulds, who told Chris about her, and to their coauthor Lisa Halvorsen, a consummate travel writer. Thanks also to the many people she spoke to, stayed with, called back for information, emailed, and called again. She is truly grateful. And thanks to her granddaughter, Greer, who sometimes let her grandmother have quiet time to work.

All three authors are grateful to Róisín Cameron and Michael Tizzano for shepherding this manuscript to fruition.

—Christina Tree
Lisa Halvorsen
Pat Goudey O'Brien

# WHAT'S WHERE IN VERMONT

What follows is an alphabetical listing of the many things that make Vermont special.

We have attempted to impose a semblance of order by dividing it into categories: *Travel Information Basics, Getting There & Getting Around, Arts, Food & Drink, Nature, Outdoor Activities, Shopping, Sights to See, What's More,* and *Further Reading.*

But first, a bit of history that you can see. The shape of this long, skinny land between Lake Champlain and the Connecticut River valleys was determined by a series of overlapping turf claims by the royal governors of New Hampshire and New York.

Bennington, chartered by the avaricious Governor Benning Wentworth in 1749, was the first chartered town west of the Connecticut River in the New Hampshire Grants, and it became the tinderbox for settlers' resistance to New York's rival claims, confirmed by King George in 1764. The desperate grantees found a champion in the protean Ethan Allen from Connecticut. This frontier rebel—land speculator, firebrand, and philosopher—recruited the boisterous Green Mountain Boys, militiamen who pledged defiance of the 'Yorkers, and then fought the British.

Independence was first formally declared in July 1778 in Windsor, where delegates gathered in Elijah West's tavern (now **The Old Constitution House**) to adopt a model constitution, the country's first to abolish slavery. They then rushed off to Lake Champlain to attack the British, who had retaken Fort Ticonderoga, which the Green Mountain Boys had captured in 1775.

Only in 1791—after 14 years as an Independent Republic and after the competing land claims between New Hampshire and New York were settled—was Vermont finally admitted as the 14th state. But its feisty and fiercely independent settlers had done their part to secure independence from Great Britain.

The only battle of the Revolution actually fought on Vermont soil is commemorated at the **Hubbardton Battlefield** near Castleton, where a small force of Green Mountain Boys under Colonel Seth Warner stopped a far larger British contingent. The invaders were soon repulsed again by General John Stark in the **Battle of Bennington**, actually fought on New York soil, but commemorated by the 306-foot-high **Bennington Battle Monument** and celebrated every August 16th as **Bennington Battle Day**, a state holiday.

One Vermont contribution to the Revolution was a flop as a military effort but proved useful in the decades that followed. In 1772 the **Bayley-Hazen Military Road** had been conceived as an invasion route to Canada, but after some 50 miles were completed, it became obvious that the road could as easily aid an invasion from Canada. It eventually became a significant route for settlers heading from the Connecticut River Valley up into the Northeast Kingdom, and it remains a popular mountain-biking route.

In the 1790s settlers began pouring into the new state. The population nearly tripled, from 85,000 in 1791 to 235,000 in 1820; in the process the many graceful homes and churches seen throughout Vermont were built. Notable showcases for sophisticated Federal-style houses include Dorset, Castleton, Middlebury, Brandon, Woodstock, and Norwich. The imprint of this era goes far beyond architecture. It established Vermont's still-distinctive landscape of wooded hills as well as valleys patched with small farms, salted with interconnected villages. The majority of Vermont's 14,000 miles of road date back to the early nineteenth century, and almost half of these miles remain unpaved.

By the 1840s, merino sheep had transformed the Vermont landscape, greatly expanding its open pasture land, much of it subsequently preserved as dairy farmland. William Jarvis is largely forgotten today, but it was Jarvis who, as the US Consul in Lisbon, managed to smuggle 4,000 merino sheep out of Spain and into the US, settling them in Weathersfield. Spain had closely guarded its herds of merinos, a more productive breed and with water-shedding wool and longer fibers than other sheep. That was in 1811, and the War of 1812 sent prices for domestic wool soaring. Burgeoning textile mills gobbled up the wool and merino sheep became the state's main livestock; by 1840 there were upward of two million in Vermont, bringing prosperity preserved in handsome brick and clapboard farmhouses.

Vermont's self-contained villages flourished in the decades before the Civil War, but with the advent of textile mills and the railroad, the population began shifting from hilltops to river valleys. So it happens that many Vermont towns contain several distinct villages, and in many—Bellows Falls and Randolph are prime examples—the nineteenth-century brick "village" is now what we think of as the town, while the original "center" is small, sleepy, and worth finding.

Evidence of the state's extraordinary record in the **Civil War** and its greater-than-average number of casualties per capita may be seen in the memorials that dot most town and village greens. The way Vermonters turned the tide of the battle at Cedar Creek is portrayed in Julian Scott's huge painting hanging in the **Statehouse in Montpelier.** The anniversary of the October 1864 **St. Albans**

**Raid**, the northernmost engagement of the Civil War, is observed annually.

Vermont's congressional delegations have always had more influence in Washington than the state's size might suggest. The **Justin Morrill Homestead in Strafford**, a spacious Gothic Revival house, reminds us of the distinguished career of the originator of the Land-Grant College Act of 1862, who served in Congress from 1855 to 1898. This lively legislative tradition continues with present senators Patrick Leahy and Bernie Sanders.

## Travel Information Basics

**Vermont Department of Tourism and Marketing** (800-VERMONT) offers vacation planning, information packets, seasonal highlights, and an excellent website (**vermontvacation.com**) with links to every aspect of exploration of the state. A Vacation Planning packet can be requested through an online form on the website or by calling the toll-free number above. The standard packet includes the *Official Vermont Road Map & Guide to Vermont Attractions* (a detailed road map with symbols identifying attractions, covered bridges, golf courses, state parks and historic sites, ski areas, public boat and fishing access ramps, and more); request *The Vermont Vacation Guide*, a helpful and current magazine-format guide published by the Vermont Chamber of Commerce (vtchamber.com). You may also want to request the *Vermont Historic Sites Guide* or the *Vermont Campground Guide.* All of these publications and more are available at Vermont's numerous welcome and information centers, once you arrive in the state.

The **Vermont Information Centers Division** maintains highway welcome and information centers with pay phones, Wi-Fi, and restroom facilities. At the Massachusetts border, northbound at

Guilford on **I-91**, the state's largest and most complete **Welcome Center** (802-258-4503; facilities open 24 hours) showcases Vermont products. Other I-91 rest areas open daily are located southbound at **Hartford**, **Bradford**, and **Lyndon**. Along I-89 your first stop should be the **Sharon Welcome Center** (802-281-5216), which is also the Vermont Vietnam Veterans Memorial, an architecturally striking building that tells its story well and also includes an octagonal greenhouse filled with exotic vegetation watered by recycled wastewater.

Less elaborate rest areas are found southbound in **Randolph**, and both north- and southbound in **Williston**, and **Georgia**. There's also an inviting welcome center just over the state line from New Hampshire on **I-93** at **Waterford** (802-751-0472), as well as visitor centers at the New York–Canada border on US 2 in **Alburgh** (802-796-3980) and on the New York border on VT 4A in **Fair Haven** (802-265-4763). In **Montpelier**, the **Capital Region Visitor Center**, 134 State Street (802-828-5981), is the source of statewide information. The **Derby Line Welcome Center** (802-873-3311) on I-91

southbound also welcomes visitors from Canada.

**Waypoint Visitor Centers**, along the Connecticut River Byway (ctriverbyways .org), serve communities on both sides of the river. Look for them in Brattleboro, Bellows Falls, Windsor, White River Junction, St. Johnsbury, and Wells River.

**AAA Emergency Road Service:** 800-222-4357. For **road conditions** dial 511 or click on 511vt.com.

VERMONT SCENIC BYWAYS (vermont -byways.us). Most Vermont roads would qualify as byways anywhere else, but 10 are now officially recognized for their archaeological, cultural, historic, natural, recreational, or scenic qualities. Download a map/guide from the website.

WEATHER REPORTS The Vermont Agency of Transportation's weather line is 511 or 800-ICY-ROAD, (511vt.com). *An Eye on the Sky* on Vermont Public Radio (also at fairbanksmuseum.org) reports detailed daily forecasts.

*Note:* In Vermont's **Travel Information System** of directional signs, which replace billboards (banned since 1968, another Vermont first), stylized symbols for lodging, food, recreation, antiques and crafts, and other services are located at intersections off major highways.

EMERGENCIES Try **911** first. This simple SOS has finally reached most corners of Vermont. For state police, phone 802-878-7111; for poison, 800-222-1222; and for help with dental emergencies, 800-640-5099.

## Getting There & Getting Around

AIR SERVICE **Burlington International Airport** (802-863-1889; btv.aero) offers by far the most scheduled service in

VERMONT WELCOME CENTER, I-89 IN SHARON   CHRISTINA TREE

Vermont, with flights to Atlanta, Chicago, Detroit, Newark, New York City, Philadelphia, and Washington, DC. Carriers include **Delta**, **United Airlines**, **American Airlines**, **JetBlue**, and **Porter** (seasonal), which offer some good deals. Curiously, at this writing, the only commuter service to Boston is from the **Rutland-Southern Vermont Regional Airport** (flyrutlandvt.com) and the **Lebanon Municipal Airport** (flyleb.com) in New Hampshire, serving the Upper Connecticut River Valley. For national service to southern Vermont, check **Bradley International Airport** in Windsor Locks, Connecticut (bradleyairport.com), and **Albany Airport** (albanyairport.com) in New York, convenient for much of the western part of the state.

**Manchester (New Hampshire) Airport** (flymanchester.com) is the largest airport in northern New England, with many domestic and some international flights.

AIRPORTS Click on **vtrans.vermont .gov/aviation** for details about Vermont's 16 airports, just two (see above) with scheduled flights but all accessible to private and some to charter planes. Request a copy of the *Vermont Airport Directory* from the Vermont Agency of Transportation (802-828-2657).

AMTRAK (800-USA-RAIL; amtrak .com). Amtrak's **Vermonter** runs from Washington, DC, to St. Albans with stops (at decent hours both north- and southbound) in Brattleboro, Bellows Falls, Claremont (NH), Windsor, White River Junction, Randolph, Montpelier, Waterbury, and Essex Junction (Burlington). The **Adirondack** runs up the western shore of Lake Champlain en route from Manhattan to Montreal and stops at Port Kent, NY, on dates the ferry to Burlington operates. The **Ethan Allen Express** connects Rutland with New York City via Albany—but it's a long haul. All Vermont trains accept skis as baggage. Carry-on

bike service is available on the **Vermonter**.

BUS SERVICE "You can't get there from here" is no joke for would-be transit passengers to, from, and around Vermont. **Vermont Transit** has been absorbed by **Greyhound** (greyhound.com), which still maintains a Boston–Burlington run via White River Junction and Montpelier and New York City via Brattleboro and Bellows Falls to White River Junction. Regional bus services are taking up the slack. Bennington-based **Green Mountain Express** (greenmtncn.org) serves Bennington County, including Manchester and Pownal, with stops in between. Rutland-based **Marble Valley Transit** (thebus.com) serves Manchester, Killington, Middlebury, Fair Haven, and points in between. **Green Mountain Transit** (ridegmt.com) serves commuter routes and additional options in Chittenden County, the Capital District, Franklin and Grand Isle Counties, Stowe and Lamoille County, and the Mad River Valley. **Chittenden County Transportation Authority** has regular bus service in Burlington, Essex, South Burlington, Shelburne, Williston, Winooski, Milton, and a portion of Colchester. **Rural Community Transportation** (riderct.org) serves the Northeast Kingdom. See *Getting There* under each destination.

CUSTOMS INFORMATION Vermont shares a 90.3-mile border with the Canadian province of Quebec. Since the September 11 terrorist attacks, all border crossings have become far stricter. Even in Derby Line (Vermont), where it's tempting to walk the few steps into Stanstead (Quebec) to a restaurant, repercussions can be serious. Travelers must present a passport, a passport card, a Trusted Traveler Card, or an Enhanced Driver's License, or valid tourist visas, if required. Pets are required to have a veterinarian's certificate showing a recent vaccination against rabies. At this writing, it's possible to bring in Canadian cheese, but check on your entry into Canada. For detailed information, contact the US Customs District Offices in St. Albans (802-524-6527), in Montreal (514-636-3875), or in Toronto (905-676-2606). For US customs information, visit cbp.gov/travel; for Canadian, cbsa-asfc.gc.ca.

FERRIES A number of car-carrying ferries ply Lake Champlain between the Vermont and New York shores, offering splendid views of both the Green Mountains and the Adirondacks. The northernmost crosses to Plattsburgh, NY, from **Grand Isle** on VT 314 (year-round; 14 minutes). From **Burlington**, they cross to Port Kent, NY (one hour); a third ferry travels between Charlotte and Essex, NY (25 minutes). All three are operated by the **Lake Champlain Transportation Company**. Near the southern end of the lake, the car-carrying **Fort Ticonderoga Ferry** provides a seasonal, scenic shortcut (seven minutes) between Larrabees Point and Ticonderoga, NY. The Fort Ti Ferry has held a franchise from the New York and Vermont legislatures since circa 1800.

MAPS The *Official Vermont Road Map & Guide to Vermont Attractions* (see *Information*) is free and extremely helpful for general motoring but will not suffice for finding your way around the webs of dirt roads that connect some of the most beautiful corners of the state. Among our favorite areas where you will need more detail: the high farming country between Albany, Craftsbury, and West Glover; similar country between Chelsea and Williamstown; south from Plainfield to Orange; and the country between Plymouth and Healdville. We strongly suggest securing a copy of the *New Hampshire/Vermont Atlas & Gazetteer* (DeLorme) if you want to do any serious backroad exploring. Among the best regional maps for anyone planning to do much hiking or biking are those published by

Map Adventures (mapadventures.com). Also see *Hiking and Walking*.

## Arts

ART GALLERIES Vermont's art collections (painting, sculpture, and decorative arts) are small, diverse, and widely scattered. The **Bennington Museum** is known for its works by Grandma Moses; there is also the **Robert Hull Fleming Museum** at the University of Vermont, Burlington; the **Middlebury College Museum of Art**; the **St. Johnsbury Athenaeum and Art Gallery**; the **T. W. Wood Art Gallery and Arts Center** in Montpelier; and the **Shelburne Museum**. While they lack permanent collections, the best changing exhibits in the state are usually found at the **Southern Vermont Arts Center** in Manchester, the **Brattleboro Museum & Art Center**, and the **Helen Day Art Center** in Stowe; also check out the nonprofit **Firehouse Center for the Visual Arts** in Burlington and the **Chaffee Art Center** in Rutland. Brattleboro, Woodstock, Brandon, and Bellows Falls offer the greatest number of private galleries. **Burlington** and **Brattleboro** hold open **Gallery Walks** the first Friday of every month.

FIDDLING Vermont is the fiddling capital of the East. Fiddlers include concert violinists, rural carpenters, farmers, and heavy-equipment operators who come from throughout the East to gather in beautiful natural settings. The newsletter of the **Northeast Fiddlers Association** (nefiddlers.org) lists fiddling meetups around the state.

FILM Hollywood hits have been filmed in Vermont, including *The Cider House Rules*, *Forrest Gump*, *The Spitfire Grill*, and *What Lies Beneath*. But Vermont filmmakers have produced independent hits of their own in recent years. Jay Craven's dramatizations of Howard Frank Mosher's novels—*Where the Rivers Flow*

CHANDLER CENTER FOR THE ARTS, RANDOLPH

*North, A Stranger in the Kingdom*, and *Disappearances*—evoke life as it was in the Northeast Kingdom not so long ago. Nora Jacobson's *My Mother's Early Lovers* and *Nothing Like Dreaming* are absorbing narratives. By the same token, Tunbridge sheep farmer John O'Brien's film trilogy, *Vermont Is for Lovers, Man with a Plan*, and *Nosey Parker*, goes right to Vermont's still very real rural core. *Man with a Plan* launched its hero's real-life political campaign, and, to the amazement of the country, retired Tunbridge dairy farmer Fred Tuttle not only defeated a wealthy carpetbagger for the Republican nomination but won a respectable percentage of the vote for a US senatorial seat.

MUSIC The Green Mountains are filled with the sounds of music each summer, beginning with the **Burlington Discover Jazz Festival** (discoverjazz.com), more than 100 concerts held during the course of a week in different locations around Burlington in early June. In Putney, a late-June–July series consisting of three evening chamber music concerts each week is presented in the **Yellow Barn Festival** (yellowbarn.org). In July and August, options include the internationally famous **Marlboro Music Festival** (marlboromusic.org) at Marlboro College, presenting chamber music on weekends. The **Killington Music Festival** (killingtonmusicfestival.org) is a series of Sunday concerts at Rams Head Lodge in June and July, and the **Manchester Music Festival** (mmfvt.org) brings leading performers to various venues around Manchester in July and August. Also well worth noting: the **Central Vermont Chamber Music Festival** (centralvt chambermusicfest.org) at the Chandler Music Hall in Randolph in mid- to late August, and concerts at the Town House in Hardwick by the **Craftsbury Chamber Players** (craftsburychamberplayers.org) in July and August. The **Vermont Symphony Orchestra** (vso.org), the oldest of the state symphonies, figures in a number of the series noted above and in performances throughout the state. In Weston, the **Kinhaven Music School** (kinhaven.org) offers free concerts on summer weekends, and in Brattleboro the **Brattleboro Music Center** (bmcvt .org) brings in world-renowned classical groups for its year-round Chamber Music Series. See also *Fiddling*.

OPERA HOUSES Northern New England opera houses are a turn-of-the-twentieth-century phenomenon: theaters built as cultural centers for the surrounding area, stages on which lecturers, musicians, and vaudeville acts as well as opera singers performed. The 1910 **Hyde Park Opera House** has been restored by the Lamoille County Players; the 1899 **Barre Opera House** is an elegant, acoustically outstanding, second-floor theater, year-round home of the Barre Players. In the neoclassical Derby Line **Opera House**, the audience sits in Vermont, looking at a stage located in Canada. Tom Thumb and Houdini performed at Rutland's restored vintage 1914 **Paramount Theater**, which offers a full repertory from cabaret to jazz, comedy, and musicals. The **Chandler Center for the Arts** in Randolph and the opera houses in **Vergennes** and **Enosburg Falls** have all been restored for cultural events. Each of these is described under *Entertainment* within respective chapters.

THEATER  Vermont's two long-established summer theaters are both in the Manchester area: the **Dorset Playhouse** and the **Weston Playhouse**. Other summer theaters can be found in Colchester (**St. Michael's Playhouse** offering equity productions), Stowe (**Stowe Theatre Guild**), and Hyde Park (**Lamoille County Players**), as well as in Castleton, Saxtons River, Waitsfield (the **Valley Players**), and White River Junction. **Northern Stage** in White River Junction stages performances October–May. There's also the **Lost Nation Theater**, a year-round resident company in Montpelier and **Unadilla Theatre** in East Calais. In Brattleboro you can catch performances by the **New England Youth Theatre** and the **Vermont Theatre Company**. The **Flynn Theater** in Burlington and the **Paramount Theater** in Rutland offer live year-round performances as well as film screenings.

## Food & Drink

APPLES  During fall harvest season, the demand is not only for bushel baskets already filled with apples, but also for an empty basket and the chance to climb a ladder and pick the many varieties grown in Vermont—primarily in the Champlain Islands, the Champlain Valley around Shoreham, and the Lower Connecticut River Valley between Springfield and Brattleboro. Listings of orchards and apple festivals can be found under descriptions of these areas in this book and by requesting a map/guide to farms from the Vermont Apple Marketing Board (**vermontapples.org**). From the earliest days of settlement through the mid-1800s, more apples, it's said, were used for making hard cider and brandy than for eating and cooking. In 1810 some 125 distilleries were producing more than 173,000 gallons of

VERMONT AGENCY OF AGRICULTURE, FOOD, AND MARKETS

apple brandy annually. Today wineries and cideries are once more making apple brandy.

BREWERIES  Civil War–era Vermont was New England's leading hops-producing state, but the late nineteenth-century temperance movements and other factors virtually eliminated its beer industry. Now, Vermont brewing is back and growing with a vengeance. There are more breweries here per capita than in any other state. Check out **vermontbrewers.com** for a map/guide of the dozens of small breweries that seem to bloom across Vermont's hillsides on a weekly basis. Beer geeks travel long distances to the **Alchemist Brewery** in Stowe, to **Lawson's Finest Liquids** in Waitsfield, and to **Hill Farmstead Brewery** in Greensboro Bend. The popular **Switchback Brewing Company** in Burlington, **Magic Hat Brewing Co.** in South Burlington, **Otter Creek Brewing** in Middlebury, **Long Trail Brewing** in West Bridgewater, **Rock Art Brewery** in Morrisville, and **Trout River Brewing Co.** in Lyndonville are all widely distributed and worth a visit, as is **Harpoon Brewery** (with a popular pub/restaurant) in Windsor.

CHEESE  Vermont's production of cheese rivals even its overactive mojo for beer. Similarly, there's more artisan cheese made per capita in this state than in any other state in the Union. It's not just quantity, either. The quality is legendary, leading to international garlands for cheeses made from sheep's, goat's, and cow's milk. The **Vermont Cheese Council**'s downloadable **Vermont Cheese Trail map** (vtcheese.com) lists and locates approximately 50 cheesemakers, indicating if/when visitors are welcome. Within their locations' respective chapters, we describe many of these establishments. The best known are **Crowley Cheese** (crowleycheese.com), established in 1882 and billed as "the oldest continuously operated cheese factory in the US," which still operates in its original wooden factory near Ludlow; **Cabot Creamery** (cabotcreamery .com), the state's largest producer, a farmers' cooperative owned since 1919 in Cabot with outlets in Waterbury and Quechee; the **Grafton Village Cheese Company** (graftonvillagecheese.com) in Grafton and Brattleboro; and **Sugarbush Farm** (sugarbushfarm.com), high on a hill in Woodstock. The **Plymouth Cheese Factory**, the second oldest working cheese factory in the country, is still in operation in Plymouth Notch. We also describe and recommend searching out smaller operations, like **Neighborly**

**Farms of Vermont** (neighborlyfarms .com) in Randolph Center.

CIDERIES  Records indicate that cider found its way to Vermont in the form of frozen blocks transported by Samuel de Champlain. Production decreased during Prohibition, but the art of hard cider is thriving once more today. Check **vermontapples.org** for a listing of more than a dozen sources of hard cider. Among them: **Woodchuck Cider** (woodchuck.com) launched its hard cider revival in 1991 and welcomes visitors to its Middlebury Cider House. **Citizen Cider** (citizencider.com) is a Burlington destination, known for its ever-expanding roster of bubbly beverages but also for its tasting room, which serves pub fare. **Champlain Orchards Cidery** (champlainorchardscidery.com) in Shoreham creates hard cider and ice cider in numerous varieties from fruit grown on site. **Eden Ice Cider** (edenicecider.com) in West Charleston turns frozen apples into sweet dessert wines and has a tasting room in Newport. In Cambridge, **Boyden Valley Winery & Spirits** (boydenvalley.com) produces Vermont ice ciders, as well as hard cider. **Shelburne Orchards** (shelburneorchards.com) makes apple brandy but also fine juices that don't contain booze (including spicy Ginger Jack).

COMMUNITY SUPPERS  No website serves this elusive but ubiquitous Vermont institution. Check local papers and bulletin boards and try to catch at least one supper for a sense of local community as well as for regional food.

DINERS  Vermont will not disappoint old-fashioned diner buffs. Still, offerings tend to be on the simple side—be prepared to pay cash in some locations. Hearty meals at reasonable prices can be found in Burlington at **Henry's Diner** on Bank Street, a landmark since 1925. The South Burlington Worcester dining car known as the **Parkway Diner** serves the

CHRISTINA TREE

best hot turkey sandwiches in the state. Fare tends toward the modern at Middlebury's **The Diner**, where Korean beef-filled naan bread and jalapeño popper French toast might be the order of the day. **T. J. Buckley's** in Brattleboro looks like the vintage Worcester diner it is, but inside, oak paneling gleams and the upscale, dinner-only cuisine represents some of the best in the state. Also in Brattleboro, former Ed's Diner is now **Three Stones Restaurant**, serving Mayan cuisine. West Brattleboro is home to the **Chelsea Royal Diner**, a find for families, and in Bennington, **The Blue Benn Diner** serves imaginative vegetarian as well as standard diner fare. Traveling up the Connecticut River Valley, the **Miss Bellows Falls Diner**, **Windsor Diner**, and the **Fairlee Diner** are all vintage classics and the real deal. In Chester, there's the friendly **Country Girl Diner**. In the Northeast Kingdom there is **Martha's Diner**, a chrome classic in Coventry, the **Village Restaurant** in Hardwick, **Miss Lyndonville Diner** in Lyndonville, and **Anthony's Diner** in St. Johnsbury.

DISTILLERIES Check **distilledvermont .org** for the Vermont Tasting Tour map, published by the Distilled Spirits Council of Vermont. Look for detailed descriptions in the book as they appear geographically.

HIGHWAY ROAD FOOD Cruising Vermont's interstates, we have learned where to find good food less than a mile from the exit. We strongly favor diners (see *Diners* in this listing) and local eateries. All the following restaurants are described in their respective chapters. In addition, along **I-91**, **Isabell's Café** is just off Exit 14 in Thetford, **Colatina Exit** off Exit 16 in Bradford's business block, and, just off Exit 17 in Wells River, the **P&H Truck Stop** is a genuine trucker's oasis, open 24 hours. Along **I-89**: right off Exit 3, **Eaton's Sugar House** is a find, and off Exit 7, the **Wayside Restaurant and Bakery** is another one. **The Red Hen Café** is a bakery (great breads) and café just west of Exit 10. At Exit 14E: Turn east onto Williston Road and head away from town to find **Al's French Frys**. Also see *Diners*.

ICE CREAM, CREEMEES, AND GELATO Vermont's quality milk is used to produce some outstanding ice cream as well as cheese. The big name is, of course, **Ben & Jerry's**, proud producers of what *Time* once billed "the best ice cream in the world." Their plant on VT 100 in Waterbury (factory tours, free samples, real cows) is one of the state's most popular tourist attractions, but it is now owned by Unilever. Look for **Wilcox Ice Cream** in Sunderland and throughout the state in local places like **Cassie's Corner** in Greensboro, just up from the beach on Caspian Lake. Soft-serve is known in Vermont as a "creemee" and is easy to find at any snack bar in the summer.

Stowe Ice Cream (formerly known as I. C. Scoops) is worth seeking out in Stowe for uncommon homemade flavors; **Depot Street Malt Shop** around the corner is the place for sundaes and an old-fashioned experience. All in all, it's hard to beat the World's Fair Sundae at the **Whippi Dip** in Fairlee: fried dough topped with vanilla ice cream, maple syrup, mixed nuts, and whipped cream.

As all artisan food production has grown, so has homemade ice cream, crafted from local ingredients. The **Sweet Spot** in Waitsfield is ideally located next to the Mad River for an afternoon of lolling by the water with the most intense chocolate ice cream ever tasted. **lu•lu Ice Cream** in Vergennes offers flavors like curried peanut and basil, as well as classics like maple, fully flavored and not too sweet. In Burlington, the **Chubby Muffin** features garden-fresh varieties such as strawberry-basil. Grabbing a scoop at **Artesano Mead** ice cream is plenty of reason to find your way east from St. Johnsbury to Groton.

The state capital is also Vermont's top source for gelato. At **Chill Gelato**, scoops are more whimsical, including flavors from flowers and tea, but there's Belgian chocolate as well. We also have to include **Morano Gelato** in Hanover, NH, offering a creamy concoction hailed by *Forbes* magazine as the best gelato in America.

MAPLE SUGARING (vermontmaple .org). We urge visitors to buy syrup directly from the producer any time of the year (finding the farm is half the fun!). During March and April the sugar maples really perform in a show that can't be seen through a windshield. Sugaring season begins quietly in February, as thousands of Vermonters wade, snowshoe, and snowmobile into their woods and begin "tapping," a ritual that has changed since plastic tubing replaced buckets. But the timing is the same. Traditionally, sugaring itself begins on Town Meeting Day (the first Tuesday in March). But sap runs only on those days when temperatures rise to 40 and 50 degrees during the day and drop into the 20s at night. When the sap does run, it must be boiled down quickly. What you want to see is the boiling process: sap churning madly through the large, flat evaporator pan, darkening as you watch. You are enveloped in fragrant steam, listening to the bubbling of the sap, sampling the end result on snow or in tiny paper cups. Sugaring is Vermont's rite of spring. Don't miss a sugar-on-snow party: plates of snow dribbled with viscous hot syrup, accompanied by plain doughnuts and dill pickles. Vermont maple syrup is 100 percent pure, no additives. The **Vermont Maple Festival**, held in late April in St. Albans, is a three-day event that includes tours of local sugarhouses (vtmaplefestival.org). Most sugarhouses welcome visitors on **Maple Open House Weekend** in late March. Vermont produces more than a third of the national maple syrup supply and more than any other state. About a quart of syrup is made per tap; it takes 30 to 40 gallons of sap to make each gallon of

syrup. The process of tapping trees and boiling sap is stubbornly known as sugaring rather than syruping because the end product for early settlers was sugar. Production flagged when imported cane sugar became accessible, but the Civil War revived the maple sugar industry. Union supporters were urged to consume sugar made by free men and to plant more and more maples.

PICK YOUR OWN Strawberry season is mid- to late June. Cherries, plums, raspberries, and blueberries can be picked in July and August. Apples ripen by mid-September and can be picked through foliage season. See **pickyourown.org /vt.htm**.

VERMONT FRESH NETWORK (vermontfresh.net). This green sign on restaurant menus and walls show affiliation with the nonprofit that partners chefs with local farmers.

WINE Vermont has traditionally made apple and other fruit wines, but grape has become the fruit of choice. Grape vineyards and wines are proliferating so quickly that it's best to check **vermont grapeandwinecouncil.com** to keep abreast. Download a map/guide to more

MARCH IS MAPLE SUGARING SEASON  RUTLAND CHAMBER OF COMMERCE

# TOURISM IN VERMONT

Tourism has been an integral part of Vermont's history for more than 150 years. Before the Civil War, southerners patronized mineral spas in every part of the Green Mountain State, from Brattleboro to Brunswick Springs. After the war, Vermont's burgeoning railroads teamed up with the state's Board of Agriculture to promote farm vacations. Railroad guides also promoted specific destinations like Newport, spawning an elegant four-story Lake Memphremagog House ("one of the largest and finest hotels in New England"), and Lake Willoughby ("one of the most remarkable places on the continent"). Carriage roads were built to the tops of Jay Peak, Mount Mansfield, and Mount Equinox.

In the 1860s the Equinox House would attract the president's family. By 1862 the *Manchester Journal* could report that during the previous summer, "Every house in the village was as full as a Third Avenue car, almost entirely New Yorkers." Woodstock was equally well known in the right Manhattan circles.

By the late nineteenth century the Vermont Board of Agriculture recognized that "[t]here is no crop more profitable than the crop from the city," and an 1890s pamphlet advised farm wives on how to decorate and what to serve when city guests were in town. The state was also promoting the sale of farms that had been abandoned by their owners, who headed West after the Civil War. Many urbanites snapped up the farms, triggering the state's ongoing second home industry.

"Tourism" as such began after World War I. "Auto touring" had come into vogue earlier but Vermont roads were known as the worst in New England. It wasn't until after the flood of 1927—which washed out a number of major highways and more than 100 covered bridges—that the state focused on highway improvement.

The 1930s saw the state publicity bureau inviting tourists to explore "Unspoiled Vermont;" the decade would also include the publication of Vermont's first serious guidebooks, the Federally funded *WPA Guide to Vermont* and *Let Me Show You Vermont* by Charles Edward Crane. These books focused on touring Vermont by road rather than train; there was a push to eliminate billboards and to improve views from roadsides. Homes and farms throughout the state hung out signs, inviting passing tourists to spend the night. Clearly, however, Vermonters were only willing to welcome the kind of visitors who took the trouble to navigate their roads.

In 1936 a proposal for building a federally funded, 260-mile Green Mountain Parkway that spanned the length of the state—passing just below the crests of Pico, Killington, and several other peaks—was roundly defeated in a public referendum.

After World War II, however, Vermont launched what may be the world's first and most successful campaign to turn off-season into peak season. "If you can pick and choose, there

than 20 vineyards and orchards, along with the **Vermont Wine Passport**. Get your passport stamped at 10 or more wineries to be eligible for the annual prize drawing.

## Nature

CATAMOUNT TRAIL (catamounttrail .org). You may not want to ski the 300 miles from Massachusetts to Canada, but it's nice to know you can—along the longest cross-country ski trail in this country. Since 1984, when three young skiers bushwhacked their way the length of Vermont, the Catamount Trail has been evolving. The nonprofit Catamount Trail Association now has more than 1,800 paying members. Over the years, countless permits and dozens of easements have secured the use of private and

NATURE

is no better time for a motor trip through Vermont than in autumn," Abner W. Coleman wrote in the first issue of *Vermont Life*, a state publication. The autumn 1946 article continued: "To the color photographer, Vermont during the autumn months offers delights indescribable. Should film become more plentiful this year, hundreds of camera enthusiasts will be roaming around these hills, knocking themselves out in a happy frenzy of artistic endeavor. For the autumn woods run the entire spectrum's course, from the blazing reds of the maple through the pale yellows of beech and birch to the violet of far-off mountain walls."

While Vermonters can't claim to have invented skiing, the state does boast America's oldest ski resorts. In the 1930s skiers began riding rope tows up slopes in Woodstock, at Pico, and on Mount Mansfield; after World War II, Stowe became the "Ski Capital of the East." Patrons at Mad River Glen built the country's first slope-side lodging, and in the early '60s, nearby Sugarbush opened with the East's first bottom-of-the-lifts village. In ensuing decades, more than a dozen Vermont ski areas have evolved into year-round resorts and offshoot communities. Ironically, Vermont's ski towns mirror the story of its mill towns. Whereas mills were positioned at waterfalls—and no longer need the water to generate power—ski resorts have grown around mountains chosen for their good terrain and "dependable" snowfall, but it's now apparent that access to enough water to make snow is crucial.

Many visitors still come searching for the proverbial "Vermont mystique," that indefinable quality of life and character that is alive and well, especially along the back roads and in villages in which "neighboring" still reigns. While the portrait of the legendary Vermont Yankee—frugal, wary, taciturn, and sardonic—has faded somewhat, independent-minded Vermonters (many formerly "tourists") take care of one another, tolerate eccentricities, and regard the world with a healthy skepticism.

public lands. Bridges have been built, trailhead parking created, and *The Catamount Trail Guidebook* written with maps and descriptions of each of the trail's 31 segments. The excellent website includes a "trip planning" section with suggested places to stay along the way. Members receive a regular newsletter and discounts at participating touring centers and retailers. Also see *Skiing, Cross-Country.*

CONNECTICUT RIVER New England's longest river rises near the Canada–New Hampshire border and forms the boundary between New Hampshire and Vermont for some 255 miles. Not far below its source are a series of lakes: five in New Hampshire's North Country town of Pittsburg, and two—Moore and Comerford—near St. Johnsbury. The 145 miles between Barnet and Brattleboro are punctuated by four dams, each creating deeper pools that turn the river into a series of slow-moving, narrow lakes. But of the 275 miles the river runs from its source to the Massachusetts border, 134 miles are free-flowing. The entire river is now the centerpiece of the 7.2-million-acre, four-state Silvio O. Conte National Fish and Wildlife Refuge. The **Connecticut River Byway** includes 10 bi-state "waypoint" information centers between Brattleboro and Colebrook, NH. Click onto **ctriverbyways.org** for a historical and cultural guide. Note that we include information about river towns in both states in The Connecticut River Valley chapter.

FOLIAGE Vermont is credited with inventing foliage season, first aggressively promoted just after World War II in the initial issues of *Vermont Life*. The Vermont Department of Tourism and Marketing sends out weekly bulletins on color progress, which is always earlier than assumed by those of us who live south of Montpelier. Those in the know usually head for northern Vermont in late September and the first week of October, a period that coincides with peak color in that area as well as with the **Northeast Kingdom Fall Foliage Festival**. By the following weekend, central Vermont is usually ablaze, but visitors should be sure to have a bed reserved long before coming, because organized tours converge on the state. By the Columbus Day weekend, your chances of finding a bed are slim. During peak color, we recommend visiting midweek and avoiding Vermont's most congested tourist routes; there is plenty of room on the back roads, especially those unsuited to buses. We strongly suggest exploring the high roads through Vermont's "gaps" (see *Gaps, Gulfs, and Gorges*) during this time of year.

GAPS, GULFS, AND GORGES Vermont's mountains were much higher before they were pummeled some 100,000 years ago by a mile-high sheet of ice. Glacial forces contoured the landscape we recognize today, notching the mountains with a number of handy "gaps" through which humans inevitably built roads. Gaps frequently offer superb views and access to ridge trails. This is true of the **Appalachian**, **Lincoln**, **Middlebury**, and **Brandon gaps**, all crossing the Long Trail and linking VT 100 with the Champlain Valley, and of the **Roxbury Gap**, east of the Mad River Valley. Note, however, that the state's highest and most scenic gap of all is called a notch (**Smugglers' Notch** between Stowe and Jeffersonville), the New Hampshire name for a mountain pass. Gaps at lower elevations are gulfs, scenic places that make ideal picnic sites: Note **Granville Gulf** on VT 100, **Brookfield Gulf** on VT 12, **Proctorsville Gulf** on VT 103 between Proctorsville and Chester, and **Williamstown Gulf** on VT 14. The state's outstanding gorges include 163-foot-deep **Quechee Gorge**, which can be viewed from US 4 east of Woodstock; **Brockway Mills Gorge** in Rockingham (off VT 103); **Cavendish Gorge**, Springfield; **Clarendon Gorge**, Shrewsbury (traversed by the Long Trail via footbridge); **Brewster River Gorge**, south of Jeffersonville off

BRATTLEBORO BANDSTAND GREG LESCH

VT 108; **Jay Branch Gorge** off VT 105; and (probably the most photographed of all) the **Brown River** churning through the gorge below the Old Red Mill in Jericho.

GARDENS Vermont's growing season is all the more intense for its brevity. Commercial herb and flower gardens are themselves the fastest-growing form of agriculture in the state, and many inns and B&Bs pride themselves on their gardens. **Hildene** in Manchester also features formal gardens with thousands of peonies, and the **Shelburne Museum** holds an annual Lilac Festival in mid- to late May. Within this book we describe our favorite commercial gardens in *Selective Shopping*. For a listing of commercial nurseries, log onto greenworks vermont.org.

THE GREEN MOUNTAINS Running 160 miles up the spine of this narrow state, the Green Mountains themselves range in width from 20 to 36 miles, with peaks rising to more than 4,000 feet. A part of the Appalachian Mountain chain, which extends from Alabama to Canada's Gaspé Peninsula, they were once far higher. The Long Trail runs the length of the range, and VT 100 shadows its eastern base. Also see *Hiking and Walking* and *Gaps, Gulfs, and Gorges*.

GREEN MOUNTAIN NATIONAL FOREST The Green Mountain National Forest encompasses more than 400,000 acres, spread across nearly two-thirds of Vermont's length and traversed by 900 miles of trails, including the **Appalachian Trail** and the **Long Trail**, which follows the ridgeline of the main range of the Green Mountains (see *Hiking and Walking*). The forest contains six wilderness areas. Use of off-road recreational vehicles is regulated. Information—printed as well as verbal—about hiking, camping, skiing, berry picking, and birding is available from the ranger stations in

CIDER HILL GARDENS, WINDSOR   CHRISTINA TREE

**Manchester Center** (802-362-2307) and **Rochester** (802-767-4261). Request a free "mini map" from the **Green Mountain National Forest** (802-747-6700; 231 North Main Street, Rutland). All three offices maintain visitor centers, open weekdays 8–4:30; Rochester is open Saturdays from late May to early October.

LAKES The state famed for green mountains and white villages also contains more than 400 relatively blue lakes: big lakes like **Champlain** (110 miles long) and **Memphremagog** (boasting 88 miles of coastline, but most of it in Canada), and smaller lakes like **Morey**, **Dunmore**, **Willoughby**, **Bomoseen**, and **Seymour**. A century ago there were many more lakeside hotels; today just a handful of these classic summer resorts survive: **Quimby Country** in Averill, **Highland Lodge** in Greensboro, the **Tyler Place Family Resort** in Highgate Springs, the **Basin Harbor Club** near Vergennes, and the **Lake Morey Resort** in Fairlee. Lakes are particularly plentiful and rentals are reasonable in Vermont's Northeast Kingdom. There are also state parks with campsites on **Groton Lake**, **Emerald Lake**, **Island Pond**, **Maidstone Lake**, **Lake Bomoseen**, **Lake Carmi**, **Lake Elmore**, **Lake St. Catherine**, and **Silver Lake** (in Barnard). On **Lake Champlain** there are a number of state campgrounds, including those on **Grand Isle** (accessible by car) and **Burton Island** (accessible by public launch from St. Albans Bay). See *Campgrounds* for details about these locations, private campgrounds (we recommend Harvey's Lake Cabins and Campground in West Barnet), and sites maintained by the Army Corps of Engineers on **Ball Mountain Lake** and **North Hartland Lake**. The **Green Mountain Club** (see *Hiking*) maintains two cabins for rental on Wheeler Pond near Lake Willoughby. There is public boat access to virtually every Vermont pond and lake of any size. Boat launches are listed on the official state highway map.

MOUNTAINTOPS While Vermont can boast only seven peaks above 4,000 feet, there are 80 mountains that rise more than 3,000 feet and any number of spectacular views, several of them accessible in summer and during foliage season for those people who prefer riding to walking up mountains. **Mount Mansfield**, which at 4,393 feet is the state's highest summit, can be reached via the Toll Road and a gondola. The mid-nineteenth-century road brings you to the small Summit Station at 4,235 feet, from which the 0.5-mile Tundra Trail brings you to the actual summit. The Mount Mansfield gondola, an eight-passenger enclosed lift, hoists you from the main base area up to the Cliff House Restaurant, from which a trail also heads up to the Chin. The big news about **Killington Peak**, Vermont's second highest at 4,241 feet, is **Peak Lodge**, a state-of-the-art glass-walled summit lodge, open year-round, accessible via a 1.2-mile gondola ride. The gondola carries mountain bikes, and there are trails for both hiking and biking back down. **Jay Peak**, a 3,150-foot summit towering

**SILVER LAKE** ADDISON COUNTY CHAMBER OF COMMERCE

**THE VIEW FROM CAMEL'S HUMP** RACHEL CARTER

like a lone sentinel near the Canadian border, is accessible via a 60-passenger tram, and a "four-state view" from the top of **Stratton Mountain** is accessible via the ski resort's six-passenger gondola (daily in fall). Honestly, we don't recommend the Auto Road to the 3,267-foot **Burke Mountain** in East Burke—too rough on the gears coming down. We love the Toll "Parkway" to the parking area below the 3,150-foot summit of **Mount Ascutney** in Mount Ascutney State Park. It has been nicely upgraded, and there is a turnout for picnicking with a view up the Connecticut River, as well as a summit fire tower with a view that sweeps from New Hampshire's White Mountains to Mount Monadnock on the east and up the spine of the Green Mountains to the west. From Sunderland, southwest of Manchester in southern Vermont, Skyline Drive snakes up **Mount Equinox** to an observatory maintained by the Carthusian monks. There are also chairlift rides to the tops of **Bromley** (you don't have to take the alpine slide down) and **Mount Snow**.

MUD SEASON  The period from snowmelt (around the middle of March) through early May (it varies each year) is known throughout the state as mud season for reasons that few visitors want to explore too deeply. Dirt roads can turn quickly into boggy quagmires.

NATURE PRESERVES  The **Vermont Land Trust** (vlt.org), dedicated to preserving Vermont's traditional landscape of farms as well as forests (it has helped protect more than 700 operating farms), and many local land trusts have acquired numerous parcels of land throughout the state. Many of the most visitor-friendly preserves are owned by **The Nature Conservancy** (nature.org), a national nonprofit that has preserved close to 7 million acres throughout the United States since its founding in 1951. Its Vermont branch is at 575 Stone Cutters Way, Montpelier.

STATE PARKS  Vermont's more than 50 exceptionally well-groomed state parks include camping and/or day-use facilities and are so diverse an assortment of properties that no one characterization applies. Within this book we attempt to describe each as it appears geographically. Vermont state parks are also detailed at an exceptional website (vtstateparks.com) and are part of the **Department of Forests, Parks and Recreation** (vtfpr.org), which manages more than 157,000 acres of state land, offering opportunities for hunting, fishing, cross-country skiing, mountain biking, snow-mobiling, and primitive as well as supervised camping. Also see *Campgrounds.*

WATERFALLS Those most accessible and worth seeing include (north to south): the falls at **Brewster River Gorge**, VT 108 in Jeffersonville, and, farther south off VT 108 (the Mountain Road) in Stowe. At **Bingham Falls** (an unmarked pull-off on the north side of the road), a trail leads downhill to the falls and gorge, recently conserved and deeded to the state. In Stowe, also look for **Moss Glen Falls**, a 125-foot drop off VT 100. (About 3 miles north of the village, turn right onto Randolph Road, then right again on Moss Glen Falls Road; park at the area on your left just before a 90-degree turn across from a narrow bridge, and look for the well-worn trail.) Beware **Big Falls** in Troy (directions are in our Jay Peak chapter): The top of this series of drops and cascades is a dramatic but rather scary spot, representing the largest undammed waterfall on any major Vermont river (the **Missisquoi**). Also in northern Vermont: the **Great Falls of the Clyde River** in Charleston; **Duck Brook Cascades** in Bolton; **Little Otter Creek Falls** in Ferrisburgh; the seven falls on the **Huntington River** in Hanksville; **Shelburne Falls** in Shelburne; and **Cady's Falls** in Morrisville.

On the east–west roads linking the Champlain Valley with VT 100 (see *Gaps, Gulfs, and Gorges*), several falls are worth noting. On VT 17 look for the parking area, picnic table, and a short trail leading to the 45-foot **Burnham's Falls** (also known as Bristol Memorial Park Falls) in Bristol Memorial Park. Nearby, on Lincoln Gap Road, just off VT 116, you'll find Bartlett Falls, a 14-foot cascade plunging into a deep swimming hole. On VT 125 check out **Middlebury Gorge** in East Middlebury; off Dugway Road note the scenic **Huntington Gorge** in Huntington

MOSS GLEN FALLS CHRISTINA TREE

(responsible for more than 20 drowning deaths); and in Hancock you'll find the 35-foot **Texas Falls**. North on VT 100 from Hancock, also look for 45-foot **Moss Glen Falls** in Granville Gulf (yes, it shares a name with the falls in Stowe). Here a boardwalk leads back to the falls, passing **Little Moss Glen Falls**. In the Upper Valley of the Connecticut River, look for **Cow Meadows Ledges** in Newbury; the falls on the **Waits River** by US 5 in the village of Bradford; and **Glen Falls**, a 75-foot drop in Fairlee almost opposite the fishing access on Lake Morey Road.

In southern Vermont look for **Buttermilk Falls** (a popular swimming hole) in Ludlow; **Old City Falls** in Strafford off Old City Falls Road; the **East Putney Falls** and **Pot Holes**; and, our favorite of all, 125-foot **Hamilton Falls** in Jamaica, cascading down a schist wall with pools (responsible for more than one death over the years). Ask locally for directions to 160-foot **Lye Brook Falls** in Manchester. Most of these sites can be located on the invaluable *New Hampshire/ Vermont Atlas & Gazetteer* (DeLorme); also check Dean Goss's fact-filled northeastwaterfalls.com and the colorful newenglandwaterfalls.com.

# Outdoor Activities

BALLOONING  Year-round flights are offered by **Balloons of Vermont** (balloonsofvermont.com), based in Quechee, also the base for **Balloons Over New England** (balloonsovernewengland .com). **Brian Boland** at Post Mills Airport (802-333-9254) designs and makes his own balloons as well as offers ascents over the Upper Connecticut River Valley; he also showcases more than 100 balloons and many unlikely things that fly in his private museum. **Above Reality** (balloonvermont.com) operates year-round over northern Lake Champlain and the Champlain Valley. The **Quechee Hot Air Balloon Festival** is held in June during Father's Day weekend, while the

**Stoweflake Hot Air Balloon Festival** (stoweflake.com) is a mid-July event with a balloon launch and tethers.

BICYCLE TOURING  In Vermont the distance via back roads from swimming hole to antiques shop to the next inn is never long. Woodstock-based **Discovery Bicycle Tours** (discoverybicycletours .com), formerly Bike Vermont, is the state's most respected inn-to-inn tour outfitter, providing a "sag wagon" (a support vehicle with spare parts and snacks), renting 27-gear hybrid bikes, specializing in small (under 20) groups, and heading to a wide variety of Vermont and foreign destinations. **POMG (Peace of Mind Guaranteed) Bike Tours of Vermont** (pomgbike.com) and **Vermont Bicycle Touring** (vbt.com) specialize in "affordable" B&B-based biking tours throughout the state. In southern Vermont, **Diverse Directions** (vtcycling .com) offers self-guided tour packages that include baggage transfer, lodging, and routing, as does **Vermont Inn-to-Inn Walking** (vermontinntoinnwalking .com)—an association of innkeepers whose establishments are a comfortable bike ride (or hike) from one another. Participants are largely on their own, but rental equipment is available and baggage is transferred from inn to inn. **Craftsbury Outdoor Center** (craftsbury.com) in Craftsbury Common rents fat-tire bikes and serves as a popular base for cycling some 200 miles of surrounding farm roads.

Bicycle paths continue to grow and multiply in Vermont. Stowe's **"Rec" Path** is 5.3 miles with convenient rentals nearby. The **Burlington Bike Path** follows the shore of Lake Champlain for 12 miles (rentals available). It connects six different parks, continuing across the Winooski River on a bike bridge and through Colchester to a seasonal bike ferry that links it with the Champlain Islands, arguably the most popular corner of Vermont for bicyclists. Check out the **Lake Champlain**

**Bikeways** site (champlainbikeways.org) for an overview of 1,100 miles of routes on both shores of the lake that extend into Canada; also check localmotion .org for additional information about bike routes. The 26-mile **Missisquoi Rail Trail** follows an old rail bed from St. Albans to Richford, and the 34-mile **D&H Rail Trail** follows an abandoned railroad bed almost 20 miles from Castleton to West Rupert, with the remainder in New York State. Check individual chapters for long-distance races. Also see **trailfinder.info** for an overview of all Vermont rec trails. Within each chapter we have described sources for local bike rentals. Also see *Mountain Biking*.

**BIRDING** While the hermit thrush, the state bird, is reclusive and not too easy to spot, Vermont offers ample opportunities for observing herons and ducks, as well as raptors like owls, hawks, falcons, ospreys, even bald eagles. It's home to more than 380 species of birds. Stop at the **Missisquoi National Wildlife Refuge** in Swanton, even if you don't have time to walk the trails. The visitor center is a must-see, with exhibits showcasing local geology and the history of human habitation as well as bird and animal life. Other outstanding birding areas include the **Dead Creek Wildlife Management Area** in Addison and the 4,970-acre **Victory Basin** east of St. Johnsbury. The 255-acre **Green Mountain Audubon Nature Center** in Huntington (vt.audubon.org) is open year-round; inquire about guided walks and special programs. The neighboring **Birds of Vermont Museum** (birdsofvermont.org) in Huntington features close to 500 lifelike carvings of birds, both male and female, displayed in their natural habitats, almost all the work of the late master carver Bob Spear. The **Vermont Institute of Natural Science (VINS)** maintains a nature center beside Quechee Gorge (vinsweb.org) open year-round, with owls, hawks, eagles, and other raptors in residence and a full program of naturalist walks and demonstrations.

**BOAT EXCURSIONS** If you don't own a yacht, there are still plenty of ways to get onto Vermont rivers and lakes. In Burlington book a cruise on the *Spirit of Ethan Allen III* (soea.com), a 500-passenger excursion boat. Farther south, the *M/V Carillon* (fortticonderoga.org) sails out of Fort Ticonderoga between New York and Vermont. For details, check under respective locations in this book. See also *Ferries*.

**BOATING RULES** For information about boating in Vermont, including boating safety and laws, see vsp.vermont.gov/ auxillary/marine.

**CAMPS, FOR CHILDREN** For information about both day and residential Vermont summer camps for boys and girls, contact the **Vermont Camp Association** (vermontcamps.org).

**CAMPGROUNDS** The *Vermont Campground Guide*, covering both private and public facilities, is published by the Vermont Campground Association and available online (**campvermont.com**), as well as at the welcome centers on Vermont interstates. Private campgrounds offer creature comforts such as snack bars, stores, playgrounds, electricity, cable TV, and Wi-Fi. For those same reasons, the state parks are quieter.

A map/guide to Vermont's 55 state parks is available from **Vermont State Parks** (802-241-3655; vtstateparks.com). The excellent website describes each park in detail with maps of the camping areas. Facilities include furnished cottages, unfurnished cabins, lean-tos, and tent and trailer sites. Fees vary with the class of the area. For reservations call the Reservation Call Center at 888-409-7579, weekdays 9–4; reserve online; or call the park directly (during the season). Reservations may be made up to 11 months in advance. Many parks offer organized programs such as hikes, campfire singalongs, films, and lectures. Most parks are relatively uncrowded, especially midweek; the most popular are Branbury, Stillwater, Groton Forest, Grand Isle, and Lake St. Catherine. This book describes state parks as they appear geographically.

Within the 400,000-acre **Green Mountain National Forest**, seven designated camping areas are available on a first-come, first-served basis for a maximum of 14 days in a 30-day period for $10–16 per night. Camping is also permitted in the wilds without fee or prior permission unless otherwise posted, but before you pitch your tent, visit one of the district ranger offices; see *Green Mountain National Forest*. The **US Army Corps of Engineers**, New England District, also maintains campsites close to flush toilets, showers, and swimming at the **Winhall Brook Camping Area** at Ball Mountain Lake in Jamaica and at **North Hartland Lake** near Quechee. For details, click on corpslakes.us.

CANOEING AND KAYAKING **Clearwater Sports** (clearwatersports.com) in Waitsfield offers guided tours, instruction, and special expeditions, as does **Umiak Outdoor Outfitters** (umiak.com) in Stowe. **Vermont Canoe Touring Center** (vermontcanoetouringcenter.com) in Brattleboro offers canoe rentals, shuttle service, and river camping on the Connecticut. **Wilderness Trails** in Quechee offers similar trips on the neighboring stretch of the river, on nearby ponds, and on the White River; so does **Great River Outfitters** (greatriver outfitters.com) in Windsor. For the upper reaches of the Connecticut, check **Passumpsic River Outfitters** near St. Johnsbury. For canoeing and kayaking elsewhere in the Northeast Kingdom, see **Clyde River Recreation** (clyderiver recreation.com) in West Charleston and Newport, and **Montgomery Adventures** (montgomeryadventures.com) near Jay Peak.

Check out the **Vermont Fish and Wildlife Department** website (vtfishand wildlife.com) for put-in places. **Recommended books:** Roioli Schweiker's *Canoe Camping Vermont and New Hampshire Rivers* (The Countryman Press) is a handy guide, and the *AMC River Guide: Vermont/New Hampshire* (AMC Books) is good for detailed information on canoeable rivers, as is *The Connecticut River Boating Guide, Source to the Sea* (Falcon Press), published in cooperation with the Connecticut River Watershed Council. The 740-mile **Northern Forest Canoe Trail** (northernforestcanoetrail.org), which begins in Old Forge, NY, dips in and out of Vermont on its way to Fort Kent, ME. The organization is headquartered in Waitsfield (802-496-2285).

DOGSLEDDING **Eden Dog Sledding** (edendogsledding.com) in Eden is sited in some of the snowiest backwoods of northern Vermont, a 75-acre property surrounded by protected wilderness with tours and lodging offered year-round. **Great River Outfitters** (greatriver outfitters.com) in Windsor provides mushing by the Connecticut River, snow permitting, and shuttles patrons to snowier venues when necessary.

FISHING Almost every Vermont river and pond, certainly any body of water serious enough to call itself a lake, is stocked with fish and has one or more access areas. Brook trout are the most widely distributed game fish. Visitors ages 15 and over must have a 5-day, a 14-day, or a nonresident license good for a year, available at any town clerk's office, from the local fish and game warden, or from assorted commercial outlets. Because these sources may be closed or time consuming to track down on weekends, it's wise to obtain the license in advance from the **Vermont Fish and Wildlife Department** (802-241-3700; vtfishandwildlife.com). Request an application form and ask for a copy of the *Vermont Guide to Hunting, Fishing and*

*Trapping,* which details every species of fish and where to find it on a map of the state's rivers and streams, ponds, and lakes. Boat access, fish hatcheries, and canoe routes are also noted on the *Fish Vermont Official Map & Guide.* To prevent the spread of invasive aquatic species, felt-soled waders and boots are banned in Vermont.

**The Orvis Company,** which has been in the business of making fishing rods and selling them to city people for more than a century, has its flagship store in Manchester. Also in Manchester is the outstanding **American Museum of Fly-Fishing** (amff.com). Many inns, notably along Lake Champlain and in the Northeast Kingdom, offer tackle, boats, and advice on where to catch what.

**Quimby Country** (quimbycountry .com), with a lodge and cabins on Forest and Great Averill ponds, and **Seyon Ranch** (vtstateparks.com) on Noyes Pond in Groton State Forest, have all catered to serious fishermen since the nineteenth century. Landlocked salmon as well as rainbow, brown, brook, and lake trout are all cold-water species plentiful in the Northeast Kingdom's 37,575 acres of public ponds and 3,840 miles of rivers and streams. For guiding services, check in those chapters. Warm-water species found elsewhere in the state include smallmouth bass, walleye, northern pike, and yellow perch.

Ice anglers can legally take every species of fish (trout only in a limited number of designated waters) and can actually hook smelt and some varieties of whitefish that are hard to come by during warmer months; the **Great Benson Fishing Derby** held annually in mid-February on Lake Champlain draws thousands of contestants from throughout New England. The **Lake Champlain International Fishing Derby**, based in Burlington, is a big summer draw. Books to buy include the *New Hampshire/ Vermont Atlas & Gazetteer* (DeLorme), with details about fishing species and access; the *Atlas of Vermont Trout Ponds* and *Vermont Trout Streams*, both from Northern Cartographics Inc.; and *Fishing Vermont's Streams and Lakes* by Peter F. Cammann (The Countryman Press). Within this book we have listed shops, outfitters, and guides as they appear within each region. **Vermont Outdoor Guide Association** (voga.org) represents qualified guides throughout the state; check out their informative website.

GOLF More than 60 Vermont golf courses are open to the public, and more than half of these have 18 holes, half a dozen of them justly praised throughout the country. A full program of lodging, meals, and lessons is available at Mount Snow, Killington, Okemo, Stratton Mountain, Sugarbush, and Stowe. The Woodstock Inn, Lake Morey Resort, and others also offer golf packages. The Manchester area boasts the greatest concentration of courses. More than 60 courses are identified on the *Official Vermont Road Map & Guide to Vermont Attractions*; also see vermontvacation.com and vtga.org.

HIKING AND WALKING More than 700 miles of hiking trails run across Vermont—which is 162 miles long as the crow flies but 255 miles long as the hiker trudges, following the **Long Trail** up and down the spine of the Green Mountains.

DOGSLEDDING RACHEL CARTER

**FLY-FISHING** STOWE AREA ASSOCIATION

But few hikers are out to set distance records on the Long Trail. The path from Massachusetts to the Canadian border, which was completed in 1930, has a way of slowing people down. It opens up eyes and lungs and drains compulsiveness. Even die-hard backpackers tend to linger on rocky outcrops, looking down on farms and steeples. A total of 98 side trails (175 miles) meander off to wilderness ponds or abandoned villages; these trails are mostly maintained, along with the Long Trail, by the **Green Mountain Club** (802-244-7037; greenmountainclub .org), founded in 1910. The club also maintains about 66 shelters and 70 campsites, many of them staffed by caretakers during summer months. The club publishes the *Long Trail Guide*, which gives details on trails and shelters throughout the system, as well as the *Day Hiker's Guide to Vermont*. These and other guides are sold in the club's visitor center (4711 Waterbury Stowe Road, Waterbury; open 9–5 daily; closed weekends off-season). **The Appalachian Trail Conservancy** (appalachiantrail.org) includes detailed information in its

*Appalachian Trail Guide to Vermont and New Hampshire*, and *50 Hikes in Vermont* (The Countryman Press).

Backpackers who are hesitant to set out on their own can take a wide variety of guided hikes and walks. Vermont Outdoor Guide Association (voga .org) can put you in touch with guides and adventure-geared packages. For those who prefer to have their baggage transferred and to combine hiking with fine dining and lodging, **Country Inns Along the Trail** (inntoinn.com) has been offering guided and self-guiding packages since 1975. Also see **Vermont Inn to Inn** (vermontinntoinnwalking .com) for four-night, inn-to-inn walking tours (3–10 miles per day) with luggage transported.

Within this book we suggest hiking trails as they appear geographically. Also note the recent proliferation of trail systems: in the Northeast Kingdom, check out the **NorthWoods Stewardship Center** near Island Pond, and the **Hazen's Notch Association Trails** (hazensnotch .org). (See also *Birding, State Parks, Mountain Biking*, and *Nature Preserves*.)

TRAILHEAD AT PUTNEY MOUNTAIN  CHRISTINA TREE

**HORSEBACK RIDING, MORGAN HORSES, AND EQUESTRIAN SPORTS** Morgan horses are as much a symbol of the Vermont landscape as black-and-white Holsteins. The Vermont state animal is a distinctive breed of saddle horse popular throughout America. The first "Morgan" was born in the late 1790s to singing teacher Justin Morgan of Randolph. Colonel Joseph Battell began breeding Morgans on his Weybridge farm in the 1870s and is credited with saving the breed (America's first developed breed of horse) from extinction. The farm is now a breeding and training center operated by the **University of Vermont** (uvm.edu/morgan), open to the public. For more about Morgan horse sites and events, visit vtmorgan horse.com. The best options for trail rides around the state are **Vermont Icelandic Horse Farm** in Waitsfield, **Mountain Top Inn & Resort** in Chittenden, **Open Acre Ranch** in Fairlee, **Mountain View Ranch** in Danby, **Kimberly Farms** in North Bennington, and **D-N-D Stables** in East Burke. The **Green Mountain Horse Association** (gmhainc.org) in South Woodstock holds Dressage Days and

other equestrian events May–September, and the **Manchester Summer Festival Horse Show** is followed by a series of other horse shows in East Dorset. See their respective chapters for details.

**HUNTING** *The Vermont Digest of Hunting, Fishing and Trapping Laws* and a useful State of Vermont Hunting Map are available from the Vermont Fish and Wildlife Department (802-241-3700; vtfishandwildlife.com). Of special interest to nonresidents: a reasonably priced, 5-day small-game license. The ruffed grouse or "partridge" is the state's most abundant game bird, while woodcocks, or "timberdoodles," are found throughout the state. The wild turkey is considered "big game"—as hunters will understand when they try to bag them (in-season in October and May). October is bow-and-arrow season for white-tailed deer, and November is buck season. Hunting regulations for black bear and moose populations vary with the year.

**MOUNTAIN BIKING** In recent years Vermont mountain biking options have dramatically broadened as the potential for the state's hundreds of miles of dirt and Class 4 roads as well as for cross-county trail systems has been recognized. The nonprofit **Kingdom Trails Association** (kingdomtrails.org) in East Burke maintains a more-than-100-mile mix of trails across woods and meadows, including lift-serviced trails at Burke Mountain, also geared to fat tire biking in winter; **Mad River Valley** trails also include lift service at Sugarbush and a link with a 60-mile network maintained by the Mad River Riders. In Windsor, **Sport Trails at Ascutney** (stabvt.org) is an evolving network of trails. **Sleepy Hollow Inn, Ski, and Bike Center** (skisleepyhollow.com) in Huntington offers extensive cross-country trail networks and bike rentals. **Blueberry Hill Inn** (blueberryhillinn.com) is set high in Goshen with easy access to trails in the Moosalamoo region of the Green

Mountain National Forest and to Silver Lake. **Trapp Family Lodge** (trappfamily .com) rents bikes for use on its extensive cross-country trails.

Several more ski areas offer lift-assisted mountain biking. The **Mount Snow Mountain Bike School** (mountsnow .com) offers 45 miles of trails, some served by lifts Memorial Day to Columbus Day. **Stratton Mountain** (stratton .com) offers more than 100 miles of trail, primarily in its Sun Bowl; lifts accessing trails off the summit run during foliage season. The 45 miles of trails at **Mountain Bike Park at Killington** (killington .com) are accessed by lift from US 4 from July through Columbus Day weekend (weather permitting). **Jay Peak Resort** (jaypeakresort.com) also permits mountain biking on ski trails, accessible via its tramway. The **Craftsbury Outdoor Center** (craftsbury.com), also in the Northeast Kingdom, offers fat-tire bike rentals for exploring more than 200 miles of dirt roads through glorious farm country, as well 20 km of single-track snowshoeing trails on its own 400 acres. In Websterville, **Millstone Hill Touring and Recreation Center** (millstonehill .com) offers 42 km of single-track trail in 350 acres of wooded terrain, spotted with abandoned-granite quarries. In Putney, the **West Hill Shop** (westhillshop.com) publishes its own map of an extensive network of single-track trails and forgotten roads.

The nominally priced Topographic Maps & Guides produced by **Map Adventures** (mapadventures.com) are useful map/guides outlining rides in various parts of Vermont: the Burlington and Stowe areas, the White River Valley, the Upper Valley, and southern Vermont, among others. Also check out the **Vermont Mountain Bike Association** (vmba.org).

ROCKHOUNDING The most obvious sites are the **Rock of Ages Quarry and Visitor Center** in Barre and the **Vermont Marble Museum** in Proctor, both with interactive exhibits. Vermont fossils, minerals, and rocks (including dinosaur footprints) may be viewed at the **Perkins Museum of Geology** at the University of Vermont, Burlington, and the **Fairbanks Museum** in St. Johnsbury. The 480-million-year-old coral reef at Fisk Quarry on Isle La Motte is another must-see. And the annual **Champlain Valley Gem, Mineral, and Fossil Show** is held in summer, sponsored by the Burlington Gem and Mineral Club (burlingtongemand mineralclub.org). Gold, incidentally, can be panned in a number of rivers, notably Broad Brook in Plymouth; the Rock River in Newfane and Dover; the Williams River in Ludlow; the Ottauquechee River in Bridgewater; the White River in Stockbridge and Rochester; the Mad River in Warren, Waitsfield, and Moretown; the Little River in Stowe and Waterbury; and the Missisquoi in Lowell and Troy.

SKIING, CROSS-COUNTRY The **Vermont Ski Areas Association** (skivermont .com) lists some 20 cross-country ski centers on its website and profiles them in its useful free *Ski Vermont Alpine and Nordic Directory* and *Ski Vermont Magazine*. Centers are also listed in the *Vermont Winter Guide*, published by the Vermont Chamber of Commerce and available free by phoning 800-VERMONT. Within this book we have described each commercial touring center as it appears geographically. It's important to check conditions before you jump in the car. Vermont's most dependable snow can be found on high-elevation trails in **Stowe**, at **Craftsbury Outdoor Center** in Craftsbury Common, **Hazen's Notch** in Montgomery Center, **Bolton Valley Resort** between Burlington and Stowe, **Burke Mountain Cross-Country** in East Burke, and **Blueberry Hill** in Goshen. **Mountain Top Inn** in Chittenden and **Grafton Trails & Outdoor Center** in Grafton offer some snowmaking. All the cross-country ski centers mentioned above are located on the 300-mile **Catamount Trail**, a marked ski trail that runs

SKI VERMONT ASSOCIATION

the length of the state (see *Catamount Trail*). **Prospect Mountain Nordic Ski Center** (prospectmountain.com), a former alpine area in the southwestern corner of the state, also tends to have reliable conditions because of its site in the state's highest town. **Mad River Glen** specializes in telemarking. **Blueberry Lake Cross-Country Ski Center** and **Ole's Cross-Country Center** are also in Warren.

Also see *State Parks* and *Green Mountain National Forest*.

SKIING, DOWNHILL  Since the 1930s, when America's commercial skiing began with a Model T Ford engine pulling skiers up a hill in Woodstock, skiing has been a Vermont specialty. Twenty ski areas are members of the **Vermont Ski Areas Association**, accessible with daily updated snow conditions and weather on the website **skivermont.com**. Request a free *Ski Vermont Alpine and Nordic Directory* and a *Ski Vermont Magazine* and/or phone 800-VERMONT for a glossy *Vermont Winter Guide*. Daily lift tickets are,

of course, not the cheapest way to ski. A season's pass aside, there are always deeply discounted multiday lift and lodging packages, and there are frequently discounts for ordering ahead online.

The areas vary widely in size and character. **Killington/Pico** boasts the longest ski season in the East. **Mount Snow** is the most convenient to New York City; **Stratton** is a close second. **Stowe** remains the Ski Capital of the East when it comes to the quantity and quality of inns, restaurants, and shops. **Sugarbush**, with a lower profile and almost equal options on and off the slopes, is preferred by many New England skiers, especially given the option of skiing at neighboring **Mad River Glen**, a cooperatively owned ski area with minimal snowmaking and a ban (the only one in the East) against snowboarders. **Okemo** is known for its outstanding snow grooming and facilities, and **Jay Peak**, near the Canadian border, for its natural snow, off-piste and glade skiing, and facilities including a water park, an ice arena, and a large slope-side bed base; **Burke** has a loyal following and some great trails and lodging, also a mid-mountain condo-style lodge.

SLEIGH RIDES  Sleigh rides are listed under *To Do* as they appear geographically in the book.

CROSS-COUNTRY SKIER  BURKE MOUNTAIN SKI RESORT

SNOWBOARDING  This international sport was first popularized by Burton Snowboards (born in Manchester, long since moved to Burlington). Snowboarding lessons, rentals, and special terrain parks are offered at every major Vermont ski area except Mad River Glen.

SNOWMOBILING  Vermont's roughly 6,000 miles of well-marked, groomed trails interlace in a system maintained by the **Vermont Association of Snow Travelers** (vast.com). VAST's corridor trails are up to 8 feet wide and are maintained by 140 local snowmobile clubs; for detailed maps and suggestions for routes, activities, and guided tours, check the website. Due to insurance laws, snowmobile rentals and tours are relatively few. The Northeast Kingdom in general and Island Pond in particular are best geared to snowmobiling, with storage facilities and a wide choice of lodging handy to trails. The **Northeast Kingdom Chamber of Commerce** (nekchamber.com) publishes a snowmobiling map/guide to the area. Within the book we list snowmobile rentals and tours as they appear geographically.

SNOWSHOEING  Snowshoeing is experiencing a rebirth in Vermont, thanks to the new lightweight equipment. Virtually all ski-touring centers now offer snowshoe rentals, and many inns stock a few pairs for guests.

SOARING  **Sugarbush Soaring**, in the Mad River Valley, is known as one of the prime spots in the East for riding thermal and ridge waves. The Sugarbush Airport is a well-established place to take glider lessons or rides or simply to watch the planes come and go. The **Fall Wave Soaring Encampment** held in early October (weather permitting) draws glider pilots from throughout the country. Glider and airplane rides are also available at the **Stowe-Morrisville Airport** (802-888-7845) and from the **Post Mills Soaring Club** at the Post Mills Airport (802-333-9992), where soaring lessons are also a specialty.

SWIMMING  On the *Official Vermont Road Map & Guide to Vermont Attractions*, you can pick out the day-use areas that offer swimming, most with changing facilities. Similar facilities are provided by the Green Mountain National Forest at **Hapgood Pond** in Peru, and the **US Army Corps of Engineers** maintains beaches and recreation facilities at its flood-control dam in Thetford, Townshend, Jamaica, and North Springfield. There are also public beaches on roughly one-third of Vermont's 400 lakes and ponds. Add to these all the town recreation areas and pools available to visitors—and you still haven't gone swimming Vermont-style until you've sampled a Vermont swimming hole. These range from deep spots in the state's ubiquitous streams to deep quarries in Dorset and West Rutland and freezing pools between waterfalls. We have included some of our favorite swimming holes but could not bring ourselves to reveal them all. Look for cars parked along the road on a hot day.

TENNIS  Vermont claims as many tennis courts per capita as any other state in the Union. These include town recreation facilities and sports centers as well as private facilities. For a listing of both public and private facilities, see **ustavermont.com**. Summer tennis programs, combining lessons, lodging, and meals, are offered at **Bolton Valley**, **Killington**, the **Village at Smugglers' Notch**, **Stratton**, **Topnotch Resort** in Stowe, and both the **Bridges Family Resort and Tennis Club** and **Sugarbush Resort** in Warren. Check *Tennis* in each area.

## Shopping

ANTIQUES  The pamphlet *Antiquing in Vermont* lists more than 100 of the state's most prestigious dealers, members of the

**Vermont Antiques Dealers' Association,** at **vermontada.com.** The association sponsors an **annual antiques show** in July in Woodstock. Major concentrations of dealers can be found in Bennington, Burlington, Dorset, Manchester, Middlebury, Woodstock, and along VT 30 in the West River Valley. The **Weston Antiques Show** (westonantiquesshow.org), usually the first weekend in October, is the state's oldest and still one of its best. Look for large group dealerships in Quechee, Danby, East Arlington, Bellows Falls, and East Barre.

AUCTIONS  Most major upcoming auctions are announced in the Thursday edition of Vermont daily newspapers, with a listing of items that will be up for bid. Auctions may be scheduled at any time, however, during summer months. Check local chapters for details.

BOOKSTORES  At this writing, Vermont counts 20 healthy and inviting independent bookstores. The **Vermont Antiquarian Booksellers Association** (VABA) lists its members at **vermontisbookcountry .com.**

CHRISTMAS TREES  Vermont's many Christmas tree farms generally open after Thanksgiving, inviting customers to come tag the tree they want, leaving it until the last moment to cut, so it will be fresh when they take it home. Check the website **vermontchristmastrees.org** and **vtfarms.org** for a list of the more imaginative marketers. For a do-it-yourself experience, contact the **Green Mountain National Forest Service** in Rochester (802-767-4261) and inquire about cutting your own tree for a nominal fee.

COUNTRY STORES,  also called "general stores," are a distinct species that is both endangered and evolving to fill the changing needs of the hundreds of villages for which they still serve as hubs. Most now offer hot food and a deli. Some invite patrons to linger at tables or on couches. Within the book we have lovingly described the state's iconic general stores such as **Currier's** in Glover, **Willey's** in Greensboro, **Hastings** in West Danville, **Dan & Whit's** in Norwich, and **D&K's Jamaica Grocery** in Jamaica. We also note variations on the old model that offer eat-in options. Some of our favorites are **The Warren Store, Putney General Store, H. N. Williams General Store** in Dorset, **Craftsbury General Store,** and **Newbury Village Store.** In recent years, preservation and community groups have salvaged and revamped these community hubs; for examples, visit **Guilford, Shrewsbury, West Townshend,** and **Barnard.** For a complete list of independently owned markets and a map, check out the **Vermont Alliance of Independent Country Stores** website (vaics.org). **The Vermont Country Stores** in Weston and Rockingham that publish a thick catalog—a source of long underwear, garter belts, and Healthy Feet Cream—and are major tourist destinations. **Farm-Way, Inc.,** in Bradford, billed as "complete outfitters for man and beast" is Vermont's answer to L. L. Bean but without a catalog.

CRAFTS  More than 1,500 Vermonters make their living from crafts. There are also more than 100 retail craft venues in

SHOPPING FOR ANTIQUES  CHRISTINA TREE

GALAXY BOOKSTORE, HARDWICK  CHRISTINA TREE

the state. During Vermont's **Open Studio Weekend** on Memorial Day weekend, and again the first weekend in October, hundreds of artisans welcome visitors in almost as many locations. Request a copy of the Vermont Crafts Studio Tour Map, available at information centers and on request from the **Vermont Crafts Council** (802-223-3380; vermontcrafts .com). It's worth keeping year-round, as many craftspeople welcome visitors informally. Within this book we have described studios, galleries, and shops and have also included major craft tours and fairs. The outstanding galleries are **Frog Hollow Vermont State Craft Center** in Burlington (froghollow.org), **The Artisans Hand Craft Gallery** (artisanshand .com) in Montpelier, **Art on Main** (artonmain.net) in Bristol, **The Collective** (collective-theartofcraft.com) in Woodstock, **Vermont Artisan Designs** (vtart.com) in Brattleboro, and the **Brandon Artists Guild** (brandonartistsguild .com). The **Northeast Kingdom Artisans Guild** on Railroad Street in St.

Johnsbury (nekartisansguild.com), a Vermont State Craft Center, has been in operation for 20 years. On Thanksgiving weekend **Putney Craft Tour** (putneycrafts.com) and the **Walpole Artisan Open Studios Tour** (walpole artisans.com) add up to a great way to explore back roads and take care of holiday shopping. Also see **craftcenter .vermont.gov.**

FACTORY OUTLETS  Our bias leans toward distinctly made-in-Vermont products. Among our favorites: **Johnson Woolen Mills** (quality wool clothing for all ages) in Johnson; **Bennington Potters** (dinnerware, housewares, and more) in Bennington and Burlington; and **Vermont Marble** in Proctor. **Charles Shackleton** and **Miranda Thomas** produce outstanding furniture and ceramics in an old mill in Bridgewater. **Copeland Furniture** in Bradford also has some seconds in its showroom. **Simon Pearce** in Quechee and Windsor sells seconds of his gorgeous glassware at affordable prices. **The Outlet Center** just off I-91, Exit 1, in Brattleboro offers some genuine finds. In addition to its many factory name brand stores, Manchester is home base to **Orvis**, both its flagship retail store and outlet.

D&K'S JAMAICA GROCERY  CHRISTINA TREE

FARMERS' MARKETS Farmers' markets can be found in almost every Vermont community mid-June–early October and monthly throughout winter in some areas. Count on finding fresh vegetables, fruit, honey, meat, eggs, flowers, crafts, wine, preserves, and much more at farm prices in commercial centers throughout the state. Look for listings within each chapter. Click on the website (vtfma.org) for the Vermont Farmers' Markets Association for a listing of more than 50 members.

## Sights to See

BARNS, ROUND A number of round barns were built between 1899 and World War I. The most striking and easily accessible survivors include the **Moore barn** in Barnet, the **Hastings Barn** in Waterford, the **Metcalf barn** (Robillard Flats) in Irasburg, and the **Joslin round barn**, now a cultural center attached to the **Inn at Round Barn Farm**. The **Welch Barn** on VT 12 in Morristown just north of Lake Elmore rises into view as you drive the beautiful stretch north from Montpelier; in the Upper Valley, the **Buston Barn** is off US 5 south of Wells River and the photogenic 1906 round barn and its goats in Piermont, NH, are backed by Vermont hills across the river. The Shelburne Museum includes a handsome round barn from Passumpsic and at neighboring Shelburne Farms, the vast, five-story, Norman-style **Farm Barn**, the acre-large **Breeding Barn**, as well as the handsome **Coach Barn** are on view.

CEMETERIES There's no better way to get close to Vermont's history than through its cemeteries. The Vermont Old Cemetery Association (voca58.org) provides a helpful starting point with its online listings of historical burial grounds, complete with maps and mentions of prominent people interred in different locations. International website findagrave.org is a good next step for

ROUND BARN, PIERMONT, NEW HAMPSHIRE CHRISTINA TREE

research—many graves are listed with photographs, and some pages have detailed histories of the deceased. The **Old Bennington Cemetery** may be best known as Robert Frost's final resting place, but its denizens are a tightly packed group of Revolutionary War heroes and early Vermont governors. Near Putney, the **Westminster Old Cemetery** is uncommonly well preserved, making it an approachable ground zero for learning about the 1775 Westminster Massacre, viewed by some historians as the first battle of the Revolution. **Laurel Glen Cemetery** in Cuttingsville—down VT 103 in Rutland County—is home to Bowman Mausoleum, with a sculpture of John Porter Bowman on its steps, and inside, statues of three female Bowmans and the unsettling inscription, A COUCH OF DREAMLESS SLEEP. In New Haven, near Middlebury, **Evergreen Cemetery** is eternal host to Timothy Clark Smith, buried beneath a glass window, with a bell to alert passersby in case he was accidentally interred alive. Smith's neighbors, many buried in the eighteenth century, benefited from a poetic stonecutter with a penchant for dark verse. In Middlebury proper, **West Cemetery** is the location of Vermont's oldest burial. Museum founder Henry Sheldon committed the remains of 2-year-old Amum-Her-Kephesh-Ef to Vermont soil after discovering the Egyptian mummy was too decayed to display. His stone marker lists his death date as 1883 BC. **Hope Cemetery** in Barre is deservedly Vermont's most famous for its monuments carved for stonecutters by stonecutters. But **Green Mount Cemetery** in nearby Montpelier should not be overlooked. Positioned on a steep incline just past the city center, the memorials have a distinctly English Victorian feel in contrast with the lush Italianate design at Hope. Burlington has a **Green Mount Cemetery** of its own, and it's filled with members of the revolutionary Allen family, although it's uncertain whether Ethan Allen's earthly form lies under the soaring monument to him. Other Burlington luminaries repose at **Lakeview Cemetery**. The biggest name therein is that of Civil War general George Stannard, but the greatest attraction is the lakeside cemetery's diversity. There are specially consecrated Jewish and Muslim

sections, as well as stones emblazoned with missives in Vietnamese and Chinese.

COVERED BRIDGES  The state's 100 surviving covered bridges are marked on the official state map and on our maps and appear in the appropriate chapters of this book under *Must See*. Also see covered**bridgemap.com/vt**. Bridge buffs should buy a copy of *Covered Bridges of Vermont* by Ed Barna (The Countryman Press). The **Vermont Covered Bridge Museum** (artcenter.svu.edu/covered-bridge) at the Laumeister Art Center at Southern Vermont College in Bennington features a theater production, dioramas, interactive exhibits, and a model railroad with covered railroad bridges.

MARBLE  **Vermont Marble Museum** (vermontmarblemuseum.org) exhibits in Proctor dramatize the history and ongoing importance of marble quarrying in Vermont. The **Dorset Historical Society's Bley House Museum** also has impressive

GREEN RIVER COVERED BRIDGE, GUILFORD  CHRISTINA TREE

exhibits and a diorama pinpointing all the one-time quarries in that area, some of which are now popular swimming holes. The **Vermont Marble Trail** goes from Bennington via Dorset and Danby to Rutland.

MUSEUMS  Within this book, we have listed museums in their geographic areas. They vary from the small but memorable **Bread and Puppet Theater Museum** in Glover to the immense **Shelburne Museum**—with its 39 buildings, many housing priceless collections of art and Americana. A number of outstanding historical museums are found in Vermont (our favorites are the **Bennington Museum** in Bennington, the **Henry Sheldon Museum** in Middlebury, the **Old Stone House Museum** in Brownington , and the **Dana House** in Woodstock), some with collections that go beyond the purely historical. The **Bennington Museum** is famed for its collection of Grandma Moses paintings as well as

early American glass and relics from the Revolution, and the **Fairbanks Museum & Planetarium** in St. Johnsbury has vaulted wooden halls filled with a mix of vintage and local environmental exhibits that place it in a class of its own. The **Billings Farm & Museum** in Woodstock shows off its blue-ribbon dairy and has a fascinating, beautifully mounted display of nineteenth-century farm life and tools, and the adjacent **Marsh-Billings-Rockefeller National Historical Park** traces the state's environmental history.

## What's More

ABENAKI  The Abenaki Native American presence in Vermont is far more pervasive than was historically acknowledged; only relatively recently has the tribe's importance become known. In present-day Swanton, the Indian village of Missisquoi became a mission village, a way station for Abenaki headed for

BREAD AND PUPPET THEATER MUSEUM, GLOVER CHRISTINA TREE

Canada. Abenaki life is presented in an exhibit at the **Abenaki Tribal Museum and Cultural Center**. Native American settlements are also recorded at Otter Creek, and the eighteenth-century tavern at **Chimney Point State Historic Site** in Addison has a well-mounted display explaining the territory's Native American and French colonial heritage.

AGRICULTURE AND AGRITOURISM
Some 1.25 million acres of the state's total of 6 million acres are devoted to agriculture. The farmhouse and barn are still symbols of Vermont, and a Vermont vacation can include a farm visit, whether to buy syrup, cheese, wool, or wine; maybe pick apples or berries; tour a dairy operation; or stay for a night or a week. Finding farms can be an excuse to explore unexpectedly beautiful backcountry.

Of course a "farm" isn't what it used to be. Fewer than 1,100 of Vermont's 6,400 farms are now dairy, compared with 10,000 dairy farms 40 years ago. Even so, the average size of dairy herds has increased: With just 15 percent as many dairy farms, the state produces more than twice as much milk as it did 45 years ago. Vermont remains New England's largest milk-producing state; gross sales of cheese, ice cream, dips, cream cheese, yogurt, milk, and milk powder total $1.2 billion per year.

Before cows, there were sheep. In the 1830s and '40s, meadowland was grazed by millions of merino sheep, but when the Civil War ended, so did the demand for wool blankets, and many sheep farms went under. Current Vermont farmers raise goats and llamas, beef cattle, miniature donkeys, Christmas trees, flowers, vegetables, and fruit, as well as brewing beer and distilling spirits. For a list of farms open to the public for tours, to sell their products, or for farm stays, check on the Vermont Farms Association website, **vtfarms.org**.

AGRICULTURAL FAIRS  The **Champlain Valley Exposition** (cvexpo.org) in Essex Junction (lasting an entire week before Labor Day) is by far the state's largest agricultural fair. **Addison County Fair and Field Days** (addisoncountyfielddays .com) in early August in New Haven, as well as the **Orleans County Fair** in Barton (orleanscountyfair.net), five days in mid-August, and the **Caledonia County Fair** (caledoniacountyfair.com), always the following weekend in nearby Lyndonville, all feature ox, pony, and horse pulls as well as a midway, live entertainment, and plenty to please all ages. The **Bondville Fair** (bondvillefair.org), three days in late August, claims to be Vermont's oldest continuous fair and is also the real thing. The **Vermont State Fair** (vermont statefair.org) in Rutland lasts five days in mid-August. The **Tunbridge World's Fair** (tunbridgefair.com), held four days in mid-September, is the oldest (even though its organizers did skip 1918) and most colorful of them all.

CHILDREN, ESPECIALLY FOR  Look for the 🦋 symbol throughout this book; it designates child-friendly attractions as well as lodging and dining. Of particular note:

The **Montshire Museum of Science** (montshire.org) in Norwich is largely hands-on and kids-geared, explaining many basic scientific mysteries indoors

CHILDREN'S FARM AND FOREST AT RETREAT FARM

and out. **ECHO, Leahy Center for Lake Champlain** (echovermont.org) is another hands-on science center with an aquarium featuring 2,200 live fish, amphibians, and reptiles. The **Billings Farm & Museum** (billingsfarm.org) and **Vermont Institute of Natural Science** (vinsweb .org), both in the Woodstock area, and the **Fairbanks Museum & Planetarium** (fairbanksmuseum.org) in St. Johnsbury are also all geared to stimulate and please youngsters.

Many ski resorts compete for family business, especially during their off-seasons. **Smugglers' Notch** offers the largest, most extensive family summer day camp and ski programs. Resorts with kids' programs include the **Tyler Place Family Resort** in Highgate Springs, **Basin Harbor Club** in Vergennes, and **Quimby Country** in Averill in the northeastern corner of the state. A century ago, hundreds of Vermont farms took in visitors for weeks at a time. **Liberty Hill Farm** in Rochester is a standout, successfully combining a

working dairy farm with family-friendly hospitality.

COLLEGES  For information about all the state's colleges and universities, contact **Vermont State Colleges** (vsc.edu) and the **Consortium of Vermont Colleges** (vtcolleges.org).

EVENTS  Almost every day of the year, some special event is happening somewhere in Vermont, such as a church supper, a theatrical production, a concert, or a crafts fair. We list *Special Events* for each chapter, and major listings can also be found at **vermontvacation.com**, but many of the best events only surface on local bulletin boards. In northern and central Vermont, check out the free and information-rich *Seven Days,* covering local arts and entertainment.

HISTORICAL SOCIETIES  Historical societies are frequently worth seeking out, but because most are staffed by volunteers, they tend to be open just a few hours a week, usually in summer. Of Vermont's 251 towns, 200 have historical societies. Check out the map/listing for members of the **League of Local Historical Societies and Museums** at **The Vermont Historical Society** website (vermonthistory.org).

LIBRARIES  Along with general stores, libraries are central to Vermont communities. The 189 or so libraries in the state range from the one-room cottage at Joe's Pond in West Danville to opulent late nineteenth-century buildings gifted by wealthy native sons. Notable examples are the **Aldrich Public Library** in Barre, the **Kellogg-Hubbard Library** in Montpelier, the **Norman Williams Public Library** in Woodstock, and the **St. Johnsbury Athenaeum and Art Gallery**. Some of our favorites are, however, found in very small places. The **Lincoln Library**, destroyed by flooding two decades ago, has been replaced with a new building with porch rockers. **Craftsbury Public Library**, with its handsome interior, has rockers on the porch, too. In Peacham, the library marks the center of the village and is also an art center. The **Grafton Public Library** is an elegant but also homey vintage 1822 house. The **Tunbridge Public Library** is in a renovated historic brick house, as is the **Alice M. Ward Memorial Library** (with historical exhibits upstairs) on the green in Canaan. The **Pope Memorial Library** on the common in Danville is said to have ghosts; the small **Fairlee Public Library** has an excellent collection. For research, the **Vermont Historical Society Library** in Barre is a treasure trove of Vermontiana and genealogical resources; likewise, the **Wilbur Collection** of the Bailey-Howe Library at the University of Vermont and the **Russell Vermontania Collection** at the Martha Canfield Library in Arlington are excellent resources.

VERMONT PUBLIC RADIO  Stations for those addicted to National Public Radio

can be found throughout the state on the FM dial (or click on vpr.net). In the Burlington area, tune in to WVPS (107.9); in the Windsor area WVPR (89.5); in the Rutland area WRVT (88.7); in St. Johnsbury WVPA (88.5); in Manchester 106.9; in Brattleboro 88.9; in Bennington WBTN (94.3); in Middlebury 99.5; in Montpelier 94.1; and in Rupert 101.1. Check the website for VPR Classical music stations.

QUILTS  A revival of interest in this craft is especially strong in Vermont, where quilting supply and made-to-order stores pepper the state. The **Vermont Quilt Festival** (vqf.org) is held for three days in late June in Essex Junction, including exhibits of antique quilts, classes and lectures, vendors, and appraisals. **Shelburne Museum** has an outstanding quilt collection, and the **Billings Farm & Museum** holds an annual show.

RAILROAD EXCURSIONS  **The Green Mountain Railroad** (rails-vt.com) runs several excursion trains around the state. Check the website for current info.

WEDDINGS  Destination weddings have become a big business in Vermont, so big and so ubiquitous that we use the wedding-ring symbol in this book to designate establishments that specialize in them. Same-sex marriages are now officially recognized in Vermont, helping this booming industry.

# Further Reading

BOOKS  Basic tools for serious explorers include *New Hampshire/Vermont Atlas & Gazetteer* (DeLorme) and *Vermont Place Names: Footprints in History*, by Esther Swift (Vermont Historical Society, 1996). Another useful classic is *The Nature of Vermont*, by Charles Johnson (University Press of New England). Civil War buffs will be rewarded by Howard Coffin's *Full*

*Duty: Vermonters in the Civil War* (The Countryman Press). We also recommend *The View from Vermont,* subtitled *Tourism and the Making of an American Rural Landscape,* by Blake Harrison (University of Vermont Press). For children, *Vermont: The State with the Storybook Past* by Cora Cheney (New England Press) is the best.

Our favorite Vermont fiction writer is the late Howard Frank Mosher, whose evocative novels include *On Kingdom Mountain, Disappearances, Northern Borders, Where the Rivers Flow North,* and *A Stranger in the Kingdom* (the last two are also films). The Brattleboro-based mysteries of Archer Mayor, including *Open Season* and many other titles in his Joe Gunther police-procedural series, are gaining momentum. Joseph Citro is the author of several books about occult occurrences and folk legends in the state, including *Green Mountains, Dark Tales* (University Press of New England) and *Ghosts, Ghouls, and Unsolved Mysteries* (Houghton Mifflin). *Art of the State: Vermont* by Suzanne Mantell (Abrams) is a small gem. Also, please check out *Backroads & Byways of Vermont* (The Countryman Press, 2018) by the authors of this guide.

MAGAZINES ***Vermont Magazine*** (vermontmagazine.com) is a lively state-wide bimonthly that focuses on the state's townscapes, products, and personalities. ***Seven Days*** (sevendaysvt .com) is Vermont's alternative weekly newspaper, available online and free throughout the state. Great food and arts coverage, also events. ***SO Vermont Arts & Living*** (vermontartsliving.com) is an enjoyable quarterly magazine that covers galleries, museums, and arts happenings throughout southern Vermont.

# SOUTHERN VERMONT

■

## BRATTLEBORO, PUTNEY, AND THE WEST RIVER VALLEY

## THE MOUNT SNOW VALLEY

## BENNINGTON AND THE SOUTHSHIRE

## MANCHESTER AND THE MOUNTAINS

Including Arlington, Dorset, Danby, Peru, Londonderry, and Pawlet

## OKEMO VALLEY REGION

Including Ludlow, Chester, Cavendish, Mount Holly, Andover, Plymouth, and Weston

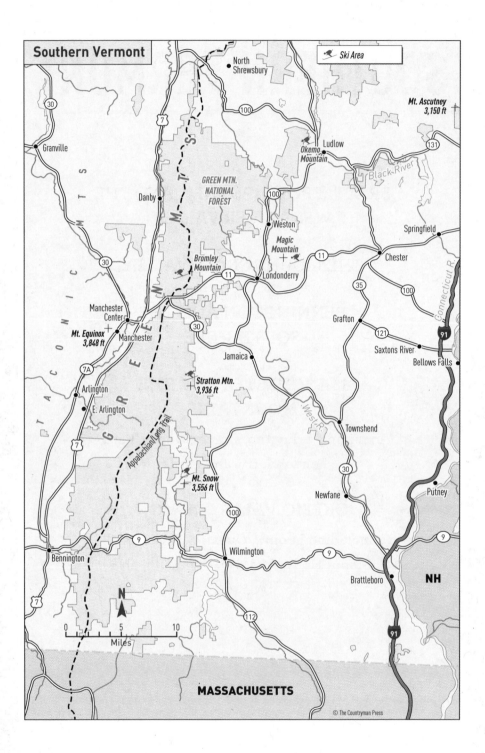

**Southern Vermont**

⛷ *Ski Area*

*Mt. Ascutney*
*3,150 ft*

North
Shrewsbury

Granville

Danby

GREEN MTN.
NATIONAL
FOREST

*Okemo*
*Mountain*
Ludlow

Black River

Springfield

Weston

*Magic*
*Mountain*

Chester

*Bromley*
*Mountain*

Londonderry

Manchester
Center

Grafton

*Mt. Equinox*
*3,848 ft*
Manchester

Jamaica

Saxtons River

Bellows Falls

*Stratton Mtn.*
*3,936 ft*

Arlington

Appalachian/Long Trail

E. Arlington

West R.

Townshend

*Mt. Snow*
*3,556 ft*

Newfane

Putney

Bennington

Wilmington

Brattleboro

**NH**

N

0          5          10
Miles

Connecticut R.

**MASSACHUSETTS**

© The Countryman Press

# BRATTLEBORO, PUTNEY, AND THE WEST RIVER VALLEY

Vermont's southeastern corner is a major gateway, and many visitors—a number of them now residents—get no farther. It's said that Vermont is a state of mind; in Brattleboro, the area's commercial and cultural hub, you quickly understand why. The world's only Brattleboro is home to a vibrant artistic and activist community with the contagious energy of a community many times its size.

Brattleboro has repeatedly shown amazing resiliency, bouncing back from a fire, flood, and recession. After a devastating fire, the iconic Brooks House, built in the 1870s as an eighty-room hotel in the heart of downtown, has been not only renovated but reinvented to house branches of two state colleges as well as residents, shops, and restaurants. Another Main Street icon, the 1930s art deco Latchis Theater and Hotel, has been lovingly restored, the former rail station (where Amtrak still stops) is an art museum, the downtown supermarket is an expansive state-of-the-art co-op with a café, and several Main Street buildings are honeycombed with artists' studios. Along with Elliot and High streets, it's a rich mix of traditional stores and galleries, restaurants and cafés, owner-operated bookstores, and boutiques. Its twice-weekly seasonal farmers' markets are among the liveliest in New England; as is the first Friday Gallery Walk. Frequent concerts, dance and circus performances, and a film festival take place without hoopla.

Smaller, rural Putney, a dozen miles up the Connecticut River, is closely linked to Brattleboro in spirit. It's home to the nationally recognized Putney School and Landmark College, also to the Yellow Barn Music School and Festival, Sandglass Theater, Next Stage (live performances and films), and the annual Thanksgiving Putney Craft Tour, the country's oldest continuing craft tour.

Northwest of Brattleboro, VT 30 shadows the West River, threading the white-clapboard villages of Newfane, Townshend, and Jamaica—strung like pearls along a couple dozen miles with unpaved back roads branching off to widely scattered inns and B&Bs, antiques dealers, galleries and shops, swimming holes, and hiking trails to unexpected vistas.

Despite its accessibility, this is far from the most visited corner of Vermont. The confluence of the Connecticut and West rivers at Brattleboro is itself a beautiful, placid place to paddle.

GUIDANCE (ꙮ) **The Southeast Vermont Welcome Center**, I-91 northbound, just south of Brattleboro's Exit 1 (open daily 7 a.m.–1 a.m.), is Vermont's largest visitor center, with displays on all parts of the state, featuring local attractions and events. **Restrooms** are open 24 hours.

**Brattleboro Area Chamber of Commerce** (802-254-4565; brattleborochamber.org), 180 Main Street, is good for walk-in information (Mon.–Fri. 9–5).

(ꙮ) **The River Garden** (157 Main Street) is a weatherproofed downtown public space overlooking the river; **public restrooms**, local brochures. Home base for Strolling of the Heifers (strollingoftheheifers.com), it is a venue for weekday brown-bag lunch

PADDLING ON THE WEST RIVER  JASON HENSK

programs and the Winter Farmers' Market. (Sat.).

*Newspapers:* The **Brattleboro Reformer** (802-254-2311; reformer.com) publishes a special Thursday calendar that's the best source of current arts and entertainment. **The Commons** (commonsnews.org). **SO Vermont Arts & Living** are also well worth checking.

GETTING THERE *By bus:* **Greyhound** (800-231-2222; greyhound.com) stops at the Shell Station, 429 Canal Street.

*By train:* **Amtrak** (800-USA-RAIL; amtrak.com) trains from Washington, DC, and New York City stop twice daily at Brattleboro's vintage railroad station, now a museum.

*By air:* **Bradley International Airport** (bradleyairport.com) in Connecticut and **Manchester Airport** (flymanchester.com) in New Hampshire offer connections with all parts of the country; both are one-and-a-half hours.

GETTING AROUND **Adventure Taxi** (802-254-8400) offers taxi services to airports, bus, and train. **Connecticut River Transit** (802-885-5162; crtransit.org), the local bus service, connects Brattleboro, Putney, Westminster, and Bellows Falls.

*Parking* Meters are plentiful and closely monitored along Main and side streets, in **Harmony Place** in the rear of the Brooks House (access from Elliot Street), also off High Street and in Brattleboro's **Transportation Center** with multilevel parking (access from Flat Street).

# ✳ Towns and Villages

**Brattleboro** (population 12,046). This largely 1870s brick and cast-iron town is the commercial hub for rural corners of three states. A number of the residents arrived in the 1970s to join communes that flourished in this area. Artists, musicians, and social activists continue to be drawn by local educational institutions (see the chapter introduction). The town's old landmark stores like Sam's Outdoor Outfitters and Brown & Roberts Hardware continue to thrive, but art galleries, crafts stores, and dozens of other independently owned, one-of-a-kind shops and restaurants are the rule, not the exception.

Brattleboro has long drawn earnest young people. World Learning, founded more than 50 years ago, has morphed into SIT Graduate Institute, granting degrees in subjects such as sustainable development and social justice. Marlboro College's downtown graduate center grants similar degrees. Branches of two state colleges, the Brattleboro Music Center, and the New England Center for Circus Arts, add to the mix.

During its long history, this town has shed many skins. The site of Fort Dummer, built in 1724 just south of town, has been flooded by the Vernon Dam. Gone too are the

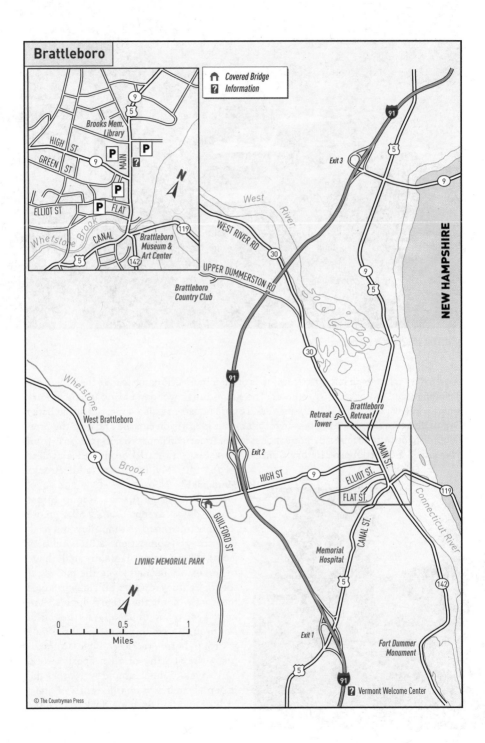

BRATTLEBORO OVERVIEW  GREG LESCH

pre-Civil War hotels that lodged trainloads of customers who came to take the water cure developed by Dr. Robert Wesselhoeft. The gingerbread wooden casino in Island Park and the fine brick town hall, with its gilded opera house, are also gone, but at the **Estey Organ Museum** (802-246-8366; esteyorganmuseum.org) you can see and hear the Brattleboro-made organs found in many thousands of American homes during the post-Civil War era. The **Brattleboro History Center** (802-258-4957; brattleborohistoricalsociety .org), 196 Main Street, and **Brooks Memorial Library** (802-254-5290; brookslibraryvt.org), 224 Main Street (open daily except Sun.), offer more insights into the town's multilayered past.

PUTNEY VILLAGE COMMON  CHRISTINA TREE

**Putney** (population 2,616; iputney .com). This town's riverside fields have been heavily farmed since the mid-eighteenth century, and its hillsides produce one-tenth of all the state's apples. Putney is also an unusually fertile place for progressive thinking. In the 1840s a group here practiced Bible Communism, the sharing of all property, work, and wives. John Humphrey Noyes, the group's leader, was charged with adultery in 1847 and fled with his flock to Oneida, NY, where he founded a famous silver plate company. Putney is known today for **The Putney School**, a coed, college

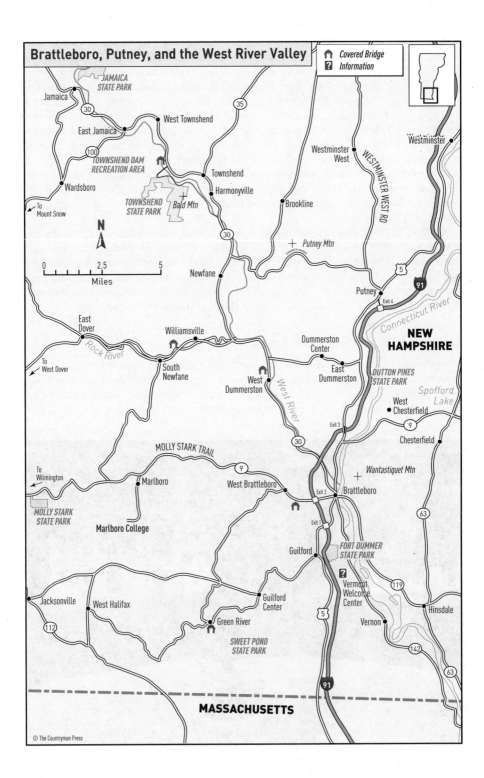

# Brattleboro, Putney, and the West River Valley

Covered Bridge
Information

JAMAICA
STATE PARK

Jamaica

30

East Jamaica

100

West Townshend

35

TOWNSHEND DAM
RECREATION AREA

Wardsboro

To
Mount Snow

Townshend

Harmonyville

TOWNSHEND
STATE PARK    Bald Mtn

N

0        2.5        5
Miles

East
Dover

Williamsville

To
West Dover

Rock River

South
Newfane

MOLLY STARK TRAIL

To
Wilmington

Marlboro

MOLLY STARK
STATE PARK

Marlboro College

Jacksonville    West Halifax

112

Brookline

Putney Mtn

Newfane

West
Dummerston

West River

Dummerston
Center

East
Dummerston

9

West Brattleboro

Exit 2

Guilford

Exit 1

Guilford
Center

Green River

SWEET POND
STATE PARK

30

Exit 3

30

Brattleboro

FORT DUMMER
STATE PARK

Vermont
Welcome
Center

Vernon

Westminster
West

WESTMINSTER WEST RD

Westminster

5

91

Exit 4

Putney

Connecticut River

NEW
HAMPSHIRE

DUTTON PINES
STATE PARK

West
Chesterfield

Spofford
Lake

9

Chesterfield

Wantastiquet Mtn

63

119

Hinsdale

142

63

91

MASSACHUSETTS

© The Countryman Press

preparatory school founded in 1935, with a regimen that entails helping with chores, including raising animals. **Landmark College** is a fully accredited college for dyslexic students and those with other learning disabilities. In July, the **Yellow Barn Music School and Festival** is housed in a barn behind the library; concerts are staged there and at other local venues throughout the month. **Sandglass Theater** (serious puppetry) and **Next Stage** (frequent live performances and films) are in Putney Village. During the three days following Thanksgiving, some two dozen local studios are open for the **Putney Craft Tour** (putneycrafts.com). Putney's scenic roads are also well known to serious bicyclists, and **Putney Mountain** (see *Hiking*) is beloved by both hikers and mountain bikers. Native sons include the late George Aiken, who served as governor before serving in Washington as a senator from 1941 to 1975, and Frank Wilson, a genuine Yankee trader who was one of the first merchants to enter Red China and founded popular **Basketville**. The **Putney Historical Society** (802-387-4411; putneyhistory.us) is housed in the town hall.

Guilford (population 2,121; guildfordvt.org). Backroaded by I-91, this agricultural town rewards with quiet rural scenery anyone who drives or pedals its roads. Hard to believe that it was the largest town in Vermont in 1817, the year the **Guilford Country Store** opened (see *Eating Out*). Labor Day weekend is big here, the time for the old-fashioned **Guilford Fair** and for the annual two-day free concerts sponsored for more than 40 years by **Friends of Music at Guilford** (802-254-3600; fomag.org) in and around the **Organ Barn**.

## ALONG VT 30 IN THE WEST RIVER VALLEY

Newfane (population 1,700). A columned courthouse, matching Congregational church, and town hall—all grouped on a handsome green—are framed by dignified, white-clapboard houses and a four-columned inn. When Windham County's court sessions began meeting in Newfane in 1787, the village was about the same size as it is now, but it was

THE VILLAGE GREEN IN NEWFANE  CHRISTINA TREE

2 miles up on Newfane Hill. Beams were unpegged and homes moved to the more protected valley by ox-drawn sleighs in the winter of 1824. Check out the exceptional **Historical Society of Windham County** (see *Must See*) with its **West River Railroad Museum**.

**Brookline** (population 467; brookline vt.com). Half as wide as it is long, Brookline is sequestered in a narrow valley bounded by steep hills and the West River. Its population is a fraction of what it was in the 1820s and '30s, when it supported three stores, three schools, two hotels, and a doctor. Its surviving landmark is a round schoolhouse, designed by John Wilson, a schoolteacher who never mentioned his previous career as Thunderbolt, an infamous Scottish high-

BROOKLINE'S ROUND SCHOOLHOUSE  CHRISTINA TREE

wayman. He gave the schoolhouse six large windows, the better to allow him to see whomever approached from any side. Wilson later added "Dr." to his name and practiced medicine in Newfane, then in Brattleboro, where he married, fathering a son before his wife divorced him "because of certain facts she learned." When he died in 1847, scars on Wilson's ankles and neck suggested chains and a rope. Today, several of Thunderbolt's pistols are preserved in local museums.

**Townshend** (population 1,150; townshendvermont.org). The village green is a splendid 2 acres, complete with a Victorian-style gazebo. The classic white 1790 Congregational church is flanked by clapboard houses and a former brick tavern, and there's a columned and tower-topped stucco hall belonging to Leland and Gray Union High School (founded as a Baptist seminary in 1834). On the first Saturday in August, the common fills with booths and games to benefit Grace Cottage Hospital, a complex that has grown out of the back of a rambling old village home and now includes assisted living buildings. VT 30 continues through West Townshend, with its recently restored country store, past Vermont's largest single-span covered bridge, and past a public swim beach. The town includes 15 cemeteries and several good places to stay and to eat.

TOWNSHEND VILLAGE GREEN  CHRISTINA TREE

**Jamaica** (population 1,035; jamaica vermont.org). The small village includes a white Congregational church (1808), another nineteenth-century church that's now the red-clapboard town hall, a standout country store, an art gallery, and an inn. **Jamaica State Park** also offers swimming, camping, and extensive hiking trails. While the village of Jamaica is small, the town is large, with many hidden corners—Hamilton Falls, Ball Mountain Dam, Pikes Falls, and the Our Lady of Ephesus shrine—to name a few to be found using the hand-drawn maps that Karen Ameden dispenses at D&K's Jamaica Grocery, the village nerve center. The **Jamaica Historical Foundation** (jamaicahf.info), housed in the village's former bank, is open mid-May–mid-October, Thurs. 1–3 and Sat. 10–1, or by appointment.

## ✳ Must See

MUSEUMS **Brattleboro Museum & Art Center** (802-257-0124; brattleboromuseum .org), 10 Vernon Street (corner of Canal and VT 119), Brattleboro. Open Sun.–Thurs. 11–5, Fri. 11–7, Sat. 10–5. Admission charged. The town's 1915 rail station makes a handsome home for increasingly compelling changing exhibits with an emphasis on contemporary art. Check the website for the current exhibit and a lively calendar of receptions, readings, music, lectures, and more.

**Estey Organ Museum** (802-246-8366; esteyorganmuseum.org), 108 Birge Street (rear), Brattleboro (turn off Canal Street at the Sunoco station). Open mid-May–October, Sat., Sun. 2–4. Visits are also available by special arrangement; call 802-246-8366. Admission. For many years Brattleboro's largest employer, the Estey Organ Co. produced thousands of organs each year between 1846 and its demise in 1960. This evolving museum is housed in a former engine house, a large, airy, well-lit space in which exhibits trace the history of organs in general and of Estey organs in particular. There are examples of reed organs from the 1860s as well as the ornately carved parlor organs found in countless Victorian homes. There are also the pipe organs Estey made for small churches throughout the county, and finally there are electronic organs, highly innovative when they first appeared. Inquire about frequent special events.

**Historical Society of Windham County** (802-365-4148; historicalsocietyofwindham county.org), 574 VT 30, Newfane; south of the common. Open Memorial Day–Columbus Day, Wed., Sat., Sun. noon–5. Exhibits fill both the main floor and the second-floor gallery. In addition to changing shows, there are permanent displays on the West River Railroad, which once operated between Brattleboro and South Londonderry (1880s–1927) and is remembered as "36 miles of trouble"; Porter Thayer's photographs of local turn-of-the-twentieth-century scenes; and the saga of John Wilson (see Brookline under *Towns and Villages*).

COVERED BRIDGES In Brattleboro the reconstructed **Creamery Bridge** forms the entrance to Living Memorial Park on VT 9. North on VT 30 in West Dummerston, a town lattice bridge across the West River is the longest still-used covered bridge in the state (for the best view, jump into the cool waters on either side; this is a popular swimming hole on a hot summer day). The **Green River** in Guilford also boasts a photogenic red covered bridge below a waterfall. The **Scott Bridge**, Vermont's longest single-span bridge, stands by VT 30 in West Townshend, just below the Townshend Dam, but it's closed to traffic. The region's oldest covered bridge spans the **Rock River** between Williamsville and South Newfane.

FOR FAMILIES **Children's Farm and Forest at Retreat Farm** (802-579-1327; retreatfarm.org), 45 Farmhouse Square, Brattleboro. Check the website for current hours. This is a working farm, originally established in 1837 as part of the neighboring Brattleboro Retreat and currently managed by a local nonprofit. The calf barn houses an education center and resident cows, as well as sheep, chicks, donkeys, goats, and rabbits. Check out the children's garden, nature trail, and workshops. *See Hiking* for more about the **Retreat Trails**, a 9-mile network with an entrance at the farm.

Also see the **Southern Vermont Natural History Museum** at Hogback Mountain (west of Brattleboro) in "The Mount Snow Valley" and the **Nature Museum** of Grafton in "The Lower Connecticut River Valley."

# ✳ To Do

BICYCLING Hundreds of miles of dirt and abandoned roads, plus many miles of off-road trails, make this a mecca for cyclists. Download maps from the Windham Regional Commission: windhamregional.org/bikemap. Amtrak's Vermonter, which stops in Brattleboro, offers carry-on service for bikes. Or you can rent a hybrid at the **Brattleboro Bicycle Shop** (802-254-8644; bratbike.com), 178 Main Street, and pick up plenty of advice about where to use it. Road biking is popular in this area, thanks to many interlinking back roads and river roads. In Putney the **West Hill Shop** (802-387-5718; westhillshop.com), open daily, just off I-91, Exit 4, offers mountain and road bike rentals. It's also home to the **Putney Bicycle Club**, which organizes races and (hard-core) tours. The **Ranney-Crawford House** in Putney (*Lodging*) is geared toward bicyclists.

BOATING **Vermont Canoe Touring Center** (802-257-5008; vermontcanoetouring center.com), 451 Putney Road, Brattleboro. Located on the West River at the cove at Veterans Memorial Bridge, US 5, just north of the junction with VT 30. Open daily Memorial Day weekend–Labor Day weekend, 9–dusk; also spring and fall weekends, weather permitting. Rental canoes, kayaks, and paddleboards; cash only.

**Whitewater on the West River**. Periodically the Army Corps of Engineers releases water from the **Ball Mountain Dam** (802-874-4881) in Jamaica, allowing whitewater rafters as well as kayakers and canoeists to take advantage of the flow.

FISHING In the **Connecticut River**, you can catch bass, trout, pike, pickerel, and yellow perch. There is an access on Old Ferry Road, 2 miles north of Brattleboro on US 5; another is from River Road on the New Hampshire shore in Westmoreland (VT 9 east, then north on VT 63). The **West River** is a source of trout and smallmouth bass; access is from any number of places along VT 30. In Vernon there is a boat access on **Lily Pond**, and in Guilford on **Weatherhead Hollow Pond** (see the *New Hampshire/Vermont Atlas & Gazetteer*, DeLorme).

GOLF **Brattleboro Country Club** (802-257-7380; brattleborocountryclub.com), 58 Senator Gannett Drive, Brattleboro. Offers 18 holes along the contours of rolling hilltops and includes a full driving range, practice areas, and an instructional range. Also see **Mount Snow** and **Stratton** ski resorts under *Downhill Skiing*; both offer golf schools and 27 holes.

HIKING **The Retreat Trails** (retreatfarm.org). In Brattleboro, 9 miles of well-maintained, mostly wooded trails web this 457-acre property, now owned by a local nonprofit. The trails were built in the nineteenth century by patients and staff of the Retreat, a pioneering mental hospital first opened in 1836. The Retreat Farm (see *Must See*) is the obvious access point, but there are many others. Popular paths lead to a nineteenth-century observation tower (now closed but still good views), a former ice pond, and the Harris Hill Ski Jump.

**Putney Mountain** between Putney and Brookline, off Putney Mountain Road (see *Scenic Drives*), is one of the most rewarding .6-mile (one way) hikes anywhere. There is ample parking and a posted map at the Putney Mountain trailhead, (see putneymountain.org). Follow the Ridgeline Trail as it heads gently uphill through birches and maples then continues through firs and vegetation that changes remarkably quickly into the stunted growth usually found only at higher elevations. Suddenly you emerge on the mountain's broad crown; it's only 1,667 feet up but is circled by a deep-down satisfying panorama. The view to the east is of Mount Monadnock, rising in lonely magnificence above the roll of southern New Hampshire, but more spectacular is the spread of Green Mountain peaks to the west. You can pick out the ski trails on Haystack, Mount Snow, and Stratton.

**The West River Trail** (WestRiverTrail.org) follows the abandoned rail bed of the West River Railroad (1879–1927), known in its time as "36 miles of trouble." Access to its first stretch is off US 5 north of town; take the second left turn after crossing the bridge. Other sections are found from Jamaica State Park to Ball Mountain Dam (3.5 miles) and from East Jamaica to Townshend Dam (3 miles). Jamaica State Park (see *Green Space*) offers a choice of three interesting trails. The most intriguing and theoretically the shortest is to Hamilton Falls, a 125-foot cascade through a series of wondrous potholes. It's an obvious mile (30-minute) hike up, but the return can be confusing. Beware of straying onto Turkey Mountain Road.

**Wantastiquet Mountain,** overlooking Brattleboro from across the Connecticut River in New Hampshire, is a good one-and-a-half-hour hike. From Main Street take VT 119 across the Connecticut and immediately after the second bridge turn left; the parking area is on your right.

**Black Mountain Natural Area,** maintained by **The Nature Conservancy of Vermont** (802-229-4425). Cross the covered bridge on VT 30 in West Dummerston and turn south on Quarry Road for 1.4 miles. The road changes to Rice Farm Road; go another 0.5 mile to a pull-off on your right. The marked trail begins across the road and abruptly rises 1,280 feet to a ridge, traversing it before dropping back down, passing

SALMON SWIMMING HOLE, JAMAICA STATE PARK  CHRISTINA TREE

a beaver dam on the way back to the river. The loop is best done clockwise. Beautiful in laurel season.

SWIMMING **Living Memorial Park**, west of downtown Brattleboro on VT 9, offers an Olympic-size public pool (mid-June–Labor Day). In the West River Valley at the **Townshend Lake Recreation Area** (802-365-7703) off VT 30 in West Townshend, you drive across the top of the massive dam, completed in 1961 as a major flood-prevention measure. Call first to check whether this is open. Its opening times vary with the quality of the water, which is affected by upstream runoff. It's a man-made beach and a gradual drop-off, good for children. **The West River** swimming holes include the West Dummerston covered bridge on VT 30 and Salmon Hole in Jamaica State Park. The river below **Hamilton Falls**, accessible from the park, is a favorite, but beware of the pools in the falls themselves; many people have died there. **Pikes Falls**, also in Jamaica, is also popular but not advisable for children. Just off VT 30, a mile or so up (on South Newfane Road), the **Rock River** swirls through a series of shallow swimming spots; look for cars. Also handy to Brattleboro, **Wares Grove** is across the Connecticut River in Chesterfield, NH (9 miles east on VT 9, the next left after the junction with VT 63). This pleasant beach on Spofford Lake is good for children; you'll find a snack bar and makeshift changing facilities.

## ✳ Winter Sports

CROSS-COUNTRY SKIING **Brattleboro Outing Club Ski Hut** (802-254-4081; brattleborooutingclub.org), 348 Upper Dummerston Road, Brattleboro. Warming hut open weekends, trails open daily in-season. Trails through woods and a golf course, 33 km machine tracked, plus rentals, lessons, and moonlit ski tours. **West Hill Shop** (802-387-5718), just off I-91, Exit 4, in Putney, rents cross-country skis and snowshoes. **Jamaica State Park** in Jamaica (see *Green Space*) offers marked trails.
    See also **Grafton Trails & Outdoor Center** in *The Lower Connecticut River Valley*.

DOWNHILL SKIING The big ski areas are a short drive west into the Green Mountains, either to **Mount Snow** (see "The Mount Snow Valley") or up VT 30 to **Stratton** (see "Manchester and the Mountains").

ICE SKATING **Nelson Withington Skating Facility at Living Memorial Park** (802-257-2311), VT 9 West, Brattleboro. Open late October–mid-March. with skate rentals. A seasonal weatherproofed rink. Call for public skate times.

SCENIC DRIVES The hilly, heavily wooded country between the West and Connecticut River valleys is webbed with roads, many of them dirt roads. Our favorites include the following:
    **West Dummerston to West Dover**: Beautiful in a car or on a bike, the 13 paved miles between VT 30 and VT 100 form a shortcut from Newfane to Mount Snow. Turn west off VT 30, 2 miles north of the covered bridge. Follow the Rock River (in summer, clumps of cars indicate swimming holes) west from West Dummerston and Williamsville, on through the picturesque village of South Newfane; detour 0.5 mile into the old hill village of Dover, very different from West Dover, down on busy VT 100.
    **VT 30 from Brattleboro to Jamaica**: VT 30 (you can loop back on VT 100) shadows the West River, passing two covered bridges and threading together the photogenic

OUR LADY OF EPHESUS SHRINE, JAMAICA CHRISTINA TREE

villages of Newfane and Townshend, as well as passing Townshend Dam (good for swimming). Plenty of places to stop along the way to shop for crafts and antiques.

**Jamaica to Wardsboro:** This is a shortcut from Jamaica to VT 100 and rewarding in its own right. It begins on VT 30, directly across from D&K's Jamaica Grocery, as Pikes Falls Road, but it quickly branches left into South Hill Road. After a few miles, keep an eye out for Mowrey Road (a dirt road), leading to an exact replica of a first-century stone house that sits on a similar hillside in Ephesus, Turkey, which is a shrine said to be the final residence of Mary, mother of Jesus. The door is usually open. The property was part of an extensive horse farm, and a short ways up the road, the stables and riding ring have been transformed into Our Lady of Ephesus House of Prayer (802-896-6000; ourladyofephesushouseofprayer.org). The retreat center is set high, with a sweeping view of surrounding hills. There is a story here, and Mary Tarinelli, who, with her husband (now deceased), created the shrine and center, is frequently on hand to tell it.

**East Dummerston to West Dummerston:** A handy shortcut from US 5 to VT 30 (or vice versa), just 2 miles up one side of a hill to picturesque Dummerston Center and 2 miles down the other. This was long known in our family as the Gnome Road because of the way it winds through the woods, the typical home for these little beings, to Vermont's longest (refitted) traffic-bearing covered bridge. It's generally known as the East/West Road.

✪ **Putney Mountain Road to Brookline and Newfane:** (Closed in winter.) From US 5 in the middle of Putney, turn left onto Westminster West Road and left again about a mile up the hill onto West Hill Road; follow this road past Green Mountain Orchards for another mile, turn right (3.3 miles from US 5) onto Putney Mountain Road, a dirt road. It forks immediately; bear right to get to Putney Mountain. The trees thicken and the sunlight dapples through in a way that never seems to occur on paved roads. The road curves up and up—and up—cresting after 2.1 miles. Note the parking area on your right for the popular hike to a fabulous view (see Putney Mountain under *Hiking*). The road then snakes down the other side into Brookline. The road turns to hardtop and ends at Grassy Brook Road. Fork left, and it's five miles to VT 30 in Newfane, or you can stay straight to find the Round Schoolhouse in the tiny village of Brookline (see our description of the village's amazing story). Heading south from Brookline Village, a right on Hill Road and another at its junction with Grassy Brook Road will bring you to VT 30.

**Brattleboro to Guilford Center to Halifax and back**: This can be a 46-mile loop to Wilmington and back; ask locally for shortcuts back up to VT 9. Take US 5 south from Brattleboro to the Guilford Country Store, then right into Guilford Center. Continue for 0.5 mile and bear right on Stage Road to the hamlet of Green River, with its covered bridge, church, and crib dam, a type of house-like dam popular during the eighteenth and nineteenth centuries. Bear right at the church (before the bridge) and then left at the Y; follow Green River Road (along the river) and then Hatch School Road into Jacksonville. To complete the loop, see *Scenic Drives* in "The Mount Snow Valley."

**The Molly Stark Scenic Byway**: VT 9 between Brattleboro and Bennington is dedicated to the wife of General John Stark, hero of the Battle of Bennington. The 20-mile stretch west from Brattleboro bypasses the village of **Marlboro**, climbing high over **Hogback Mountain,** with its **Southern Vermont Natural History Museum**, before winding down into Wilmington. For details about Marlboro and Hogback, see *Scenic Drives* in the Mount Snow chapter. Note that this route is heavily trafficked during foliage season.

SNOWMOBILING  See **Mount Snow** (in "The Mount Snow Valley") and **Stratton** (in "Manchester and the Mountains") ski resorts for tours and rentals. The VAST (Vermont Area Snow Travelers; vtvast.org) trail system can be accessed in West Brattleboro.

## ✳ Green Space

**Fort Dummer State Park** (802-254-2610; vtstateparks.com), Guilford. Located 2 miles south of Brattleboro but on the other side of I-91. Surrounded by a 217-acre forest, overlooking the site of its namesake fort, built in 1724 to protect settlements along the Connecticut River. It was flooded by the Vernon Dam in 1908. There are 50 tent/trailer sites and 10 lean-tos, hot showers, and a dump station but no hookups, also hiking trails and a playing field.

**Jamaica State Park** (802-874-4600; vtstateparks.com), Jamaica. This 772-acre wooded area offers riverside camping, swimming in a great swimming hole, a picnic area, and an organized program of guided hikes. An old railroad bed along the river serves as a 3-mile trail to the Ball Mountain Dam, and an offshoot mile-long trail leads to Hamilton Falls. There are 41 tent/trailer sites and 18 lean-tos. A large picnic shelter is handy to the swimming hole and there is a playground.

**Townshend State Park** (802-365-7500; vtstateparks.com), Townshend. Open early May–Columbus Day, best accessed from VT 30 across the Dam Road. Underused because it was sequestered in an 856-acre state forest. The camping area (30 tent/trailer campsites, four lean-tos) is near the start of the 2.7-mile steep but rewarding trail to the summit of Bald Mountain. There is also a picnic pavilion.

**Ball Mountain Lake** (802-874-4881; vtstateparks.com), Jamaica. This 85-acre lake, created and maintained by the US Army Corps of Engineers, is a dramatic sight among the wooded, steep mountains, conveniently viewed from the access road off VT 30. Over 100 campsites are available on Winhall Brook at the other end of the reservoir, accessible off VT 100 in South Londonderry.

See also *Hiking* and *Swimming*.

# ✳ Lodging

**COUNTRY INNS AND A DOWNTOWN HOTEL** 🐟 **Latchis Hotel** (802-254-6300; latchishotel.com), 50 Main Street, Brattleboro. This is a downtown, vintage 1938 art deco–style hotel. There's a small but spiffy lobby with polished terrazzo marble floors and an elevator that accesses 30 air-conditioned rooms; request one with views down Main Street and across to Wantastiquet Mountain. The rooms are comfortably furnished in art deco style, some individually themed, all with private bath, phone, fridge, and coffeemaker. The hotel is built solidly enough to muffle the sound of traffic below. For more about the theater/performance center, which is part of the Latchis, see *Entertainment*. $, $$ for the three-room suite; rates includes continental breakfast.

♂ **Windham Hill Inn** (802-874-4080; windhamhill.com), 31 Lawrence Drive, West Townshend. Set high above the West River Valley, this is a luxurious retreat, a member of the well-regarded Relais & Chateaux association. The 22 guest rooms are divided between the 1825 brick farmhouse, the White Barn Annex (some with a deck looking down the valley), and a cottage. Ample common space includes a living room, an airy sunporch, and a sitting room, and the inn throughout is country elegant; many rooms have gas fireplaces and balconies. A landscaped pool looks out over the mountains and tennis court. The 160-acre property also includes a network of hiking paths, groomed as snowshoe trails in winter. Also see *Dining Out*. $$–$$$.

🐾 ♂ **Four Columns Inn** (802-365-7713; fourcolumnsvt.com), 21 West Street, Newfane. Set back behind Newfane's magnificent green, this white pillared mansion was built in 1830 to remind the owner's wife of her girlhood home in the South. An inn since the 1960s, it has recently been totally renovated. There are 15 queen and king-bedded guest rooms, plus a cottage and village house, all new, sparely but professionally decorated, with an eye to comfort without clutter. Amenities include a Wellness Center with spa treatments (outdoors, weather permitting) and a private steam shower and bath. Common space includes an inviting marble-topped bar. $$–$$$. Also see *Dining Out*.

🐾 ♻ **Three Mountain Inn** (802-874-4140; threemountaininn.com), 30 Depot Street (corner of VT 30), Jamaica. Ed and Jennifer Dorta-Duque welcome you to their 1790s inn in the middle of a classic Vermont village. There are seven rooms upstairs and seven in neighboring Robinson House, all nicely decorated, several with a whirlpool tub, a fireplace, or a stove. Sage Cottage in the garden has skylights and a stained-glass window. Common space includes the old tavern room with its large hearth and a small bar and two small but elegant dining rooms (inn guests only). Jamaica State Park and its trails are a walk away. From $ for an off-season room in the inn to $$$ in high-season for Sage Cottage, which includes a three-course breakfast.

🐾 **Chesterfield Inn** (603-256-3211; chesterfieldinn.com) 20 Cross Road, West Chesterfield, NH. On VT 9, 2 miles east of Brattleboro. The original house served as a tavern from 1798 to 1811, but the present facility is contemporary, with a large, attractive dining room and a spacious parlor. All rooms have a sitting area, a phone, controlled heat and air-conditioning, optional TV, and a wet bar, and some have a working fireplace or Jacuzzi. Innkeepers Phil and Judy Hueber have created a popular dining room and a comfortable, romantic getaway spot that's well positioned for exploring southern Vermont as well as New Hampshire's Monadnock region. $–$$$ rates depend on room and season; all include a full breakfast.

## BED & BREAKFASTS

### IN BRATTLEBORO

✪ **1868 Crosby House** (802-257-7145; crosbyhouse.com), 175 Western Avenue. Lynn Kuralt welcomes you to her gem of an inn, a spacious Italianate mansion built by a major mill owner. The three second-floor guest rooms have marble and slate mantels, with gas hearths, luxurious baths, and built-in cupboards crafted by Tom Kuralt to hide TVs, VCRs, and CD players. Two attractive suites and cooking facilities share a porch with garden views. A sunny breakfast room overlooks the patio, and the lily pond and landscaped gardens are stepped into the hillside. The property adjoins conservation land webbed with trails and downtown and is an easy walk away. $$ includes a choice of a full sweet or savory breakfast.

**The Inn on Putney Road** (802-254-6268; vermontbandbinn.com), 192 Putney Road. Just north of the town common and within walking distance of downtown shops and restaurants, this house, with its steeply pitched, gabled roof, resembles a French château and was built splendidly in 1930 for the director of the nearby Brattleboro Retreat. Innkeepers John and Cindy Becker have redecorated and renovated the house, creating a sunny breakfast room and a second-floor sunroom, as well as adding a billiard table and appealing decor to the living room. We would recommend requesting a guest room in the rear, overlooking landscaped grounds that border the West River. $$ for rooms, more for the two-room suite, including a multicourse breakfast.

### IN PUTNEY

**Hickory Ridge House** (802-387-5709; hickoryridgehouse.com), 53 Hickory Ridge Road South. An 1808 brick mansion, complete with Palladian window, set on 12 acres with walking/cross-country ski trails. Gillian and Dennis Petit offer six softly, authentically colored guest rooms in the inn. Pets and children are welcome in the neighboring cottage, available either as two rooms or together. Inn rooms come with and without gas fireplaces, but all have private baths, phones, and TV/VCRs. The original Federal-era bedrooms are large, and there's an upstairs sitting room. The cottage consists of a room and a separate suite with its own living room and kitchen; it can also be rented as a whole. A swimming hole is within walking distance, and cross-country touring trails can be found just out the back door. Rates include a full breakfast. $$–$$$$

**Ranney-Crawford House** (802-387-4150; ranney-crawford.com), 1097 Westminster West Road. Another handsome brick Federal (1810) homestead on a quiet country road, surrounded by fields. Innkeeper Arnie Glim is an enthusiastic bicyclist who knows all the local possibilities for both touring and mountain biking. Four attractive guest rooms—two spacious front rooms with a hearth, along with two smaller back rooms, all with private bath—are $$, which includes a three-course breakfast.

### IN GUILFORD

✪ **Green River Bridge House** (802-257-5771; greenriverbridgehouse.com), 2435 Stage Road, Green River. Technically just 7 miles south of Brattleboro, this 1830s house with three guest rooms is one of the most remote-feeling and peaceful places to stay in Vermont. It's tucked into the slope just above its riverside gardens and below a covered bridge with a gentle waterfall that you can sit in. Longtime host Joan Seymour has filled the house with whimsical touches and amenities. Bicycle, walk, or run along an

# RUDYARD KIPLING AND NAULAKHA

Rudyard Kipling first visited Brattleboro in the winter of 1892 and subsequently built a house high on a hill in Dummerston (just north of the Brattleboro line). "Naulakha" is a Hindi word meaning 900 lakhas, or approximately $900,000. The shingled house is 90 feet long but only 22 feet wide, designed to resemble a ship riding the hillside like a wave. Its many windows face east across the valley to the New Hampshire hills, with a glimpse of the summit of Mount Monadnock.

Just 26 years old, Kipling was already one of the world's best-known writers, and the four years he spent here were among the happiest in his life. Here he wrote the *Jungle Books*. Here the local doctor, James Conland, a former fisherman, inspired him to write *Captains Courageous* and also delivered his two daughters. Kipling's guests included Sir Arthur Conan Doyle, who brought with him a pair of Nordic skis, said to be the first in Vermont. Unfortunately, in 1896, a highly publicized falling-out with Kipling's dissolute brother-in-law drove the family back to England. They took relatively few belongings from Naulakha; most of what is now in Naulakha once belonged to the Kiplings.

The four-bedroom house has been restored and is maintained by The Landmark Trust USA, which has preserved every detail of the home as Rudyard and Carrie Kipling knew it. The house is available year-round for short-term vacation rentals; there is a three-night minimum. Tours can be arranged with advance planning, as long as the house is not rented. Some 60 percent of the present furnishings are original, including a third-floor pool table. How about curling up with the *Jungle Books* on a sofa by the fire, only a few feet from where they were written? Or steeping in Kipling's own deep tub? Or a game of tennis on the Kiplings' court?

The Kipling Carriage House, just down the driveway, makes a great weekend retreat; it sleeps four and has also been restored to Kipling's original design. The Landmark Trust USA also restored two more historic buildings at the neighboring 571-acre Scott Farm (scottfarmvermont .com). The classic century-old sugarhouse Sugarhouse (🐾), sleeping two, and the Dutton Farmhouse, an 1837 Greek Revival, four-bedroom homestead, are set near the highest point of the farm's acreage, with 30-mile views. Both properties offer access to hiking and to the tennis courts at Naulakha. There is also the Amos Brown House, a brick Cape-style, three-bedroom home, built circa 1802 and set on 30 acres of meadow and forest in Whitingham, approximately 45 minutes west of Brattleboro(🐾).

**RUDYARD KIPLING IN HIS STUDY** COURTESY OF THE LANDMARK TRUST, USA

adjoining network of dirt roads. The $$ rate includes a full breakfast.

## IN THE WEST RIVER VALLEY (LISTED GEOGRAPHICALLY ALONG VT 30)

✪ ✎ **Fieldstone Lodge** (802-365-0265; fieldstonelodgevt.com), 51 West Street, Newfane. Hidden away across Smith Brook from Newfane's West Street, this is a handsome, 1930s Adirondack-style shingle lodge with a massive fieldstone hearth in its art-hung, open-timbered common room. Veteran innkeepers Bob and Gary offer three appealing guest rooms and two cottages. Squirrel Cottage (sleeping four to six), with a woodstove in its common room and a full kitchen, is a beauty. Walk to the village and jump from the grounds into a popular swimming hole in the brook. $$.

**Stone Boat Farm Bed and Breakfast** (802-297-9929; stoneboatfarm.com), 7240 VT 30, Jamaica. This roadside B&B is particularly popular in winter, probably the reason its five units are named for the four nearby ski areas. Joseph and Jeffrey have transformed this longtime motel into something more, especially in summer, when their extensive flower gardens are in bloom and walking trails lead down through the property to the river. In winter, cross-country skis and snowshoes are available. $–$$ per night.

**Cold Moon Farm** (802-297-3258; coldmoonfarm.com), 251 Pratt Bridge Road, Jamaica. This is not your typical Vermont farm or B&B. High on a wooded back road a few miles from Stratton, it's Irene and Ed Glazer's contemporary-style dream home, one with guest rooms (private baths) and plenty of space to relax. Brooklyn born and bred, the Glazers are now enthusiastic farmers who delight in introducing guests to their goats, chickens, and veggie garden. Irene is also a professional bread maker. Amenities include a pool table and a hot tub; breakfast features freshly laid eggs. The family-size rooms and suites are $$$–$$$$ per night.

OTHER LODGING **Colonial Motel & Spa** (802-257-7733; colonialmotelspa.com), 889 Putney Road (US 5),

**A COUNTRY BARN** CHRISTINA TREE

Brattleboro. This 65-room, two-story motel is family owned. Facilities include lap and standard-size pools in a glass greenhouse, as well as a fitness center, a steam room, and an attractive restaurant. $–$$.

CAMPGROUNDS See *Green Space* for information about camping in Fort Dummer, in Jamaica and Townshend State Parks, and at Ball Mountain Lake.

## ✳ Where to Eat

### DINING OUT

#### IN BRATTLEBORO

✪ **T.J. Buckley's** (802-257-4922; tjbuckleysuptowndining.com), 132 Elliot Street. Open Wed.–Sun. 6–9. Closed Wed. off-season. Reservations a must. This small (eight tables) but classic red-and-black 1920s Worcester diner is the best place to eat in Brattleboro. Inside, fresh flowers and mismatched settings brighten the tables, the walls are oak paneled, and chef-owner Michael Fuller prepares the night's fish, fowl, and beef (vegetarian is also possible) in the open kitchen behind the counter. The night's menu depends on what's available locally. The $45 entrée includes a salad; appetizers and desserts are extra.

**duo** (802-254-4141; duorestaurants .com), 136 Main Street. Open daily for dinner from 5, for brunch Sat., Sun. Occupying a star space in Brooks House in the heart of town, this is the Vermont companion to a well-known Denver restaurant. The a la carte menu is locally sourced, contemporary American. Entrées: $$.

✪ **Three Stones Restaurant** (802-246-1035; 3stonesrestaurant.com), 105 Canal Street. Reservations (by phone only) recommended. Open Wed.–Sat. 5–9. Who knew that a former diner styling itself a "Mexican Mayan Cocina" would be so crowded on a winter Wednesday night? Luckily there was room at the bar (beer and wine). The attractive interior space and menu are limited. No guacamole or Tex-Mex; rather, this is simple, fresh, and authentic fare from the Yucatán. The name is from the three stones on which Mayan Indians still place their outdoor cooking griddle with a fire underneath. A choice of tortillas, tamales, and empanadas come with rice, beans, greens, and freshly made salsa. Chef and co-owner Mucuy Bolles gets her culinary enthusiasm and skill from her Mayan mother. Entrées: $.

#### IN PUTNEY

**The Gleanery Café** (802-387-3052; thegleanery.com), 133 Main Street. Open Wed.–Sat. for lunch and dinner. Housed in the historic, exposed-beamed Putney Tavern, with added seasonal porch dining overlooking the common. The menu changes daily, dictated by what's available from local farms. Inquire about family-style Sunday suppers. Dinner: $$–$$$.

#### ALONG VT 30

**Artisan Restaurant and Tavern at the Four Columns Inn** (802-365-7713; fourcolumnsvt.com), 21 West Street, Newfane. Dinner except Mon.; lunch seasonally Wed.–Sat; Sun. brunch. The dining room is rustically elegant (no tablecloths), and the menu is locally and seasonally sourced. A moderately priced pub menu is available in the tavern and, weather permitting, on the pleasant patio. $$–$$$.

**Williamsville Eatery** (802-365-9600; williamsvilleeatery.com), 26 Dover Road, Williamsville. Dinner Thurs.–Sun. from 5. Just far enough off the main drag to feel like a find, this former village store has an open kitchen and features craft beers and ciders, wood-fired pizzas Thurs. and Sun., and a mix of inventive starters and entrées the remaining evenings. Reservations recommended. $–$$.

**Windham Hill Inn** (802-874-4080; windhamhill.com), 31 Lawrence Drive, West Townshend. The attractive, candlelit dining room, overlooking a pond, is open to the public for dinner (6–8:30) by reservation. Entrées are $$–$$$.

LUNCH ON THE PORCH OF THE GLEANERY CAFÉ, PUTNEY  CHRISTINA TREE

## EATING OUT

### IN BRATTLEBORO

✪ ✎ 🐟 **The Marina Restaurant** (802-257-7563; marina.com), 28 Spring Tree Road (US 5), Brattleboro. Open year-round, daily 11:30–10; Sunday brunch 10–1, dinner until 9. Sited at the confluence of the West and Connecticut rivers, with windows to maximize the view as well as seasonal patio and dockside tables. The reasonably priced menu includes plenty of seafood and vegetarian, lunch salads, pizza, and a standout Middle Eastern plate. Dinner favorites include New York strip steak and broiled sea scallops. Sunday brunch buffet.

✪ (((ψ))) **Amy's Bakery Arts Café** (802-251-1071), 113 Main Street. Open 8–6. Order from the blackboard menu up front and/or select something freshly baked from the counter display. Lunchtime salads, daily soups, and amazing sandwiches and breads; otherwise the cafe is a quiet haven—with river views.

**Whetstone Station Restaurant & Brewery** (802-490-2354; whetstone station.com), 36 Bridge Street. Open daily for lunch and dinner. A large, welcoming fish-and-chips kind of menu and pub atmosphere with a fireplace, a long bar facing out on the river, a rooftop "Biergarten" in summer, and 17 beers on tap, featuring local brews.

✎ ✪ (((ψ))) **Superfresh! Organic Café** (802-579-1751; superfreshcafe.com), 30 Main Street. Open Mon.–Wed. 9–3; Thurs., Fri. 9 a.m.–10 p.m.; Sat. 10–10; Sun. 10–9. A vegetarian's delight with many gluten-free options, from breakfast hash browns to pizzas with a "raw" grain-free/nut-free crust, and much more. The colorful dining room overlooks Whetstone Brook.

**Shin La Restaurant** (802-257-5226; shinlarestaurant.com), 57 Main Street. Open 11–9, closed Sun. A downtown mainstay for more than 30 years, known for fresh, homemade soups, dumplings, and kimchi among other Korean fare. Want Japanese instead? There's a sushi bar, too.

**Tulip Café** (802-490-2061; tulipcafe vermont.com), 126 Main Street. Open weekdays 8–4, weekends 9–4. A pleasant, laid-back lunch spot with a standout menu, from breakfast crepes to a large and mouth-watering selection of flatbreads, salads, and wraps.

**Turquoise Grille** (802-254-2327; turquoisegrille.com), 128 Main Street. Open Mon.–Fri., 11–3, 5–9; bar menu Thurs.–Sat. 9–11. Turkish specialties: kebabs, mini lamb burgers, Mediterranean salads, all fresh and tasty, plus pleasant ambiance and creative cocktails.

**Hazel** (802-579-1092; hazelpizza .com), 75 Elliot Street. Open Tues.–Sun. at 4 p.m., also Thurs.–Sat. for lunch. Specialty pies, applewood-smoked barbecue, craft beer, and signature cocktails combine to make this a popular local gathering place.

**Echo Restaurant & Lounge** (802-254-2073; echofoodanddrink.com), 73 Main Street. Open for lunch Thurs.–Sat., dinner nightly. Handy to Latchis Theater for before or after, specializing in craft cocktails, brews, and tasty small plates. Seasonal outdoor seating.

✿ ✪ **Top of the Hill Grill** (802-258-9178; topofthehillgrill.com), 632 Putney Road. Open mid-April–October, 11–9. This local barbecue mecca is just north of the bridge as you head up US 5 out of town. Indiana-born Jonathan Julian hickory-smokes his brisket and pork ribs and apple-smokes his turkey. He also makes corn bread and coleslaw from scratch. The extensive menu includes Mexican and Cajun specialties. Picnic tables and a screened deckhouse (with restrooms) overlook the river and the Retreat Meadows.

## EATING OUT BEYOND BRATTLEBORO

### IN AND AROUND PUTNEY

**JD McCliment's Pub** (802-387-4499; jdmcclimentspub.com), 26 Bellows Falls Road (US 5, just north of the village). Open Tues.–Sat. 5–midnight. Cozy in cool weather with a pure pub atmosphere, a piano and fireplace, and an upstairs area with booths. In summer,

a large deck is open, a great spot with umbrella-shaded tables. There is a house root beer as well as a choice of brews on tap, classic pub grub, flatbread pizza, summer dinner salads, and veggie options.

✿ ✪ **Putney Diner** (802-387-5433), 82 Main Street. Open 6–3 daily. The real diner deal with daily fresh eggs and no grease. Good for corned beef hash or kielbasa and eggs, gravy and hand-cut fries, grilled liver and onions, and juicy big burgers.

✪ ✿ **Curtis' All American Bar-Be-Cue** (802-387-5474), 7 Putney Landing Road. Summer through fall, Wed.–Sun. 10–dusk. Follow your nose to the blue school bus parked behind the Mobil station on US 5 in Putney, just off I-91, Exit 4. Curtis Tuff and his family cook up pork ribs and chicken, seasoned with his secret barbecue sauce; also check out the foil-wrapped potatoes, grilled corn, and beans flavored with Vermont maple syrup. There are picnic tables and a weatherproofed pavilion.

((•)) **Putney General Store** (802-387-4692; putneygeneralstore.com), 4 Kimball Hill Road. Open 7 a.m.–9 p.m. Looking much as it always has, this red-clapboard landmark was actually rebuilt from scratch after it burned to the ground in 2009. It had been rehabbed after a fire the previous year. It remains the village center, now more than ever, given the serious deli and blackboard menu, coffees, and plenty of seating.

**Putney Food Co-op** (802-387-5866; putneyfoodcoop.com), 8 Carol Brown Way, off VT 5, south of the village. Deli closes one hour before the store closes. A quick stop for great deli sandwiches, soups, and salads; tables in a pleasant café area.

### ALONG VT 9 WEST

✿ **Chelsea Royal Diner** (802-254-8399; chelsearoyaldiner.com), 487 Marlboro Road (VT 9), West Brattleboro. Open 6

CURTIS' ALL AMERICAN BAR-BE-CUE, PUTNEY  CHRISTINA TREE

a.m.–9 p.m. A genuine '30s diner a mile west of I-91, Exit 2. Plenty of parking and diner decor. Serving breakfast all day as part of a big menu that includes pizza, burgers, platters, daily blue plate specials, and great ice cream.

**Vermont Country Deli** (802-257-9254), 436 Western Avenue. Open 7–7. A great to-go deli, full stock of Vermont specialty foods.

## ALONG US 5 SOUTH

🐾 ✪ ((ᵖ)) **Guilford Country Store** (802-490-2233; guilfordcountrystore.com), 475 Coolidge Highway, Guilford. Open 7–7, Sat. 7:30–6, Sun. 8–5. Renovated and restored through community fundraising, this vintage 1817 general store with its sunny, inviting café is the hub of this rural community. Chef-owner Marc Tessitore and wife Suzanne have created an appealing oasis, good for all three meals—breakfast off the grill and then exceptional blackboard deli offerings until closing. Plenty of Wi-Fi users in between. The store also offers a wide choice of wine and Vermont beers.

## ALONG VT 30

**Rick's Tavern** (802-365-4310; rickstavern vt.com), 386 VT 30 south of Newfane Village. Open except Tues. for lunch and dinner, live jazz Thurs., and acoustic music Sat. night. The bar was built around 1890 in Bismarck, North Dakota, but the draft beers are Vermont microbrews. Daily blackboard specials, pizza, and homemade desserts.

**West Townshend Country Store & Café** (802-874-4800), 6573 VT 30, West Townshend. Open daily 7–7. This 1848 general store/post office has been restored through community financing and features an attractive café, hung with local art—good for locally sourced breakfast through lunch and onward. Frequent music. Friday clay-oven pizza parties coincide with the adjacent local farmers' market. Note the thrift store upstairs.

🍴 **The Townshend Dam Diner** (802-874-4107), 5929 VT 30, Townshend. Open daily except Tues. 5 a.m.–8 p.m. Breakfast all day. There's a big U-shaped counter and plenty of table seating and

GUILFORD COUNTRY STORE  CHRISTINA TREE

the waitresses are friendly. Specialties include homemade French toast, home fries, muffins and biscuits, the "best dam chili," soups, and bison burgers (from the nearby East Hill Bison Farm). Dinner staples include roast turkey, spaghetti, and garlic bread; daily specials. We recommend the fudge sundae.

✪ **D&K's Jamaica Grocery** (802-874-4151; dksjamaicavermont.com), 3816 VT 30, Jamaica. Open daily 7 a.m.–8 p.m. Dale and Karen Ameden's friendly, genuine, old-fashioned country store is the heart of Jamaica Village, source of sandwiches and salads for picnics in Jamaica State Park, also soups and hot food, pastries (including breakfast sandwiches), and wines. In 2008 "D&K" bought back this store, which they sold in 1990 but missed almost immediately.

**North Country General** (802-444-0269; northcountrygeneral.com), 3796 VT 30. Open Thu.–Sat. 8 a.m.–9 p.m., otherwise 8–4; closed Wed. Dan Fraser's informal eatery offers a limited menu—seasonal flatbreads, burgers, and drinks—as well as smoothies, wine, and craft beer.

BREWS ✪ (((•))) **Mocha Joe's Coffee House and Coffee Roasters** (802-257-7794), 82 Main Street, Brattleboro. Open daily weekdays from 7 a.m., 7:30 on weekends, until 8 p.m. weekdays, 9:30 Fri. and Sat. There's a funky, friendly feel to this basement-level landmark that's a must-stop in town. The coffee that's been roasted here for more than 20 years is now sold throughout the country, but this original Mocha Joe's remains its own place. The free-trade, certified-organic coffee itself—from espressos to pumpkin spice lattes—is the best. Chai, hot chocolate, and more are also served, along with pastries and light food.

**Hermit Thrush Brewery** (802-257-2337; hermitthrushbrewery.com), 28 High Street, Brattleboro. Belgian-inspired ales brewed using green technology and aged in oak casks. Tours and tastings.

WINE AND SPIRITS **Putney Mountain Winery** (802-387-5925; putneywine .com). Winery and tasting room inside Basketville, 8 Bellows Falls Road (US 5), 11–5 daily. Music professor and composer Charles Dodge has established a reputation for the quality of his sparkling fruit wines.

**Saxtons River Distillery** (802-246-1128; saxtonsriverdistillery.com), 485 West River Road (VT 30), Brattleboro. Open for tastings 9–5 Mon.–Fri., 10–5 Sat., Sun. Christian Stromberg's family fled Lithuania in 1906, bringing with them the family tradition of crafting fine liqueurs.

## ✳ Entertainment

**Latchis Theatre** (802-246-2020; latchistheatre.com), 50 Main Street, Brattleboro, shows first-run and art films as well as the Metropolitan Opera in HD plus concerts and live performances. For film buffs, this 900-seat art deco movie house with three screens is a destination. Apollo still drives his chariot through the firmament on the ceiling, the walls are graced with Doric columns, and the lobby floor bears the zodiac signs in multicolored terrazzo. Along with the Latchis Hotel in which it's housed, the theater is owned by the Brattleboro Arts Initiative.

**The New England Center for Circus Arts** (802-254-9780; necenterforcircusarts.org), 10 Town Crier Circle Drive, Brattleboro. A full program of circus arts is offered year-round in the Cotton Mill; check the website for performances.

**Brattleboro Music Center** (802-257-4523; bmcvt.org), 72 Blanche Moyse Way, Brattleboro. Housed in expanded quarters across from Living Memorial Park, this burgeoning music school sponsors a wide variety of local musical events and festivals as well as a fall–spring Chamber Music Series.

**New England Youth Theatre** (802-246-6398; neyt.org), 100 Flat Street, Brattleboro. Year-round productions of children's and all-time classics in a state-of-the-art theater. Check the website for performances.

**Marlboro Music** (802-258-9331; marlboromusic.org), Persons Auditorium, Marlboro College, 10 miles west of Brattleboro, off VT 9. This internationally famous series of chamber music concerts has been performed Fri.–Sun., mid-July–mid-August, since 1951. The festival is a seven-week gathering of world-class musicians who come to work together. It is held on this rural campus because Rudolf Serkin, one of its founders, owned a nearby farm. Pablo Casals came every year from 1960 to 1973. There are (almost) always bargain-priced seats in the tent just outside the auditorium's sliding glass door.

**Vermont Jazz Center** (802-254-9088; vtjazz.org), 72 Cotton Mill Hill, Studio 222, Brattleboro, stages frequent musical, vocal, and jazz happenings.

**Friends of Music at Guilford** (802-254-3600; fomag.org), 39 Church Drive, Guilford. A series of concerts throughout the year at various locations. Note the free Labor Day weekend concerts under *Special Events*.

### IN PUTNEY

**Next Stage Arts** (802-387-0102; nextstagearts.org), 15 Kimball Hill. A former 1841 Congregational church owned by the Putney Historical Society is now the home of the 160-seat **Next Stage Theater**, a year-round performing arts center with a full schedule of classical and folk/rock music as well as film (**Next Stage Cinema**).

**Sandglass Theater** (802-387-4051; sandglasstheater.org), 17 Kimball Hill. A resident theater company performs original work combining live theater with puppetry performances. When not on tour, they perform in a 60-seat renovated barn theater in Putney Village.

**Yellow Barn Music Festival** (802-387-6637; yellowbarn.org), 63 Main Street. Begun in 1969, this is a center for chamber music study and performance, presenting a series of chamber music concerts in July and early August. Most concerts are staged in a 150-seat, air-conditioned barn in Putney Village. Artists include well-known professionals.

# ✻ Selective Shopping

ANTIQUES **Twice Upon a Time** (802-254-2261; twicetime.com), 133 Main Street, Brattleboro. Open Mon.–Wed. 10–6, Thurs.–Sat. 10–7, Sun. 11–6. This shop's 100 dealers and many more consigners fill the entire three-level space created in 1906 for the E. J. Fenton Department Store, with its two-story-high Corinthian columns, bubble glass, and wooden gallery as a setting for clothing, antique furniture, and furnishings. The markdown schedule is modeled after the late Filene's Basement.

**Townshend Auction Gallery** (802-365-4388), 129 Riverdale Road, Townshend. Over the past 30 years, Kit Martin and Art Monette have established a solid reputation for their frequent auctions, usually Saturday mornings. Previews Friday.

ART AND CRAFTS GALLERIES *Note:* The first Friday of each month is **Gallery Walk** (802-257-2616; gallerywalk.org) **in Brattleboro**: open house with refreshments and music at dozens of downtown businesses that hang works by local artists and at studios as well as at formal galleries, usually 5:30–8:30.

♟ **Vermont Artisan Designs** (802-257-7044; vtart.com), 106 Main Street, Brattleboro. Open daily. This was the town's department store when Greg Worden acquired a portion of the space more than 20 years ago to establish the town's first quality gallery. It showcases the well-chosen work of hundreds of artisans; an upstairs gallery displays Vermont's best artists and photographers. Special exhibits change with every Gallery Walk (first Friday). There's also a kitchen store.

✪ **Gallery in the Woods** (802-257-4777; galleryinthewoods.com), 145 Main Street, Brattleboro. For decades Dante and Suzanne Corsano's gallery has been a standout, featuring folk art, finely crafted furniture, and well-known painters and artists in a variety of media from throughout the world. Changing exhibits.

**Mitchell-Giddings Fine Arts** (802-251-8290; mitchellgiddingsfinearts.com), 183 Main Street, Brattleboro. Open Wed.–Sun. 11–5. Hidden downstairs below A Candle in the Night, this is a serious contemporary gallery.

**Fire Arts Vermont** (802-257-2787; fulcrumarts.com), 485 West River Road (VT 30), Brattleboro. Open Mon.–Sat. 10–6. This big blue metal former candy-making factory houses a gallery and workspace for two well-established artists, Randi Solin and Natalie Blake. Worth a stop to see Solin's colorful glass and Blake's striking tile mosaics as well as the work of juried artists in varied media. Glass is blown in the adjoining open hot shop, and clay is shaped in an equally open studio.

IN PUTNEY

**Robert Burch Glass** (802-387-4032; robertburchglass.com), 3 Great Meadows Ridge, Putney. Visitors welcome, but call first. Robert Burch, a pioneer in art glass, hand-blows his signature cobalt perfume bottles and vases, veiled with delicate silver bubbles, as well as amber and ruby swirling paperweights in a 200-year-old barn beside his home. Seconds are available.

**Green Mountain Spinnery** (802-387-4528; spinnery.com), 7 Brickyard Lane, Putney. Open daily. Founded as a cooperative more than 30 years ago and now worker owned, this is a real spinning mill, in which undyed, unbleached fibers—alpaca, mohair, wool, and organic cotton—are carded, spun, skeined, and labeled. You can buy the resulting yarn in natural and dyed colors, and in many original patterns. The store also carries buttons and knitting supplies. Inquire about guided mill tours.

WEST RIVER VALLEY, ALONG VT 30

**Robert DuGrenier Glass Art Gallery** (802-365-4400; dugrenier.com), 1096

VT 30, Townshend. Open weekdays and most Saturdays 10–5. Robert DuGrenier's work can be seen in custom installations throughout the United States and Europe. The gallery features DuGrenier's glasswork, handblown on site, including colorful glasses, decanters, and small seashells; inquire about weekly glassblowing demonstrations.

**Elaine Beckwith Gallery** (802-874-7234; beckwithgallery.com), 3923 VT 30, Jamaica Village. Open daily (except Tues.) 10–5:30. This is a long-established, destination gallery with a strong contemporary collection, representing some 30 artists in a variety of styles and media, including painting, sculpture, and hand-pulled prints. Superb artist-printmaker Joel Beckwith is also featured. A must for art lovers.

*Note:* Also check **rockriverartists .com** (802-348-7865 or 802-348-7440) for information about a collective of artists who welcome visitors by appointment any time of year and host an open studio tour in mid-July.

BOOKSTORES ✪ **Everyone's Books** (802-254-8160; everyonesbks.com), 25 Elliot Street, Brattleboro. This is an earnest and interesting alternative bookstore, specializing in women's books; it also has a great selection of children's and multicultural titles.

**Brattleboro Books** (802-257-7777; brattleborobooks.com), 36 Elliot Street, Brattleboro. Open 10–6 daily except Sunday. An extensive selection of used and out-of-print books; over 60,000 titles fill a storefront and a basement. Browsing strongly encouraged.

**Mystery on Main Street** (802-258-2211; mysteryonmain.com), 119 Main Street, Brattleboro. Open daily 10–6 except Wednesday. The Brattleboro area is home to Archer Mayor, Vermont's most famous detective novelist, making the town a fitting location for its first mystery bookstore. Many special events.

**Old & New England Books** (802-365-7074; oldandnewenglandbooks.com),

47 West Street, Newfane. Open late May–October, Fri.–Mon. noon–5; also by appointment. Delightful browsing with an interesting stock of books old and new, cards, and posters.

SPECIAL SHOPS

IN BRATTLEBORO

**Sam's Outdoor Outfitters** (802-254-2933; samsoutfitters.com), 74 Main Street. Open daily, varying hours. The business that Sam Borofsky started in 1934 now fills two floors of two buildings, with a full stock of hunting, camping, and sports equipment. Skilled service in selecting the right fishing rod, tennis racket, or gun is a point of pride. Also a

DOWNTOWN BRATTLEBORO LYNN BARRETT

## LOCAL MARKETS

The Brattleboro Area Farmers' Market (802-254-8885; brattleboroarea farmersmarket.com) is southern Vermont's premier farmers' market, with over 50 vendors. Saturday is the big day just west of town by the Creamery Bridge (May–October). A live band and crafts, as well as produce vendors, are usually on hand. On Wednesday, there is a Downtown Market (late May–September), Tuesday, 4–9 is downtown. There's also a winter market, on Saturday at the River Garden, Main Street.

source of name brand sports and regular clothing, fishing and hunting licenses, and free popcorn.

**Delectable Mountain** (802-257-4456; delectablemountain.com), 125 Main Street. Fine-fabric lovers make pilgrimages to Jan Norris's store, widely known for its selection of fine silks, all-natural imported laces, velvets, cottons, and upholstery jacquards. It also offers a wide selection of unusual buttons.

**Borter's Jewelry Studio** (802-254-3452; bortersjewelry.com), 22 High Street. Tues.–Fri. noon–5:30, Sat. noon–4, and by appointment. Gemstones; silver and gold jewelry handcrafted into stunning settings on the premises.

**Altiplano** (802-257-1562; altiplano.com), 42 Elliot Street. Open daily. This standout shop features women's contemporary clothing and other crafted products, some with the store's own widely distributed label, designed in-house but made in Guatemala.

**Penelope Wurr** (802-246-3015; penelopewurr.com), 167 Main Street. Open Thurs.–Sun. noon–5. A two-story shop filled with furnishings, crafted items, gifts, and cards—a great place to browse.

**Beadniks** (802-257-5114; Beadniksvt .com), 115 Main Street. Beads, baubles, and whimsical wonders. A must-stop if only for the eye candy of the zillions of brightly colored beads that owner

Brian Robertshaw travels the world to find. He has been collecting and researching as well as selling beads for more than 40 years, and his base-ment-level Museum of Beads and Cultural Artifacts, open Fri.–Sat. noon–4, displays beads from as long ago as 10,000 B.C.E.

**Renaissance Fine Jewelry** (802-251-0600; vermontjewel.com), 151 Main Street. A handsome shop in a former bank, showcasing quality designer and estate jewelry.

**Brattleboro Food Co-op** (802-257-0236; brattleborofoodcoop.coop), 2 Main Street, Brookside Plaza. Open Mon.–Sat. 8 a.m.–9 p.m., Sun. 9–9; deli and freshly baked products. Recently rebuilt, better than ever. The cheese counter showcases Vermont cheeses; local produce, grains, and wines; and a café.

**Grafton Village Cheese** (802-254-2221; graftonvillagecheese.com), 400 Linden Street, (VT 30), Brattleboro. Open Mon.–Sat. 10–6, Sun. 10–5. This large red, barn-like cheese factory adjoins the Retreat Farm (see *For Families*). The shop features its own nationally distributed handcrafted cheeses along with Vermont microbrews, specialty foods, and gifts. Visitors can watch cheesemaking and receive samples.

**Brattleboro Outlet Center** (802-254-4594), 580 Canal Street, Exit 1 off I-91. Open daily. This former factory building that once produced handbags is now an old-fashioned factory outlet center with varied stores worth checking out, including Carter's Children's Wear and locally based Northeast Mountain Footwear.

### IN PUTNEY

**Basketville** (802-387-5509; basketville .com), 8 Bellows Falls Road, VT 5. Open daily 9–6. Founded by Frank Wilson, an enterprising Yankee trader in the real sense, this is a family-run business. The vast store features woodenware, wicker

# STROLLING OF THE HEIFERS

Local educational consultant Orly Munzing had recently witnessed the Running of the Bulls in Pamplona when she conceived of the idea of a slower, friendlier version—a parade of heifers and calves led by their owners up Brattleboro's Main Street—as a way of honoring and supporting local farmers. That first parade in 2002 has since expanded into a full weekend (the first in June) of farm-geared events. Sunday begins with a Farmers Breakfast and features **Tour de Heifer** cycling tours (not races) geared to all abilities, kids included, along with farm tours. Nonprofit Strolling of the Heifers is based at the River Garden, downtown Brattleboro's weatherproofed public space (see *Guidance*), with a program of weekday brown-bag presentations and performances. See strollingoftheheifers.com.

furniture (filling the entire upstairs), wooden toys, and exquisite artificial flowers as well as traditional baskets and myriad other things, large and small. *Note:* Check out the Columbus Day weekend Basketville Seconds Sale. This is also the venue for Putney Mountain Winery tastings.

FARMS TO VISIT One of the state's concentrations of farms and orchards is here in the Lower Connecticut River Valley, some offering "pick your own," others welcoming visitors to their farm stands, sugaring houses, or barns. Call before coming.

**Robb Family Farm** (802-257-0163; robbfamilyfarm.com), 822 Ames Hill Road, Brattleboro. This farm has been in the same family since 1907, and their shop features their maple syrup and candy, gift baskets,and farm-raised beef.

**Olallie Daylily Gardens** (802-348-6614; daylilygarden.com), 129 Augur Hole Road, South Newfane. Open late June–September. Grass paths crisscross the bed of blooms in many colors; ask about "evening strolls" during peak season, July-August.

**Dutton Berry Farm Stand** (802-365-4168; duttonberryfarm.com), farm stands at 407 VT 30, Newfane, and 308 VT 9, West Brattleboro (also VT 11 and 30, Manchester). Open daily, 9–7 year-round. This is a local institution; these farm stands are year-round shops with delis and freshly baked goods but also fruit and veggies from Paul and Wendy

Dutton's local orchards and farms; the stand is also a source of Christmas trees, PYO, and more.

♂ **Dwight Miller Orchards** (802-254-9111; dwightmillerorchards.com), 511 Miller Road, East Dummerston. Open seasonally, 9–5. One of Vermont's oldest family farms. A retail stand with the farm's own organic fruit and vegetables, preserves, and syrup; seasonal PYO.

**The Scott Farm** (802-254-6868; scottfarmvermont.com), 707 Kipling Road, Dummerston. Open seasonally. This historic 571-acre farm, now owned by The Landmark Trust USA (see the Rudyard Kipling sidebar for lodging on the property), includes an extensive orchard, producing 125 varieties of apples as well as peaches, plums, pears, and other fruit, for sale along with the farm's heirloom apple cider.

🌺 **Walker Farm** (802-254-2051; walkerfarm.com), 1190 Putney Road (US 5), Dummerston. A destination farm and garden center (open mid-April–Thanksgiving, 10–6) that's been in the Mannix family since 1770. Hard-to-find annuals and perennials are the specialty, but you can choose from 125 kinds of tomatoes as well as a peerless selection of flowers (started from seed), plus hundreds of other plants nurtured in the farm's greenhouses. The farm stand is open June–Thanksgiving.

♂ **Green Mountain Orchards** (802-387-5851; greenmtorchards.com), 130 West Hill Road, Putney. Open daily in-season. Pick-your-own apples and

PUTNEY CRAFT TOUR, COURTESY OF KEN PICK   LYNN BARRETT

blueberries; freshly baked pies and cider doughnuts, apple cider.

**Harlow's Sugar House** (802-387-5852), 563 Bellows Falls Road (US 5), Putney. Open seasonally. Watch maple production in-season; the store sells its own syrup, honey, and apples; PYO apples and blueberries.

## ✳ Special Events

*Note:* See **Brattleboro Area Farmers' Market** under Farms.

✿ **Gallery Walk** (gallerywalk.org) in Brattleboro, the first Friday of every month, is one of New England's oldest and most extensive art walks, regularly featuring 30 or more venues.

*February:* **Brattleboro Winter Carnival** (brattleborowintercarnival.org), a full week of celebrations, climaxed by the Washington's birthday cross-country ski race. The annual **Harris Hill Jumping Competition** (harrishillskijump

.org) may or may not coincide with the carnival.

*July 4:* A big parade winds through Brattleboro at 10 a.m.; games, exhibits, refreshments in Living Memorial Park; fireworks at 9 p.m.

*Mid-July:* **Rock River Artists Open Studio Tour** (rockriverartists.com)— open studios sponsored by artists in Williamsville and South Newfane. **Southern Vermont Dance Festival** (southernvermontdancefestival.com) is a weekend of performances and classes in and around Brattleboro.

*August:* **Free concert** on the Newfane common every Wednesday. **Grace Cottage Hospital Fair Day**—held the first Saturday, with exhibits, booths, games, and rides on the green in Townshend.

*September:* Labor Day weekend in Guilford is observed both with the old-style **Guilford Fair** (guilfordfair.org) and also with the annual two-day music festival in **Guilford's Organ Barn** (fomag.org). Concerts are free.

*Late September:* **Annual Tour de Grace**—a 21-mile expert ride from Stratton Mountain to Grace Cottage Hospital, Townshend. **Brattleboro–West Arts Studio Tour** (brattleboro-west-arts.com).

*October:* The **Newfane Heritage Festival** (newfaneheritagefestival.org), Columbus Day weekend—crafts, dancing, and raffle, sponsored by the Newfane Congregational church.

*Late October:* **Brattleboro Film Festival** (brattleborofilmfestival.org), a 10-day extravaganza based at Latchis Theater.

*November, Thanksgiving weekend:* The **Putney Craft Tour** (putneycrafts .com), held for 40 years on the three days after Thanksgiving, is an annual destination for New England families. Given the number of outstanding craftspeople and artists with homes/studios salted along the area's scenic back roads, it's a refreshing antithesis to online shopping as visitors connect with glassblowers, weavers, potters, jewelry-makers, artists, cheesemakers, and more.

*Early December:* **Christmas Bazaar** on the common, Newfane. **Cotton Mill Open Studio & Holiday Sale** (thecottonmill .org), featuring some 50 resident artists, also in Brattleboro.

*December 31:* **Last Night Brattleboro**. Fun family day and night with fireworks at the Retreat Meadows at about 9 p.m.

# THE MOUNT SNOW VALLEY

n 1954, lifts, trails, and lodges transformed Reuben Snow's West Dover farm into Mount Snow, and, in the decades since, both the resort and its steep-sided valley have been evolving as a year-round destination and a logical hub for exploring much of southern Vermont.

In the 1960s, development here was intense enough to trigger Vermont's Act 250 to help regulate growth. The Valley has long since mellowed. Driving the six miles of VT 100 south from West Dover to Wilmington, what you notice are spreading fields of multigenerational farms and the north branch of the Deerfield River. An unusual number of condominiums, as well as inns and restaurants, are salted along back roads, along with resort facilities that include two golf courses, a small airport, and a 14-mile recreational trail meandering south from Mount Snow to VT 9.

Flatlanders began summering in this area in the 1890s, arriving via the Hoosac Tunnel and Wilmington Railroad, staying in now-vanished hotels on Lake Raponda and Sadawga Lake and transforming farms into second homes. In 1902, the shingle-style hotel that's now the Crafts Inn opened in Wilmington Center and soon became part of New England's "Ideal Tour," which was widely promoted for "pleasure driving," promising pioneering auto travelers "A First Class Hotel at the End of Each Day's Run." Sited midway along VT 9 between Brattleboro and Bennington, at the junction of VT 100 north, and at the confluence of the Deerfield River and its north branch, the village of Wilmington Center still anchors the area (also known as the Deerfield Valley). During Hurricane Irene in 2011, many independently owned shops and restaurants here were flooded, but the village has recouped its losses and then some. A trail from the parking area now follows the Deerfield to Lake Whitingham.

These surrounding hills were once lumbered extensively, and Mountain Mills, a former logging village, lies at the bottom of this eight-mile-long lake, which is also known as Harriman Reservoir and was created in the 1920s by the regional power company. With hiking trails as well as multiple access points along its pristine shores, this is a popular spot for fishing, boating, and swimming. Nearby nine mile-long Somerset Reservoir is quieter, given its more remote access.

With its 3,600-foot-high summit, 1,700-foot vertical drop, and 37 miles of trails, Mount Snow has a loyal following and a reputation for being particularly friendly to families and to snowboarders; its Carinthia Park, once an independent ski area, is now a freestylers' domain, with eight terrain parks and a superpipe with 18-foot-high walls. In summer, the resort offers programs geared to golf, families, and mountain biking, and the summit with its restaurant and magnificent view can be accessed with a bubble-enclosed chairlift.

The abundance of reasonably priced condominium units appeals to families, and lodging runs the gamut, from state parks and singles'-geared lodges to high-end inns. In summer, and even in fall, most of the area's lodging prices are at "off-season" rates.

Beyond this valley corridor, forested hills and mountains rise on all sides, and the towns of Jacksonville and Whitingham to the south have long been backroaded.

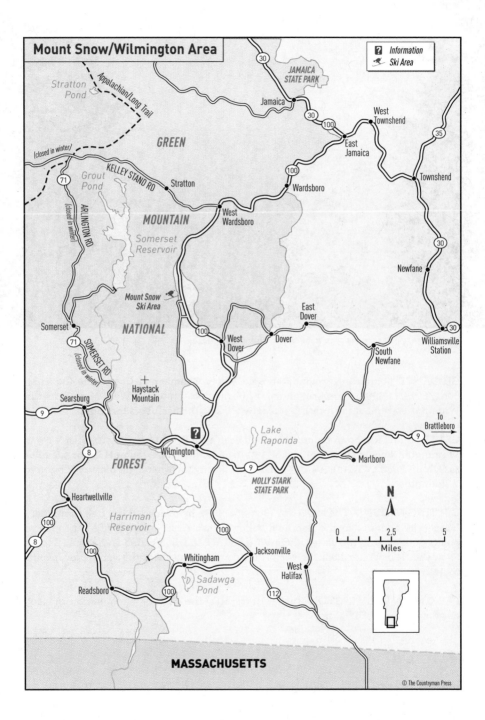

Mount Snow/Wilmington Area

? Information
🎿 Ski Area

MASSACHUSETTS

© The Countryman Press

VIEW OF SOMERSET RESERVOIR FROM MOUNT SNOW SUMMIT CHRISTINA TREE

GUIDANCE **Southern Vermont Deerfield Valley Chamber of Commerce** (802-464-8092; 877-887-6884; visitvermont.com) Information Center, 21 West Main Street in Wilmington (right at the light). Open daily. Pick up the useful visitors guide.

GETTING THERE From points south and east, take I-91 to Brattleboro, then VT 9 to Wilmington. **Scenic shortcut**: turn off I-91 in Greenfield, MA; follow US 2 for 3.6 miles to Colrain Road (VT 112); it's 17.3 miles to Jacksonville, where you pick up VT 100 to Wilmington.

GETTING AROUND **The MOO-ver** (802-464-8487; moover.com) is a free community bus service operated by the Deerfield Valley Transit Association (DVTA). It connects points of interest in the valley along VT 9 and VT 100 year-round and offers a Mount Snow shuttle in winter. Look for its Holstein cow logo and check the website for specific routes.

PARKING IN WILMINGTON Turn west (right) at the VT 100/VT 9 junction and look on your left for the "P" sign.

## ✳ To Do

BIKING  See *Mount Snow* sidebar; Zoar Outdoor (see *Boating*) also rents dirt bikes.

BOATING  Both **Lake Whitingham** (Harriman Reservoir) and **Somerset Reservoir** are spectacular boating lakes. Whitingham, easily accessible from VT 9 west of

Wilmington Center, is popular with power boaters but there is room for everyone. More remote **Somerset Reservoir** is geared toward sailboats, paddlers, and fishermen; access from VT 9 is five miles west of Wilmington Center, 10 miles up a woods road. Smaller bodies of water such as Grout Pond, Lake Raponda, and Sadawga are also excellent for canoeing and kayaking.

**Zoar Adventure Center** (802-464-2450; zoaroutdoor.com), 36 Main Street, Wilmington, rents kayaks and stand-up paddleboards and offers guided kayaking. Since 1989 ZAC has offered whitewater rafting on the Deerfield River, timed for regular dam releases south of the state line in Massachusetts.

**High Country Marine** (802-476-2108; highcountrymarine.com), 403 VT 9 West, two miles west of Wilmington Center on VT 9 at the boat launch for Lake Harriman, rents a variety of pontoon boats and Waverunners.

CHAIRLIFT  See *Mount Snow* sidebar.

FISHING  The **Deerfield River** is known for rainbow and brook trout (the season runs from the second Saturday in April through October). The remote Harriman Bypass Reach, a 4.5-mile stretch of the river between the dam in Whitingham and Readsboro, is a good bet. **Somerset Reservoir**, 6.5 miles west of Wilmington then 10 miles north on Somerset Road, offers bass, trout, and pike. There is a boat launch at the foot of the 9-mile-long lake. Smaller **Sadawga Pond** in Whitingham and **Lake Raponda** in Wilmington are also good for bass, trout, perch, salmon, pickerel, northern pike, and smelt. **Harriman Reservoir (Lake Whitingham)** is stocked with trout, bass, perch, and salmon; a boat launch is located off Fairview Avenue.

FOR FAMILIES **Southern Vermont Natural History Museum** (802-464-0048; vermontmuseum.org), 7599 VT 9. Open daily. Admission charged. Sited at the most dramatic pullout along VT 9, formerly the summit of Hogback Mountain ski area, the view here can stretch for 100 miles. Bigger than it looks from the outside, the museum began with the extensive collection of taxidermist Luman R. Nelson, which includes more than 500 stuffed New England birds and mammals in 80 dioramas. It has expanded to include live birds of prey, fish, and reptiles. The museum continues to evolve with local and environmentally focused exhibits. More than 600 acres of adjacent preservation land offer extensive hiking.

**Adams Farm** (802-464-3762; adamsfamilyfarm.com), 15 Higley Hill Road, off VT 100, Wilmington. A sixth-generation, visitor-friendly farm with livestock, a farm store featuring its own meat, a petting farm, trail rides, and sleigh and wagon rides. Inquire about special events.

GOLF  **Mount Snow Golf Club** See *Mount Snow* sidebar.

HIKING/WALKING  The *Wilmington Trail Map* depicting parking and an ever-evolving trail network. We especially recommend the two-mile **Hoot, Toot & Whistle Trail** from the village, over the Reardon pedestrian bridge and along the Deerfield River to a swim spot on Lake Whitingham. Another local favorite is the 5-mile, round-trip hike through the woods up to a great view from the summit of Haystack Mountain. Pick up or download a *Valley Trail* map, detailing the 14-mile recreational trail with multiple linked sections between Mount Snow and VT 9. These and many more local hiking and regional hikes are at visitvermont.com (see *Guidance*). The **Hogback Mountain Overlook** on VT 9 is the starting point for a hike up the old ski area access road to the Mount Olga fire tower. Trails along the shore of Lake **Whitingham** are also popular.

VIEW OF THE DEERFIELD RIVER, WILMINGTON CHRISTINA TREE

HORSEBACK RIDING **Flames Stables** (802-464-8329), 657 Boyd Hill Road, off VT 100 South, Wilmington. Reasonably priced Western saddle trail guided rides on woods trails offered year-round, pony rides for children.

**Adams Farm** (802-464-3762; adamsfamilyfarm.com), 15 Higley Hill Road, off VT 100, Wilmington. (See *For Families*) offers guided trail rides and sleigh rides on the property. Inquire about special events.

SWIMMING **Lake Whitingham** offers a number of semi-sandy designated swim spots with picnic tables and porta potties. **Mountain Mills Beach** is 1 mile south through the lights at Wilmington Center on Castle Hill Road, right on Fairview Avenue to a parking area near a sandy spot (and a boat launch) at the end. **Ward's Cove Beach** is off VT 100 south of Wilmington; turn right on Boyd Hill Road (at Flames Stables) and continue straight when the road curves. Good for swimming and kayak launching. Inquire locally about less-publicized places. Medburyville: From VT 9, 2.7 miles west of Wilmington Center, left on Woods Road over the river and left to the end of the road. Rocky, but good swimming, picnicking, and kayak launch.

TENNIS Municipal courts at **Baker Field** off School Street in Wilmington are open to the public.

## ❄ Winter Sports

See *Mount Snow* sidebar for *Downhill Skiing/Snowboarding/Snowmobiling*

CROSS-COUNTRY SKIING **Timber Creek Cross-Country Ski Area** (802-464-0999; timbercreekxc.com), West Dover. Just across VT 100 from the entrance to Mount Snow, a high-elevation, 14-km wooded system of mostly easy and intermediate trails that hold their snow cover, including access to backwoods trails and an additional 6 km of snowshoe trails. Ski and snowshoe rentals, instruction available. Full- and half-day trail fees and special packages.

**Prospect Mountain Nordic Ski Center** (802-442-2575; prospectmountain.com), 204 Prospect Access (VT 9), Woodford. A dozen miles west of Wilmington, this former downhill ski area features more than 30 km of high-elevation, groomed trails with access to backcountry trails; special trails for snowshoeing; and a comfortable base lodge with a fireplace, rentals, and good food.

SCENIC DRIVES **Molly Stark Scenic Byway** (mollystarkbyway.org). Between Wilmington and Brattleboro, the 18 miles of this VT 9 route are a twisty and heavily trafficked but rewarding ride. Five miles bring you to **Hogback Mountain**, a major overlook, said to offer a 100-mile, south-facing view. This is also the site of the **Southern Vermont Natural History Museum** (see *For Families*). Continue another 5 miles to the turnoff to **Marlboro Village**, home of Marlboro College, the mid-July until mid-August venue for the **Marlboro Music Festival** (marlboromusic.org).

**Jacksonville and Whitingham.** From VT 9 east of Wilmington Center, follow VT 100 south 6 miles, past **Flames Stables** (see *Horseback Riding*) and the turnoff for Ward's Cove, to the village of Jacksonville. At the junction of VT 100 and VT 112, check out **Spoonwood Cabin Creamery** (*Selective Shopping*) just beyond the general store, then turn and follow VT 112 a mile to the **Stone Soldier Pottery** and on to **Honora Winery & Vineyard** (see *Wineries*). Follow VT 112 another 1.5 miles south and turn onto the road marked for the **Brigham Young Monument**, following it into Whitingham. At the top of Town Hill, a monument commemorates the Mormon prophet who led his people into Utah and is hailed as the founder of Salt Lake City. He was born on a hill farm here, the son of a poor basket maker. The view takes in surrounding hills; there are picnic benches, grills, a playground, and a parking area. Ask locally for directions to Stimpson Hill where you'll find a small marker that proclaims this to be the homestead site of Brigham Young: BORN ON THIS SPOT 1801 . . . A MAN OF MUCH COURAGE AND SUPERB EQUIPMENT. (Young fathered 56 children by 17 of his 52 wives.) Before leaving the village, note the 25-acre "floating island" in the middle of Sadawga Pond. Whitingham was once a busy resort, thanks to a mineral spring and its accessibility via the Hoosac Tunnel and Wilmington Railroad. The old railroad bed is now a **12-mile walking trail** along this remote shore of Lake Whitingham.

**Valley View Road** from VT 100 in the middle of the village of West Dover climbs steeply, becoming Cooper Hill Road for a few miles to take in the panorama of mountains from the pullout at the crest, across the grounds of the Cooper Hill Inn. Continue to the original village of Dover Common—the school, library, and town hall. Loop back down to VT 100 via Dover Hill Road or follow Augur Hole Road south to VT 9.

**Handle Road** runs south from Mount Snow, paralleling VT 100, turning into Cold Brook Road when it crosses the Wilmington line. The old farmhouses along this high, wooded road were bought up by city people to form a summer colony in the late 1880s. It's still a beautiful road, retaining some of the old houses and views.

**Arlington–Kelley Stand Road** heads west from West Wardsboro through the tiny village of Stratton. At 6.3 miles the Grout Pond turnoff is clearly marked and leads 1.3 miles to the pond. Hiking trails loop around the pond, through the woods, and on to **Somerset Reservoir**. Beyond this turnoff is the monument to Daniel Webster, who spoke here to 1,600 people at an 1840 Whig rally.

Also see the **West River Valley** chapter for the scenic shortcut from West Dummerston (VT 30) to West Dover, through Williamsville and South Newfane.

## A BIG, FAMILY-FRIENDLY MOUNTAIN

**M**ount Snow (information 802-464-3333; snow report 802-464-2151; reservations 800-245-SNOW; mountsnow.com), 45 Cross Town Road, West Dover.

**WINTER SKIING AND SNOWBOARDING** Peak Resorts, the mountain's owner, has invested heavily in snowmaking and new chairlift technology, which has enhanced this 600-acre area, one of the largest mountain resorts in the Northeast. Lifts and trails connect four distinct areas: the Main Face, the expert North Face, the intermediate Sunbrook, and Carinthia, which is home to eight different terrain parks and a half-pipe. Base area facilities include three lodges, rental/repair shops, retail stores, and restaurants, plus the Ski and Snowboard School at the Discovery Center, a dedicated instruction area with a learning slope and special lifts where beginners can go at their own pace. See the chapter introduction for the resort's history. Mount Snow's Carinthia Park

KIDS' SKI CLASS AT MOUNT SNOW   MOUNT SNOW RESORT

(once an independently owned ski area) is now a 100-acre freestylers' domain with eight terrain parks. This is one big mountain with plenty of skiing challenges on its 86 trails and 100+ acres of hand-cleared "tree terrain."

*Lifts:* 20 chairlifts—1 high-speed, 6-passenger bubble lift, 3 high-speed and 1 fixed quad, 6 triples, 4 doubles. There is 1 surface lift and 4 Magic Carpets.

*Ski/snowboard trails:* 86 including 14 percent "easier," 73 percent "more difficult," 13 percent "advanced," and one "double black diamond" trail. There are numerous hand-cleared tree skiing areas on all four mountain faces.

*Snowmaking:* 80 percent of the mountain.

*Facilities:* Three base lodges, a summit lodge, the Snow Barn (nightclub with entertainment, dancing), and a nature spa at the Grand Summit Resort Hotel.

*Ski and Snowboard School:* Over 400 instructors and dozens of clinics.

*For children:* Ski and Snowboard School: Burton Riglet Program (3- to 6-year-olds), Cub Camp (3-year-olds), Snow Camp (4- to 6-year-olds), and Mountain Camp and Mountain Riders (7- to 14-year-olds).

*Rates:* See mountsnow.com for lift ticket prices, which vary with the day. The earlier you book, the more you save.

**SNOWMOBILING** Snowmobile Vermont at Mount Snow (802-464-2108). Backcountry tours in the Green Mountain National Forest daily during ski season; two-passenger machines can hold up to 350 pounds.

## SUMMER/FALL

**BIKING Mountain Biking at Mount Snow** (802-464-6640; mountsnow.com) offers mountain biking clinics, tours, rentals, and maps for its 16 miles of trails. The Canyon Express lift services a portion daily July–mid-October, then weekends until Columbus Day weekend. Lift-serviced trails are designed for everyone from beginners to experienced mountain bikers. Inquire about lodging/biking packages.

**CHAIRLIFT** (800-464-4040; mountsnow.com). Weekends in summer and daily in foliage season (weather permitting, so you might want to check ahead). A bird's-eye view of the valley and surrounding hills is offered via the six-passenger, bubble-enclosed Bluebird Express chairlift, operating from Mount Snow's main base lodge to the summit on weekends in summer and daily in peak foliage season. When the chair is operating, so is the Bullwheel at the summit, offering sandwiches, craft beers, a deck, and sweeping views across the hills to the east and north over Somerset Reservoir. You can ride or hike back down.

**Mount Snow Day Camps** (802-464-3333; mountsnow.com), Mount Snow. Mini Camp (ages 6 weeks–12 months), Kids Camp (ages 5–8), and Sports Camp (ages 9–12) run during summer, Mon.–Fri. 9–4. Activities include swimming, chairlift rides, arts and crafts, nature hikes, and field trips.

**Mount Snow Golf Club** (802-464-4254; mountsnow.com), Country Club Road, West Dover. Billing itself as "The Original Golf School," this program has been evolving since 1978. Weekend and two- to five-day midweek golf school packages are offered May–September; the 18-hole, Cornish-designed championship golf course is also open on a daily basis.

**LODGING The Grand Summit Resort Hotel at Mount Snow** (802-464-8501). At the base of the ski lifts, this sprawling, 198-room, ski-in, ski-out condo hotel and conference center features one- to three-bedroom suites (many with kitchen) as well as the usual hotel rooms. Amenities include a heated outdoor pool and hot tubs, an arcade, a spa and fitness center, and, of course, ski lifts. In summer there are golf and mountain biking programs. **Harriman's Restaurant** serves breakfast and dinner, and the **Grand Country Deli & Convenience Store** has a deli menu for dine-in or take-out. Rooms range from a basic two-person studio to a two-bedroom deluxe suite. A three-bed-

**MOUNTAIN BIKER** MOUNT SNOW RESORT

room, three-bath penthouse on the top floor sleeps 12. The standard rooms and one-bedroom suites (bedroom, bath, living room, and galley kitchen) run $–$$$, depending on the season.

Farther down by a small lake is older and modest **Snow Lake Lodge**, popular with college students and young families. The vast majority of the area's 2,100 "on-mountain" beds are rentals and multibedroom condos spread out around the foot of the mountain. **Mount Snow Central Reservations** (800-451-4211) offers lodges, inns, and condos that are slope-side or at the base of the mountain; from studios to three-bedroom units.

## ✻ Green Space

🏕 **Molly Stark State Park** (802-464-5460; vtstateparks.com), 705 VT 9, east of Wilmington Village. Open Memorial Day–Columbus Day. This 158-acre preserve features a hiking trail to the Mount Olga fire tower, at 2,415 feet, from which there is a panoramic view. The 34 campsites include 11 lean-tos.

**Lake Raponda**, Wilmington. Swimming is restricted to residents, but there is a public boat launch, good for fishing and paddleboats.

## ✻ Lodging

### INNS AND BED & BREAKFASTS

### IN WILMINGTON/WEST DOVER

✪ **Deerhill Inn** (802-464-3100; deerhill inn.com), 14 Valley View Road, West Dover. Ariane Burgess and Scott Kocher maintain this delightful inn, a nineteenth-century farmhouse with an added lodge wing known both for luxurious accommodations and fine dining. Most of the 13 rooms offer balconies, and they include suites, jetted tubs, and fireplaces. One sitting room adjoins a small bar and two spacious dining rooms, their walls decorated with the work of local artists; upstairs is another lounge for guests, plus a library nook. In summer, flowers abound inside and out, and around the patio of the swimming pool. Dinner and spa treatments can be arranged. Rates include a very full breakfast; $–$$$.

✐ ✪ **Wilmington Inn** (802-464-3768; thewilmingtoninn.com), 41 West Main Street, Wilmington. A big, gracious 1894 house set back above VT 9 on the edge of the village, within walking distance of shops and restaurants and just across the road from the riverside trail to Lake Whitingham. Innkeepers Megan and Charlie Foster have brought this 10-room B&B to a new level, replacing a former public dining room with a spacious living room. Ten guest rooms include two suites with fireplaces, and there is a comfortable "Great Room" as well

as a lounge. From-scratch breakfasts are served overlooking the garden and included in the rates ($–$$) Children welcome by prior arrangement.

✪ ✐ ✐ **Cooper Hill Inn** (802-348-6333; cooperhillinn.com), 117 Cooper Hill Road, East Dorset. This much-expanded farmhouse is 3.5 miles from the middle of West Dover but high on a hilltop with panoramic views. Innkeepers Lee and Charles Wheeler offer 10 bright, tastefully decorated guest rooms, all with private bath, divided between two wings, one family-geared and the other designed for romantic getaways. Dating in part from 1797, the inn can sleep 24 and is frequently rented in its entirety for retreats ranging in purpose from yoga to storytelling. Common space includes a spacious living room (with fireplace), a dining room, a game room, and a deck. Extensive grounds include formal flower gardens and a landscaped hollow for weddings. You can watch the sun rise on one side of the house and see it set on the other. $$ per room includes breakfast.

**Nutmeg Inn** (802-380-6101; thenutmegvermont.com), 153 West Main Street, Wilmington. Just west of Wilmington Center, this expanded farmhouse offers ten guest rooms and four suites, all with central air-conditioning. Common space includes a living room, a library, a bar, and breakfast rooms. The resident food truck is open for ribs, chicken, and similar take-home meals on Fri.-Sun., from 4 p.m. Rates ($–$$) include a full breakfast.

**West Dover Inn** (802-464-5207; westdoverinn.com), 108 VT 100, West Dover. Built in 1846 as the village inn and now on the National Register of Historic Places, Phil and Kathy Gilpin offer modern amenities and country-style appointments in each of the 11 guest rooms, some fireplace suites with jetted tubs. The homey common room has a fireplace, as well as the popular **1846 Tavern & Restaurant**. Rates include breakfast. Some minimum stays are required during holidays. Children welcome (pets not). $–$$$$.

  &#9854; &#9960; **Layla's Riverside Lodge** (802-464-7400; laylasriversidelodge.com), 145 VT 100, West Dover. This is a great place to stay if you are traveling with your dog. Grounds include an in-ground pool, a gazebo, flower gardens, quiet sitting areas along the Deerfield River, outdoor dining, a dog kennel, and access to the Valley Trail. The two-story inn has 17 guest rooms, from standard hotel rooms to luxury suites, each individually furnished. Dinner is served (see *Dining Out*). The $$–$$$ rates include breakfast.

  &#9854; **Shearer Hill Farm** (802-464-3253; shearerhillfarm.com), 297 Shearer Hill Road off VT 9, 2 miles southeast of Wilmington. This is a small working farm, just off the beaten path. Bill and Patti Pusey offer guests a pleasant living room and six guest rooms with private bath in their restored 200-year-old farmhouse and carriage house. They also raise cows and make maple syrup. The full breakfast features baked apples. $.

**Brass Bed B&B** (802-464-5523; brassbedbb.com), 30 Not-A-Road, Wilmington. Laraine and Skip Morrow's house is set among shade gardens, trails, and sculptures. The two third-floor guest rooms share a bathroom and sitting room, with its small fridge, microwave, toaster, and TV. The second room is only rented along with the first. Breakfast is brought up to your room. Snowshoes are available in winter. Both hosts are talented artists and musicians: Check out Skip's on-site **The Art of Humor** gallery.

Rates (with breakfast) are $ for the room; $$ if a suite. Children over 12 welcome.

**Candlelight Inn Bed & Breakfast** (802-368-2004; candlelightbandb.com), 3358 VT 100, Jacksonville. Mark and Pam Peterson welcome guests to their 1850s farmhouse on a quiet stretch of VT 100, six miles south of Wilmington. There are three rooms, two of which share a bath and are rented as a suite; $–$$ includes a full breakfast. The house sleeps ten and is frequently rented as a whole.

MOTELS &#9962; &#9960; **Austrian Haus Lodge** (802-464-3911; austrianhaus.com), 6 Abroad Road, West Dover, off VT 100. This attractive lodge is geared mostly to families; amenities include an indoor heated pool, a sauna, a game room, a BYOB gathering lounge with a fireplace, and a common space for kids. High-season rates of $–$$ include a continental breakfast.

  &#9962; &#9960; &#9960; **Viking Motel** (802-464-5608; vikingmotel.net), 88 East Main Street (VT 9), Wilmington. Owned by the Spiesicke family since 1978, this is the best value in Wilmington. It's also within walking distance of village shops and restaurants. Eleven nicely decorated units have two double beds each, four rooms have a queen-size bed, and all have cable TV, microwave, a coffeemaker, a fridge, AC, direct-dial phones, and full baths. $.

CONDOS/RENTALS **Mountain Resort Rentals** (802-464-1445; mountainresortrentals.com). Some 200 rentals, condos and houses.

CAMPGROUND See **Molly Stark State Park** in *Green Space*.

## &#10052; Where to Eat

DINING OUT **Folly** (802-464-1333; vtfolly.com) 33 West Main Street, Wilmington. Open for dinner Fri., Sat., Sun. 5:30–close. Reservations advised for this intimate, attractive fine-dining spot that styles itself "a modern neighborhood bistro." The a la carte menu changes weekly but might include a Spanish octopus starter and duck breast with French lentils and roasted garlic or cider-brined rabbit with polenta. Entrée prices: $$–$$$.

**Deerhill Inn** (802-464-3100; deerhillinn.com), 14 Valley View Road, West Dover. Open nightly 6–9. Reservations. The dining rooms are casually elegant, and Chef Ryan O'Connor gets high marks for locally sourced dishes like Cioppino (traditional Italian seafood stew), beef Bourguignon, and roasted Cavendish. Entrées $$–$$$.

**Cask & Kiln Kitchen** (802-464-2275; caskandkiln.com), 4 North Main Street, corner of VT 100 & 9, Wilmington. Open Thurs.–Sun. Dining room. Reservations suggested. This is a popular dining spot with a casually elegant ambiance and a seasonally inspired, locally sourced changing menu; the upstairs lounge (open Fri., Sat.) offers a full pub food menu and specialty cocktail menu. $$–$$$$.

**Two Tannery Road** (802-464-2707; twotannery.com), 2 Tannery Road, VT 100, West Dover. Open for dinner Tues.–Sun. Reservations suggested. Highly rated, creative, and flavorful food, as well as nightly specials! The building is said to date in part from the late 1700s, when it stood in Marlboro, MA. It has moved several times within this valley, serving for a while as a summer home for Theodore Roosevelt's son. The bar began service in the original Waldorf-Astoria (present site of the Empire State Building). $$–$$$.

& **The Roadhouse** (802-464-5017; wilmingtonroadhouse.com), 4 Old Ark Road, Wilmington. Dinner nightly and Sunday brunch. The name and exterior disguise the elegant atmosphere, generally fine food, and inviting bar. Crab-stuffed trout is a staple, along with traditional dishes such as the Roadhouse burger or filet mignon. Light bite menus. The bread is homemade. $–$$$.

((·)) **Anchor Seafood House & Grille** (802-464-2112; anchorseafood.com), 8 South Main Street, Wilmington. Daily lunch and dinner, Sunday brunch. Fresh seafood specialties include fresh Maine lobsters and steamers in spaces ranging from the dining room with fireplace to outside porches and a marble-topped bar with sports on the large flat screen. Daily specials. Dinner entrées $–$$$; a children's menu and a varied lunch menu are offered, including chowder and lobster rolls.

EATING OUT ✪ **Dot's Restaurant** (802-464-7284; dotsofvermont.com), 3 West Main Street, Wilmington. Open 5:30 a.m.–8 p.m., until 9 Fri. and Sat. The real center of Wilmington, called a "National Treasure" by *Gourmet* magazine. The long Formica counter, also seating in the side room, overlooks the river. Breakfast (5:30–3) includes great omelets, waffles, and corned beef hash. Then for lunch, there are house-made soups and blue-plate specials; dinner from 4 p.m. on offers plenty of choices. Try the Vermont maple berry chicken. Pies are a must. Beer and wine served. Also see **Betsey's Dots of Dover** (802-464-6476; betseysdotsofdovervt.com), 2 Mountain Park Plaza, VT 100, West Dover; the restaurant is Dot's offspring. (Open daily for breakfast and lunch, also dinner on winter weekends.)

✪ **Jezebel's Eatery** (802-464-7774; jezebelseatery.com), 28 West Main Street, Wilmington Village. Open for breakfast, lunch, and dinner, serving farm-fresh comfort food. Lunch specials include panini, soups, and salads, with freshly baked desserts a specialty; also inquire about occasional dinner seatings, which are well worth it. Full bar, craft beers. Patio seating, weather permitting.

**The Village Roost** (802-464-3344; villageroost.com), 20 West Main Street, Wilmington. Open 8–6. Pleasant atmosphere. The restaurant specializes in sandwiches, soups from organic and local ingredients, no GMO, gluten-free and vegan options, house-made bagels, and yogurt.

☙ ✿ **Wahoos Eatery** (802-464-0110; wahooseatery.com), 2 White's Road, Wilmington. Open daily for lunch and dinner May–September. Local entrepreneur Adam Grinold started Wahoos in 2000 and has turned this colorful roadside fast-food stop into a successful franchise. Food is fresh and made to order; the ability to use social media applications to order ahead makes the establishment extra "fast." Burgers, wraps, and ice cream, as well as daily specials.

## ✳ Entertainment

*Note:* Be sure to check out the **Marlboro Music Festival** (marlboromusic.org) under *Entertainment* in the Brattleboro chapter.

**MHC Dover Cinema (formerly Memorial Hall Center for the Arts)** (802-464-8411; memhall.org), 4 Mountain Park Plaza, VT 100, Dover. First-run films in high definition, also year-round live performances and community events.

## ✳ Selective Shopping

ANTIQUES **Wilmington Antique & Flea Market** (802-464-3345), 217 VT 9 East, Wilmington. Open May–October, Sat. and Sun. Bills itself as southern Vermont's largest outdoor flea market.

**Chapman's Antiques Barn** (802-464-8344; chapmansantiques.com), 38 New England Power Road, three miles west of Wilmington traffic light; sign at the bridge. Open Memorial Day–Columbus Day, Sat., Sun. Large barn filled with antiques, vintage collectibles, and handmade crafts. Chapman's Downtown Antiques, 7 West Main Street. Closed Tues. and Wed.

ART GALLERIES AND CRAFTS SHOPS ✪ **Quaigh Design Centre** (802-464-2780), 11 West Main Street, Wilmington. Open daily except Wed. May–October, noon–5; Thanksgiving–New Year's, Fri., Sat., Sun. A real gem in its own right, this is a long-established showcase for top Vermont crafts, pottery, and artwork; imported Scottish woolens and British handiwork are also specialties. Owner Lilias Hart has produced a Vermont tartan. There are also many woodcuts by Vermont artist Mary Azarian.

**The Vermont Bowl Company** (802-464-5296; vermontbowl.com), 111 West Main Street, VT 9, Wilmington. Hardwood bowls, clocks, mirrors, cutting boards, and furniture, on the western edge of the village; open daily 10–6.

**Gallery Wright** (802-464-9922; gallerywright.com), 103 West Main Street, Wilmington. Open Thurs.–Mon. 11–6. Landscapes, figures, and still lifes in oil, pastels, and prints.

**Stone Soldier Pottery** (802-368-7077), 64 Gates Road, Jacksonville Village. Call ahead. Connie Burnell is the second generation of her family to handcraft functional stoneware pottery in this classic pottery shed/showroom. Known for dinnerware, mugs, vases, and bakeware; most pieces are hand-decorated and all are hand-glazed, some with deep colors.

BOOKSTORES ✪ **Bartleby's Books** (802-464-5425; myvermontbookstore .com), 17 West Main Street, Wilmington. Open daily. An exceptional two-story independent bookstore featuring a well-chosen assortment of titles, featuring Vermont and local-interest books, cookbooks, and children's books. Owners Lisa Sullivan and Phil Taylor were in the store that Sunday morning in 2011 when the floodwaters from Hurricane Irene came surging in. Lisa now downplays the effort it took to build the store back up, instead talking about the sense of community the flood inspired. The store itself is a community gathering place, with self-serve coffee, frequent author events, and monthly openings for the changing art upstairs. Greeting cards, CDs, art supplies, stationery, games, and music.

**Austin's Antiquarian Books** (802-464-8438; austinsbooks.com), 123 West Main Street on VT 9, 0.5 mile west of downtown Wilmington. Open daily. Maps, prints, and 15,000 used, rare, and out-of-print books.

CHEESE **Spoonwood Cabin Creamery** (802-386-2802; spoonwoodcabin.com), 3090 VT 100, Jacksonville (just up from the general store). Open Sat.-Sun. noon–5. The Creamery's Wine & Cheese Shop features its own semi-soft, French-style cheese made with milk from Jersey cows at a nearby farm as well as some goat milk varities. The store also sells wines, brews, ciders, baguettes, and daily specials to-go.

FARMS ♂ **Adams Farm** (802-464-3762; adamsfamilyfarm.com), 15 Higley Hill Road, off VT 100, Wilmington. A sixth-generation, visitor-friendly farm with livestock, a farm store featuring its own meat, a petting farm, trail rides, and sleigh and wagon rides. Inquire about special events.

♂ **Boyd Family Farm** (802-464-5618; boydfamilyfarm.com), 125 East Dover Road, Wilmington. A fifth-generation working hillside farm, with pick-your-own flowers, raspberries, and blueberries June–September, then pumpkins, gourds, mums, kale, and cabbage in the fall. Homemade wreaths are always available, and the hillside gardens are a popular wedding venue.

**Wheeler Farm** (802-464-5225), 36 Woffenden Road (VT 100) north of Wilmington Village. A third-generation working farm with Jersey and Dutch belted cows, part of the cooperative that produces Cabot cheese. Maple syrup

MAIN STREET, WILMINGTON CHRISTINA TREE

is produced and sold, along with maple cream and sugar.

SPECIALTY SHOPS **1836 Country Store Village** (802-464-5102; 1836countrystore.com), 28 West Main Street, Wilmington, has an eclectic stock of decorative brasses, pierced-tin lanterns, toys and games, Vermont specialty foods, and the usual souvenirs. Note the amazing old floors.

**Norton House Quilting** (802-464-7213; nortonhousequilting.com), adjacent to the 1836 Country Store at 30 West Main Street, Wilmington. Oxen pulled the house here in the 1830s; the structure dates from 1760, making it Wilmington's oldest. A quilter's mecca with over 3,000 fabrics and every quilting accessory. Note the yawning brick hearth and the historical objects upstairs in the windowed closet.

**Pickwell's Barn** (802-464-3198; pickwellsbarn.com), 22B West Main Street, Wilmington, has pottery, clocks, prints, colorful glassware, Vermont wines, and specialty foods.

WINE AND SPIRITS **Honora Winery & Vineyard** (802-368-2226; honorawinery.com), 201 VT 112, Jacksonville. Open daily. Honora specializes in cold-weather varieties of both red and white wines. The tasting room and store are open Wed.–Sun. 11–6. A few miles down the road, visitors can tour the vineyards (best to call), a great site for weddings.

## ✳ Special Events

*July 4 weekend:* A very big celebration in these parts, with fireworks at

LISA SULLIVAN OF BARTLEBY'S BOOKS   CHRISTINA TREE

Mount Snow, parades, and other events (visitvermont.com). The most famous parade is in the tiny village of Wardsboro, 12 miles north of Mount Snow on VT 100.

*Late July–mid-August:* **Marlboro Music Festival** (marlboromusic.org).

*Early August:* Annual **Deerfield Valley Farmers' Day Fair** (dvfair.com) includes midway games, rides, horse pull, and demolition derby.

*Late September:* **Vermont Wine & Harvest Grand Tasting**, Mount Snow (thevermontfestival.com).

# BENNINGTON AND THE SOUTHSHIRE

**B**ennington is both the name of Vermont's southwesternmost town and of its southwesternmost county. It's the only county divided into North and South "shires," each with a venerable courthouse, one in Manchester and one in the town of Bennington, whose name honors Benning Wentworth, the avaricious governor of the New Hampshire Grants. The town, settled in 1749, was the first he designated west of the Connecticut River. In 1770 Bennington, the "Bennington Mob"—better known as the Green Mountain Boys—formed at Fay's Catamount Tavern, led by Seth Warner and Ethan Allen, vowing to expel the "Yorkers" who claimed the territory and, eventually, the British.

The August 16, 1777, Battle of Bennington—more precisely, the Battle for Bennington—prevented General Burgoyne's occupation of the area, helped by New Hampshire's General John Stark's hastily mobilized militiamen. They beat the tar out of the Hessians on high ground near the Walloomsac River, across the New York border. The story is memorialized in the Bennington Battle Monument, a 306-foot-high obelisk towering over Old Bennington and the surrounding countryside. Paintings and memorabilia in the Bennington Museum depict the era, and the human toll is evident in the memorials of soldiers at the Old Bennington Cemetery.

Major old north–south and east–west highways (Historic VT 7A and VT 9) cross at downtown Bennington's "Four Corners." However, limited-access highways (US 7 and VT 279) now circumvent the town. Along with outlying commercial strips and loop roads, these have backroaded the community's three distinctive centers: Old Bennington, North Bennington, and downtown. All are worth finding.

North Bennington is a gem of a former mill village with mansions hidden down leafy side roads. The most ornate of these, the Park-McCullough House, is open to visitors for tours or events; another estate forms the core of the Bennington College campus. The town also offers a choice of B&Bs, fine and casual dining, three of the county's five covered bridges, several waterfalls, extensive walking paths, and Lake Paran.

GUIDANCE  The **Bennington Area Chamber of Commerce** (802-447-3311; bennington .com), 100 Veterans Memorial Drive (US 7), maintains a cheerfully staffed, well-stocked information center, open year-round Mon.–Fri. 9–5; also on weekends mid-May–mid-October. Their free Bennington guide and their fold-out map/guides are both excellent.

**Downtown Bennington Visitor Center** (802-442-5758; betterbennington.com), 215 South Street. Open year-round Mon.–Sat. 9–5. Beautiful nineteenth-century stone building, originally a smithy, then a police station, now an information center.

Also check the **Shires of Vermont** regional tourism website: shiresofvermont.com.

GETTING THERE  *By car:* From New York City/New Jersey: Take I-87 to Exit 23, then I-787 to Exit 9E; continue to US 7 east to Bennington.

From Boston: I-90 to I-91 to Brattleboro and VT 9 (the Molly Stark Scenic Byway).

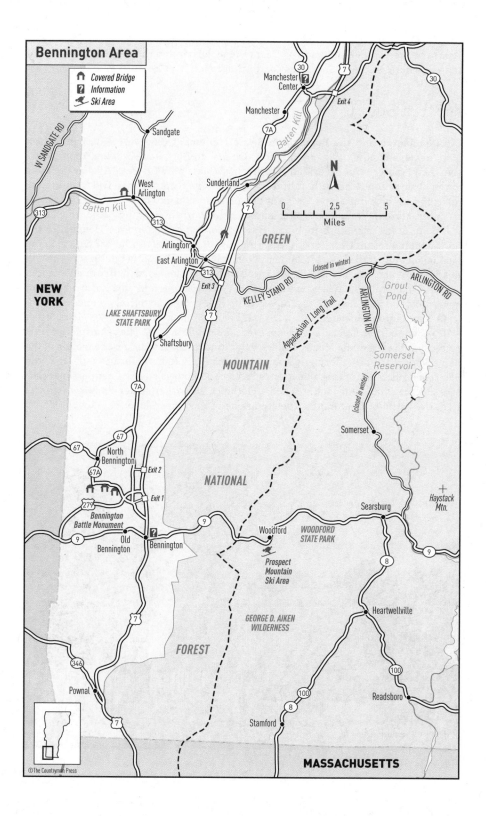

**GETTING AROUND** Going north can be confusing; watch the signs carefully to choose between the limited-access US 7 to Manchester and the more interesting but slower Historic VT 7A to Shaftsbury and Arlington.

## ✳ Must See

**Old Bennington and the Bennington Battle Monument** (802-447-0550; bennington battlemonument.com), Old Bennington. Open late-April–late-October, daily 9:30–5:30. Admission charged. Parking area at its base, just off VT 9 west. An elevator rises to the observation floor, with a three-state view. The focal point in Old Bennington, this 306-foot, blue limestone shaft was dedicated in 1891 and remains the tallest man-made structure in Vermont. It commemorates the Battle of Bennington, in which General John Stark repelled British and Hessian forces at Walloomsac Heights, to the northwest in present New York State, on August 16, 1777. Leave your car parked at the monument and stroll down Monument Avenue past the fine early houses and the Old Academy to the imposing **Old First Church** with its triple-decker belfry and Palladian windows, built in 1806. A slew of Revolutionary War heroes and villains, five Vermont governors, and poet Robert Frost repose in its well-preserved burial ground.

○ **Bennington Museum** (802-447-1571; benningtonmuseum.org), 75 Main Street (VT 9), Bennington. Open daily except Wed. and holidays 10–5. The centerpiece of this museum is the Grandma Moses Gallery, exhibiting the world's largest collection of the naive work of the artist formerly known as Anna Mary Robertson. Down the hall, the one-room schoolhouse that she attended as a child houses some of her personal possessions and a hands-on look at schools, clothing, and toys from her era. View artifacts from the Battle of Bennington, including one of the oldest American Revolutionary

BENNINGTON OLD FIRST CHURCH ERICA HOUSKEEPER

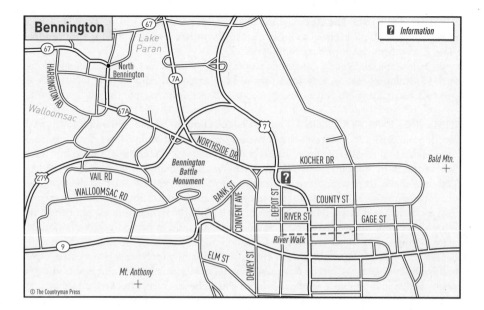

flags in existence, before visiting Old Bennington. Also in the collection are medical tools, hair jewelry, modern art, and an extraordinary 10-foot ceramic piece of Bennington Pottery created for the 1853 Crystal Palace Exhibition in London. Give yourself a few hours to absorb it all. Admission charged; students/seniors and under 18 are free.

# ✳ To Do

**CULTURAL ATTRACTIONS** **Southern Vermont College's Laumeister Art Center** (previously the Bennington Center for the Arts and Vermont Covered Bridge Museum; 802-442-7158; artcenter.svc.edu), 44 Gypsy Lane, Bennington. Open every day but Tues., 10–5. Admission charged, children under 12 free. These adjoining museums are very different. The Art Center includes fine-art galleries with Native American arts and fine-art bird carvings, changing exhibits, wind sculptures, and an ongoing performance schedule. The Covered Bridge Museum presents Vermont's covered bridges and their lore, delivered through videos, dioramas, and interactive exhibits.

*𝒮* **The Dollhouse and Toy Museum of Vermont** (802-681-3767; dollhouseandtoy museumofvermont.com), 212 Union Street, Bennington. Open Sat.–Sun. 1–4 p.m. or by appointment. Nominal admission. The museum is in a lovely Victorian house that looks like a dollhouse itself. Dollhouses and dolls of many styles, as well as photographs, trains, trucks, and other educational toys. Open every day during the week between Christmas and New Year's.

**DISC GOLF** **Willow Park Disc Golf Course**, 472 East Road, Bennington (gmdgc.org).

**GOLF** *𝒮* **Mount Anthony Country Club** (802-442-2617; mtanthonycc.com), 180 Country Club Drive (just below the Battle Monument), Bennington. Eighteen-hole golf course with pro shop and clinics, open April–November; also, weddings, events. The Grille restaurant is open year-round. See *Dining Out.*

HIKING/WALKING **The Appalachian Trail** crosses VT 9 several miles east of Bennington. There's a parking area and an easy hike south to Harmon Hill for a 360-degree view. Allow three or four hours round-trip.

✐ **Mile-Around Woods** (northbennington.org), North Bennington. West of the Park-McCullough House, look for a break in the stone wall and a marked entrance to this foot and bridle path across lovely woods and meadows, part of the original estate.

HISTORICAL ATTRACTIONS **The Park-McCullough House** (802-442-5441; park mccullough.org), 1 Park Street, North Bennington, just off Main Street. Grounds open daily, dawn to dusk. House open for tours Fri–Sat. 10–2, Sun. noon–4, closed in winter. Special tours by appointment. The 35-room Victorian mansion was built in 1865 by Trenor W. Park. Born poor, Park was a self-educated lawyer who married the daughter of a former governor. In 1852, he took his young family to California, where he made a fortune in the Gold Rush. Back in Vermont, he bought his father-in-law's farm and built this three-story, mansard-roofed mansion with a grand staircase and hall, stained-glass skylight, and richly paneled woodwork. Park's son-in-law, John G. McCullough, became governor of Vermont in 1902 and raised his family in the capacious home. Open to the public since 1965, on the National Register of Historic Places, and functioning as a community arts center. The house is filled with artwork, furniture, artifacts, clothing, and toys, more than 100,000 items in total belonging to the Hall-Park-McCullough family. There's an appealing children's playhouse replica of the mansion as well as a gift shop. The **Carriage Barn** houses a collection of carriages and doubles as an events and reception site. Inquire about concerts and lectures.

**Robert Frost Stone House and Museum** (802-447-6200; bennington.edu/robert-frost-stone-house-and-museum), 121 VT 7A, Shaftsbury. Gifted to Bennington College at the end of 2017, the house and museum remain a public resource for studying the life of the iconic poet; the college is currently planning new programs and activities there. Frost lived and worked for a time in the 1920s in this stone-house-turned-museum; it was here that he wrote "Stopping by Woods on a Snowy Evening." Through the windows, you can still see the apple trees, stone walls, and country lanes that inspired him. Biographical exhibits and a few of his personal belongings are on display.

**The Shaftsbury Historical Society** (802-375-2776; shaftsburyhistoricalsociety.org), 3871 VT 7A, Shaftsbury. Open Tues., Thurs., and weekends by appointment. This gradually developing cluster of historic buildings includes two schools and an 1846 Baptist meetinghouse. Free.

HORSEBACK RIDING **Kimberly Farms** (802-442-5454; kimberlyfarms.org), 1214 Cross Hill Road, North Bennington, offers trail rides, lessons, and an overnight horse camp on its 60-acre farm.

✐ **Lively's Livery** (802-447-7612; livelyslivery.com), 193 Crossover Road, Bennington. Horse-drawn carriage service (weddings a specialty), wagon rides, trail rides, sleigh rides, bridge tours.

SCENIC DRIVES **Bennington County's five covered bridges.** Three of them, the **Silk Road Bridge** (1840), the **Paper Mill Village Bridge** (1840s), and the **Henry Bridge** (rebuilt 1989) are all an easy drive just off VT 67A, south of North Bennington. Continue north on VT 67A as it turns into Main Street, then left on VT 67 to VT 7A, following it north past the Robert Frost House and **Lake Shaftsbury State Park** to the village of Arlington. Note the historic marker in front of the home of writer Dorothy Canfield Fisher. Turn left onto VT 313 and follow the Batten Kill for 4.4 miles through woods

# ANNA MARY ROBERTSON "GRANDMA" MOSES

When Mary Robertson Moses entered her first agricultural fair, she won a prize for her fruit and jam. "But no pictures," she recalled. Moses began painting in Bennington in 1932, when she moved to the city to care for her daughter Anna, who had tuberculosis. Painting replaced pictures embroidered with wool when Moses's arthritis prevented her from stitching. Holding a paintbrush was gentler on her joints. Her naive depictions of her childhood in Greenwich, NY, attracted no notice, and once her daughter healed, Moses returned to her farm in Hoosick Falls, NY. There, wealthy art collector Louis J. Caldor first spied Moses' work in the window of a drugstore. What attracted him isn't clear. Perhaps the sparkles? More likely, it was a vogue for outsider art, and Moses's candy-colored representations of what she called "old-timey" fit the bill. At first her Yankee pragmatism kept her from attending exhibitions. Once won over, though, she made the big-city scene complete with baked goods and jam to share with fans.

The Bennington Museum hosts the world's largest public collection of Moses's paintings. Almost completely lacking in perspective or depth, faces are pink blobs that resemble smiley faces. And winter scenes are speckled with glitter, much to the chagrin of Moses's art handlers. A pair of paintings on display at the museum depicts the town of Bennington, neither bearing a resemblance to the city. One was painted from life, another from a photograph, but Moses admitted that she had little regard for accuracy. Instead, her paintings capture a feeling. *A Country Wedding* is a more accurate time capsule of a sunny late-nineteenth-century wedding day than any photograph. *Sugaring Off* conjures every sensation: of boiling maple sap around an outdoor fire, or the taste of sugar on snow.

At the Bennington Museum, the sensory experience of Moses's life isn't limited to her canvases. The schoolhouse she attended until becoming a "hired girl" at age 12 has been transported to Bennington and installed down a short hallway from the gallery devoted to Moses's work. There her early years, including items she owned and contemporary clothing and dolls, come to three-dimensional life.

Moses was born nearly a year before Abraham Lincoln took office. She died at 101, having enjoyed TV appearances, an Oscar-nominated biographical documentary, and a *Life* magazine cover devoted to her 100th birthday. Perhaps she was less a "genuine American primitive" than one of America's first ironic celebrities.

and farmland to West Arlington. Here is the frequently photographed tableau of a classic green-shuttered church with spiky steeple, a farmhouse (painter Norman Rockwell's home from 1939 until 1953), and the red **West Arlington Bridge** (1872). Return to Arlington Village and, at the sign for East Arlington, turn north on the East Arlington Road, continuing 1.9 miles to the **Chiselville Bridge**, built high above Roaring Branch Brook in 1879. Continue along this road until it veers to join VT 7A in Sunderland, near the toll road that goes to the top of Mount Equinox.

**Readsboro.** This road less taken is our favorite way to Bennington from Massachusetts. Follow US 2 west from Greenfield, MA, for 3.6 miles to Colrain Road. Continue for 17.3 scenic miles through Colrain, MA, to Jacksonville, VT. Here VT 100 splits, the more traveled road heading north to VT 9 (see below) at Wilmington, the other branch meandering west through Whitingham and 14 miles to Readsboro—arguably the most remote town in southern Vermont and one that's become a center for artists and craftspeople. Its proximity to the Hoosac Tunnel and its status as a roundhouse for the Wilmington Railroad spawned this late-nineteenth-century mill village (population 809), which was later known for its large chair factory. The **Readsboro Inn**

(802-423-7077; readsboroinn.net) marks the center of town, with its lounge and reasonably priced dining room and lodging. **Readsboro Glassworks** (see *Selective Shopping*) is another draw. Several more studios are open periodically, and a craft festival is held every September (readsboroarts.org). The **Readsboro Historical Society** (802-423-5432; readsborohistoricalsociety.org), 152 Glen Avenue, is open by appointment. It's 11 more miles northwest through high backcountry to VT 9 at Searsburg, 14 miles east of Bennington.

**Molly Stark Byway.** For a map and details about the 48 miles of VT 9 between Bennington and Brattleboro, see the introduction to "Southern Vermont" and *Scenic Byways* in the Mount Snow chapter. Also see mollystarkbyway.org.

SWIMMING **Lake Paran**, VT 67, North Bennington. This hidden gem, a recreation area centered on a 35-acre lake with facilities for swimming, also has good fishing. Hiking on trails walked by Robert Frost. Daily rates.

Also see **Lake Shaftsbury State Park** and **Woodford State Park** under *Green Space*.

TENNIS **Bennington Tennis Center** (802-447-7557; benningtontenniscenter.com), 200 Lovers Lane, Bennington. An indoor tennis club complete with lessons.

## ❄ Winter Sports

CROSS-COUNTRY SKIING ✎ **Prospect Mountain Nordic Ski Center** (802-442-2575; prospectmountain.com), 204 Prospect Access Road, Woodford (you may need to set your GPS for Bennington). Open daily 9–5, as long as there's snow. Little Woodford has the highest elevation of any town in the state. The base at this cross-country skiing area is 2,250 feet, increasing the odds for consistent snow. Phone or check the website for conditions. A former downhill family ski area, the focus is now on 30 km of cross-country trails groomed for skating and classic skiing, plus extensive backcountry connecting with the Green Mountain National Forest trails. The base lodge has a stone hearth, a woodstove, and a modest restaurant. Moonlight dinners and ski tours during full moons.

Also see **Woodford State Park** under *Green Space*.

## ❄ Green Space

✎ **Lake Shaftsbury State Park** (802-375-9978; vtstateparks.com), 262 Lake Shaftsbury Road, Shaftsbury. Open Memorial Day weekend–Labor Day weekend. A private resort until 1974, these 84 acres surrounding Lake Shaftsbury offer swimming, picnicking, rental kayaks, rowboats and pedal boats, concession stand, lakefront cottage rental (sleeping six), and 15 lean-tos clustered for group camping. The Healing Spring Nature Trail circles the lake.

✎ **Woodford State Park** (802-447-7169; vtstateparks.com) 142 State Park Road, Bennington. This 400-acre heavily wooded area includes swimming in Adams Reservoir; a children's playground; picnic spots; and canoe, kayak, and rowboat rentals. Several hiking trails—including the 2.7-mile trail around the lake—are excellent for cross-country skiing in winter.

# ❋ Lodging

## INNS AND BED & BREAKFASTS

### IN BENNINGTON

⚙ **The Four Chimneys Inn** (802-447-3500; fourchimneys.com), 21 West Road (VT 9) in Old Bennington. Owners Pete and Lynn Green were married in this stately 1910 colonial revival home. Their inn offers 11 luxurious rooms, all spacious with private bath, TV, and phone, most with a fireplace and Jacuzzi, and two with glassed-in porch. Firewood provided. The grounds are beautifully landscaped, but the inn is not suited to pets or children under age 12. Rates include country breakfast. $–$$$$.

**South Shire Inn** (802-447-3839; southshire.com), 124 Elm Street. This attractive 1887 mansion features 10-foot ceilings and bedrooms furnished with antiques. Three of the nine guest rooms have a fireplace, and all have a private bath; two can be joined as a suite. Carriage House rooms have a whirlpool tub, a fireplace, and TV. Tea is served many afternoons, and breakfast is offered. Unable to accommodate pets or children. Senior discounts. $–$$.

### IN NORTH BENNINGTON

**The Eddington House** (802-442-1511; eddingtonhouseinn.com), 21 Main Street. This sunny vintage 1857 manse is in the middle of a picturesque village, within walking distance of a waterfall and handy to walking paths and swimming. The House has three tastefully furnished, unfussy rooms with a private bath. A full breakfast and afternoon tea are included. $–$$. Children over 12 welcome.

⚙ **Taraden Bed and Breakfast** (802-447-3434; taraden.com), 183 Park Street. The Tudor-style manor, once part of the Park-McCullough estate, now has 19 acres including a barn (for small weddings and events) and a guest cottage. Bob and Nan Lowary offer three suites:

the two-room Night Pasture sleeps four and has a fridge, microwave, and TV; the West Wing suite sleeps three (fridge and TV); and the Cottage sleeps two, with French doors opening onto a deck (fridge and microwave). Rates include a full breakfast. Children over 12 welcome. $$.

## MOTELS

### IN BENNINGTON

**Paradise Motor Inn** (800-575-5784; vermontparadiseinn.com), 141 West Main Street, close to the Bennington Museum, with 77 air-conditioned rooms, a pool, and a tennis court, set in 8 landscaped acres on a knoll above VT 9. Standard room (two king beds) or a suite with living room and kitchen in foliage season. $–$$.

🐾 **Knotty Pine Motel** (802-442-5487; knottypinemotel.com), 130 Northside Drive (VT 7A). The locals use this family-owned motel to put up their guests—not a bad sign. There's a pool and an adjacent diner. Pets are welcome as long as they are not left alone. Clean, no-frills rooms. Continental breakfast included. $.

🐾 **Harwood Hill Motel** (802-442-6278; harwoodhillmotel.com), 864 Harwood Hill Road. Perched on a hilltop north of Bennington, this motel "with the million-dollar view" is owned by four friends who are bringing art to the establishment and partnering with local museums to introduce their guests to the locale (they also have an Artist in Residence program on-site and showcase their own work and that of local artisans). Eight deluxe rooms, cottages, and economy units, all with air-conditioning, refrigerator, and cable TV. The deluxe rooms have a microwave and phone, pets with restrictions and an extra charge. $.

**CAMPING** See **Vermont State Parks** (vtstateparks.com) under *Green Space*. Also see private campgrounds listed at bennington.com.

# ✳ Where to Eat

DINING OUT **Pangaea Restaurant & Lounge** (802-442-7171; vermontfine dining.com), 1 Prospect Street, North Bennington. Dinner is served in the restaurant Tues.–Sat. 5–9. The Lounge is open nightly, 5–10. This chef-owned eatery in the center of tiny North Bennington is southern Vermont's culinary star. Nicholas Disorda and William Scully draw the best from every continent for their menu. The wine cellar has won *Wine Spectator* awards, and beers include imports from India and the Czech Republic. Most menu items can be made as starters or entrées to your own taste. In summer, seating extends to an outdoor terrace overlooking the river. Entrées $$$.

⚙ **The Grille at Mount Anthony Club** (802-442-2617; mtanthonycc.com/grille), 180 Country Club Drive, Bennington. Open year-round for lunch and dinner. With a winter hearth and seasonal terrace, it's a great place to stop after visiting the nearby Bennington Monument. Entrées $–$$.

✿ **Allegro Ristorante** (802-442-0990; allegroristorante.com), 520 Main Street, Bennington. Open seven days, 5–10 p.m. Despite being prepared with ingredients from small, local farms, which are normally expensive to acquire, the creative Italian fare here is perhaps the best value in the area. Salads and appetizers, including rabbit and ricotta sausage meatballs, are enough to satisfy a smaller appetite. $–$$.

## EATING OUT

### IN BENNINGTON

**Blue Benn Diner** (802-442-5140), 314 North Street (US 7). Open daily for breakfast and lunch. This 1940s classic diner offers copious choices for pancake breakfasts and combines "road fare" with a few surprises, including tabouleh and falafel. A 10-minute wait for a seat is not uncommon.

✿ **Lil' Britain Fish & Chip Shop** (802-442-2447), 116 North Street. Open Tues.–Sat. for lunch and dinner. The red English phone booth in the corner says it all: This is southern Vermont's only authentic chip shop. Order your fish-and-chips with mushy peas and a side of curry for dipping, then take home a sausage roll or a steak-and-kidney pie. There are Brit groceries, too.

**Madison Brewing Company** (802-442-7397; madisonbrewingco.com), 428 Main Street. Open for lunch and dinner daily. A longstanding local family, the Madisons began brewing as a hobby before opening this brewpub. It has become a destination stop for beer lovers. Outdoor seating in warm weather and a huge pub menu are the other attractions.

### IN NORTH BENNINGTON

**Kevin's Sports Pub & Restaurant** (802-442-0122; kevinssportspubandrestaurant.com), 27 Main Street. Open daily for lunch, dinner, and late night. Burger & Brew on Mondays; Italian Specials on Thursdays. Live entertainment on weekends, and the game is always on. The community gathering spot, frequently packed for dinner—but you can always find space at the bar.

⟨⟨ᵛ⟩⟩ **Powers Market** (802-442-6821; powersmarket.com), 9 Main Street. Open Mon.–Sat. 7–5; Sunday 8–4. Sited on the village's triangular square, this columned building was built in 1833 as a company store for the local paper mill. There's still an old-fashioned soda fountain, with flavors including cherry cola, root beer, and pomegranate, with or without ice cream. House specialty sandwiches are available on gluten-free bread.

⟨⟨ᵛ⟩⟩ **Marigold Kitchen Pizza** (802-445-4545; marigoldkitchen.info), 25 Main Street. Open Tues.–Sun. for dinner, lunch Fri.–Sat. Closed in winter. Pleasant atmosphere; organic, artisanal, and fresh pizzas and salads. Sit down or take out.

BAKERIES **Bakkerij Krijnen** (802-442-1001), 1001 Main Street, Bennington. Open daily. It's easy to miss this Dutch, from-scratch bakery, but don't. You'll be a happier person for having tucked into marzipan-filled pastries and naturally leavened bread stamped with the shape of Vermont. Comforting vegan soups are served at lunchtime.

## ✻ Entertainment

**Oldcastle Theatre Company** (802-447-0564; oldcastletheatre.org), 331 Main Street, Bennington. This professional theater company performs a mix of war-horses and new works alike, as well as both musicals and straight plays. Check the website for season dates, lodging, and restaurant deals available with theater tickets.

**Bennington College** (802-442-5401; bennington.edu), 1 College Drive, Bennington. This beautiful campus hosts many events open to the public; check the website for a calendar.

**Vermont Arts Exchange** (802-442-5549; vtartxchange.org), 48 Main Street, North Bennington. Basement Music Series concerts, art classes for young and old, art shows, yoga, performances, special events, facility rental.

Also see **The Laumeister Art Center** under *To Do: Cultural Attractions*.

## ✻ Selective Shopping

ART GALLERIES AND CRAFTS STUDIOS **Hawkins House Craftsmarket** (802-447-0488; hawkinshouse.net), 262 North Street (US 7), Bennington, is a craft market complex filled with the work of 400 diverse artisans, plus some new and used clothing. Open daily.

**Fiddlehead at Four Corners** (802-447-1000), 338 Main Street, Bennington. Open 7 days a week. This downtown gallery is itself a work of art, housed within the marble walls of a historic

bank, complete with high ceilings and brass chandeliers. Former teacher Joel Lentzner and his wife, Nina, produce one-of-a-kind hand-painted furniture. The fine art and contemporary crafts include Dr. Seuss art, glass, sculpture, jewelry, and ceramics.

**Mount Nebo Gallery** (518-686-4334; willmoses.com), 60 Grandma Moses Road, Eagle Bridge, NY. Open daily. Off NY 67, less than a dozen miles west of North Bennington, the original white frame farmhouse that was the home of Grandma Moses now belongs to her great-grandson, artist Will Moses. This is the place for numbered and signed prints, cards, and other products from the younger Moses.

✪ **Bennington Potters** (802-447-7531; benningtonpotters.com), 324 County Street, Bennington. Open year-round, Mon.–Sat. 9:30–6, Sun. 10–5. Bennington was known for its stoneware pottery in the early and mid-1800s, and ornate samples can be viewed in the Bennington Museum. But the brand lives on. In 1964 Bennington Potters expanded into

BENNINGTON POTTERS CHRISTINA TREE

its present home, once a business supply outlet for coal, firewood, ice, and lumber. Over the years the company has grown, retaining a dozen full-time potters. This flagship factory store also stocks specialty foods, housewares, and gifts.

Visit vermontcrafts.com for all regional artisans and note that Memorial Day weekend is **Open Studio Weekend** in Vermont.

**BOOKSTORES Bennington Bookshop** (802-442-5059; benningtonbookshop .com), 467 Main Street, Bennington. Open Mon.–Sat. 10–6, Sun. noon–4. Extended hours in summer. A full-service, independent bookstore specializing in Vermont books, adult and children's titles, and greeting cards.

**Now and Then Books** (802-442-5566; nowandthenbooksvt.com), 439 Main Street, Bennington. Open Wed.–Mon. The oldest used- and collectible-book shop in the area, with an emphasis on fiction, cookbooks, and Vermont. With more than 50,000 titles, this is one of New England's largest antiquarian collections, also active online.

**BREWERIES Northshire Brewery** (802-681-0201; northshirebrewery.org), 108 County Street, Bennington. Tours and tastings Saturday or by appointment; microbrews include Equinox Pilsner, Battenkill Ale, Chocolate Stout, and Summer Lager.

**Madison Brewing Company** (802-442-7397; madisonbrewingco.com) 428 Main Street, Bennington. See *Eating Out*.

**FARMS ✔ The Apple Barn & Country Bake Shop** (802-447-7780; theapplebarn .com), 604 US 7 south, Bennington. Open daily May–October. Up to 30 varieties of apples to pick, six types of strawberries, and blueberries; produce, candy, cheese, pies, and food specialties are also available in the farm store, complete with a bakery and coffee shop.

**Shaftsbury Alpacas** (802-447-3992; shaftsburyalpacas.com), 12 South State Line Road, North Bennington. Sandy Gordon invites you to spend a day as an alpaca farmer (nominal admission charge) or just to shop in the Alpaca Shack for throws, slippers, outerwear, and more. Open weekdays and weekends; check web for seasonal hours.

**Clear Brook Farm** (802-442-4273; clearbrookfarm.com), 47 Hidden Valley Road (VT 7A), Shaftsbury. Open 10–6 mid-May–mid-October. Bedding plants, produce, farm store, on a growing organic farm.

**Wing and a Prayer Farm** (802-233-6031; wingandaprayerfarm.com), 983 Myers Road, Shaftsbury. Visits by appointment. Bakery, farm animals, workshops. Meet the alpacas, sheep, and goats whose hair is made into wool at this small farm.

**FARMERS' MARKET Bennington Farmers' Market**, 601 Main Street, Bennington. First Baptist Church Community Room, winter quarters. Saturdays, October–April. Vegetables, local storage crops, maple syrup and honey, handcrafts, baked goods, artisanal fare. Live music. At 100 Pleasant Street for summer Tuesdays, 3–6. And at 150 Depot Street for summer Saturdays, 10–1.

**SPECIALTY SHOPS Hemmings Sunoco Filling Station** (802-442-3101; hemmings .com), 216 Main Street, Bennington. Open daily 7–7. A full-service classic Sunoco filling station and convenience store—and the home of the world's largest collector car marketplace (for buying and selling). Vintage vehicle displays include a 1937 Hudson and a 1910 Buick; there's also a quasi-museum selling auto-related memorabilia. Check the website for frequent cruise-ins and events.

**Camelot Village**, 66 Colgate Heights, located in a string of renovated eighteenth-century barns just west of the Old First Church on VT 9 in Bennington. Open 9:30–5:30 daily. The **Antique Center** (802-447-0039; antiquesatcamelot

.com), displays antiques and collectibles from more than 140 dealers.

**The Village Chocolate Shoppe** (802-447-3789; villagepeddlervt.com), 471 Main Street, Bennington. Open daily; closed Sunday, January–May. Meet Morris and Betty, a mated pair of 100-pound chocolate moose. You can't eat them, but you can learn all about chocolate and buy some to take home. Events, tastings, and make-your-own chocolate art. Check website for schedule of events.

## ✳ Special Events

*May:* **Annual Bennington Road Race** (runreg.com/zembenn)—the local marathon, starting at the Park-McCullough House, North Bennington.

*Memorial Day weekend:* **Bennington Mayfest** (betterbennington.com/may fest)—a 10–5 street festival downtown, with artisans, local food vendors, and entertainment.

*July 4:* **Annual 4th of July Celebration** (bennington.com) with evening fireworks, Willow Park.

*August, first weekend:* **Bennington Arts Weekend**. Arts, crafts, music, brews. See bennington.com for details.

*Mid-August:* **Bennington Battle Day Week of Celebrations** (bennington.com), with the annual fire department's Sunday parade. Battle reenactments, special museum events, and family activities.

*Labor Day weekend:* **Southern Vermont Garlic & Herb Festival** (bennington.com/garlicfest), Camelot Village. Sample garlic jelly and ice cream, pickled and roasted garlic, garlic golf, also crafts and music.

*Mid-September:* **Annual Bennington Car Show & Swap Meet** at Willow Park, Bennington (bennington.com). Car show, swap meet, crafts festival, car corral, tractor pull, food, and entertainment. **Annual Bennington Quilt Fest** (benningtonquiltfest.com)—an exhibit of statewide quilts, plus lectures and demonstrations at the middle school.

*Weekend before Halloween:* **Fallapalooza! Fall Festival** (betterbennington .com) held in downtown Bennington, with food, vendors, entertainment, the Walloomsac farmers' market, and activities.

*Late November–mid-December:* **Festival of the Trees**, Bennington Museum, Bennington (benningtonmuseum.org). Silent auction, food, and tour of decorated trees and wreaths throughout the museum's galleries.

# MANCHESTER AND THE MOUNTAINS

*Including Arlington, Dorset, Danby, Peru, Londonderry, and Pawlet*

Manchester, the area's largest community, has been a summer resort since the Civil War. Winter visitors started arriving in 1939, when Bromley opened, augmented in the 1960s by two more ski resorts, Stratton and Magic Mountain, and by several cross-country ski centers with dependable snow.

Manchester comprises two villages that once differed in status. Manchester Village is a gathering of mansions along marble sidewalks around the Congregational church, the gold-domed Bennington County Courthouse, and the white-columned Equinox Resort. Mary Todd Lincoln and her sons, Robert and Tad, spent two seasons at the Equinox, booking a third for the entire family for summer 1865; the president, unfortunately, never made it.

Other presidents—Ulysses S. Grant, Benjamin Harrison, Theodore Roosevelt, and William Taft—also stayed at this hotel, but it was Lincoln's family who adopted the village. Robert Todd Lincoln, president of the Pullman Palace Car Company, selected Manchester Village for his summer home, building Hildene, the lavish mansion that's open to the public. Other opulent "summer cottages" are now B&Bs.

In the nineteenth century, the opulence of Manchester Village contrasted sharply with the poverty of neighboring Factory Point down the hill, home to sawmills, marble works, and a tannery.

BENNINGTON COUNTY COURTHOUSE IN MANCHESTER  LISA HALVORSEN

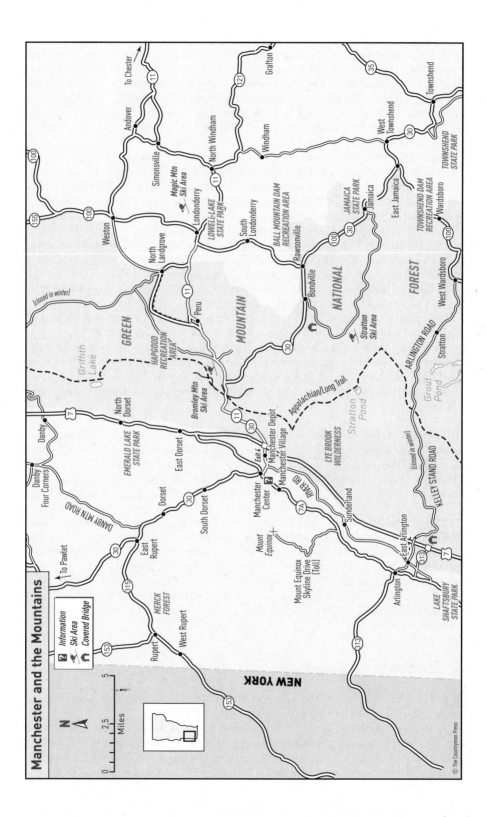

# Manchester and the Mountains

© The Countryman Press

**Legend**
- ℹ Information
- 🎿 Ski Area
- ⌂ Covered Bridge

N
↑

Miles
0    2.5    5

NEW YORK

Today Manchester Center (Factory Point) is a bustling, attractive town, a mix of factory outlets and specialty stores. While the villages retain separate zip codes and zoning, the lineup of shops and restaurants along VT 7A blur the lines between the two. Around 30 top brand outlets fill old homes and house-size compounds, blending nicely with shopping icons such as Orvis, which has been supplying the needs of anglers and other sports enthusiasts since 1856. Manchester is also a cultural center, home to the Southern Vermont Arts Center, the Manchester Music Festival, and the month-long Vermont Summer Festival Horse Show.

Fortunately, the 1930s Work Progress Administration's plan to carve ski trails on Mount Equinox never panned out, and Manchester Village retains its serene, white-clapboard good looks, at least for the time being. A stray peak from the Taconic range, 3,848-foot Mount Equinox looms over its namesake hotel. Much of the mountain is now owned by the Carthusian monks. It's accessible by hiking trails and a toll road from VT 7A in Sunderland, south of town.

The Batten Kill, beloved by anglers and paddlers, runs south from Manchester through Sunderland and Arlington, one of Vermont's oldest towns, with more than its share of covered bridges, antiques stores, and genuine beauty.

To the east, the Green Mountains rise, even within the Manchester town limits, rolling off into heavily forested uplands punctuated along VT 11 by picturesque villages, including Peru, Landgrove, and Londonderry. In winter there's skiing at Bromley and Magic Mountain and at the area's largest ski resort, Stratton Mountain.

From Manchester, VT 30 leads to the elegant village of Dorset, known for its year-round playhouse and destination dining. It then veers northeast through the Mettawee River Valley to the village of Pawlet and beyond. Heading directly north, US 7 follows Otter Creek from North Dorset to Danby through a steep-sided, wooded valley, a hiking haven.

GUIDANCE **Manchester Business Association** (802-362-6313; manchestervermont .com). The Manchester Visitor Center is located at 4826 Main Street, Manchester Center, at the rotary circle at the junction of US 7 and VT 30. Open daily. The Shires of Vermont regional tourism website (shiresofvermont.com) also has information about the area.

GETTING THERE *By car:* From Bennington, US 7 to Manchester is a limited-access highway that's speedy but dull, except for viewing Mount Equinox. You get a more interesting taste of the area, especially around Arlington, by following Historic VT 7A, now the Shires of Vermont Scenic Byway. From the southeast, the obvious access is I-91 to Brattleboro, then VT 30 north. From New York City, take I-87 to Exit 23, then take I-787 north to Exit 9E, then go east on US 7 to Bennington; continue on VT 279 (Bennington Bypass) to US 7 North to Exit 4 in Manchester or follow Historic VT 7A from Bennington.

# ✳ Towns and Villages

In addition to Manchester, the area has a number of picturesque villages, mainly located on VT 30, VT 11, and VT 7A, including the following:

**Arlington** (population 2,317). Although never formally the capital of Vermont, this was the de facto seat of government during most of the Revolutionary War period. Fearing British attacks in the north, Vermont's first governor, Thomas Chittenden, moved south from Williston, liberated a Tory property in Arlington (the area known

ARLINGTON COMMUNITY HOUSE  LISA HALVORSEN

as Tory Hollow), and conducted affairs of state from there. Dorothy Canfield Fisher, an early American author and a longtime Book-of-the-Month Club judge, made her home here. So did artist Norman Rockwell, who lived in West Arlington from 1939 to 1953 and painted small-town America. One of his models was Dr. George Russell, immortalized in Rockwell's *The Country Doctor*, who amassed a valuable collection of Vermontiana. These documents, genealogies, works by Vermont authors and artists, and late-nineteenth-century photographs are housed in the Martha Canfield Memorial Free Library (802-375-6153; marthacanfieldlibrary.org), 528 East Arlington Road.

**Dorset** (population 2,031; dorsetvt.com). A fashionable summer refuge for years, few signs of commerce mar its green lawns and marble sidewalks. Today's tranquility, making it popular with artists, writers, and the affluent, contrasts sharply with the hot-headed days of its youth. In 1776 the Green Mountain Boys gathered in Cephas Kent's tavern and issued their first declaration of independence from the New Hampshire Grants, signed by Thomas Chittenden, Ira Allen, Seth Warner, and other founding fathers of Vermont. The **Dorset Inn** (see *Lodging*), said to be Vermont's oldest continuously operating hostelry, is the village focal point, along with the

**Dorset Playhouse** (see *Entertainment*) and the Dorset Field Club, a private 18-hole golf course, the state's oldest. The first marble quarried in North America came from Dorset; one quarry—now a popular swimming hole—even supplied marble for the New York City Public Library. The Dorset Historical Society's **Bley House Museum** (802-867-0331; dorsetvthistory.org), on VT 30 at Kent Hill Road, contains displays about the area's history, including the local marble and iron industries.

## ✳ Must See

**American Museum of Fly-Fishing** (802-362-3300; amff.com), 4070 Main Street, Manchester Center, next to the Orvis Company's flagship store. Open Tues.–Sat. Admission.

OUTDOOR SCULPTURES AT THE SOUTHERN VERMONT ARTS CENTER  LISA HALVORSEN

The museum documents the history of fly-fishing through artifacts, historic fishing-related photos, prints, paintings, and ephemera. The tackle, rods, and reels owned by luminaries such as Bing Crosby, Ernest Hemingway, and Presidents Herbert Hoover and Dwight Eisenhower are the crux of the permanent collection. The fly collection numbers around 22,000, including the oldest documented flies, tied in England and Scotland in 1789.

    &#9855; **Southern Vermont Arts Center** (802-362-1405; svac.org), 930 SVAC Drive, Manchester, off West Road. Grounds open year-round. Buildings and galleries open Tues.–Sun. April–December. Free admission. Elizabeth de C. Wilson Museum and Galleries is a work of art, with its soaring, light-filled galleries housing first-class touring shows of paintings, sculpture, prints, and photography. Yester House Gallery stages a number of member shows per year. Concerts, including the summer Manchester Music Festival series, ballet performances, and lectures, take place in the 430-seat Arkell Pavilion. Visitors may picnic on the grounds, which include outdoor sculptures and trails.

## ✳ To Do

BICYCLING  Mountain bike, hybrid bike, and touring bike rentals and touring information are available from **Battenkill Bicycles** (802-362-2734; battenkillbicycles.com), open Thurs.–Mon. 10–5 at 99 Bonnet Street, Manchester Center.

    Also see sidebar for **Stratton Mountain.**

    **Equipe Sport and Mountain Riders** (802-297-2847; equipesport.com), junction of VT 30 and VT 100 in Rawsonville; also in the Village Square at Stratton Mountain (802-297-3460); sales, rentals, and bike maps.

BOATING  The Batten Kill is popular with kayakers and canoeists in spring. The Manchester-to-Arlington section is relatively flat water, but it gets difficult a mile above Arlington.

# A CELEBRATED SUMMER ESTATE

**H**ildene, the Lincoln Home (802-362-1788; hildene.org), 1005 Hildene Road, Manchester Village, off VT 7A. Open year-round, seven days a week. Admission. Limited handicapped accessibility. Built as the summer home of Robert Todd Lincoln and his wife Mary Harlan Lincoln, the estate comprises 412 acres of land with views of both the Green Mountains and the Taconic range. Bring a picnic lunch and plan to stay at least half the day.

Visits begin at the Carriage Barn, a welcome center with a museum store and video presentations on the Lincoln family and the Hildene experience, and the restoration of *Sunbeam*, a 1903 wooden Pullman Palace sleeping car. You learn that Robert, the only child of President Abraham and Mary Todd Lincoln to survive to adulthood, first came to the village in 1863 as a young man with his mother to stay at the Equinox House. Forty years later, Robert returned to Manchester to build a 24-room Georgian Revival manor he called Hildene, for "hill and valley with a stream."

Transportation is provided from the welcome center, with the first stop at *Sunbeam*. Built during Robert's tenure as president of the Pullman Palace Car Company, its story is told through the voices of Pullman Company executives, wealthy passengers, and the African-American porters.

Next stop is Hildene Farm, with its solar-powered Rowland Agricultural Center, set in an expansive meadow. At the timber-frame barn, which houses Hildene's herd of goats, you can learn about the cheesemaking process, from milking the goats to the making of artisanal cheese.

The mansion is a standout among Vermont's historic houses containing many of the family's belongings. Guides provide an introduction and then play a short piece for guests on Mr. and Mrs. Lincoln's 1,000-pipe Aeolian organ, originally playable both manually and with one of around 240 player rolls of music. The house's many treasures include President Lincoln's stovepipe hat, one of three in existence.

Behind the house are the restored French parterre-style formal gardens, featuring the family's original peonies in June and then perennials later, often beautiful well into October. Lincoln's observatory sits on the promontory near the house. Picnic tables outside the welcome center offer a pleasant view of the less formal cutting, kitchen, and butterfly gardens. Twelve miles of walking trails are also used for cross-country skiing and snowshoeing in the winter; rentals available.

The lower 100 acres, known as the Dene, contain a year-round greenhouse, a pollinator sanctuary, and a protected bobolink habitat. Guests can access this area throughout the year on foot and from spring through fall by tram or by daily guided wagon rides. The wagon also stops at the 600-foot floating wetlands boardwalk and Dene Farm to visit the animals.

*SUNBEAM*, A 1903 PULLMAN PALACE SLEEPING CAR  LISA HALVORSEN

**Stratton Mountain** (802-297-4321; stratton.com), at First Run Ski Shop. Canoe and kayak tours, rentals, and sales.

**Equipe Sport** (802-297-2847; equipesport.com), 8749 VT 30, South Londonderry (Rawsonville Marketplace). The shop offers kayak rentals.

**Emerald Lake State Park** (802-362-1655; vtstateparks.com), 65 Emerald Lake Lane, East Dorset. Canoes, kayaks, rowboats, and pedal boats for rent.

BUSHWHACKING **Land Rover Experience Driving School** (802-362-0687; equinox resort.com), Manchester Village, at the Equinox Resort. The school offers off-road driving instruction on an 80-acre course and backroad trails for more experienced drivers. Expert instructors teach driving techniques for all terrain, depending on the driver's skill level. Extra passengers are welcome; drivers must have a valid license.

**Backroad Discovery Tours** (802-362-4997; backroaddiscovery.com). The company offers small group tours on southern Vermont's back roads and byways, stopping at spots of historical significance and scenic views. Tours offered every season, including Revolutionary and Civil War tours, April–November.

FISHING Since the mid-nineteenth century, fly-fishing has been serious business on the Batten Kill, recognized as Vermont's best wild trout stream. Access is available at several places on VT 7A. Brown trout can be found in Gale Meadows Pond, accessible via a gravel road from VT 30 at Bondville. Emerald Lake in East Dorset is stocked with pike, bass, and perch; rental boats are available at Emerald Lake State Park. Fishing license info at vtfishandwildlife.com.

**Orvis Fishing Schools** (802-531-6213; orvis.com/fly-fishing), the top name in fly-fishing instruction and equipment, offers one- and two-day courses, April–October, across from the Orvis flagship store in well-stocked casting ponds and on the Batten Kill. The Fly-Fishing 101 class is free. The website has an extensive list of resources, including Orvis-endorsed fly-fishing guides.

**The Battenkill Angler** (802-379-1444; battenkillangler.com). Tom Goodman offers classes on fly-tying; fly-fishing, including techniques, strategies, and tactics for catching trout; and navigating some of New England's finest trout rivers.

**The Reel Angler** (802-362-0883; thereelangler.com), 302 Depot Street, Manchester Center. A full-service shop and outfitter with guide service on the Batten Kill, Mettawee, and other rivers and lakes.

GOLF **The Golf Club at the Equinox** (802-362-7870; playequinox.com), 108 Union Street, Manchester Village. The club was established in the 1920s for guests of the Equinox House, and then it was expanded and redesigned in 1991 by Rees Jones to incorporate 18 holes. **Dormy Grill** (see *Eating Out*) offers pleasant dining with a beautiful view of the course.

**Stratton Mountain Golf Course** See sidebar on page 119.

HIKING The Green Mountain National Forest District Office (802-362-2307; fs.usda .gov) has hiking maps for the 14,600-acre Lye Brook Wilderness preserve south of Manchester; a 2.3-mile trail leads to the Lye Brook Waterfalls and the Long Trail. Portions of the Long Trail are suitable for day hikes, either north over Bromley Mountain or south over Spruce Peak from VT 11/30. Another popular route is the Stratton Pond Trail, starting at Kelley Stand Road and stretching to Stratton Pond; one shelter is in the immediate area, and swimming is permitted. Griffith Lake, accessible from Peru and Danby, is a less-crowded swimming and camping site on the trail. For details, consult the Green Mountain Club's *Long Trail Guide*.

☀ ♞ **Merck Forest & Farmland Center** (802-394-7836; merckforest.org), 3270 VT 315, Rupert (west of Dorset). A beautiful find near the New York border. Open year-round, free admission, with unexpected birding opportunities. (See *Green Space*)

**Mount Equinox** The six-mile Burr and Burton Trail goes from Manchester Village to the summit. At 3,848 feet, this is the highest Vermont mountain not traversed by the Long Trail. Refer to the *Day Hiker's Guide to Vermont* (Green Mountain Club) for information.

See also *Green Space*.

HORSEBACK RIDING, ETC. ♞ **Taylor Farm** (802-824-5690; taylorfarmvermont.com), 825 VT 11, Londonderry, offers farm tours and carriage rides in summer and fall. In winter, Belgian draft horses pull box-style sleighs. Artisanal cheese is available for sale.

♞ **Horses for Hire** (802-297-1468; horses4hire.com), 893 South Road, Peru. Deb Hodis offers one- and two-hour and half-day trail rides, sleigh rides, and riding lessons for individuals and groups, even in winter, weather permitting.

♞ **Mountain View Ranch** (802-293-5837; mountainviewranch.biz), 502 Easy Street, Danby. In addition to trail rides (including picnic and sunset rides), the ranch offers a backcountry trek for advanced riders and Cowboy Up, a one-hour trail ride and instruction on barrel racing and other rodeo events. Donkey and pony rides are offered for young riders. Winter brings sleigh rides with hot chocolate and s'mores.

♞ **Chipman Stables** (802-293-5242; chipmanstables.com), 33 Danby-Pawlet Road, Danby. Year-round western trail rides; pony rides, fall hayrides, winter sleigh rides, riding lessons, and kids' horse camps.

SCENIC DRIVES **Mount Equinox Skyline Drive** (802-362-1114; equinoxmountain .com).

From the tollhouse on VT 7A in Sunderland, the 5.2-mile toll road, open May–October, twists and turns its way to the summit of 3,848-foot high Mount Equinox. There are picnic areas and turnouts for scenic views along the way. Visit the Saint Bruno Scenic Viewing Center at the top to explore the history of Mount Equinox and to learn more about the Carthusian monks who own the mountaintop and about the Mount Equinox Annual Hill Climb sports car race. Enjoy one of the most panoramic views in southern Vermont before driving back downhill—in low gear.

**Green Mountain National Forest Road Number 10**, Danby to Landgrove. Closed in winter. Beginning in Danby, this 14-mile byway climbs through the Robert T. Stafford White Rocks National Recreation Area, crossing a number of tempting hiking paths and the Long Trail. The road follows Tabor Brook down into Landgrove, a tiny, picturesque village.

**East Rupert to Danby**. Danby Mountain Road is the logical shortcut from Dorset to Danby, and it's quite beautiful, winding up and over a saddle between Woodlawn Mountain and Dorset Peak. Well-surfaced dirt, with long views in places. If you're coming from East Rupert, turn right at Danby Four Corners and follow Mill Brook into Danby.

**Kelley Stand Road**. From VT 7A, follow East Arlington Road and continue until you cross a bridge. Turn right onto Kelley Stand Road, which is a great foliage-viewing trip all the way to Stratton. Closed in winter.

SWIMMING **Dorset Quarry**, VT 30 between Manchester and Dorset. Look for the historic marker. Popular swimming place with limited off-road parking. Although privately owned, the owners allow access. Not suitable for small children, given the rough terrain and deep pool.

✆ ♿ **Hapgood Pond Recreation Area** (802-362-2307; fs.usda.gov), 1615 Hapgood Pond Road, Peru. This Green Mountain National Forest site has a sandy beach and pond with a shallow drop-off, ideal for families with young children; picnic tables; handicapped-accessible fishing pier; and wooded camping area with 28 sites.

✆ **Emerald Lake State Park** (802-362-1655; vtstateparks.com), 65 Emerald Lake Lane, East Dorset, has a beach and clear lake for swimming.

See also *Green Space*.

TENNIS **Cliff Drysdale Tennis School at Stratton Mountain** (802-297-4230; stratton .com), 5 Village Lodge Road. Tennis legend Cliff Drysdale offers tennis weekends in summer; clinics, camps, programs, and instruction offered for players of all ages.

**Equinox Hotel Tennis** (802-362-4700; equinoxresort.com), 3567 Main Street, Manchester Village. Three plexicushion all-weather outdoor courts are open to the public for an hourly fee and private lessons.

## ❄ Winter Sports

CROSS-COUNTRY SKIING AND SNOWSHOEING ✆ **Viking Nordic Center** (802-824-3933; vikingnordic.com), 615 Little Pond Road, Londonderry. The 39-km trail system includes 35 km of groomed trails (3 km lighted for night skiing) and 4 km of dedicated snowshoe trails. You'll also find instruction, rentals, a retail shop, and a café serving drinks, light breakfasts, soups, and sandwiches. Lodging includes The Apartment, ideal for two families, and The Farmhouse, a home with a library, a hearth, and four bedrooms that sleep 10. Both are available for rent by the weekend or by the week and come with free trail passes.

✆ **Wild Wings Ski & Yoga** (802-824-6793; wildwingsski.com), 246 Styles Lane, Peru. A family-oriented touring and yoga center located within the Green Mountain National Forest, 2.5 miles north of Peru. The 28 km of groomed one-way trails, appropriate for beginning and intermediate skiers, are at elevations between 1,650 and 2,040 feet. This area tends to get heavier snowfall than other local touring centers. Instruction and rentals (skis and snowshoes); no skate skiing or dogs.

**Nordic Center at Stratton Mountain** (802-297-4567; stratton.com). Based at the Sun Bowl, the touring center has a 12-km series of groomed loops plus adjoining backcountry trails. Guided backcountry ski and snowshoe tours offered. Hot lunches and snacks available at the Sun Bowl Base Lodge.

**Hildene** (802-362-1788; hildene.org), 1005 Hildene Road, Manchester Village. The historic Lincoln estate and working farm has cross-country skiing trails and rentals. Trail fee.

DOWNHILL SKIING See sidebar for Bromley Mountain Resort and Stratton Mountain Resort on page 119.

🎿 ✆ **Magic Mountain Ski Area** (802-824-5645; magicmtn.com), 495 Magic Mountain Access, Londonderry. Open Thurs.–Sun. and holidays. It may not be the biggest of southern Vermont's ski areas, but Magic Mountain might be the area's most challenging spot. Its 43 trails are twisty and narrow, and almost half of its 1,700 vertical feet are steep drops. The 190-acre area was developed in 1960 by Swiss ski instructor Hans Thorner, who hoped to re-create the atmosphere of a Swiss Alpine village. He chose this mountain for the sheer drama of its terrain. Magic remains relatively overlooked, making it a perfect destination to escape the crowds (and expense) of the larger resorts. Although it lacks the indulgences and amenities of the larger resorts, the commercial

# STRATTON AND BROMLEY: YEAR-ROUND RESORTS

## STRATTON

(800-STRATTON; ski report: 802-297-4211; stratton.com). Located atop a 4-mile access road from VT 30 in Bondville, Stratton is a popular, well-groomed mountain. It was here that Jake Burton invented the snowboard, and today Stratton is noted for its terrain parks, for both skiers and snowboarders. Stratton keeps a loyal following by harvesting a steady crop of snow for what are predominantly intermediate-level runs, but plenty of opportunities also exist for advanced skiers along its 97 trails, including some good moguls and long top-to-bottom runs of 2,000 vertical feet.

VIEW OF STRATTON MOUNTAIN RESORT FROM THE GONDOLA   LISA HALVORSEN

The mountain itself rises to 3,936 feet, with two separate areas: the original North Face, and the distinctly sunnier Sun Bowl. Thanks to a large number of lifts, skiers are generally dispersed over the trail network. Stratton Village includes a variety of shops, restaurants, and spas; the resort offers a range of accommodations, including a hotel and 300 condominiums within walking distance or a short shuttle ride from the slopes. Activities include cross-country skiing and snowshoeing at the Nordic Center, dog sledding, lift-served snow tubing, and snowmobiling.

*Mountain Profile: Lifts:* 11, including a 12-passenger gondola and four six-passenger, high-speed detachable chairlifts. *Trails and slopes:* 97. *Vertical drop:* 2,003 feet. *Snowmaking:* 95 percent. *Ski school:* Ski and snowboard lessons. *For children:* Childcare center for ages 6 weeks–3 years, including combined ski and play programs; slopeside meeting place for Kids-Kamp (ski and snowboard full-day programs for ages 4–12).

*Facilities:* Restaurant and cafeteria in the base lodge; cafeterias can also be found mid-mountain

SKIING AT STRATTON   STRATTON MOUNTAIN RESORT

and in the Sun Bowl. The Bavarian-style Village Square at the base contains shops and restaurants; there is also a sports center.

**SUMMER/FALL** A lot happens here in summer, including golf; hiking; mountain biking; fishing; kayaking at Gale Meadows, Lowell Lake, and Stratton Pond; scenic gondola rides; and tennis and golf schools. Kids ages 6 weeks–12 years can attend KidsKamp for half or full days, late June–early September.

**Stratton Mountain Golf Course** is a 27-hole championship course with a full clubhouse, including the Green Apron restaurant (802-297-4295; open seasonally for lunch and for farm-to-table dinners), a pro shop, and a practice facility. **The Stratton Golf School** offers weekend and midweek sessions, including professional instruction, and has a special 22-acre training facility.

**Summit Views** are accessible by gondola in summer and fall.

**First Run Ski Shop** (802-297-4321) rents mountain and road bikes. Inquire about guided tours.

## BROMLEY

🖊 (802-824-5522; bromley .com), 3984 VT 11, Peru, 6 miles east of Manchester. Founded in 1936 by Fred Pabst of the Milwaukee brewing family, this is among the oldest ski areas in the country. The only southern-facing ski mountain in Vermont, it also was one of the first to develop snowmaking, chairlifts, and condominiums. Pabst is credited with inventing the J-bar, which pulled skiers up the mountain rather than requiring them to clutch a rope. Bromley's next owner brought the first alpine slide to North America, establishing Bromley as a summer destination. This popular family mountain has many trails suited to beginners and intermediates, but the eastern slopes have more challenging runs, including the legendary Pabst Peril. In winter there's a reservations service for condominiums.

**SKIING AT BROMLEY** BROMLEY MOUNTAIN RESORT

**Mountain Profile:** *Lifts:* 9: 1 high-speed detachable quad, 1 fixed-grip quad, 4 doubles, 1 T-bar, 1 Kids Carpet, and 1 covered Magic Carpet. *Trails:* 47 trails—evenly divided among beginner, intermediate, and expert. *Terrain Parks:* Designed and tailored for a progressive freestyle experience. It's not all big air, or all rails, or even all in one line, just all fun. *Vertical drop:* 1,334 feet. *Snowmaking:* 86 percent of the terrain, from base to summit. Facilities include a cafeteria, a tavern, a sandwich shop, and an outdoor Waffle Shack. *Ski school:* Both ski and snowboard schools have been recognized nationally.

**SUMMER/FALL** Bromley is a popular stop on the **Long Trail**, which is accessible from the same chairlift that serves the **Bromley Alpine Slide** (open Memorial Day–mid-October, weather permitting). The **Big Splash** waterslide (biggest in Vermont) and the **Giant Swing** are huge draws for the teen set. You'll also find miniature golf, a 24-foot climbing wall, space bikes, bounce house, bungee trampoline, and the **Sun Mountain Flyer**, a four-track zipline, the longest in New England. The **Aerial Adventure Park** with 23 "adventures" has a fully equipped ropes course, with 65 unique elements spread over five course levels in the trees.

THE BROMLEY ALPINE SLIDE  BROMLEY MOUNTAIN RESORT

hype and sprawling condos are refreshingly absent, too. The advanced trails are the real draw here, but there is plenty of good, well-groomed terrain for beginners and intermediates. The two chairlifts, the bottom-to-top red double and the black triple, are long and comparatively slow, reminiscent of what it was like to ski and socialize before high-speed detachable chairs were invented.

**Mountain Profile**: *Lifts:* 4: 1 triple chair, 1 double, and 2 surface; *Trails and slopes:* 43; *Vertical drop:* 1,700 feet; *Terrain park:* 11 features; *Facilities:* Cafeteria, bar, restaurant, and entertainment at the base lodge. The Black Line Tavern, where this community hangs out for a little après-ski fun and music, serves great food. *Ski school:* Ski and snowboard lessons. Ask about special events and lift packages. *Tubing Park:* The region's only tubing park with its own tow; illuminated Friday, Saturday, and holiday nights. Summer activities gear up at Magic Mountain, with 4th of July fireworks, outdoor music events, and a nine-hole disc golf course.

RIDING MAGIC MOUNTAIN'S RED DOUBLE CHAIRLIFT  MAGIC MOUNTAIN

ICE SKATING ⚘ **Riley Rink at Hunter Park** (802-362-0150; rileyrink.com), 410 Hunter Park Road, Manchester Center, is an Olympic-size indoor ice-skating rink off VT 7A. The rink is open late October–early March. Check the website for public skating hours and fees; rentals available.

SLEIGH RIDES  See *Horseback Riding.*

SNOWMOBILING The Winter Recreation Map, free from the Green Mountain National Forest District Office (802-362-2307; fs.usda.gov), Manchester, shows trails presently maintained in this area by the Vermont Association of Snow Travelers (vtvast.org).

**Stratton Snowmobile Tours** (802-379-1483; stratton.com). Nighttime one-hour snowmobile tours are available at Stratton Mountain, with mini-snowmobile tours offering instruction for kids.

# ✳ Green Space

⚘ **Equinox Preservation Trust** (802-366-1400; equinoxpreservationtrust.org), Manchester Village. This nonprofit organization was formed in 1996 to preserve 914 acres on Mount Equinox and the surrounding area. The parcel is open to the public for hiking, mountain biking, cross-country skiing, and snowshoeing. Horseback riding is permitted on the lower sections of the mountain. A downloadable trail map and user's guide with detailed trail descriptions—the 1.2-mile Equinox Pond loop trail is a must—and parking information is available on the website. The trust offers special events and nature walks year-round, some geared to children.

🐾 🎣 **Merck Forest & Farmland Center** (802-394-7836; merckforest.org), 3270 VT 315, Rupert. Open year-round, dawn to dusk; free. This 3,162-acre forest and farming area, set aside in the 1950s as a model for conservation and sustainable land use, is a nonprofit environmental education organization with an organic farm with crops and livestock, an organic sugarbush, and a gift shop/online store selling farm products. The center has 28 miles of trails for walking, hiking, skiing, snowshoeing, and horseback riding, and a spring-fed swimming pond at the end of a 2-mile hike. Eight rustic cabins that sleep from 6 to 15 are available year-round (by reservation) for a modest fee. Each has a wood-burning stove, bunks, and a nearby outhouse. Shelters and tent sites also are available. The center offers nature programs, workshops, and educational day programs and camping trips for ages 4–20.

🐾 **Grout Pond Recreation Area** (802-362-2307; fs.usda.gov), west of the village of Stratton, with an entrance on Kelley Stand Road. Deep in the Green Mountain National Forest, this area offers fishing, swimming, picnicking, and camping on a first-come, first-served basis. Eleven of the 17 sites are walk-ins; some are accessible by boat. Ten miles of multipurpose trails link to another trail system. The popular 2.6-mile Pond Loop Trail can be completed in a few hours.

🐾 🎣 **Lowell Lake State Park** (802-824-4035; vtstateparks.com), 260 Ice House Road, Londonderry, off VT 11 east of Magic Mountain. A former summer camp with a rustic lodge, the park is currently undeveloped with no facilities. A 3.5-mile loop hiking trail encircles the pristine 100-acre lake, passing by a Revolutionary War–era cemetery. One section of the trail is open to mountain bikes and horses, and there's a boat launch for kayaks and canoes. Open year-round; entry is free.

Also see *Hiking* and Emerald Lake State Park and Hapgood Pond under *Lodging—Campgrounds*.

# ✳ Lodging

RESORTS 🎣 🐾 🎣 ♿ **The Equinox Resort & Spa** (802-362-4700; equinoxresort.com), 3567 Main Street, Manchester Village. One of Vermont's most historic hotels—it's on the National Register of Historic Places—has grown incrementally over the centuries, beginning as a pre–Revolutionary War tavern and recognized as a premier summer resort by 1863, the first year Mary Todd Lincoln vacationed here. Its 195 guest rooms are spread out in 4 buildings: the main hotel; neighboring Charles Orvis Inn (the nineteenth-century residence of the founder of the Orvis fly-fishing empire); the Townhomes; and the historic 1811 House, dating from the Revolutionary War era. The hotel's many dining options include

**Marsh Tavern**, which occupies the shell of the 1769 tavern by the same name and serves lunch and dinner daily, with live music on weekends. The **Spa at Equinox** has a fitness center, an indoor pool, and a full menu of services. In addition to tennis, golf, and touring bikes, guests can register for the **Land Rover Experience Driving School** (see *Bushwhacking*) and the **Green Mountain Falconry School**. Guests enjoy a full concierge service. $$–$$$$.

INNS AND BED & BREAKFASTS

IN MANCHESTER

**The Barnstead Inn** (802-362-1619; barnsteadinn.com), 349 Bonnet Street, Manchester Center. Neil and Cynthia Humphrey host guests in an 1830s carriage house with 14 attractive rooms,

THE EQUINOX LISA HALVORSEN

some with private entrance, fireplace, and exposed wooden beams. The Green River suite has hand-laid bluestone floors with a native rubble stone fireplace. The inn, located close to the village center, has a secluded outdoor pool and a pond. No meals are served, but it's an easy walk to good breakfast places. $–$$$$.

**The Inn at Manchester** (802-362-1793; innatmanchester.com), 3967 Main Street, Manchester Village. This gracious late-nineteenth-century home with its inviting front porch is set back from Main Street. Longtime hosts Frank and Julie Hanes provide 21 guest rooms, including 12 suites, with 4 in the restored, 1867 carriage house by the pool. Three rooms, including one suite, are located upstairs in the Celebration Barn, also used as a venue for weddings, accommodating 150 guests. The inn has a fully licensed bar and a self-service pantry with drinks and freshly baked goods. Breakfasts are full and hearty, including homemade breads and the inn's signature cottage cakes, served with warm apricot sauce. $$–$$$$.

**The Inn at Ormsby Hill** (802-362-1163; ormsbyhill.com), 1842 Main Street, Manchester Center. For a century, this elegant manor with spectacular mountain views was the summer home of Edward Isham, Robert Todd Lincoln's law partner. Today innkeepers MaryAnn and Jack Orlando welcome guests to this gracious inn, one of only 12 Four-Diamond Inns and Hotels in Vermont. The eight guest rooms and two suites have a queen or king four-poster bed, fireplace, and two-person whirlpool tubs. Some also have two-person steam saunas. The Frances Suite is over the top, with its private second-floor deck, wood-burning fireplace, and two bathrooms. Common space includes a serene living room, the conservatory where breakfast is served, and an informal gathering room with a massive fireplace, original to the 1764 house. $$–$$$$.

**The Inn at Willow Pond** (802-362-4733; innatwillowpond.com), 74 Willow Pond Road (VT 7A), Manchester Center. Located 2.3 miles north of town and owned by the Bauer family, this inn offers 40 spacious guest rooms and suites in three separate, contemporary condo-like buildings on a hillside overlooking the Manchester Country Club's golf course. The eighteenth-century Meeting House reception building contains a lofty main lounge, conference facilities, a fitness center with exercise equipment, two saunas, a library, and an outdoor lap pool. The suites feature a living room with a wood-burning fireplace. Continental breakfast included. $$–$$$$.

🐾 Ɛ **Reluctant Panther Inn & Restaurant** (802-362-2568; reluctantpanther.com), 39 West Road, Manchester Center. Styling itself as Vermont's premier small luxury hotel, the property, owned by Peter Sharpe and Jeff Ferrar, has 20 elegant rooms in three buildings: the Main House, the Mary Porter House, and the Carriage House. All have fireplaces and marble baths and are furnished with antiques and original artwork. A made-to-order breakfast is included. Options for dinner include the **Panther Restaurant** or the more informal **Panther Pub** and, in warmer months, **The Patio** for alfresco dining. $$–$$$$.

**Seth Warner Inn** (802-362-3830; sethwarnerinn.com), 2353 Main Street, Manchester Center. This historic 1800 house is set back from VT 7A, southwest of Manchester Village. Ask innkeeper Stasia Tetreault to see the thank-you note Robert Todd Lincoln wrote after staying here in 1911. Five bright guest rooms with exposed beams and stenciling are furnished in antiques and curtained in lace. Common space includes a gracious living room, a small library, and a dining room, in which guests gather for a full breakfast. The deck overlooks a duck pond. Children 13 and over. $–$$.

♂ 🐾 Ɛ **Wilburton Inn** (802-362-2500; wilburton.com), 257 Wilburton Drive, Manchester. This 30-acre hilltop estate is Manchester's most secluded inn and a popular wedding venue. The brick, Tudor-style mansion offers 11 spacious upstairs suites and bedrooms. Accommodations also are available in seven widely scattered buildings, including a two-bedroom innkeeper's cottage and a 15-bedroom mansion with ballroom that sleeps 34. In 1987, psychiatrist Albert Levis and his late wife Georgette bought the property, which is now managed by Melissa Levis and her brother Max. Melissa and sister Tajlei, a playwright, stage theatrical events, including murder mystery weekends. Every Wednesday in summer is Farm Night (open to the public), featuring outdoor dining with music and artisanal vegetarian cuisine from brother Oliver's **Earth Sky Time Community Farm** (802-384-1400; earthskytime.com). The grounds include a pool, tennis court, striking outdoor sculptures, and the Museum of the Creative Process, founded by Dr. Levis as a center for creative discovery and research. Ask about special events, including doggie slumber parties. $–$$$$.

## IN ARLINGTON

♂ Ɛ 🚹 **Arlington Inn** (802-375-6532; arlingtoninn.com), 3904 VT 7A. This stunning 1848 Greek Revival mansion was built by Martin Chester Deming, a Vermont railroad magnate. Owners Eric (a noted chef) and Elizabeth Berger offer 16 spacious rooms in the main house, carriage house, and adjacent 1830 parsonage, many with four-poster or sleigh beds, fireplaces, and antiques befitting the historic ambience. The inn also is a popular spot for dinner (see *Dining Out*), and the barn and gardens make an ideal venue for weddings. Made-to-order breakfast is included in the rate. $$–$$$$.

WILBURTON INN  LISA HALVORSEN

♂ ⚲ **West Mountain Inn** (802-375-6516; westmountaininn.com), 144 West Mountain Inn Road. The Carlson family has presided over this rambling, century-old, white-clapboard hillside home since 1978. The suites and rooms are country elegant, named for famous people associated with Arlington; a copy of Dorothy Canfield Fisher's *Vermont Tradition* is in every room. The property's Historic Mill has three two-bedroom townhouses with cooking facilities. Common rooms have fireplaces, and there's a children's playroom. Breakfast and dinner are served daily (see *Dining Out*). The inn's 150 acres contain walking and snowshoeing trails, gardens, and llamas in residence. Inquire about special events. $$–$$$$.

🐾 **Inn on Covered Bridge Green** (802-375-9489; coveredbridgegreen.com), 3587 River Road. Clint and Julia Dickens invite fans of Norman Rockwell to stay in his former home, built in 1792 across from the Arlington Green Covered Bridge and the village green where Ethan Allen mustered his Green Mountain Boys. The inn has seven nicely appointed guest rooms in the main house; a full country breakfast is included. Pets are permitted in the two housekeeping cottages; one was converted to a small art studio for Rockwell's son Jarvis, and the other was the artist-illustrator's studio. Guests can go swimming, canoeing, and fly-fishing in the Batten Kill, just a few hundred feet from the inn. The setting is quintessentially Vermont. $–$$$$.

## IN DORSET

♂ 🐾 ⚲ & **The Barrows House** (802-867-4455; barrowshouse.com), 3156 Main Street. In the heart of the village, this petite resort became a member of the Dorset Inn family in 2012. The property features a pool, two tennis courts, 6 acres of manicured grounds and gardens, a restaurant and taproom, and an outdoor dining terrace. The 27 guest rooms, suites, and cottages are a great fit for wedding parties, families, or special events. The central building is Dorset's first parsonage, built in 1796. Walk to town along marble sidewalks, but return for dinner at the exquisite gastropub. Rates include an elegant breakfast at the Dorset Inn. $$–$$$$.

♂ 🐾 ⚲ **Dorset Inn** (802-867-5500; dorsetinn.com), 8 Church Street. The inn, in continuous operation since 1796, faces Dorset's pristine town green. Known for its cuisine (see *Dining Out*) and relaxing atmosphere, the inn has 25 guest rooms, including six two-room luxury suites with a fireplace and whirlpool bath; all come with full breakfast. It's within walking distance of the Dorset Playhouse, the Bley House Museum, an art gallery, and a general store. The day spa offers facials and massages. $$–$$$$.

🐾 **Dovetail Inn** (802-867-5747; dovetailinn.com), 3370 VT 30. This gracious 1800s inn, facing Dorset's green, has 11 guest rooms ranging from cozy to luxurious. The Hearthside Room has a fireplace, a wet bar, and a deck. Guests have access to a butler's pantry, with a fridge, a microwave, and a sink. An expanded continental breakfast is served in the Keeping Room. $–$$$.

& **Inn at West View Farm** (802-867-5715; innatwestviewfarm.com), 2928 VT 30, Dorset, is a small lodge on a former farm with an appealing personality. Locally recognized for its exceptional cuisine (see *Dining Out*), the inn has 10 rooms, including one suite and one handicapped-accessible downstairs room, and inviting common spaces, including a wicker furniture-filled sun porch and a living room with a wood-burning fireplace. Full breakfast included. Children must be over 12. $$.

⚲ **Marble West Inn** (802-867-0400; themarblewestinn.com), 1847 Dorset West Road. This well-maintained historic inn with expansive mountain views has seven contemporary yet stylish guest rooms. Guests rave about the gourmet multicourse breakfasts prepared by innkeepers and Le Cordon Bleu–trained chefs Julia and Paul VanDerWielen, who

DOVETAIL INN LISA HALVORSEN

have taken locally sourced, farm-to-table cuisine to a new level. The couple also serves a four-course prix fixe dinner on Friday and Saturday evenings, by reservation. Seating is limited to 16; open to the public. $$–$$$.

## IN LANDGROVE

✪ ♂ ♨ 🐾 ♂ ♿ **The Landgrove Inn** (802-824-6673; landgroveinn.com), 132 Landgrove Road. This rambling country inn—a fine example of "Vermont continuous architecture"—on a quiet dirt road has 18 rooms, two with shared bath, many of which are well suited to families. The 32-acre property has a heated pool, tennis courts, a stocked trout pond (catch and release), and lawn games. Innkeepers Tom and Maureen Checchia also opened the InView Center for the Arts (802-824-6700) in a studio behind the inn, which offers multiday art workshops. In winter you can take a sleigh ride or ski the 10-km groomed cross-country trail system that leads to the picturesque village of Landgrove. Bromley Mountain Resort and Stratton Mountain Resort are close by. Breakfast is an event here, served on oak tables in the wood-beamed dining room overlooking the garden. The dining room is open to the public five nights a week (see *Dining Out*). $–$$$.

## IN SOUTH LONDONDERRY

♂ **The Londonderry Inn** (802-824-5226; londonderryinn.com), 8 Melendy Hill Road. On a knoll overlooking the West River, this large historic home has been a country inn since 1941. Innkeeper Maya Drummond has decorated the 27 guest rooms with folk-art-painted furniture and walls. The bright common rooms include a huge stone fireplace, a billiards room, a movie room, and Maya's antique bell collection. Freshly baked cookies are served every afternoon. Children will enjoy the resident corgis and the many nooks to explore. Breakfast included. $–$$.

## IN SUNDERLAND

♂ ♂ ♿ **Hill Farm Inn** (802-375-2269; hillfarminn.com), 458 Hill Farm Road. Located off VT 7A north of the village, this historic farmstead is set on 50 acres of land with walking trails bordering the Batten Kill. The 1830 main building and farmhouse comprise 11 guest rooms, including several suites. Cuddle up to goats, sheep, and potbellied pigs in the barn after enjoying a full country breakfast prepared by the on-site chef. A renovated farmhouse, sleeping eight, is also available to rent. $$–$$$.

♂ **Ira Allen House** (802-362-2284; iraallenhouse.com), 6311 VT 7A. Kevin Marvelli and Michael Garvey are the innkeepers of this roadside tavern built by Ethan Allen (his brother Ira was the surveyor) in 1779 with a "new" wing added in 1846. One of Vermont's oldest inns, it has four guest rooms and historic features, including hand-hewn beams, a fireplace of handmade bricks, wide-board floors, and original hand-blown glass windowpanes. The Batten Kill, popular for trout fishing and kayaking, runs through the property. Two-night minimum on weekends (Fri.–Sat.) Breakfast is included. $–$$.

MOTELS ♿ **Palmer House Resort** (802-362-3600; palmerhouse.com), 5383 Main

Street (VT 7A), Manchester Center. A family-owned motel with 50 rooms/suites: some with a fireplace, a Jacuzzi, and a refrigerator. Facilities include indoor and outdoor pools, a fitness center, a stocked trout pond, tennis courts, and a nine-hole golf course, all on 16 acres adjacent to the Green Mountain National Forest. Ye Olde Tavern restaurant (see *Dining Out*) is adjacent. $–$$.

🌀 ✒ **Olympia Lodge** (802-362-1700; olympia-vt.com), 7259 Main Street (VT 7A), Manchester Center. Its motto is "the motel that feels like an inn." Trish and Sal Asciutto have turned this 24-room lodge into an extension of their home and family. Accommodations are basic motel rooms, but most guests don't come for the rooms. They come to ski and play, and when they're through, they like to spend time in the lounge, with its full bar and fireplace. There is a pool and tennis in summer, and a hot breakfast served daily year-round. $–$$.

CAMPGROUNDS **Green Mountain National Forest District Office** (802-362-2307; fs.usda.gov), Manchester. A public information office serving the southern half of the 400,000-acre Green Mountain National Forest is located on VT 30/11 east of Manchester at 2538 Depot Street; open year-round, Mon.–Fri. Maps and information are available on places to fish, hike, cross-country ski, and camp. All national forest campsites are available on a first-come, first-served basis.

♻ ✒ **Emerald Lake State Park** (802-362-1655; vtstateparks.com), 65 Emerald Lake Lane, East Dorset, just off US 7. Open Memorial Day–Columbus Day weekend. This 430-acre park, with 67 campsites and 37 lean-tos, surrounds the 20-acre Emerald Lake, named for the color of its water. There's a beach, a snack bar, paddle- and pedal-boat rentals, three picnic areas, and hiking and nature trails.

🐾 ✒ **Hapgood Pond Recreation Area** (802-362-2307), 1615 Hapgood Pond Road, Peru. Acquired in 1931, this was the beginning of the Green Mountain National Forest. Visitors can swim, fish, and boat on the 7-acre pond, or they can hike the 8-mile forest trail. The camping area, with 28 sites (first come, first served), is separate from the picnic grounds and beach. See also *Swimming*.

🐾 ✒ **Merck Forest & Farmland Center** (802-394-7836; merckforest.org), 3270 VT 315, Rupert. Rustic cabins, lean-tos, and tent sites can be found in this 3,162-acre forest in the Taconic Mountains west of Dorset. See also *Green Space*.

## ✳ Where to Eat

DINING OUT

TOPS

**The Chantecleer Restaurant** (802-362-1616; chanteceerrestaurant.com), 8 Read Farm Lane, East Dorset. Open for dinner Wed.–Sun. The setting is an elegantly remodeled old dairy barn with a massive fieldstone fireplace. Long regarded as one of Vermont's top restaurants, Swiss chef Michael Baumann's establishment is known for nightly game specials and roast rack of lamb. Leave room for Bananas Chantecleer, premium

FISHING AT EMERALD LAKE STATE PARK  RACHEL CARTER

vanilla ice cream smothered with warm bananas and caramel-rum sauce. The wine list is extensive. Reservations essential. $$$–$$$$.

**Mistral's at Toll Gate** (802-362-1779; mistralsattollgate.com), 10 Tollgate Road, Manchester. Open for dinner daily except Wed. Reservations recommended. Chef Dana Markey and his wife Cheryl own this dining landmark, housed in the old tollhouse that once served the Boston-to-Saratoga road. The menu is French, from the pâté maison, escargots, and frog legs through the roast duckling and stuffed chateaubriand Béarnaise. All can be paired with wine from the *Wine Spectator* Award of Excellence–recognized wine list. $$$–$$$$.

**Silver Fork** (802-768-8444; thesilver forkvt.com), 4201 Main Street, Manchester. Open Tues.–Sat. for dinner. Reservations are needed far in advance for this intimate six-table restaurant with a large following. Menu choices are surprisingly large, too. Chef Mark French is originally from Baltimore, and you'll usually find oysters on the menu here, possibly pan fried with homemade tartar sauce, and crabcakes with house-made shoestring potatoes. He trained under a German chef, so expect dishes such as veal sautéed with onions and mushrooms, served with house-made spaetzle. For 13 years Mark and his wife Melody, who runs everything but the kitchen, had a restaurant in Puerto Rico, which explains the imaginative seafood, including salmon strudel, a house specialty. $$$.

✪ **SoLo Farm & Table** (802-824-6327; solofarmandtable.com), 95 Middletown Road, South Londonderry. Open nightly for dinner, except Tues.–Wed. Chef Wesley Genovart, who started the restaurant in 2011 with his wife Chloe, sources natural, mostly local ingredients for his inventive farm-to-table cuisine, pairing unexpected ingredients. He grew up in Spain, she is local, and the menus reflect both heritages. House-made, hand-rolled pasta is always on the menu, and choices could be russet potato-ricotta cheese gnocchi or a dill and rye seed pappardelle with rabbit and pork sausage. Entrées one night might include a wood-grilled Casco Bay monkfish and spring lamb, pork ramen and a moulard duck cassoulet the next. The restaurant's wine list is impressive. $$$.

✪ **Verdé** (802-297-9200; verde stratton.com), 19 Village Lodge Road, Stratton. Open daily for dinner, Fri.–Sun. for lunch. Dinner reservations recommended. The restaurant focuses on Mediterranean-inspired cuisine with a Vermont flare. Chef Aaron Mitchell-Patrick pushes boundaries to create dishes such as guinea hen cassoulet with stewed heirloom beans and house chorizo and Spanish turbot with a gold potato puree. Desserts include house-made ice creams and sorbets and a pistachio crème brûlée. Whatever you choose, it will be made from local ingredients with exceptional craft. $$$–$$$$.

*More fine dining*

**The Copper Grouse Restaurant and Bar** (802-362-0176; coppergrouse.com), 3835 Main Street, Manchester. Breakfast and dinner daily, lunch Mon.–Sat., Sunday brunch. Among the newest restaurant arrivals on Manchester's eclectic culinary scene, The Copper Grouse, located at the Kimpton Taconic Hotel, serves innovative tavern fare. Entrées range from the Cooper Grouse burger to lamb ravioli and beef tenderloin, all featuring products from Vermont purveyors. Or you can make a meal of small plates—confit chicken eggrolls, hand-cut truffle fries, or maple sriracha chicken wings, for example—with a signature cocktail, of course. $$–$$$$.

**The Perfect Wife Restaurant & Tavern** (802-362-2817; perfectwife.com), 2594 Depot Street, Manchester. Open Tues.–Sat. for dinner; tavern open later. Manchester native Amy Chamberlain credits her stint at Arrows in Ogunquit, ME, as the source of two of her specialties, sautéed crabcakes served with rémoulade on mixed greens as an appetizer and sesame-crusted yellow fin tuna, seared medium rare and served over stir-fried vegetables as an entrée—a house favorite since the restaurant opened in 1996. The menu changes regularly, dictated by what's fresh and seasonal, but also in keeping with Chef Amy's creative freestyle cuisine. Dining is in the cobble-walled dining room or the nicely lit greenhouse garden room. **The Other Woman Tavern** is a totally different and equally inviting scene, a lively local gathering place with music on weekends and a pub menu ranging from salads, sandwiches, and burgers to grilled strip steak. $$–$$$.

**Reluctant Panther** (802-362-2568; reluctantpanther.com), 39 West Road (VT 7A), Manchester Village. Open for dinner nightly except Sunday. The inn's relatively formal Main House dining room features two fireplaces with views of Mount Equinox and a landscaped backyard with a pond, gardens, and gazebo. The exquisite gourmet cuisine is seasonal, with an ever-changing menu, and the wine list is impressive. $$–$$$.

🍴 **Ye Olde Tavern** (802-362-0611; yeoldetavern.net), 5183 Main Street, Manchester Center. Open daily for dinner. This genuine 1790 tavern, with stenciled walls and period-perfect furnishings, specializes in "authentic American" dishes such as Yankee pot roast and roast tom turkey, but filet mignon and lobster bisque also are on the menu. Early-bird menu before 6, Sun.–Thurs. $$–$$$.

## IN DORSET

**The Barrows House** (802-867-4455; barrowshouse.com), 3156 VT 30. Open for dinner, Wed.–Sun. Although this is a gastropub, don't expect simple—this is still Dorset, after all. Start with sambal aioli or duck wings in mango sweet chili sauce. For your main course, seared scallops or veal Milanese might be in order. Ask to see the dessert menu. If it's available, order the s'mores pie with blowtorched marshmallows on top, although the mixed berry crepe brûlée is also a winner. Cocktails made from local spirits are key, too. In summer, sit outside by the fire pit. $–$$$.

**Dorset Inn** (802-867-5500; dorsetinn .com), 8 Church Street. Breakfast, lunch, and dinner served daily. Popular for pre-theater dining, as it is within walking distance of the Dorset Playhouse. Tavern classics such as turkey croquettes and liver with bacon and onions are offered beside short rib poutine and rainbow beet salad. $$–$$$.

**Inn at West View Farm** (802-867-5715; innatwestviewfarm.com), 2928 VT 30. Open for dinner Thurs.–Mon. Chef Raymond Chen describes his cuisine as contemporary American with French and Asian influences. Salads on any given night might include classic Vermont beets with goat cheese or a sesame-dressed seaweed salad. Pork belly sliders, dumplings, and other small plates are available, and for bigger appetites there are coriander-flavored, braised short ribs or a grilled hanger steak with asparagus. $–$$$.

## ELSEWHERE

**The Arlington Inn** (802-375-6532; arlingtoninn.com), 3904 VT 7A, Arlington. Chef Eric Berger has a reputation for serving reliably fine food in his magnificent 1847 mansion, open for dinner Tues.–Sat. Choose between the formal dining room and the more casual Deming Tavern. The Arlington Inn mixed grill, with petit mignon, duck breast, and loin lamb chop, is the house special, served with a white cheddar eggroll potato. A vegetarian dish is always available, perhaps porcini mushroom ravioli. $$$.

**The Landgrove Inn** (802-824-6673; landgroveinn.com), 132 Landgrove Road, Landgrove. Dinner by reservation; hours vary by season, so call ahead. This is relaxed fine dining at its best with meals by candlelight, overlooking the lovely garden at this country inn. The Vermont

Night special, a prix fixe three-course dinner, is offered every evening in summer and fall, Sun.–Thurs. in winter. Or choose from one of a half-dozen entrées on the menu such as crispy roast duckling or grilled lamb chops. Chef Katie Schneider is happy to accommodate vegetarians and vegans with advance notice. $$–$$$.

**West Mountain Inn** (802-375-6516; westmountaininn.com), 144 West Mountain Inn Road, Arlington. Open daily for breakfast and dinner. Hidden away on a hillside overlooking the Batten Kill Valley and Mount Equinox, this gracious inn is well worth seeking out. Fruit and cheese are served in the bar, followed by upscale, chef-driven meals that accentuate the beautiful food grown nearby, particularly local cheeses. $$.

## EATING OUT

### IN AND AROUND MANCHESTER

*Bob's Diner* (802-362-4681), 2279 Depot Street, Manchester Depot. Open daily for breakfast, lunch, and dinner. A shining chrome diner with very good food (the milkshakes are the best). Give it a try, especially with kids.

**Depot Bistro Café** (802-366-8181; depot62.com/cafe), 515 Depot Street, Manchester. The surroundings at this furniture store can best be described as futuristic Turkish shabby chic. The wonderful secret (other than the eclectic furnishings) is the wood-fired oven, which turns out pita, flatbreads, and kebabs straight from the fire. Ingredients are all organic, even those in the nutty, honey-rich baklava.

**Dormy Grill** (802-362-7870; playequinox.com), in the Golf Club at the Equinox, 108 Union Street, Manchester Village, serves lunch daily May–October, dinner May–Labor Day, with outdoor deck seating overlooking the ninth green. Enjoy tasty soups, salads, burgers, and paninis while feasting your eyes on the spectacular mountain vistas. Reservations are advised.

*Gringo Jack's* (802-362-0836; gringojacks.com), 5103 Main Street, Manchester Center, is a southwestern bar and grill with its own barbecue smokehouse on the premises. Open daily for lunch and dinner. Chips and salsa when you sit down, over 40 tequilas, a children's menu, and a pleasant outdoor patio in summer. Margaritas are half-price on Thurs.; seasonal specials. Check out their extensive product line.

*Mulligan's Manchester* (802-362-3663; mulligans-vt.com), 3912 VT 7A, Manchester Village. Open daily for lunch and dinner. A convenient, moderately priced, family-geared place featuring flame-grilled steaks, seafood, and pastas. Children's menu and daily specials. The restaurant has a second location at Stratton Mountain.

**Seasons Restaurant** (802-362-7272; seasonsvt.com), 4566 Main Street, Manchester Center. Open Tues.–Sun. for lunch and dinner. A local favorite for basics from pizza, a Reuben sandwich, or a fish taco to more expensive entrées, including miso honey-glazed salmon and New York strip steak.

*Zoey's Double Hex Restaurant* (802-362-4600; zoeys.com), 1568 Depot Street, Manchester Center. Open daily for lunch and dinner, closed Tues. Just what you may be looking for—a cheery, informal atmosphere with roomy booths, a screened porch, and famous burgers—but plenty of other choices as well, from meatloaf and chicken potpie to sage-rubbed grilled rib-eye. Also visit **Zoey's Deli and Bakery** (802-362-0005) at 539 Depot Street for dine-in or take-out lunch.

### IN LONDONDERRY

*The New American Grill* (802-824-9844; newamericangrill.com), 5700 VT 100. Open daily for lunch and dinner. Chef-owner Max Turner has put this cheerful eatery with friendly service and decent prices on the culinary map. The menu is big, varied, and reasonably priced, with the area's best burgers. Starters may include venison chili and mussels steamed in lemon broth, white wine, and lemon. The menu continues with salads, pastas, fish tacos, lobster risotto, jambalaya, veggie stir-fry, grilled sandwiches, and desserts. Daily specials and kids' menu.

**Swiss Inn** (802-824-3442; swissinn .com) 249 VT 11. Open to the public for dinner nightly during ski season, less often other times of the year. Raclette and fondues complement Swiss and German entrées, such as Geschnetzeltes (veal in a white wine and cream sauce), beef stroganov, and chicken Lugano (chicken breast dipped in a Gruyère cheese and egg batter); also continental dishes such as pasta with marinara and filet mignon.

## ELSEWHERE

**The Barn Restaurant and Tavern** (802-325-3088; barnrestaurant.com), 5581 VT 30, Pawlet. Open for dinner Wed.–Sun. The classics menu—everything is priced at $14—offers salmon, filet mignon, scallops broiled or grilled, and other "classic" dishes. But you aren't limited to these. The menu includes a number of shared plates, salads, and entrées, including ribeye. The restaurant is in a vintage dairy barn with a huge stone hearth and a view of the Mettawee River.

## BREAKFAST & LUNCH

### IN AND AROUND MANCHESTER

**Al Ducci's Italian Pantry** (802-362-4449; alduccis.com), 133 Elm Street, Manchester Center. Open daily. Eat-in or take-out at this authentic Italian deli. The menu includes several customizable sandwich choices. Salads and dinner entrées are available by the pound for take-out. The eatery also sells artisanal cheeses, breads, and Italian specialty foods.

**Gourmet Café and Deli** (802-362-1254; manchestergourmetdeli.com), 4961 Main Street, Manchester Center.

Open daily for breakfast and lunch in Manchester Center's Green Mountain Village shopping center. This café is a real find, with a pleasant atmosphere and service, reasonable prices, great salads, sandwiches, and Vermont craft beers.

**Little Rooster Café** (802-362-3496), 4645 Main Street, Manchester Center. Breakfast and lunch; closed Wed. This pleasant chef-owned café is one of the hottest lunch spots in town, offering daily specials and the ultimate corned beef hash, signature Maine crabcakes served on watercress with French bread, and delicious tuna Niçoise. Full liquor license. If you come at noon, be prepared to wait. No credit cards.

**Spiral Press Café** (802-362-9944; spiralpresscafevt.com), 15 Bonnet Street, at the Northshire Bookstore (see *Selective Shopping*). Open daily. A comfortable oasis for book lovers, with teas and specialty coffees, good sandwiches, and freshly baked cookies and treats.

**Up for Breakfast** (802-362-4204), 4935 Main Street. Open daily. Cheerful, small upstairs eatery with a huge menu and reputation. Be prepared for fanciful omelets with avocado crabcakes and salmon, wild turkey hash, or Belgian waffles. The orange juice is freshly squeezed, and the coffee can be cappuccino or latte.

MORE FOOD AND DRINK ✎ **Mother Myrick's Confectionary** (802-362-1560; mothermyricks.com), 4367 Main Street, Manchester Center. Open daily. Famous for its buttercrunch toffee, handmade chocolates, and Lemon Lulu cake.

✎ **Village Peddler and Chocolatorium** (802-375-6037; villagepeddlervt .com), 261 Old Mill Road, East Arlington. Located just off VT 7A, this shop sells chocolate, fudge, and Vermont products, although its big draw is its Chocolatorium, where you can watch a video on chocolate, from harvest to processing; sample chocolate or make your own chocolate bar (for a fee); and view displays of vintage chocolate-making equipment, chocolate sculptures, and a 100-pound bear made of chocolate.

🍦 **Wilcox Ice Cream** (802-362-1223; wilcox-ice-cream.com), 6354 VT 7A, Sunderland. Some of the creamiest, most delectable flavors (try the maple gingersnap) in Vermont are made by the Wilcox family. Although this ice cream stand is only open in summer, Wilcox ice cream is available in retail sizes at grocery stores and served at local restaurants.

GENERAL STORES **Dorset Union Store** (802-867-4400; dorsetunionstore.com), 31 Church Street, Dorset, opposite the Dorset Inn. Open daily. A village landmark since 1816, it carries general provisions and then some, including deli sandwiches; house-made cookies; and an extensive selection of wines, cheeses, and Vermont products, all perfect for a picnic on the green.

**H. N. Williams General Store** (802-867-5353; hnwilliams.com), 2732 VT 30, Dorset. Open daily. A large white barn of a store housed in what started out as an 1840 harness shop, one of Vermont's oldest family-run businesses. The deli/café here is one of the best places around for a sandwich (hot or cold), panini, soup, pie, or daily special; eat-in or take-out. The store also sells clothing, specializing in US-made apparel, along with everything from yard equipment to toys, fertilizer, tools, and pet food and supplies.

**J. J. Hapgood General Store and Eatery** (802-824-4800; jjhapgoodgeneralstore.com), 305 Main Street, Peru. Open daily, serving breakfast and lunch. The store, established in 1827, is the longest continuously operating general store in the state. Owners Juliette and Tim Britton bought it in 2013, turning the store into a gathering space with tables, an open kitchen, and a full deli. Breakfast on organic oatmeal and corned beef hash. Sandwiches are on house-made wheat bread, soups are made daily, and all meat and produce is locally sourced. The store also sells specialty pizzas, Vermont products, freshly baked goods, and more.

DORSET UNION STORE LISA HALVORSEN

# ✳ Entertainment

&#9855; **Dorset Playhouse** (802-867-5777; dorsetplayers.org), 104 Cheney Road, Dorset. The Dorset Players, a community theater group formed in 1927, own and perform in this beautiful playhouse in the center of Dorset. In summer the Dorset Theatre Festival stages new plays and classics, performed by well-known actors and resident professionals, six days a week, June–early September.

**Manchester Music Festival** (802-362-1956; mmfvt.org) hosts a series of chamber music concerts in early July–mid-August with performances at the Southern Vermont Arts Center.

**Village Picture Shows** (802-362-4771; villagepictureshows.com), 263 Depot Street, Manchester Center. Mainstream and art films.

Also see the Weston Playhouse (westonplayhouse.org) in "Okemo Valley Region."

# ✳ Selective Shopping

LOCAL LANDMARKS **Orvis Retail Store** (802-362-3750; orvis.com), 4200 Main Street, Manchester Center, supplying the needs of anglers and other sportsmen since 1856. Known widely for its mail-order catalog and retail shops throughout the US and UK, the Orvis flagship store is styled as a luxury country lodge but still specializes in the fishing rods made in the factory out back. It also sells fishing tackle and gear, country clothes, and other small luxury items—from silk underwear to welcome mats—that make the difference in country, or would-be country, living. Open daily year-round. **Orvis Outlet** is at 4382 Main Street.

✿ **The Northshire Bookstore** (802-362-2200; northshire.com), 4869 Main Street, Manchester Center. Open daily. One of Vermont's most browse-worthy bookstores, with a broad selection of

adult titles, children's books, and DVDs. The Morrows have stocked the venerable Colburn House with a wide range of volumes, including used and antiquarian. They schedule frequent author lectures, book signings, and co-sponsored events, offering breakfast, lunch, and snacks in their **Spiral Press Café** (see *Eating Out*).

ART GALLERIES AND CRAFTS STUDIOS *Note:* Memorial Day weekend is Open Studio Weekend (vermontcrafts.com; see *Special Events*). Southern Vermont Arts Center (see *Must See*) hosts multiple rotating exhibits.

IN THE MANCHESTER AREA

✪ **Epoch** (802-768-9711; epochvermont.com), 4927 Main Street, Manchester Center. This is a standout cooperative gallery, showcasing works by 18 top-tier members that include glass, wooden creations, furniture, jewelry, paintings, sculpture and woven work, painted floor mats, and much more. Open daily.

**Helmholtz Fine Art** (802-855-1678; helmholzfineart.com), 442 Depot Street, Manchester Center. Open Wed.–Sun. Lisa Helmholtz-Adams launched the gallery in 2014 and represents several artists, primarily from Vermont. The gallery hosts regular events throughout the year for the public to meet the artists and learn about their work.

✿ **Manchester Arts Studio and Gallery** (802-768-8593; manchesterartsvt.com), 4497 Main Street, Manchester Center. The venue, which includes both fully equipped pottery and sewing studios, encourages artistic exploration and creativity through weekly classes, workshops, events, and open studio time in various media for adults and kids. The Create 'n Sip painting parties (adults) and pizza and paint parties (kids) are popular.

**Manchester Hot Glass** (802-362-2227; manchesterhotglass.com), 79 Elm Street, Manchester Center, is a full-service glassblowing studio and gallery. Usually open Thurs.–Mon., but call ahead.

**Tilting at Windmills Gallery** (802-362-3022; tilting.com), 24 Highland Avenue (VT 11/30), Manchester Center. Open daily. An unusually large gallery with national and international works in oils and egg tempera, mostly realism and impressionism.

## IN DORSET

**3 Pears Gallery** (802-770-8820), 41 Church Street, Dorset. Located on Dorset's green, the gallery is a well-curated showcase for the work of 30 local artists and artisans, in media ranging from fine art to ceramics, artisan jewelry, and garden art.

**Flower Brook Pottery** (802-867-2409; flowerbrookpottery.com), 3210 VT 30. Open Tues.–Sat. Potter Janno Gay creates whimsical, handcrafted, hand-painted pieces, specializing in collectible pottery, for sale in her shop. She has a paint-your-own studio and will ship your art home (for a fee).

**Gallery on the Marsh** (802-867-5565; westinpitcherart.com), 2237 VT 30. Open most days. The gallery beside the artists' home displays realistic wildlife paintings by John Pitcher and farm life landscapes and portraits by his wife, Sue Westin.

## ELSEWHERE

**Bob Gasperetti Furniture Maker** (802-293-5195; gasperetti.com), 848 South End Road, Mount Tabor. Shaker-, Mission-, and Arts & Crafts–inspired furniture; call for appointment.

✪ **D. Lasser Ceramics** (802-824-6183; lasserceramics.com), 6405 VT 100, Londonderry. Open daily. At this studio showroom, you can observe artisans at work, creating colorful and original dishware, vases, and other pottery pieces in more than 30 different color patterns.

**Lake's Lampshades** (802-325-6308; lakeslampshades.com), 60 School Street, Pawlet. Open Mon.–Sat. Judy Sawyer Lake's studio/shop is a riot of fabrics and colors, all shaped into lampshades. If you can't find something here to brighten a corner of your life, Judy will make it to order.

**FACTORY OUTLETS** The cluster of designer discount stores in Manchester Center evokes mixed feelings from Vermonters. Some chafe at what they consider to be corporate intrusion into a once-quiet village. Others welcome the increased exposure, not to mention the acres of quality goods. In general, the prices are not rock-bottom, but they are better than you'd find in the city. Most are open 10–6 daily, later in summer.

**Manchester Designer Outlets** (manchesterdesigneroutlets.com). The glass-and-wood anchor complex at and near the junction of VT 7A and VT 11/30 in Manchester Center houses several designer outlets: Ann Taylor, Armani, J. Crew, Brooks Brothers, Crabtree & Evelyn, Eddie Bauer, Michael Kors, Marimekko, Polo Ralph Lauren, and many more.

**J. K. Adams Co. and The Kitchen Store** (802-362-4422; jkadams.com), 1430 VT 30, Dorset. Open daily. A three-floor cornucopia of top-quality kitchen gear from butcher blocks to knife racks, tableware, and cookbooks, with an observation deck overlooking the woodworking factory. Everything a foodie could want. The Dorset Farmers' Market is held here Sundays in winter.

**SPECIALTY SHOPS** **Long Ago & Far Away** (802-362-3435; longagoandfaraway.com), 4963 Main Street, Manchester Center. Grant and Betsy Turner own this gallery, which specializes in Canadian Inuit, Native Alaskan, and Native American art, including sculpture and jewelry with many one-of-a-kind pieces. Open daily.

&. **The Mountain Goat** (802-362-5159; mountaingoat.com), 4886 Main Street, Manchester Center. Open daily. Quality outdoor clothing and gear are the hallmarks of this and other Mountain Goat stores (in Northampton and Williamstown, MA). Owner Ron Houser really knows which shoe is good for your foot. Houser specializes in orthotics "for athletes, hikers, and everyday victims of gravity."

ANTIQUES SHOPS **1820 House of Antiques** (802-293-2820), 82 South Main Street, Danby. Open year-round, daily in summer, closed Tues.–Wed. in winter. A number of dealers sell through this shop, which features American country and formal furniture and accessories.

**Brewster Antiques** (802-362-1579), 152 Bonnet Street, Manchester Center. Just off VT 7A, open Mon.–Sat. The shop carries a wide assortment of antiques, including estate jewelry, mainly from the 1850s–1960s.

**Comollo Antiques** (802-362-7188; vtantiques.com), 4686 Main Street, Manchester Center. Open daily. Furniture, fine art, estate jewelry, folk art, toys, and international wines.

**East Arlington Antiques Center** (802-375-6144), 1223 East Arlington Road, Arlington. Open daily. More than 70 dealers sell everything from linens to silver, furniture, art, and other collectibles at this antiques center, located in a vintage former movie theater on a scenic byway. Continue along this road to the Chiselville Covered Bridge, built in 1870 and named for the chisel factory that once stood nearby.

**Marie Miller Antique Quilts** (802-867-5969; antiquequilts.com), 1489 VT 30, Dorset. Open daily. Over 200 antique and vintage quilts, dating from the nineteenth and early-twentieth centuries, for sale, plus hooked rugs, antique Quimper, and faience (tin-glazed pottery).

FARMS *Note:* The Vermont Maple Open House Weekend (vermontmaple.org) is held in late March. See *Special Events*.

✪ ✿ ✿ **Consider Bardwell Farm** (802-645-9928; considerbardwellfarm.com), 1333 VT 153, West Pawlet. Consider Stebbins Bardwell opened Vermont's first cheesemaking co-op here in 1864; more than a century later, current owners Angela Miller and Russell Glover make award-winning artisanal cheeses by hand, using milk from their herd of Oberhasli goats and from Jersey cows on neighboring farms. Cheese is available for sale, or you can take a self-guided tour of the farm, visit the pastured animals, or picnic on the grounds. Check the website for on-farm events.

✿ **Dutton Berry Farm** (802-362-3083; duttonberryfarm.com), 2083 Depot Street (VT 11/30), Manchester. This is one of three farm stands (the original is in Newfane) featuring local produce, much of it grown in 14 greenhouses on Paul Dutton's farms in the West River Valley. In winter it's a good spot for locally grown Christmas trees and wreaths. Open daily year-round. Pick-your-own in summer.

✿ **Taylor Farm** (802-824-5690; taylorfarmvermont.com), 825 VT 11, Londonderry. Holstein and Jersey milk cows provide milk for the farm's famous Gouda cheeses and baked goods. Wagon and sleigh rides, farm animal visits. Open daily.

✿ **Equinox Valley Nursery** (802-362-2610; equinoxvalleynursery.com), 1158 Main Street, Manchester. Open daily, closed Thurs.–Sun., January–April. An outstanding nursery and farm stand managed by three generations of the Preuss family; good for picking vegetables, berries in-season, and Christmas tree sales—they'll even deliver, set up, and add lights. The nursery is famous for its Pumpkin Patch, with its autumn-themed displays, corn maze, wagon rides, and pumpkin-carving festival.

✿ **Mad Tom Orchard** (802-366-8107; madtomorchard.com), 2615 Mad Tom Road, East Dorset. A seasonal farm stand and pick-your-own farm with raspberries and tart cherries, beginning in July, and apples September–mid-October. Open daily in-season, except Mon.

# ✳ Special Events

*March:* **US Open Snowboarding Championships**, Stratton Mountain Resort (stratton.com). **Vermont Maple Open House Weekend**, late March, at local sugarhouses (vermontmaple.org).

*Memorial Day weekend:* **Vermont Open Studio Weekend**. See vermontcrafts.com for list of participating area art and crafts studios and galleries.

*June:* **Manchester Antique & Classic Car Show** (manchestercarshow.com) at Dorr Farm with a vintage sports car climb to the Mount Equinox summit. **Wanderlust** (wanderlust.com/festivals/stratton), Stratton Mountain, combining yoga, music, and wellness and nature activities.

*Mid-June–early September:* **Dorset Theatre Festival** summer season (dorsettheatrefestival.org).

*July 4:* Manchester (manchestervermont.com) and Dorset (dorsetvt.com) both host an old-fashioned Fourth, a daylong celebration that culminates in fireworks.

*July–mid-August:* The **Vermont Summer Festival Horse Show** comes to Manchester for six weeks (vt-summerfestival .com). **Summer Concert Series** on the Manchester town green, Tues. evenings in July and August (manchestervermont .com)

*Late August:* **Bondville Fair** (bondvillefair.org), one of Vermont's oldest and most colorful country fairs.

*Late September:* **Peru Fair** (perufair .org), old-fashioned country fair with pig roast, crafts, food, and entertainment.

*October:* **Manchester Fall Art and Craft Festival** (craftproducers.com) at Riley Rink, Manchester Center.

*December:* **Manchester Merriment** (manchestervermont.com)—historic inns tour, tree lighting, annual lighted tractor parade, horse and wagon rides.

*Thanksgiving weekend through New Year's:* **Hildene Holiday Tours** (hildene .org) of the mansion, decorated for Christmas.

# OKEMO VALLEY REGION

*Including Ludlow, Chester, Cavendish,*
*Mount Holly, Andover, Plymouth, and Weston*

The area is anchored by Okemo, a major ski resort, in the village of Ludlow, the area's largest community. East of town, VT 131 follows the Black River—once the power source, with Jewell Brook, for the nineteenth-century mills—through the smaller mill villages of Proctorsville and Cavendish. VT 103 branches south, following the Williams River to Chester, a handsome old crossroads community at the confluence of five roads and comprising three distinctive villages, all within walking distance. It offers an exceptional choice of lodging, dining, and shopping and easy access to much of southern and central Vermont.

Given its central location and lodging both on and off the mountain, Ludlow is a good base from which to explore. VT 103 climbs west into hill towns and down into the Lower Champlain Valley. VT 100 climbs south up Terrible Mountain and down into Weston. North of town VT 100 follows the river and ponds to Plymouth Notch, birthplace of Calvin Coolidge. His village, now preserved as a state historic site (see *Coolidge* sidebar), looks much as it did in 1923, when he was sworn in as the 30th president of the United States by his father in his kerosene-lit home. Coolidge attended Ludlow's Black River Academy, now a great little museum. (See *Must See*.)

**GUIDANCE** **Okemo Valley Regional Chamber of Commerce** (802-228-5830; yourplace invermont.com), 57 Pond Street, Ludlow. Closed Sunday. This walk-in information office in the Marketplace, across from Okemo Mountain Access Road on VT 103 (look for the clock tower), has regional menus, events listings, and lodging brochures. The chamber also publishes the *Okemo Valley Regional Guide*.

**GETTING THERE** *By air*: Ludlow is approximately a two-hour drive from several airports, including Albany, Hartford, Burlington, and Manchester, NH. Cape Air has a one-hour flight from Boston to Rutland (Rutland-Southern Vermont Regional Airport), which is 25 minutes from Ludlow.

*By car*: From points southeast, take I-91 to Vermont Exit 6 to VT 103 north to Chester and Ludlow. The area can be accessed from I-91, Exits 7 and 8. From New York and western Massachusetts, take I-87 north to New York Exit 23, then follow I-787 to Troy to Exit 9 toward Bennington.

*By rail*: Amtrak's **Ethan Allen Express** (800-USA-RAIL; amtrak.com) offers daily service from New York City's Penn Station to Rutland via Albany. In winter, Amtrak's **Thruway Bus** transports passengers from the Rutland train station to Okemo.

**GETTING AROUND** **Okemo Mountain Resort** (802-228-4041; okemo.com) offers a free shuttle to the village on weekends and during holiday periods, December–March. Buses make frequent stops at several locations in the Ludlow/Proctorsville area. The resort provides round-trip shuttle service from the Rutland-Southern Vermont Regional Airport and the Rutland Amtrak terminal when booked with lodging reservations. **Okemo Mountain Resort Properties** provides free shuttle service for owners and

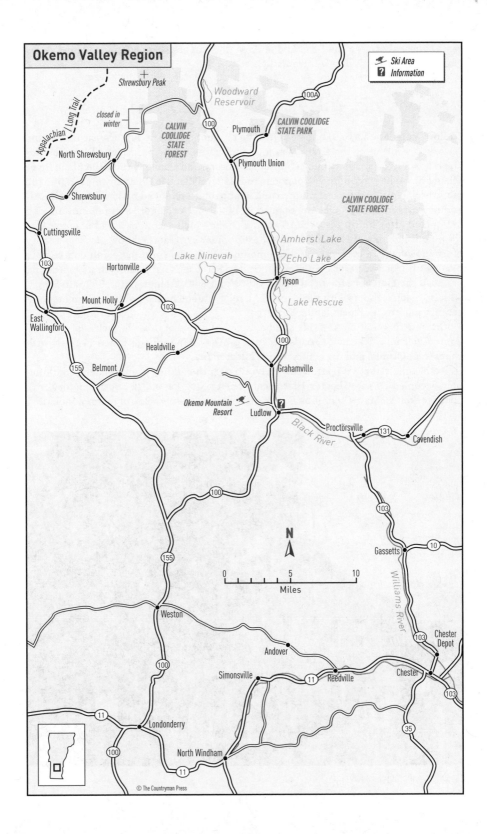

# Okemo Valley Region

Ski Area
? Information

Shrewsbury Peak

Woodward Reservoir

closed in winter

100

CALVIN COOLIDGE STATE FOREST

Plymouth

100A

CALVIN COOLIDGE STATE PARK

North Shrewsbury

Plymouth Union

Appalachian / Long Trail

Shrewsbury

CALVIN COOLIDGE STATE FOREST

Cuttingsville

103

Amherst Lake

Hortonville

Lake Ninevah

Echo Lake

Tyson

Mount Holly

103

Lake Rescue

East Wallingford

Healdville

100

Belmont

155

Grahamville

Okemo Mountain Resort

Ludlow

?

Black River

Proctorsville

131

Cavendish

100

103

N

Gassetts

10

0    5    10
Miles

155

Williams River

Weston

Andover

103

Chester Depot

100

Simonsville

11

Reedville

Chester

103

11

Londonderry

35

100

North Windham

11

© The Countryman Press

rental guests between the Base Lodge Area, the Inn at Jackson Gore, Okemo Valley Nordic Center, and Willie Dunn's Grille.

## ✳ Towns and Villages

**Ludlow** (population 2,640) boomed with the production of "shoddy" (fabric made from reworked wool) after the Civil War, a period frozen in the red brick of its commercial block, Victorian mansions, magnificent library, and academy (now the Black River Museum). In the wake of the wool boom, the General Electric Company moved into the picturesque mill at the heart of town and kept people employed making small-aircraft engine parts until 1977. Okemo, opened in 1956, was a sleeper—a big mountain with antiquated lifts—until 1982, when Tim and Diane Mueller bought it and began transforming it into one of New England's most popular ski resorts, known for the quality of its snowmaking, grooming, and on-mountain lodging. An 18-hole golf course doubles as a full-service cross-country ski center. For a sense of Ludlow in its pre-skiing era, visit the **Fletcher Memorial Library** (802-228-8921; fmlnews.org), 88 Main Street, with its reading rooms with fireplaces; old-style, green-shaded lights; and nineteenth-century paintings of local landscapes.

**Chester** (population 3,154) is sited at the confluence of three branches of the Williams River and five major roads. Its string-bean-shape village green is lined with shops, restaurants, and the centerpiece **Fullerton Inn**.

Across the street (VT 11) is the early nineteenth-century brick academy building now occupied by the **Chester Historical Society** (802-875-5459; chesterhistory.org), open weekends, May–Columbus Day. It presents the town's colorful history, including

THE CHESTER HISTORICAL SOCIETY LISA HALVORSEN

the story of Clarence Adams, a prominent citizen who broke into more than 50 businesses and homes between 1886 and 1902 before being apprehended. VT 103 forks north from the village center to **Chester Depot**, a cluster of homes and public buildings around the well-kept Victorian depot and the town hall. Follow VT 103 past the vintage 1879 red wooden Yosemite Fire House with its two towers (one for the bell, the tall one for drying hoses) to the **Stone Village**, a double line of early-nineteenth-century houses built from locally quarried granite. Built by two brothers in the pre–Civil War decade, the buildings later played a role in the Underground Railroad. Chester offers more than its share of local lodging, dining, and shopping. The town is handy to skiing at **Magic Mountain**, **Bromley**, and **Okemo** and to cross-country skiing and biking at **Grafton Trails & Outdoor Center** (see the "Lower Connecticut River Valley" chapter).

**Weston** (population 630). A logical hub for exploring southern Vermont, this village is home to the **Weston Playhouse**, one of the country's oldest and best summer theaters, and the original **Vermont Country Store**. Majestic maples shade the oval common, and a band plays regularly in the bandstand in summer. Weston was one of the first villages in Vermont to be consciously preserved. Like the theater, the unusually fine historical collection in the **Farrar Mansur House** and (indirectly) **The Vermont Country Store** all date from the "Weston Revival" of the 1930s. Visitors are very welcome at **Weston Priory** (802-824-5409; westonpriory.org), a community of Benedictine monks, nationally known for the Gregorian chant in their daily common prayer and other music sung and played during Sunday liturgies. There's a gift shop, a retreat house, and a rare sense of peace both inside and outside the monastery. Free summer concerts are presented by the **Kinhaven Music School** (see *Entertainment*).

## Must See

**Black River Academy Museum** (802-228-5050; bramvt.org), 14 High Street, Ludlow, open Memorial Day–Columbus Day, Tues.–Sat.; winter by appointment. Built in 1889, the academy's reputation drew students from throughout New England. President Calvin Coolidge was a member of the class of 1890. Now a museum, exhibits about "Main Street" circa 1900, a Ludlow home circa 1870, and an early twentieth-century classroom offer a sense of what it meant (and still means) to live in the Black River Valley. Another exhibit, created by local elementary school students, focuses on Ludlow's barns. The museum contains a restored painted theater curtain and a collection of clothing, tools, and other artifacts from Finnish families who settled in the area in the early 1900s.

**The Museums of Weston** (802-824-5294; weston-vermont.com/weston-vermont-historic-museums). A trio of museums, open seasonally, depict life in eighteenth- and nineteenth-century Weston. Even if you have never set foot inside a historic house, make an exception for the **Farrar Mansur House** (658 Main Street), built in 1797 as a tavern with a classic old taproom. (Open for tours and demonstrations late June–mid-October.) Thanks to 1930s Work Progress Administration artists, murals

WESTON'S OLD MILL MUSEUM LISA HALVORSEN

# CALVIN COOLIDGE AND PLYMOUTH NOTCH

Calvin Coolidge (1872–1933) is best remembered for his dry wit and thrift, his integrity and common sense, all famously Vermont virtues. The village of Plymouth Notch—where Coolidge was born, assumed the presidency, briefly governed the country (in summer 1924), and is buried—is said to be the best-preserved presidential birthplace in the nation. It also may be the best-preserved Vermont village, offering an in-depth sense of the people who once lived there.

The **President Calvin Coolidge State Historic Site** (802-672-3773; historicsites.vermont.gov/coolidge) is open late May–mid-October, daily. Admission charged. During the off-season, the Aldrich House, which doubles as an office and exhibit space, is open weekdays (no charge, but call ahead).

In the **President Calvin Coolidge Museum and Education Center**, the main entrance to the village, the permanent exhibit, *More Than Two Words: The Life & Legacy of Calvin Coolidge*, dramatizes the story of how a boy from Plymouth Notch became president, using Coolidge's own words and interactive media.

The village at the foot of East Mountain remains low-key, much as it looked in the 1920s, although roads have been paved. Power lines are buried (electricity didn't reach Plymouth until after Calvin's death). You can visit the still-operating Plymouth Cheese factory (see *Cheese*) built by John Coolidge, the president's father, and the general store where he became storekeeper in 1868. The store sells, among other things, Moxie, the president's favorite soft drink, as well as penny candy, maple syrup, and Coolidge memorabilia.

Calvin was born on the Fourth of July, 1872, in the modest attached house. The family moved across the street to the larger Coolidge Homestead (inquire about guided tours) when he was 4 years old. It was there, when he was home to help with haying, that Vice President

CALVIN COOLIDGE'S BIRTHPLACE  LISA HALVORSEN

Coolidge learned of President Warren Harding's unexpected death. At 2:47 a.m. on August 3, 1923, he was sworn in, by his father, as 30th president of the United States.

"I didn't know I couldn't" was the reply Coolidge Sr. gave when reporters asked how he knew he could administer the presidential oath of office. "Colonel John" was a former state senator, notary public, and village sheriff, as well as shopkeeper. His terse response typifies the dry wit for which his son would later become known.

The population of Plymouth Notch during Coolidge's presidency was 29, with most of these residents comprising

CALVIN COOLIDGE'S GRAVESITE LISA HALVORSEN

the Old-Time Dance Orchestra, which played in the dance hall above the general store. This same room served as the Summer White House for a dozen days in 1924. At the time Calvin and his wife Grace were grieving the death of their son Calvin Jr., a promising 16-year-old who died due to a complication from an infected blister he acquired while playing tennis at the White House.

Plymouth resident Ruth ("Midge") Aldrich opened several tourist cabins (prefab jobs brought up from Boston) to accommodate the Secret Service and the Top of the Notch Tea Room to serve a steady stream of curious visitors. Plymouth Notch, however, never really hit the big time as a tourist attraction, perhaps because, while he continued to visit "The Notch," President Coolidge retired to private life not here but in his adopted home of Northampton, MA.

After graduating from nearby Amherst College, Coolidge opened a law practice in Northampton and served as mayor, and it was there that he met his wife, fellow Vermonter Grace Anna Goodhue, who was teaching at the Clarke School for the Deaf. He represented Northampton in the Massachusetts Legislature before becoming governor of the Bay State, and he died in Northampton as well.

It was Aurora Pierce, the family housekeeper, who fiercely preserved the Coolidge Homestead, adamantly opposing even minor changes like plumbing or electricity. Not until Aurora's death in 1956 did Vermont's Historic Sites Commission assume management of the house and its contents.

The historic site presently comprises 25 buildings, the majority of the village, including the square-steepled Union Christian Church, the setting for frequent concerts and lectures; a one-room schoolhouse; and barns housing farm implements and horse-drawn vehicles. The Wilder House Restaurant (open daily for breakfast and lunch) was the childhood home of Calvin Coolidge's mother. Coolidge is buried with seven generations of his family in the small graveyard across the road from the village.

Also see *Special Events*.

of Weston in its prime cover the living room walls, and a number of primitive portraits hang in the adjacent rooms over period furniture and furnishings donated by Weston families. The upstairs ballroom displays 1820s stenciling. In the attic, a rendition of townspeople dancing—each face is painted to resemble a specific resident—conjures the spirit of a town that knew how to have fun. Next door is the **Craft Building**, the town's first firehouse, which houses a Concord coach used by the Weston Cornet Band as a bandwagon from 1880 to 1930. A reproduction 1780 **Old Mill** stands by a dam and waterfall. You can see many vintage tools and demonstrations here, including grain grinding.

The **Vermont Scale Museum** is located inside **The Vermont Country Store** (802-824-3184; vermontcountrystore.com), 657 Main Street, Weston. This collection, which numbers more than 150 scales and devices made from 1850 to 1950, includes several Fairbanks and Howe scales used for sales, science, medicine, and other industries.

# ✳ To Do

ARTS AND CRAFTS **Fletcher Farm School for the Arts and Crafts** (802-228-8770; fletcherfarm.org), 611 VT 103 South, Ludlow. Operated since 1947 by the Society of Vermont Artists and Craftsmen, the school is headquartered in an old farmstead on the eastern edge of town. It offers courses throughout the year in traditional crafts, contemporary crafts, and fine art. In summer, lodging and meals are available on campus. In fall through spring, multiday workshops are offered at area inns. Crafts include fiber arts, stained glass, weaving, woodcarving, quilting, painting, rug hooking and braiding, and more. Open to all ages.

BIKING See *Okemo Mountain* sidebar for rentals, lift-served trails, and programs. **Mountain Cycology** (802-228-2722), 106 Main Street, Ludlow. No rentals, but store owners Rick and Pam Trainer sell and repair bikes and can advise on local bike routes.

BOATING **Echo Lake Inn** (802-228-8602; echolakeinn.com), 2 Dublin Road, Ludlow (VT 100), rents canoes and other boats to guests only. **Camp Plymouth State Park** (802-228-2025; vtstateparks.com), 2008 Scout Camp Road, Ludlow, off VT 100, offers seasonal canoe, kayak, and rowboat rentals (see *Swimming* for directions). Nearby **Lake Ninevah** is quiet, with some beautiful marshes and woods.

FISHING Lake Rescue, Echo Lake, Lake Ninevah, Woodward Reservoir, and Amherst Lake all have public access. Fishing licenses are required for anyone 15 or older. The catch includes rainbow trout, bass, perch, and pickerel. The Black River along VT 131 in Cavendish is good for fly-fishing. The 6-mile stretch from the covered bridge in Downers to a second covered bridge is a trophy-trout section, stocked each spring with 1.5-pound brown trout and 18-inch rainbows.

FITNESS CENTERS AND SPAS See sidebar for **Okemo Mountain Resort**.
**Castle Hill Spa** (802-226-7419; castlehillresortvt.com), 2910 VT 103, Proctorsville, (junction of VT 103 and VT 131). This spa in a historic carriage house on the Castle Hill Resort grounds is the only full-service spa in the Okemo/Ludlow area. It offers a range of exercise options, including tennis courts and a heated outdoor pool and hot tub for year-round use.
**Tater Hill Golf Club** (802-875-2517; taterhillgolfclub.com), 6802 Popple Dungeon Road, North Windham (off VT 11, not far from Chester). An 18-hole course with a pro

shop and practice range, now owned by Okemo. The full-service Clubhouse Restaurant has daily lunch specials.

SCENIC TRAIN RIDES **The Green Mountain Railroad** (802-463-3069; rails-vt.com/chester) offers fall foliage and dinner train excursions, mid-September–mid-October, leaving from Chester Depot, 539 Depot Street, Chester.

SWIMMING ✑ **West Hill Recreation Area** (802-228-2849), 37 Depot Street, Ludlow (West Hill off VT 103), includes a beach and a small, spring-fed reservoir, popular with kayakers and anglers.

**Buttermilk Falls**, at the end of Buttermilk Falls Road off VT 103 (just west of the junction of VT 100 and VT 103). This secluded swimming hole has a series of small, but beautiful, falls.

✑ **Camp Plymouth State Park** (802-228-2025; vtstateparks.com), 2008 Scout Camp Road, Ludlow. Turn east over the bridge off VT 100 across from Echo Lake Inn at Tyson. Continue 1 mile to the crossroads, then turn left onto Scout Camp Road. The park has a sandy beach on Echo Lake, a picnic area, boat rentals, volleyball, horseshoes, and a playground.

CHESTER DEPOT  LISA HALVORSEN

WALKING **Vermont Inn to Inn** (802-875-4288; vermontinntoinnwalking.com). Four-night, inn-to-inn walking tours (6–10 miles per day) are offered among four area inns. Luggage is transported for you, and a trail snack is provided, along with lodging, breakfast, and dinner.

SCENIC DRIVES **Okemo Mountain Road** in downtown Ludlow (off VT 100/103) follows the Okemo Mountain Access Road beyond the base lodge (stay left). Although it is a ski trail in winter, in summer and fall it's a hard-topped, 2.5-mile route to the summit. From the parking lot, take the half-mile trail through the woods to a former fire tower. On a clear day, you will have 360-degree views.

**Shrewsbury Loop.** From Ludlow, head north for 2 miles on VT 100, then northwest on VT 103 for 5 miles to Healdville. Watch for the sign for the **Crowley Cheese Factory** (802-259-2340; crowleycheese.com). The three-story wooden building, built in 1882 by Winfield Crowley, is America's oldest continuously operating cheese factory. In the 1880s, every Vermont town had a cheese factory to process surplus milk, but Crowley Cheese was distributed up and down the East Coast. Getting there requires a 2-mile detour down a side road, but it's well worth the effort. Visitors are welcome daily, although cheese usually is made only Tues.–Thurs. (See *Cheese*.) VT 103 climbs to Mount Holly, and then it continues another 5 miles to Cuttingsville. Turn at the

# A FAMILY-FRIENDLY SKI RESORT

Okemo Mountain Resort (802-228-1600; snow report: 802-228-5222; okemo.com), 77 Okemo Ridge Road or 111 Jackson Gore Road, Ludlow. A big mountain with southern Vermont's highest vertical drop, Okemo is a destination ski and snowboard resort with summer attractions and a family-friendly appeal.

The ski area has five distinct areas: Jackson Gore Peak, Solitude Peak, South Face, Glades Peak, and South Ridge. Jackson Gore has its own entrance, base area, lodging, and restaurants. Accommodations include 700 slope-side condominium units and the Jackson Gore Inn, with 245 condo-style units.

From the summit, beginners can run a full 4.5 miles to the base. There are a number of wide, central fall-line runs down the face of the mountain. World Cup is a long and steep, but forgiving, run with sweeping views down the Black River Valley to the Connecticut River.

Mountain Profile: Lifts: 20, including 5 high-speed quads (one is a 6-passenger bubble chair with heated seats—the first of its kind in the US); Trails and slopes: 121 trails and glades—32 percent novice, 37 percent intermediate, 31 percent advanced/expert. Vertical drop: 2,200 feet (the greatest vertical drop in southern Vermont); Snowmaking: covers 98 percent of trails; Ski school: Okemo's Ski + Ride School is staffed by 450 instructors. Children's programs are offered for ages 3-14. Ski and snowboard programs include Women's Alpine Adventures (1-3-day intensive programs). The Penguin Day Care Center for kids 6 months to 6 years provides supervised indoor and outdoor activities. Inquire about Kids' Night Out programs, available 6–9 p.m. in-season. Restaurants: The resort has a number of dining options from snack bars and cafés to fine dining restaurants, including Coleman Brook Tavern located at the Jackson Gore Inn. (see Dining Out).

CROSS-COUNTRY SKIING AND SNOWSHOEING Okemo Valley Nordic Center (802-228-1396; okemo.com), 89 Fox Lane, Ludlow, 1 mile from Okemo Mountain Resort's Jackson Gore. The center, located at the Okemo Valley Golf Club, has 22 km of tracked and skate-groomed trails plus 13 km of snowshoe trails. Instruction and rentals available. There's also a snack bar and a fully-stocked Nordic shop.

SNOWMOBILE RIDES Okemo Snowmobile Tours (802-422-2121; snowmobilevermont.com). The "Mountain Tour" is a one-hour guided tour through the woods, while the more adventurous "Back Country Tour" is a 25-mile ride through the Calvin Coolidge State Forest. Special tours for little ones on kid-size snowmobiles offered.

## SUMMER/FALL

ADVENTURE ZONE offers a summer/fall play center (for all ages). The big attraction here is the Timber Ripper Mountain Coaster, which also operates in ski season. Riders can control the speed of the sled-like cars that travel along 3,100 feet of track following the contours of the mountain, looping along down a 375-verti-

JACKSON GORE INN AT OKEMO MOUNTAIN   LISA HALVORSEN

FAMILY RIDING QUAD CHAIRLIFT AT OKEMO  COURTESY OF OKEMO MOUNTAIN RESORT

cal-foot descent. The Zone also includes an 18-hole miniature golf course, zipline tours, a treetop challenge course, a bungee trampoline, a climbing wall, and other activities. Best deal: Purchase an Adventure Zone wristband, good all day with unlimited access to many of the activities—including a scenic chairlift ride and a full-day pass to the **Spring House Pool and Fitness Center** (802-228-1419; okemo.com), a two-level fitness and aquatic center at Jackson Gore Inn, offering year-round swimming, racquetball, fitness classes, weights and cardio equipment, a hot tub, and a sauna. Wristbands are available at the Jackson Gore Resort Services desk or the Adventure Zone booth. Okemo's **Haulback Challenge Course** (combine with the Adventure Zone wristband and save) features three different courses of varying levels of difficulty. Or take a Segway tour. Both a one-hour introductory tour and a more challenging off-road tour are offered.

**BIKING** The **Spring House Pool and Fitness Center** offers seasonal hybrid bike rentals with map guides to local swimming holes as well as lift-served mountain biking with several miles of trails from the top of the South Ridge Quad chairlift (late May–early October). Mountain Outfitters (802-228-1450) offers fat bike rentals for use in the Jackson Gore base area, including on designated mountain areas. Bikes are designed for use on all surfaces, especially snow. Trail map provided.

**GOLF Okemo Valley Golf Club** (802-228-1396; okemo.com/golf), 89 Fox Lane, Ludlow. An 18-hole championship "heathland-style" course said to suggest Scottish links. Facilities include an 18-acre outdoor Golf Learning Center with a 370-yard-long driving range, four practice greens, and a 6,000-square-foot indoor practice area with a nine-hole putting green and a full-swing golf simulator. The club also has a pro shop and Willie Dunn's Grille (see *Eating Out*).

## YEAR-ROUND FUN

The **Ice House** sports pavilion transitions from a winter skating rink to a warm-weather complex with tennis courts, basketball courts, and a jogging track. A full massage menu is offered. Day passes are available.

road ("Town Hill") posted for **Shrewsbury**, and right again at the T toward Shrewsbury Center, with its white wooden church on a knoll beside two old taverns, now both B&Bs. One of these, **Smith Maple Crest Farm** (802-492-2151; smithmaplecrestfarm .com), has been in the same family since the early 1800s. Stop to buy some maple syrup and to take in the view. In North Shrewsbury, 2 more miles up the hill, the nineteenth-century **W. E. Pierce General Store** (802-492-3326; piercesstore.com) has been restored by the Preservation Trust of Vermont and is a community cooperative that sells soups, sandwiches, baked goods, local products, and groceries. Check out the signs tacked to the big old fir tree nearby. They point west to Rutland and east to Plymouth Union, giving the impression that you are standing on the peaked roof over this entire region. Fasten your seat belt and, conditions permitting, plunge east down the vintage 1930s CCC Road, one of Vermont's steepest and most scenic routes. It's 6 miles straight down (seemingly)—with superlative mountain and valley views—to VT 100 in Plymouth. Note the pullout for Shrewsbury Peak, the trailhead for a steep 1.2-mile path that connects with the Long Trail. This was the site of Vermont's second rope tow, installed in 1935 by the Rutland Ski Club. Around 2,400 spectators came up this road (now closed in snow season) to watch the skiers. Continue to VT 100A to Plymouth Union, perhaps the first rural Vermont village to be mentioned in publications throughout the world—on August 3, 1923. (See Calvin Coolidge sidebar on page 142.) Make your way back to VT 100. From Plymouth, it's a scenic 9-mile ride south past a chain of lakes to Ludlow.

**VT 100 Scenic Byway and loop**. VT 100 from Andover to Plymouth includes Plymouth Union and extends south through Ludlow. Head over Terrible Mountain to Weston (see *Towns and Villages*), then follow the Andover Road for 11 miles west to Chester (see *Towns and Villages*) and loop back to Ludlow (12 miles) on VT 103, detouring into the village of Proctorsville. Be sure to stop at Singleton's General Store.

# ✳ Lodging

RESORTS  See Okemo Mountain Resort sidebar on page 146.

♂ **The Castle Hill Resort and Spa** (802-226-7361; castlehillresortvt.com), 2910 VT 103, Proctorsville. The English Cotswold-style inn, a member of Historic Hotels of America, was built in 1901 for quarry and timber baron Allen Miller Fletcher, who was later elected governor of Vermont. It was the first home in the state to be fully wired for electricity, and today it has original woodwork, lighting fixtures, and other features. Accommodations include 10 luxuriously appointed rooms, many with mountain views. The dining room features a three-course prix fixe menu, and there's a full-service spa (see *Fitness Centers and Spas*). One- to three-bedroom condo units on-site, each with handcrafted furniture and a Jacuzzi tub,

are ideal for families, as are the family suites and rooms at the resort's Pointe Hotel (see *Motels*). Ask about spa, ski, and other packages. $$$–$$$$.

INNS

IN CHESTER

♂ **The Fullerton Inn** (802-875-2444; fullertoninn.com), 40 The Common. Bret and Nancy Rugg are the innkeepers of this big, old-fashioned inn on the Chester green. The Ruggs have renovated all 20 guest rooms, decorating each one individually, adding country quilts and fabrics and sitting rooms. Common spaces include the handsome lobby around the stone hearth, a tavern with its own hearth, a formal dining room (See *Dining Out*), and a sunny breakfast room. Ask about the Brewery Tour, which includes stops at five breweries or brewpubs and concludes with a beer-themed dinner in the inn's tavern. Packages are available with lodging, breakfast, dinner, and the tour. $–$$.

## IN LUDLOW

⚲ **Echo Lake Inn** (802-228-8602; echolakeinn.com), 2 Dublin Road (VT 100). Built in 1840 as a Victorian summer hotel, this four-story, white-clapboard inn has 23 rooms with an additional seven condo units in the adjacent Cheese Factory and Carriage House. Guest rooms vary far more widely than in most inns, from country traditional (with genuine nineteenth-century cottage furnishings) to romantic come-ons, with king-size beds and in-room jetted tubs, to family suites. Amenities include a spa room, tennis courts, an outdoor pool, and a dock on Echo Lake across the road, with rowboats and canoes. The inviting pub and dining room are open to the public (see *Dining Out*). Tom Gianola is your innkeeper. $–$$$$.

⚲ ♿ **The Inn at Water's Edge** (802-228-8143; innatwatersedge.com), 45 Kingdom Road. Bruce and Tina Verdrager have taken full advantage of the inn's location on Echo Lake, offering canoeing and fly-fishing, as well as bicycles and an outdoor hot tub for guests. The expansive Victorian house has 11 individually decorated rooms and suites with Jacuzzis and gas fireplaces. Doc's Place, a restored English pub, is ideal for an après-ski drink or a nightcap. Rates include a full breakfast and a four-course candlelit dinner, although B&B options are available. $–$$$.

**The Pettigrew Inn** (802-228-4846; pettigrewinn.com), 13 Pleasant Street. The former Andrie Rose Inn was purchased by Courtenay Dundy in July 2017, who renamed it for the Pettigrew family, prominent nineteenth-century Ludlow merchants. The 13 luxurious rooms, some with fireplaces, skylights, and spa tubs, are named after other historic local residents. Accommodations are in two historic nineteenth-century buildings and include a full gourmet breakfast. The

inn is handy both to Okemo and to village shops. $–$$.

## IN WESTON

🐾 ⚲ ♿ **Colonial House Inn & Motel** (802-824-6286; cohoinn.com), 287 VT 100. A rare and delightful combination of nine motel units and five traditional inn rooms (shared baths), connected by a pleasant dining room, a sunken sitting room, and a solarium overlooking the lawn. Second-generation innkeepers Kim and Jeff Seymour make all ages feel welcome, and most guests are repeats. Rates include a multicourse breakfast. The inn is 2 miles south of the village, with lawn chairs facing a classic farmscape across the road; most guest rooms overlook a meadow. Complimentary afternoon cookies. Dinner, served family style, available on weekends. $.

⚲ 🐾 ♿ **Inn at Weston** (802-824-6789; innweston.com), 630 Main Street (VT 100). Innkeepers Bob and Linda Aldrich have made this one of Vermont's outstanding inns. Enthusiastic gardeners, they maintain the fabulous gardens on the 6 acres surrounding this vintage 1848 inn on the edge of Weston Village. The 13 guest rooms are divided among the main inn, the Coleman House (with its own library/sitting room) across the road, and the Carriage House, with the most luxurious suites. All are delightfully furnished in antiques; some have a deck, whirlpool tub, and fireplace. The dining room (see *Dining Out*) is open to the public and justifiably popular, especially in summer on show nights at the nearby Weston Playhouse. $$–$$$.

## BED & BREAKFASTS

### IN CHESTER

⚲ ♿ **Chester House Inn** (802-875-2205; chesterhouseinn.com), 266 Main Street. A gracious village house dating from 1780, now with seven guest rooms, including a handicapped-accessible first-floor room with a canopy queen bed, a gas fireplace, and a steam shower. Four other rooms have a fireplace, another front room has a two-person Jacuzzi, and the family suite can sleep six. The inn is ideal for small weddings. Hosts Bob and Jan Francis offer a full breakfast. Well-behaved children over 10 are welcome. $–$$.

○ ✹ 🐾 🖋 **Henry Farm Inn** (802-875-2674; henryfarminn.com), 2206 Green Mountain Turnpike. This old tavern, set on 56 rolling acres, has a nice out-in-the-country feel. Larger than other farmhouses of the period, it was built in 1760 as a stagecoach stop on the Green Mountain Turnpike, now a quiet dirt road only minutes from the Chester green. The nine-room inn retains its pine floors, beehive oven, hand-hewn beams, and other original features. A path leads to the spring-fed pond up the hill, and a swimming hole in the Williams River is just across the road. In winter, ski out the back door through the woods and meadow or skate on the pond. Inquire about frequent quilting workshop

weekends. Your hosts are Paul and Patricia Dexter. Rates include a full country breakfast. $–$$.

🖋 **The Hugging Bear Bed & Breakfast and Shoppe** (875-2412; huggingbear .com), 244 Main Street. The centrally located inn, which overlooks the town green, is convenient to shops and restaurants. Each of the six rooms in this Italian Colonnade home, built in 1850, blends nineteenth-century charm with modern amenities. In keeping with the theme, innkeeper and shop owner Laura Thomas has tastefully tucked teddy bears throughout the inn. The adjoining shop, which has the largest selection of Steiff collectibles and Muffy Vanderbears in the Northeast, has 10,000 teddy bears in stock. Full country breakfast made to order. Two-night minimum on holiday weekends. $–$$.

♂ ♿ **Inn Victoria** (802-875-4288; innvictoria.com), 321 Main Street. With its mansard roof and columned porch, this is a showy Victorian on the Chester green. All six rooms are named for

HUGGING BEAR INN  LISA HALVORSEN

Queen Victoria's children. The Princess Victoria Room fills almost the entire third floor and features a queen-size bed in front of a gas fireplace, a separate sitting room, a mini-fridge, and a deluxe bath with the works. Request the Prince Albert Room (fully handicapped accessible) or the Princess Helena Room, the only two rooms with access to the hot tub on the back deck. Innkeepers Dan and Penny Cote stock a guest fridge, serve a three-course gourmet breakfast, and offer high teas (see *Tea* under *Where to Eat*). $–$$$.

## IN THE LUDLOW AREA

♂ ♿ **Golden Stage Inn** (802-226-7744; goldenstageinn.com), 399 Depot Street, Proctorsville. A stagecoach stop in the eighteenth century, Universalist minister Reverend Warren Skinner purchased the inn in 1830, and it stayed in the family for 100 years. Rumor has it that this was a stop on the Underground Railroad. There are six bright, comfortable guest rooms and two suites, one named for the writer and performer Cornelia Otis Skinner, a descendant of the reverend. Innkeepers Michael and Julie-Lynn Wood provide a full breakfast, afternoon treats, Saturday night chocolate cake, winter soups, and a bottomless cookie jar. Eggs are from their chickens and honey comes from their hives. Room discounts offered for Fletcher Farm students, April–August. $–$$$.

**The Okemo Inn** (802-228-8834; okemoinn.com), 61 Locust Hill Road, Ludlow, near the junction of VT 100 North and VT 103. Open year-round except for two weeks in April and November. Ron and Toni Parry have been the innkeepers here since 1972, and their 1810 home has the feeling of a well-kept lodge, effortlessly welcoming. There are 10 nicely furnished guest rooms, including one much-requested room in a poolside cottage; full breakfast included. Ask about the golf, ski and

stay, crafts school, and other seasonal packages. $–$$.

## IN WESTON

**Apple Knoll Inn** (802-824-0051; appleknollinn.com), 815 VT 100. Architecturally, 1830 was a good year, judging from the graceful lines of this farmhouse. Interior detailing includes Indian shutters, paneling, and wide-plank floors; there's a wood-burning Rumford fireplace and a piano in the parlor, also a library with a woodstove and a pool in the garden. Known for many years as the Darling Inn, it was given a new name and a new life by current proprietors Wes and Lisa Hupp. The four rooms vary in size and bed choice (from twins to king), but all are comfortably furnished with antiques and include a full breakfast. Two-night minimum stay required. A one-bedroom cottage that sleeps four is available for rent. $–$$.

MOTELS **Brandmeyer's Mountainside Lodge** (802-824-5851; brandmeyerslodge .com), 913 VT 100, Weston. Bob and Lisa Brandmeyer operate a cheery 10-unit motor lodge with a comfortable pub, serving a hot complimentary breakfast daily. Discounted room rates for Weston Priory visitors and clergy. $.

🐾 ♪ **Motel in the Meadow** (802-875-2626; motelinthemeadow.com), 936 VT 11 West, Chester. A former nurse, Pat Budnick is accustomed to caring for people as guests will attest. The motel with country decor is conveniently located near three ski areas—Okemo, Bromley, and Magic Mountain—with easy access to snowmobile trails. Two rooms have kitchenettes. The family room has two queen-size beds and twin bunk beds. Rates include a continental breakfast. Inquire about Music in the Meadow, held in July, and be sure to check out the gift shop with its many handmade items. $.

🐾 ♪ **The Pointe at Castle Hill Resort & Spa** (802-226-7361; castlehillresortvt.com),

2940 VT 103, Proctorsville. This contemporary motor inn has 70 fairly large rooms equipped with fridge and coffeemaker and 26 suites, some with full kitchen and sitting room with gas fireplace. The inn offers an indoor pool, a hot tub/spa room, business and fitness centers, and a game room. This is the check-in point for the **Castle Hill Resort and Spa** (see *Inns*), and guests have easy access (for a fee) to the Castle's full-service spa. $$–$$$.

🐾 🖋 **Timber Inn Motel** (802-228-8666; timberinnmotel.com), 112 VT 103, Ludlow. A family-run motel since 1986, this 18-unit motel with newly refurbished rooms is a favorite with skiers on a budget for its affordable rooms and convenient location as a winter shuttle bus stop for Okemo. It has a hot tub and sauna in winter and a heated outdoor pool in summer. Owners Glenn and Donna Heitsmith also rent a two-bedroom apartment that sleeps six and has a full kitchen and deck overlooking the Black River. $–$$.

## ❋ Where to Eat

### DINING OUT

#### IN CHESTER

**The Free Range** (802-875-3346; thefreerangevt.com), 90 The Common. Open Tues.–Sun. for dinner; lunch, Sat.; brunch, Sun. New in the fall of 2014, this is the right restaurant in the right place—imaginative comfort food in an 1895 Victorian house on the common. When Anne and Rick Paterno ditched the corporate life to open the restaurant, they chose a name inspired by Rick's childhood nickname of "Ranger Rick" or "Range" for short. But Executive Chef and Managing Partner Jason Tostrup also has free range when developing his seasonal menus, which include variations on grass-fed burgers and choices such as braised beef short ribs with a creamy bleu cheese polenta and vegetarian buckwheat gnocchi. $–$$.

**Fullerton Inn** (802-875-2444; fullertoninn.com), 40 The Common. Open nightly except Sunday. This classic old inn's dining room is surprisingly casual, with a varied menu and reliably good food, ranging from mac 'n cheese to roast half-duck cassoulet and trout meunier. Also serves lunch, Wed.–Sat. $–$$$.

(((•))) **Tokai-Tei Japanese Restaurant at the Old Town Farm Inn** (802-875-2346; otfi.com), 665 VT 10. Open Thurs.–Sat. for dinner by reservation. Halfway between Chester and Ludlow isn't exactly where you'd expect to find a first-rate Japanese restaurant, but that's where Michiko Yoshida-Hunter presides over the kitchen of this family-geared lodge, turning out tantalizing and reasonably priced sushi and entrées such as "Unagi Kabayaki" (marinated eel), the house speciality; "gyu-aspara maki" (beef asparagus roll); and a choice of tempura and sushi dishes. Entrées include miso soup and garden salad and steamed tamanishiki rice. The restaurant is BYOB, and desserts include green tea or red bean ice cream, made in-house.

#### IN LUDLOW

(((•))) **Coleman Brook Tavern** (802-228-1435; okemo.com/dining), Jackson Gore Inn at Okemo Mountain Resort, 111

DINING AT COLEMAN BROOK TAVERN  COURTESY OF OKEMO MOUNTAIN RESORT

Jackson Gore Road. Open Wed.–Sun. for dinner. This is the signature restaurant in Okemo's base complex, and it's sleekly comfortable, with sofas, wing chairs, and dim lighting to mitigate its size. The cherrywood-paneled Wine Room is its most intimate setting. The restaurant's award-winning wine list features nearly 800 wines. Reservations recommended. $–$$$.

✪ **The Downtown Grocery** (802-228-7566; thedowntowngrocery.com), 41 South Depot Street. Serves dinner nightly except Tues. and Wed. (also closed Thurs. in November) Weston native chef Rogan Lechthaler and wife Abby have created a deservedly popular farm-to-table dining venue in town (formerly Cappuccino's). The blackboard menu lists the night's specials, but the entrées on the printed menu are also as locally sourced as possible. The pasta is house-made, as are the sorbets and ice cream (flavors change daily). Meats are cured in-house. Reservations recommended. $$–$$$.

**Echo Lake Inn** (802-228-8602; echolakeinn.com), 2 Dublin Road (VT 100). Open to the public for dinner. Casual elegance best describes the inn's inspired menu. Head chef Christopher Vincent and Chef Phil Lewis combine their talents to offer an à la carte menu that changes seasonally, with choices such as pan-roasted Black Pearl Scottish Salmon and Pork Normandy. Vegetarian options typically include a freshly made pasta dish, such as cranberry sage ravioli with smoked cheddar and caramelized onions. Specialties include pan-seared-then-roasted boneless duck breast, served with the day's sauce. $$–$$$.

🍴 ✎ **Harry's Cafe** (802-228-2996; harryscafe.com), 68 VT 100 North. Open for dinner, Wed.–Sun. Trip Pearce has been one of the area's most colorful chefs since 1989 when he opened his café (named for his father). His present venue (formerly Bella Luna) is far more expansive (140 seats) and central (junction of VT 103 and VT 100) but retains the same airy, informal feel as the original venue. The eclectic menu offers a wide range of choices. You might dine on a mix of appetizers—hand-rolled spring rolls and grilled Caesar salad—or split an antipasto with Harry's smoked seafood chowder. A former lobsterman, Pearce is serious—and creative—with fish. The fish-and-chips (dipped in beer batter) are a perennial favorite, as is the Pad Thai (add shrimp or chicken), the eatery's signature dish. $$–$$$.

## IN WESTON

**Inn at Weston** (802-824-6789; innweston .com), 630 Main Street (VT 100). Open June–late February for dinner. The candlelit dining room and adjacent pub are delightful in any season—and in summer, there is dining on the deck and orchid-filled gazebo. The menu changes seasonally, and Chef John Pirrello uses local ingredients whenever possible. $$–$$$.

## EATING OUT

## IN CHESTER

✎ **Country Girl Diner** (802-875-1003; countrygirldiner.com), 46 VT 103 South. Open daily for breakfast and lunch, Fri. nights in summer for dinner. Cash only. Don't let the quaint appearance of this 1944 dining car fool you. The staff is friendly, and the food goes beyond typical diner fare. Soups are freshly made, and burgers get a creative twist. Try the Smashburger with caramelized onions and Swiss cheese, or the Reuben burger topped with sauerkraut, Thousand Island dressing, and Swiss cheese.

((•)) **Heritage Deli & Bakery** (802-875-3550), 642 VT 103 South. Open daily. A warmly attractive café/gourmet food shop. Owner Michele Wilcox is the baker, and soups are made from scratch, too. The café has Provençal-print tablecloths, bright colors, booths, and fresh flowers whenever possible. At lunch, try a soup or salad combo with one of more than a dozen signature sandwiches named for folks like Grandma Moses (tarragon turkey salad on a croissant) and Ira Allen (turkey, sun-dried tomato cream cheese, and lettuce on a baguette).

((ꜛ)) **MacLaomainn's Scottish Pub** (802-875-6227; maclaomainns.com), 52 South Main Street. Open daily for lunch and dinner. Scotsman Alan Brown and Chester resident Deb Brown first met playing cribbage online, then met in person, built this cozy pub, and were married in it. Haggis, a dish so peculiarly Scottish it's a national symbol, has been a surprising big hit, along with steak and fish pies and bangers and mash. Late-night bites. The bar is fully licensed and offers a wide choice of beers (including Scottish) and whiskeys.

((ꜛ)) **Stone Hearth Inn** (802-875-2525; stonehearthinnvermont.com), 698 VT 11 West. Open Thurs.–Mon. The feel here is of a classic, old-style ski lodge with a large, inviting family-geared lounge including a wood-fired hearth and plenty to keep kids happy. Begin with baked Brie or the smoked salmon, and dine on the flatiron steak, an eggplant stack layered with homemade pesto, or the "tart du jour." Sandwiches and burgers are always available. Fully licensed, beers on tap.

## IN LUDLOW

& ✍ **D. J.'s Restaurant** (802-228-5374; djsrestaurantvermont.com), 146 Main Street. Open daily for dinner. A first-rate family restaurant; a separate lounge has booths for diners. The burger with hand-cut fries and fixings in the pub is probably the best value in town. The menu is large; the crispy roast duckling is a house favorite. Nightly specials and kid's menu.

((ꜛ)) **The Hatchery** (802-228-2311; thehatcheryvt.com), 164 Main Street. Open daily. Cash only. This restaurant, which opened in 1978, serves breakfast and lunch all day. Breads are from a local bakery, with other ingredients also locally sourced as much as possible.

((ꜛ)) ✍ **Java Baba's Slow Food Café** (802-228-7810; javababas.com), 57 Pond Street (Okemo Marketplace, VT 100 across from the Okemo Access Road). Open daily. An all-day oasis, good for breakfast bagels through creative sandwiches, salads, wraps, house-made quiche, pizza, soups, freshly baked muffins, and cookies. It's a great space to chill with a latte and a laptop.

& **Mojo Café** (802-228-6656; mojocafevt.com), 106 Main Street. Open Tues.–Sat. for dinner, Fri.–Sat. for lunch. Literally the hottest spot to eat in town, with an extensive blackboard menu of spicy Mexican, Cajun, Creole, and southern specialties. Go for the poblano rings. Owners John and Jodi Seward also offer a rotating selection of hard-to-find brews.

✍ **Pot Belly Pub and Restaurant** (802-228-8989; thepotbelly.com), 130 Main Street. Open for lunch and dinner daily. Dining here has been a Ludlow tradition since 1974. The ambience is casual, with live music on busy weekends. The restaurant offers an extensive dinner menu with small plates and a kids' menu. At lunch, try a Pot Belly Burger and jazz it up with chili, mushrooms, or bacon.

((ꜛ)) **Stemwinder** (802-228-5200; stemwindervt.com), 46 Depot Street. Open Wed.–Sat. for dinner. Located behind the Wine & Cheese Depot, also owned by Leslie Stuart, co-owner of Stemwinder with chef Wendy Neal, this attractive wine bar serves small plates and soups, although you'll also find beef sliders, seasonal pasta dishes, thin-crust pizzas, and a cheese and meat board on the menu.

**Willie Dunn's Grille** (802-228-1387; okemo.com/dining), 89 Fox Lane at the Okemo Valley Golf Club. Open summer and fall for lunch and dinner. A great lunch bet for its sandwiches, paninis, and burgers. The dining room has views of the pond and the 18th green; outside patio dining is also available.

## IN PROCTORSVILLE

✪ 🍴 ((ɢ)) **Crows Bakery and Opera House Café** (802-226-7007; crowsbakeryand cafe.com), 73 Depot Street (off VT 103). Open for breakfast and lunch, Tues.–Sun. An attractive café serving full breakfasts and exotic wraps such as Veggie Wrapsody and Tuna Kahuna, plus a choice of sandwiches. The house specialty is vegetarian chili, made with quinoa, although the place is known for its made-from-scratch pastries, breads, and desserts.

**Vermont Apple Pie** (802-554-0040), 265 Depot Street. Open daily. A homey, authentic eatery in the middle of the village, it is best known for its apple pie but is also a great breakfast spot, serving filling portions of home-cooked food.

## IN WESTON

♿ 🍴 **The Bryant House** (802-824-6287; vermontcountrystore.com), 657 Main Street. Open daily for lunch; brunch on Sunday. Owned by the neighboring **Vermont Country Store**, this fine old house dates from 1827, with an 1885 tavern. Lunch includes Yankee pot roast, chicken pie, and other hearty New England regional foods. The signature dessert is Indian pudding. The bar is a beauty, made of solid mahogany with a brass rail, transported from the Hudson Valley and a perfect fit. Check out the antique soda fountain and the Bryant family's nineteenth-century–style bedroom, preserved upstairs. In summer, **Mildred's Dairy Bar**, at the rear of the restaurant, serves casual fare such as made-to-order grass-fed burgers, hot dogs, pulled pork sandwiches, and, for dessert, maple creemees and Vermont's own Wilcox ice cream.

**Hartness Tavern** at the Weston Playhouse (802-824-5288; westonplayhouse .org), 12 Park Street. Open for dinner and drinks on main stage show evenings beginning at 5 for theater patrons. This is a pleasant dining room overlooking a waterfall, less formal dining than at the inn. The menu typically includes a few starters, four or five entrées, and desserts. Reservations can be made when booking tickets. (See also *Entertainment*.)

((ɢ)) **The Village Green Gallery** (802-824-3669; villagegreengallery.com), 661 Main Street. A delightful coffee bar with comfortable seating to gather your thoughts and/or check email surrounded by art and fine crafts. See *Selective Shopping—Art Galleries*.

Also see *High Teas*.

HIGH TEAS 🍴 **Inn Victoria** (802-875-4288; innvictoria.com), 321 Main Street, Weston. High tea featuring pastries, scones, sweets, clotted cream, and a choice of 50 teas is served by reservation, Fri.–Sun., in the inn's elegant Victorian guest parlor or dining room. Discounts for guests of the inn. Inquire about special tea tastings.

**Rose Arbour Tea Room** (802-875-4767; rosearbour.net), 55 School Street, Chester, just off the green. Open seasonally, Wed.–Sat. This tearoom, gift shop, and gallery has specialized in multicourse high teas for 20 years. Chef Suzanne Nielson is known for her scones and pastries; tea also includes finger sandwiches, petits fours, and a choice of sandwiches. Reservations required.

## ✳ Entertainment

**Jackson Gore Summer Music Series** at Okemo Mountain Resort, (802-228-1600; okemo.com), 77 Okemo Ridge Road, Ludlow. Summer-long series of free concerts on the lawn, Fri. nights. Okemo's Adventure Zone stays open late for concertgoers.

✪ **Kinhaven Music School** (802-824-4332; kinhaven.org), 354 Lawrence Hill Road, Weston, a nationally recognized summer camp for young musicians, presents free concerts by students on weekends in July and August. Faculty perform on Saturday nights in July. Performances are held in the Concert Hall, high in the meadow of the school's

31-acre campus, which looks more like a farm than a school. Picnics are encouraged.

**Sundays on the Hill Concerts** (sundaysonthehill.org), 37 Lawrence Hill Road, Weston. Concerts (mostly chamber music) are held in a historic 1838 church, now nondenominational, on summer Sundays through mid-September.

✪ ♿ ⟨⟨ᵠ⟩⟩ **Weston Playhouse Theatre Company** (802-824-5288; westonplay house.org), 12 Park Street, Weston. Billed as "the oldest professional theater in Vermont," the Weston Playhouse has a company composed largely of professional Equity actors and routinely draws rave reviews. Quality aside, Weston couldn't be more off-Broadway. The pillared theater—the façade is that of an old church—fronts on a classic village common and backs on the West River, complete with a waterfall and Holsteins grazing in the meadow beyond. Many patrons arrive early to dine at the **Hartness Tavern** (see *Eating Out*) at the Playhouse and linger after the show to join cast members at the **Weston Playhouse's Act IV Cabaret** (reservations required). Performances are Tues.–Sat. night with matinees, Wed., Sat. and Sun., late June–Labor Day weekend. Plays are also staged at a second venue, Weston Playhouse at Walker Farm (703 Main Street, Weston).

## ✳ Selective Shopping

ANTIQUES SHOPS **William Austin's Antiques** (802-875-3032), 42 Maple Street, Chester. A full line (more than 600 pieces) of period and country antique furniture and collectibles.

ART GALLERIES

IN CHESTER

**Chasse Fine Art Gallery** (802-875-5585; chasseart.com), 558 Main Street. Open daily. The gallery showcases the paintings of Denis Chasse and the photography of Katheryn Chasse. Work is primarily New England–themed.

**Crow Hill Gallery** (802-875-3763; crowhillgallery.com), 729 Flamstead Road. Call for hours. Watercolorist Jeanne Carbonetti welcomes visitors to the home and studio/gallery that she and her husband designed and built on a rise above the meadows, a great setting for her vibrant paintings. The author of several books, she also offers group and private instruction in painting and the creative process.

IN WESTON

⟨⟨ᵠ⟩⟩ **The Village Green Gallery** (802-824-3669), 661 Main Street. The walls are hung with original art, with a corner devoted to children's book illustrations. The newly renovated space also features fine locally crafted items. Coffee bar, seating space.

BOOKS ⟨⟨ᵠ⟩⟩ **The Book Nook** (802-228-3238; thebooknookvt.com), 136 Main Street, Ludlow. Open Wed.–Mon. This owner-operated independent bookstore has a wide selection of books, including many by Vermont authors, some of whom are invited to visit the store to read from their work.

**Phoenix Books Misty Valley** (802-875-3400; phoenixbooks.biz/misty valley), 58 Common Street, Chester. Open daily. Michael DeSanto and Renee Reiner maintain a friendly, well-stocked bookshop; browsing is encouraged, and author readings are frequent.

CRAFTS

IN CHESTER

**103 Artisans Marketplace** (802-875-7400; 103artisansmarketplace.com), 7 Pineview Drive (VT 103). Open Wed.–Sun. Just east of town, this sizable gallery is easy to miss. Don't miss it. Turn around if you pass by it. The wrought iron and fanciful metalwork are by

**PHOENIX BOOKS MISTY VALLEY** LISA HALVORSEN

owners Elise and Payne Junker, who also showcase the crafted pottery, blown glass, jewelry, prints, clothing, and chocolate, of more than 200 artisans.

✪ ✎ **Bonnie's Bundles Dolls** (802-875-2114; bonniesbundlesdolls.com), 250 North Street (VT 103). Look for the OPEN flag on this 1814 house in the middle of Chester's Stone Village. It's usually out. Bonnie Watters doesn't like to sell her handmade cloth dolls to retail shops, so she welcomes visitors to her parlor, home to roughly 100 one-of-a-kind dolls, each copyrighted, signed, and registered. She also takes custom orders, including creating monogrammed portrait dolls from a photo. In business for more than 40 years, Bonnie has stitched more than 14,000 dolls. For many families, buying dolls from Bonnie is a multigenerational tradition.

**DaVallia Art and Accents** (802-875-1203; thedavallia.com), 78 The Common. Open Thurs.–Sun. Michael and Jessie Alon showcase the work of more than 60 Vermont and nationally recognized artists at DaVallia's Art Boutique on the village green. Great stuff—from jewelry

to wall art and handcrafted furniture, this is a gem of a shop. They also own **39 North Gallery** (802-895-8900) in the historic Chester Stone Village.

**Six Loose Ladies** (802-875-7373; sixlooseladies.com), 287 Main Street. Open Wed.–Sun. The unlikely name for this totally wholesome cooperative fiber arts store comes from the nineteenth-century practice of teaching streetwalkers to spin, weave, and knit as an alternative to their lifestyles. The store carries knitting, spinning, and felting supplies, as well as a large selection of locally produced yarns and items made by members.

### IN LUDLOW

**Clearlake Furniture** (802-228-8395; clearlakefurniture.com), 322 VT 100 North. Artisan-crafted hardwood furniture, made one piece at a time; also upholstered pieces and decorative accents.

**Craft and Gift Shoppe at Fletcher Farm** (802-228-4348), 611 VT 103 South.

Open late June–early September, closed Mon. Handcrafted items by members of the Society of Vermont Artists and Craftsmen are for sale, including stained glass, patchwork quilts, sterling silver, and paper products. (See *To Do*).

**The Silver Spoon** (802-228-4753; silverwareart.com), 44 Depot Street. Steve Manning fashions an amazing variety of objects from antique silverware, including jewelry, wind chimes, candleholders, and art objects. The shop is located in the **Depot Street Gallery**, which features the work of more than 150 artists and sculptors.

CHEESE ✪ **Crowley Cheese Factory** (802-259-2340; crowleycheese.com), 14 Crowley Lane, Mount Holly. 1.8 miles up the Healdville Road, a left off VT 103, 5 miles northwest of the junction with VT 100 in Ludlow. Open daily. Check for hours. See *Scenic Drives* for the history of Vermont's oldest cheese factory, which began in 1824 in the Crowley family kitchen, and this exceptional cheese, made by hand and sharper and creamier than cheddar.

✐ **Plymouth Artisan Cheese** (802-672-3650; plymouthartisancheese.com), 106 Messer Hill Road, Plymouth, in the President Calvin Coolidge State Historic Site in Plymouth Notch, off VT 100A. Open

daily. The cheese factory was started in 1890 by John Coolidge, father of the president. The equipment is modern, but traditional methods produce a distinctive granular-curd cheese, available here in waxed blocks and rounds. Sample the cheeses and take a self-guided tour of the second-floor museum to view vintage equipment and to learn the history of cheesemaking in the area.

**Wine & Cheese Depot** (802-228-4128), 46 Depot Street, Ludlow. A serious wine store. Owner Leslie Stuart knows Vermont cheese, too, showcasing many of them, including both Crowley and Plymouth. See Stemwinder, the store's wine bar, under *Eating Out*.

COUNTRY STORES **Belmont General Store** (802-259-2292; belmontgeneralstore.com), 2400 Belmont Road, Belmont. Open Mon–Sat.; open occasional Sundays. The store, in continuous operation since 1843, provides all the necessities: groceries, wine, apparel, licenses, and meals. Stop by the deli, which offers everything from breakfast options to burgers, wraps, and pizza.

**Singleton's General Store** (802-226-7666; singletonsvt.com), 356 Main Street (VT 131), Proctorsville. Best known for its smoked meats. This much-expanded, family-run (for three generations) grocery store has kept abreast of the demands of the area's ski condo owners while continuing to cover the basics expected by its loyal local clientele. The store, which has a great wine selection, a Vermont liquor store, and an outstanding deli, also sells fishing and hunting licenses, rods and reels, guns and ammo, sporting goods, Johnson Woolen Mills and other sturdy outdoor wear and boots, and Vermont products. Note the antique guns and stuffed trophies on display. But why the camel?

**The Vermont Country Store** (802-824-3184; vermontcountrystore.com), 657 Main Street, Weston. Open year-round, daily. Established by Vrest Orton in 1946, the original store has

PLYMOUTH ARTISAN CHEESE MUSEUM  LISA HALVORSEN

since quintupled in size and spilled into four adjacent buildings. It's still in the family—Lyman, the present Orton patriarch, and his sons Gardner, Cabot, and Eliot are all involved—and still follows the founder's creed that every product sold must "work, be useful, and make sense." The inventory of the store and its catalog (accounting for most of the company's business) focuses on practical items that make life easy, including many nostalgic brands. The store's own line of edibles features the Vermont Common Cracker, unchanged since 1812, still stamped out in a patented nineteenth-century machine. For most patrons, this is destination shopping, and they stay to eat at the store's **Bryant House** next door. The store has a second location in Rockingham at 1292 Rockingham Road (VT 103).

SHOPPERS AT THE VERMONT COUNTRY STORE  CHRISTINA TREE

**The Weston Village Store** (802-824-5477), 660 Main Street, Weston. Open daily. A tourist-geared emporium, boasting the state's largest collection of weather vanes, it's also known for its many varieties of fudge, maple products, great Vermont cheese selection, and puzzles, with more than 200 in stock.

FARMS AND FARMERS' MARKETS  **Jersey Girls Farm Café and Market** (802-875-3663), 32 VT 10 (junction with VT 103), Gassetts. Open Fri.–Sun., selling local family-farm milk, eggs, produce (in season), and other natural products.

**Chester Farmers' Market** (802-875-2703), 1292 Rockingham Road, Rockingham (VT 103 South). Open Memorial Day–Columbus Day weekends, Sundays.

**Ludlow Farmers' Market** (802-230-7706; ludlowfarmersmarket.org), 53 Main Street, Ludlow, late May–early October, Fridays.

SPECIAL SHOPS  **Conrad Delia, Windsor Chair Maker** (802-875-4219; popplefields.com), 1300 Popple Dungeon Road, Chester. After a long career as a home builder on Long Island, Conrad Delia

studied with several New England chair makers before opening his own shop. Call to schedule a visit or a one-on-one chair-making workshop.

**Country on the Common** (802-875-3000; countryonthecommon.com), 80 The Common, Chester. A great selection of reasonably priced clothing, one-of-a-kind infinity scarves, and craft items by regional artists.

**Next Chapter** (802-770-4848), 6 Andover Street, Ludlow. A women's clothing boutique with handmade clothing, accessories, and jewelry.

MORE FOOD  **Green Mountain Sugar House** (802-228-7151; gmsh.com), 820 VT 100 North, Ludlow. Open daily, year-round. You can watch syrup being produced in March and April; maple candy is made throughout the year on a weekly basis. This is also a place to find freshly pressed cider in September. Shop for specialty smoked meats, Vermont cheese, and gift baskets of Vermont food products. The shop is open daily 9–6 "most of the time," according to longtime owners Doug and Ann Rose.

WILDER BARN AT THE PRESIDENT CALVIN COOLIDGE STATE HISTORIC SITE  LISA HALVORSEN

## ✳ Special Events

*February:* **Chester Winter Carnival** (meetchestervermont.com), genuine old-fashioned family fun with public skating, broom hockey, dogsled rides, music, and food.

*Late March:* **Vermont Maple Open House Weekend** (vermontmaple.org).

*April:* Okemo's annual **Slush Cup** (okemo.com). A wacky competition where crazily costumed competitors attempt to skim across a slush pond in the Jackson Gore Base Area without falling in.

*Early July:* **Fletcher Farm Arts and Crafts Fair, Ludlow** (fletcherfarm.org).

*July 4:* **President Calvin Coolidge Birthday Memorial**, Plymouth (historicsites.vermont.gov/coolidge).

*Late July:* Annual **Music in the Meadow Festival**, Chester (motelinthemeadow.com).

*Late July/early August:* **Plymouth Old Home Day** at President Calvin Coolidge State Historic Site (historicsites.vermont.gov/coolidge)—a longstanding tradition with wagon rides, sheep shearing, music, crafts, and games.

*July–August:* **Okemo Valley Music Festival**—free concerts in Ludlow, Cavendish, and Chester (yourplaceinvermont.org); **Kinhaven Music School concert series** (kinhaven.org/concerts).

*Late September:* **Fall Fair on the Green**, Chester (chesterfallfestival.org). **Plymouth Cheese and Harvest Festival** (historicsites.vermont.gov/coolidge).

*Late September/earlyOctober:* **Weston Antiques Show,** Weston (westonantiquesshow.org). One of the state's oldest and most respected antiques shows, staged in the Weston Playhouse, featuring more than 200 dealers.

*Columbus Day weekend:* The **Weston Crafts Fair**, Weston (westoncraftshow.com), juried show, all media. **Cider Days in Mount Holly** (mounthollyvt.org) features a 100-year-old cider press, crafts show, and community supper.

*Late November-mid-December:* **Overture to Christmas**, Chester (meetchestervermont.com). Events include a Children's Day with Santa and Mrs. Claus, tree lighting, concerts, and candlelight caroling.

*December*: **Torchlight Parade and Fireworks Display** at Okemo Mountain Resort, Ludlow (okemo.com); **Inndulgence Tour** (yourplaceinvermont.com), two-day, self-guided open house tour of Okemo Valley inns with festive food and drinks.

# THE CONNECTICUT RIVER VALLEY

■

## THE CONNECTICUT RIVER VALLEY

### LOWER VALLEY RIVER TOWNS

Including Bellows Falls, Saxtons River, Grafton, Springfield, Weathersfield, and Windsor

### UPPER VALLEY RIVER TOWNS

Including White River Junction, Norwich, Thetford, Fairlee, Bradford, Newbury, and Wells River, VT; also Hanover, Orford, Piermont, Haverhill, and Woodsville, NH

# THE CONNECTICUT RIVER VALLEY

The Connecticut River flows 410 miles from its high source on the New Hampshire–Quebec border to Long Island Sound in the state of Connecticut. What concerns us here are its 270 miles as a boundary—and bond—between the states of New Hampshire and Vermont. Defying state lines, it forms one of New England's most beautiful and distinctive regions, shaped by a shared history.

Judging from more than 130 archaeological sites along this stretch of the river, people have occupied its banks for many thousands of years. Evidence of Western Abenaki villages has been found at Newbury, at Claremont (NH), and at the Great Falls at present-day Bellows Falls. By the late seventeenth century, English settlements had spread from the mouth of the Connecticut up to Deerfield, MA, just below the present New Hampshire–Vermont border. Fort Dummer was built in 1724 in what, at the time, was Massachusetts (and now is Vernon, VT); the Fort at No. 4 was built 50 miles upriver in 1743 in present-day Charlestown, NH. Settlers and Native Americans lived side by side. However, during this period, former friends and neighbors also frequently faced each other in battles to the death.

At the reconstructed Fort at No. 4, you learn that five adults and three children were abducted by a band of Abenaki in 1754 (all survived), and that in 1759, Major Robert Rodgers and his Rangers retaliated for the many raids from the Indian village of St. Francis (near Montreal) by killing many more than 100 residents, including many women and children. The suffering of "Rodgers' Rangers" on their winter return home is legendary. A historic marker on NH 10 in Haverhill, NH, offers a sobering description.

After the 1763 Peace of Paris, France withdrew its claims to New France, and English settlers surged up the Connecticut River, naming their new communities for their old towns in Connecticut and Massachusetts: Walpole, Haverhill, Windsor, Norwich, and more. This was, however, no-man's-land.

In 1749 New Hampshire governor Benning Wentworth had begun granting land on both sides of the river (present-day Vermont was known as "The New Hampshire Grants"), a policy that New York's Governor George Clinton refused to recognize. In 1777, when Vermont declared itself a republic, 16 towns on the New Hampshire side opted to join it. In December 1778, at a meeting in Cornish, NH, towns from both sides of the river voted to form their own state of "New Connecticut," but neither burgeoning state wanted to lose so rich a region. In 1779 New Hampshire claimed all of Vermont.

In 1781 delegates from both sides of the river met in Charlestown, NH, and agreed to stick together. Vermont's Governor Chittenden wrote to General Washington asking to be admitted to the Union, incorporating towns contested both by New Hampshire and New York. Washington replied in the affirmative, but requested that the contested baggage be left out.

In 1782 New Hampshire sent 1,000 soldiers to enforce their jurisdiction. Not long thereafter Washington asked Vermont to give in—and it did. Needless to say, the river towns were unhappy about this verdict.

The Valley itself prospered in the late eighteenth and early nineteenth centuries, as evidenced by the exquisite Federal-era (1790s–1830s) meetinghouses and mansions still to be seen in river towns. With New Hampshire's Dartmouth College, established in 1769, at its heart, and rich floodplain farmland stretching its length, this valley differed far more dramatically than today from the unsettled mountainous regions walling it in on either side.

The river remained the Valley's highway in the early nineteenth century. A transportation canal was built to circumvent the Great Falls at present-day Bellows Falls, and Samuel Morey of Orford, NH, built a steamboat in 1793. Unfortunately Robert Fulton scooped up his invention, but the upshot was increased river transport—at least until the 1840s, when railroads changed everything.

"It is an extraordinary era in which we live," Daniel Webster remarked in 1847, watching the first train roll into Lebanon, NH, the first rail link between the Connecticut River and the Atlantic. "It is altogether new," he continued. "The world has seen nothing like it before."

In this "anything's possible" era, the Valley boomed. At the Robbins, Kendall & Lawrence Armory in Windsor, gun makers developed machines to do the repetitive tasks required to produce each part of a gun. This meant that for the first time an army could buy a shipment of guns and know that if one was damaged, it could be repaired with similar parts. In the vintage 1846 armory, now the **American Precision Museum**, you learn that this novel production of interchangeable parts became known as the American System of precision manufacturing. Springfield too became known for precision toolmaking. Until recently, this area was known as Precision Valley.

In places the railroad totally transformed the landscape, creating towns where there had been none, shifting populations from high old town centers like Rockingham and Walpole, NH, to the riverside. This shift was most dramatic in the town of Hartford, where White River Junction became the hub of north–south and east–west rail traffic.

The river itself was put to new uses. It became a sluiceway, down which logs were floated from the northern forest to paper mills in Bellows Falls and farther downriver. Its falls had long powered small mills, but now a series of hydro dams were constructed, including the massive dam between Barnet, VT, and Monroe, NH, in 1930. This flooded several communities to create both Comerford Reservoir and the visual illusion that the Connecticut River stops there. At present, 16 dams stagger the river's flow between the Second Connecticut Lake above Pittsburg, NH, and Enfield, CT, harnessing the river to provide power for much of the Northeast.

By the 1950s many people compared the river to an open sewer and towns turned their backs on it, depositing refuse along its banks. Still, beyond towns, the river slid by fields of corn and meadows filled with cows. In 1952 the nonprofit Connecticut River Watershed Council was founded to "promote and protect wise use of the Connecticut Valley's resources." Thanks to the 1970s Clean Water Act and to acquisitions, greenups, and cleanups by numerous conservation groups, the river itself began to enjoy a genuine renewal. Visitors and residents alike discovered its beauty; campsites for canoeists were spaced along the shore. At present, kayaks and canoes can be rented along several stretches.

The cultural fabric of towns on either side of the river has remained close-knit. Although the hurricane of 1927 destroyed many bridges, the 21 that survive include one of the longest covered bridges in the United States (connecting Windsor, VT, and Cornish, NH). It's only because tourism promotional budgets are financed by individual state taxes that this stretch of the river valley itself has not, until recently, been recognized as a destination by either New Hampshire or Vermont.

The Connecticut River corridor is now officially the **Connecticut River Byway** as well as one of ten **Vermont Scenic Byways**. See **ctriverbyways.org** for an interactive map and excellent coverage of the cultural history as well as present attractions in towns along both sides of the Connecticut River.

Visually visitors see a river, not state lines. Interstate 91 on the Vermont side has backroaded US 5, as it has NH 10 on the New Hampshire side. Following these "byways," travelers can explore historic towns, farm stands, and local scenic spots, finding their way to quiet river roads along both riverbanks. Access to the river via canoe and kayak has increased in recent years, thanks to outfitters and conservation groups that maintain launch areas and campsites. Within each chapter of this book, prime sights to see shift from one side of the river to the other; the same holds true for places to eat, stay, hike, and generally explore this very distinctive region.

# LOWER VALLEY RIVER TOWNS

*Including Bellows Falls, Saxtons River, Grafton, Springfield, Weathersfield, and Windsor*

**B**ellows Falls, sited at one of the largest drops in the entire length of the river, itself cascades down glacial terraces so steep that steps connect the brick downtown with Victorian homes above and with riverside mill buildings below. Below and above Bellows Falls, old roads follow the Connecticut's tributaries to visitor-friendly villages like Saxtons River and Grafton, to Springfield and to proudly built old meeting-houses, the core of now almost vanished villages like Weathersfield Center.

In the town of Windsor, 26 miles north of Bellows Falls, the layerings of history are compressed along a Main Street that includes the eighteenth-century "Constitution House" (the official birthplace of Vermont), a 1950s diner, and a white-pillared 1790s Asher Benjamin–designed church. Down the road is a brick armory, the 1840s venue for perfecting the concept of interchangeable parts, a process that revolutionized the gun and tool industry globally. North of town a former riverside dairy farm is now Artisan's Park, combining shopping, dining, and outdoor activities.

New England's longest covered bridge links the communities of Windsor, VT, and Cornish, NH, site of the nineteenth-century summer home of sculptor Augustus Saint-Gaudens. Now a national historic site, the estate evokes the era (1885–1935) in which prominent artists, writers, and landscape architects transformed many of the Valley's former farms into summer homes, commuting to New York by the train line that still stops in Windsor.

**GUIDANCE Great Falls Regional Chamber of Commerce** (802-463-4280; gfrcc.org). 17 Depot Street, Bellows Falls. Open Mon.–Fri. varying hours. Well worth finding, housed in the Waypoint Center and representing Charlestown and Walpole, NH, as well as the town of Rockingham, with its villages of Bellows Falls and Saxtons River, also neighboring Grafton.

The **Springfield Regional Chamber of Commerce** (802-885-2779; springfieldvt.com), 56 Main Street, answers phone queries year-round (weekdays 9–5) and maintains the eighteenth-century Eureka Schoolhouse (VT 11, near I-91) as a seasonal information booth.

**GETTING THERE** *By bus:* **Greyhound** (800-231-2222; greyhound.com) buses from points in Connecticut and Massachusetts stop in Bellows Falls at the rail station, 54 Depot Street.

*By train:* **Amtrak** (800-USA-RAIL; amtrak.com). The *Vermonter* stops at Bellows Falls en route from New York City and Washington to Essex Junction and St. Albans.

**GETTING AROUND** I-91 provides a quick way north and south, with exits at Putney, Westminster, Rockingham, and Springfield. US 5 and NH 12 are the old, mostly scenic river highways; there are fewer connecting bridges than there once were. Note the bridge from Walpole, NH, to North Westminster at I-91, Exit 5. In Bellows Falls the Vilas Bridge from the square to VT 12 is closed indefinitely, but the Arch Bridge at the

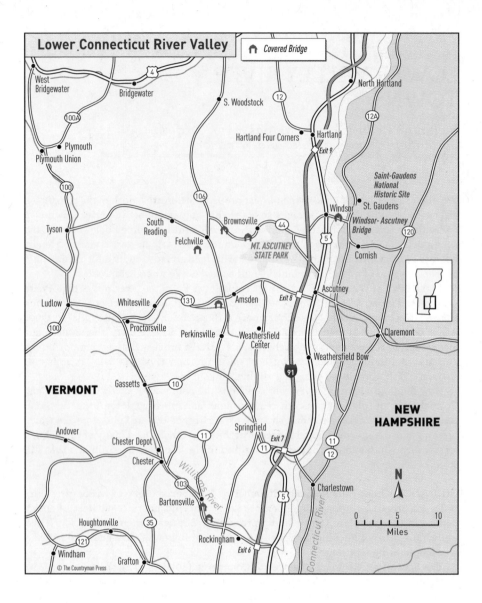

## Lower Connecticut River Valley

🏠 *Covered Bridge*

West Bridgewater
Bridgewater
S. Woodstock
North Hartland
Hartland Four Corners
Hartland
Exit 9
Plymouth
Plymouth Union
Saint-Gaudens National Historic Site
Windsor
St. Gaudens
Windsor-Ascutney Bridge
Tyson
South Reading
Brownsville
Felchville
MT. ASCUTNEY STATE PARK
Cornish
Ludlow
Whitesville
Amsden
Exit 8
Ascutney
Claremont
Proctorsville
Perkinsville
Weathersfield Center
Weathersfield Bow
VERMONT
Gassetts
NEW HAMPSHIRE
Andover
Chester Depot
Springfield
Exit 7
Chester
Williams River
Bartonsville
Charlestown
Houghtonville
Rockingham
Exit 6
Windham
Grafton
Connecticut River
© The Countryman Press

N

0    5    10
Miles

northern end of the village connects with North Walpole. A bridge also links Springfield and Charlestown at I-91, Exit 7, and in Windsor the Windsor/Cornish covered bridge remains the link.

## ✳ Towns and Villages

**Bellows Falls** (a village, population 3,061) The Bellows Falls Canal, completed in 1802, eased flatboats through a series of locks, substantially expanding navigation up the Connecticut. The creation of the canal also formed the island (site of the **Amtrak** station) separating the village from the river, which drops through the half-mile gorge below the dam.

This was a sacred place for Native Americans, as evidenced by **petroglyphs** visible from the Vilas Bridge (open to pedestrians only). Look for a series of round heads, said to date in age anywhere from 300 to 2,000 years ago, now painted yellow.

In 1869 William Russell developed a way of making paper from wood pulp, using logs floated down from both sides of the river; the canal was put to work powering mills and a building boom followed, evidenced by **Rockingham Town Hall**, with its Florentine-style tower, and a restored, town-owned 500-seat **Opera House** used for frequent live performances as well as for films. The surrounding square is lined with a lively mix of shops and restaurants. Just off the square the cheerily yellow-painted **Exner Block** houses studios and shops for artists and craftspeople, thanks to the Rockingham Arts and Museum Project (RAMP). The **Bellows Falls Historical Society, Inc.** (802-376-6789), maintains the vintage 1831 **Adams Grist Mill** (open June–October, weekends 1–4 p.m.) and has developed the **Bellows Falls Historic Riverfront Park**. Bellows Falls is known as the home of Hetty Green (1835–1916), who parlayed a substantial inheritance into a $100 million fortune, dressed like a bag lady, and was known as the "Witch of Wall Street."

**Saxtons River** (population 555) is a village in the town of Rockingham. It's the home of the **Vermont Academy**, founded in 1876, now a private prep school with students from throughout the world. Along its main street look for **Main Street Arts** (mainstreetarts.org) and the seasonal **River Artisans** cooperative, as well as the striking **Saxtons River Inn**.

ROCKINGHAM TOWN HALL, BELLOWS FALLS  CHRISTINA TREE

**Springfield** (population 9,213; springfieldvt.com). Sited near the confluence of the Connecticut and Black rivers, Springfield boomed with Vermont's tool industry in the nineteenth and first half of the twentieth centuries, but it has suffered along with the decline of that industry. Beyond the powerful falls, the town's compact downtown offers several places to eat and shop. Gracious nineteenth-century mansions in residential neighborhoods include **Hartness House** (see *Lodging, Dining Out*).

**Weathersfield** (population 2,825; weathersfieldvt.org). The community is composed of several small villages, including Perkinsville, Ascutney, Weathersfield Bow, and the original settlement at Weathersfield Center (see sidebar)

**Windsor** (population 3553; windsorvt .org). Windsor's mid-nineteenth-century prosperity is reflected in the handsome lines of the columned Windsor House, once considered the best public house between Boston and Montreal. The Italianate building across the street was designed in 1850 by Ammi Young as a post office with an upstairs courtroom that served as Woodrow Wilson's summer White House from 1913 to 1915; the

# VINTAGE VILLAGE

Grafton (population approximately 669; graftonvermont.org). Prior to the Civil War, Grafton boasted more than 1,480 residents and 10,000 sheep. Wool was turned into 75,000 yards of Grafton cloth annually; soapstone from 13 local quarries left town in the shape of sinks, stoves, inkwells, and foot warmers. But then one in three of Grafton's men marched off to the Civil War, and few returned. Sheep farming, too, "went west." An 1869 flood destroyed the town's six dams and its road. The new highway bypassed Grafton. The town's tavern, however, built in 1801, entered a golden era. Innkeeper Harlan Phelps invested his entire California gold rush fortune in adding a third floor and double porches, and his brother Francis organized a still-extant cornet band. Guests included Emerson, Thoreau, and Kipling; later, both Woodrow Wilson and Teddy Roosevelt visited. However, the tavern was sagging, and nearly all the 80-some houses in town were selling cheap with plenty of acreage in the 1960s, when the **Windham Foundation** (802-843-2211; windhamfoundation.org), funded by a resident summer family, bought much of the town and set about restoring it. **The Grafton Inn** was renovated (see *Lodging*), cheesemaking was revived, the village wiring was buried, and the **Grafton Trails & Outdoor Center** (see *To Do*) was established, a destination for both cross-country skiing and mountain biking. Within its few streets, Grafton can pleasantly fill a day. Both the **Nature Museum** (802-843-2111; nature-museum.org) and the **Vermont Museum of Mining & Minerals** (802-875-3562; vtm3.org) offer plenty for families to do. The vintage 1811 Butterfield House is now the inviting **Grafton Public Library** (802-843-2404; graftonpubliclibrary.org) and the **Grafton History Museum** (802-843-2584), open seasonally, has extensive exhibits. At **Grafton Forge** (802-843-1029), Aaron Andersen demonstrates his craft. You watch cheesemaking in the original **The Grafton Village Cheese Company** (802-843-2255; graftonvillagecheese.com) factory and can buy cheese in the village general store/eatery (Mktgrafton.com), which offers breakfast and lunch through a supper deli menu and tables but is also a great picnic source. The town's independently owned **Gallery North Star** and **Jud Hartmann Gallery** (see *Shopping*) are destinations for art lovers. The town's coronet band, founded in 1867, still performs in the village and neighboring towns.

**GRAFTON INN** CHRISTINA TREE

CONNECTICUT RIVER ABOVE THE CORNISH–WINDSOR BRIDGE WITH MT. ASCUTNEY  CHRISTINA TREE

president spent his summers in Cornish, across the **Cornish–Windsor Covered Bridge**. Cornish was at the time an artists' and writers' colony that had evolved around sculptor Augustus Saint-Gaudens. The colony nurtured artist Maxfield Parrish; his painting *Templed Hills* hangs in the Peoples United Bank, 50 Main Street. Parrish left it in perpetuity to the bank's tellers for "keeping my account balanced." It depicts a mountain that resembles Mount Ascutney, towering above water that resembles Lake Runnemede. The lake is now the town-owned conservation area **Paradise Park**. For another overview of Windsor, see the chapter. Unfortunately, many visitors get no nearer to Windsor than **Artisans Park** (see sidebar).

## ACROSS THE RIVER

**Walpole, NH** (population 3,711). Along the length of the Connecticut River, few communities are more closely historically and physically linked, yet more different, than Walpole and Bellows Falls. Walpole's village is a white wooden New England classic, set high above NH 12, graced by fine old churches and mansions, most from the early and mid-nineteenth century, when this was a popular summer haven. Louisa May Alcott summered here and Emily Dickinson visited. In the twentieth century, James Michener came to research the lifestyle of New England-born missionaries for the opening chapter of *Hawaii*. Current creative residents include filmmaker Ken Burns and chocolate maker Lawrence Burdick, who together have transformed the village Post Office Block, now housing the original **Burdick Chocolate Shop and Café**. The **Walpole Historical Society** (walpolehistory.org) displays a significant collection and changing exhibits on three floors of the tower-topped Academy Building.

    **Charleston, NH** (population, 5,101) was a stockaded outpost during the French and Indian Wars. Its Main Street was laid out in 1763, 200 feet wide and a mile long, with more than five dozen structures that now make up a National Historic District; 10 buildings predate 1800. Also see **Fort at No. 4** under *Must See*.

# WEATHERSFIELD CENTER, A SMALL TREASURE

Sited on a scenic old north–south byway between Springfield and VT 131, **Weathersfield Center is a gem of a hamlet. The Weathersfield Meeting House** (802-263-9497), completed in 1821, is one of Vermont's most elegant Federal-era buildings (open regularly only for Congregational church Sunday services late June through Labor Day). It's set on a knoll-top green that was planted in the 1860s with maples, now a stately grove shading a tall granite shaft commemorating "the men who have volunteered to serve their country in the late war of rebellion, begun in 1862 and surpassed in 1865." Farther along the green, an eighteenth-century millstone commemorates "all those who have served our country in time of stress in its first 200 years." The **Weathersfield Historical Society** (802-263-5230) is housed in the Reverend Dan Foster House across the road (open by appointment). It displays Civil War memorabilia, archival photos, and the last wildcat killed in town (1867). It was Weathersfield native William Jarvis who transformed the economy of Vermont—and the rest of northern New England—by smuggling 4,000 merino sheep out of Spain in 1811. By 1840 there were upward of two million sheep in Vermont.

WEATHERSFIELD MEETING HOUSE  CHRISTINA TREE

## ✳ Must See

**The Saint-Gaudens National Historic Site** (603-675-2175; nps.gov/saga), 139 Saint Gardens Road, Cornish, NH. Grounds open daily, dawn–dusk. Buildings open daily Memorial Day–late October; a modest admission fee is good for a week; free under age 16. This glorious property with a view of Mount Ascutney includes the sculptor's summer home and studio, sculpture galleries, and formal gardens, which he developed and occupied between 1885 and his death in 1907. A visitor center features a 15-minute orientation film about the artist and his work. Augustus Saint-Gaudens (1848–1907) is remembered primarily for public pieces: the Shaw Memorial on Boston Common, the statue of Admiral Farragut in New York's Madison Park, the equestrian statue of General William T. Sherman at the Fifth Avenue entrance to Central Park, and the Abraham Lincoln in Chicago's Lincoln Park. He was also the first sculptor to design an American coin (the $10 and $20 gold pieces of 1907). His home, Aspet, is furnished much as it was when he lived there. Copies of some of the most famous works, such as the Shaw Memorial, cast with the original molds, are displayed around the grounds. Augustus Saint-Gaudens loved the Ravine Trail, a quarter-mile cart path to his swimming hole along Blow-Me-Up Brook, now marked for visitors, and other walks laid out through the woodlands and wetlands of the Blow-Me-Down Natural Area. Saint-Gaudens was the center of the "Cornish Colony," a group of poets, artists, landscape designers, actors, architects, and writers including Ethel Barrymore, Charles Dana Gibson, Finley Peter Dunne, and Maxfield Parrish; President Woodrow Wilson's first wife, Ellen, a painter, was drawn into this circle, and the president summered at a nearby home from 1913 to 1915. *Note:* Bring a picnic lunch for Sunday-afternoon chamber music concerts, at 2 p.m. in July and August.

**American Precision Museum** (802-674-5781; americanprecision.org), 196 Main Street, Windsor. Open Memorial Day weekend–October, 10–5 daily. Admission charged, free on Sunday. In *Roadside History of Vermont*, Peter Jennison notes that while it is known as the "Birthplace of Vermont," Windsor can also claim to be the midwife of the state's machine tool industry. Windsor resident Lemuel Hedge devised a machine for ruling paper in 1815 and dividing scales in 1827. Asahel Hubbard produced a revolving pump in 1828, and Niconar Kendall designed an "under hammer" rifle in the 1830s, the first use of interchangeable parts, in this picturesque old mill. The 1846 Robbins & Lawrence Armory, a National Historic Landmark, holds the largest collection of historically significant machine tools in the nation. In 1987 the American Society of Mechanical Engineers designated the museum an International Mechanical Engineering Heritage Site and Collection. At the 1851 Great Exposition in London's Crystal Palace, the firm demonstrated rifles made with interchangeable parts, the concept perfected at the Windsor armory. Based on that presentation, the British

CARITAS SCULPTURE BY AUGUSTUS SAINT-GAUDENS  GREG SCHWARZ FOR THE NATIONAL PARK SERVICE

# A PIECE OF HISTORY IN ROCKINGHAM

Rockingham Meeting House, Meetinghouse Road, off VT 103, about 1 mile west of I-91, Exit 6. Open daily Memorial Day–Columbus Day, 10–4 but manned by volunteers. Donations appreciated. Vermont's oldest unchanged public building was constructed as a combination church and town hall in 1790 and 1801. The simply lined, clapboard structure stands on a rise, and its extensive graveyard spreads out behind. Inside, light streams through two tiers of twenty-over-twenty windows, and the natural wooden interior seems to glow. Box pews fill the floor and more pews line the gallery, all with seats and backs worn shiny from use.

ROCKINGHAM MEETING HOUSE   CHRISTINA TREE

government ordered 25,000 rifles and 141 metal-working machines and coined the term *American System* for this revolutionary approach to gun-making. Special exhibits feature machine tools from the collection, tracing their impact on today's world.

**Views from Mount Ascutney State Park** (802-674-2060; vtstateparks.com), 1826 Back Mountain Road (VT 44), Windsor. Open late May–mid-October; day-use fee. A well-surfaced 3.8-mile "parkway" spirals gently up through hardwoods from VT 44A (off US 5) between Ascutney and Weathersfield. Note the pullout with picnic facilities and a great view up the valley. A parking lot in the saddle between the mountain's south peak and its summit accesses an 0.8-mile foot trail that takes you the additional 344 vertical feet to the summit. It's well worth the effort for a 360-degree panorama, sweeping from the White Mountains to the northeast and west across Vermont farms and forests rolling into the Green Mountains. A former fire tower has been shortened and offers an observation platform. The road, built in the 1930s by the Civilian Conservation Corps, offers pull-outs with varying views and places to picnic. This is one of Vermont's first state parks and a popular launch spot for hang gliders; also see *Biking, Hiking, and Camping.*

**Cornish–Windsor covered bridge,** linking US 5, Windsor, and VT 12A, Cornish, is the country's longest two-span covered bridge and is certainly the most photographed in New England. A lattice truss design built in 1866, it was rebuilt in 1989. For the best view, turn left on VT 12A and look for the marked boat launch area a short way upstream.

AMERICAN PRECISION MUSEUM

**Old Constitution House** (802-674-6628), 16 North Main Street, Windsor. Open Memorial Day–Columbus Day, weekends and Mon. holidays 11–5. Nominal admission. This is Elijah West's tavern (but not in its original location), where delegates gathered on July 2, 1777 to adopt Vermont's constitution, America's first to prohibit slavery, establish universal voting rights for all males, and authorize a public school system. Excellent first-floor displays trace the history of the formation of the Republic of Vermont; upstairs is the town's collection of antiques, prints, documents, tools and cooking utensils, tableware, toys, and early fabrics. Special exhibits vary each year. A path out the back door leads to Lake Runnemede.

**Fort at No. 4** (603-826-5700; fortat4.org), 267 Springfield Road, Charleston, NH, open seasonally; admission. Set on 20 riverside acres on the Connecticut River, this stockade fort replicates the way the settlement looked in the 1740s. A full 50 miles north of any other town on the Connecticut River, the original fort served first as a trading post in which Native Americans and newcomers lived together peaceably until the outbreak of the French and Indian Wars, during which it withstood repeated attacks. The complex includes the Great Hall and furnished living quarters. Costumed interpreters demonstrate eighteenth-century life, a small museum displays locally found settler and Native American artifacts, and the gift store carries historical books for all ages. Inquire about frequent battle reenactments.

## ✳ To Do

GRAFTON INN  THE WINDHAM FOUNDATION

BIKING Road biking is popular in this area, thanks to many interlinking back roads and river roads. **Grafton Trails & Outdoor Center** (802-843-2400; graftontrails.com) in Grafton rents mountain bikes and offers mountain biking on its cross-country trails, as well as offering lessons.

**Ascutney Trails** (ascutneytrails.com) is a 30-mile network of interconnected trails accessed from the former Ascutney Mountain Ski Area (now Holiday Inn Club Vacations) in the village of Brownsville, VT 44. It was hand-built and is maintained by volunteer members of the Sport Trails of the Ascutney Basin (STAB). Paradise Sports (802-674-6742; paradisesportsshop.com), 25 Depot Avenue, Windsor, rents, fixes, and sells mountain bikes.

BOATING **Great River Outfitters** (802-674-9933; greatriveroutfitters.com), 36 Park Road, Windsor. Open daily offering kayaking, canoeing, and tubing on a placid and popular paddling stretch of the river, ending here. The company also offers camping and a variety of other ways of experiencing the Garden.

*Boat access to the Connecticut River:* **Herricks Cove**. Picnic area, boat landing, and bird sanctuary, a good picnic spot off US 5 near I-91, Exit 6, in Rockingham, above Bellows Falls.

**Hoyt's Landing**. Off VT 11 and I-91, Exit 7, in Springfield, a recently upgraded put-in that's also good for fishing and picnicking.

GOLF **Bellows Falls Country Club** (802-463-9809; bellowsfallscountryclub.com), 12 Country Club Road (VT 103), Rockingham. Scenic nine-hole course; clubhouse with bar and lunchroom. **Crown Point Country Club** (802-885-1010; crownpointcountryclub.com), 2 Weathersfield Center Road, Springfield. A gem of an 18-hole course with pro shop, golf lessons, driving range, restaurant, and banquet facilities. **Hooper Golf Course** (603-756-4080; hoopergolfcourse.com), 166 Prospect Hill Road, Walpole, NH. This vintage course offers nine holes and a clubhouse, serving lunch.

HIKING/WALKING **Bellows Falls Historic Riverfront Park and Trail System**. This trail begins at the Bellows Falls Historical Society property on Mill Street and runs along the Connecticut River. Also see the **Windham Hill Pinnacle Association** (802-869-1681; windhamhillpinnacle.org) for a map and access points for this well-maintained ridge trail running south through Westminster to connect with Putney Mountain.

**Mount Ascutney** offers the area's most dramatic hiking. Of the four trails to the summit, we recommend the 2.9-mile ascent from Weathersfield with an 84-foot waterfall about halfway up (the trailhead is on Cascade Falls Road, 3.5 miles north off VT 131). The 3.2-mile Brownsville Trail begins on VT 44 between Windsor and Brownsville; the 2.7-mile Windsor Trail starts on VT 44A in Windsor. The 4.4-mile Futures Trail begins in Windsor State Park and links up with the Windsor Trail.

SWIMMING **Grafton Swimming Pond**, VT 121, 1 mile west of the village, is an oasis for children. **Grafton Trails & Outdoor Center**, VT 35, also offers swimming and a wooden float.

**Stoughton Pond Recreation Area** (802-886-2775), 98 Reservoir Road off VT 106 in Weathersfield, north of Springfield, not to be confused with the swimming hole in Perkinsville (also VT 106), where the **Black River** cascades into delicious pools at an old power site. **Kennedy's Pond** (VT 44 west) in Windsor has a small beach, great for kids. Inquire locally about numerous other swimming holes in the Black and Williams rivers and about **Twenty-Foot Hole** (a series of cataracts and pools in a wooded gorge) in Reading.

# ✳ Winter Sports

CROSS-COUNTRY SKIING, SNOWSHOEING, DOG SLEDDING **Grafton Trails & Outdoor Center** (802-843-2400; graftontrails.com), 783 Townshend Road, Grafton.

Fifteen km of trails, groomed both for skating and classic strides, meander off from a log cabin warming hut, over meadows, and into the woods on Bear Hill. Snowmaking on 5 km, rentals, instruction, snowtubing, and 10 km of snowshoeing trails.

**Great River Outfitters** (802-674-9933; greatriveroutfitters.com), 36 Park Road, Windsor, in Artisans Park (see sidebar), Windsor, rents cross-country skis and snowshoes and maintains cross-country and snowshoeing trails in the riverside Path of Life Garden, also offering access to trails on neighboring acres. Dogsledding rides with or without snow; sleigh and wagon rides and winter tepee camping also offered. Check the website for scheduled guided tours and other adventures.

SCENIC DRIVES  The national **Connecticut River Byway** (ctriverbyways.org) encompasses both sides of the river. From I-91, take Exit 5 (**Westminster**) and turn south to cross the river to **Walpole, NH** (see *Towns and Villages*) and turn at the sign for the village center. Back on NH 12, head north to **Charlestown** to see reconstructed **Fort at No. 4** (see *Must See*). Cross back to Vermont on US 11 at **Hoyt's Landing** (just off I-91, Exit 7). Zip back down I-91 to Exit 6 and follow VT 103 for roughly 1 mile to the turnoff for the **Rockingham Meeting House** (see sidebar). Return to US 5 and turn south to **Bellows Falls** (see *Towns and Villages*).

**Rockingham to Weathersfield.** From the **Rockingham Meeting House** (see sidebar) follow Meetinghouse Road to VT 102, and after The **Vermont Country Store**, take the first real right-hand turn on Brockway Mills Road and an immediate left on Williams Road, following it through the Worrall Covered Bridge (1870) and back to VT 103 but just for a fraction of a mile. Turn right again on the Lower Bartsonville Road and follow it through the new Bartonsville covered bridge, rebuilt after its predecessor was wiped out in 2012. This scenic byway becomes Pleasant Valley Road, rejoining VT 11 after 5.2 miles. Turn right on VT 11 and follow it into downtown Springfield, turning left beyond the Springfield River onto Valley Street, which turns into Brook Road as it climbs past the **Springfield Country Club** (see *Golf*) and on into Weathersfield Center. Be sure to stop at the **Weathersfield Meeting House** (see sidebar). Continue on to VT 131. Here you can take Exit 8 to return to Bellows Falls or turn north on US 5 for Windsor (5 miles). Or detour the mile up VT 44 to **Ascutney State Park**, with its 3.8-mile parkway spiraling up almost to the 3,144-foot-high summit, itself one of the most scenic drives in the state.

# ✻ Green Space

**Wilgus State Park** (802-674-5422; vtstate parks.com), 1.5 miles south of I-91, Exit 8,

GRAFTON TRAILS & OUTDOOR CENTER THEWINDHAM FOUNDATION

LAKE RUNNEMEDE, WINDSOR  CHRISTINA TREE

US 5, Windsor. Open Memorial Day–Columbus Day. This small, quiet campground on the Connecticut River is ideal for canoeists—the 17 tent sites, six lean-tos, and four cabins are on the riverbank. Playground, picnic tables, hiking trails; also canoe, kayak, and rowboat rentals.

**Ascutney State Park** *Must See, Hiking,* and *Scenic Drives.* A total of 49 tent sites, trailer sites, and lean-tos can be reserved. Also see *Hiking.*

**Paradise Park.** A 177-acre preserve with a network of trails for walking, snowshoeing, and skiing through woods, around fields, and along the shoreline of Lake Runnemede in the heart of Windsor. It's best accessed from County Road, off State Street.

**Path of Life Garden** (pathoflifegarden.com), 36 Park Way in Artisans Park (see sidebar), Windsor. Open year-round. Admission. The path leads to a 14-acre riverside "garden" with distinct "rooms"—some resembling sculpture gardens, but including a maze

PATH OF LIFE GARDEN  CHRISTINA TREE

lined with 800 hemlock trees and a 90-foot rock labyrinth, and a natural amphitheater for summer bonfires and drumming. Inquire about teepee camping.

## ✳ Lodging

INNS ♿ ♂ **The Inn at Weathersfield** (802-263-9217; weathersfieldinn.com), 1342 VT 106, Perkinsville. Best known for fine dining (see *Dining Out*), the inn also offers luxurious guest rooms and suites. They range in size and locale (from the original 1792 to newer wings); baths vary from shower to Jacuzzi; many rooms have fireplaces. The inn is set back from the road, just south of the village of Perkinsville, in 21 wooded acres with an amphitheater used as a wedding venue. Innkeepers Richard and Marlee Spanjian host cooking classes and programs at their specially designed Hidden Kitchen. $$–$$ rates include full breakfast.

   &#x26; ♂ ❅ **Grafton Inn** (802-843-2248; graftoninnvermont.com), 92 Main Street, Grafton. The brick core of this splendid building dates from 1801, but the double-porched façade is mid-nineteenth century. The early-nineteenth-century-style interior is country elegant but unstuffy and comfortable (a discreet elevator accesses the second and third floors). There are 45 guest rooms, 11 (including 3 suites) in the old inn itself, the remainder divided between the Windham and Homestead cottages. Four rental houses with full kitchens and common space, some with working fireplace, sleep between 6 and 10 people apiece. In total, the inn can accommodate 90 people. $$$$$, depending on season. See *Grafton* sidebar in this chapter for the inn's history. There's candlelit dining in the **Old Tavern Restaurant** (see *Dining Out*). The inn's **Phelps Barn Pub** offers a pub menu: $$–$$$

   ❅ **Saxtons River Inn** (802-869-2110; innsaxtonsriver.com), 27 Main Street, Saxtons River. The vintage 1903 village inn with a distinctive square, five-story tower once again belongs to the family who restored and put it on the culinary map (see *Dining Out*) and the cheery pub at the front of the house is a popular gathering place. The 16 pleasant rooms all have a private bath and phone; continental breakfast is included in $–$$ per couple.

   ✪ **Hartness House** (802-885-2115; hartnesshouseinn.com), 30 Orchard Street. This landmark vintage mansion, set high on a hill above downtown Springfield, offers 40 rooms, 11 in the original house and the remainder divided between later additions. Since a change of ownership in 2015, renovations have been ongoing; rooms vary widely. The mansion was built by James Hartness, an inventor, pioneer aviator, president of Springfield's leading tool company, and Vermont governor. However, he is best remembered as an astronomer who installed one of the first tracking telescopes in the country, now part of a museum connected to the house by an underground tunnel (tours open to guests). See *Dining Out*. Rates: $–$$ include full breakfast.

## BED & BREAKFASTS

### IN GRAFTON

✪ ❧ **The Inn at Woodchuck Hill Farm** (802-843-2398; woodchuckhill.com), 275 Woodchuck Hill Road. Open May–November. Originally a 1780s farmhouse, high on a hill, off a back road, this is a comfortable, longtime lodging operated by Mark and Marilyn Gabriel. The comfortable porch, living, and dining rooms all offer long views, as do many of the three rooms and three suites. By the pond, the old barn has been revamped to offer two attractive, self-catering, family-size units and a handicapped suite, along with Spruce Cottage, furnished in antiques and fully equipped; sleeps up to seven people. There is a sauna in the woods next to the pond, which is good for swimming, fishing, and canoeing, and the 200 rolling acres are laced with walking trails. Inquire about Kundalini yoga classes and retreats. Inn room rates are $–$$, full breakfast included; $$ for barn suites.

### IN BELLOWS FALLS/SAXTONS RIVER

❧ **Harvest Barn Inn** (802-732-8254; harvestbarninn.com), 16 Webb Terrace, Bellows Falls. Sited high on a steep hillside north of the village, this is a casual, comfortable place with river views and an expansive back meadow with a pond. Check the website for views of the seven rooms, all cheerful and comfortable with private bath, sharing a sunny common space in the front of the house. A full breakfast is included in the rate. $.

**Moore's Inn** (802-869-2020; mooresinn.com), 57 Main Street (VT 121), Saxtons River. Dave Moore is a sixth-generation Vermonter who grew up in this Victorian house, with its fine woodwork and spacious veranda. It remains very much Dave and Carol's family home, as well as a guesthouse. The guest rooms—six on the second floor and three on the third—are all self-contained, six with a private bath, TV, refrigerator, coffeemaker, and breakfast cereal. The three third-floor guest rooms share a living room and can be rented together. The kitchen, living room, and bath are shared. Coffee and breakfast cereals are provided. Bicyclists are especially welcome; maps, advice, and guided tours are available. $.

### IN WINDSOR

✪ **Snapdragon Inn** (802-227-0008; snapdragoninn.com), 26 Main Street, Windsor. This graceful brick mansion was built in 1815 and eventually formed the core of an estate that included several homes and 1,000 acres. Its best-remembered owner was Max Perkins, legendary editor to Thomas Wolfe, Ernest Hemingway (both stayed in room #8), and F. Scott Fitzgerald. You can read their work in the library, a spacious, comfortable, fireplace-centered room that's also stocked with board games. The nine second- and third-floor guest rooms are spacious and sparely furnished with an eye to light and comfort; the king or queen beds are fitted with feather comforters, and there are desks and fresh flowers. A generous buffet breakfast is set out in the rose-colored dining room, included in the rates. A path leads from the garden to Lake Runnemede (see Paradise Park in *Green Space*). $$$–$$$$.

**Windsor Mansion Inn** (802-674-4112; windsormansioninn.com), 153 Pembroke Road, Windsor. Set high on a hill above

SNAPDRAGON INN, WINDSOR   CHRISTINA TREE

town with a view of Mount Ascutney, this genuine old mansion (it hosted both Theodore Roosevelt and Woodrow Wilson) is a longtime inn, recently renovated and renamed. With 17 guest rooms, spacious living and dining, and landscaped grounds, it lends itself to wedding and meetings but welcomes overnight guests. $$–$$$.

**CAMPING** See Wilgus and Mount Ascutney State Parks under *Green Space*. The Vermont State Parks reservation line operates weekdays: 888-409-7579.

## ✱ Where to Eat

### SOUTH TO NORTH

**DINING OUT** ❧ **The Old Tavern** (802-843-2248; graftoninnvermont.com), 92 Main Street, Grafton, serves dinner to the public by reservation; closed Mon., Tues. off-season. Candlelit dinner is served in the formal old dining room amid fine portraits and Chippendale chairs in this beautifully restored old tavern (see *Grafton* sidebar and *Lodging*). Entrées $$–$$; the inn's **Phelps Barn Pub** offers informal dining.

✪ ❧ **Leslie's – The Tavern at Rockingham** (802-463-4929; lesliestavern.com), 60 Rockingham Road, Rockingham,

US 5 just south of I-91, Exit 6. Open nightly except Mon.–Tues. Reservations appreciated. John Marston opened his restaurant in a 1790s tavern back in 1986, and he continues to create new and eclectic dishes, fusing many influences with experience and using as much homegrown produce as possible. The menu changes nightly and Leslie Marston makes desserts from scratch daily. Entrées $$; children's menu. Check for upcoming cooking classes.

**The Inn at Weathersfield** (802-263-9217; weathersfieldinn.com), 1342 VT 106, Perkinsville. Open to the public for dinner Wed.–Sun., nightly in foliage season. Reservations suggested. The dining room is a former carriage house, candlelit, with windows overlooking the garden. Check the website for seasonal menus with 75 percent of ingredients sourced within 25 miles. $$–$$$.

**Popolo** (802-460-7676; popolomeans people.com), 36 the Square, Bellows Falls. Open for dinner except Mon.; for lunch Fri., brunch Sun. *Popolo* means "people" in Italian, and the spirit of this place is bringing people together for good food, drink, and live entertainment at the heart of town. Housed in the renovated Windham Hotel, the pleasant street side space is hung with full-size copies of 1930s Federal Arts Program murals depicting Vermont farm scenes (the originals are in the former St. Albans post office). The limited but nicely varied menu is Italian-inspired farm to table. Frequent live music and other performances. Dinner entrée: $$; note the 6 percent added to ensure a living wage ($15 per hour) for waitstaff.

**Saxtons River Inn** (802-869-2110; innsaxtonsriver.com), 27 Main Street, Saxtons River. Open for dinner except Tues. A winter menu in the cheery, old-fashioned dining room offers a choice of a dozen entrées, from burgers to rack of lamb. $–$$$.

**Hartness House Tavern** (802-885-2115; hartnesshouse.com), 30 Orchard Street, Springfield. Open for dinner; Wed.–Sun). The tavern in this expansive vintage inn has been totally renovated under current owners and specializes in

INN AT WEATHERSFIELD, PERKINSVILLE  INN AT WEATHERSFIELD

**SAXTONS RIVER INN** CHRISTINA TREE

farm-to-table dining with a menu featuring small plates, appetizers, and cocktails. Check the website for expanded hours, music, and special events. Saturday night guests are invited to tour the telescope museum (see *Lodging*).

✪ **Skunk Hollow Tavern** (802-436-2139; skunkhollowtavern.com), 12 Brownsville Road, Hartland Four Corners (off VT 12, north of I-91, Exit 9). Dinner Wed.–Sun. Reservations suggested. This split-personality restaurant, hidden away in a small village, is a local favorite. Patrons gather downstairs to munch on fish-and-chips or pizza; the more formal dining is upstairs in the inn's original parlor. The menu changes seasonally but has dependably excellent salad of the day and from-scratch soups. Open-mic night Wed. and Fri. Entrées from grass-fed burgers to filet mignon. $–$$$.

## WORTH CROSSING THE RIVER

**The Restaurant at Burdick's** (603-756-9058; 47mainwalpole.com), 47 Main Street, Walpole, NH. Open Tues.–Sat. for lunch, dinner; Monday lunch; Sunday brunch. Reservations suggested. Chocolatier extraordinaire Larry Burdick and his friend, filmmaker Ken Burns, have transformed the town's former IGA into a chic dining spot. With its warm yellow walls, soft lighting, and artfully placed mirrors and paintings, the ambiance as well as menu evokes a French bistro. Specialties include onion soup gratinee, quiche, Provençal beef stew, and seared duck breast. The bread is fresh and crusty, and the chocolate desserts are to die for. Entrées: $$–$$$. But you can always get a bistro burger. A less expensive bistro menu is served 3–5:30.

**EATING OUT** Listed from south to north.

**IN AND AROUND BELLOWS FALLS**

✪ **Café Loco at Harlow Farm Stand** (802-376-9626), 6365 US 5 north of I-91, Exit 5, Westminster. Open Mon.–Sat., 7–4, Sun. 8–4, May–December. It's easy to miss this delightful café surrounded by the Harlow family's organic farm. The café at this mega-farm stand, orchestrated by Michael Lenox, features freshly made soups, sandwiches, homemade pies, and daily specials.

🦞 **Father's Restaurant** (802-463-3909; fathersrestaurant.com), 7079 US 5, 1 mile south of Bellows Falls. Open Sun. 7–3, Tues.–Sat. 6 a.m.–8 p.m. A local family restaurant with a salad bar, kids' menu, wine, and beer.

✪ **Flat Iron Exchange** (802-460-0357; flatironexchangevt.com), 51 the Square, Bellows Falls. Open 6 a.m.–9 p.m. This attractive coffeehouse is an all-day gathering spot with comfortable couches as well as tables, papers, a choice of coffees, teas, and home-baked pastries. Art changes frequently, and there's often live music.

**Miss Bellows Falls Diner** (802-463-9800), 90 Rockingham Street, Bellows Falls. Open daily 6–2, Sun. 7–2. Inside and out this Worcester diner is still pure, unhokey 1920s.

(((•))) **Café 7 on the Square** (802-460-1051), 7 Square Drive, Bellows Falls. Open daily 8–3. Great for breakfast, lunch, and Wi-Fi in between.

**Moon Dog Cafe** (802-732-8453), 24 Rockingham Street. Open daily. Known for soups and healthy, tasty sandwiches, salads, and desserts. Espresso drinks, smoothies, and juices also served.

WINDSOR

**Windsor Station Restaurant and Barroom** (802-674-4130; windsorstationvt.com), 26 Depot Avenue. Open for lunch Thurs.–Sat.; dinner Tues.–Sun. The interior of this 1902 railroad station is darkly paneled, brightened with art, and divided between the Lounge Car, with pub food, and the more formal Dining and Parlor Cars with an Italian-accented menu. Produce is locally sourced; locally crafted beers are a specialty, and dinner reservations are advisable. $–$$.

**Windsor Diner** (802-674-5555), 135 Main Street. Open daily 6 a.m.–8 p.m. This classic 1952 Worcester diner (#835) serves good, honest diner food: meatloaf, liver and onions, and macaroni and cheese, along with omelets, burger baskets, pies, and more.

BREWS **Harpoon Riverbend Taps and Beer Garden** (802-674-5491; harpoonbrewery.com), 336 Ruth Carney Drive (see *Artisans Park* sidebar). Open daily May–October, Sun.–Wed. 10–6, Thurs.–Sat. 10–9; November–April, closed Mon. Boston-based, Harpoon has transformed the former Catamount Brewery into a popular gathering place/informal restaurant. In summer it expands with outside tables. Brews on tap change with the season. The menu is basic pub with daily specials. Patrons (over 21 years of age) are welcome to sample up to four kinds. It's an attractive space with a glass wall overlooking the lawn and picnic tables, a two-sided hearth, and tables as well as bar seating. Frequent music, special events, and brewery tours.

(((•))) **Boston Dreams** (802-230-4107; bostondreams.com), 7 State Street, Windsor. Freshly ground coffees, pastries, bagels, chili, and a blackboard menu. Also 12 flavors of Gifford's ice cream. The walls are hung with Red Sox photos and other sports memorabilia (for sale).

## ✳ Entertainment

✪ **Bellows Falls Opera House** (802-463-4766;), in Rockingham Town Hall, on the square in Bellows Falls. This vintage, 1926 vaudeville house has been beautifully refurbished and serves as a venue for live performances as well as Fri.–Tues. films; tickets $5.

**Main Street Arts** (802-869-2960; mainstreetarts.org), 35 Main Street, Saxtons River. This local arts council sponsors dance and musical performances, cabarets, and recitals, as well as art classes.

**Springfield Theater** (802-885-2929), 26 Main Street, downtown Springfield. First-run films.

## ✳ Selective Shopping

ANTIQUES SHOPS **Windham Antique Center** (802-732-8081; windhamantiquecenter.com), 5 the Square. Open 10–7 daily, until 5 Sunday. This is a destination multi-group store in the heart of Bellows Falls.

**S. B. & Company Antiques/Auctioneers** (802-460-1190; sbauctioneers.com), 46 Canal Street, Bellows Falls. Check the website for frequent auctions.

ARTS AND CRAFTS *Note:* **Bellows Falls Art Walk**, featuring local art and music, takes place in Bellows Falls the third Friday of every month.

*Note:* **The Putney Craft Tour** (putneycrafts.com), held for more than 30 years for three days after Thanksgiving, showcases the work of more than two dozen craftspeople within a dozen miles of Putney. **The Walpole Artisans Cooperative** also sponsors an open studio tour on Thanksgiving weekend (walpoleartisans.org).

## IN BELLOWS FALLS/WALPOLE

✪ **Sherwin Art Glass Studio/Gallery** (802-376-5744; sherwinartglass.com), 33 Bridge Street, Bellows Falls. Chris Sherwin usually can be found here, creating colored art glass.

**River Artisans** (802-460-0059; riverartisans.com), 28 Village Square. Check website for hours. Formerly in Saxtons River, this exceptional cooperative showcases work by local artisans, crafted in a wide variety of media.

**Walpole Artisans Cooperative** (603-756-3020; walpoleartisans.org), 52 Main Street, Walpole, NH (across from Burdick's Café). Open daily. A juried cooperative showcasing local craftspeople.

## IN GRAFTON

**Gallery North Star** (802-843-2465; gnsgrafton.com), 151 Townshend Road. Open daily 10–5. An outstanding, long-established gallery. Six rooms in a nineteenth-century Grafton Village house are hung with landscapes and graphic prints, oils, watercolors, and sculpture.

**Jud Hartmann Gallery** (802-843-2018; judhartmanngallery.com), 6 Main Street. Open mid-September–Christmas holidays 10–5. Hartmann began his career as a sculptor in Grafton and has since won national acclaim for his bronze portrayals of Native Americans. If not in his gallery, look for him on the ski trails at Grafton Pond, which he founded years back. In summer, look for his gallery in Blue Hill, ME.

## IN SPRINGFIELD

**Gallery at the Vault** (802-885-7111; galleryvault.org), 68 Main Street. This quality crafts store is all about Visual Art Using Local Talent (hence its name) and is definitely worth checking out.

**Great Hall**, 100 River Street. A magnificent atrium space, a venue for public art and frequent special exhibits in the former Fellows Gear Sharper Factory building.

## IN WINDSOR

✪ **Cider Hill Gardens & Art Gallery** (802-674-6825; ciderhillgardens.com), 1747 Hunt Road, 2.5 miles west of State Street, Windsor. Open May–September, Thurs.–Sun. 10–5.; October–November Fri.–Sun. Sarah Milek's display garden specializes in hundreds of varieties of peonies, hosta, and daylilies. It's the setting for Gary Milek's studio (garymilek.com), showcasing striking Vermont landscapes done in egg tempera, as well as botanically correct floral prints and stunning cards made from them. Check the website for talks, tours, and exhibits.

**Simon Pearce Glass** (802-230-2402; simonpearce.com), 109 Park Road, see *Artisans Park* sidebar. Open daily 10–5. After establishing his original glass-blowing facility in Quechee, Simon Pearce built this additional, 32,000-square-foot factory down by the Connecticut River. Designed to be visitor friendly, it includes a catwalk above the factory floor from which you can watch glass being blown and shaped. The shop features seconds as well as first-quality glass and pottery.

**Rockledge Farm Woodworks** (800-653-2700; rockledgefarm.com), 58 Ascutney Basin Road, Weathersfield. Open Tues.–Sat., 9–5, Sun. noon–4. This is a 200-year old farm with a long, family woodworking tradition. Visitors are welcome to watch as Vermont hardwoods and burls are crafted into nationally distributed furniture and woodenware that's also sold here. Bring a picnic for the tables under the apple trees.

SPECIAL SHOPS **The Vermont Country Store** (802-463-2224; vermontcountryst ore.com), 1292 Rockingham Road (VT 103), Rockingham Village. An offshoot of the Weston store known for its catalog featuring hard-to-find old-timey gadgets. The license plates on cars, trucks, and RVs parked by this big red barn of a place are from all over the country. Walls and aisles inside are filled with a wild and wonderful mix of products from the past: cotton sleepwear and nature-based tonics, Vermont Common Crackers, American-made lawn chairs, weather sticks, and cat clocks with moving eyes. In a corner beyond the free cheese samples, women make sandwiches to take to the shaded picnic tables outside, near the dairy bar.

**Village Square Booksellers** (802-463-9404; villagesquarebooks.com), 32 the Square, Bellows Falls. Open Mon.–Thurs. 9–5, Fri. 9–6, Sat. 9–4, and Sun. 10–3. Patricia and Alan Fowler's independent, full-service bookstore also carries music, cards, toys, local photography by Alan, and changing work by local artists. It's the main venue for author readings and special programs. This is also a source of tickets for performances at the Opera House (see *Entertainment*) and other local events.

**J&H Hardware** (802-463-4140; jandhhardware.doitbest.com), 20 the Square, Bellows Falls. An old-style hardware store, also carrying toys, sporting goods, and men's and women's clothing.

FOOD, FLOWERS, AND FARM STANDS *Also see:* Cider Hill Gardens & Art Gallery under *Art & Craft.*

**Allen Brothers Farms & Orchards** (802-722-3395), 6023 US 5, 2 miles south of Bellows Falls. Open year-round, daily 6 a.m.–9 p.m. Offers pick-your-own apples and potatoes in-season; also sells vegetables, plants and seeds, honey, syrup, and Vermont gifts; great to-go sandwiches, also cider doughnuts.

**Harlow Farm Stand** (802-722-3515; harlowfarm.com), US 5, less than a mile north of I-91, Exit 5. Open May–December, daily 9–6. A century-old farm in the same family. Organic produce, bedding plants, flowers, and baked goods. Also see Café Loco under *Eating Out.*

**Plummer's Sugar House** (802-843-2207; plummerssugarhouse.com), 3 miles south of Grafton Village on Townshend Road. Open all year. A third-generation maple producer, making pure syrup for more than 30 years; also maple candy and sugar; ships anywhere in the US.

**Morning Star Perennials** (802-463-3433; morningstarflowers.com), 221 Darby Hill Road, Rockingham (off US 5). More than 300 varieties of organically grown perennials, including many rare ones.

✐ **Wellwood Orchards** (802-263-5200; wellwoodorchards.com), 529 Wellwood Orchard Road, Springfield. Pick-your-own strawberries (June and July), then raspberries and blueberries (mid- to late July), and finally apples (mid-August–October). Petting zoo, country store, and food tent (weather permitting).

**Vermont Shepherd Farm Store** (802-387-4473; vermontshepherd.com), 281 Patch Road, Westminster West; open daily 9–5. Vermont Shepherd has won top awards for its distinctive, hand-pressed, sweet creamy sheep's-milk cheese. It's made April–October, then aged 4 to 8 months. The self-serve shop is open daily 9–5.

**Halladay's Flowers & Harvest Barn** (802-463-3331; halladays.com), 59 the Square, Bellows Falls. A village flower store that's also an outlet for herb blends, dip mixes, and cake mixes all made in town from natural ingredients, as well as wines, local hard cider, and cheese.

**Green Mountain Smokehouse** (802-674-6653), 341 US 5, Windsor. Open Mon.–Fri. 9–5, Sat. 9–4. A destination for maple-smoked bacon lovers, with many varieties of sausage, ham, and more.

FARMERS' MARKETS In **Bellows Falls** (bffarmersmarket.com) on Fri. 4–7, June–mid-September, Hetty Green Park;

## NOT YOUR USUAL PARK

**A**rtisans Park (artisanspark.net), US 5 , one mile south of I-91, Exit 9. Tourist traffic in Windsor has shifted from downtown to a clustering of enterprises spaced in a park-like riverside setting several miles north of downtown. The commercial anchors of Artisans Park are **Simon Pearce** (see *Art and Craft*) and the **Harpoon Brewery** (see *Brews*). This visitor-friendly commercial campus is the brainchild of local therapist Terry McDonnell, who bought a former farm on the Connecticut here in the 1990s and set about creating the **Path of Life Garden**, which now contains 18 distinct landscaped and sculpted areas, each designed to portray a step in the cycle of human life. Patterned on a vintage garden in Ireland, it includes a maze lined with 800 hemlock trees and a 90-foot rock labyrinth. Admission is through **Great River Outfitters** (*Boating*). The Park also includes **Silo Distillery** (silodistillery.com), with tours and tastings of its vodka, whisky, and bourbon, and several shops selling Vermont-made cheese, preserves, and more; **Blake Hill Preserves** (blakehillpreserves.com) is an outlet for widely respected, locally made fruit jam and marmalade makers; and the **Vermont Farmstead Cheese Company Market** (vermontfarmstead.com), featuring Vermont cheese and food products, also wine; outdoor seating for grilled cheese sandwiches and wood-fired pizza on weekends.

Winter Market, third Fridays, at the train station, 50 Depot Street.

**Springfield** (springfieldvtfarmers market.), seasonal, Sat., 10–1:30, Lower Clinton Street by the bike path. **Windsor Farmers' Market** (802-359-2557), State Street Green, 51 Main Street, Sat., late May–mid-October. Wintermarket, first and third Sat., December–May at the Windsor Welcome Center, 3 Railroad Avenue.

## ✳ Special Events

*Note:* Check bellowsfallsvt.org for current happenings, and see Art Walk under *Art Galleries.*

*June:* **Roots on the River**, second weekend (rootsontheriver.com).

*July 3:* **Annual VSO Concert Under the Stars and Fireworks** at Grafton Trails & Outdoor Center, part of the Grafton Music Festival.

*July 4 weekend:* A big **parade** in Saxtons River with fireworks. **Windsor County Agricultural Fair**, Barlow's Field, Springfield.

*August:* **Rockingham Old Home Days**, Bellows Falls (gfrcc.org). A full weekend of events: railroad excursions, live entertainment, art show, Rockingham Meeting House Pilgrimage, and fireworks. Annual **Stellafane Convention of Amateur Telescope Makers** (stellafane .com), Springfield.

*Thanksgiving weekend:* **Putney Craft Tour** (putneycrafts.com; see *West River Valley*) and the **Walpole Artisan Open Studios Tour** (walpoleartisans.com) add up to a great way to explore back roads and take care of holiday shopping.

# UPPER VALLEY RIVER TOWNS

*Including White River Junction, Norwich, Thetford, Fairlee, Bradford, Newbury, and Wells River, VT; also Hanover, Orford, Piermont, Haverhill, and Woodsville, NH*

The Upper Valley ignores state lines to form one of New England's most rewarding and distinctive regions.

*Upper Valley* is a name coined in the 1950s by a local daily, the *Valley News*, to define its two-state circulation area. The label has stuck to a group of towns that tried to form the state of "New Connecticut" (see the introduction to "The Connecticut River Valley") in the 1770s.

The Valley itself prospered in the late eighteenth and early nineteenth centuries, as evidenced by the exquisite Federal-era meetinghouses and mansions still salted throughout this area. The river was the area's only highway in the eighteenth and early nineteenth centuries and was still a popular steamboat route in the years before the Civil War.

The river remains more a bond than a boundary. The Upper Valley phone book includes towns on both sides of the river, and Hanover's Dresden School District reaches into Vermont (this was the first bistate school district in the United States). The Rivendell School District to the north stretches from Vershire, VT, on the west to Orford, NH. The Montshire Museum, founded in Hanover, NH, but now located in Norwich, combines the two states in its very name.

The Connecticut and White rivers converge at White River Junction, also the hub from which rail lines once radiated and now the junction point for the region's interstates (I-89 and I-93) as well as its historic highways (US 4 and US 5). As many as 100 steam locomotives per day chugged into this station (still an Amtrak stop) at the height of nineteenth-century rail usage, an era that spawned a compact brick village, currently experiencing a renaissance as a lively arts, shopping, and dining hub.

North along the river, villages are spaced along both sides, each with its special appeal. Stately Norwich, VT, seems a sleepy sister to Hanover, just across the Ledyard Bridge. Home to Dartmouth College, Hanover's few but busy blocks are studded with shops and restaurants, but in Norwich harbors there's the Montshire Museum, hidden down by the river, and the King Arthur Flour campus has a following among bakers from all over the country.

The 36 miles north from Norwich and Hanover are an exceptionally beautiful stretch of the entire bistate Connecticut River Byway. I-91, set high above the Vermont bank of the river, has backroaded US 5 and NH 10. Both alternately hug the river and thread farmland. The attractions are farm stands, river landings, swim beaches, and unexpected discoveries like the *Vermontasaurus* dinosaur in a grassy airfield in Post Mills and Farm-way, a vast and varied emporium hidden down near the river in Bradford. The 15 riverside miles north from Bradford have an even more off-the-beaten track feel to them, and the scenery just gets better, backed by New Hampshire's White Mountains. This is its own special area, dubbed *Cohase*—an Abenaki word meaning

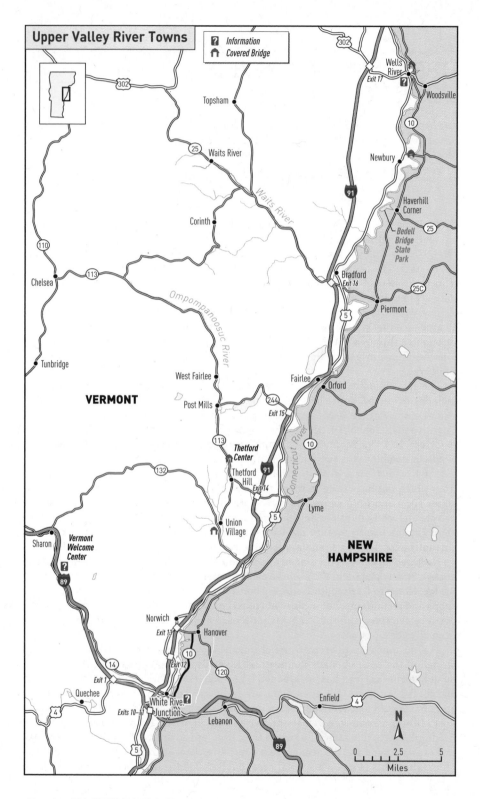

# Upper Valley River Towns

**?** Information
**⌂** Covered Bridge

302

Topsham

25 Waits River

*Waits River*

Corinth

110

113 Chelsea

*Ompompanoosuc River*

Tunbridge

**VERMONT**

West Fairlee

Post Mills

113

132

**Thetford Center**

Thetford Hill
*Exit 14*

Union Village

Sharon

**Vermont Welcome Center**

**?**

89

Norwich
*Exit 13*

14

*Exit 1*

Quechee

4

5

White Rive.
Junction **?**
*Exits 10–11*

Lebanon

89

Hanover

10

*Exit 12*

120

Enfield

4

302

Wells River
*Exit 17* **?**

Woodsville

10

Newbury

91

Haverhill Corner

*Bedell Bridge State Park*

25

Bradford
*Exit 16*

25C

5

Piermont

244
*Exit 15*

Fairlee
Orford

10

91

5

Lyme

**NEW HAMPSHIRE**

*Connecticut River*

N

0    2.5    5
Miles

"wide valley"—by the Wells River–based chamber of commerce that embraces both sides of the river.

We especially love the stretch north from Bradford to Newbury, a handsome village with a welcoming general store. The bridge just south of the village leads to Haverhill, NH. Turn south on NH 10, to the hauntingly beautiful village of Haverhill Corner. The way back is through Piermont, NH, to Orford, with its aristocratic "Ridge Houses" and the vintage bridge back to visitor-friendly Fairlee. Local bicyclists loop back and forth across the bridges between Fairlee and Newbury. Their well-known advice is "Take 5 (north) and Hang 10 (back south)."

GUIDANCE **White River Junction Welcome Center** (802-281-5050), 100 Railroad Row in the Amtrak station, White River Junction. Open 10–5 daily. A friendly, information-packed center with restrooms. From I-91 and I-89 exits to US 5, follow the signs.

GUIDANCE **Cohase Regional Chamber of Commerce** (802-518-0030; cohase.org) publishes a helpful map/guide and maintains a seasonal welcome center in Wells River, just west of the bridge on US 302.

GETTING THERE *By car:* Interstates 91 (north/south) and 89 intersect at White River Junction as do US 5 (north/south) and US 4, the old east–west highway through central Vermont and New Hampshire.

*By bus:* **Greyhound** (800-231-2222; greyhound.com) stops in White River Junction, with service to Boston, Burlington, New York City, and Montreal. **Dartmouth Coach** (603-228-3300; dartmouthcoach.com) offers great service from Boston and Logan Airport to Hanover, NH.

*By air:* The **Lebanon Municipal Airport** (603-298-8878;), West Lebanon (marked from the junction of I-89 and VT 10), offers flights to Boston and New York City. Rental cars are available, and the airport is also served by **Big Yellow Taxi** (603-643-8294).

*By train:* **Amtrak** (800-USA-RAIL; amtrak.com) serves White River Junction, en route to and from New York City/Washington, DC, and St. Albans, VT.

GETTING AROUND Visitors can easily explore both sides of the river. I-91 offers a quick route up and down the Valley with multiple exits to the old highways, NH 10 and 12, and US 5. Many of the bridges are long gone but they survive between the villages of White River Junction and West Lebanon, Norwich and Hanover, Thetford and Lyme, Fairlee and Orford, Bradford and Piermont, Newbury and Haverhill, and Wells River and Woodsville.

## ✳ Towns and Villages

### LISTED FROM SOUTH TO NORTH

**White River Junction** (population 2,569; whiteriverjunction.org) one of five villages within the town of Hartford and one of the liveliest downtowns in the Upper Valley. The vintage **Hotel Coolidge**, one of the last of New England's railroad hotels, is in the welcoming heart of a compact downtown that's enjoying a renaissance as a performance, dining, and shopping destination. **Northern Stage** offers professional performances in a state-of-the-art theater, while the Briggs Opera Company remains a venue for local music and theater, and several village restaurants and shops are themselves destinations. The **Center for Cartoon Studies** (a two-year program with a library endowed by Charles M. Schulz, creator of *Peanuts*) offers changing exhibits, and the free **Main Street Museum** (802-356-2776; mainstreetmuseum.org), housed in a former firehouse, is a true "cabinet of curiosities," almost a parody of the museum genre.

**Norwich** (population 3,844; norwichvt.us). The village is an architectural showcase for fine brick and frame Federal homes. Just across the bridge from Dartmouth College campus, this was itself the original home of Norwich University (founded in 1819), which moved to Northfield after the Civil War. The **Norwich Inn**, with its popular brewpub and dining room, is the hospitable heart of town. Hidden down between I-91 and the river, the **Montshire Museum** offers insights into ways the world and universe go 'round as well as into how the river shapes the immediate environment; also, there are riverside walking trails. **King Arthur Flour Company's** flagship Baker's Store and Baking Education Center on US 5, south of town, draw devotees from throughout the country. Check norwichhistory.org for exhibits and hours at the **Norwich Historical Society** (802-649-0124), housed in the vintage 1807 Lewis House.

**Hanover, NH** (population 11,266), is synonymous with Ivy League **Dartmouth College** (dartmouth.edu), chartered in 1769 and one of the most prestigious colleges in the country. Few college towns are as visitor-friendly. Maple and elm-shaded Dartmouth Green doubles as the town common and includes a staffed information kiosk (open June–September). Here, Dartmouth College buildings include a hospitable hotel, a major performance center, and an outstanding art museum. **Dartmouth Row**, a file of four striking white colonial buildings on the rise along the eastern side of the green, represents all there was to Dartmouth College until 1845. Campus tours are offered.

**Lyme, NH** (population 1,716) is known for its splendid, vintage, 1812 **Congregational church** with numbered horse stalls at the head of a handsome green. Take **River Road** north by old farms and cemeteries, over an 1880s-period covered bridge.

**Thetford** (population 2,784). Thetford Hill, a short detour up VT 113 from US 5, is a beauty, the site of Thetford Academy and an elegant Congregational church. Union Village Dam, a recreation area maintained by the Army Corps of Engineers, offers a sandy swim beach and shaded picnic facilities.

**Fairlee Village**, shelved between the Palisades and a bend in the Connecticut River, is a plain cousin to aristocratic Orford, NH (well known for its lineup of elegant Federal-era houses), just across the river, but it's a better stop given a choice of places to eat: the wonderfully eclectic **Chapman's Country Store** and the **Fairlee Drive-In**. **Lake Morey**, site of **Lake Morey Resort** and its golf course, is just west of the village. It's named for Samuel Morey, who is said to have invented the first steamboat in 1793, 14 years before Robert Fulton launched his craft. Many believe the remains of his little steamer lie at the bottom of Lake Morey, scuttled after Morey was swindled by Fulton. **Lake Fairlee**, south of town off VT 244, offers a public swim beach.

**Orford, NH** (population 1,044) is known for its **Ridge Houses**, a center-of-town lineup of seven houses so strikingly handsome that Charles Bulfinch has been erroneously credited as architect. Its southernmost towns are sleepy Piermont, NH, and (relatively) bustling Bradford, VT, built on terraced land at the confluence of the Waits River and the Connecticut.

**Bradford**, built on terraced land at the confluence of the Waits River and the Connecticut, a nineteenth-century mill village that produced plows, paper, and James Wilson, an ingenious farmer who made America's first geographic globes. Low's Grist Mill across from the falls now houses a restaurant and there are more options in the business block. From Bradford, the view across the river encompasses Mount Moosilauke, easternmost of the White Mountains.

**Newbury** is one of Vermont's oldest towns, founded in 1761 by Jacob Bayley, a Revolutionary War general still remembered as the force behind the Bayley–Hazen Road, conceived as an invasion route northwest to Canada. It was abandoned two-thirds of the way along, but after the Revolution it served as a prime settlement route. The village of Newbury was a Native American settlement for many thousands of years, and in the early 1800s its mineral springs drew travelers. Five miles north, the village of **Wells River** (also in the town of Newbury) marked the head of navigation on the Connecticut through the 1830s.

**Haverhill, NH,** is immense, comprising seven very distinct villages, including classic examples of both the Federal and railroad eras. Nineteenth-century **Woodsville** retains its ornate 1890s brick Opera Block and three-story railroad station, and it is a good road-food stop. The Haverhill–Bath covered bridge, built in 1829 and billed as the oldest covered bridge in New England, is just beyond the railroad underpass (NH 135 North). It's roughly eight miles south on NH 10 to the **Haverhill Corner** Historic District, a time-frozen village sited at the junction with NH 25, the old Coos Turnpike that goes east to Plymouth. It was the Grafton County seat from 1791 to 1891 and its graceful nineteenth-century courthouse is now Court Street Arts (603-989-5500), a performance center with frequent programs and exhibits. The village itself is a gem: a grouping of Federal-era and Greek Revival homes and public buildings around a double, white-fenced common.

## ✲ Must See

✐ ♿ **Montshire Museum of Science** (802-649-2200; montshire.org), Exit 13, I-91, Montshire Road, Norwich. Open daily 10–5 except Thanksgiving and Christmas; June–Labor Day. Admission charged.
Use of the outdoor exhibit areas, Woodland Garden, and trails is included with admission. Few cities have a science museum of this quality. This award-winning, hands-on science center with more than 140 exhibits is sited on 110 trail-webbed acres beside the Connecticut River. The name *Montshire* derives from blending *Vermont* and *New Hampshire*. The focus is on demystifying scientific phenomena, engaging your senses, and learning about the world around you. The elaborate 2.5-acre Science Park features water bubbling from a 7-foot Barre granite boulder, and from this "headwater" a 250-foot "rill" flows downhill, snaking over a series of terraces, inviting you to manipulate dams and sluices to change its flow and direction (visitors are advised to bring bathing suits and towels). You can also shape fountains, cast shadows to tell time, and push a button to identify the calls of birds and insects. Note Ed Kahn's *Wind Wall*, an outdoor sculpture attached to the museum's

MONTSHIRE INTERIOR MONTSHIRE MUSEUM

BOLAND BALLOON MUSEUM, POST MILLS CHRISTINA TREE

tower, composed of thousands of silver flutter discs that shimmer in the breeze, resembling patterns on a pond riffled by wind. In the Hughes Pavilion overlooking Science Park, visitors may enjoy their picnic lunch or they may purchase lunch and snacks at the outdoor café (summer only).

Some of our favorite exhibits: the fog machine up in the tower, the see-through beehive, leaf-cutter ants, the physics of bubbles, and the planet walk. There are also astounding displays on moths, insects, and birds. Most exhibits are hands-on. While there's a corner for toddlers and many demonstrations geared to youngsters, this is as stimulating a place for adults as it is for their offspring. The Museum Store alone is worth stopping for. Inquire about special events, programs, summer camp, and visiting exhibitions.

## ✳ To Do

BALLOONING **Boland Balloons** (802-333-9254), Post Mills Airport, West Fairlee. Mid-May–mid-November. Brian Boland offers morning and sunset balloon rides. Boland builds as well as flies hot-air balloons (he's known internationally as a hot-air balloon designer), and he maintains a museum with more than 150 balloons and airships—one of the largest collections in the world, with flying contraptions you might never believe could fly, along with antique cars. Boland also maintains rustic cabins on the premises for patrons ($) and offers packages in conjunction with nearby Silver Maple Lodge (see *Bed & Breakfasts*). The last summer evening we were there, we floated above Lake Fairlee, over green shores and kids' summer camps and down over woods patched with cornfields, on toward the Connecticut River. Even if you don't go for a ride it's worth taking a drive out VT 244 to Post Mills to see *Vermontasaurus*, a 122-foot-long, 25-foot-high dinosaur, and its offspring, fashioned by Brian Boland, with

LAKE FAIRLEE CHRISTINA TREE

the help of local students, using wood from his collapsed barn roof; when Boland is around, he permits visitors to tour the neighboring museum.

ROAD BIKING Given its unusually flat and scenic roads and well-spaced inns, this area is beloved by bicyclists. Search out the river roads: from VT 12A (just north of the Saint-Gaudens site) on through Plainfield, NH, until it rejoins VT 12A; from VT 10 north of Hanover, NH (just north of the Chieftain Motel), through Lyme, NH, rejoining VT 10 in Orford, NH. A classic, 36-mile loop is Hanover to Orford on VT 10 and back on the river road. The loop to Lyme and back is 22 miles. For inn-to-inn guided tours in this area, contact **Discovery Bicycle Tours** (802-457-3553; discoverybicycletours.com).

BOATING With its usually placid water and scenery, the Connecticut River through much of the Upper Valley is ideal for easygoing canoeists and kayakers.

**Fairlee Marine** (802-333-9745; fairleemarine.com), US 5 in Fairlee, rents pontoons, canoes, rowboats, and small motors for use on the Connecticut River and two local lakes.

Information on seven primitive campsites along this stretch of the Connecticut can be found on the **Upper Valley Land Trust**'s website: uvlt.org.

FISHING You can eat the fish you catch in the Connecticut River—it yields brown and rainbow trout above Orford. There's a boat launch on the Vermont side at the Wilder Dam, another just north of Hanover, NH, and another across the river in North Thetford. Lake Mascoma (look for boat launches along VT 4A in Enfield, NH) and Post Pond in Lyme, NH, are other popular angling spots.

FITNESS CENTER **Upper Valley Aquatic Center** (802-296-2850; uvac-swim.org), 100 Arboretum Lane, junction of I-89 and I-91, White River Junction. Featuring a 25-meter competition training pool, three-lane lap pool, splash park with children's area, fitness center, and café. Open to the public.

GOLF **Hanover Country Club** (603-646-2000), Rope Ferry Road, off VT 10, Hanover. Open May–October. Founded in 1899, an 18-hole facility with 4 practice holes, pro shop, and PGA instructors.

 **Lake Morey Country Club** (802-333-4800; lakemoreyresort.com/golf), Fairlee, has 18 holes.

HANG GLIDING **Mount Ascutney State Park**, VT 44A off US 5, Windsor. Brownsville Rock, less than a mile by trail northwest of the Mount Ascutney summit, is a popular launch site. Note that a paved summit road accesses the trail.

HIKING **Cross Rivendell Trail** (crossrivendelltrail.org). Check the website for details and a map of this 36-mile trail across the Connecticut River valley, from the Vermont hills above Vershire, then running through West Fairlee, Fairlee, and Orford, NH, four towns that make up the bistate Rivendell School District. Pick up a map at Chapman's in Fairlee (see *Selective Shopping*).

 **Smarts Mountain** via the Appalachian Trail. It's roughly 3.5 miles to the summit from the parking area on Dorchester Road in Lyme, NH. The parking area lies just before the iron bridge. From the trailhead (marked in orange), follow the white blazes up the Lambert Ridge Trail (the AT) or the more gradual blue-blazed Ranger Trail. Both bring you to a point with a spectacular view out across the valley. You can do a loop.

 **Fairlee Forest Trails**. Fairlee boasts over 35 miles of public trails with stunning mountain views, rushing streams, and an 80-plus-acre network of wetlands, with many songbirds. Trail maps are available at Chapman's Country Store, Fairlee (see *Selective Shopping*).

HORSEBACK RIDING **Open Acre Ranch** (802-333-9196), 1478 Blood Brook Road, Fairlee. Rebecca Guilette offers the increasingly rare chance to ride out through rolling farmland and back roads. Reasonably priced one-, two-, and four-hour trails rides are offered for riders of varying abilities; small children and beginner riders can ride in the ring. Private and group lessons. Trails web the 400-acre ranch and adjacent town forest.

SWIMMING Ask locally about swimming holes in the Connecticut River.

 **Storrs Pond Recreation Area** (603-643-2134; storrspond.org), NH 10 north of Hanover, NH (Reservoir Road, then left). Open June–Labor Day, 10–8. Bathhouse with showers and lockers, lifeguards at both the (unheated) Olympic-size pool and the 15-acre pond. Fee for nonmembers.

 **Treasure Island** (802-333-9615), VT 244 on Lake Fairlee, Thetford. This town's swimming area, open seasonally 9–8, offers a sand beach, picnic tables, and a playground. Admission charged.

 **Union Village Dam Recreation Area** (802-649-1606), East Thetford. Open Memorial Day–mid-September. The Army Corps of Engineers maintains the popular area with its swim beach and picnic area, also walking and cross-country trails.

# ✳ Winter Sports

CROSS-COUNTRY SKIING AND SNOWSHOEING **Dartmouth Cross-Country Ski Center** (603-643-6534), Rope Ferry Road (off VT 10 just before the country club), Hanover, NH. Open in snow season Tues., Thurs., Fri. 10–6, Wed. 9–5, weekends 9–5. Twenty-five km of varied trails, some geared to skating, through the Storrs Pond and Oak Hill areas; rental skis, skates, and snowshoes.

DOWNHILL SKIING **Dartmouth Skiway** (603-795-2143; skiway.dartmouth.edu), 39 Grafton Turnpike, Lyme Center, NH. An amenity for families as well as the college, with a snazzy 16,000-square-foot timber base lodge. Open 9–4 daily in-season; rentals and ski school. More than 100 skiable acres spread over 2 mountains, 30 trails: 1 quad chair, 1 double chair, a beginners' J-bar. Vertical drop: 968 feet. Snowmaking: 70 percent. Reasonable rates.

SKATING **Lake Morey Resort** (802-333-4311; lakemoreyresort.com), 1 Club House Road, Fairlee. The Upper Valley Trails Association, the Hulbert Outdoor Center, and the resort share maintenance of a 4.5-mile skate and broom trail; the resort rents skates and also maintains smaller rinks for recreation and hockey games.

# ✳ Green Space

**Pine Park**, just north of the Dartmouth campus between the Hanover Country Club and the Connecticut River, Hanover, NH. Take North Main Street to Rope Ferry Road Park at the trail sign above the clubhouse. These tall pines provide one of the beauty spots of the Valley. The 125-year-old trees were saved from the Diamond Match Company in 1900 by a group of local citizens. The walk is 1.5 miles.

**Montshire Museum of Science Trails**, Norwich. The museum's 110 acres include a 12-acre promontory between the Connecticut River and the marshy bay at the mouth of Bloody Brook. The 0.25-mile trail leading down through tall white pines to the bay is quite magical. The 1.5-mile Hazen Trail runs all the way to Wilder Village. These trails are hard-packed, accessible to strollers and wheelchairs. See the museum sidebar for details about admission.

**Union Village Dam Recreation Area** (802-649-1606). Maintained by the Army Corps of Engineers, 3.0 miles off US 5 at Pompanoosuc, offers a sandy beach and shaded picnic facilities.

**Thetford Hill State Park** (802-289-0603; vtstateparks.com), 622 Academy Road, Thetford Center. Developed by the Civilian Conservation Corps in the 1930s, this state park is open for day use only for picnics and hiking on its cross-country trails (maintained by Thetford Academy).

**Bedell Bridge State Historic Site** (603-227-8745; nhstateparks.com), 880 Meadow Lane, Haverhill, off NH 10, just north of Haverhill Four Corners. A sign points the way down through a cornfield and along the river to this 74-acre park, the site of the former 1866 covered bridge, one of the longest in the country until it was destroyed in 1979. The stone buttresses survive, and this is still a peaceful riverside spot, ideal for a picnic; there is also a boat launch.

# ✳ Lodging

## LISTED GEOGRAPHICALLY, SOUTH TO NORTH

✪ ◉ ✦ ♿ **Hotel Coolidge** (802-295-3118; hotelcoolidge.com), 39 South Main Street, White River Junction. A beloved icon, being New England's last railroad hotel, the Coolidge is also comfortable, clean, and reasonably priced. The hotel sits across the way from the Welcome Center/Amtrak station, adjacent to the Briggs Opera House, steps from shops and restaurants and the Northern Stage local buses to Hanover and Lebanon stop at the door, and rental cars can be arranged. All 30 elevator-served guest rooms have a private bath, a phone, and a TV and have been tastefully furnished; the family suites (two rooms connected by a bath) are a terrific value. The large, inviting lobby with its wood-burning fireplace doubles as a gallery for local art and offers a guest computer. Search out the splendid Peter Michael Gish murals in the Vermont Room, painted in 1949 in exchange for room and board. Owner-manager David Briggs, a seventh-generation Vermonter, takes his role as innkeeper seriously and will arrange for special needs. Most double rooms $, two-room suites $$. Also see *Hostel*.

✪ ◉ 🐾 ✦ ♿ **Norwich Inn** (802-649-1143; norwichinn.com), 325 Main Street, Norwich. Just across the river from Hanover and less formal and expensive than the Hanover Inn (below), this is very much a gathering place for Dartmouth parents, faculty, and students. Innkeepers Joe and Jill Lavin have preserved all the 1890s graciousness and charm of the parlors and dining rooms in the 16-guest, three-story, tower-topped inn. They have also added annexes with tasteful decor and contemporary comforts: gas fireplaces, spacious baths, and central air. Walker House, with 16 rooms, has an elevator and in Ivy Lodge, two of the four luxurious suites

are pet friendly. The inn's **Jasper Murdock's Alehouse** features 15 varieties of inn-made brews (see *Eating Out*). The dining rooms are open for breakfast, lunch, and dinner. All three meals are served but not included. $–$$.

♿ **Hanover Inn** (603-643-4300; hanoverinn.com), 2 East Wheelock Street, Hanover, NH. The 108-room brick Dartmouth-owned hotel on the green has been renovated down to its 1902 studs, the decor transformed from neo-colonial to sleekly, comfortably contemporary, featuring locally made furniture, furnishings, and art. It represents the ultimate luxury in Upper Valley lodging. Handicapped accessible. See *Dining Out* for Pine, the inn's street-side restaurant. $$–$$$.

**Six South Street** (603-643-0600; sixsouth.com), 6 South Street, Hanover, NH, is an attractive, 69-room hotel, a short walk from Dartmouth Green. $$.

**The Lyme Inn** (603-795-4824; thelymeinn.com) 1 Market Street, Lyme, NH. An elevator now accesses nine rooms and five suites on the top three floors. Amenities include central air, gas fireplaces, and jetted tubs. There's a parlor on the first floor, as well as **The Tavern** and the more formal **Garden Dining Room**. $$–$$$ includes full breakfast. $–$$.

INKEEPER DAVID BRIGGS WELCOMES GUESTS TO THE HOTEL COOLIDGE   CHRISTINA TREE

♂ ✍ **Lake Morey Resort** (802-333-4311; lakemoreyresort.com), 1 Club House Road, Fairlee. On the shore of Lake Morey, this sprawling, lakeside landmark best known for its golf course is also a winter destination for ice skaters. In summer, supervised children's programs are included with MAP. Landscaped grounds and reception areas make this a nice wedding venue. The resort dates from the early 1900s and was owned by the Avery family for some 20 years beginning in the 1970s; it was then sold but since reclaimed. The 130 rooms and suites vary from cozy and old-fashioned in the original building to spacious and balconied in the newest wing. The splendid lake view remains key, along with a player-friendly 18-hole golf course. Facilities include an indoor swimming pool, Jacuzzi, sauna, fitness center, and spa. There are also tennis courts. All three meals are served. Winter EP rates include up to two children sharing a room with parent: $–$$. Inquire about MAP per-person summer and fall rates, also golf packages, and cottage rentals.

🏕 🐾 ♿ **Silver Maple Lodge & Cottages** (802-333-4326; silvermaplelodge.com), 520 US 5 South, Fairlee. Just south of the village on US 5, Silver Maple was built as a farmhouse in 1855 and has been welcoming travelers since 1925; it has a comfortable feel. There are also cottages; even those with fireplaces and kitchenettes are reasonably priced. Native Vermonters Scott and Sharon Wright enjoy tuning guests into local sights and restaurants; they also offer a ballooning package with Boland Balloons. $ per couple includes a continental breakfast.

🐾 ✪ **The Gibson House** (603-989-3125; gibsonhousebb.com), 341 Dartmouth College Highway (VT 10), Haverhill, NH. Open June–October. Innkeepers Susie Klein and Marty Cohen offer eight imaginatively decorated rooms in one of the Valley's finest Greek Revival homes, built in 1850 on the green in Haverhill Corner. While the house fronts on VT 10, the 50-foot-long sunny back porch with wicker seats and swing takes full advantage of the splendid view west across the terraced garden and the Connecticut River. $ weekdays, $$ weekends includes a full breakfast.

HOSTEL **The Hotel Coolidge** (802-295-3118). A wing of the Coolidge, described under *Hotels*, is a Hostelling International facility with dorm-style beds and access to a self-service kitchen and laundry. Private family rooms are also available by reservation. $.

# ✳ Where to Eat

LISTED GEOGRAPHICALLY, SOUTH TO NORTH

DINING OUT  In White River Junction
✪ 🐾 **Thyme** (802-295-3312; thymevermont.com), 85 North Main Street, White River Junction. Open Tues.–Sat. 11:30–2:30 and 5–9. Reservations recommended for dinner, especially on Northern Stage performance nights. This remains essentially the elegantly casual bistro that was long known as Tip Top Café. According to chef-owner Eileen McGuckin, the change in name and decor (there's more green), reflects the increased focus on locally sourced ingredients during her half-dozen years in this kitchen. Point taken. Whether it's a soup and half sandwich for lunch ($) or a delectable vegetarian, meat, or fish dinner entrée ($$), the distinct flavors of each fresh ingredient come through, imaginatively paired and nicely plated.

**Elixir Restaurant and Lounge** (802-281-7009; elixirrestaurant.com), 188 South Main Street, White River Junction. Tues.–Sat. 5–10:30. A casual but "night out" kind of place known for both cocktails and food, handy to Northern Stage in a renovated railroad freight house to simply sip wine, beer, or cocktails as well as to dine at. $$

*Also see* **Tuckerbox** under *Eating Out*.

## IN NORWICH

**Carpenter and Main** (802-649-2922; carpenterandmain.com), 326 Main Street, Norwich. Open for dinner except Tues. and Wed.; tavern 5:30–10, dining room 6–9; reservations suggested. An 1820s building at the heart of this village houses the venue for chef-owner Bruce MacLeod's celebrated, locally sourced fare. Entrées $–$$ in the bistro and $$–$$$ in the dining rooms.

✪ **Jasper Murdock's Alehouse at the Norwich Inn** (802-649-1143; norwichinn.com), 225 Main Street, Norwich. Open for dinner and for lunch on weekends. The same menu is available both in the inn's formal dining room and in the green-walled, comfortable pub, with seating that expands seasonally onto the flowery deck. The dinner menu might include vegetable strudel and ale-braised lamb shank. The varied house brews are available nowhere else in town. Dinner entrées $–$$.

✪ **Canoe Club Bistro** (603-643-9660; canoeclub.us), 27 South Main Street, Hanover, NH. Open daily for lunch and dinner with light fare between meals (2–5 p.m.) and a bistro menu until 11:30 p.m., a real rarity in these parts. Reservations suggested for dinner. Acoustic music nightly, also Sunday jazz brunch. Decor includes vintage canoes and Dartmouth memorabilia, and the food is dependably delectable. Dinner entrées $–$$.

**Pine** (603-643-4300; hanoverinn.com), 2 East Wheelock Street, Hanover. Open daily for all three meals. Named for the lone tree in the Dartmouth College logo, this casually elegant street-side restaurant is a popular rendezvous. There's an inviting bar just inside the door, a leather sofa and armchairs by the open hearth at its center, and large Palladian-style windows overlooking both the green and South Main Street. The menu ranges from sandwiches to memorable, locally sourced feasts. Dinner entrées $$–$$$.

**Peyton Place** (603-353-9100; peytonplacerestaurant.com), 454 Main Street (VT 10), Orford, NH. Open for dinner Wed.–Sun. 5:30–9; closed Sun. off-season. Reservations a must. Destination dining, this restaurant (named for owners Jim and Heidi Peyton) is housed in a 1773 tavern with a genuine old pub room—and a pub menu—as well as more formal dining rooms. Dinner entrées might range from house-made vegetarian ravioli to rack of lamb with wild mushrooms. The blackboard pub menu might include house-made duck and chorizo dumplings or quesadillas with tortillas made in-house. Dinner entrées $–$$. Check the website for a mouth-watering illustrated menu and live music.

✪ **Ariana's Restaurant at The Lyme Inn** (603-795-4824; arianasrestaurant .com), 1 Market Street, Lyme, NH. Open Thurs.–Mon. 5–8 p.m. Check the website for Wednesday Wine Dinners. Reservations suggested, a must on weekends. This popular dining destination has moved downriver from an Orford barn to The Lyme Inn (see *Lodging*) and Chef Martin Murphy has expanded his menu as well as seating. The menu remains locally sourced and you can still sup on potato soup and mushroom crepes or dine on duck confit. The menu might range from shepherd's pie (with local veal and cheddar), vegan curried rice, and a choice of pastas to veal cassoulet (local veal osso buco and sausage) and sirloin steak. Entrées $–$$.

## EATING OUT

### IN WHITE RIVER JUNCTION

✪ 🖉 🐾 «(¶)» **Tuckerbox** (802-359-4041; tuckerboxvermont.com), 1 South Main Street. Open Tues.–Sat. 7 a.m.–9 p.m., Fri., Sat. until 10, Mon. 7–5, Sun. 10:30–9. From a corner café, this oasis has expanded into an attractive dining destination (dinner reservations recommended), still retaining its role as a local gathering spot. Turkish specialty options begin with breakfast, in addition to freshly baked pastries and homemade granola; the choices increase at lunch and dinner. The barista menu is a draw throughout the day, and with the sleek new dining area comes a full bar. Anyone for a fig martini? $–$$.

**Piecemeal Pies** (802-281-6910; piecemealpies.com), 5 South Main Street. Open Tue.–Thur. 9–6:30, Fri. 9–8, Sat. brunch 10–3. British-inspired individual savory meat pies and hard cider are the specialty in this bright and spacious "pie shop." Rabbit and bacon is the signature pie, but there are veggie options as well as soups, salads, and traditional fruit pies. Ingredients are locally sourced, and the back of the shop is an open kitchen.

Also see **Thyme** under *Dining Out*; it's a pleasant, reasonably priced lunch option.

**Big Fatty's BBQ** (802-295-5513; bigfattybbq.com), 186 South Main Street. Open. 11–9, closed Tues. Wide choice of beers and barbecue; order at the counter and eat at two large shared tables or some smaller ones; seasonal outside seating. A great local atmosphere when there's music; mixed reviews for food. $–$$.

## IN NORWICH

✿ **King Arthur Flour Baker's Store** (802-649-3361; kingarthurflour.com), 135 US 5. Open daily 7:30–6. Inside this flagship campus, best known for its store and baking classes, a large café is filled with the aroma of warm, fresh breads, pizza, and tasty pastry pickings. Hot breakfast choices and a full lunch that includes soups and salads; espresso bar and kids' menu.

*Note:* **The Norwich Farmers' Market** (norwichfarmersmarket.org) is Sat. 9–1, May–October, on US 5, 1 mile south of the village. It's unusually big and colorful, with 50 vendors and many baked goods. Winter markets are indoors at Tracy Hall, Sat. bi-monthly in winter. Check the website.

## IN HANOVER, NEW HAMPSHIRE

✪ ✿ **Lou's Restaurant and Bakery** (603-643-3321; lousrestaurant.net), 30 South Main Street. Open for breakfast weekdays from 6 a.m., Sat. and Sun. from 7. Lunch Mon.–Sat. until 3. Since 1947, this has been a student and local hangout, and it's great: a long Formica counter, tables and booths, fast, friendly service, good soups, sandwiches, pies, daily specials, and irresistible peanut butter cookies at the register. At breakfast, go for artery cloggers like poached eggs on corned beef hash or a virtuous egg white and goat cheese omelet. Lots of choices here.

✿ **Molly's Restaurant & Bar** (603-643-2570; mollysrestaurant.com), 43 South Main Street. Open daily for lunch and dinner. The greenhouse up front shelters a big, inviting bar that encourages single dining. The menu is immense: big salads, enchiladas, burgers, everything from pasta to steak at dinner.

**Sushiya** (603-643-4000; hanoversushi.com), 72 South Main Street. Authentic Korean bibimbap and kimchi, also better-than-average sushi.

✪ ✿ **Morano Gelato** (603-643-4233; moranogelato.com). 56 South Main Street. This is Morgan Morano's original showcase for her exceptionally creamy and flavorful gelato, hailed by *Forbes* magazine as the best in America.

✪ **Umpleby's Bakery & Café** (603-643-3030; umplebys.com), 3 South Street. A Vermont migrant from the Bridgewater Mill, still offering flaky croissants, from-scratch soups, and sandwiches on homemade bread.

Also see the **Canoe Club** under *Dining Out*, a great spot for lunch.

## IN EAST THETFORD

**Isabell's Café** (802-785-4300), 3052 US 5. Open Tues.–Sat. 7–2. Beverly and Don Hogdon work together in this bright and cheery breakfast/lunch oasis just off I-91, Exit 14. A shelf of toys keeps young diners happy.

## IN FAIRLEE

**Samurai** (802-331-1041), 176 US 5. Open Tues.–Sun. 3–9 p.m. A blend of locally sourced ingredients in an unlikely but wildly successful fusion of Asian, Tex-Mex, and basic comfort food.

    **Whippi Dip** (802-331-1313), 158 US 5. Open seasonally 7 a.m.–9 p.m. A take-out known for barbecue as well as hard and soft ice cream. Try the World's Fair Sundae: fried dough topped with vanilla ice cream, maple syrup, mixed nuts, and whipped cream.

    ✪ **Fairlee Diner** (802-333-3569), 256 Main Street. Closed Tues., otherwise 5:30–2. Turn left (north) on US 5 if you are coming off I-91. This is a classic 1930s diner, with wooden booths, worn-shiny wooden stool tops, and great breakfasts. The mashed potato dough-nuts are special, also standout pan-cakes and French fries; the soup and pie are dependably good. Daily specials. No credit cards.

    See the **Fairlee Drive-In** under *Entertainment* for the best burgers in town.

## IN BRADFORD

**Alexander's Restaurant** (802-222-5505; alexandersrestaurantandpub.com), 48 Main Street, Bradford. Open daily, Tues.–Sat. 11:30–9. Housed in a historic brick mill by the falls in the Waits River as you approach Bradford from the south. Leb-anese-style skewered beef and chicken are specialties. The best tables overlook the falls.

    **The Hungry Bear Pub & Grill** (802-222-5288; hungrybearpubandgrill.com), 776 Lower Plains Road, Bradford (US 5 and I-91, Exit 16). Open for lunch through dinner. A sports bar and a casual dining room known for its burgers and steaks—but it's a big menu.

    ✪ **Colatina Exit** (802-222-9008), 164 Main Street, Bradford. Open daily from 11. An expansive trattoria, best known for wood-fired oven pizzas and a large, locally sourced Italian menu: plenty of antipasto, insalata, and pasta choices as well as traditional Italian dishes like chicken Marsala. Try the Robie Farm veal cannelloni and sausage served with fresh pasta. Plenty of pizza choices, panini, and calzones. The upstairs pub offers river views.

    **Bliss Village Store and Deli** (802-222-4617), 158 South Main Street, Bradford. Open 6 a.m.–7 p.m. This is a classic general store but with Crock-Pots full of soup, chili, or stew-fried chicken and a deli with daily specials. Tables are in the back—including a booth overlooking the river.

## FARTHER NORTH

**Newbury Village Store** (802-866-5681; newburyvillagestore.com), 4991 US 5, Newbury. Open 6 a.m.–8 p.m. most days. This is an inviting general store with com-fortable seating near the periodicals, daily baked muffins and cookies, and a deli that features hot breakfast as well as other sandwiches. There are staple groceries, also a selection of wine and Vermont prod-ucts. The **Thistle Café** in back overlooks the Connecticut. Burgers, pizzas, cheese steak, and supper menu from 5:30.

    ✪ **P&H Truck Stop** (802-429-2141; pandhtruckstop.com), just off I-91, Exit 17, on US 302, Wells River. Open 6 a.m.–10 p.m. for hot meals, 24 hours for to-go premade sandwiches, pies, and the like. This is a classic truck stop with speedy service, friendly servers, and heaping portions at amazing prices. Plus, the bread is homemade; ATM and phone available (cell phones don't tend to work around here).

    ✎ **The Happy Hour Restaurant** (802-757-3466; happyhourrestaurant.net), 42 Main Street (US 5), Wells River. Open lunch–dinner except Mon. This large, pine-paneled family restaurant in the middle of town boasts a sense of friendly service and satisfied patrons. Most specials include the salad bar—and servings are generous. Children's menu.

**Saltwater Bar & Bistro** (603-747-2365), 85 Central Street, Woodsville, NH. Open Wed.–Thurs. 11–7, Fri.–Sat. until 9. This attractive restaurant features fresh fish from lobster rolls and fish sandwiches to blackened swordfish. Wine and beer.

**Little Grille Comida Mexicana** (603-747-2777; thelittlegrille.com), 50 Smith Street, Woodsville, NH. A good road-food stop with the feel of a neighborhood favorite, best for burritos and burgers. Full bar.

## ✳ Entertainment

MUSIC AND THEATER **Northern Stage** (802-296-7000; northernstage .org), Barrette Center for the Arts, 74 Gates Street, White River Junction. Northern Stage is a professional non-profit regional theater company with performances October–May in a new, state-of-the-art, 308-seat theater.

Productions include dramas, comedies, musicals, as well as lesser-known works and new plays fresh from Broadway and London's West End.

**Hopkins Center for the Arts** (603-646-2422; hop.dartmouth.edu/online /performances), on the Dartmouth green, Hanover, NH. Sponsors musical and theater productions and films, all open to the public.

FILM **Nugget Theater** (603-643-2769), nugget-theaters.com 575 Main Street, Hanover, NH. First-run films.

✪ **Fairlee Drive-In** (802-333-9192; fairleedrivein.com), 1809 US 5, Fairlee. Summer only. This 1950 icon, thanks to local support, now has a digital projector as well as stereo sound. It's attached to the family-run **Fairlee Motel**; its snack bar features "thunderburgers," with beef from the family's farm across the river. Gates open at 7 p.m.; films begin at dusk.

NEWBURY VILLAGE STORE  CHRISTINA TREE

# ✳ Selective Shopping

*Note:* First Fridays of every month, galleries and other venues in White River Junction offer music and refreshments.

## IN WHITE RIVER JUNCTION

✪ **Long River Gallery & Gifts** (802-295-4567; longrivergallery.com), 49 South Main Street. Open Tue.–Mon. 9–6, Sun. 11–3. An exceptional gallery showcasing the work of 150 juried Vermont and New Hampshire artisans, crafted sculpture, furniture pottery, hand knits, jewelry, glassware, wooden ware, original artwork, prints, and much more, from cards to whimsical multimedia sculptures.

**Lampscapes** (802-295-8044), 77 Gates Street, White River Junction. Open Tues.–Sat. 11–5. Kenneth Blaisdell is a former engineer and a serious landscape artist whose combination studio/shop is a find. The metal floor and table lamps themselves are striking, and the shades are works of art, each one of a kind, ranging from luminescent and literal to semi-abstract, detailed landscapes, priced within reasonable reach.

**Scavenger** (802-295-0808), 41 South Main Street. Open Tue.–Sat. 11–6. A small gallery featuring jewelry sculpted from natural objects, as well as contemporary art, artisanal wine, and craft beer.

**Revolution, Vintage & Urban Used Clothing** (802-295-6487; shoptherev .com), 25 North Main Street, White River Junction. The decor alone is worth a visit. Kim Sousa offers an exceptional mix of eclectic, funky vintage, designer, and Vermont-made clothing, plus footwear, jewelry, and accessories. Free espresso.

## IN NORWICH

**King Arthur Flour Baker's Store** (802-649-3361; kingarthurflour.com), 135 US 5. Open daily 7:30–6. Home as well as prime outlet for the country's oldest family-owned flour company (since 1790), this store draws serious bakers and would-be bakers. The store features every conceivable kind of flour, baking ingredient, and a selection of equipment and cookbooks, not to mention bread and there are pastries made in the adjacent bakery (visible through a glass connector). The neighboring **King Arthur Baking Education Center** offers baking classes, from beginner to expert, from piecrust to braided breads and elegant pastries. Also see the café under *Eating Out*.

✪ **Dan & Whit's General Store** (802-649-1602), 319 Main Street. The quintessential Vermont country store. Hardware, groceries, housewares, boots and clothing, farm and garden supplies, and a great community bulletin board: If they don't have it, you don't need it.

**The Norwich Bookstore** (802-649-1114; norwichbookstore.com), 291 Main Street, next to the post office. This is a light, airy store with well-selected titles and comfortable places to sit. Staff are very knowledgeable. Frequent readings and a good children's section.

## HEADING NORTH

**Pompanoosuc Mills** (802-785-4851; pompy.com), 3184 US 5, East Thetford. Showroom open daily 9–6, Sat., Sun. 11–5. Workshop tours offered Mon.–Sat. Dartmouth graduate Dwight Sargeant began building furniture in this riverside house, a cottage industry that has evolved into a riverside corporate headquarters/factory with showrooms throughout New England.

(((•))) **Cedar Circle Farm** (802-785-4737; cedarcirclefarm.org), 225 Pavillion Road, just off US 5, East Thetford. September–October, closed Mon.; otherwise open daily. A major farm stand selling the farm's vegetables and flowers, offering PYO strawberries in June, blueberries in July, herbs June–September, and

CHAPMAN'S COUNTRY STORE, FAIRLEE  CHRISTINA TREE

pumpkins in October. The farm store also carries local cheeses, honey, syrup, organic milk, yogurt, and ice cream, books, note cards, and more. Coffee and Wi-Fi in its **Hello Café**.

✪ **Chapman's Country Store** (802-333-9709; chapmansstore.com), 491 Main Street, Fairlee. Open daily 8:30–6, until 5 on Sun. Since 1924 members of the Chapman family have expanded the stock of this old pharmacy to include 10,000 hand-tied flies, wines, Mexican silver and Indonesian jewelry, used books, maple syrup, and an unusual selection of toys. It also incorporates Lee's Sport Center, selling fishing licenses, USGS maps, and stand-up paddleboards as well as dispensing information about local hiking trails.

**Farmer Hodge's** (802-333-4483), 2112 US 5 North, Fairlee. Open daily, a working dairy farm with registered Holsteins, homemade jams, jellies, pickles, maple, beans, and pancake mix, plus seasonal produce and gifts.

✪ **Farm-Way, Inc.** (800-222-9316; vermontgear.com), 286 Waits River Road (VT 25), Bradford. One mile east of I-91, Exit 16. Open Mon.–Sat. 8:30–5:30, until 8 Fri. Billed as "complete outfitters for man and beast," this is a phenomenon: a family-run source of work boots and rugged clothing that now includes a stock of more than two million products spread over 11 acres: tack, furniture, pet supplies, syrup, whatever. Now substantially solar powered. Shoes and boots remain a specialty, from size 4E to 16; 25,000 shoes, boots, clogs, sandals, and sneakers in stock; also kayaks, sporting equipment, furnishings, and gifts.

**Copeland Furniture** (802-222-5300; copelandfurniture.com), 64 Main Street, Bradford. Open Mon.–Fri. 10–6, Sat. 10–5. Contemporary, cleanly lined, locally made furniture in native hardwoods displayed in a handsome showroom in the converted nineteenth-century brick mill across from Bradford Falls. Seconds.

**Star Cat Books** (802-222-5826; starcatbooks.com), 157 Main Street, Bradford. A browsing-friendly bookstore, both new and used titles.

✪ **South Road Pottery** (802-222-5798; brucemurraypotter.com), 3458 South Road, Bradford. Open May–October, 10–5. Bruce Murray is an established, nationally known potter whose studio/showroom is in a timber-frame eighteenth-century barn surrounded by farm fields. It's well worth the scenic drive to this exceptional studio with its wide variety of handmade and hand-decorated stoneware, both functional

BRUCE MURRAY OF SOUTH ROAD POTTERY  CHRISTINA TREE

(lamps, vases, unusual butter dishes—really mini crocks that keep butter soft) and decorative wall tiles and plaques. His work continues to evolve and gain wide recognition. Inquire about workshops and about the **Barn Bridge Guest Room,** an attractive guest unit with a private deck, bath, and galley kitchen.

*Note:* This area is studded with artists and craftspeople who keep irregular studio hours but open for the Memorial Day statewide crafts tour and again the first weekend in October.

FARMS **Robie Farm & Store** (603-272-4872; robiefarmnh.com), 25 NH 10, Piermont, NH. Six generations of Robies have farmed this property. The farm store sells dairy beef, free from antibiotics and hormones; also low-fat and skim raw milk as well as pints of cream, plus eggs from free-range chickens. There's a variety of cheese, including Toma from their own raw milk and ice cream made in small batches. Check the website for farm tours, hiking trails, and pontoon boat cruises.

✪ **Four Corners Farm** (802-866-3342; 4cornersfarm.com), 306 Doe Hill Road, just off US 5, South Newbury. Bob and Kim Gray sell their own produce and flowers. An exceptionally pretty farm with Jersey milk cows, Scottish Highland beef cows, and 50 acres of fruit and vegetables. The big farm stand, housed in a vintage barn, is just off and up above the highway. Known for strawberries, but always a trove of seasonal fruits and vegetables with year-round produce from their greenhouses, Christmas trees, and PYO berries in-season.

✦ **Windy Ridge Orchard** (603-787-6377; windyridgeorchard.com), 1775 Benton Road, North Haverhill, NH. Open daily Labor Day–Thanksgiving, 9–6; weekends Thanksgiving to Christmas, 9–4. Pick-your-own apples and pumpkins, farm animals, kids' corral playground, nature trails, picnic tables, **Cider House Café,** and gift shop. Apple picking begins in mid-August and lasts through mid-October depending on the variety. There are 3,500 apple trees on 20 acres, overlooking the Valley and Green Mountains; also cut-your-own Christmas trees.

Visit the **Bradford Farmers' Market** (Sun. 10–2), May–October.

## ✳ Special Events

For details about any of these events, phone the town clerk, listed with information.

*July* **Connecticut Valley Fair** (bradfordfair.org), mid-July, Bradford. Ox and horse pulling, sheep show, midway, and demolition derby. The **North Haverhill (NH) Fair** (nohaverhillfair .com), last weekend, is an old-style fair with ox and tractor pulls, pig races, and more.

*October:* First weekend: **Vermont North Studio Tours** (vermont northbyhand.org). Craftspeople hold open studios with outstanding arts and crafts; also a great excuse to explore back roads during peak foliage season in this area.

OPPOSITE: VERMONT STATEHOUSE, MONTPELIER. ISTOCK

# CENTRAL VERMONT

## WOODSTOCK/QUECHEE AREA

## THE WHITE RIVER VALLEYS

Including Randolph, Sharon, Royalton,
Bethel, Rochester, Hancock, Braintree,
Brookfield, Chelsea, Tunbridge, and Strafford

## SUGARBUSH/MAD RIVER VALLEY

## BARRE/MONTPELIER AREA

## KILLINGTON/RUTLAND AREA

# WOODSTOCK/QUECHEE AREA

Cradled between Mount Peg and Mount Tom and circled by the Ottauquechee (pronounced *otto-KWEE-chee*) River, Woodstock is repeatedly named among the prettiest towns in America. Its story, including the history of the landscape as well as buildings, is told at the Marsh-Billings-Rockefeller National Historical Park, the country's only national park to focus on the concept of conservation.

The Ottauquechee River flows east through Woodstock along US 4 toward the Connecticut River, generating electricity as it tumbles over falls beneath the covered bridge at Taftsville and powers Simon Pearce's glass factory a few miles downstream in Quechee Village. Below Quechee, the river has carved Vermont's "Grand Canyon," Quechee Gorge, spanned by US 4.

The Woodstock Railroad carried passengers and freight the 20 miles between Woodstock and White River Junction between 1875 and 1933. Easing traffic congestion, which includes 18-wheelers headed for Rutland as well as tour buses year-round, is an enormous challenge. US 4 is the shortest trek across "Vermont's waist," and a constant stream of vehicles winds up the valley, files through Woodstock, circles around its exquisite green, and moves on along the river, west into Bridgewater.

Our advice for Quechee and Woodstock: Walk. Park at the picnic area just beyond Quechee Gorge and savor the view of the river churning below 163-foot-high walls. Walk the path down to the water's edge or around Vermont Institute of Natural Science (VINS), the neighboring raptor and nature sanctuary. In Woodstock Village, stroll the green and the streets, then walk Mountain Avenue through Faulkner Park, on up to the top of Mount Tom, then back down the Pogue Carriage Road to Billings Farm.

Like most of the world's famously beautiful and heavily touristed areas, especially those that are also home to sophisticated people who could live anywhere, the Ottauquechee River Valley offers visitors plenty to see and do, and still more, the more you explore.

GUIDANCE **The Quechee Gorge Visitors Information Center** (802-295-6852; hartford vtchamber.com) is maintained by the Hartford Area Chamber of Commerce, US 4 at Quechee Gorge. Open year-round, 9–5 May–October, 10–4 off-season. This is a nice, well-stocked center with restrooms and helpful staff.

**The Woodstock Area Chamber of Commerce** (802-457-3555; 888-496-6378; woodstockvt.com) maintains a friendly, staffed information center with restrooms on Mechanic Street, marked on Central Street (the main shopping block), open weekdays, year-round, 9–5, 9–4 in winter. The chamber publishes *Window on Woodstock*, a useful free pamphlet guide. Lodging places post available rooms on the website of the chamber, which has been known to find beds during foliage season for stranded leaf-peepers. Restrooms are also available weekdays in the town hall, west of the green. Check the **Town Crier** blackboard at the corner of Elm and Central Streets for current happenings.

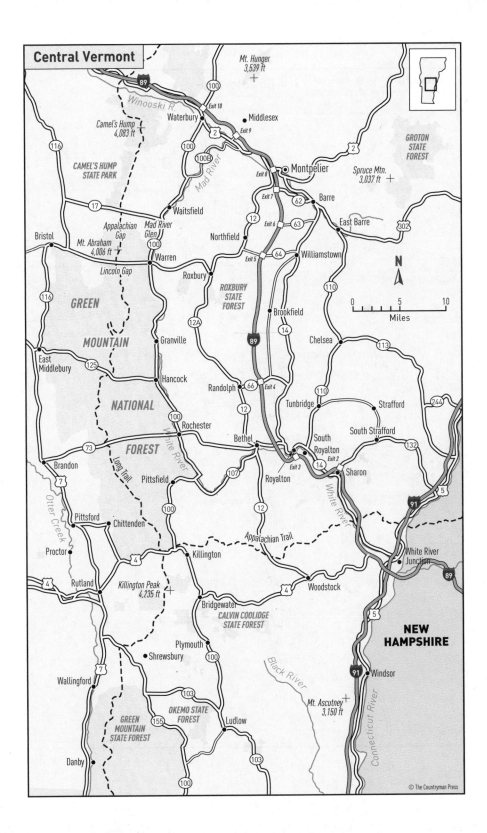

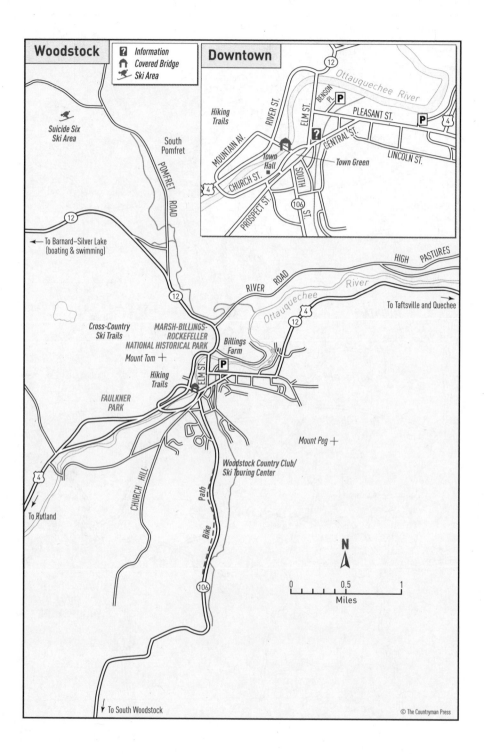

**Woodstock**

Information
Covered Bridge
Ski Area

**Downtown**

Ottauquechee River

Hiking Trails

MOUNTAIN AV.

RIVER ST.

ELM ST.

BENSON PL.

PLEASANT ST.

CENTRAL ST.

LINCOLN ST.

Town Hall

Town Green

CHURCH ST.

SOUTH ST.

PROSPECT ST.

106

12

4

Suicide Six
Ski Area

South
Pomfret

POMFRET ROAD

12

← To Barnard–Silver Lake
(boating & swimming)

12

RIVER ROAD

HIGH PASTURES

Ottauquechee River

12

4

To Taftsville and Quechee →

Cross-Country
Ski Trails

MARSH–BILLINGS–
ROCKEFELLER
NATIONAL HISTORICAL PARK

Mount Tom +

Billings
Farm

Hiking
Trails

ELM ST.

P

FAULKNER
PARK

Mount Peg +

4

Woodstock Country Club/
Ski Touring Center

CHURCH HILL

Bike Path

↓
To Rutland

106

N

0     0.5     1
Miles

↓ To South Woodstock

© The Countryman Press

GETTING THERE  *By car:* US 4 west from I-91 and I-89.

For details about train, bus, and air, see *Getting There* in "Upper Valley River Towns" on page 187.

PARKING  These are walk-around towns in which the first thing you do is park. In Woodstock, two-hour meters on Central and Elm streets, and four-hour meters on Mechanic off Central are closely monitored 10–4, Mon.–Sat., 25¢ per half hour. Red drop boxes in front of the town's two pharmacies are provided to pay fines—but you can also bring a ticket to a merchant or restaurant in town and they will validate it (no fine!). There are free lots by the river on Pleasant Street behind the Norman Williams Public Library and—on weekends only—at the elementary school on VT 106 south of the green.

WHEN TO GO  This area is as genuinely year-round as Vermont gets. **Marsh-Billings-Rockefeller National Historical Park** and the **Billings Farm & Museum** are open May through mid-October, but Woodstock's early-December **Wassail Weekend** is its most colorful happening, and January through March bring cross-country and alpine skiing. The **Quechee Hot Air Balloon Festival** in June is the area's most famous event.

## ✳ Towns and Villages

**Woodstock** (population 3,048, including the village of South Woodstock and Taftsville). In the 1790s, when it became the shire town of Windsor County, Woodstock began attracting prosperous professionals, who, with local merchants and bankers, built the concentration of distinguished Federal houses that surround the elliptical green, forming an architectural showcase that has been meticulously preserved. In the nineteenth century it produced more than its share of celebrities, including Hiram

WOODSTOCK'S BUSIEST CORNER, CENTRAL & ELM, DOWNTOWN  CHRISTINA TREE

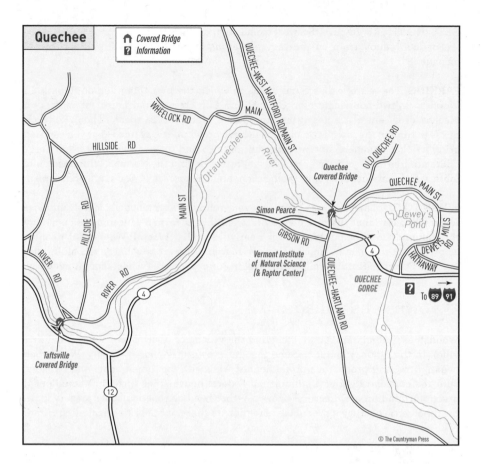

**Quechee**

🏠 Covered Bridge
❓ Information

QUECHEE-WEST HARTFORD RD

MAIN ST

WHEELOCK RD

MAIN

HILLSIDE RD

OLD QUECHEE RD

Ottauquechee River

Quechee Covered Bridge

QUECHEE MAIN ST

HILLSIDE RD

MAIN ST

Simon Pearce

Dewey's Pond

DEWEY'S MILLS RD

HATHAWAY

RIVER RD

GIBSON RD

Vermont Institute
of Natural Science
(& Raptor Center)

4

RIVER RD

QUECHEE-HARTLAND RD

QUECHEE GORGE

❓ To 89 91

4

Taftsville
Covered Bridge

12

© The Countryman Press

Powers, the sculptor whose nude *Greek Slave* scandalized the nation in 1847, and Senator Jacob Collamer (1791–1865), President Lincoln's confidant, who declared, "The good people of Woodstock have less incentive than others to yearn for heaven."

Three eminent residents in particular—all of whom lived in the same house but in different eras—helped shape the current Woodstock (see the box in *Must See* on page 210).

"Innkeeping has always been the backbone of Woodstock's economy, most importantly since 1892 when the town's business leaders and bankers decided to build a new hotel grand enough to rival the White Mountain resorts," said local historian Peter Jennison. By the turn of the twentieth century, in addition to several inns, Woodstock had an elaborate mineral water spa and golf course area, and it had become Vermont's first winter resort, drawing guests from Boston and New York City for snowshoeing and skating. In 1934 America's first rope tow was installed here, marking the real advent of downhill skiing.

By the early 1960s, however, the beloved Woodstock Inn was creaky, the town's small ski areas had been upstaged, and the hills were sprouting condos. Laurance Rockefeller acquired the two ski areas (upgrading Suicide Six and closing Mount Tom) and had the 18-hole golf course redesigned by Robert Trent Jones. In 1969, Rockefeller replaced the old inn. In 1992 his Woodstock Foundation opened the **Billings Farm & Museum**. **The Marsh-Billings-Rockefeller National Historical Park**, comprising the neighboring Rockefeller mansion and 550 surrounding forested acres on Mount Tom, opened in 1998.

Woodstock itself remains a real town with a lot going on. Events chalked on the Town Crier blackboard at the corner of Elm and Central streets are likely to include a supper at one of the town's several churches (four boast Paul Revere bells), the current film at the theater in the town hall, events at the historical society, and guided walks.

*Note:* The Woodstock Historical Society has published detailed pamphlets and guides, available at **Dana House** (see page 212).

**Quechee** (population 2,500) on US 4, some 6 miles east of Woodstock, is one of five villages in the township of Hartford. In the mid- and late nineteenth century, life revolved around the J. C. Parker and Co. mill, which produced a soft baby flannel made from "shoddy" (reworked rags). A neighboring mill village surrounded the Deweys Mill, which made baseball uniforms for the Boston Red Sox and the New York Yankees. In the 1950s, both mills shut down. In the 1960s, the Deweys Mill virtually disappeared beneath a federal flood-control project, and 6,000 acres straddling both villages were acquired by the Quechee Lakes Corporation, the largest second-home and condominium development company in the state. Thanks in good part to Act 250, Vermont's land-use statute, the end result is unobtrusive. Most homes are sequestered in woods; open space includes two (private) 18-hole golf courses. In Quechee Village, the mill is now **Simon Pearce**'s famous glass factory and restaurant, and the former mill owner's mansion is the **Parker House Inn**. Dramatic **Quechee Gorge** is visible from US 4 but is best appreciated if you follow the trail along the edge to the bottom of the gorge. The **VINS Center** is also here. Tourist-geared shops and eateries continue to proliferate along US 4, but, along back roads, conservation land preserves open space.

## ✳ Must See

LISTED FROM EAST TO WEST

**Quechee Gorge**, US 4, is one of Vermont's natural wonders, a 3,000-foot-long, 163-foot-deep chasm sculpted 13,000 years ago by the waters of what is now known as the Ottauquechee River. Visible from the highway, it is now part of a state park that includes hiking trails along the rim and down into the gorge. See *Green Space* on page 214.

**The Vermont Institute of Natural Science/Vermont Raptor Center** (802-359-5000; vinsweb.org), 149 Natures Way, Quechee. Open 9:30–5 April–October, 10–4 the rest of the year; also open holidays and school vacations. Admission charged. A beloved institution devoted to rehabilitating birds of prey, VINS occupies 47 acres of rolling forestland just west of Quechee Gorge. Resident raptors include bald eagles, peregrine falcons, snowy owls, hawks, and other birds of prey that have been injured. They are displayed in huge outdoor flight enclosures. There are outdoor interpretive exhibits, nature trails, and a shop. Inquire about naturalist-led walks and flight demonstration programs. Nominally priced snowshoe rentals for use on the trails.

**Visitor Center for Billings Farm & Museum and the Marsh-Billings-Rockefeller National Historical Park**, VT 12 north of Woodstock Village. Open May–October, daily 10–5. The parking lot and visitor center at Billings Farm serve both the farm and national park, with displays on Marsh, Billings, and Rockefeller, and a theater that shows *A Place in the Land*, Charles Guggenheim's award-winning documentary dramatizing the story of all three men. (There's no admission fee for the restrooms and gift shop, but a nominal fee is charged to see the film if you aren't visiting the farm or museum.) *Note:* A combination ticket to the Billings Farm & Museum and programs at Marsh-Billings-Rockefeller National Historical Park is $16 adults, $12 seniors.

# GEORGE PERKINS MARSH (1801–82), FREDERICK BILLINGS (1823–90), AND LAURANCE ROCKEFELLER (1910–2005)

Three men in particular have helped shape Woodstock's landscape. The first, George Perkins Marsh, born and raised here, damaged his eyesight by age 7 by devouring encyclopedias and books on Greek and Latin. Sent outdoors, he studied the woods, fields, birds, and animals with equal intensity. He noted the effects of logging on the landscape (60 percent of Vermont's virgin forest was harvested in the first half of the nineteenth century) and the resulting floods and destruction of fisheries. Later, traveling in the Middle East as the US ambassador to Turkey, Marsh noted how once-fertile land had become desert. He wrote: "I fear man has brought the face of the earth to a devastation almost as complete as that of the moon."

Marsh wrote *Man and Nature* at age 63, while US ambassador to Italy. Published in 1864, it is widely recognized as the first book to acknowledge civilization's effect on the environment and the first to suggest solutions. In contrast with Henry David Thoreau (whose book *Walden* appeared in 1854), Marsh didn't idealize wilderness. Instead, he attempted to address the interdependence of the environment and society as a whole.

*Man and Nature* isn't an easy read, but it greatly influenced this country's nascent sciences of forestry and agriculture as well as many of the era's movers and shakers, among them Frederick Billings. Raised in Woodstock, Billings departed at age 25 for San Francisco. That city's first lawyer, he made a fortune registering claims and speculating in land during the Gold Rush. As a returning son who had "made good," Billings spoke at the 1864 Windsor County Fair, remarking on the rawness of the local landscape, the hills denuded by logging and sheep grazing. In 1869, he bought the old Marsh farm and transformed the vintage 1805 house into a mansion. On Mount Tom, he planted more than 100,000 trees, turned a bog into Pogue Pond, and created the carriage roads. Billings's primary home was in New York, and as president of the Northern Pacific Railroad (the reason Billings, Montana, is named for him), he toured the country extensively. He continued, however, to retreat to Woodstock, creating a model dairy farm on his property, a project sustained after his death, through thick and thin, by his wife and two successive generations of Billings women.

In 1934 Frederick Billings's granddaughter Mary French (1910–97) married Laurance Rockefeller in Woodstock. John D. Rockefeller Jr. had been largely responsible for creating more than 20 state and national parks and historic sites; Laurance inherited his father's

**Marsh-Billings-Rockefeller National Historical Park** (802-457-3368; nps.gov/mabi), VT 12 north of Woodstock Village. Mount Tom carriage roads and forest trails (see *Green Space* on page 214) are open year-round, free in summer (for winter use see *Cross-Country Skiing*). The Queen Anne mansion, the centerpiece of this estate, is notable for its antiques, Tiffany glass, and especially for its American landscape art, as well as for a sense of the amazing individuals who lived there. Guided hour-plus tours, offered Memorial Day–October, are limited to a dozen visitors at a time; reservations are advised ($8 adults, $4 seniors and ages 6–15). These depart from the **Carriage Barn** (open late May–October, 10–5; free), an inviting space with dark bead-board walls and the feel of a library, with exhibits that establish Marsh, Billings, and Rockefeller within the timeline of America's conservation history. A multimedia exhibit, *People Taking Care of Places*, profiles individuals practicing conservation around the world. Visitors are invited to take advantage of the reading area with its conference-size table (crafted from wood harvested on Mount Tom) and relevant books, including children's stories.

commitment to conservation and quickly became an effective advocate of ecotourism. In the 1950s Mary Rockefeller inherited the Billings estate in Woodstock, and in the 1960s Laurance bought and replaced the old Woodstock Inn, incorporating the golf course and Suicide Six ski area into one resort. Rockefeller also created the Woodstock Foundation, a nonprofit umbrella for village projects such as acquiring and restoring dozens of historic homes, burying power lines, building a new covered bridge by the green, and collecting local antique farm tools and oral histories. He opened the **Billings Farm & Museum** in 1983. The **Marsh-Billings-Rockefeller National Historical Park** opened in 1998.

ROCKEFELLER MANSION AT MARSH-BILLINGS-ROCKEFELLER PARK  CHRISTINA TREE

**Billings Farm & Museum** (802-457-2355; billingsfarm.org), 69 Old River Road. Open May–October, daily 10–5; weekends November–February 10–4. Christmas and February vacation weeks, open 10–4. Admission charged, 2 and under free. Billed as the "Gateway to Vermont's Rural Heritage," this is one of the finest Jersey dairy farms in America and a museum dedicated to telling the story of Vermont's rural past. Established as a model farm by Frederick Billings in 1871, it became a museum under the stewardship of his granddaughter Mary French Rockefeller and her husband, Laurance Rockefeller. Exhibits demonstrate traditional ways of plowing, seeding, cultivating, harvesting, and storing crops; making cheese and butter; woodcutting; and sugaring. The restored 1890 farm manager's house reflects the farm as it was in Billings's day. Visitors can observe what happens on a modern dairy farm with a prizewinning Jersey herd. The farm's Percheron workhorses—Jim, Joe, Sue, and Lynn—welcome visitors. Almost every day, activities are geared to kids, from toddlers on up. Cows are milked daily at 3:30 p.m. Inquire about special events like the Pumpkin & Apple Celebration and Harvest Weekend in fall; Thanksgiving weekend and Christmas week celebrations; sleigh ride weekends in January and February; and periodic demonstrations and crafts exhibits. The annual quilt exhibit in August–September is worth a special trip.

**The Dana House** (home of the Woodstock Historical Society, 802-457-1822; woodstockhistorical.org), 26 Elm Street, Woodstock. Open May–October, Tues.–Sat, varying hours. Office and research library open year-round. Admission charged (free under age 6); 40-minute tours on the hour. John Cotton Dana was an eminent early-twentieth-century librarian and museum director whose innovations made books and art more accessible to the public. Completed in 1807 and occupied for the next 140 years by the Dana family, this historic house has an interesting permanent exhibit portraying the town's economic heritage and an admirable collection of antiques, locally wrought coin silver, portraits, porcelains, fabrics, costumes, and toys. The John Cotton Dana Library is a research and reference center. There is also an exhibit gallery.

**The Norman Williams Public Library** (802-457-2295; normanwilliams.org), on the Woodstock green. Open daily 10–5 except Sundays and holidays. A Romanesque gem, donated and endowed in 1883 by Dr. Edward H. Williams, general manager of the Pennsylvania Railroad and later head of Baldwin Locomotives. It offers children's story hours, poetry readings, and brown-bag summer concerts on the lawn, as well as Internet access.

COVERED BRIDGES There are three in the town of Woodstock. The **Lincoln Bridge** (1865), US 4, West Woodstock, is Vermont's only Pratt-type truss; the **Middle Bridge**, in the center of the village, was built in 1969 by Milton Graton, "last of the covered-bridge builders," in the town lattice style (partially destroyed by vandalism and rebuilt). The **Taftsville Bridge** (1836), US 4 East, the second oldest bridge in Vermont, was disabled in 2011 by Hurricane Irene, rebuilt and reopened in 2014.

SCENIC DRIVES The whole area offers delightful vistas; one of the most scenic short-cuts is North Road, which leaves VT 12 next to Silver Lake in Barnard and leads to Bethel. Also be sure to drive VT 106 to South Woodstock. This section of US 4 is now a part of the Vermont Crossroads Scenic Byway.

## ✳ To Do

BALLOONING **Balloons of Vermont** (802-369-0213; balloonsofvermont.com), based in Quechee, operates year-round (the two-person basket has a seat) and will launch from your home or inn (conditions permitting). Quechee is also the scene of the **Quechee Hot Air Balloon Festival** on Father's Day weekend in June, New England's premier balloon festival, featuring rides as well as live entertainment and crafts (see *Special Events* on page 225).

BICYCLING **Discovery Bicycle Tours** (802-457-3553; discoverybicycletours.com), Woodstock. Vermont's most experienced, most personalized, and altogether best inn-to-inn tour service, offering weekend, five-, and seven-day trips through much of Vermont. Twenty-one-speed Trek and Cannondale hybrids are available for rent.

**Wilderness Trails** (802-295-7620), Clubhouse Road at the Quechee Inn. Bike rentals for the whole family, plus maps.

**Woodstock Sports** (802-457-1568), 30 Central Street, Woodstock, has mountain and hybrid bike rentals; offers repairs and clothing; and rents snowshoes and skates.

Mountain as well as touring bikes are available at **The Woodstock Inn**, and there are (single- and doubletrack) trails on neighboring Mount Peg.

BOATING **Wilderness Trails** (802-295-7620; quecheeinn.com), Clubhouse Road at the Quechee Inn, offers guided canoe and kayak trips; as well as rentals and shuttle service on the Connecticut, White, and Ottauquechee rivers, and in the Deweys Mills Waterfowl Sanctuary. Inquire about island camping.

**Silver Lake State Park** (802-234-9451; vtstateparks.com), in Barnard rents rowboats, canoes, and kayaks.

FISHING **Vermont Fly-Fishing School** (802-295-7620), the Quechee Inn at Marshland Farm. Marty Banak offers lessons as well as providing tackle and guided fishing on Deweys Pond and the Connecticut, White, and Ottauquechee rivers.

FITNESS CENTER AND TENNIS **Woodstock Athletic Club** (802-457-6656), part of the Woodstock Inn and Resort, VT 106. Indoor tennis and racquetball, lap pool, whirlpool, aerobic and state-of-the-art fitness equipment; spa treatments, facials, massage, manicure and pedicure; flexible memberships and day-use options; pro shop. There are 10 outdoor courts (4 DecoTurf and 6 clay) that can be rented; also, there are lessons and equipment rental.

**Vail Field**, Woodstock. Two public tennis courts and a children's playground.

GOLF **Woodstock Inn and Resort Golf Club** (802-457-6674; woodstockinn.com), part of the Woodstock Inn and Resort, offers one of Vermont's oldest (1895) and most prestigious 18-hole golf courses, scenic and compact, redesigned by Robert Trent Jones Sr. in 1961. It crosses water 11 times. Tee times can be reserved just 24 hours in advance of play. Facilities include a pro shop, a putting green and practice range, lessons, electric carts, a restaurant, and a lounge.

HORSEBACK RIDING Woodstock has been an equestrian center for generations, especially for Vermont's hardy Morgans, which are making a local comeback in South Woodstock. **Kedron Valley Stables** (802-457-1480; kedron.com), VT 106, South Woodstock. Lessons, plus carriage, wagon, and sleigh rides. **The Green Mountain Horse Association** (802-457-1509; gmhainc.org), 4342 South Road (VT 106), South Woodstock, sponsors events throughout the year, including sleigh rallies, long-distance rides, and jumping and dressage competitions. Visitors are welcome at shows and other events.

*Note:* **Open Acre Ranch** (openacreranch.com) in Fairlee (see the previous chapter) offers trail rides of varying lengths for most ability levels.

POLO **Quechee Polo Club** (quecheeclub.com). Matches are held most Saturdays at 2 p.m. in July and August on the field near Quechee Gorge.

SPA **The Spa at The Woodstock Inn & Resort** (802-457-6697; woodstockinn.com), 14 the Green, Woodstock. This is a major spa with a light-filled poolside Great Room where visitors luxuriate after treatments, which include many kinds of massage, body polishes and wraps, facials, and skin care.

SWIMMING **Silver Lake State Park** (802-234-9451; vtstateparks.com), 10 miles north on VT 12 in Barnard, has a nice beach. Open Memorial Day weekend–Labor Day weekend. Another smaller beach is right next to the general store.

The **Woodstock Recreation Center** (802-457-1502; woodstockrec.com), 54 River Street, has two public pools, mostly for youngsters.

For **indoor pools** see *Fitness Center* above and in "Upper Valley River Towns" on page 192.

## ❄ Winter Sports

CROSS-COUNTRY SKIING AND SNOWSHOEING **Woodstock Inn and Resort, Tubbs Snowshoes & Nordic Adventure Center** (802-457-6674; woodstockinn.com), VT 106. A total of 60 km of some of the most varied and scenic trails for skiing and snowshoeing in New England. The network traverses 30 km of 1880s carriage roads on Mount Tom, climbing gently from the valley floor (700 feet) to the summit (1,250 feet), skirting a pond, and finally commanding a view of the village, in the Ottauquechee Valley. The center itself, a source of tickets, a map, ski (skating and classic stride) and Tubbs snowshoe rentals (as well as poles), lockers, and lessons, is at the Woodstock Racquet & Fitness Center. Right outside the door, you'll find 10 km of gentle, meadow skiing on the golf course, connecting with woodland and snowshoe trails on Mount Peg. Lessons, salesroom, lockers, soup, and sandwiches.

**Wilderness Trails** (802-295-7620; quecheeinn.com), Clubhouse Road at the Quechee Inn, has 18 km of track-set trails, including easy loops through the woods and meadows around Quechee Gorge, offering fine views of its waterfalls, also harder trails down into the gorge. Snowshoe rentals are offered.

DOWNHILL SKIING **Suicide Six Ski Area** (802-457-6661; woodstockinn.com), South Pomfret, 5 miles north of Woodstock on Pomfret Road. Heir to the first ski tow in the United States, which was cranked up in 1934 but on the other side of this hill, Suicide Six is now part of the Woodstock Inn and Resort complex and has a base lodge finished with native woodwork. Its beginners' area has a J-bar; two double chairlifts climb 655 vertical feet to reach 23 trails ranging from easy to the Show Off and Pomfret Plunge, plus a half-pipe for snowboarders. Lessons, rentals, retail shop, and restaurant/lounge.

ICE SKATING **Silver Lake**, by the general store in Barnard. **Union Arena**, at Woodstock Union High School, VT 4 west, Fri.-night skating for families. **Woodstock Sports** (802-457-1568), 30 Central Street, Woodstock, offers skate and ski rentals. **Wilderness Trails** (see above) in Quechee also rents skates and clears the pond on its property and across the road.

SLEIGH RIDES **Kedron Valley Stables** (802-457-1480; kedron.com), 4342 South Road (VT 106), South Woodstock. Weather permitting, sleigh rides are offered daily.

## ❄ Green Space

**Mount Tom**'s 1,357-foot summit towers above the village of Woodstock. It's one of Vermont's most walked and walkable mountains. From Mountain Avenue in the village itself, **Faulkner Park** (donated by Mrs. Edward Faulkner, one of Woodstock's most thoughtful philanthropists) features a trail patterned on Baden-Baden's "cardiac" walks. A marked, 1.6-mile path zigzags up to the summit (bring a picnic; a bench

WALKING THE FOREST PATH FROM THE VISITOR CENTER TO QUECHEE GORGE   PAT GOUDEY O'BRIEN

overlooks the village). The **Marsh-Billings-Rockefeller National Historical Park** encompasses more than 500 acres on the backside of Mount Tom, with 30 miles of footpaths that were originally carriage roads, including a trail to Pogue Pond. Enter on VT 12 at the park (follow signs) or at the trailhead on Prosper Road, just off VT 12. Inquire about frequent seasonal programs offered by the national park (802-457-3368). Also see *Cross-Country Skiing* for winter use on page 214.

**Mount Peg Trails** begin on Golf Avenue behind the Woodstock Inn. Open May–October. One is roughly 5 miles round-trip, a peaceful walk upward along easy switchbacks beneath pines, with a picnic bench at the summit. Views west down the valley to Killington.

**Quechee Gorge State Park** (802-295-2990; vtstateparks.com), off VT 4, Quechee. This 611-acre preserve encompasses the gorge (see *Must See* on page 209). Trails from the rim lead gently down (south of US 4) into the gorge, which should be approached carefully. On a hot day, it's tempting to wade into the shallow water at the south end of the gorge—but beware of sudden water releases that have been known to sweep swimmers away. Ditto for the rockbound swimming hole at the north end of the gorge under the spillway. Look for picnic tables under the pines on Deweys Mills Road. The campground (open mid-May–October 15) offers 47 tent/trailer sites, seven lean-tos, and a dump station. This property belonged to a local woolen mill until the 1950s, when it was acquired by the US Army Corps of Engineers as part of the Hartland Dam flood-control project.

**North Hartland Lake Recreation Area** (802-295-2855) is a 1,711-acre preserve created by the US Army Corps of Engineers to control the confluence of the Ottauquechee and Connecticut rivers and to mitigate flooding. It offers a sandy beach, a wooded picnic area with grills, and a nature trail. Access is poorly marked, so ask directions at the Quechee information booth.

**Silver Lake State Park** (802-234-9451; vtstateparks.com), VT 12, Barnard. Campground open Memorial Day–Labor Day. Silver Lake is good for fishing, swimming, and boating (rentals available). The park offers a snack bar and wooded campground with 40 tent/trailer sites and seven lean-tos. Hot showers.

**Teagle's Landing** is Woodstock's vest-pocket park, a magical oasis below the bridge in the middle of town (Central Street). Landscaping and benches invite sitting by the river, a tribute to Frank Teagle (1914–97), one of Woodstock's most dedicated residents.

**Dewey Pond Wildlife Sanctuary**, Deweys Mills Road, Quechee. Originally a mill-pond, this is a beautiful spot with nature trails and a boat launch, good for bird-watching and fishing.

**Hurricane Forest**, US 5, White River Junction. This 500-acre town forest harbors a pond and many miles of trails. Ask directions at the Quechee information booth.

**Eshqua Bog**, off Hartland Hill Road, Woodstock. A 40-acre sanctuary managed by the New England Wild Flower Society and The Nature Conservancy with a white-blazed loop trail circling through 8 acres of wetlands, with orchids blooming in summer. Ask directions locally.

Also see **Vermont Institute of Natural Science** under *Must See* on page 209.

## ✳ Lodging

RESORTS **Twin Farms** (802-234-9999; twinfarms.com), 452 Royalton Turnpike, Barnard. There's luxury and then there's luxury. Twin Farms is Vermont's premier resort. Peter Jennison, for many years this book's coauthor, noted how ironic it is that the former country home of Sinclair Lewis, whose novels satirize the materialism of American life, and Dorothy Thompson, the acerbic foreign correspondent, is now a 325-acre Shangri-La for "corporate CEOs, heads of government, royalty, and celebrities . . . to unwind, frolic, and be rich together in sybaritic privacy." That said, this is authentically a place apart, and each of the rooms and 10 sequestered "cottages" is an amazing creation. The Vermont landscape is front and center with paths winding through woods, orchards, and meadows. In winter there's cross-country and downhill skiing. In place of a spa, there's a 3,000-gallon Japanese-style soaking pool. The contemporary glass-walled, two-story aviary blurs the difference between inside and outside; a sunken, jetted bath resembles a pool below a cave-like stone hearth.

The tone throughout the resort is casual, relaxed, and friendly. There are four stylish rooms in the main house; rates include access to two bars and the use of all recreational amenities: a fully equipped fitness center, croquet equipment, tennis courts, a pond, and mountain bikes. There are minimum stays on weekends and holidays, along with an 18 percent service charge. There is a staff of 42 here for 20 rooms. Check the website for current rates. $$$$+.

**The Woodstock Inn and Resort** (802-332-6853; woodstockinn.com), 14 the Green, Woodstock, is the lineal descendant of the eighteenth-century Eagle Tavern and the famous "old" Woodstock Inn that flourished between 1893 and 1969, putting the town on the year-round resort map. Today's 142-room, air-conditioned, colonial-style 1970s edition was created by Laurance Rockefeller and has recently been thoroughly and tastefully remodeled. The main lobby is dominated by a stone hearth, a book-lined library with games of chess, and a beautiful

THE VENERABLE HEART OF THE WOODSTOCK INN    CHRISTINA TREE

conservatory invite guests to sit back and wile their time away.

The grounds include a landscaped swimming pool and a full-service spa. Resort facilities are also spread around town. See *To Do* on page 213 for details about the outstanding 18-hole **Golf Club**, the **Racquet and Fitness Club, Suicide Six Ski Area**, and the **Nordic Center**, with 60 km of trails meandering out over the golf course and around Mount Tom. The **Red Rooster** off the lobby is the inn's casually elegant restaurant. Windows overlook the garden (see *Dining Out* on page 220). The main dining room is reserved for breakfasts and functions, while richly paneled **Richardson's Tavern** is open evenings for drinks and pub fare. Current regular-season rates, depending on room and season; children 12 and under are free when staying in a room with an adult. MAP available. Check out the many packages. $$–$$$.

♻ **The Quechee Inn at Marshland Farm** (802-295-3133; quecheeinn.com), 1119 Quechee Main Street, Quechee. Off by itself on a quiet side road east of Quechee Village, this historic farm is an attractive inn with 25 guest rooms. You'll see the rough-hewn beams of the original Georgian-style house built here by Colonel Joseph Marsh in 1793. With successive centuries and owners, it expanded to include a distinctive, two-story, double-porched ell. In 1954 it moved to higher ground to escape the rising waters created by the Hartland Dam. In 1968 it became the first headquarters and accommodations for the Quechee Lakes Corporation; a decade later, the couple who acquired it established its present look and reputation, which subsequent owners have preserved. Rooms vary in size and feel. Three are suites; all have a private bath and phone. The brick-floored, raftered lounge, with its piano, books, and games, opens onto a big, sunny dining room where breakfast and dinner are served. The inn is home to the **Vermont Fly-Fishing School**, offering canoeing and kayaking tours on the Connecticut, White, and Ottauquechee rivers, along with mountain bike rentals. In winter it maintains 18 km of groomed cross-country ski trails. Guests enjoy privileges at the nearby **Quechee Club**, with its 18-hole golf course, tennis courts, health center, and pools. Rates are varied and include full breakfast. Inquire about packages. $–$$$.

INNS ♂ **The Kedron Valley Inn** (802-457-1473; kedronvalleyinn.com), 4778 South Road (VT 106), South Woodstock. This mellow brick centerpiece of South Woodstock has been welcoming visitors since 1828 and once served as a stop on the Underground Railroad. There are 27 varied guest rooms divided among the main inn, the Tavern Building (vintage 1822), and the log lodge motel. The 12-acre property includes a 2-acre swim pond with a sandy beach. All guest rooms have a TV, A/C, and a private bath; most have a fireplace. Both the pub-style tavern and the inn dining room are gathering places for local residents as well as for guests. The inn can host receptions for up to 200. Also see *Dining Out* on page 221. $$–$$$.

**Parker House Inn** (802-295-6077; theparkerhouseinn.com), 1792 Quechee Main Street, Quechee. A redbrick mansion built in 1857 by Vermont senator Joseph Parker beside his flannel mill on the Ottauquechee River, this inn is best known for food (see *Dining Out* on page 221) but is also a comfortable place to stay. Since acquiring it, chef Alexandra Adler and her husband Adam have installed new baths and revamped the rooms. The downstairs parlors are now dining rooms, but there is a small second-floor sitting room with a TV, a sunny downstairs reading nook, a breakfast room, and a riverside deck. Dine and Stay packages. Add 15 percent gratuity. Guests have access to Quechee Club facilities. $$–$$$.

**506 On the River Inn** (802-457-5000; ontheriverwoodstock.com), 1653 West Woodstock Road (US 4). This two-story,

38-room contemporary inn opened in 2014 on the 6-acre site of a former riverside motel. Spacious guest rooms have balconies or patios; upper-floor rooms overlook the Ottauquechee. Rooms and suites have king beds, armchairs, minibars, and many more amenities. A large, nicely decorated open room is divided into casual kick-back space at one end and the **506 Bistro & Bar**, with its antique bar, at the other. There's also a game room, a toddlers' playroom, a library, and a gym. In warm weather, relax in Adirondack chairs by the river or pond. In case you're wondering: "506" was the address on West Woodstock Road in a simpler, not-so-long-ago era—the one in which a family-run gem of a motel on this spot was a reasonably priced find. $$–$$$ includes breakfast.

**Lincoln Inn & Restaurant at The Covered Bridge** (802-457-7052; lincolninn.com), 2709 West Woodstock Road (US 4), Woodstock. Reopened in 2014, this 1870s farmhouse has been reincarnated as an English-style "restaurant with rooms." Along with the neighboring Lincoln Covered Bridge, it's named for Abraham, a cousin of a previous owner. Innkeeper Mara Mehlman has a culinary background but it's her partner, Jevgenija Saromova, who has the serious credentials. Rooms are comfortable and the inn is sited on 7 riverside acres. $$.

## BED & BREAKFASTS

### IN WOODSTOCK

*Note:* Warm, comfortable inns and B&Bs abound in Woodstock; we have a small sampling here. Parking can be tough, hence the advantage of the many in-town B&Bs described below. All face major thoroughfares, however; you might want to request back- or side-facing rooms.

✪ **Ardmore Inn** (802-457-3887; ardmoreinn.com), 23 Pleasant Street. One of the most convenient B&Bs to downtown shops, this is a cheery, comfortable, meticulously restored 1867 Greek revival village house with five spacious guest rooms, each with a private marble bath. Back in Southern California, innkeeper Charlotte Hollingsworth managed a bookstore; here she has named each of the rooms for a Vermont author or illustrator, fitting it with appropriate volumes. Our favorite is the spacious Archer Mayor Room, named for Brattleboro's detective novelist. There's also a well-stocked downstairs library with a fireplace and a many-windowed sunroom with rockers. In the dining room, guests gather around the antique Nantucket dining room table. Both Charlotte and husband Cary offer helpful advice about local sights and dining. Room includes a three-course breakfast and afternoon refreshments. $$.

✪ **The Charleston House** (802-457-3843; charlestonhouse.com), 21 Pleasant Street. This luxurious Federal brick townhouse (vintage 1835) in the middle of the village is especially appealing, with period furniture in nine guest rooms, all with private bath and air-conditioning, several with fireplace and Jacuzzi. Five rooms are in the original part of the house, four in the more contemporary back. Your genial hosts are Willa and Dieter (Dixi) Nohl. For many years Dixi managed Burke Mountain ski area in the Northeast Kingdom. $$–$$$ including full breakfast.

**The Jackson House Inn** (802-457-2065; jacksonhouse.com), 43 Senior Lane (just off US 4), West Woodstock. This luxuriously appointed and equipped 1890 farmhouse has been expanded to include five queen guest rooms and six spacious single-room suites furnished in period antiques, several with French doors. Our favorites are the two second-floor suites in the main house with gas fireplace and French doors opening onto a balcony over the landscaped grounds with gardens and a spring-fed pond. Common space in the inn is ample and elegant: library, dining room, and living room, as well as a fully licensed lounge with fireplace. Current innkeepers Kathy and

Rick Terwelp reserve the large, sunny dining area, formerly a restaurant, for guests and for special events. Rates include breakfast. $$–$$$.

## BEYOND THE VILLAGE

✪ 🏠 **Deer Brook Inn** (802-672-3713; deerbrookinn.com), 4548 West Woodstock Road (US 4), Woodstock. Five miles west of Woodstock and 10 miles east of Killington's Skyeship Gondola, Win Coffin and Phil Jenkins are your hosts at this restored 1820 farmhouse, set back in fields across the road from the Ottauquechee River. Each of the five rooms has a full bath and climate-controlled heat, radio/CD player, and air-conditioning. A ground-floor, two-room suite with a sitting room is good for families. Room 1 has skylights above the bed and in the bathroom. Rates include full breakfast. $–$$.

**Apple Hill Inn Bed & Breakfast** (802-457-9135; applehillinn.com), 10 Hartwood Way, Woodstock. The 30-mile view of the Ottauquechee and surrounding hills is spectacular in any season, and the spacious, many-windowed house has been designed to maximize it. Longtime innkeeper Beverlee Cook has furnished the contemporary interior with Oriental rugs and authentic eighteenth-century antiques, an elegant counterpoint to the large, light-filled rooms. An avid (organic-geared) cook and baker, Beverlee caters receptions and serves afternoon teas in the solarium. The vintage barn down the hill adds to wedding option venues. Pets are welcome—as are young children—in the Paradise Room (with a 360-degree view) above the garage. $$–$$$ includes breakfast buffet.

**Bailey's Mills Bed & Breakfast** (802-484-7809; baileysmills.com), 1347 Bailey's Mills Road, Reading. As happens so often in Vermont, surprises lurk at the end of a back road, in this case a few miles west of VT 106. With a two-story porch and fluted columns, Bailey's Mills resembles a southern antebellum mansion. The 17-room brick home includes 11 fireplaces, two beehive ovens, a dance hall, and an 1829 general store, all part of an ambitious manufacturing complex established by Levi Bailey (1766–1850) and operated by his family for a century. Today Barbara Thaeder offers several comfortable rooms, two with working fireplaces, each with a cozy sitting area and private bath, tastefully furnished with antiques. A spacious solarium makes the Honeymoon Suite especially appealing. Paths lead off across the meadows into the woods and toward a swim pond. (Ask about the adjacent Spite Cemetery.) $$.

**Maple Leaf Inn** (802-234-5342; mapleleafinn.com), 5890 VT 12, Barnard. Mike and Nancy Boyle are the innkeepers in this Victorian-style farmhouse, designed specifically as a B&B. Stenciling, stitchery, and Nancy's handmade quilts decorate the seven air-conditioned guest rooms, each with a capacious private bath, king-size bed, sitting area, telephone, and TV/VCR. Most guest rooms have wood-burning fireplaces and whirlpool baths. The parlor, library, and dining room are bright and inviting. The Country Garden Room on the main floor has easy access for anyone who needs special assistance. $$–$$$, includes breakfast.

**Farmhouse Inn** (802-672-5433; farmhouseinnvt.com), 5250 West Woodstock Road, Woodstock. Six miles west of Woodstock Village, this imposing white-clapboard farmhouse sits back from the road, across the river from the Ottauquechee River and backed by a striking five-story red barn. Barry and Tory Milstone offer five second- and third-floor guest rooms with a private bath and temperature control, furnished in antiques. Children are welcome, and there's a family suite with a sitting room, for a suite sleeping up to four; includes a full breakfast. $–$$.

Also see the **October Country Inn** in "Killington/Rutland Region" on page 292.

OTHER ✪ **Shire Riverview Motel** (802-457-2211; shiremotel.com), 46 Pleasant Street, Woodstock. Location, location. This two-story, independently owned 42-unit motel is within walking distance of downtown, and while it fronts on Pleasant Street (US 4), it backs on the river; most rooms have river views and many have deck access. A contemporary building with six upscale suites is also in back; another recently refurbished building houses three more high-end rooms. All rooms have phone and computer hookup, furnished with two queens, two doubles, or a king. All have a fridge, and some have a gas fireplace and Jacuzzi. $–$$.

Rental units range from small condos to six-bedroom houses, all with access to resort facilities, which include a small ski mountain, golf courses, and clubhouse with its indoor pool and squash courts. These can be rented through local realtors, such as **Quechee Lakes Rentals** (802-295-1970; quecheelakesrentals.com) and **Carefree Quechee Vacations** (802-295-9500; carefreequecheevacations.com).

*Note:* For camping at the area's two state parks, see *Green Space* on page 215.

## ✳ Where to Eat

DINING OUT ✪ **Simon Pearce Restaurant** (802-295-1470; simonpearce.com), The Mill, 1760 Quechee Main Street, Quechee. Open for lunch (11:30–2:45) and dinner (5–9; reservations advised), Sunday brunch (11–2:45). This is a cheerful, contemporary place for consistently superior food, served on its own pottery and glass, overlooking the waterfall and covered bridge rebuilt since Hurricane Irene. This is a high-profile tourist stop with a recently expanded viewing area to watch glass being blown in the stone mill below or to shop in the original store that remains open through dinner hours. $$$.

♂ **The Prince and the Pauper** (802-457-1818; princeandpauper.com), 24 Elm Street, Woodstock. Open nightly for dinner (reservations advised). Executive chef Charles "Gavin" Dziedziech and proprietors Heidi Talbert and Vincent Talento maintain the establishment's long-held reputation for superior food and service. The prix fixe dinner menu changes nightly, and the bistro menu offers lighter fare, including hearth-baked pizzas. $$–$$$.

♂ **The Barnard Inn Restaurant & Max's Tavern** (802-234-9961; barnardinn.com), 5518 VT 12, 10 miles north of Woodstock, Barnard. Open Tues.–Sat. 5–9 p.m. Reservations advised. Will Dodson grew up in St. Louis, graduated from the Culinary Institute of America, acquired this 1796 brick house in 2000, and has been known ever since for his exceptional, locally sourced fare. He grows 80 percent of his summer veggies and keeps chickens and ducks for their eggs. The formal dining option requires reservations and a plan for your party. In the less formal Max's Tavern, guests are welcome without prior notice. A large selection of wines and beers is available by the glass. Desserts are irresistible in both venues. $$–$$$.

♬ **The Red Rooster at The Woodstock Inn and Resort** (802-332-6853; woodstockinn.com), 14 the Green, Woodstock. Open daily noon–10. This casually elegant restaurant is airy and inviting. The menu stresses locally sourced products and produce. Lunch options feature specialty sandwiches and salads. The à la carte dinner menu includes a plate of regional cheeses. There's a reasonably priced children's menu. Pub fare is available in Richardson's Tavern (see *Eating Out* on page 222). $$–$$$.

**Lincoln Inn & Restaurant** (802-457-7052; lincolninn.com), 2709 West Woodstock Road (US 4), West Woodstock. Open for dinner, by reservation only. Latvian-born Jevgenija Saromova is the chef orchestrating this serious new dining option. The venue is an 1870s farmhouse by the river. $$$.

**Parker House Inn** (802-295-6077; theparkerhouseinn.com), 1792 Quechee Main Street, Quechee. Open for dinner daily (reservations, please); also for lunch summer weekends. Chef Alexandra Adler continues to get good reviews for her French-accented bistro in a classic brick Victorian mill owner's mansion. Light fare and cocktails are served in the riverside back bar. Lunch, when served, is on the riverside deck. $–$$.

**The Kedron Valley Inn** (802-457-1473; kedronvalleyinn.com), 4778 South Road (VT 106), 5 miles south of Woodstock. Open for dinner Thurs.–Mon. 5:30–9. The large, low-beamed dining room is country elegant and casual. Entrées might range from a Cloudland Farm beef burger to New York strip steak. $–$$.

**Cloudland Farm** (802-457-2599; cloudlandfarm.com), 1101 Cloudland Road, Woodstock. Open by reservation for dinner Thurs., Fri., and Sat. Closed in mud season. This is a new twist on farm-to-table: the tables are at the farm. Drive 3.8 miles up and up and up Cloudland Road and you come to a many-windowed, post-and-beam building constructed from wood harvested on this farm. Come on a Thursday night and you sit down to an informal dinner featuring the farm's own meat. Fridays and Saturdays are more formal, with tables draped in linen. The three-course menu is still served family-style. Prices vary slightly with the menu, which you can check online before reserving. There's also a big wood-fired hearth. Children are half price. It's BYOB $$–$$$.

Also see **Norwich Inn, Carpenter & Main**, and **Skunk Hollow Tavern** in "Upper Valley River Towns" on page 180.

EATING OUT

IN WOODSTOCK

**Bentley's Restaurant** (802-457-3232; bentleysrestaurant.com), 3 Elm Street, Woodstock. Open daily for lunch and dinner. The 1970s restaurant here, an oasis of Victoriana and plants, has been expanded and updated by new owners, and both service and quality have improved. A lifesaver in the middle of town, good for burgers or specialty sandwiches and flatbreads at lunch; dinner choices range from fish-and-chips to crispy roasted duck. Frequent live music.

**Worthy Kitchen** (802-457-7281), 442 East Woodstock Road. This companion piece to the Worthy Burger in South Royalton is Woodstock's current hot spot. Craft beers (18 and counting) and hard ciders are the big draw, along with a blackboard menu and good-vibes atmosphere. You order and wait to be buzzed. Fresh, local ingredients, gluten-free, all the right things, and delicious. Try the fried chicken.

**Fairways Grille** (802-457-6672), Woodstock Inn and Resort Golf Club, VT 106 south. Open in summer for lunch 11:30–3. This is a Woodstock insider's meeting spot but open to the public, especially appealing on sunny days when you can dine on the deck. Designer sandwiches and salads, burgers, a good grilled Reuben. During ski season, hot chili and snacks are available for cross-country skiers in the fireside lounge.

**Mon Vert Café** (802-457-7143; monvertcafe.com), 69 Central Street. Open 7:30–11:30 for breakfast, until 4 for lunch. This bright, attractive café fills the need for a light, locally sourced, imaginative café in the middle of the village. The yogurt and pesto are homemade. Breads are from Red Hen, and even the chicken in the chicken salad sandwich has its provenance noted.

**Melaza Caribbean Bistro** (802-457-7110; melazabistro.com), 71 Central Street. Open five days a week, Wed.–Sun. 5 p.m. Meat and vegetarian specials with a Caribbean flair.

**Mountain Creamery** (802-457-1715), 33 Central Street, serves breakfast daily 7–11:30, lunch until 3, pastry and espresso until 6. Soups, sandwiches, salads, daily specials, and their own handmade ice cream as well as apple pie. Pies and cakes are also for sale.

**Richardson's Tavern at the Woodstock Inn** (802-332-6853; woodstockinn .com), 14 the Green. Usually open evenings for pub fare in a casual dining and tavern setting, but check. This is a delightful find, a richly paneled tavern room with a wood-fired hearth, wing chairs, and all the accoutrements of an exclusive club, including reading lights beside tables. Entrées include reasonably priced comfort food and burgers.

**White Cottage Snack Bar** (802-457-3455; whitecottagesnackbar.com), 863 West Woodstock Road. Open May–October, 11–10. Hurricane Irene did a job on this local legend, but it bounced back, better than ever. The classic 1950s take-out has reopened with expanded indoor as well as outdoor seating overlooking the river. The lobster bisque and chowder (Ipswich clams are delivered daily) are housemade. We recommend the Jamaican pulled pork. The menu is large. Gifford's ice cream. Closed in winter.

**Barnard General Store** (802-234-9688), 6134 VT 12, Barnard. Open 7–7. Sited beside Silver Lake and in the middle of a small village, this is a beloved landmark. When it closed in 2013, the community raised funds and, with the help of the Preservation Trust of Vermont, bought it back. It continues to be a great spot for breakfast and lunch as well as milkshakes, coffee, and sandwiches to take to the lake across the street. This is also a full general store, selling ethanol-free gas and groceries.

**South Woodstock General Store** (802-457-3050; southwoodstockcountrystore .com), 4800 South Road (VT 106), South Woodstock. Open daily for staples, great breakfast, lunch (order and grab a table), take-out foods, freshly baked bread, and Vermont gifts.

**Out of Bounds—Suicide Six Ski Area** (802-457-6661; woodstockinn .com), South Pomfret, 5 miles north of Woodstock on Pomfret Road. During the winter months, enjoy savory homemade soups, hearty sandwiches, fresh salads—and don't forget the bar for a warm-up

COZY INTERIOR AT BENTLEY'S RESTAURANT IN WOODSTOCK  PAT GOUDEY O'BRIEN

hot chocolate or hot toddy. Located slope-slide at Suicide Six.

PICNICS  On a beautiful summer or fall day the best place to lunch is outside. In Woodstock itself there's Teagle's Landing, right on Central Street by the river, and Faulkner Park on Monument Avenue. See *Green Space* on page 214 for other ideas.

**Woodstock Farmers' Market** (802-457-3658; woodstockfarmersmarket .com), 979 Woodstock Road (US 4), Woodstock. Deli hours: Tues.–Sun. 10–4. Rebuilt after a hit from Hurricane Irene, this is the town's standout place for locally sourced organic produce. It also has soups, sandwiches, and salads to go and lots of veggie options. (We recommend The Garden of Eden on multigrain bread.) The store also sells fresh fish, free-range chicken, local produce, meals to go, and Baba À Louis bread.

**The Village Butcher** (802-457-2756; thebutcher.biz), 18 Elm Street, Woodstock. A superb butcher and a deli with sandwiches, soups, and specials to go, along with its top-flight meats, wines, and baked goods, plus homemade fudge.

## ✴ Entertainment

**Pentangle Arts** (802-457-3981; pentanglearts.org), Town Hall Theater,

31 the Green, Woodstock. First-run films are shown Fri.–Mon. evenings at 7:30 in the Town Hall Theater. Live presentations at the town hall and at Woodstock Union High School include a variety of musical and other live entertainment. Check the **Town Crier** blackboard at the corner of Elm and Central Sts. for current happenings. Inquire about the Woodstock Film Society.

## ✳ Selective Shopping

**ANTIQUES SHOPS** The Woodstock area is a mecca for antiques buffs. There are two big group galleries. **Vermont Antique Mall** (802-281-4147), 5573 Woodstock Road (US 4) in the Quechee Gorge Village, open daily, is one of New England's largest antiques collectives, with two floors full of dealers. The **Antiques Collaborative** (802-296-5858; antiquescollaborative.com), Waterman Place, 6931 Woodstock Road (US 4), at the blinking light in Quechee, is also open daily (10–5) and shows representative stock from more than 150 dealers: period furniture (usually in good condition), silver, Oriental rugs, and more.

Among the more than a dozen individual dealers: **Wigren & Barlow** (802-457-2453; wigrenandbarlow.com), 29 Pleasant Street, is Woodstock's most elegant antiques shop, with a large selection of fine country and formal furniture, decorative accessories, and garden appointments (open daily 10–5).

*Note:* **The Vermont Antique Dealers' Association** (vermontantiquesdealers .com) holds its annual show in July at Woodstock Union High School. A pamphlet guide to *Antiquing in and around Woodstock* is available from the information center.

**ART GALLERIES** The following are all in Woodstock: **Woodstock Gallery** (802-457-2012; woodstockgalleryvt.com), 6 Elm Street, specializes in contemporary carvings, prints, and antiquities. **Gallery on the Green** (802-457-4956; galleryon thegreen.com), 1 The Green, features original art, limited-edition prints, photography, and occasionally sculpture from New England artists. **The Fox Gallery** (802-457-1250; thefoxgallery.com), 5 The Green. Neil and Janice Drevitson have maintained this gallery in their house for more than 40 years, exhibiting primarily their own traditional, highly realistic landscapes, portraits, and still lifes, as well as a select number of sculptors and other artists.

**The Collective** (802-457-1298; collective-theartofcraft.com), 47 Central Street, Woodstock. An outstanding artisan-run gallery showcasing a mix of contemporary art and fine craft in the old riverside linseed mill.

**ARTISANS Simon Pearce Glass** (802-295-1470; simonpearce.com), The Mill, 1760 Quechee Main Street, Quechee. The shop (802-295-2711) is open 10–9 daily. The brick mill by the falls in the Ottauquechee was the nineteenth-century home of J. C. Parker and Co., producing "shoddy"—wool reworked from soft rags. In 1981 Simon Pearce opened a glass factory here, harnessing the dam's hydropower for his furnace. Pearce established a national reputation for his distinctive production pieces: tableware, vases, lamps, candlesticks, and more. In the rebuild after Hurricane Irene, the glass-blowing viewing from the Simon Pearce Restaurant (see *Dining Out* on page 220) has been expanded and is a must-see. Simon Pearce now also operates a large, visitor-friendly glass and pottery factory in nearby Windsor (see "Upper Valley River Towns" on page 182).

**Charles Shackleton Furniture** and **Miranda Thomas Pottery** (802-672-5175; shackletonthomas.com), 102 Mill Road (VT 4), The Mill, Bridgewater. Open daily 10–5. This couple met at art school in England and again at Simon Pearce Glass. Charles was an apprentice glassblower before he switched to furniture making; Miranda founded the pottery studio there. They have since acquired much of the Bridgewater Mill, and Charles works with fellow crafters to produce exquisite furniture. It's made to order, but models are displayed (along with seconds at the mill), complemented by Miranda's distinctive pottery, hand thrown and carved with traditional designs, such as rabbits, fish, and trees. Her pottery is housed in a former worker's cottage in the mill's parking lot. Inquire about furniture workshops and pottery studios.

**Farmhouse Pottery** (802-774-8373; farmhousepottery.com), 1837 West Woodstock Road (US 4), Woodstock. Open Wed.–Sun. The store showcases partially rough-finished, elegantly simple tableware, vases, and small useful pieces that you can watch being crafted in the adjoining workshop. Zoe and James Zilian see their distinctive work as expressing "farm-to-table values." James, with a long background at Simon Pearce, is obviously a skilled marketer. Prices are high, and Farmhouse Pottery is already a hot gift item.

**Danforth Pewter** (802-457-7269; danforthpewter.com), 9 Central Street, Woodstock. Now nationally known and distributed, known for pewter work that includes lamps, jewelry, kitchen items, and much more, Danforth was founded in Woodstock in 1975 but its workshop has long since moved to Middlebury. This new store is a trove of likely gifts.

BOOKSTORES **The Yankee Bookshop** (802-457-2411; yankeebookshop.com), 12 Central Street, Woodstock. Established in 1935, this is Vermont's oldest continuously operated independent bookshop. It carries an unusually large stock of hardbound and paperback books for adults and children, plus cards; it features the work of local authors and publishers. It also carries toys and learning tools, kites and spinners.

SPECIAL SHOPS

IN WOODSTOCK VILLAGE

**F. H. Gillingham & Sons** General Store (802-457-2100), 16 Elm Street, owned and run by the same family since 1886, is something of an institution, retaining a lot of its old-fashioned general store flavor. You'll find plain and fancy groceries; wine; housewares; hardware for home, garden, and farm; books; Vermont products, and much more.

**Woodstock Pharmacy** (802-457-1306), 19 Central Street. Open daily 8–6, Sundays until 1 p.m. Another Woodstock institution that has branched out well beyond the basics, especially good for stationery and (downstairs) for children's toys and books.

**Who Is Sylvia?** (802-457-1110), 26 Central Street, in the old village firehouse, houses two floors of great vintage clothing and accessories for men as well as for women.

**Red Wagon Toy Company** (802-457-9300; redwagontoy.com), 41 Central Street, specializes in creative toys and children's clothing, from infant to size 16.

**Whippletree Yarn Shop** (802-457-1325), 7 Central Street, has yarns, knitting patterns, sample sweaters, and gifts. Inquire about knitting classes.

IN AND NEAR QUECHEE

**Fat Hat Clothing Co.** (802-296-6646; fathat.com), 1 Quechee Main Street (corner of US 4). A business that has evolved over more than 30 years from making floppy "fat hats" to a variety of comfortable, colorful clothing, most designed and made right here. Check out the markdowns upstairs.

**Quechee Gorge Village** (802-295-1550; quecheegorge.com), 5573 Woodstock Road (US 4) at Quechee Gorge. A long, weatherproofed shopping complex housing a number of quality enterprises, among them the vast **Vermont Antique Mall** (see *Antiques Shops* on page 223); **Vermont Spirits Distilling Company**

(vodka); the **Cabot Quechee Store**, a Cabot Cheese outlet with Putney Mountain Winery tastings; and the **Vermont Toy Museum and Gift Shop**, with seasonal rides on a miniature train and carousel.

**Taftsville Country Store** (802-457-1135), 404 Woodstock Road (US 4), Taftsville. This 1840 landmark is also still the post office and carries Vermont products; cheeses, maple products, jams, jellies, smoked ham, and bacon, plus staples, wine, books, and more. Mail-order catalog.

ELSEWHERE

FARMS **Sugarbush Farm** (802-457-1757; sugarbushfarm.com), 591 Sugarbush Farm Road, Woodstock, but located in Pomfret: Take US 4 to Taftsville, cross the covered bridge, go up the hill, turn left onto Hillside Road, then follow signs. Warning: It's steep. Beware in mud season, but it's well worth the effort: Sample seven Vermont cheeses, all packaged here along with gift boxes, geared to sending products to far corners of the world. In-season you can watch maple sugaring, walk the maple and nature trail, or visit with the farm animals.

**On the Edge Farm** (802-457-4510; ontheedgefarm.com), 49 VT 12, Woodstock (2.5 miles north of Woodstock Village). An outstanding farm stand open year-round but just Fri.–Sun. in January. Locally raised and smoked meat as well as seasonal fruit and veggies, fresh eggs, jams, pickles, pies, and flowers.

**Seasonal farmers' markets** in Woodstock take place on Wed. (3–6) on the village green.

## ✳ Special Events

*Note:* Check the **Town Crier** blackboard on Elm Street for Woodstock weekly happenings.

*Washington's birthday:* **Winter Carnival** events sponsored by the Woodstock Recreation Center (woodstockrec.com).

*March:* **Maple Madness**, sponsored by the Woodstock Area Chamber of Commerce. (woodstockvt.com).

Late May: Annual **Sheep Shearing and Herding Weekend** at Billings Farm & Museum, Woodstock (billingsfarm.org). The **Memorial Day Parade** in downtown Woodstock is worth a trip.

*First Sunday in June:* **Covered Bridges Half Marathon**, Woodstock area.

*Father's Day weekend:* **Quechee Hot Air Balloon Festival** (quecheeballoon festival.com)—a gathering of more than two dozen balloons with ascensions, flights, races, crafts show, and entertainment.

*July:* **An Old Fashioned 4th** at Billings Farm & Museum (billingsfarm.org) includes a noon reading of the Declaration of Independence, nineteenth-century-style debates, games, and wagon rides. **Bookstock** (bookstockvt.org), last weekend in Woodstock.

*August:* **Quechee Games** (quechee games.com), late August, Highland games and dancing, pipe bands, sheepdog trials. Billings Farm & Museum (billingsfarm.org) hosts the **Billings Farm Quilt Show** all month, and the **Antique Tractor Day** with a parade, first Sunday. **Taste of Woodstock** (woodstockvt.com), second Saturday.

*September:* **Woodstock Art Festival**, weekend after Labor Day.

*Mid-October:* **Vermont Antiques Festival**, Quechee. **Apples & Crafts Fair** (woodstockrec.com) Columbus Day weekend, Woodstock—more than 100 juried craftspeople and specialty food producers.

*Second weekend of December:* **Wassail Weekend** (woodstockvt.com), Woodstock includes a grand parade of carriages around the Village Green, holiday house tour, a Wassail feast, Yule-log lighting, and concerts.

# THE WHITE RIVER VALLEYS

*Including Randolph, Sharon, Royalton, Bethel,*
*Rochester, Hancock, Braintree, Brookfield,*
*Chelsea, Tunbridge, and Strafford*

As I-89 sweeps up through central Vermont in a grand 52-mile arc—from White River Junction to Montpelier—it offers a series of panoramas. Motorists see the high wall of the Green Mountains beyond the Braintree Range on the west and catch glimpses of an occasional valley village. What they don't see is one of Vermont's best-kept secrets: the classic old villages, abrupt valleys, and hill farms along the White River and its three branches.

The White River rises high in the Green Mountains in Granville Gulf and rushes down through Hancock, widening and slowing among farms in Rochester, keeping company with VT 100 until Stockbridge, where it turns east, carving a narrow valley for VT 107. At Bethel the river begins to parallel VT 14 and I-89. As it courses through the Royaltons and Sharon, it's joined by its three northern branches.

Each of these streams, rising some 20 miles north of the main stem of the river, has carved its own valley. The First Branch, shadowed by VT 110, threads six covered bridges, lush farmland, and the unselfconsciously beautiful villages of Chelsea and Tunbridge. The Second Branch begins above picturesque Pond Village in Brookfield, known for its floating bridge, and flows south along VT 14. The Third Branch rises in Roxbury and flows south through a lonely valley (along VT 12A) to Randolph, one of the area's few I-89 exits and an Amtrak stop as well as the only commercial center of any size in this entire area.

Beautiful as these valleys are, the high east–west roads that connect them, climbing up over hills and down into the next valley, are more rewarding still. See *Scenic Drives* on page 231 for tours that can pleasantly fill many days. In the absence of any major resort hub, a variety of widely scattered farms and B&Bs offer lodging and many good reasons to explore this rural region, genuinely as well as geographically the heart of Vermont.

GUIDANCE **White River Valley Area Chamber of Commerce** (802-728-9027; whiterivervalleychamber.com), 31 VT 66, Randolph. Phone answered year-round; seasonal information center at State Plaza just off I-89, Exit 4; website and printed directory cover this area.

**Sharon Northbound Information Center and Vermont Vietnam Veterans' Memorial** (802-281-5216), I-89, Sharon. Open 7 a.m.–11 p.m. Not what you expect to find at a roadside rest area. The 7,000 names on the memorial itself represent all the Vermonters who served in the Vietnam War, which is evoked through exhibits that include a time line and film clips. Also unexpected here: a "living greenhouse" filled with plants and descriptions of how they recycle waste. The staffed center is a source of local information; restrooms are outstanding.

**Green Mountain National Forest Ranger District Office and Visitor Center** (802-767-4261), VT 100 in Rochester. Open Sundays from late May to early October. A major

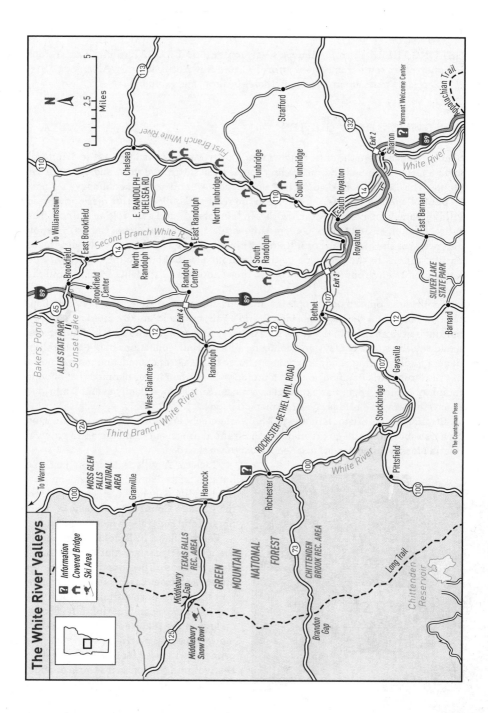

# The White River Valleys

**Legend:**
- 🛈 Information
- ⌒ Covered Bridge
- ⌒ Ski Area

N

0  2.5  5
Miles

To Williamstown

To Warren

110

113

First Branch White River

Chelsea

E. RANDOLPH–
CHELSEA RD

Strafford

Tunbridge

132

South Tunbridge

North Tunbridge

Vermont Welcome Center

Exit 2

Sharon

89

White River

110

East Randolph

East Brookfield

Second Branch White R.

14

North Randolph

South Royalton

14

Brookfield

89

65

Brookfield Center

ALLIS STATE PARK

Sunset Lake

Bakers Pond

Randolph Center

South Randolph

Exit 4

89

Royalton

Exit 3

East Barnard

SILVER LAKE STATE PARK

12

Bethel

107

West Braintree

12

Randolph

Barnard

124

Third Branch White River

12

Gaysville

107

MOSS GLEN FALLS NATURAL AREA

Stockbridge

Granville

ROCHESTER–BETHEL MTN. ROAD

Hancock

White River

100

Rochester

Pittsfield

100

© The Countryman Press

100

Middlebury Gap

TEXAS FALLS REC. AREA

GREEN MOUNTAIN NATIONAL FOREST

73

CHITTENDEN BROOK REC. AREA

125

Middlebury Snow Bowl

Brandon Gap

Long Trail

Chittenden Reservoir

center (restrooms) with detailed information on hiking, biking, picnicking, bird-watching, camping, and other recreation in this part of the GMNF.

*Herald of Randolph* (ourherald.com), published Thursdays, covers this area.

GETTING THERE *By train:* **Amtrak's Vermonter** (800-USA-RAIL; amtrak.com) stops in Randolph en route from Washington, DC, and New York City to St. Albans.

*By car:* I-89 exits are in Sharon, Bethel/Royalton, and Randolph.

## ✱ Towns and Villages

**Sharon Village.** Here the river road (VT 14) meets the high road (VT 131 to Strafford) and I-89. The columned **Sharon Trading Post** is a classic general store, and there are gas pumps. The **Sharon Historical Society** across the way is open summer Sundays 1–3 p.m.

**South Royalton Village.** On a bend in the river and off VT 14, this classic railroad village frames an oversize green with two bandstands and a Civil War cannon. The railroad hotel, an 1887 brick Queen Anne–style commercial block, the train depot, and many of the clapboard buildings within eyeshot have all received a new lease on life, thanks to the presence of the **Vermont Law School**. Founded in 1973 and known for its environmental law center, the school draws students from around the world.

**Tunbridge.** Some 20,000 people jam into this village of 400 over four days each September. They come for the Tunbridge World's Fair, first held in 1867. Sited in a grassy, natural bowl by a bend in the river, it has everything an agricultural fair should have: a midway, livestock displays and contests, a Floral Hall, collections of old-time relics, dancing, sulky racing, a fiddling contest, horse pulls, a grandstand, and more. Known as "the Drunkards Reunion" during a prolonged era when it was claimed that anyone found sober after 3 p.m. was expelled as a nuisance, it's now a family event. Tunbridge boasts four covered bridges (see our map on page 227).

**Strafford** is an aristocratic town. The white-clapboard Town House, built in 1799 on a rise above the village green in South Strafford, is a beauty, and the gothic revival **Justin Morrill Homestead** (*Must See*) is just down the road.

MILL HOLLOW, TUNBRIDGE CHRISTINA TREE

**Chelsea.** A village with not just one but two picturesque commons. Noteworthy buildings include a steepled church, the Orange County Courthouse, a brick library, and Federal-era homes and stores.

**Pond Village in Brookfield** is one of the most picturesque four-corners in all New England. The "pond" here, better known as **Sunset Lake**, is too deep to support the pillars of an ordinary bridge. The 330-foot-long span was initially floated on logs in the 1820s and has been rebuilt many times since. In January it's the prime viewing spot for the Ice Harvesting Festival, and as soon as it's warm enough, someone is almost always fishing here for smallmouth bass and yellow perch. The phone lines above it are festooned with fishing lines and sinkers from aborted

THE FLOATING BRIDGE IN POND VILLAGE, BROOKFIELD  CHRISTINA TREE

castings. **Allis State Park**, a few miles west, offers camping, picnicking, and a sweeping view.

**Bethel** (population 1,968). At the confluence of the White River and its Third Branch as well as the intersection of VT 107 (east–west) and VT 12 (north–south), with access to I-89 and a Victorian business block, Bethel is currently enjoying a renaissance. Look for new enterprises in the Blossom and Arnold blocks and in the Depot. Note the enormous rainbow and brook trout mural on the wall at the intersection.

**Randolph** (population 4,800). In **Randolph Center** (east on VT 66 from I-89, Exit 4) brick and clapboard Federal-era mansions line a main street that was cut unusually wide with the idea that this might be the state capital. Instead it's now a quiet village, home to **Vermont Technical College**, established 1806. A historic marker recounts the arrival in town of a young stallion from Massachusetts in 1789, the progenitor of Vermont's beloved Morgan horse breed. Randolph remains a horsey community, but with the arrival of the railroad in the mid-nineteenth century, population shifted from the center down to the valley, 3 miles west (now the other side of I-89). Amtrak now stops here, and **Chandler Center for the Arts** serves the town as the area's lively performance center. Randolph's Independence Day parade is one of the biggest around.

**Rochester** (population 1,200) straddles VT 100 in a quiet valley between the Green Mountains and the Braintree Range. The village centerpiece is 4-acre Rochester Park, a classic green with a bandstand, the scene of Sunday concerts. Just north of the park, a walkable lineup of mismatched buildings is full of surprises. There's a locally owned supermarket (Mac's), a heavy-duty hardware store/laundry, a serious bike shop, a contemporary art gallery, a bookstore/cafe, and two restaurants. Lodging options include **Huntington House**, this area's only inn and **Liberty Hill Farm** (see the sidebar on page 235), a family-geared working dairy. North of the village on VT 100, the **Green Mountain National Forest Visitor Center** orients sportsmen, picnickers, and hikers to the largely uninhabited western portion of the town that lies within the GMNF.

Summer brings a variety of music, inside and out, but everything about Rochester is very low-key.

## ✳ Must See

**Justin Morrill Homestead** (802-765-4288; morrillhomestead.org), 214 VT 132, Strafford Village. Open Memorial Day–Columbus Day, Wed.–Sun. 11–5; tours on the hour. Admission charged. Justin Morrill never went to college but is remembered as the congressman who sponsored the Land Grant Colleges Acts (one in 1862 and another in 1890) that created more than 76 present institutions, currently enrolling some 2.9 million students. Many have evolved into state universities. The son of a Strafford blacksmith, Morrill made enough money as a country storekeeper (which he parlayed into a chain of stores) to retire at age 38 and enter politics on an antislavery and temperance platform. He served in Congress for 44 years (1855–98), never finding much time to spend in his striking, 17-room Gothic Revival mansion because he kept getting reelected. A man who was instrumental in the design and construction of the Wash-

TEXAS FALLS  CHRISTINA TREE

ington Monument and the Library of Congress, Justin Morrill helped design his own house and the now-restored gardens and orchard. The icehouse and carriage barn are fitted with interpretive panels about Morrill and the many national events in which he played a role. Inside and out, this is a fascinating house, well maintained by the Vermont Division for Historic Preservation and Friends of the Morrill Homestead. Check the website for frequent programs and events.

**Floating Bridge at Sunset Lake**, Pond Village. See Brookfield under *Towns and Villages* on page 228.

**Texas Falls**, Hancock. On VT 125 west of VT 100 in Hancock; a Green Mountain National Forest sign points to the road to the falls. It's a quarter-mile. The falls are an exceptional series of shoots and pools, rimmed by interesting rock formations. A short, steep (be careful) trail still leads down to the falls. A quarter-mile farther up the road is a pleasant riverside picnic area with grills and outhouses.

COVERED BRIDGES There are five covered bridges in Tunbridge: the **Cilley Bridge**, south of the junction of VT 110 with Strafford Road and built in 1883; the **Howe Bridge** (1879), east off VT 110 in South Tunbridge; and in North Tunbridge, the 1845 **Flint Bridge** and 1902 **Larkin Bridge**, both east of VT 110. The

# JOSEPH SMITH MEMORIAL

The Joseph Smith Memorial and Birthplace (802-763-7742), 357 LDS Lane (off Dairy Hill Road), South Royalton, is open year-round: May–October, 9–7 daily, 1:30–7 p.m. Sunday; otherwise closing at 5. A marker on VT 14 points up a steep, 2-mile hill to a complex maintained by the Church of Jesus Christ of the Latter-Day Saints. This is the site of the farm on which the Mormon Church founder was born in 1805 and where he lived until he was 10 years old. Each foot of a 38.5-foot-high granite obelisk marks a year in the life of the prophet, who was murdered by a mob in Carthage, Illinois, in 1844. Exhibits at the hilltop visitor center complex include paintings, sculpture, and a film; the property also offers picnic tables.

photogenic **Mill Bridge** (rebuilt) lies just north of the general store. Continuing north along VT 101, look for the 1883 **Moxley Bridge**, just off VT 110, 2.5 miles south of Chelsea. In Randolph, two multiple kingpost bridges, both built in 1904, are just off VT 14 between East Randolph and South Randolph.

SCENIC DRIVES **The Quickie Tour: Sharon to South Royalton via Strafford and Tunbridge** (22 miles). Take I-89 to Exit 2, Sharon, and climb VT 132 to Strafford, site of the **Justin Morrill Homestead** and the Town House. Continue up and over the hills and down into **Tunbridge**. If time permits, turn north on VT 110 for 5 miles and past three **covered bridges** to **Chelsea**. Otherwise, turn south on VT 110 for the 5 scenic miles back (past one covered bridge) to VT 14 at South Royalton and pick up I-89 again at Exit 3 in Royalton, or turn back down VT 14 to Sharon. En route you pass the turnoff for the **Joseph Smith Memorial.**

 **A Longer Loop: Randolph Center, Brookfield, Chelsea** (27 miles). At I-89, Exit 4 turn east into Randolph Center, then north along a glorious Ridge Road (marked TO BROOKFIELD) to VT 65 and hang a left to Pond Village with its floating bridge across Sunset Lake (see *Towns and Villages* on page 228). Then turn back to follow VT 65 east to VT 14, and then south 6 miles to East Randolph, and Chelsea Mountain Road east to VT 110, north for the mile into Chelsea; return south on 110 through Tunbridge, passing six covered bridges on the way back to VT 14 and I-89.

## ✳ To Do

BIKING **Green Mountain Bikes** (802-767-4464; greenmountainbikes.com), VT 100 in Rochester Village. A source of information about local trails in and beyond the national forest. Also rentals, sales, and repairs. Also check with the **Green Mountain National Forest Visitor Center** (*Guidance*) and see *Scenic Drives* above.

BOATING AND TUBING  While most of the White River is navigable in high water (May–August), the 20-mile stretch from Rochester to Stockbridge and Bethel is especially popular with canoeists, tubers, and kayakers. A good place to put in is at the cement bridge just south of Rochester. In Stockbridge, **Vermont River Tubing** (802-746-8106; vermontrivertubing.net), VT 100, just below the junction with VT 107: rentals, organized tubing trips, and shuttle service. Phone for river conditions. In the wake of 2011 Hurricane Irene, much of VT 107 has been rebuilt, offering more river pullouts and access. The **Sharon Trading Post** (802-763-7404), just off I-89, at the junction of VT 14 and VT 132, also rents tubes.

FISHING Trout abound at the junction of the Tweed and White rivers, downstream of Bethel, above Randolph, and below Royalton. Fly-fishing enthusiasts find the Bethel area good for large rainbow and brown trout, while below Royalton there are bass, spring walleye, and trout. **Bakers Pond** on VT 12 in Brookfield has a parking area and boat launch, good for trout fishing, and Brookfield's **Floating Bridge** in Pond Village is a popular fishing spot. Visitors are welcome at the **White River National Fish Hatchery** (802-234-5241) in Bethel, VT 107, near the junction of VT 12; it raises salmon for the Connecticut River restoration program. The **Roxbury State Fish Hatchery** (802-485-7568) in Roxbury raises brookies and Atlantic salmon, explaining some great fishing downstream.

GOLF **Montague Golf Club** (802-728-3806; montaguegold.com), 50 Randolph Avenue, Randolph. One of the oldest courses in Vermont, 18 holes. The Second Branch of the White River winds through it.

    **The White River Golf Club** (802-767-GOLF; whiterivergold.com), 3070 VT 100, Rochester. Nine holes, clubhouse with a restaurant serving lunch (dinner by arrangement). Open May–October. Affordable, great for families, and a historic and beautiful course.

HIKING **The Green Mountain National Forest** (see *Guidance* on page 226) harbors numerous trails. **Allis State Park**, Brookfield (off VT 12; see page 229). A 2.5-mile trail circles down through meadows and back up through woods. A trail leads from the picnic area to a fire tower with a great view.

PICNICKING **Brookfield Gulf**, VT 12 west of Brookfield. Picnic facility, nature trail.

    **Braintree Hill**, Braintree Hill Road (off VT 12A just west of downtown Randolph). A great picnic spot with an early cemetery and sweeping views to the White Mountains. Note the handsome Braintree Meeting House. In the GMNF, **Bingo Brook** in Rochester offers picnic sites with grills by a mountain stream, good for fishing and swimming.

    **VT 100 picnic sites** in Rochester beckon down by the White River; check at the GMNF visitor center. **Texas Falls** (see *Must See* on page 230), Hancock, offers picnic sites.

SWIMMING Ask locally about swimming holes in the First, Second, and Third Branches and the main stem of the White River. One of the deepest swimming holes is under the bridge in Stockbridge; just off VT 107, look for parking and a trail. In Randolph Center there is a man-made beach, a bathhouse, and a picnic area.

## ✳ Winter Sports

CROSS-COUNTRY SKIING AND SNOWSHOEING ✪ **Nordic Adventures** (802-767-3272), 3485 VT 100, south of Rochester Village. Dean Mendell offers a full line of cross-country and backcountry ski equipment and snowshoes. He offers rentals and lessons as well. He is also the go-to source for information about trails in the **GMNF** and beyond, including those maintained by **Rochester Area Ski Trail Association** (RASTA.org).

    **Strafford Nordic Center** (802-765-0016; straffordnordicskiing.com), 53 Rockbottom Road, Strafford. Check the website for conditions and directions. The lodge is at an elevation of 1,400 feet and the 30 km of trails through woods and open meadow climb to 1900 feet. They are groomed and tracked primarily for skating but an additional 10,000 km are untracked, designed for classic stride.

# ✳ Lodging

**INNS** **Huntington House Inn** (802-767-9140; huntingtonhouseinn.com), 19 Huntington Place, Rochester. Sited on Rochester's large, leafy park and dating from 1806, this is an inviting inn. There are six comfortable guest rooms (private baths) in the inn itself, and a former general store next door houses three luxurious, two-bedroom condo-style units, each with a full kitchen, dining area, and living room. Also see the **1806 Cocoa Pub** (*Dining Out* on page 236) and **Doc's Tavern** (*Eating Out* on page 238). Rates: $–$$ for inn rooms, $$ for condos.

**BED & BREAKFASTS** ✪ 🐾 **Green Trails Inn and Fork Shop** (802-276-3412), Pond Village, Brookfield. Open mid-May–November. This is a genuinely hospitable country inn, a handsome 1840 farmhouse at the heart of Pond Village. Innkeeper

Jane Doerfer is an accomplished cook and cookbook author. The eight attractive guest rooms have beds with high-quality mattresses and linens, well-chosen antiques, and books; three work well as family suites with their own entrances. Guests stroll across the road to Sunset Lake with its Floating Bridge, and there's swimming from the grassy little park, shaded by a willow tree. The gracious parlor and dining room overlook the pond. Reasonable rates include a generous buffet-style breakfast, with fresh fruit, local cheeses, and a hot dish, maybe sausage apple cobbler. Inquire about cooking classes, solo rates, and whole-house rental (it sleeps 18); the neighboring **Fork Shop**, usually rented as a whole, was built in 1839 as a pitchfork factory, with a waterfall churning musically down along one side. It offers five bedrooms and features a common room with walled-in windows, also a private patio on the lake. Rates $ per couple.

GREEN TRAILS INN, BROOKFIELD  CHRISTINA TREE

**FARMS** *Note:* **Liberty Hill Farm,** described in the sidebar, is an outstanding farmstay.

**Devil's Den Farm Homestay Bed & Breakfast** (802-685-4582), 396 VT 110, Chelsea. Rhoda and Bill Ackerman welcome guests to the rambling farmhouse built by Rhoda's grandparents. There's plenty of sitting space inside and out on the flower- and rocker-lined porch, and guests have access to the kitchen as well; five bedrooms, all are furnished with family antiques, quilts, and hand-woven rag rugs. Rhoda and Bill are on hand in the farmstead's new addition and offer breakfast, if requested. The farm includes 65 acres of fields, pastures, and woods and includes the cave for which it's named. $.

**Grand View Farm** (802-685-4693; grandviewfarmvt.com), 1638 Scales Hill Road, Washington. Kim Goodling and her husband, Chuck, raise Gotland sheep on their hilltop farm. The B&B part of the farmhouse is divided from the family house by the kitchen. Dating from the 1700s, it consists of a sitting room and two bedrooms, one with twin beds and the other with a four-poster queen. Breakfast can be full or self-serve, continental. $$. Inquire about felting classes.

🖉 **Four Springs Farm, Campground and Learning Center** (802-763-7296; fourspringsfarm.com), 776 Gee Road, Royalton. Jinny Hardy Cleland raises fruit, vegetables, herbs, flowers, and poultry on her 70-acre farm, open to the public for exploration, programs, celebrations, and cabin and tent camping (just eight privately located sites, a central wash house, and picnic pavilion). Visitors are welcome to tag along on chores, walk the trails, explore the streams, or be a part of one of the custom programs set up for families and groups who stay on the farm. $.

**CAMPGROUNDS** **Chittenden Brook Campground in the Green Mountain National Forest** (802-767-4261), 5.3 miles

BARN AT DEVIL'S DEN HOMESTAY BED & BREAKFAST  CHRISTINA TREE

# VERMONT'S BEST FAMILY FARM STAY

**L**iberty Hill Farm (802-767-3926; libertyhillfarm.com), 511 Liberty Hill, Rochester. This is the real thing: a working dairy farm with more than 100 Holsteins, set in a broad meadow, backed by mountains. Its much-photographed 1890s red barn, one of the most photographed in Vermont, was built by Dr. Charles Wesley Emerson, founder of Boston's Emerson College. There's a capacious white-clapboard 1825 farmhouse, and, best of all, there is farm wife-host par excellence Beth Kennett. Since 1984, Beth and her husband Bob have been welcoming guests of all ages. Kids quickly get to know the cows, each with a name tag in her ear. They can help milk, bottle-feed the calves, and collect eggs. Meals are served family style, and dinner is as delicious as it is prodigious, much of it sourced from the garden and/or

R. M. EMMY

baked from scratch; ice cream is homemade. There are seven guest rooms (five with queen beds, one with two single beds, and a room with four single beds) and four shared baths; families can spread into two rooms sharing a sitting room and bath. In summer you can hear the gurgle of the White River (good for trout fishing as well as for swimming and tubing). Added to these options is **Harvest House**, a walk across the meadow. Built in 1782, it retains its eighteenth-century feel and four hearths but offers three comfortable bedrooms, a contemporary kitchen, and gracious common space. It accommodates overflow from the farm and can be rented as a whole. $$

**LIBERTY HILL FARM BARNS** COURTESY OF LIBERTY HILL FARM

west of Rochester on VT 73. The 17 camp-sites are fitted with picnic tables and grills; there are hand-operated water pumps and vault toilets. The surround-ing forest provides good fishing, hiking, and birding. No trailers over 18 feet. No hookups or showers. *Note:* Primitive camping is permitted almost everywhere in the GMNF.

**Allis State Park** (802-276-3175; vtstateparks.com). Open mid-May–Labor Day. Named for Wallace Allis, who deeded his Bear Mountain Farm to the state as a campground and recre-ational area. Sited on the summit of Bear Mountain, it includes a picnic area and trail to the fire tower, as well as 18 tent and 8 lean-to sites, each with a picnic table and fireplace. Hot showers but no hookups. Handy to several good fishing ponds.

## ✳ Where to Eat

DINING OUT ✪ **Wild Roots Restaurant** (802-763-0440; wildrootsvt.com), 5615 VT 14, South Royalton. Reservations suggested. Housed in a vintage, 1818 brick tavern (formerly the Fox Stand Inn), this gem of a restaurant gets rave reviews for genuine farm-to-table din-ners. The a la carte menu includes start-ers "to share," tantalizing fish, meat, and vegetarian entrée choices and sides, local beers, and spirits. The dining room seats just 20 and is drawing patrons from throughout the region. $$–$$$.

### IN RANDOLPH

**Black Krim Tavern** (802-728-6776; theblackkrimtavern.com), 21 Merchants Row. Open for dinner Tues.–Sat. Named for a variety of tomato, this is a small, colorful restaurant with a weekly-changing menu. The focus is on fresh, creative, and locally sourced ingredients. Cocktails, local brews on tap. $$.

✪ **Saap** (802-565-8292; saap restaurant.com), 50 Randolph Avenue.

Open Mon.–Sat. noon–9. Not your ordi-nary Thai restaurant. The ambiance in this spacious, hilltop restaurant is casual and pleasant and the owners are well-established Vermont chef Steve Morgan and his wife, Rung, an experienced Bangkok chef. Both have a passion for the wild, fresh, and fiery flavors of Thailand's northeaster Isaan region and both are sticklers for local as well as authentic Thai ingredients. Full bar. $.

✪ **One Main Tap & Grill** (802-865-8117; onemaintg.com) 2 Merchants Row. Open daily from 4 p.m. An attractive space with seasonal sidewalk tables. Local beers are a specialty, with more than a dozen on tap, as well as other not-so-local brews plus Citizen (hard) Cider and a thoughtful choice of wines. The food isn't an afterthought either: from burgers to Winner Winner (local) Chicken dinner. Entrées $–$$.

### IN ROCHESTER

**1806 Cocoa Pub at the Hunting-ton House Inn** (802-767-9140; huntingtonhouseinn.com), Huntington Place, Rochester. Open for dinner Fri.–Sun. This small restaurant with a formal feel has a seriously sweet menu, from cocoa-rubbed tenderloin to chocolate fondue. $–$$.

### ELSEWHERE

**Stone Soup Restaurant** (802-765-4301), 7 Brook Road, Strafford. Reservations requested. Open Thurs.–Sun. 6–9 p.m. No credit cards. There is no sign outside this distinguished old house in Strafford Village, just down from the striking 1799 Town House. The chef-owners continue to earn rave reviews for signature dishes ranging from quail to scallops to Bur-mese stew. $$–$$$.

**Tozier's Restaurant** (802-234-9400; toziersrestaurantvt.com), VT 107 west of Bethel. Open May–October, in summer 11–8, Thurs.–Sun. in shoulder seasons. A classic road-food stop with pine paneling and a river view. Seafood (mostly fried, some broiled) is a dinner specialty, along with a turkey dinner. Take-out window for ice cream and basics, picnic tables overlooking the river. $–$$$.

**Tessie's Tavern** (802-392-8042; tessiestavern.com), 88 North Road (just off VT 107), west of downtown Bethel. Closed Monday. Housed on the ground floor of a Victorian mansion, this place offers an eclectic menu to satisfy all palates. $–$$$.

EATING OUT  Road food, listed geographically from south to north, off I-89.

## IN SOUTH ROYALTON

**Worthy Burger** (802-763-2575; worthyvermont.com), 56 Rainbow Street. Open from 4 p.m. Wed., Thurs., from 11 a.m. Fri.–Sun. Styled as "a craft beer and burger bar" and housed in the former railroad freight house, this is a hot spot for this town full of law students. It's across the tracks from the green, and more than a dozen microbrews were on tap when we stopped by.

**5 Olde Tavern & Grill** (802-763-8600; fiveolde.com), 192 Chelsea Street. Open daily 11–11. A casual, student-geared coffeehouse/pub, good for pizza, burgers, and quesadillas along with veggie stir-fry and ribs. Check out the salmon burgers.

✪ **Chelsea Station Restaurant** (802-763-8685), 108 Chelsea Street. Open 6–3. Look for the striped awning and houseplants in the window. Inside there's a counter and row of deep booths. Most people know one another, but visitors feel welcome. Better-than-average diner food, freshly baked bread; on our last visit the soup was made from fresh, local asparagus.

## AT I-89, EXIT 3

✪ **Eaton's Sugar House, Inc.** (802-763-8809). Located at the junction of VT 14

and VT 107 in Royalton, just off I-89, Exit 3. Open daily 7–2. Don't be put off by the funky exterior. This is a good old-fashioned family restaurant featuring pancakes and local syrup, sandwiches, burgers, and reasonably priced daily specials. Try the turkey club made with freshly carved turkey on homemade bread. Vermont maple syrup, cheese, and other products are also sold.

## IN BETHEL

✪ **Bethel Village Sandwich Shop** (802-234-9910), 269 Main Street. Open except Mondays for breakfast through mid-afternoon, until 6 Fri., Sat. David Sambor's pleasant café offers full breakfast and lunch with special house-baked muffins—maybe raspberry cheesecake—each morning, and hot lunch specials, from-scratch soups, also dinners-to-go. On a day in October, it was pumpkin-ginger soup with a steak, avocado, and cheese wrap.

🍴 **Cockadoodle Pizza Café** (802-234-9666; cockadoodlepizza.com), 235 Main Street. Open daily for lunch and dinner, serving a wide choice of mouth-watering signature pizzas plus panini and sandwiches on "rustic rolls," each named for a different Vermont town. Closed Sundays.

## ALONG VT 107

✪ 🍴 **Creek House Diner** (802-234-9191), 1837 River Street, Bethel, at junction of VT 107 and VT 12. Open daily 7 a.m.–8 p.m. A clean, handy road-food stop with booths, a salad bar, liver and onions, prime rib, friendly service, beer, and wine. Great daily specials. Children's menu.

## AT I-89, EXIT 4, RANDOLPH

**Chef's Market** (802-728-4202; chefsmarketvt.com), 839 VT 12 South. Open weekdays 9–6, Sat. 9–5, Sun. 10–3. Featuring local and organic produce, this is also a source of great sandwiches and prepared foods. New in 2017: **Chef's Downtown Deli** (802-565-8130), 29 North Main Street, open 7–4. Hung with local art, a cheerful, satisfying stop for breakfast and lunch.

### ALONG VT 100

**Doc's Tavern at the Huntington House Inn** (802-767-9140; huntingtonhouseinn .com), 19 Huntington Place, Rochester. Open except Tuesdays. Housed in a newly renovated barn, this is an informal sports bar with booths, a pool table, a pub menu, and a dozen local beers on tap.

✪ **Rochester Café & Country Store** (802-767-4302; rochestercafe.com), 100 Main Street, Rochester Village. Breakfast 7–11:30, lunch until 5. Good fries and burgers, pleasant atmosphere. Great soda fountain, booths, and the town gathering place. Try the maple cream pie.

✪ **Sandy's Books & Bakery** (802-767-4258), 30 North Main Street (VT 100), Rochester. Open 7:30–6. Just north of the gas pumps. Good in the morning for espresso, freshly made whole-grain breads and muffins, and at lunch for soups, salads, and sandwiches, vegetarian choices, cookies all day, beer, and wine. Light dinner served but only until 6.

## ✳ Entertainment

### IN RANDOLPH

**Chandler Center for the Arts** (802-728-6464; chandler-arts.org), 71–73 Main Street, Randolph. This community-based arts organization, housed in **Chandler Music Hall,** includes a 575-seat theater with outstanding acoustics and handsome stenciling. It's open year-round for performances that include chamber music, traditional and heritage music, folksingers, family performances, and the Vermont Symphony Orchestra, as well as several annual festivals. **Playhouse Theatre** (802-728-4012; playhouseflicks.webplus.net), 11 South Main Street, Randolph. The oldest movie house in the state, updated for 3D and surround sound and first-run flicks. Check the website for programs and ticketing.

### IN ROCHESTER

Check out the **Rochester Chamber Music Society Concert Series** (802-767-9234; rcmsvt.org) schedule and the **Summer Park Concert Series,** Sunday evenings. **The White River Valley Players** (whiterivervalleyplayers.org), a community theater, stages spring and fall performances in the high school.

## ✳ Selective Shopping

**BigTown Gallery** (802-767-9670; bigtowngallery.com), 99 North Main Street, Rochester Village. Open Wed.–Sat. 10–5, Sun. 11–4. This exceptional gallery showcases an eclectic, ever-changing mix of paintings and sculpture. It's also a setting for piano rehearsals and plays performed in the backyard amphitheater.

**Green Mountain Glassworks** (802-767-4547; michaeleganglass.com), 5523 VT 100, Granville. Open Wed.–Mon. 9–5 most of the year. Don't pass up this exceptional roadside studio and gallery. Vermont natives Michael and Angela Egan shape Venetian-style freehand-blown glass into spectacular vases, pitchers, and a variety of artworks in glass and reasonably priced glass earrings.

**Sandy's Books & Bakery** (see *Eating Out*). Librarian Sandy Lincoln has expanded her well chosen line of new and used books in the inviting "Bookery" beside her popular cafe, which also sells a line of Vermont Soap Organics, crafted items, and more.

FARMS **Neighborly Farms of Vermont** (802-728-4700; neighborlyfarms.com), 1362 Curtis Road, Randolph Center.

Open Mon.–Thurs. 8–2. Rob and Linda Dimmick and their three children run an organic dairy and make organic cheeses that they sell at the farm store and through area stores. Visitors are welcome to see the cows and to watch cheesemaking (call ahead for days/hours) through the viewing window in the store, which also features products from other local farms.

**Vermont Technical College Farm** (802-728-1000), VT 66 east off I-89, Exit 4, Randolph Center. Tour the sugarhouse, apple orchard (pick your own in-season), and dairy barn.

**Maple Ridge Sheep Farm** (802-728-3081; mrsf.com) in Braintree, said to be the oldest and largest Shetland sheep farm in the country, produces fleece, machine-washable sheepskin, yarn, knit and woven items, and meat. Call first.

**Sunshine Valley Organic Berry Farm** (802-767-3989), 129 Ranger Road, Rochester. Organic blueberries and raspberries, pre-picked or PYO in-season.

Check out **Green Mountain Girls Farm** in Northfield, offering lodging as well as a variety of vegetables and herbs. **Fat Toad Farm**, in Brookfield, is a family-run business that produces goat's-milk caramel sauces. **L. H. Stowell & Son Christmas Trees** in Brookfield is a 200-acre Christmas tree farm offering choose-and-cut trees, and **Pagoda Pond Gardens**, high on a hill in East Braintree, features hardy varieties of daylilies in display gardens.

## ✷ Special Events

*Last Saturday in January:* **Brookfield Ice Harvest Festival**—ice cutting, ice sculpting, hot food, sledding, and skating.

*March:* **Maple Open House Weekend** (vermontmaple.org), local sugarhouses.

*July:* **July 4 parades** in Strafford and Rochester, a bigger one in Randolph (usually over 5,000 spectators), with food and crafts.

*July–August* Band concerts: South Royalton (srtownband.org) Thursday evenings and in Rochester (rochestervermont.org) Sunday evenings.

*September:* **New World Festival** (newworldfestival.com), Sunday before Labor Day at Chandler Music Hall in Randolph, a major gathering of traditional New England and Celtic musicians, also food and crafts. **Tunbridge World's Fair** (tunbridgefair.com), Tunbridge, four days at midmonth, ongoing for more than 130 years in a superb setting, definitely one of the country's most colorful agricultural fairs, with horse and oxen pulling, contra dancing, sheepdog trials, livestock and produce judging, horse racing, amusement rides, pig races, pony rides, and more. **Harvest Fair** (rochestervermont.org) in the park in Rochester, second Saturday.

*Late September–early October:* **Vermont Sheep and Wool Festival** (vtsheepandwoolfest.com) first weekend, at the Tunbridge Fairgrounds.

# SUGARBUSH/MAD RIVER VALLEY

Seven miles wide and named for the river down its center, the Mad River Valley is walled on the west by some of the highest peaks in the Green Mountains, with meadows stretching across the valley floor to the Roxbury Range in the east. In summer and fall, visitors hike the Long Trail, soar in gliders above the Valley, mountain bike on ski trails and high woods roads, horseback ride, fish and swim in the Mad River, or play golf and tennis. In August, the month-long Vermont Festival of the Arts offers daily events.

Mad River Glen began attracting skiers to this farming and lumbering valley in 1948, but the look and lifestyle of the present community center on its ski areas. The '60s brought ski-struck urbanites to Sugarbush, Glen Ellen (the two have since merged), and Mad River Glen. They played polo in addition to building an airport and gliding school, specialty shops, and fine restaurants. Young architects designed some of New England's first trailside homes and clustered condominium complexes. This commitment to efficient design means several thousand visitors can bed down here on any given night, but it's far from obvious where.

Physically just 4 miles apart, Sugarbush and Mad River Glen are nothing alike. By the 1990s it had become clear that northern New England's natural snowfall is

MAD RIVER SWIMMING HOLE OFF MEADOWS ROAD IN WAITSFIELD  PAT GOUDEY O'BRIEN

too fickle a base for the big business that skiing had become for the ski industry to depend on. With limited artificial snowmaking, Mad River Glen, the "ski it if you can" mountain, kept its demands and lift prices modest, becoming the country's first cooperatively owned ski area (divided among some 2,000 shareholders). It also remains the only area in the East that bars snowboarders, featuring telemarking and animal tracking instead.

Sugarbush has its own snowmaking pond and has upgraded its snowmaking system to be more energy efficient, with no man-made cover on the majority of its 111 trails, remaining one of the most ecologically sensitive of the East's mega ski resorts. Back in the '90s, when its multi-resort-owner proposed building a signature "grand" hotel at the base of Lincoln Peak, the community balked. Sugar-

MAD RIVER VALLEY CHAMBER OF COMMERCE VISITOR CENTER, BRIDGE STREET, WAITSFIELD  MADRIVER VALLEY.COM

bush Resort is now owned by a locally based partnership that maintains vibrant local connections.

Christmas week through February is high season. Midweek during this same period is cheaper and far quieter. Ditto for March, when the man-made snow base at Sugarbush is deep and weekend crowds have eased. By mid-April, skiing is done. May and June appeal to birders (spring migration before trees are in full leaf). Warren's Fourth of July parade and celebration, small but famous, kicks off a series of summer events. As noted above, thanks to the gap roads this is an ideal hub for foliage season. After the leaves fall it's dead until mid-December.

With direct links to the Champlain Valley via scenic roads through the Appalachian and Lincoln gaps on the west, this is a logical lodging and dining hub from which to explore some of Vermont's most magnificent and varied landscapes. Dining and shopping are outstanding but uncrowded.

GUIDANCE **Mad River Valley Chamber of Commerce** (802-496-3409; madrivervalley .com), 4403 Main Street, Waitsfield. The visitor center at the corner of Bridge Street is open Wed.–Fri. 9–5, Sat.–Sun. noon–5.

**Green Mountain National Forest Rochester Ranger District Station and Visitor Center** (802-767-4261), VT 100 in Rochester. Open Saturdays from late May to early October. While this excellent information center is 25 miles south of Warren, it's worth knowing it's there (see "White River Valleys" on page 226) as a resource for exploring much of the area immediately west and south of the Valley.

GETTING THERE *By air:* Burlington International Airport is 45 miles away; see "Burlington Region" for carriers.

*By bus and train:* Montpelier is the nearest Vermont Transit/Greyhound stop. Waterbury, 12 miles north of Waitsfield, is the closest Amtrak station.

*By car:* Valley residents will tell you that the quickest route from points south is I-89 to Randolph, 15 miles up VT 12A to Roxbury, then 8 miles over the Roxbury Gap to

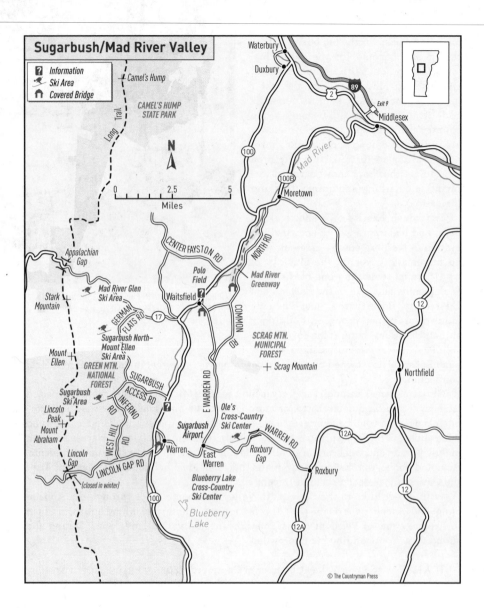

**Sugarbush/Mad River Valley**

Warren. This is also the most scenic route (the view from the top of the gap is spectacular), but this steep road can be treacherous in winter. In snow, play it safe and take I-89 to Middlesex, Exit 9, then VT 100B for 13 miles south to Waitsfield.

GETTING AROUND During ski season Green Mountain Transit's **Mad Bus** fleet circles among condos at the top of Sugarbush Access Road, as well as restaurants and nightspots around the valley. Free 26-passenger buses link the Valley floor to all three mountain base areas, running daily on a regular schedule. Evenings and some late weekend routes, too. See madrivervalley.com/about/mad-bus for details.

**Alpine Limousine** (802-793-3543) and **C&L Taxi** (802-496-4056) offer local and long-distance service.

## ✳ Towns and Villages

The Mad River Valley includes **Moretown** (population 1,658) to the north and **Fayston** (population 1,353), an elusive town (it's easy to get to, just hard to find!) without a center that was an important lumber industry presence into the early twentieth century. It's home to the former Mount Ellen (now part of Sugarbush Resort) and Mad River Glen ski areas, and to inns and restaurants along VT 17 and the German Flats Road.

**Warren Village.** The village center of the long-established farm town of Warren (population 1,700) is a compact clapboard cluster of town hall, historic meetinghouse, bandstand, and general store across from an inn. The village has had a recent face-lift, but still looks very much like it did in the 1950s when VT 100 passed through its center, but the effect of Sugarbush, the ski resort that's way up an access road at the other end of town, has been total. The **Pitcher Inn**'s plain face masks an elegant restaurant and some of the most elaborate (and expensive) themed rooms in Vermont; the **Warren Store** (once a stagecoach inn) stocks a mix of gourmet food and upscale clothing and gifts. Arts, antiques, and crafts are within an easy walk, and a covered bridge spans the Mad River. The village is the setting for one of Vermont's most colorful July 4 parades.

**Waitsfield** (population 1,719) is the Valley's commercial center, with two small, well-designed shopping centers flanking VT 100 on land that was farmed until the 1960s. The main shopping area is called Irasville, but that's just the area designation. It's still Waitsfield. The historic district north on VT 100, a gathering of eighteenth- and nineteenth-century buildings, includes a library and steepled church, and more shopping on and around Bridge Street (leading to the Great Eddy Covered Bridge). Larger and denser than it first looks, the village offers a sophisticated mix of boutiques and services and several first-rate restaurants. Changing historical exhibits from the Waitsfield Historical Society (waitsfieldhistoricalsociety.com) are displayed in the General Wait House, which shares office space with The Mad River Path Association. Benjamin Wait, one of Vermont's famed Rodgers' Rangers, fought in the French and Indian Wars and the Revolutionary War before founding the town at age 53 in 1789. He later argued with fellow settlers over where to put the town common. He preferred it close to where the commercial center is today; the original common remains high on Joslin Hill Road. Check out the **Madsonian Museum of Industrial Design** (802-496-6611; madsonian.org), 45 Bridge Street. Open Fri.–Sun., noon–4, with exhibits ranging from cars to toasters, a project of Valley architect David Sellers.

## ✳ Must See

In winter, the Valley's magnets are its alpine and cross-country ski areas, but summers are busy with activities to pursue. See below for more descriptions and at **madriver valley.com/vt/activities.**

## ✳ To Do

### SUMMER/FALL

BICYCLING—ROAD & MOUNTAIN The area's outstanding scenery and variety of hard-topped roads have long drawn serious cyclists. A network of technical single-track trails—a total of 60 miles over a vertical variance of 3,000 feet—has gained traction in mountain biking circles. Sugarbush Resort's lift-serviced trails connect with a Valley-wide network. **Mad River Riders**, a local organization with both mountain and roadie members, connects about 30 miles of trails through a mix of public forest and private farmland, and lists hundreds of miles of road rides through the valley and to nearby landscapes (madriverriders.com). Their 5-mile network at **Blueberry Lake**, banked and pitched for beginners as well as for experienced riders, is a local favorite because you can ride and then cool off in the lake. Another fave is the **Revolution Trail**, looping from Lareau Farm into the Camel's Hump State Forest. For maps and events, check the website for **Sugarbush Adventure Center** (sugarbush.com) about offers on rentals with pads and helmets as well as clinics, kids' and adult mountain bike camps, and lift service to its trails. For questions and repairs, check with **Clearwater Sports** (802-496-2708; clearwatersports.com), **Infinite Sports** (802-496-3343; infinitesportsvt.com), or **Stark Mountain Bike Works** (802-496-4800). The possible tours for road cyclists are spectacularly varied—from quiet river roads to two of the highest gaps (mountain passes) in Vermont. This is the hub of the four-day Labor Day weekend **Green Mountain Stage Race** (gmsr.info), which attracts some of the country's most serious cyclists. Check madrivervalley.com for suggested routes, along with those listed here under *Scenic Drives*. **Fit Werx** (802-496-7570; fitwerx.com), 4312 Main Street, Waitsfield, is nationally famed for fitting serious cyclists to their bikes.

CANOEING AND KAYAKING **Clearwater Sports** (802-496-2708; clearwatersports .com), 4147 Main Street, Waitsfield. Barry Bender offers rentals and learn-to-canoe, -kayak and -stand-up programs including guided river trips and paddleboard yoga. Tubing rentals are available, as are put-ins and pickups. The local paddling pond is man-made **Blueberry Lake** in Warren.

FISHING Numerous streams offer good fly-fishing. The chamber of commerce keeps a list of half a dozen guide services. Vermont fishing licenses are required for anyone 15 and older, and can be obtained at the **Village Grocery** (802-496-3354), Waitsfield; **Moretown General Store** (802-496-6580); and **Bisbee Hardware** (802-496-3635), Waitsfield. **Fly Fish Vermont Service** (802-253-3964) in Stowe provides guided trips. Rob Shannon, based at the Fly Rod Shop in Stowe (802-253-7346; flyrodshop.com), offers year-round instructional, guided tours.

FITNESS CENTERS *See* **Sugarbush Resort** sidebar on page 248.
   **Bridges Family Resort and Tennis Club** (802-583-2922; bridgesresort.com), Sugarbush Access Road, Warren. A year-round health and tennis club with indoor and outdoor tennis, heated pools, fitness center, hot tub, and sauna.

FOR FAMILIES *See* **Sugarbush Resort** sidebar on page 248. Summer day camps are also offered at **The Bridges Family Resort and Tennis Club** (802-583-2922), Warren. For ages 13 and up, there's a weeklong **Youth Soaring Camp** (802-496-2290) at **Sugarbush Airport** (see *Soaring* on page 245). **Mad River Glen** offers nature-geared day camps in summer. Climbing wall for anyone over 6 years old (instruction available at the **Valley Rock Gym**, 802-583-6700).

GOLF *See* **Sugarbush Resort** sidebar on page 248.

HIKING Pick up a copy of *Trails, Paths & Long Trail Hikes Guide*, available at the chamber of commerce, which unlocks the area's many superb hiking secrets.
   The **Long Trail** runs along the ridge of the Green Mountains and is easily accessible from three places: two gap roads and the Sugarbush Bravo chairlift. From Lincoln Gap

Road, the gap itself is 4.7 miles west of VT 100. Hike a short way south to Sunset Ledge for a view of the Champlain Valley and Adirondacks. A more popular hike is north from the gap (start early; parking is limited) over to the Battell Shelter and on to Mount Abraham (5 miles round-trip), a 4,006-foot summit with spectacular views west, south as far as Killington Peak, and north as far as Belvidere Mountain. From Mount Abraham north to Lincoln Peak (accessible by Sugarbush chairlift) and on to Mount Ellen (4,083 feet) is largely above tree line. The 3,637-foot General Stark Mountain to the north is best accessed (still a steep 2.6-mile hike) from VT 17 at Appalachian Gap. For details about shelters, contact the **Green**

SWIMMING AT WARREN FALLS   PAT GOUDEY O'BRIEN

**Mountain Club** (802-244-7037; greenmountainclub.org). **Mill Brook Inn**'s Joan Gorman also recommends beginning 2.1 miles up Tucker Hill Road at the small parking area (on the left) at the CAMEL'S HUMP STATE FOREST sign. Follow the blue blazes through the stand of pines known as "the Enchanted Forest" to the top of Dana Hill Road (approximately one-hour round-trip, good for skiing and snowshoeing).

**Mad River Glen** (802-496-3551; madriverglen.com) offers a full schedule of guided backcountry trips and bird-watching tours. The ski trails are a popular route up to the summit of Stark Mountain, with spectacular views west to Lake Champlain and the Adirondacks. Also see *Walking and Running* on page 246 for the **Mad River Path Association** trails.

HORSEBACK RIDING  **Vermont Icelandic Horse Farm** (802-496-7141; icelandichorses .com), 3061 North Fayston Road, Waitsfield. Year-round. These strong, pony-size mounts brought to Iceland by Vikings are still relatively rare in this country. Karen Winhold offers one- and two-hour, half- and full-day trail rides and (seasonal) inn-to-inn treks from her stable. The horses have an unusually smooth gait (faster than a walk, gentler than a trot).

ROCK CLIMBING  See the **Valley Rock Gym** (802-583-6700), under *For Families*, on page 244.

SOARING  **Sugarbush Soaring** (802-496-2290; sugarbushsoaring.org), Warren. Open daily May–October. One of the East's prime spots for riding thermal and ridge waves, solo and private glider lessons, rides, vacations are available for all ages. Come to watch.

SPAS  **MadRiver Massage** (802-496-5638; madrivermassage.com), Starch House overlooking the Mill Brook, VT 100, Waitsfield (just north of the VT 17 junction). Open daily 10–5, Sundays seasonally. A full range of massage, including shiatsu, reflexology, Reiki, and "stress-diffuser," plus body and bath products.

SWIMMING  South of Warren Village, the Mad River becomes a series of dramatic falls and whirlpools cascading through a gorge. The most secluded swimming hole is by

MAD RIVER SWIMMING HOLE AT WARD ACCESS AREA ON VT 100B IN MORETOWN PAT GOUDEY O'BRIEN

the **Bobbin Mill** (the first right off VT 100 after Lincoln Gap Road, heading south); park by the gravel pit and follow the path through the pines to a series of pools, all icy cold. Ask locally about **Warren Falls** and the best spot for skinny-dipping. The **Lareau Farm swimming hole** (now a town park) in the Mad River, south of Waitsfield on VT 100, is best for kids. **Blueberry Lake** in Warren is now owned by the Green Mountain National Forest; the **Ward Fishing Access area** on VT 100B in Moretown is another good bet. **Bristol Falls** is just about 10 miles from Warren via Lincoln Gap Road. The **Sugarbush Sports Center** features a large, L-shape outdoor pool with adjacent changing facilities, café, bar, and Jacuzzi; **The Bridges Family Resort and Tennis Club** offers indoor and outdoor pools and swimming lessons. Many inns also have outdoor pools. The **Punch Bowl** swimming hole off VT 100 north of Warren is clothing-optional; inquire.

TENNIS See **The Bridges Family Resort and Tennis Club** (802-583-2922) under *Fitness* and *For Families*. Also see **Sugarbush Health and Racquet Club**, in the sidebar on page 248.

WALKING AND RUNNING The **Mad River Path Association** (madriverpath.com) maintains several evolving recreation paths in the Valley, namely: the **Warren Path**, beginning near Brooks Field at Warren Elementary School (Brook Road, Warren); the **Millbrook Path** in Fayston, running through the woods (blue blazes) between Millbrook Inn and Tucker Hill Lodge, up across German Flats Road to the Inn at Mad River Barn; the **Mad River Greenway**, following the Mad River from a parking area on Meadow Road; and the **Village Path**, beginning at Fiddlers' Green and heading south to the Irasville Cemetery and beyond. The Association hosts the annual Mad Dash, an eclectic collection of walks and races for all comers. See madriverpath.com for details.

WEDDINGS The Mad River Valley area probably represents the state's largest concentration of wedding venues and related services. Look for information from the chamber of commerce at madrivervalley.com/vermont-wedding.

## Winter Sports

CROSS-COUNTRY AND SNOWSHOEING **Ole's Cross-Country Center** (802-496-3430; olesxc.com), 2355 Airport Road, Warren. More than 30 miles of groomed trails radiate out across the meadows and into the woods with elevations ranging from 1,120 to 1,640 feet. Reservations requested for lessons and tours. The center is downstairs in a small airport building.

**Blueberry Lake Cross-Country Ski Center** (802-496-6687; blueberrylakeskivt.com), 424 Plunkton Road, Warren. A hidden treasure, not far from Ole's on the east side of the

Valley, this is a homey, old-style touring center with snacks, drinks, and a wood-fired hearth as well as rentals and some 30 km of secluded and protected trails with elevations of 1,300–1,500 feet, groomed to skating width, set single-track.

**Clearwater Sports** (802-496-2708; clearwatersports.com), VT 100, Waitsfield, offers rentals, along with custom and group tours, backcountry skis, and "skins" for attempting local stretches of the Catamount Trail (below).

## LOCAL TRAILS

**Puddledock** in Granville Gulf State Reservation on VT 100, south of Warren, has 3.5 miles of ungroomed trails marked with red metal triangles; a map is available at the registration box.

**Catamount Trail** (catamounttrail.org). Check the guidebook (see *What's Where* on page 28) and website for stretches of the trail in the Valley. The most popular begins at the Battleground condominiums on VT 17 and climbs steadily uphill to the Beaver Ponds in the **Phen Basin Wilderness** area. Also see **Stark Mountain by Snowshoe** in the **Mad River Glen** sidebar on page 252. Stop at the visitor center at the corner of VT 100 and Bridge Street for more options.

ICE SKATING **The Skatium** (802-496-8845) at Mad River Green Shopping Center in Waitsfield (lighted) offers rentals, also available from neighboring **Inverness Ski Shop** (802-496-3343); free day and night skating on the groomed hockey rink at **Brooks Recreation Field** off Brook Road in Warren.

SNOWMOBILING Eighty miles of local trails through forests and across fields are maintained by the **Mad River Ridge Runners**; snowmobile registration can be purchased at **Kenyon's Store**, VT 100, Waitsfield. No rentals.

SCENIC DRIVES **East Warren Road**. If you miss this road, you miss the heart of the Valley. From Bridge Street in Waitsfield Village, cross the covered bridge, bear right onto East Warren Road, and continue the 6 miles to East Warren. The Green Mountains are set back across open farmland, and views stretch across the valley to the ski resorts. For a full view of the Valley, take the Roxbury Gap Road up to the pullout (be careful, it's steep and has few places to turn around). From East Warren, continue down 2 miles to Warren Village and VT 100.

**Bragg Hill Road**. The views from this peerless old farm road are unrivaled across pastures and narrow valley cut by the Mill Brook to Mount Ellen. Begin at Bragg Hill Road (off VT 100 north of the VT 17 junction) and drive uphill, continue as it turns to dirt, and follow it around (bearing left); it turns into Number 9 Road and rejoins VT 17.

**Granville Gulf** (see the map in "The White River Valleys" on page 227). Drive VT 100 south from Warren and up into a dark, narrow, twisting pass, the heart of the Granville Gulf State Reservation. At the height-of-land, the Mad River begins

A BARRED OWL NEAR BLUEBERRY LAKE CONTEMPLATES HIS WORLD IN THE HILLS OVER WARREN  PAT GOUDEY O'BRIEN

# WINTER, SUMMER, AND FALL AT SUGARBUSH

**S**ugarbush Resort (802-583-6300; 800-53-SUGAR; sugarbush.com), 1840 Sugarbush Access Road, Warren. With two mountains, sixteen lifts, nearly thirty wooded areas, and 111 trails, Sugarbush is one of New England's biggest ski destinations. The primary base area for the resort is Lincoln Peak Village at Sugarbush South with the barn-red and Clay Brook Hotel as its centerpiece. Ski services are in the Farmhouse and kids' programs, in the Schoolhouse. The Mount Ellen base area is less extensive but user-friendly and a good place to begin on a busy weekend. Mount Ellen is the resort's highest lift-accessed peak and offers varied terrain, expansive views, and the Reimergasse Terrain Park (for riders and freestyle skiers). The two base areas are connected by chairlift and sandwich the Slide Brook Basin, with over 2,000 acres of backcountry. There is also an 18-hole Robert Trent Jones Sr.-designed golf course, downhill and cross-country mountain biking, and hiking along Vermont's Long Trail.

*Lifts:* 16: 10 quads, 2 triples, 1 doubles, and 3 surface. The resort typically runs 9–4 on weekdays and 8–4 on weekends/holidays.

*Trails:* 111 trails and 28 wooded areas: 484 on-trail acres plus another 97 wooded area acres.

*Vertical drop:* 2,600 feet. *Snowmaking:* 70 percent of terrain.

*Facilities:* At Lincoln Peak, the Gate House, Schoolhouse (children's programs), and Farmhouse lodges offer cafeterias, lounges, ski shops, rentals, and restaurants; the centerpiece here is the slope-side Clay Brook Hotel and Residences. Pisten Bully access to Allyn's Lodge on Lincoln Peak for dinner and for Powder Morning First Tracks. *Sugarbush Ski and Ride School:* Headed by Terry Barbour and John Egan, the emphasis is on learning by doing. Clinics, special teen program; women's clinics, guided backcountry skiing. *Snowboarding:* Rentals, lessons, terrain parks. *For children:* Nursery from infancy; children's ski school with Micro, Mini, and SugarBear programs. *Rates:* The best prices can be found

**WINTER FUN ON THE SLOPES AT SUGARBUSH RESORT** JOHN ATKINSON, COURTESY OF SUGARBUSH RESORT

**SUGARBUSH PANORAMA** HANS JONATHON VON BRIESEN

online. Sugarbush's SugarXpress Card enables purchasing and loading lift tickets on computer or mobile device. *Tips:* Favorite intermediate runs are Jester and Snowball at Lincoln Peak and Rim Run and Cruiser at Mount Ellen.

## SUMMER/FALL

**MOUNTAIN BIKING** Sugarbush Resort's lift-serviced trails connect with a Valley-wide network. A total of 60 miles over a vertical variance of 3,000 feet.

**FOR FAMILIES** **Sugarbush Summer Adventure Center** Open seasonally. An 800-foot zipline; two disc-golf courses, including the Peak Course (chairlift access); and mountain biking with kids' programs, instruction for all ages, and a bungee trampoline that can send you soaring. The **Sugarbush Health & Recreation Center** (802-583-6700) has a climbing wall, for children 6 years and up.

**GOLF** **Sugarbush Resort Golf Club** (802-583-6725), 1091 Golf Road, Warren. An 18-hole, Robert Trent Jones Sr. course, PGA rated 42, par 72; cart and club rentals, lessons, practice range, and pub. Inquire about golf/lodging packages.

**FITNESS CENTERS** **Sugarbush Health & Recreation Center** (802-583-6700; sugarbush.com), Sugarbush Village, features indoor and outdoor pools, indoor and outdoor Jacuzzis, whirlpool, sauna, steam room, indoor squash, tennis, and racquetball courts, massage room, and aerobics studio.

## *LODGING*

🐾 **Clay Brook at Sugarbush**, red with a central silver silo, is a full-service, 110-room condohotel at the hub of lifts. Units range from studios to five rooms with Shaker-style decor, fireplace, and granite-topped kitchen; 61 units are in the rental pool; some are pet friendly.

LIFT-ASSISTED MOUNTAIN BIKING AT SUGARBUSH RESORT  JOHN ATKINSON

Facilities include an outdoor pool and whirlpools and **Rumble's Kitchen** (see below). **Sugarbush Inn** (802-583-6100). Handy (via shuttle and car) to lifts at both Lincoln Peak and Mount Ellen, and across the road from the golf course, is an inviting 42-room inn. Amenities include the use of the Health and Recreation Center, room phones, air-conditioning, a library, and a sitting room.

**Sugarbush Resort Condos** (802-583-6160; sugarbush.com). The number of resort-managed units available varies and usually averages around 100—some slope side, most walk-to-the-slopes—with health club access. From $ to $$$$. Prices vary with unit size and season. **Sugarbush Village Condominiums** (800-451-4326; sugarbushvillage.com) represents a similar range of condos and homes around Sugarbush.

### DINING

**Timbers Restaurant** (802-583-6800) A post-and-beam round "barn" at the base of the lifts is a full-service restaurant serving three squares, including a serious dinner menu with a commitment to fresh and local. Dinner might include an empanada filled with homemade chorizo, pork belly tacos, and a porcine entrée, all originating from the same pig cut up on site. $$$-$$$$.

**Rumble's Kitchen** (802-583-6800) at Lincoln Peak. A post-and-beam round barn at the base of the lifts, serving breakfast, lunch, and dinner, depending on the season, with a commitment to fresh and local food. **Allyn's Lodge** (802-583-6590), midmountain at Lincoln Peak. Open only in season. By day (10–2 in ski season) this is a pleasant stop and after dark it is literally the height of dining out in the Valley. Reservations are required and limited. Access is via the Lincoln Limo (snowcat). There's candle- and firelight, a four-course, locally sourced meal, and optional wine. Guests can don headlamps and ski down, conditions permitting, or take the cat. $$$.

its course north to the Gulf of St. Lawrence, and the White River flows south toward Long Island Sound. A few miles south, **Moss Glen Falls** spill down a steep cliff by the road. To turn this 20-mile drive into a day trip, continue to Hancock and across the Middlebury Gap to Middlebury, then back across Appalachian or Lincoln Gap to the Mad River Valley.

**Mad River Byway.** VT 100 and VT 100B from Granville Gulf to Middlesex Village has been designated the "Mad River Byway," an unparalleled scenic drive from the hills of Granville, along the valley floor, to US 2 in Middlesex; pick up a pamphlet guide at the chamber office or check it out on the website madrivervalley.com.

## ✳ Lodging

*Note*: The website madrivervalley.com offers an overview of Valley lodging. Inquire about the "Ski the Valley Passport" with discounted tickets at both ski areas, as well as cross-country and other perks. *Note also:* Many Valley lodgings request a two-night minimum stay on winter and other popular weekends.

INNS AND LODGES The Valley has one of Vermont's largest concentrations of distinctive inns and bed & breakfasts. These are a sampling of what the Valley has to offer. More information on inns, B&Bs, and other lodging is at madrivervalley.com. Inns listed here serve dinner as a matter of course; B&Bs may serve dinner on occasion.

❄ **Pitcher Inn** (802-496-6350; pitcherinn.com), 275 Main Street, Warren. Designed by architect David Sellers to look like it's been sitting in the middle of Warren Village for a century, the white-clapboard inn opened in the

1997–98 winter season, replacing an older inn that had burned. A member of Relais & Châteaux, this is the Valley's most luxurious inn. Common spaces include a small library, a hearth, an elegant dining room (see *Dining Out* on page 255), and the downstairs pub. Each of the nine guest rooms was designed by a different architect to convey an aspect of local history. The Lodges suggests a Masonic lodge (once a major social force in the Valley), with a midnight-blue ceiling studded with stars and obelisk-shaped posts on the king-size bed. From a bedside switch in the Mountain Room, make the sun rise and set over the mountains painted on the facing wall. The bathrooms are splendid. In the neighboring annex, the rate includes breakfast and afternoon tea (Sun.–Thurs. is less); a 13 percent service charge is added. Dogs are permitted in the Stable Suite. Inquire about packages. $$$–$$$$.

**The Bridges Family Resort and Tennis Club** (802-583-2922; bridgesresort .com), 202 Bridges Circle, Warren. A self-contained, family-geared resort near the Sugarbush main lifts and base lodge. Facilities include indoor tennis and outdoor courts; an indoor pool, saunas, hot tub and fitness room; and 100 attractive condo-style units ranging from one to three bedrooms, each with fireplace, sundeck, TV, and phone, some with washer/dryer. Cheaper off-season and for longer stays; inquire about ski and tennis packages. $$–$$$+.

**Mad River Barn** (802-496-3310; madriverbarn.com), 2849 Mill Brook Road, Waitsfield. Heather and Andrew Lynds took the legendary lodge building down to the studs and put it back together with new plumbing, wiring, central air, and an ambience that appeals to families and sports-minded singles and couples with echoes of the old icon. The large game room and bar, as well as the guest rooms, are bright and fresh with lots of details recycled from the old lodge. The eighteen rooms are divided

between the main Barn (built as lodging for the Civilian Conservation Corps in the '30s, becoming a ski lodge in the '40s) and the adjoining "Farmhouse" that houses two amazing bunk rooms, each with six beds and one bath. Each can be rented as a whole (minimum four people) or per bed. In the old Annex (1980s), family-size rooms are clean and comfortable. For more about the bar and restaurant, open to the public, see *Eating Out* on page 255. $–$$.

**The Waitsfield Inn** (802-496-3979; waitsfieldinn.com), 5267 Main Street (VT 100), Waitsfield. Innkeepers Jon and Vickie Walluck host this middle-of-the-village inn, an 1825 parsonage with a "great room"—offering plenty of space to relax in front of the hearth—in the attached (former) carriage and horse barn. The dining rooms (serving buffet dinners to groups Thurs.–Sun.) are well away from spaces reserved for guests. The 14 guest rooms (all with private bath) vary from cozy doubles to family rooms with lofts. Appropriate for children ages 6 and older. During regular summer and winter seasons, the rate includes a full breakfast. $$.

**Weathertop Mountain Inn** (802-496-4909; weathertopmountaininn.com), 755 Mill Brook Road, Waitsfield. Simple on the outside, the inside of Weathertop is filled with Asian art, Persian carpets, and souvenirs from the years innkeepers Lisa and Michael Lang spent traveling while based in Singapore. In addition to a full breakfast, they offer guests an optional dinner menu with entrée choices such as spiced minced lamb with yogurt and mint sauce or venison medallions in black pepper. The common space includes a large living room with a fieldstone fireplace and piano, as well as a TV with a DVD/video player and a library of old movies. Off the patio there's a hot tub and sauna, and a fourth-floor game room has a fireplace. The eight air-conditioned rooms have either two double beds, a queen, or a king. All have a fridge and full bath. $–$$.

# WINNER ONLY

**Mad River Glen** (802-496-3551; madriverglen.com). The ubiquitous red-and-white bumper sticker challenges MAD RIVER GLEN: SKI IT IF YOU CAN, but the mountain is one of the friendliest as well as one of the most challenging places to ski. It's also the only one in New England to prohibit snowboarding. One of the region's oldest major ski areas, it became the first to be owned cooperatively by its skiers, who are dedicated to preserving its narrow, continuously vertical trails, cut to the contours of the mountain. Access to the summit of Stark Mountain (3,637 feet) is via the vintage 1948 single chair, the only one left in the country. It's been rehabbed rather than replaced. All trails funnel into the central base lodge area, the better for families, many of whom are now third-generation Mad River skiers. Some long-popular woods trails are off the ski map, a phenomenon that has since been aped by many other ski areas. A popular place for telemarking, this is also the only major ski mountain with a serious snowshoe trail system and full program of snowshoeing/nature treks. On a good snow day, it's the region's best ski buy.

*Lifts:* 4 chairs, including the single plus the Callie's Corner Handle Tow.

*Trails and slopes:* 21 expert, 8 intermediate, 16 novice, a total of 800 skiable acres.

*Vertical drop:* 2,037 feet. *Snowmaking:* 15 percent, which includes top-to-bottom on the Practice Slope, also other high-volume, low-elevation areas. *Facilities:* Base lodge, cafeteria, and pub; also the newly restored Birdcage, halfway up the mountain, serving sandwiches, and drinks; ski shop, rentals, and ski school. *For children:* Cricket Club Nursery for 6 weeks–6 years; programs for ages 3–17 include Junior Racing and Junior Mogul.

*Rates* are affordable and under 6/over 70 ski free.

*Tip:* According to frequent MRG skier Joan Gorman, intermediates can experience the same kind of terrain the experts enjoy without the steeps or mogulspin Porcupine, a wide trail with some pitch and length to it. It is often groomed, but with moguls allowed to build up along the edges. Snail, a long, winding, almost cross-country-ski-type trail, is entirely different, lined with trees and with twists and turns that keep you paying attention. Off the single chair, intermediates can enjoy the narrow, beautiful cruiser Antelope to the mid-station and then cross over to continue down the mountain on Bunny, not quite what its name implies.

BED & BREAKFASTS ♂ **The Inn at Round Barn Farm** (802-496-2276; theroundbarn.com), 1661 East Warren Road, Waitsfield. Named for its remarkable round (12-sided) barn built in 1910 and now housing the **Green Mountain Cultural Center** (see *Entertainment* on page 256), with a lap pool and a greenhouse on its ground floor, this old farmhouse is one of New England's most elegant bed & breakfasts. There are 12 antiques-furnished rooms, 7 with gas fireplace, several with steam shower and/or Jacuzzi, all overlooking meadows and mountains. Winter guests are asked to leave shoes at the door and don slippers to protect the hardwood floors. Common space includes a sun-filled breakfast room, stone terrace, book-lined library, and lower-level game room with a pool table, a TV, a VCR, and a fridge stocked with complimentary soda and juices. Prices include a gourmet breakfast and afternoon edibles. Weddings are a specialty of the barn, which also serves as a venue for events, summer concerts, and opera. In winter, the inn maintains extensive snowshoe trails (snowshoes are complimentary to guests). Appropriate for children 15 and older. The inn hosts an Opera Festival in June, a photo exhibit in August, and a juried art show in foliage season. Rooms range from a double with a regular shower to a suite with marble fireplace, a canopy king bed, a Jacuzzi, and a steam shower. $$–$$$.

✪ ☗ **Millbrook Inn** (802-496-2405; millbrookinn.com), 533 Mill Brook Road (VT 17), Waitsfield. Open year-round except April, May, and

**Stark Mountain by Snowshoe** Half a dozen trails ranging in length from a short spur to 2.2 miles are marked, with a program of guided tracking treks, 10:30 a.m. weekend days, along with other special events during the season. An on-mountain nature center is an added attraction.

**Telemarking:** Rentals, lesson and lift packages, and special events.

**SINGLE LIFT UP MAD RIVER GLEN** COURTESY MAD RIVER GLEN

mid-October–mid-December This nineteenth-century farmhouse has two inviting living rooms, one with a fireplace. Seven guest rooms have stenciled walls, bureaus, antique beds with twin, queen-, or king-size mattresses, and private baths. One of the Valley's first ski lodges, Millbrook is open in summer as well. Pets by prior arrangement, no charge. Inquire about the two-bedroom, two-bath Octagon House where children are welcome (there's a crib), a short walk away but on the wooded hillside behind the inn (minimum two days). Longtime innkeeper Joan Gorman, a serious chef, offers an optional four-course dinner to guests. Full breakfast is included with rooms, $–$$.

**Wilder Farm Inn** (802-496-9935; wilderfarminn.com), 1460 Main Street, Waitsfield. A handsome, yellow 1850s farmhouse sits across the road from the Mad River and one of its better swimming holes north of the village. There's plenty to please here: A parlor with a TV, floor-to-ceiling windows, and a library with a big stone hearth that, like the one in the dining room, burns real logs. Breakfast is an organic production with ingredients from the garden, fresh eggs from the inn's own chickens, and more, sourced as locally as possible. Its eight rooms are tastefully decorated. Owners Ryan and Rebecca moved to Vermont and purchased the inn in 2016, and are adding features like a solar-panel-covered car parking bay with electric recharging stations. $–$$

**The Mad River Inn** (802-496-7900; madriverinn.com), 243 Tremblay Road, off VT 100, Waitsfield. A renovated 1860s structure with fine woodwork and large picture windows overlooking meadows that invite snowshoeing in winter. Just steps from the recreation path and a good swimming hole, it also serves as a lodging base for the Vermont Icelandic Horse Farm a short drive away. Inquire about two- to five-day riding packages. The seven guest rooms and two-bedroom suite all have featherbed or memory-foam mattress toppers and a private bath. Facilities include an outdoor hot tub and a downstairs game room with a pool table. A three-course breakfast and afternoon tea are included. Children 5 years and older are welcome. $-$$.

✆ **1824 House** (802-496-7555; 1824house.com), 2150 Main Street (VT 100), Waitsfield. North of the village, the eight guest rooms vary, but all have a private bath. There are gracious drawing and dining rooms with fireplaces. The 15-acre property invites walking, and there's a good swimming hole in the Mad River just across the road. The 1870s post-and-beam barn is a frequent wedding venue. Two-day minimum on weekends, three on winter holidays. Full breakfast included in $-$$.

**Mountain View Inn** (802-496-2426; vtmountainviewinn.com), 1912 Mill Brook Road (VT17), Fayston. This very Vermont house is bigger than it looks, with seven nicely decorated guest rooms (private baths). It's been geared to guests since it became one of the Valley's first ski lodges in 1948, since 1978 under ownership by Fred and Susan Spencer. Guests gather around the wood-burning stove in the living room and at the long, three-century-old pumpkin pine harvest table for breakfast. Handy to Sugarbush, Mad River Glen, and the Mill Brook Path. $ per couple.

✆ **The Featherbed Inn** (802-496-7151; featherbedinn.com), 5864 Main Street (VT 100), Waitsfield. Tom and Linda Gardner are the innkeepers in this nicely restored 1806 inn, with exposed beams, pine floors, and a formal living room as well as an informal "lodge room" with

fieldstone fireplace, games, and books. It's set far back from VT 100, overlooking flower gardens and fields, perfect for weddings. Ten guest rooms are divided between the main house, which includes two family-friendly suites, and a garden cottage with three more rooms, all with featherbed mattresses.

A full breakfast is included in $-$$.

✆ **Tucker Hill Inn** (802-496-3983; tuckerhill.com), 65 Marble Hill Road, Waitsfield. A classic 1940s ski lodge with a fieldstone hearth in the pine-paneled living room, it's a Valley favorite. Kevin and Patti Begin offer 15 rooms and suites, some suitable for families, all with private bath, phone, TV. Most rooms have a queen or king bed and are accessed off one hall in the main house. Enjoy gourmet meals in the pub or upstairs in the dining room, open to the public Wednesday to Saturday, 5:30–9:00 p.m. Weddings are a specialty. Rooms and suites, $$-$$$ includes breakfast.

✆ **Inn at Lareau Farm** (802-496-4949; lareaufarminn.com), 48 Lareau Road at VT 100, Waitsfield. This classic old farm includes a red barn that houses the American Flatbread (pizza) Restaurant, which now owns it. The 13-room inn has spacious grounds stretching to a swimming hole and back to a wooded hill, and it includes an outdoor pavilion popular for weddings. $.

**Hostel Tevere** (802-496-9222; hosteltevere.com), 203 Powderhound Road, off VT 100, Warren. The creation of Sarah (from Cape Cod) and Giles (from Milwaukee), who met in Rome, Sarah (a UVM grad who grew up skiing at Sugarbush) saw the need for reasonably priced, hostel-style lodging in the Valley. Sarah is surprised by the number of older (20s-plus) folks and families who are frequent repeaters. $.

CONDOMINIUMS The Valley harbors upward of 1,000 condominium units, but only 350 or so are available for rental. Many are clustered around Sugarbush South (Lincoln Peak), more are scattered along the access road, and some are squirreled away in the woods. No one reservation service represents them all. *Also see* the **Sugarbush Resort** sidebar on page 248.

## ✳ Where to Eat

DINING OUT *Note:* The Valley restaurants are unusual in both quality and longevity. Most have been around for quite some time.

**275 Main at the Pitcher Inn** (802-496-6350; pitcherinn.com), 275 Main Street, Warren Village. Open for dinner Wed.–Mon. Reservations essential. The elegant dining room features an à la carte menu orchestrated by chef Michael Bove. The bill of fare leans toward the rich and comforting but is dictated by the local ingredients available that day. The choice of wines by the glass is large, and the wine list itself is long and widely priced. Entrées: $$–$$$.

✪ ✔ **Chez Henri** (802-583-2600; chezhenrisugarbush.com), Sugarbush Village. Open only during ski season from 11:30 for a bistro/bar menu and from 5:30 for dinner. A genuine bistro, opened in 1964 by Henri Borel, former food controller for Air France. You're paying more for coddling and a room full of antiques than the high-priced, fusty fare, including fondue, French onion soup, and steak au poivre. $$–$$$.

**The Common Man Restaurant** (802-583-2800; commonmanrestaurant.com), 3209 German Flats Road, Warren. Dinner only. Reservations recommended. The ultramodern cuisine from Adam Longworth, a Vermont native, and transplant Lorien Wroten is at delicious odds with the chandelier-bedecked, mid-nineteenth-century barn in which it's served. Thursday is pasta night, featuring dinners that are less expensive. Order the soup! Longworth layers flavors and textures. $$–$$$.

**Peasant** (802-496-6856, peasantvt .com), 40 Bridge Street, Waitsfield. Dinner Thurs.–Mon. The name tells you what you

need to know about the aesthetic here. Co-owner with his wife, Mary Ellen, Chris Alberti walked out of his World Trade Center office 20 minutes before the first plane hit on 9/11. His well-earned joie de vivre is palpable in his simple food. Pastas, meatballs, and a hearty cassoulet are typical of his rustic, pan-European menu. $$.

*Also see* **Timbers Restaurant** in the **Sugarbush Resort** sidebar on page 248.

EATING OUT **American Flatbread Restaurant** (802-496-8856; americanflatbread.com), 40 Lareau Road, VT 100, Waitsfield. Open Thurs.–Sun. 5–9:30 p.m., year-round (more or less). George Schenk's distinctive flatbread is baked in a primitive, wood-fired oven made of local materials. Flatbread toppings include cheese and herbs, sun-dried tomatoes, homemade sausage with mushrooms, accompanied by salads whose dressing boasts homemade fruit vinegar. Also specials such as grilled vegetables with garlic-herb sauce and oven-roasted chicken.

**Big Picture Café** (802-496-8994; big-picturetheater.info), 48 Carroll Road, off VT 100, Waitsfield. Breakfast and lunch, Mon.–Sat. 8–2:30; Sunday brunch, 8–2; dinner, Tues.–Sat., 5–9. Eat and drink while you take in a film, or enjoy your meal in the adjacent cafe that's an all-day gathering spot. The international menu ranges from huevos rancheros through croque monsieur to homemade shepherd's pie. There's also an espresso bar with Italian and French sodas, a Biergarten in summer, a full bar, and an authentic soda fountain. Kid's menu.

✔ **Mad River Barn and Pub** (802-496-3310; madriverbarn.com), 2849 Mill Brook Road, Waitsfield. Open from 5 nightly. Families, skiers, hikers, and cyclists all fit comfortably and mingle in the pub and adjacent game room with its classic pinball and hand shuffleboard. You can always build your own burger or dine on Vermont-raised elk and venison stew. $–$$.

**MINT Restaurant** (802-496-5514; mintvermont.com), 4403 Main Street (enter from Bridge Street), Waitsfield. Open Thur.–Sun. for dinner (5:30–8:30). Vegetarians and carnivores alike rave about the taste of everything here. Lunch on a toasted cheese quesadilla with soy mozzarella, sweet corn, avocado, salsa fresca, and salad greens tossed in lavender herb vinaigrette. The tea selection is the best in the Valley (and beyond). Wine and beer at dinner. Chef Iliyan is from Bulgaria; he and his wife, Savitri, from Budapest, met in California.

☙ **Tucker Hill Inn** (802-496-3983; tuckerhill.com), 65 Marble Hill Road, Waitsfield. Open for dinner to nonguests Wed.–Sat. Under present ownership the inn's cozy pub and renovated restaurant get top reviews from locals and visitors alike. Nightly specials.

**Localfolk Smokehouse** (802-496-5623), jct. of VT 17 and VT 100, Waitsfield. Open Tues.–Sat. from 5 p.m. for food. Trusted local foodies rave about the hickory-smoked barbecued ribs and chicken, also Tex-Mex staples. A wide choice of draft beers, funky atmosphere, a pool table, outdoor deck, and frequent live music.

**Hostel Tevere** (802-496-9222) 203 Powderhound Road, just off VT 100, Warren. Breakfast daily, dinner Wed.–Sat. 6–10:30. Breakfasts have an enthusiastic local following.

**The Mad Taco** (802-496-3832), 2 Village Square, Waitsfield. Open 11–9 daily. Don't ask for nachos here—they don't have them at this authentic Mexican eatery. House-smoked, local meats find their way into tacos, tortas, and burritos that taste more Oaxaca than Waitsfield, especially when doused with one of the colorful homemade hot sauces. Wash down with craft beer.

**The Warren Store** (802-496-3864; warrenstore.com), Warren Village. Open daily 8–7; on Sundays and in winter until 6. Year-round the bakery produces French and health breads, plus croissants and great deli food and sandwiches, panini specials, breakfast till noon, daily specials; inside tables plus (in summer) a deck overlooking the Mad River.

## ✳ Entertainment

♂ **The Big Picture Theater & Café** (802-496-8994; bigpicturetheater.info), VT 100, Waitsfield. Mainstream and independent films. Annual film festival.

**Green Mountain Cultural Center** (802-496-7722; theroundbarn.com) at the Round Barn Farm, East Warren Road, Waitsfield. This concert and exhibit space in a classic round barn is the setting for a series of summer concerts and operas, along with workshops and a major foliage-season art exhibit.

The **Valley Players** (802-583-1674; valleyplayers.com), a community theater company housed in the Waitsfield Odd Fellows Building, produces three or four plays a year in its own theater in Waitsfield Village, VT 100.

The **Phantom Theater** (802-496-5997 in summer), a local group with New York City theater community members, presents original plays and improvisational performances for children and adults at Edgecomb Barn in Warren.

**The Commons Group** (802-496-4422; theskinnerbarn.com), the Skinner Barn, 609 Common Road, Waitsfield. Founded by Broadway and TV performer Peer Boynton, presenting theater, concerts, and a cabaret series.

Also note **Mad River Chorale** performances in late fall or early winter and late spring or early summer (madriverchorale.net).

APRÈS-SKI **The Hyde Away** (802-496-2322; hydeawayinn.com) is the hot spot near Mad River Glen (VT 17). Literally hidden away behind the inn, **Zach's Tavern** offers a fireplace, a big friendly bar, and a pool table, as well as dimly lit corners for pub food or the inn's full menu; many microbrews and nightly specials.

**Castlerock Pub** at Gatehouse Lodge, Lincoln Peak base area, is the Sugarbush gathering spot at the base of the lifts. Also see **Localfolk Smokehouse** in *Eating Out* on page 256.

# ✳ Selective Shopping

ART GALLERIES **Artisans' Gallery**
(802-496-6256; vtartisansgallery.com),
20 Bridge Street, Waitsfield. Open daily
11–6. A selective collection of crafted
items from throughout Vermont: clothing, pottery, crafts, decoys, photography,
and much more.

**Parade Gallery** (802-496-5445) in
Warren Village is a longstanding and
widely respected source of affordable
prints and original art, sculpture, and
photography, featuring Gary Eckhart
watercolors and Sabra Field prints.

**The Bundy Modern** (802-583-5832),
361 Bundy Road, Waitsfield (off VT 100
just north of Warren). Open Sat.–Sun.
12–5. Art and sculpture exhibits spring
through early fall.

CRAFTS SHOPS AND GALLERIES **Mad
River Glass Gallery** (802-496-9388),
4237 Main Street (VT 100), Waitsfield
Village. Melanie and Dave Leppia's
handsome gallery is a must-stop. The
glass is deeply colored, highly original,
and created (blown and cast) on the
premises.

**Waitsfield Pottery** (802-496-7155;
waitsfieldpottery.com), VT 100 across
from Bridge Street. Ulrike Tesmer makes
functional, hand-thrown stoneware
pieces, well worth a stop.

**Luminosity Stained Glass Studio**
(802-496-2231; luminositystudios.com),
the Old Church, VT 100, Waitsfield. Open
except Tues. This is a very special shop.
Since 1975 this former church has served
as the studio in which Barry Friedman
fashions Tiffany-style lampshades and a
variety of designs in leaded and stained
glass. Now he devotes most of his time to
custom work, but he keeps a selection of
opulent lighting, also showcasing Arroyo
craftsmen and mica lamps.

Also see **Green Mountain Glassworks** (michaeleganglass.com), studio
in Granville, on VT 100 south of Warren
and the Granville Gulf. The sign outside
invites you in to watch the artist at work.
Michael Egan's hand-blown glass creations are worth the short, scenic trip.

SPECIAL SHOPS **The Warren Store** (802-
496-3864; warrenstore.com), Warren Village. Open 8–6 in winter, until 7 in
summer. Staples, good wine selection, Vermont specialty items, and the deli and
bakery are downstairs (see *Eating Out* on
page 256). Upstairs the More Store is one
of Vermont's best-kept secrets, an eclectic
selection of clothing, jewelry, hardware,
and gifts.

**All Things Bright and Beautiful**
(802-496-3997; allthingsbright.com),
Bridge Street, Waitsfield. You'll find an
incredible number of stuffed animals
and unusual toys on two floors of this old
village house.

**The Store** (802-496-4465;
vermontstore.com), 5275 Main Street
(VT 100), Waitsfield. Since its 1965 opening, this shop has grown tenfold, now
filling two floors of an 1834 former Methodist meetinghouse with antiques, cookware, tabletop gifts, collectibles, lifestyle
books, Vermont gourmet products, and
children's toys and books from around
the world. Inquire about cooking in the
test kitchen out back.

**Tempest Book Shop** (802-496-
2022; tempestbookshop.com), Village
Square, Waitsfield. Model trains circle
above in this bookstore, a trove of
titles in most categories, including
children's books. We like their motto:
"A house without books is like a room
without windows" (Horace Mann). Also
CDs and posters.

**Alpine Options** (802-583-1763; alpine
options.com), with locations at Sugarbush (on the access road) and at Mad
River Glen. Open daily, Fri. until 11 p.m.
during ski season. Ski and snowboard
rentals, demos, and repair: the best-qual-
ity, all-around service according to
locals.

**East Warren Community Market**
(802-496-6758; eastwarrenmarket.com),
42 Roxbury Mountain Road. Open daily.

Housed in the former East Warren schoolhouse, a market and food co-op specializing in local and organic, staples, wines, baked goods.

## FARMS AND A FARMERS' MARKET

*Note:* Of all Vermont's ski resort areas, the Mad River Valley remains the most visually and genuinely committed to supporting its food producers, with names and products listed in the Mad River Valley Four Seasons Guide, including a map to locations, free from the chamber.

**Waitsfield Farmers' Market** (802-472-8027; waitsfieldfarmersmarket .com), mid-May–mid-October at the Mad River green, Sat. 9–1. A real standout with a wide selection of herbs, veggies, fruits and flowers, breads, cheese, syrup, meats, crafts, and music.

### YEAR-ROUND

**Mountain Valley Farm** (802-496-9255), 1719 Common Road, Waitsfield. Set high on an open shoulder of the Valley with a classic red cupolaed barn, the farm welcomes visitors for wagon and sleigh rides, weddings, birthday parties, or simply to meet the barnyard animals and walk or cross-country ski. Inquire about the guest suite.

**Gaylord Farm** (802-496-5054), 6405 Main Street, Waitsfield. The farm store is open year-round. Call for hours. A long-time family farm, formerly dairy, presently 600 acres with 250 belted Angus beef, 400 laying hens, 600 meat birds, plus seasonal produce. Look for the farm shop and house beside Hap's Garage (also part of the family).

**Hartshorn Organic Farm** (802-279-8054; hartshornfarm.com), VT 100, Waitsfield. Organic farm produce is sold in the farm stand on site, featuring vegetables and fruits, as well as CSA shares and pick-your-own strawberries and blueberries in season. Watch sap boil in the maple sugarhouse, or buy local jams and pickled veggies.

**SUGARHOUSES Eastman Long & Sons** (802-496-3448), 1188 Tucker Hill Road, Fayston. "Sonny" Long sets 6,000 taps on 100 high wooded acres that have been in his family for generations. He welcomes visitors to his roadside sugar-house during sugaring season.

**Palmer Maple Products** (802-496-3696), 75 Maple Lane, Waitsfield. Delbert and Sharlia Palmer sell syrup from their farm on this scenic road.

Also check with the chamber of commerce.

## ✳ Special Events

*Note:* Check with the chamber of commerce and its website (madrivervalley .com) for weekly listings of special events.

*January:* **Mountain Top Film Festival** (mountaintopfilmfestival.com), at the Big Picture Theater, Waitsfield.

*July 4:* Outstanding **parade and community celebration**, Warren Village. **Mad Marathon** (madmarathon.com), Mad River Valley, early July.

*July–August:* **Summer productions** by the Valley Players, the Commons Group, and by the Phantom Theater (see *Entertainment* on page 256).

*August:* **Vermont Festival of the Arts** (valleyartsvt.com/arts) throughout the Valley: daily happenings, open studios. **Mad River Valley Century Ride** (mrvcenturyride.com), third Saturday.

*August/early September:* **Green Mountain Stage Race** (gmsr.info), four days of bicycle racing.

*September:* **Vermont Barns and Bridges Festival** (vtbarnsandbridges festival.com), barn and farm tours, art exhibitions, other events at various locations in the Mad River Valley.

*November:* **Waitsfield Ski and Skate Sale** is huge, at the elementary school.

*Early December:* **Country Christmas** (madrivervalley.com), a weekend of art, entertainment, shopping specials, holiday events throughout the valley.

# BARRE/MONTPELIER AREA

Any serious attempt to understand the character of Vermont entails a visit to Montpelier, the state capital. This disarmingly small, bohemian college town has a vibrant culinary landscape and one-of-a-kind shops and restaurants along State and Main streets. The back streets are a jumble of bridges, narrow lanes, and mansard roofs. Montpelier is nicely positioned for travelers on I-89 and US 2 and VT 302, which run all the way to Maine, and it provides access to Central Vermont's "commercial strip," known as the Barre-Montpelier Road, where several businesses are located.

The region's other large community is Barre (pronounced *berry*), which is billed as "the granite capital of the world" for its many quarries, where high-quality gray Barre granite, now used primarily for memorial stones, is cut, shaped, and sculpted. The big area attraction is the **Rock of Ages Quarry** in Graniteville, southeast of town, although **Hope Cemetery** and **Elmwood Cemetery**, with their elaborately carved gravestones, the work of generations of skilled stone carvers, are worth visiting. The **Vermont History Center** (headquarters of the Vermont Historical Society) and the **Barre Opera House**, one of Vermont's most beautiful historic theaters, are right downtown.

Southwest of Montpelier is the proud old town of Northfield, home of Norwich University, the oldest private military college in the United States, and several well-preserved covered bridges. East Barre, East Montpelier, Marshfield, and Plainfield—home to Goddard College—are popular with travelers for their rural character and charm.

GUIDANCE **The Capital Region Visitor Center** (802-828-5981; informationcenter.vermont.gov/centers/capital_region), 134 State Street, Montpelier, is open daily. Housed in a red brick building across from the Vermont Statehouse, it has knowledgeable, friendly staff and a restroom.

**Central Vermont Chamber of Commerce** (802-229-5711; 877-887-3678; centralvt.com) has information on lodging, dining, and attractions.

**Montpelier Alive** (802-223-9604; montpelieralive.com), Montpelier's Downtown Association, has a useful website specific to downtown Montpelier, including many art, music, and food events.

**Downtown Barre Partnership** (802-477-2967; thebarrepartnership.com) produces events throughout the year, including the Barre Heritage Festival, and is a useful source for local business information and the area's attractions.

GETTING THERE *By bus:* **Greyhound** (800-231-2222; greyhound.com) from

YOUTH TRIUMPHANT  LISA HALVORSEN

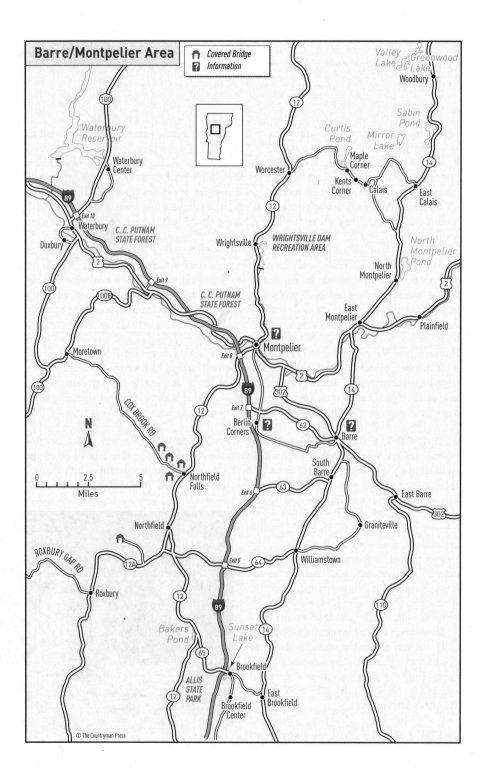

Boston to Montreal, connecting with New York and Connecticut service, stops in Montpelier in front of city hall on Main Street.

*By train:* **Amtrak** (800-USA-RAIL; amtrak.com) stops in Montpelier Junction, a mile west of town on the other side of I-89. Amtrak's Vermonter line offers carry-on bike service.

*By car:* For **Montpelier** take I-89, Exit 8, then follow Memorial Drive. Turn left at the traffic light onto Bailey Avenue, then right onto State Street, which will bring you to the statehouse and downtown area. Paid parking is available on the street and in several municipal parking lots.

To reach **Barre**, take I-89 to Exit 7, and follow signs for VT 62, a divided highway, to Main Street.

## ✳ Towns and Villages

**Montpelier** (population 7,855). Precisely why this narrow floodplain of the Winooski River was chosen in favor of Burlington or the more centrally located town of Randolph as Vermont's capital in 1805 is uncertain, as is the reason why it was named for a small city in the Languedoc region of France. The fact is, however, that Vermont's first legislators picked a place noted for its unusual number of whiskey distilleries—it's still famous for its legislative watering holes—and named it for a town renowned for its wine and brandy. The gold-domed **Vermont Statehouse** dominates the downtown, which is chock-a-block with independent shops, award-winning restaurants, arts venues, and a thriving year-round farmers' market. The smallest and possibly the most livable of the nation's state capitals, Montpelier has the impressive **Vermont Historical Society Museum** and **Hubbard Park**, a 194-acre green oasis on the hill behind the statehouse.

VERMONT STATEHOUSE LISA HALVORSEN

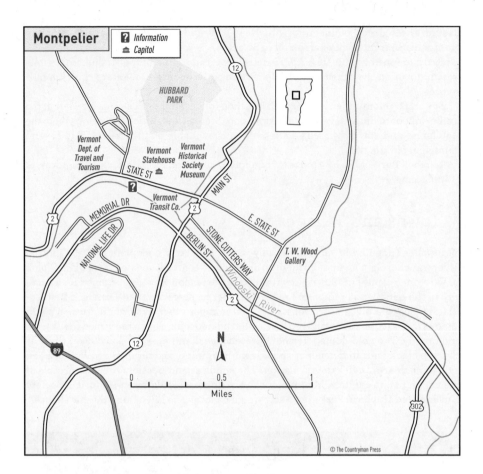

**Barre** (population 9,052). The architecture of what was historically a working-class city is a testament to the talents of the legions of stonecutters who settled here. Most of the buildings date from 1880–1910, a period when the population swelled from 2,000 to 12,000 with the arrival of quarry men and stone carvers primarily from Italy and Scotland, although also from Spain, Eastern Europe, and other countries. The **Socialist Labor Party Hall** at 46 Granite Street was built in 1900 with local granite by Italian stonecutters for the grand sum of $7,000. It served as a community hall and place where many anarchists and socialists spoke. Today it's a popular event space (802-331-0013; oldlaborhall.com). Barre's memorial stone business escalated after 1888, when the railroad finally linked the quarries to finishing sheds in the valley and to outlets beyond. **Rock of Ages** has long welcomed visitors to view the process from pit to finished product with quarry and factory tours. The **Vermont Granite Museum**, housed in a former granite shed, provides fascinating insight into the industry's history.

**Northfield** (population 6,207). This town's mid-nineteenth-century commercial blocks suggest the prosperity that it enjoyed while native son Charles Paine served as Vermont's governor. Paine actually brought the Vermont Central Railway through his hometown instead of Barre, the more logical choice. The old depot, built in 1852, is believed to be Vermont's oldest surviving railroad station. Today the town's pride is Norwich University, a private, coed college, which is the oldest private military college in the United States. The exhibits in the **Sullivan Museum and History Center**

(802-485-2183; academics.norwich.edu/museum) on campus trace the 200-year history of the college. Here you will learn that this institution sent more than 300 officers into battle during the Civil War. Changing exhibits at the **Northfield Historical Society Museum** (see *Historical Attractions* on page 268) provide a glimpse into the town's history. Northfield also has a number of accessible covered bridges.

MORSE FARM MAPLE SUGARWORKS  LISA HALVORSEN

## ✳ Must See

**Morse Farm Maple Sugarworks** (802-223-2740; morsefarm.com), 1168 County Road, Montpelier. Open year-round, daily except holidays. Sugar-on-snow parties March–April; cross-country skiing in winter; antiques and crafts fairs in summer; and hayrides and foliage walks in fall. The farm has been in the same family for eight generations. The store features its own syrup and maple products, Vermont crafts, and a free sugarhouse tour with tastings and an outdoor museum devoted to Vermont farm life. Check out the whimsical folksy characters carved by owner Burr Morse. Also see *Cross-Country Skiing* on page 269.

    **Rock of Ages Visitor Center and Tours** (802-476-3119; rockofages.com), 558 Graniteville Road, Graniteville. The visitor center is open May–October, Mon.–Sat.; factory tours year-round, weekdays. Narrated shuttle tours are offered for a nominal fee May–October to Smith Granite Quarry, a working, 50-acre, 600-foot-deep quarry. Self-guided factory tours are free. From the observation deck of the Manufacturing

ROCK OF AGES QUARRY  LISA HALVORSEN

Unions

VERMONT GRANITE MUSEUM   LISA HALVORSEN

Division, you can watch master sculptors polish and sculpt blocks of granite. The visitor center features interactive exhibits and a retail store with granite gifts, although many visitors come with a different type of purchase in mind: their gravestones. You also can test your prowess on the outdoor granite bowling lane.

🖉 ♿ The **Vermont Granite Museum and Stone Arts School** (802-476-4605; stoneartsschool.org), 7 Jones Brothers Way, Barre. Open June–October, Wed.–Sat. Housed in the former Jones Brothers Granite Shed, the museum tells the story of Vermont's granite industry through photos, vintage equipment, sculptures, and interactive exhibits on history, geology, and technology. Try your hand at etching or freehand sculpting. The **Stone Arts School** teaches stone-carving techniques, sandblasting, and stonewall construction; students learn from experienced sculptors and stone workers.

🖉 The **Vermont Historical Society Museum** (802-828-2291; vermonthistory.org), 109 State Street, Montpelier. Open year-round, Tues.–Sat. Admission charged. (Fee also includes admission to the **Vermont Heritage Galleries** at the **Vermont History Center** in Barre.) This outstanding state history museum, maintained by the Vermont Historical Society, occupies the ground floor of the replica of the Pavilion Hotel, a five-story, mansard-roofed landmark that occupied this site between 1870 and 1966. *Freedom & Unity: One Ideal, Many Stories*—the permanent exhibition—chronicles Vermont from the year 1600 to the present time. It dramatizes Abenaki Indian life, draws visitors into Bennington's Catamount Tavern to explore the state's beginnings, and explores life in the nineteenth century through interactive exhibits and re-created buildings.

## ❋ To Do

### SUMMER/FALL

BIKING **The Vermont Bicycle Shop** (802-622-8222; vermontbicycleshop.com), 105 North Main Street, Barre, rents, sells, and repairs mountain bikes. **Bicycle Express** (802-485-5424; bikeexpressvt.com), 56 Depot Square, Northfield, has sales and service. **Freeride Montpelier** (802-552-3521; freeridemontpelier.org), 89 Barre Street, Montpelier, a volunteer-run bicycle cooperative, provides community access to tools and expert mechanics for do-it-yourselfers and hosts bike rides and events. The **Central Vermont Chamber of Commerce** website (centralvt.com) has extensive biking resources, including mountain bike clubs, tours, and races. Download a copy of *Central Vermont Back Road Bike Tours*, which provides a detailed description for several suggested routes. The 2-mile **Montpelier Bike Path** runs from the Stone Cutter's Way and Granite Street intersection to Junction Road, just past the intersection with Dog River Road. **Millstone Hill Touring and Recreation Center** (802-479-1000; millstonetrails.com), 34 Church Hill Road, Websterville, is a superb biking destination. The Millstone Hill Trail Association maintains the trail system, 42 km of single-track trails that wind through 1,500 acres of wooded terrain, with dozens of abandoned quarries. Nominal day-use fee for bikers. Accommodations available at **The Lodge at Millstone Hill** (see *Lodging* on page 271).

MOUNTAIN BIKING AT MILLSTONE HILL  CENTRAL VERMONT CHAMBER OF COMMERCE

BOATING AND FISHING **Wrightsville Beach Recreation Area** (802-552-3471; wrightsvillebeachvt.com), created by the **Wrightsville Dam,** just north of Montpelier on rural VT 12, is popular for swimming, boating, fishing, and picnicking. Canoe, kayak, and stand-up paddleboard rentals are available. See the "Mad River Valley" and "Stowe and Waterbury" chapters for boat tours, on pages 240 and 395, respectively.

The area has dozens of ponds with good fishing spots, including **North Montpelier Pond**, with a fishing access off VT 14; and **Curtis Pond** and **Mirror Lake** in Calais (pronounced *CAL-lus*). **Nelson Pond** and **Sabin Pond** in Woodbury are both accessible from VT 14, as are **Valley Lake** and **Greenwood Lake** (good for bass and pike). The **Stevens Branch** south of Barre and the **Dog River** in Northfield offer brook trout. Fishing licenses are required. Info can be found at vtfishandwildlife.com. **R&L Archery** (802-479-9151; rlarchery.com), 70 Smith Street, Barre, is the best local source for fishing and hunting supplies, licenses, and information. It also sells archery, kayaking, geocaching, paintball, and even gold prospecting equipment.

COVERED BRIDGES Three covered bridges are on Cox Brook Road in Northfield Falls (off VT 12 at the Falls General Store). The **Northfield Falls Covered Bridge** (or **Station Covered Bridge**), and the **Lower Cox Brook Covered Bridge** are within sight of each other. Continue on this road to the **Upper Cox Brook Covered Bridge,** a queenpost-truss bridge with a 51.5-foot span. A fourth bridge, the **Slaughter House Bridge,** crosses Dog River on Slaughter House Road nearby, while the **Stony Brook Covered Bridge** can be viewed on VT 12A in Northfield Center. Built in 1899, the latter was the last kingpost-truss covered bridge constructed on a public highway in Vermont.

COX BROOK ROAD COVERED BRIDGES  LISA HALVORSEN

# A SHRINE TO BARRE'S STONECUTTERS

**H**ope Cemetery (802-476-6245), 201 Maple Avenue, Barre. You would be forgiven if you mistook Hope Cemetery for an outdoor sculpture park. This 65-acre cemetery, established in 1895 in a park-like setting on a hill above Barre, has more than 10,500 beautifully carved grave markers and ornate crypts.

Its original 53 acres were designed by the renowned landscape architect Edward P. Adams, although as much care went into planning future sections as the cemetery expanded. But it's the headstones and mausoleums sculpted from locally quarried granite that set this cemetery apart. Many have floral patterns, bas-reliefs, or other elaborate designs, or are cut in unusual shapes, a lasting testament to the talented stone carvers who created these—and who, in many cases, are buried beneath their final work.

**HOPE CEMETERY** LISA HALVORSEN

**DISC GOLF** The area's three disc-golf courses are located in North Calais, Websterville, and the **Wrightsville Beach Recreation Area**. Check the Green Mountain Disc Golf Club website (gmdgc.org) for details.

**GOLF Montpelier Elks Country Club** (802-223-7457; montpelierelkscc.com), 203 Country Club Road, Montpelier. This active country club of the local Elks Lodge has a nine-hole public golf course laid out over 124 acres with views of the Green Mountains.

**Barre Country Club** (802-476-7658; ccofbarre.net), 142 Drake Road, Barre. This is a hilly, affordable 18-hole course with a restaurant run by the restaurateurs behind Cornerstone Pub & Kitchen (see *Dining Out* on page 272). Dinner reservations are recommended.

In the early twentieth century these master craftsmen began arriving in the Barre area, lured by the promise of good money to work in the granite industry. Most came from Italy, although many were from Scotland and other European countries.

There was a growing need for these workers' talents as the demand for Barre granite grew. But with their work came the added risk of early death from unsafe working conditions, particularly from silicosis, also known as potter's rot, a disease caused by inhalation of silica dust. It became tradition for each man to carve his own headstone, and if he passed before it was done, then a family member or friend would complete the work.

One of the most poignant stories is that of Louis Brusa, who died of silicosis after successfully fighting to make ventilation systems mandatory in granite sheds. He commissioned fellow carver Don Colletti to carve his gravestone—Brusa cradled in his wife's arms as he sits near death in an armchair. Brusa posed for the sculpture himself. Although it's rumored that Mary's image was replaced by that of his mistress, in the end she triumphed. She was buried beneath the stone in 1957, 20 years after her husband's untimely passing at 51.

Other notable stones are that of an elderly couple sitting in bed holding hands for all eternity and a replica of Michelangelo's *Pietá*. Newer monuments reflect what was important to the deceased, with gravestones in the shape of a racecar, soccer ball, biplane, and cat. Although these monuments honor the dead, for the living, Hope Cemetery is an open-air museum of granite artistry.

LOUIS BRUSA GRAVESTONE  LISA HALVORSEN

**Northfield Country Club** (802-485-4515; northfieldcountryclub.com), 2066 Roxbury Road, Northfield. This course is considered one of the best nine-hole courses in the state. The Clubhouse Café serves deli-style grub.

HIKING/WALKING *Guidance:* **The Green Mountain Club** (802-244-7037; greenmountainclub.org). The club encourages general inquiries and trail description updates. Its visitor center, located at 4711 Waterbury Stowe Road, Waterbury Center, is open daily from mid-May to mid-October, weekdays the rest of the year. For descriptions of local hikes purchase a copy of *Day Hiker's Guide to Vermont* (Green Mountain Club) or *50 Hikes in Vermont* (The Countryman Press). Suggested hikes include:

**Spruce Mountain**, Plainfield. An unusually undeveloped state holding of 500 acres, rich in bird life. The trail begins in **L. R. Jones State Forest**, 4.2 miles south of the village. The three-hour, 4.4-mile round trip hike has 360-degree views from the fire tower at the summit.

**Worcester Range**, north of Montpelier, notably **Elmore Mountain** in Elmore State Park (802-888-2982; vtstateparks.com), a 3-mile trek yielding a panorama of lakes, farms, and rolling hills—see "North of the Notch" on page 414; **Mount Worcester** (approached from the village of Worcester); and **Mount Hunger**.

**Groton State Forest**, east of Montpelier. This 25,000-acre forest offers an extensive year-round trail system. See "St. Johnsbury and Burke Mountain" on page 432.

**Allis State Park** (802-276-3175; vtstateparks.com), Randolph. See "The White River Valleys" on page 226.

**Hubbard Park** and **North Branch River Park** in Montpelier are both accessible from **North Branch Nature Center** (802-229-6206; northbranchnaturecenter.org), 713 Elm Street (VT 12 North). The nature center hosts year-round birding programs and other events, including several for children.

**Hubbard Park** also may be reached by a 20-minute walk on a trail behind the statehouse. It has a 54-foot stone observation tower and an off-leash area for dogs. North Branch River Park offers gentle trails along this fork of the Winooski River, as well as more challenging, higher-altitude trails. Both parks are used for cross-country skiing and snowshoeing. Also see **Millstone Hill** under *Biking* on page 265.

HISTORICAL ATTRACTIONS **Kellogg-Hubbard Library** (802-223-3338; kellogg hubbard.org), 135 Main Street, Montpelier. Open Mon.–Sat., hours vary. This lovely Italianate structure, built in 1895 of rough granite blocks, is as palatial inside as out. Behind its two-story columned entrance, you'll find a second-floor balcony, ornate fireplaces, a fine oak-and-marble staircase, classical friezes, and a central skylight that fills the hall with light.

**Northfield Historical Society Museum** (802-485-4792; nhsvt.org), 75 South Main Street, Northfield. Housed in the former Governor Charles Paine House, the museum explores the history of the town through exhibits, photographs, manuscripts, and scrapbooks. Call for hours or to make an appointment.

**USS *Montpelier* Museum** (802-223-9502; montpelier-vt.org), 39 Main Street, Montpelier. Open weekdays. Free. Tucked upstairs in a few back rooms of the city hall is this unexpected display of ship models, uniforms, medals, and diaries documenting the life of Admiral George Dewey, a native son who inspired the christening of at least three US Navy ships named after his hometown. The most recent was a nuclear attack submarine, commissioned in 1993.

**Vermont History Center** (802-479-8500; vermonthistory.org), 60 Washington Street, Barre. Open year-round. Admission charged. **Heritage Galleries** open Mon.–Fri., Leahy Library, Tues.–Fri., second Sat. Daily research fee. Housed in the former Spaulding School, an exquisite Victorian building designed in 1891 by Lambert Packard—the architect of St. Johnsbury's Fairbanks Museum—the Vermont Historical Society headquarters includes galleries with changing exhibits on the state's history and a research library.

HORSEBACK RIDING ✐ **T-N-T Stables** (802-476-3097; tntstables1.webs.com), 75 Pine Hill Road, Barre. Tina and Tiffany Poulin offer hour-long trail rides, pony rides, and instruction for those 8 and older.

**VERMONT HISTORY CENTER** LISA HALVORSEN

STOCK CAR RACING **Thunder Road International Speedbowl** (802-244-6963; thunderroadvt.com), 80 Fisher Road, Barre, off Quarry Hill Road. Check the website for the schedule of races and other events at this family-friendly venue.

SWIMMING ✐ **Wrightsville Beach Recreation Area** (802-552-3471; wrightsville beachvt.com), VT 12, Middlesex—6 miles north of downtown Montpelier. The Maple Corner area of Calais also has a number of swimming holes.

## ✳ Winter Sports

CROSS-COUNTRY SKIING **Millstone Hill Touring and Recreation Center** (802-479-1000; millstonetrails.com), 34 Church Hill Road, Websterville, has 40 km of groomed cross-country and snowshoe trails that weave through abandoned quarries. No trail fee. The touring center is located in a restored general store, around the corner from **The Lodge at Millstone Hill** (see *Lodging* on page 271), with trail maps and rentals; open daily, weather permitting.

  **Morse Farm Ski Touring Center** (802-223-0560; skimorsefarm.com), 1168 County Road, Montpelier. Open daily, weather permitting. At an elevation of 1,200 feet, the farm offers a series of loops ranging from 0.7 to 3.9 km—more than 25 km of trails in all. Rentals, lessons, and a warming hut attached to the gift shop with snacks available. Separate snowshoe trails.

ICE SKATING ✐ **The Central Vermont Civic Center** (802-229-5900; cvmcc.org) at 268 Gallison Hill Road, Montpelier, off VT 302. Public skating and rentals; public skating hours vary, so check website.

**Barre City** ♦ **BOR Ice Arena** (802-476-0258; barrecity.org/bor), 25 Auditorium Hill, Barre, in the Civic Center. Open for public skating November–mid-March. Call ahead for days/hours. No skate rentals are available.

SNOWMOBILING A large number of **VAST trails** (Vermont Association of Snow Travelers—in other words, snowmobile trails) can be found in Washington and Orange counties extending through the Barre/Montpelier area. VAST trails are primarily on private land and are open to responsible snowmobilers from mid-December (after hunting season) to mid-April (depending on snow conditions). Check the VAST (vtvast .org) or Central Vermont Chamber of Commerce website (centralvt.com) for trail information.

*Note:* For more on winter sports, see "Sugarbush/Mad River Valley" and "Stowe and Waterbury" on pages 240 and 395, respectively.

SCENIC DRIVES **Roxbury to Warren.** The road through Roxbury Gap, while not recommended in winter, is spectacular in summer and fall, commanding a breathtaking view of the Green Mountains from the crest of the Roxbury Range. Do not resist the urge to stop, get out, and enjoy this vista. Ask locally about the hiking trail that follows the ridgeline from the road's highest point.

**Northfield to Moretown.** Cox Brook Road connects Northfield Falls with the village of Moretown. It's dirt part of the way, offering views in both directions near the crest and passing through three covered bridges at the Northfield Falls end. In Northfield, Turkey Hill Road begins across from Depot Square and climbs up to panoramic views.

# ✳ Lodging

## IN MONTPELIER

♂ **Capitol Plaza Hotel and Conference Center** (802-223-5252; capitolplaza.com), 100 State Street. The former landmark tavern is now a four-story downtown hotel with more than 60 guest rooms and suites, some with jet hot tubs or spa showers. Amenities include a fitness room, golf privileges to the Country Club of Vermont (private course), and room service from J. Morgan's Steakhouse (see *Dining Out* on page 272). Located almost across the street from the Vermont Statehouse, the hotel is often booked for state-related conferences and events and weddings. $–$$$$.

⚘ **The Inn at Montpelier** (802-223-2727; innatmontpelier.com), 147 Main Street. Accommodations are in two adjacent stately Federal-style manses that have been renovated and furnished with antiques and Oriental carpets. Both belonged to James Langdon, a prominent local businessman. The Lamb-Langdon house has a wraparound veranda, the perfect place to rest after an afternoon stroll. Some of the 19 rooms have fireplaces, and one has a huge private deck. Innkeepers John and Karol Underwood keep the 24-hour guest pantry well

CAPITOL PLAZA HOTEL  CAPITOL PLAZA HOTEL

stocked with coffee, tea, and freshly baked cookies. $$–$$$.

## IN BARRE

⌀ **Maplecroft Bed & Breakfast** (802-477-5050; maplecroftvermont.com), 70 Washington Street (VT 302). This striking Victorian house and the Vermont History Center are neighbors, making this a convenient choice for anyone researching Vermont history or genealogy at the center. Built by George Mackie, a Scottish granite shed owner, in 1887 to resemble castles at home, this five-room inn is distinctive for its circular tower, high ceilings, and period furnishings. Guests are greeted by Dan Jones and Yasunari Ishii, and their West Highland white terrier, Barney. Children 12 and older welcome. Rates include a hearty breakfast. English and Japanese spoken. $–$$.

⌀ ⌀ ⌀ ⌀ **The Lodge at Millstone Hill** (802-479-1000; millstonehill.com), 59 Little John Road, East Barre. Owner Pierre Couture is a walking encyclopedia about Millstone Hill and its historic granite quarries, now part of a trail-webbed recreation area for mountain biking and cross-country skiing. Accommodations range from rooms in the main lodge (converted barn), farmhouse, or cottage (some rooms have shared bath) to a luxury loft suite with full kitchen and solarium (two-night minimum). Primitive campsites have direct access to the trail system. $–$$.

## BEYOND

⌀ **Green Mountain Girls Farm** (802-505-9840; eatstayfarm.com), 923 Loop Road, Northfield. The barn guesthouse, available June–mid-October, can accommodate up to five people. The three-bedroom Farmhouse Inn, for rent November–May in entirety only, sleeps six. Rates for both include a farm tour, breakfast starter basket, and access to a private kitchen to make your own farm

breakfast. $$$–$$$$. For information on guided farm tours and other activities, see *Farms* on page 277.

⌀ **Hollister Hill Farm B&B** (802-454-7725; hollisterhillfarm.com), 2193 Hollister Hill Road, Marshfield. Bob and Lee Light fled New Jersey for Vermont in 1972 and milked cows for 25 years, eventually replacing them with beefalo, pigs, chickens, and turkeys. In 1983 they moved to their present property, an 1825 Federal-style brick farmhouse set on 204 acres, and continue to farm, selling naturally raised meats, raw milk from four Jersey cows, maple syrup, honey, and other farm products at their farm store in the barn. They started the B&B in 1999, naming it after Josiah Hollister, the original landowner. Rates include a hearty country breakfast. In winter, guests are encouraged to bring cross-country skis or to borrow snowshoes; snowmobile trails traverse the property. $–$$.

⌀ ⌀ **Marshfield Inn & Motel** (802-426-3383; marshfieldinn.com), 5630 US 2, Marshfield. Closed January–March. A flat-roofed Victorian farmhouse overlooking the Winooski River Valley forms the centerpiece of this complex. Lodging is in the 10 neighboring motel units with queen or two doubles, two with kitchenettes. Innkeepers Tracey Hambleton and Diana Batzel serve a nominally priced breakfast (there's a full menu) in the main house six days a week. Located halfway between Montpelier and St. Johnsbury, this is a good base for exploring many of the area's attractions. $.

⌀ ⌀ **Pie-in-the-Sky Farm Bed & Breakfast and Retreat** (802-426-3777; pieinsky.com), 93 Dwinell Road, Marshfield. This rambling Civil War–era farmhouse was home for a time to the Pie-in-the-Sky commune but has been a dairy and sheep farm and home for Jay Moore, Jude Sargent, and their cats for many years. Singles or doubles with shared baths are available, or rent the six-room suite with three bedrooms, two baths, kitchen, parlor with woodstove, and greenhouse with hot tub.

The 120-acre property has trails for cross-country skiing, snowshoeing, or walking. Groton State Forest, with hiking trails and swimming, is nearby. Breakfast included. Inquire about retreats and weekly rentals. $–$$.

## ✲ Where to Eat

DINING OUT **Cornerstone Pub & Kitchen** (802-476-2121; cornerstonepk.com), 47 North Main Street, Barre. Open Tues.–Sat. for lunch and dinner. Several local beers are on tap at this spacious restaurant, but the ambience is local, too. The walls are decorated with early-twentieth-century road signs and posters including advertisements for Barre's Magnet Theatre, which closed in the 1950s. But hearty food is the main attraction. Try one of their signature burgers or the barbecue pork shank with smoked bacon jalapeño mac 'n cheese. $$.

**J. Morgan's Steakhouse** (802-223-5222; capitolplaza.com), 100 State Street, Montpelier. Breakfast, lunch, and dinner daily year-round; extensive Sunday brunch buffet. The restaurant has earned accolades as one of Vermont's best steakhouses for its aged and hand-cut steaks and steak burgers. Seafood also plays a starring role on the menu. Try the blackened jumbo scallops with grilled fresh pineapple and cilantro sour cream or the Billionaire's Cake, a pan-seared patty of Maine lobster, lump crabmeat, and shrimp, topped with a lemon-caper butter sauce. Kids will love the model trains that chug their way around the dining room at this hotel restaurant. $$–$$$$.

**Kismet** (802-223-8646; kismetkitchens.com), 52 State Street, Montpelier. Open for dinner Wed.–Sat. and brunch on weekends. Chef-owner Crystal Maderia changes menus as the season's produce dictates. What doesn't budge is her brilliant palate and taste for innovation. Plates have varied from Lebanese tartare kibbeh and grilled octopus with peaches to an indulgent burger served with fries drizzled in truffle honey. Brunch is unapologetically hearty, with several takes on Eggs Benedict alongside Portuguese baked eggs

J. MORGAN'S STEAKHOUSE CAPITOL PLAZA HOTEL

and bread pudding topped with poached eggs. $–$$.

**NECI on Main** (802-223-3188; neci .edu), 118 Main Street, Montpelier. Open for dinner Tues.–Sat. Culinary students and their chef-instructors collaborate on preparation and presentation of dishes featuring Vermont farm products, many locally sourced, to offer diners a memorable dining experience. The menu includes several entrées plus small plates and shareables, including tapas and cheese boards. $–$$.

(ꞷ) **Sarducci's Restaurant & Bar** (802-223-0229; sarduccis.com), 3 Main Street, Montpelier. Open for lunch Mon.–Sat.; dinner nightly. This spacious Mediterranean-style Italian restaurant, famous for its wood-fired pizzas and pasta dishes, is popular with legislators and families alike. Reservations are recommended, especially on weekends. In summer enjoy outdoor dining with views of the Winooski River. $–$$.

## EATING OUT

### IN MONTPELIER

✪ ✎ **Chill Gelato** (802-223-2445), 32 State Street. Open Tues.–Sun. The gelato here is made fresh daily in small batches using local milk. Making only a bit at a time allows owners Theo and Nora Kennedy freedom to explore quirky tastes to create new flavors such as chocolate lavender, chai, and rose (vanilla flavored with rose water).

✎ **The Mad Taco** (802-225-6038; themadtaco.com), 72 Main Street. Lunch and dinner every day. The menu changes daily at this tiny taco counter, which has a larger branch in Waitsfield. Just don't expect nachos. This locavore establishment is devoted to roasted or smoked meats and veggies, stuffed into tacos, burritos, and quesadillas. Try the homemade hot sauces.

✎ ⴖ (ꞷ) **Skinny Pancake** (802-262-2253; skinnypancake.com), 89 Main Street. Open daily. In addition to its savory and sweet crepes, this centrally

located eatery serves paninis, salads, and munchies, including sweet potato fries and crepe chips served with pico de gallo; full coffee and espresso bar.

(ꞷ) **Three Penny Taproom** (802-223-8277; threepennytaproom.com), 108 Main Street. Open daily. The impressive tap list at this unpretentious gastropub includes many hard-to-find beers, including a nice selection of local and international craft beers. Pair these with elevated versions of bar food, such as the smoked trout rillettes or a meaty chili cheeseburger with house-made cheese sauce.

**Wilaiwan's Kitchen** (802-505-8111), 34 State Street. Open Mon.–Fri. for lunch only. You'll feel like you stepped into a roadside eatery in Thailand when you wait for a seat at this popular restaurant. The menu is limited—only three main entrées, although dishes change weekly—but the portions are ample and freshly prepared as you watch.

### BEYOND

(ꞷ) **Cornerstone Burger Co.** (802-485-4300; cornerstoneburger.com), 21 East Street, Northfield. Serves dinner Wed.–Sun., lunch on weekends. While burgers made from beef, turkey, duck, venison, and pork—combined with an array of creative toppings—are the mainstay of the menu, the restaurant also serves soups, salads, and entrées, including salmon and a fried chicken bowl.

ⴖ ✎ **Positive Pie** (802-454-0133; positivepie.com), 65–69 Main Street, Plainfield. Open daily for lunch and dinner; breakfast on weekends. This is the place to gather in Plainfield. Twenty craft beers, ciders, and root beers on tap go down easy alongside locavore pizza, pasta, and eclectic sandwiches.

✎ **Wayside Restaurant and Bakery** (802-223-6611; waysiderestaurant.com), 1873 VT 302 (Barre–Montpelier Road), Berlin. Open daily for breakfast, lunch, and dinner. This family restaurant has been serving comfort food since 1918.

The menu hasn't changed much since then, including holdovers such as grilled beef liver and onions, salt pork and milk gravy, and in-season, locally caught perch. For dessert, try their signature Grapenut custard pudding or freshly baked apple pie with homemade ice cream.

BREAKFAST/LUNCH

IN MONTPELIER

**Birchgrove Baking Café** (802-223-0200; birchgrovebaking.com), 279 Elm Street. Breakfast and lunch daily. Savory pastries always are available for a meal, but you'll be tempted to skip them in favor of a s'mores tart, crackling caramel monkey bread, and a homemade floral soda. Planning a celebration? The bakers specialize in beautifully decorated cakes for all occasions.

   **Capitol Grounds Café** (802-223-7800; capitolgrounds.com), 27 State Street. Open daily with made-to-order breakfast available until 2 p.m. The café roasts its own coffee, sold under the brand name of 802 Coffee, although it also offers a wide selection of teas, smoothies, and other beverages. It serves soups, vegetarian and meat chilis, and sandwiches (including breakfast ones) using locally sourced ingredients.

   & **Hunger Mountain Food Co-op** (802-223-8000; hungermountain.coop), 623 Stone Cutters Way. Open daily. Hidden in a corner of this cooperative market is a glass-sided café overlooking the river; the café features daily specials, a hot bar, salad bar, hot and cold sandwiches, and several vegetarian and vegan options. Ingredients are organic or locally sourced. Breakfast served all day.

   **La Brioche Bakery & Cafe** (802-229-0443; neci.edu), 89 Main Street. Open Mon.–Sat. for breakfast and lunch. New England Culinary Institute instructors and students bake everything in this European-style bakery and café. Pastries are an appealing mix of French-inspired classics and highly original experiments.

At mealtime, get freshly made salads, soups, and made-to-order sandwiches. Eat in the dining room, on the patio, or grab a bagged lunch to go.

   & **National Life Cafeteria** (802-229-3397; neci.edu), 1 National Life Drive. Open for breakfast and lunch, weekdays. The cafeteria partners with the New England Culinary Institute and has views through plate-glass windows of the mountains. Pick up a dining room pass in the lobby. There's a big salad bar, a choice of made-to-order sandwiches, grill items, specials like Eggs Benedict with steak, locally raised barbecued pork over pasta with Cabot cheddar, and a wide choice of desserts.

BEYOND

   ✪ **Rainbow Sweets** (802-426-3531), 1689 US 2, Marshfield. Open Wed.–Sun., June–February, for breakfast, lunch, and dinner. This village café, owned by Bill Tecosky and Trish Halloran, has been a landmark foodie destination for more than 40 years. Stop by in the morning for empanadas and espresso, or for a lunch of Moroccan b'stilla or a savory brioche. Homemade pizza is available on weekend nights. The bakery, which sells European sweet and savory pastries, is perhaps most famous for "Johnny Depps on a Plate," a custard-filled profiterole dipped in caramel.

   ((ŗ)) **Red Hen Bakery & Café** (802-223-5200; redhenbaking.com), 961 US 2, Middlesex, just off I-89 Exit 9. Open seven days, for breakfast and lunch. Husband-and-wife team Randy George and Liza Cain are Vermont bread barons, famous for their crusty, organic loaves. These artisan breads are served with just about everything at this combination bakery, café, and gourmet foods store. The blackboard menu lists house-made soups and signature sandwiches. Sweet and savory pastries crowd the cases and counter. For breakfast, grab an espresso and maple-frosted cinnamon bun or breakfast sandwich. Or purchase a bag of

Vermont granola at **Nutty Steph's** (802-229-2090; nuttystephs.com), located in the same building and open daily. In addition to granola and trail mix, the company's other handcrafted products include chocolate confections, chocolate bars, and specialty candies.

## ✱ Entertainment

THEATER ♿ **Barre Opera House** (802-476-8188; barreoperahouse.org), 6 North Main Street, Barre. Built in 1899 after fire destroyed the original 1866 opera hall, this intimate, acoustically outstanding, 650-seat theater occupies the upper floors of city hall. Year-round programming ranges from local theater productions and dance to international music, symphonies, and opera.

♿ **Lost Nation Theater** (802-229-0492; lostnationtheater.org), Montpelier City Hall Arts Center, 39 Main Street, Montpelier. More than 100 events are staged each year including cabarets, concerts, and black-box productions of contemporary plays, classics, and original works.

**☉ Unadilla Theater** (802-456-8968; unadilla.org), 501 Blachly Road, Marshfield, on the Marshfield-East Calais town line. Part of the charm of this performing arts theater is its unconventional pastoral setting. Bill Blachly launched his 100-seat theater in a Quonset hut dairy barn in rural Vermont in 1979, adding a second venue on his rural property in 2012. Several plays are presented in repertory, Thurs.–Sun., in summer. Patrons are invited to picnic on the grounds before the performance and to browse the perpetual used-book sale during intermission. Silent and classic films are shown Monday nights.

## MUSIC

### IN MONTPELIER

**Brown Bag Music Series** (802-223-9604; montpelieralive.com). Free lunchtime concerts Thursdays in the summer at the Christ Church Courtyard, 64 State Street.

**Capital City Concerts** (capitalcityconcerts.org), a classical chamber music series in Montpelier, stages five concerts per year. The main venue is the Unitarian Church of Montpelier, with additional concerts at the Champlain Valley Unitarian Universalist Society, Middlebury, and Paramount Theater, Rutland.

**Farmers Night Concert Series** (802-828-2228; leg.state.vt.us). Free concerts are given on Wednesdays in the House Chamber at the statehouse, January–April, when the legislature is in session. The series began in the nineteenth century for lawmakers who found themselves far from home with little to do in the evening after a day's session. At first the men performed for one another. Today the entertainment is a mix of talks and music by various Vermont performing groups.

### BEYOND

**Adamant Music School** (802-223-3347; adamant.org), 1241 Haggett Road, Adamant. Piano students perform public concerts throughout the summer at Waterside Hall at this bucolic spot between East Montpelier and Calais. Concertgoers are welcome to view the paintings displayed in the hall and the sculptures in the outdoor Meditation Garden.

**QuarryWorks Theater** (802-229-6978; quarryworks.org), 743 Quarry Road, Adamant. The Adamant Community Cultural Foundation offers free summer theater productions at its QuarryWorks Theater near the Adamant Music School. Reservations are a must—the theater only seats 50—and may be made two weeks in advance. Playgoers may arrive early to picnic on the grounds.

FILM **Capitol Showcase**, 93 State Street, Montpelier, and **Paramount Twin**

Cinema, 241 North Main Street, Barre, are both classic old movie houses showing first-run feature films (802-229-0343; fgbtheaters.com).

**The Savoy** (802-229-0598; savoytheater.com), 26 Main Street, Montpelier. The capital's only theater for independent, foreign, and art films also has occasional speakers and special events. Concession offerings include gourmet chocolates, craft beers and wines, and organic popcorn with real melted butter.

## ✳ Selective Shopping

ANTIQUES **East Barre Antique Mall** (802-479-5190; eastbarreantiquemallvt .com), 133 Mill Street, East Barre. Open May–October. Closed Mondays. This sprawling former furniture store houses central Vermont's largest group antiques shop with 400 consignees and dealers on three floors. A number of other antiques shops are scattered throughout the area, including along US 2 from Montpelier to Danville.

ART GALLERIES AND CRAFTS STUDIOS *Note:* Check the Montpelier Alive website (montpelieralive.com) for scheduled **Art Walks** with music and art throughout downtown.

**Ann's Weavery** (802-223-7177; annsweavery.com), 961 US 2, Middlesex, just off I-89 Exit 9. Open Tues.–Sat. This fiber arts gallery sells handcrafted wearables, wall art, crafting kits, and knitting, needle felting, and weaving supplies. Owner Ann Lovald offers weaving lessons by appointment on an Ashford rigid heddle loom.

**Artisans Hand Craft Gallery** (802-229-9492; artisanshand.com), 89 Main Street, Montpelier. Open daily. An exceptional variety of Vermont craftwork by a cooperative of more than 100 artists working in multiple media.

**Green Mountain Hooked Rugs** (802-223-1333; greenmountainhookedrugs .com), 2838 County Road, Montpelier

(near Morse Farm). Open Wed.–Sat. Stephanie Allen-Krauss comes from four generations of rug hookers and sells colorful examples of the craft at this gallery. Inquire about the Green Mountain Rug School, the nation's largest, which is held each June and offers traditional and contemporary rug-hooking classes.

**The HiVE** (802-595-4866; thehivevt .com), 961 US 2, Middlesex. Open Fri.–Tues. The HiVE, an artist collective, sells handcrafted items and up-cycled art including jewelry, felted crafts, paintings, and furniture by Vermont craftspeople.

**The Mud Studio** (802-224-7000; themudstudio.com), 961 US 2, Middlesex. Open year-round. Closed Tues. Several dozen individual potters share this studio producing stoneware and porcelain, both whimsical and functional. The studio offers pottery classes for children and adults.

✐ SPA (**Studio Place Arts**) (802-479-7069; studioplacearts.com), 201 North Main Street, Barre. Open Tues.–Sat. This visual arts center has classes for both adults and kids and showcases the work of contemporary artists in its galleries. SPA also rents studio space to artists in its historic three-story building.

((ꞏ)) **T.W. Wood Art Gallery and Arts Center** (802-262-6035; twwoodgallery .org), 46 Barre Street, Montpelier. Open Tues.–Sat. Established in 1896, but now relocated closer to downtown, this gallery houses one of the state's largest permanent art collections. Changing exhibits feature contemporary Vermont artists and craftspeople.

Also see vermontcrafts.com.

BOOKSTORES ✐ ♿ **Bear Pond Books** (802-229-0774; bearpondbooks.com), 77 Main Street, Montpelier. Open daily. One of the state's top independent bookstores stocks new and used books, including a large selection of literature, art, and children's books. Check the website for scheduled author events, including readings and workshops.

&#x267F; **The Country Bookshop** (802-454-8439; thecountrybookshop.com), 35 Mill Street (off US 2 at the blinker), Plainfield. Open daily, but it's wise to call ahead. The first floor of this 150-year-old house overflows with more than 30,000 books—everything from paperbacks to first editions—plus postcards and paper ephemera. Frequent sales with deep discounts allow owner Ben Koenig to keep the inventory fresh. Specialties include books on folk music, folklore, and bells and carillons.

✒ **Next Chapter Bookstore** (802-476-3114; nextchapterbooksvt.com), 162 North Main Street, Barre. Open Mon.–Sat. Owner Cynthia Duprey, a former first-grade teacher and in-home daycare operator, channeled her love of books and reading into a fun business venture. Her store specializes in children's books and educational games with a tree house/reading loft and regular story hours for young readers, although the establishment also has a diverse selection for adults and hosts adult book clubs.

FARMERS' MARKETS Local farmers' markets include Barre Farmers' Market, Capital City Farmers' Market (Montpelier), Northfield Farmers' Market, and Plainfield Farmers' Market. Dates, times, and details at vermontagriculture.com.

FARMS The area has a number of maple-sugaring operations, which get active once the sap starts flowing February through April. Vermont Maple Open House Weekend is held annually in late March. Information and a list of participating sugarhouses can be found at vermontmaple.org/openhouse.

✒ **Bragg Farm Sugarhouse & Gift Shop** (802-223-5757; braggfarm.com), 1005 VT 14 North, East Montpelier. Open daily year-round. This eighth-generation farm still gathers sap the old-fashioned way (in 2,200 buckets), using a wood-fired evaporator for boiling. The shop carries a variety of Vermont maple products, cheeses, crafts, and specialty foods and includes a small museum and ice cream parlor with maple creemees and milkshakes. Free guided tours of the farm are available year-round with sugar-on-snow served March–April weekends.

**Fresh Tracks Farm Vineyard and Winery** (802-223-1151; freshtracksfarm.com), 4373 VT 12, Berlin. Store and tasting room open daily. Christina Castegren and her husband Kris Tootle grow all their own grapes on 14 acres for their award-winning wines and tap 1,000 maple trees for syrup and maple wines. Live music some evenings in summer.

✪ ♂ ✒ **Green Mountain Girls Farm** (802-505-9840; eatstayfarm.com), 923 Loop Road, Northfield. Open year-round. Laura Olsen and Mari Omland offer guided farm tours and hands-on farm experiences, ranging from one hour to multiple days. These may include animal care and feeding, milking goats, cheese-making, and farm-to-plate cooking classes where participants harvest farm produce, collect eggs, and visit the farm's Omnivore Farm Stand to select meat (humanely raised and organically managed pork, chicken, lamb, turkey, and goat) to cook a meal in the barn kitchen. The farm also hosts yoga sessions and frequent community events. Farmstays are available.

**Morse Farm Maple Sugarworks** (see *Must See* and *Cross-Country Skiing* on pages 263 and 269, respectively).

SPECIAL SHOPS **Buch Spieler Records** (802-229-0449; buchspielerrecords.com), 27 Langdon Street, Montpelier. Open daily. This independent music store, in business since 1973, specializes in new and vintage vinyl, although the store also carries novelties and old school comics.

✒ **Woodbury Mountain Toys** (802-223-4272; woodburymountaintoys.com), 24 State Street, Montpelier. Open daily. Their motto is "Come in and play with us." This independent toy store carries many locally made and hard-to-find items as well as major lines. It's like a hands-on whimsical toy museum, but you can take the displays home.

## ✻ Special Events

*Mid-March:* **Green Mountain Film Festival** (gmffestival.org). Artistic, interpretive, and thought-provoking feature films and shorts are shown at several Montpelier venues during this nine-day celebration of film.

*April:* **PoemCity** (montpelieralive.com) celebrates National Poetry Month with poems, workshops, lectures, displays, readings, and other events all month.

*Mid-May:* **Black Fly Festival** (blackflyfestival.org), a quirky local celebration at the Adamant Co-op with live music, a pie-baking contest, nature walks, a parade, and a fashion show to celebrate winter's end and the start of black fly season.

*Memorial Day weekend:* **Open Studio Weekend** (vermontcrafts.com), where artisans open their studios to the public for tours and sales, takes place throughout Vermont.

*June–July:* **Vermont Mountaineers Baseball** (thevermontmountaineers .com). New England intercollegiate

baseball games at the Recreation Field, Elm Street, Montpelier. Check website for schedule.

*July 3:* **Montpelier's Independence Day Celebration** (montpelieralive.com). Live music, games, road race, parade, vendors, and a giant fireworks display; various venues including the statehouse lawn.

*Last weekend in July:* **Barre Heritage Festival and Homecoming Days** (barreheritagefestival.org). This four-day downtown festival with music, street entertainment, vintage car show, bathtub races, and street fair celebrates the community's unique cultural history and heritage.

*Labor Day weekend:* **Northfield Labor Day Weekend** (northfieldlaborday.org) is a family-fun weekend of events with music, games, car show, chicken barbecue, and parade with floats and Norwich University cadets.

*Mid-October:* **Cabot Apple Pie Festival** (cabotvermont.org/annual-events) is a daylong apple pie celebration with a serious apple pie contest, crafts fair, and silent auction.

*Last weekend in November:* **Winter Festival of Vermont Crafters** (greater barrecraftguild.com) is central Vermont's largest craft fair with more than 100 vendors and free admission.

# KILLINGTON/RUTLAND AREA

Killington Resort is among the largest ski areas in the eastern United States. It boasts seven mountain areas, including Pico Mountain, with an expansive lift network and snowmaking system. Killington Peak, at 4,235 feet, the second highest Vermont summit, is flanked by four other mountains and faces a majestic range across Sherburne Pass.

The road through this upland village has been heavily traveled since the settling of Rutland (11 miles west) and Woodstock (20 miles east), but there wasn't much here. In 1924 an elaborate, rustic-style inn was built at the junction of US 4, the Appalachian Trail, and the new Long Trail. A winter annex across the road came in 1938, when Pico Mountain (now part of Killington) installed one of the country's first T-bars. But the logging village of Sherburne Center (now the town of Killington) was practically a ghost town on December 13, 1958, when Killington Basin Ski Area opened.

Condominiums currently cluster at higher elevations, while lodges, inns, and motels are strung along the 4.5-mile length of Killington Road and west along US 4 as it slopes 9 miles down through Mendon to Rutland. Ski lodges are salted along VT 100

**VIEW OF KILLINGTON MOUNTAIN** KILLINGTON RESORT

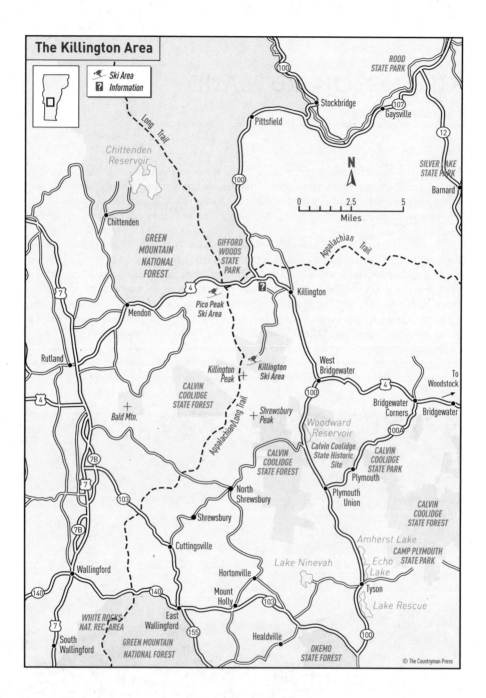

The Killington Area

Ski Area
Information

ROOD STATE PARK

100

Stockbridge

107

Pittsfield

Gaysville

12

Chittenden Reservoir

SILVER LAKE STATE PARK

100

N

Barnard

Chittenden

0    2.5    5
Miles

GREEN MOUNTAIN NATIONAL FOREST

GIFFORD WOODS STATE PARK

Appalachian Trail

7

4

Killington

Pico Peak Ski Area

Mendon

Rutland

Killington Peak

Killington Ski Area

West Bridgewater

To Woodstock

4

7

CALVIN COOLIDGE STATE FOREST

4

Bald Mtn.

Appalachian/Long Trail

100

Bridgewater Corners

Bridgewater

Shrewsbury Peak

100A

Woodward Reservoir

7B

Calvin Coolidge State Historic Site

CALVIN COOLIDGE STATE PARK

7

CALVIN COOLIDGE STATE FOREST

North Shrewsbury

Plymouth

Plymouth Union

103

Shrewsbury

CALVIN COOLIDGE STATE FOREST

7B

Cuttingsville

Amherst Lake

CAMP PLYMOUTH STATE PARK

Wallingford

Lake Ninevah

Echo Lake

140

Hortonville

Tyson

140

Mount Holly

Lake Rescue

7B

103

WHITE ROCKS NAT. REC. AREA

East Wallingford

155

Healdville

100

7

South Wallingford

GREEN MOUNTAIN NATIONAL FOREST

OKEMO STATE FOREST

© The Countryman Press

north to Pittsfield, and in the village of Chittenden, sequestered up a back road off US 4, near a mountain-backed reservoir. Forested mountains dominate the surrounding landscape in all directions. This is a major crossroads for Appalachian and Long Trail hikers as well as for vehicles.

A gem at Killington Resort is the Peak Lodge, a glass-walled summit lodge on Lincoln Peak, open year-round. It offers one of the most spectacular views in the Northeast, a destination in its own right. It marks the spot on which the Reverend Samuel Peters in 1763 is said to have christened all that he could see "Verd Monts." Even in winter non-skiers are always welcome.

With a purposeful emphasis on promoting the wider community in partnership with the ski resorts, a visitor center has been positioned at the junction of US 4 and VT 100, stocked with information about local hikes and extensive biking trails, both on and off the mountain. Summer and fall events have multiplied, and more restaurants are open year-round.

Home of the Vermont State Fair, Rutland is the business and shopping center for a large rural radius. Stolid, early-Victorian mansions and streets crisscrossed with railroad tracks testify to its nineteenth-century prosperity, when Rutland was known as "the marble city." The long-established shops along Merchants Row and Center Street, among the state's best-preserved commercial blocks, have enjoyed renewed attention.

Rutland lies in a broad, rolling corridor between the Taconic Mountains along the New York border and the Green Mountains running up through Vermont. The valley is broad enough to accommodate two major north–south routes. US 7, a major route, hugs the Green Mountains and, with the exception of the heavily trafficked strip around Rutland, is a scenic ride. VT 30 to the west is quieter, winding through farm country and past two major lakes, Lake Bomoseen and Lake St. Catherine, both popular summer meccas.

US 4 is a mountain-rimmed, four-lane highway from Fair Haven, at the New York line, to Rutland, where it joins US 7 north a bit before breaking east again, heading up and over Killington. In 2011, US 4 from West Rutland to Hartford was named the "Crossroads of Vermont Byway" by the Vermont Scenic Byway Program (vermontvacation.com/byways). VT 140 from Wallingford to Poultney is a scenic byway through Middletown Springs, where old mineral water springs form the core of a pleasant park. Bed & breakfasts are salted through farm country and the high hamlets of Shrewsbury and North Shrewsbury, in the Green Mountains, less than 10 miles from Rutland.

GUIDANCE **The Rutland Region Chamber of Commerce** (802-773-2747) maintains a website (rutlandvermont.com) and the chamber office downtown at 50 Merchants Row operates a year-round visitor center in the lobby, Mon.–Sat., 8:30–5.

**Killington Chamber of Commerce** (802-773-4181; killingtonchamber.com) provides information about the area, and the **Killington Pico Area Association** has installed a **Welcome Center** (802-773-4181) near the junction of US 4 and VT 100 across from the Killington access road, open winter/spring weekdays 9–5, weekends 10–2, and summer/fall weekends, 10–5; restrooms.

Vermont maintains the **Fair Haven Welcome Center** (802-265-4763) on US 4 near the New York line, open daily 7–7.

GETTING THERE *By air:* **Rutland-Southern Vermont Regional Airport** (flyrutlandvt .com) is served by Cape Air (800-CAPE-AIR; capeair.com), with regular flights to Boston, and charter companies. Links to rental cars and taxis are on the website.

*By train:* **Amtrak** (800-USA-RAIL; amtrak.com). Daily service to and from New York City on the Ethan Allen Express to Rutland.

*By bus:* **Marble Valley Regional Transit District** (802-773-3244; thebus.com), 158 Spruce Street, Rutland, operator of "**The Bus**," connects Rutland with Killington, the Rutland airport, Manchester, Fair Haven, and Middlebury, as well as to points within the city. In winter, **shuttle buses** run from Marble Valley in Rutland to several Killington points, including Pico Mountain on US 4 and points on Killington Road. **Vermont**

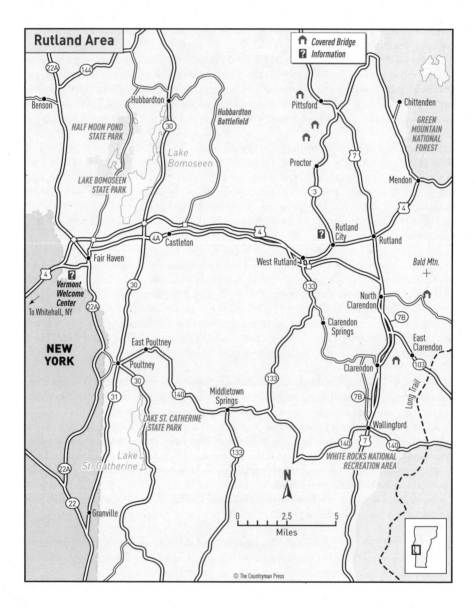

Rutland Area

Covered Bridge
Information

22A
144
Benson
Hubbardton
HALF MOON POND STATE PARK
30
Lake Bomoseen
Hubbardton Battlefield
LAKE BOMOSEEN STATE PARK
Pittsford
Chittenden
GREEN MOUNTAIN NATIONAL FOREST
Proctor
7
Mendon
3
4
4A
Castleton
4
Rutland City
Rutland
Fair Haven
West Rutland
Bald Mtn.
4
Vermont Welcome Center
22A
133
To Whitehall, NY
North Clarendon
7B
East Clarendon
NEW YORK
East Poultney
Clarendon Springs
30
Poultney
Clarendon
103
133
31
30
140
Middletown Springs
7B
LAKE ST. CATHERINE STATE PARK
Wallingford
22A
133
140
7
140
Lake St. Catherine
WHITE ROCKS NATIONAL RECREATION AREA
Long Trail
22
Granville
N
0    2.5    5
Miles

© The Countryman Press

**TransLines** (844-888-7267; vttranslines.com) stops at the Killington Pico Area Welcome Center, US 4, en route from Lebanon, NH, to Rutland.

*Getting around:* A **free shuttle** (802-422-FREE) operates nightly in ski season among lodging places and five restaurants along the access road.

## ✳ Towns and Villages

**Poultney** (population 3,432; poultneyvt.com) is on VT 30 near the New York border, north of Lake St. Catherine, home to Green Mountain College, a four-year coed liberal arts college emphasizing environmental studies. The town has significant journalistic associations: Horace Greeley, founder of the *New York Tribune*, lived at the Eagle Tavern in East Poultney (now a private home) while he learned his trade at the *East Poultney National Spectator* in the 1820s. George Jones, who helped found *The New York Times* in 1851, worked with Greeley. Attracted by the slate quarries, Vermont's first Jewish community settled here during the Civil War, and Welsh immigrants came to work in the quarries jobs. Until the 1950s, it was one of the largest Welsh-speaking communities in the country. Green Mountain College has an extensive Welsh archive, teaches Welsh heritage, and its choir still sings Welsh songs at each of its performances.

**East Poultney** is a picturesque hamlet worth visiting. The fine white Baptist church, built in 1805, is the centerpiece, standing on a small green surrounded by a cluster of historic buildings: the Melodeon Factory, Union Academy, and the Old School House. Tours are available for download at poultneyhistoricalsociety.org. **The Original Vermont Store** is located here, next to the fast-flowing Poultney River.

**Castleton** (population 4,717; castletonvt.com) at VT 4A and VT 30, is home to **Castleton University**, the oldest member of Vermont's state college system. Here, in Remington Tavern, Ethan Allen and Seth Warner planned the capture of Ticonderoga. Blacksmith Samuel Beach—Vermont's own Paul Revere—reputedly ran some 60 miles in 24 hours to recruit more men for the raid. The town grew rapidly after the Revolution, now showcasing pillared Greek Revival houses, most designed by Thomas Royal Dake, many on Main Street. Note the **Ransom-Rehlen Mansion**, with its 17 Ionic columns, and Congregational Meeting House, now the **Federated Church**, with the pulpit that Dake completed with his own funds. Between 1850 and 1870, the West Castleton Railroad and Slate Company was the largest marble plant in the country.

**Fair Haven** (population 2,952; fairhavenvt.org), located where US 4, VT 4A, and VT 22A intersect, is at the core of Vermont's slate industry. In the 1780s, the controversial Matthew Lyon started an ironworks and published a newspaper called *The Scourge of Aristocracy*, in which he lambasted the Federalists. Elected to Congress in 1796, Lyon had scuffles on the floor of the House and was jailed under the Alien and Sedition Acts for his criticism of President Adams, causing massive public uproar. Lyon was reelected to Congress while still in jail and cast the tie-breaking vote that made Thomas Jefferson president instead of Aaron Burr. Around the spacious green are three Victorian mansions (two faced with marble) built by descendants of Ira Allen, founder of the University of Vermont.

**Benson** (population 1,056; benson-vt.com), west of VT 22A, 8 miles north of Fair Haven, is one of those tiny villages "that time forgot" except as a scenic photo op. In recent years it has developed a creative personality, with artisans and special shops.

**Pittsfield** (population 546; pittsfieldvt.com) is almost completely enclosed in the Green Mountain National Forest on VT 100 north of Killington on your way to the White River and Mad River valleys. This route was one of the most severely damaged by 2011's Hurricane Irene, isolated for two weeks. Pittsfield is also known as the home of the running, biking, and snowshoe races and endurance competitions introduced by Joe De Sena, the town's major landholder, owner of the Amee Farm Lodge, the Trailside Inn, Amee Farm, and the Original General Store (see peak.com and spartanrace.com) and creator of a 20-mile trail system.

# ✳ Must See

○ **Vermont Marble Museum** (800-427-1396; vermontmarblemuseum.org), 52 Main Street, Proctor. From Business US 4 in West Rutland follow VT 3 north. Open daily mid-May–October. This is a privately maintained museum housed in a vast old marble shed on Otter Creek. Approach across a multi-arched marble bridge, built in 1915 as a memorial to Fletcher D. Proctor, scion of the family, who formed The Vermont Marble Company in 1870. An award-winning film relates the story of Vermont's part in the quarrying and carving of the Tomb of the Unknown Soldier at Arlington National Cemetery. Marble from Proctor and Danby was used for the US Supreme Court building, the Lincoln Memorial, and the Beinecke Library at Yale. Marble quarrying continues in Vermont and includes a subterranean quarry in Danby. The museum has an extensive gift shop. A quarter-mile walkway leads to the old Sutherland Falls Quarry. Pick up a sandwich or Vermont specialty treat at the Proctor Co-op or at the Museum's Cookie Barn. Admission.

**The Carving Studio and Sculpture Center** (802-438-2097; carvingstudio.org), 636 Marble Street, West Rutland. Sited at the head of a 200-acre former quarrying and manufacturing site, the center offers workshops, residencies, sculpture sales, a sculpture garden, and rotating exhibits and events. Check website for schedule.

**The New England Maple Museum** (802-483-9414; maplemuseum.com), 4578 US 7, Pittsford. Call for hours. Admission charged. Maple was originally a Native American sugar traded with European settlers. This museum illustrates the history, production, and consumption of maple syrup and its byproducts. View the Danforth Collection of antique equipment, murals, and a 10-minute media presentation. There's a tasting room, too.

**Chaffee Art Center** (802-775-0356; chaffeeartcenter.org), 16 South Main Street, Rutland. Open Tues.–Sat. In the midst of a five-year expansion and rededication project for the building's interior and new permaculture gardens outside, the Chaffee's galleries are housed in an 1896 Queen Anne Victorian building listed on the National Register of Historic Places. Permanent and periodic exhibits and youth galleries inside are intended for school displays, where students can view traditional and contemporary paintings, sculpture, crafts, graphics, and photography. Donation appreciated.

**Slate Valley Museum** (518-642-1417; slatevalleymuseum.org), 17 Water Street, Granville, NY. Open year-round, closed Sun.–Mon. Admission charged; children 12 and under are free. Just across the New York border from Poultney, it includes a quarry shanty, tools, a mural, paintings, photographs, family artifacts, and a gift shop.

**Wilson Castle** (802-773-3284; wilsoncastle.com), 2970 West Proctor Road between West Rutland and Proctor. Open for guided tours daily, late May–late October. This nineteenth-century turreted mansion was built in 1867 for the English bride of a Vermont physician, John Johnson, no expense spared. The opulent furnishings include Venetian tapestries, 400-year-old Chinese scrolls, a Louis XIV French onyx-covered table, and a gallery of classic sculpture, not to mention 84 stained-glass windows. In 1939, it was acquired by pioneering radio engineer Herbert Lee Wilson, who established AM radio towers around the world. Inquire about special Saturday-night murder mystery dinners and the Halloween Haunted House. The mansion can also be rented as a party or wedding venue.

The **Hubbardton Battlefield** (802-273-2282; historicsites.vermont.gov/hubbardton), 5696 Monument Hill Road, Hubbardton, 7 miles north of the posted US 4 exit. A hilltop visitor center is open late May–Columbus Day, Thurs.–Sun. Admission charged. Some guided tours available to sites on the grounds. Battle buffs won't want to miss the diorama and narrated 3-D map of this 1777 Revolutionary War site. Of all American battlefields, this one looks most the way it did on the day of the battle. Paths lead through wooded landscapes, signs describe events that unfolded, and the views of the Taconic Mountains to the south, Pittsford Ridge to the east, and the Adirondacks to the west are unparalleled.

## ✳ To Do

BIKING There's great biking here; check for maps at voga.org. Little-trafficked roads wind through the rolling countryside around Lake St. Catherine and Middletown Springs. Rentals are available from the **Alpine Bike Works** (802-773-0000; alpinebikeworks.com) at 2326 US 4 in Killington. Rentals and repairs are available. They also have bike skis for winter fun.

**Pine Hill Park** (pinehillpark.org), located entirely in the city of Rutland, with its trailhead at the Giorgetti Athletic Complex, 2 Oak Street Extension, Rutland. The park offers a unique 300-acre, highly refined 16-mile single-track trail system for mountain biking, running, hiking, walking, geocaching, and snowshoeing. No motorized vehicles allowed in park.

**Green Mountain Trails** (gmtrails.org), VT 100, Pittsfield. Accessible from Amee Farm, maps available at the Original General Store. Twenty-five miles on 750 acres, a fast-growing network of multi-use single-track trails geared to varied abilities; check the website for races and events.

See **Killington Resort** sidebar for mountain biking on page 290.

Also see *Hiking* on page 287.

BOATING Speed, ski, pontoon, and fishing boat rentals as well as canoes and kayaks for **Lake Bomoseen** are available from **Woodard Marine, Inc.** (802-265-3690; woodardmarine.com), with showroom and boat rentals at 615 Creek Road, Castleton.

**Lake St. Catherine, Half Moon,** and **Bomoseen State Parks** (vtstateparks.com) each offer canoe, kayak, and rowboat rentals. See *Green Space* on page 288.

**Chittenden Reservoir** is a sublime place to canoe or kayak, 674 acres backed by mountains. Boat access is at the end of Chittenden Dam Road. **Woodward Reservoir** on VT 100 south is another beautiful spot for paddling.

**Base Camp Outfitters** (802-775-0166; basecampvt.com) 2363 US 4, Killington, offers kayak rentals for use on **Kent Pond** in Killington.

**Vermont Adventure Tours** (802-773-3343; vermontadventuretours.com) 233 Woodstock Avenue, Rutland, offers canoe, kayak, and whitewater tours as well as canoe and kayak rentals.

COVERED BRIDGES There are six covered bridges in the area: the 1836 **Kingsley** or **Mill River Bridge**, East Road, off Airport Road, East Clarendon; the 1880 **Brown Bridge**, off Cold River Road, Shrewsbury; the 1840 **Depot Bridge**, off US 7 north, Pittsford; the 1849 **Cooley Bridge**, Elm Street, Pittsford; the 1843 **Gorham** or **Goodnough Bridge**, Gorham Bridge Road, off VT 3, Pittsford; and the 1830 **Twin Bridge**, East Pittsford Road, off US 7 north, Rutland.

DISC GOLF **Killington Disc Golf Course** at Killington Ski Resort (killington.com) begins at the K-1 Lodge and meanders its way through 18 holes on Snowden Mountain.

FISHING Licenses are available at vtfishandwildlife.com and additional resources at voga.org. Landlocked salmon and trout can be had in **Chittenden Reservoir**; trout in **Mendon Brook**. There is fishing in **Kent** and **Colton** ponds, and in the **White, Tweed,** and **Ottauquechee** rivers. **Woodward Reservoir** on VT 100 south and **Echo Lake** in Tyson (accessible from **Camp Plymouth State Park**) have good fishing as well.

    **Stream and Brook Fly-Fishing** (802-989-0398; streamandbrook.com) offers beginners' programs and full- and half-day guided trips. Rod Start, a Vermonter with over 30 years' fishing experience, offers **Green Mountain Fishing Guide Service** (802-446-3375; greenmtnguide.com), based in Tinmouth.

    **Dwight D. Eisenhower National Fish Hatchery** (802-483-6618; fws.gov/ddenfh), 4 Holden Road, North Chittenden. Open daily. The Fish and Wildlife Service raises landlocked salmon and lake trout here; children can feed the fish.

FITNESS CENTERS AND SPAS **New Life Hiking Spa** (802-353-2954; newlifehikingspa .com), based at Killington Mountain Lodge (see *Lodging* on page 294). Mid-May–September. Since 1978. Weight loss fitness programs that combine sensible eating and moderate exercise. Days begin with a pre-breakfast walk. Body conditioning, yoga, and hiking (all levels). Meals are varied, focused on energy and stamina (a good solo vacation).

    **The Gymnasium** (802-773-5333; thegymnasium.net), 11 Cottage Street, Rutland. Open daily. A complete wellness and cardiovascular center with a full line of equipment and classes.

    **Vermont Sport & Fitness Club** (802-775-9916; vermontsportandfitness.com), 40 Curtis Avenue, Rutland. Open daily. Full-service health club with tennis and racquet sports; classes; cardio, strength, and training equipment; nutrition programming; and personal training.

    *Also see* **Killington Resort** sidebar on page 289.

ENDURANCE RACES **Peak Races** (peakraces.com), based at Amee Farm, Pittsfield. The latest craze in adventure sports, ultramarathons, and mountain bike races on ever-expanding, single-track **Green Mountain Trails** (gmtrails.org) on 750 acres of woods and fields, some involving multiple obstacles and physical challenges, taking multiple days. The brainchild of Joe De Sena, Wall Street trader and author of the best-seller *Spartan Up.*

GOLF *See* **Killington Resort** sidebar on page 289.

    **Green Mountain National Golf Course** (802-422-4653; gmngc.com), 476 Barrows Towne Road, Killington. This highly rated 18-hole course, clubhouse, three practice teeing areas, four target greens, and an 8,000-square-foot putting green. Pro shop, restaurant, and lessons.

    **The Rutland Country Club** (802-773-3254; rutlandcountryclub.com), 275 Grove Street, Rutland, a mile north of Rutland's business section. With 18 holes, rolling terrain; restaurant, pro shop, and putting green.

    **Proctor-Pittsford Country Club** (802-483-9379; proctor-pittsford.com), 311 Country Club Drive, Pittsford. Scenic countryside, 18 holes, a lounge, and a small-town feel.

    **Lake St. Catherine Country Club** (802-287-9341; lakestcatherinecountryclub.com), 2725 VT 30, Poultney. Restaurant, pro shop, and lessons; 18 holes over varied locations.

    **Prospect Pointe Country Club** (802-468-5581), 111 Prospect Point Road, Bomoseen. Offers nine holes on Lake Bomoseen.

**Stonehedge Golf** (802-773-2666; stonehedgegolf.com), 216 Squire Road, North Clarendon, is a nine-hole, par-3 public course with great rates. Stay in form during the off-season at the **Stonehedge Indoor Golf Center** (802-779-9595), 172 South Main Street, Rutland.

HIKING Pick up a copy of the widely available, free *Killington Region Hiking Guide* (discoverkillington.com).

The **Appalachian Trail** (appalachiantrail.org) and the **Long Trail** (greenmountainclub .org), accessed north and south from US 4 in Killington. Websites offer access to maps and guidebooks. For guided hikes, check out Killington-based **Appalachian Trail Adventures** (888-855-8655; appalachiantrailadventures.com).

**Deer Leap Trail**, off US 4 behind the Inn at Long Trail, a popular short hike: 45 minutes one-way, up a winding, moderately steep path. There is a southerly panoramic view from the top of a tall cliff. For a whole-day hike, continue along the Long Trail to Chittenden Reservoir or branch east at the Maine Junction at Willard Gap onto the Appalachian Trail. This trail also connects with Gifford Woods State Park. Park a car at the other end and be sure to bring a hiking map.

**Bald Mountain.** This 3-mile, three-hour round-trip hike is in Aitken State Forest, off Notch Road from US 4 in Mendon. The blue-blazed circle trail begins just past the intersection with Wheelerville Road. On the West Haven side is the **Helen W. Buckner Memorial Preserve** (nature.org) with hiking trails and nature exploration in this Nature Conservancy tract.

**Thundering Falls Trail**, Killington. Off River Road, a 900-foot handicapped-accessible boardwalk and path through floodplain and forest lead to a platform at the base of Thundering Falls, a sheer rock face with water pouring down it, part of the Appalachian Trail.

**Robert T. Stafford White Rocks National Recreation Area**, VT 140 off US 7 in Wallingford. Follow signs from the White Rocks Picnic Area. A 2,600-foot, conical white peak surrounded by quartzite boulders that retain ice and snow into summer. Pick up a hiking guidebook before starting out.

**Delaware and Hudson Rail Trail**, Poultney–Castleton. A rail-trail enjoyed by hikers, snowmobilers, walkers, bikers, equestrians, and cross-country skiers.

HORSEBACK RIDING **Mountain Top Inn & Resort Equestrian Program** (802-483-2311; mountaintopinn.com), 195 Mountain Top Road, Chittenden, offers May–October horseback riding geared to every level, one- and two-hour guided trail rides, English and Western. Dressage, cross-country, and children's instruction are available. Trail rides for ages 8 and up.

**Pond Hill Ranch** (802-468-2449; pondhillranch.com), 1683 Pond Hill Road, Castleton, a 200-acre, family-owned ranch offering trail rides, lessons, and pony rides for children. Saturday-night **rodeos**, summer and fall.

**Chipman Stables** (802-293-5242; chipmanstables.com), 33 Danby Pawlet Road, Danby Four Corners. This family-run stable offers trail rides, hayrides, and pony rides.

ROCK CLIMBING **Green Mountain Rock Climbing Center** (802-773-3343; vermont climbing.com), based in Rutland at 223 Woodstock Avenue, offers lessons and climbs for ages 4 and up, all abilities. Inquire about winter ice climbing.

SWIMMING **Elfin Lake Beach**, off VT 140 west, 2 miles southeast of Wallingford, and **Crystal Beach**, a municipally owned white sand beach on the eastern shore of **Lake Bomoseen**. **Kent Pond** in Killington is town owned, accessible from River and

Thundering Brook roads. near the town offices. Also see state parks (vtstateparks.com) under *Green Space*. For pools, see *Fitness Centers & Spas*.

TENNIS **Summit Lodge** (802-422-3535; summitlodgevermont.com), 200 Summit Road, Killington Road, Killington. Four clay outdoor courts are available to the public if not in use by members. **Vermont Sport & Fitness Club** (802-775-9916; vermontsportandfitness.com) in Rutland has three indoor and eight outdoor courts.

**Public courts** are maintained by the city of Rutland and the towns of Chittenden, Killington, Castleton, Fair Haven, Poultney, and Proctor.

## ✳ Winter Sports

CROSS-COUNTRY SKIING AND SNOWSHOEING **Mountain Meadows Cross-Country Ski and Snowshoe Area**, operated by **Base Camp Outfitters** (802-775-7077; xcskiing.net), 2363 US 4, Killington, east of the Killington access road. Open daily (conditions permitting). Rentals and sales.

**Mountain Top Nordic Ski & Snowshoe Center** (802-483-6089; mountaintopinn .com), 195 Mountain Top Road, Chittenden. Sixty km of trails, 40 km groomed. The Nordic Center is one of the country's oldest commercial cross-country ski centers. At 1,495–2,165 feet, the center offers sweeping views of mountains and Chittenden Reservoir. Rentals, lessons, and some snowmaking.

ICE SKATING In Rutland, Castleton University's **Spartan Arena** (802-775-3100) offers public ice skating, as does **Giorgetti Arena** (802-775-7976; rutlandrec.com) for the Rutland Recreation Department.

SLEIGH RIDES **Mountain Top Inn & Resort** (802-483-6089; mountaintopinn.com). Thirty-minute, horse-drawn sleigh rides in-season.

SNOWMOBILING **Mountain Top Inn & Resort** (802-483-6089; mountaintopinn.com) also offers guided snowmobile rides.

## ✳ Green Space

*Note:* For more information about the following, see **vtstateparks.com.**

**Calvin Coolidge State Forest**. This 16,000-acre preserve is scattered through seven towns and divided by VT 100 into two districts. It includes Killington and Shrewsbury Peaks. **Coolidge State Park** (802-672-3612), VT 100A, is east of Plymouth Notch. Open late May–mid-October, these 500 acres include a campground (62 campsites including 36 lean-tos, a dump station, a picnic area, and restrooms with hot showers), picnic shelters (no hookups), and hiking and snowmobile trails. **Camp Plymouth State Park** (802-228-2025), off VT 100 in Tyson, was a camp owned by the Boy Scouts of America until ownership was transferred to the state in 1984. It offers a beach on Echo Lake (picnic area, food concession), two open-air picnic pavilions, one enclosed shelter with a full kitchen, a group camping area, and four cottages. Inquire about gold panning and trails into the abandoned village of Plymouth Five Corners. North of the turnoff for VT 100A, the steep CCC Road (marked for Meadowsweet Farm) climbs away from VT 100 into the western swatch of the forest, with beautiful views of the valley. The road is

# BEAST OF THE EAST

**K**illington Resort (802-422-3333; killington.com), 4763 Killington Road, Killington. With more than 155 interconnected trails on six mountains plus 57 at its sister resort Pico Mountain (5 miles away and connected by shuttle service), Killington is unquestionably big, worthy of its title "Beast of the East." Thanks to five (counting Pico) entry points and a far-flung network of lifts and trails, skiers are dispersed throughout almost 2,000 skiable acres. Given its size and diversity, Killington attracts ski weekers in larger numbers than other eastern mountains, making for a lively midweek atmosphere. New England's first mountain to introduce high-quality snowmaking, it boasts the longest season in the east, traditionally beginning in October and lasting into May.

**DOWNHILL SKIING AND SNOWBOARDING** *Lifts:* 22, including 9 quads (5 high-speed) plus the Skyeship and K-1 Express Gondolas, 2 doubles, 3 triples, 6 surface lifts (carrying 38,315 riders per hour).

*Trails and slopes:* 155, with 1,509 skiable acres including 73 miles of trails.

*Vertical drop:* 3,050 feet.

*Snowmaking:* 600 acres of terrain, with 2,000-plus snow guns, including 1,400+ low-energy guns.

*Snowboarding:* Two half-pipes, 7 terrain parks, and The Stash, an "all-natural" terrain park with over 50 features such as rock-wall rides, log jibs, and cliff drops, designed to challenge intermediate and advanced riders.

*Facilities:* 6 base lodges, 5 ski rental shops, 1 mountaintop lodge, 5 lounges.

*Special programs:* Ramshead Family Center with a children's Snow Sports School divided into 5 levels of programs with a maximum of 3–5 students per instructor. More than 60 ski and snowboard school instructors hold the highest level of certification.

UNPARALLELED VIEWS FROM KILLINGTON SLOPES  KILLINGTON RESORT

*Rates* Check the website or phone Killington's Central Reservations (800-621-MTNS; killington.com) for many options. The best value is always the 5-day lifts/lodging package, available at most local inns, lodges, and condo rental offices.

**Pico Mountain** (802-422-3333; picomountain.com). One of Vermont's first mountain resorts, Pico opened in 1937 with a tow hooked up to the engine of a Hudson auto. Currently under the same ownership as Killington, the winter lifts at this family-friendly resort are only open Thurs.–Mon. and holiday weeks.

*Vertical drop:* 1,967 feet.

*Skiable acres:* 468, with 57 trails adding up to 19 miles, the largest percentage intermediate, all funneling to the base lodge.

*Lifts:* 2 express quads, 2 triples, and 2 doubles, 1 rope tow.

*Snowmaking:* 75 percent of trails have snowmaking.

*Facilities:* Rentals, instruction, sports center, and condo lodging (see killington.com).

**Killington Snowmobile Tours** (802-422-2121; snowmobilevermont.com). One- and two-hour mountain and backcountry tours, plus snowcross track for kids ages 4–11. Rental helmets, clothing, and boots.

## SUMMER/FALL

**AERIAL RIDES** The **Killington K-1 Express Gondola** (800-621-MTNS; killington.com) runs ski season and late June–Columbus Day from K-1 Lodge to the Peak Lodge (see above) top of Killington Peak. Check in early September and off-season. Recently repainted in bright designs, carrying mountain bikes in summer and fall as well as skis in winter. It offers easy access to 15-plus miles of trails.

**MOUNTAIN BIKING** After the snow melts, Killington features the family-friendly Snowshed Adventure Center, 30 miles of mountain biking trails with expansion underway with Gravity Logic, plus 15 miles of hiking trails. The K-1 Express Gondola operates July–Columbus Day (weather permitting), hoisting bicyclists and their bikes from the K-1 Lodge up to Killington Peak, accessing 35 miles of trails and a 1,700-foot vertical drop spread across five mountain areas. The Snowshed Express Quad lift serves expanded beginner terrain on weekends. Guided tours, instruction, bike rentals, and packages available.

MOUNTAIN BIKING ABOUNDS IN THE KILLINGTON REGION  KILLIN... RESORT

closed in winter, harboring some of the area's snowiest cross-country trails, accessible only by going the long way around through Shrewsbury (see *Scenic Drive's* in "Okemo Valley Region" on page 145).

**Gifford Woods State Park** (802-775-5354; vtstateparks.com), half a mile north of US4 on VT 100, Killington. The campground (22 tent/trailer and 20 lean-to sites, four cabins, restrooms, and hot showers) is convenient to the Appalachian Trail, which runs through the park. Across the road is the **Gifford Woods Natural Area**, a 7-acre stand of virgin hardwoods (sugar maple, yellow birch, basswood, white ash, and hemlock).

**Killington Golf Course** (802-422-6700; killington.com), 227 East Mountain Road. Killington Resort has its own 18-hole, 6,186-yard, par-72 course designed by Geoffrey Cornish. Clinics, league nights, packages, and restaurant. PGA professional instruction, rental clubs, and popular instructional programs through their Mountain Golf School.

**YEAR-ROUND** ✪ **Peak Lodge** (killington.com). Open when the K-1 Express Gondola operates, daily during ski, foliage, and summer seasons. Check in shoulder seasons and to make sure it isn't closed for a function. In summer and fall, many patrons hike up and take the gondola back down. At 4,214 feet, this is Vermont's most spectacular view for the least effort. On a clear day, the view from the summit of the state's second highest summit encompasses five states. It sweeps northwest to the Adirondacks, east to the White Mountains, and north along the spine of the Green Mountains. On a clear summer day, we curl up with a brew in one of the inviting leather armchairs, changing seats every hour or two to take in the view from another side of the lodge. The food is worthy of its setting: the frank is Boar's Head and the cheeseburger is made out of local Angus beef, with Cabot sharp cheddar.

**FITNESS CENTERS AND SPAS Pico Sports Center** (802-747-0564; picomountain.com), 4763 US 4, Killington. Open daily. A 75-foot lap pool, aerobics and fitness classes, cardio equipment, strength training machines, free weights, saunas, tanning, and fitness evaluations. Day passes and short-term memberships available.

**Killington Grand Spa** (802-422-1050), Killington Grand, 228 East Mountain Road. Full menu of spa treatments.

## LODGING

**The Killington Grand Resort Hotel** (802-422-5001; killington.com), 228 East Mountain Road, Killington. At the base of the lifts, this 200-room, newly renovated facility offers standard hotel rooms, also studios; one-, two-, and three-bedroom suites (with kitchen); and penthouse suites. It's immense, with endless corridors and Vermont's biggest meeting space (the Grand Ballroom)—ideal for conventions. The rooms are irreproachably comfortable. Amenities include an outdoor heated pool, outdoor hot tub, sauna, health club, game room, on-site day care, a café, and walk-to-the-slopes convenience. It's close not only to the base lodge, but in summer to the golf course as well. Best values year-round if combined with a sports package.

**CONDOS/RENTALS Killington Resort's Central Reservations** (800-621-MTNS; killington.com) serves many hundreds of condo units ranging from **Sunrise Condominiums**, high on the mountain, to **Pico Resort Hotel** on US 4 beside the Pico base lodge. **The Woods Resort & Spa** (866-785-8904) offers townhouse living with a fully developed spa on the premises.

Trails lead up to **Deer Leap Mountain** and waterfalls where Kent Brook enters Kent Pond. In winter, cross-country trails connect with Mountain Meadows.

**Lake Bomoseen**, north of Castleton, is a popular local summer colony. Alexander Woollcott summered here during the 1930s, on Neshobe Island. **Bomoseen State Park** (802-265-4242; vtstateparks.com), US 4 west of Rutland, Exit 3, 5 miles north on Town Road. Its 66 campsites, including 10 lean-tos, are set in a lovely 3,576-acre wildlife refuge; beach, picnic area, nature program, trails, boat ramp, and rentals. A popular geocaching spot.

**Half Moon State Park** (802-273-2848; vtstateparks.com), between Fair Haven and Rutland on US 4; take Exit 4, go 6.5 miles north on VT 30, left on Hortonia Road and continue 2 miles, then go left on Black Pond Road for 2 miles. Wooded campsites (52 tent sites; 11 lean-tos; five cabins) around a secluded pond; boat rentals; hikes to **High Pond**.

**Lake St. Catherine State Park** (802-287-9158; vtstateparks.com), 3 miles south of Poultney on VT 30. Fifty tent or trailer campsites and 11 lean-tos, plus sandy beaches, fishing, boat rentals, and nature trails.

# ✳ Lodging

## AT AND AROUND KILLINGTON

**Killington Central Reservations** (800-621-MTNS; killington.com). Open daily; the bureau keeps a tally on vacancies and makes reservations. A wide variety of two- to five-day ski and summer packages are available.

*Note:* Killington's **Skyeship Gondola** on US 4 also puts the inns of Plymouth (to the southeast) within easy reach, and lodging in both Woodstock is within 14 miles. See *Guidance* on page 281 for central reservations numbers.

## RESORTS **Mountain Top Inn & Resort**
(802-483-2311; mountaintopinn.com), 195 Mountain Top Road, Chittenden. Set high on a hill with a spectacular view of Chittenden Reservoir and mountain backdrop, this 350-acre resort has been around since the 1940s. It hosted President Dwight Eisenhower and his entourage in 1955 for a fishing expedition. Today it offers an impressive array of activities, lessons, and sports options. Thirty-two lodge rooms (breakfast included) from classic doubles to luxury rooms and suites, many with themes. Also, four one-bedroom cabins with kitchenettes, four two- and three-bedroom cottages, and 19 chalet rentals, all with at least two bedrooms. Summer activities abound from riding (and a kid's horsemanship camp) to disc golf, with archery, fishing, boating, and more! In winter, 60 km of cross-country ski trails, snowshoeing, horse-drawn sleigh rides, ice skating, snowmobiling, and massage therapy. The events barn, a wedding and conference venue, includes yoga and massage rooms, a theater, a game room, a fitness center, an outdoor pool, and a hot tub. Equestrian and Nordic programs are based at the nearby rustic Activities Center. Dine at the **Mountain Top Tavern**. Pets are allowed in the cabin for an extra fee (they receive a dog bed, bowls, and a welcome treat). Inquire about the many special offers. Double occupancy required in high season. $$–$$$$.

INNS AND BED & BREAKFASTS **Red Clover Inn** (802-775-2290; redcloverinn .com), 7 Woodward Road, Mendon. Open year-round. Set on 5 secluded acres, minutes from Pico and Killington access roads, this 1840s farmhouse was a 200-acre summer retreat and is now a top-notch inn and restaurant (see *Dining Out* on page 295). Along with the Carriage House, 13 guest rooms, many with fireplace or Jacuzzi. For family fun in summer, check out their sister property, **Tyler Place Family Resort**, in "The Northwest Corner." Tented weddings are available for up to 150 guests. Children age 8 and older are welcome. Breakfast and afternoon tea. $$–$$$.

**The October Country Inn** (802-672-3412; octobercountryinn.com), 362 Upper Road, Bridgewater Corners. Handy to both Killington and Woodstock just off US 4 but on a small back road a block off the highway. Hiking trails lead past the swimming pool to the top of a hill for a sweeping, peaceful view, with seating provided at the top. Seasoned innkeepers Edie and Chuck Janisse are founts of information about things to do and see in the region (ask about bike tours; bring your own bike or rent nearby). They offer occasional prix fixe gourmet candlelit dinners with wine and local produce served family style. Breakfasts are included with room. Small weddings can be accommodated. $$.

**Fox Creek Inn** (802-483-6213; foxcreekinn.com), 49 Dam Road, Chittenden. Sequestered up the back road leading from Chittenden Village to the reservoir, the inn offers an away-from-it-all feel but with easy access to both Killington and downtown Rutland. It was a summer house for inventor William Barstow, who had managed to sell his various holdings for $40 million right before the 1929 stock market crash. Each of the eight guest rooms is different, many with gas fireplace, most with Jacuzzi. A two-room suite has two baths. There is swimming, canoeing, and fishing in the Chittenden Reservoir, and in winter cross-country ski or just lounge around. Children must be 12 or older. Inquire about four-course candlelight dinners and seasonal inn-to-inn walking tours. $$–$$$.

**The Vermont Inn** (802-775-0708; vermontinn.com), 78 Cream Hill Road, Mendon. Set above US 4 with a view of Killington and Pico, this nineteenth-century farmhouse has a homey feel. The living room with woodstove, the pub/lounge with fireplace, a game room, and an upstairs reading room, a sanctuary in the evening when the dining room is open to the public (see *Dining Out* on page 295). There's a sauna and hot tub; summer facilities include a pool. The 17 guest rooms range from smallish to spacious. Five have a gas fireplace; several are suites. Facilities include a fitness center and game and reading rooms. Breakfast included. $–$$$.

**Casa Bella Inn** (802-746-8943; casabellainn.com), 3911 VT 100, Pittsfield. Eight miles north of the Killington hustle-and-bustle, this double-porched 1835 inn looks over the Pittsfield town green. Innkeeper Susan Cacozza is from Britain. Her husband, Franco, is a chef from Tuscany and offers a delicious and convenient order-ahead service in the restaurant. The eight stately guest rooms, each with private bath, all come with a delicious breakfast. Children 10 and over welcome. $.

LODGES **The Inn at Long Trail** (802-775-7181; innatlongtrail.com), 709 US 4, Killington. This is the first building in New England specifically built to serve as a ski lodge, originally the annex built in 1938 beside a summer inn that has since burned. Designed to resemble a forest, the interior incorporates parts of trees and boulders in amazing ways, the furnishings are largely Adirondack style, and the fire in the large stone hearth is real. A bit of a backyard cliff can be seen in the pub and dining room. Owned by the McGrath family since 1977, the inn caters to through-hikers on the Appalachian and Long trails and to outdoorspeople of all sorts. The 14 rooms are small but cheery (two are family suites); five two-room suites have fireplaces and some have whirlpools. The redwood hot tub soothes muscles after hiking or skiing. Dinner is sometimes available in the dining room, but check hours for **McGrath's Irish Pub** (see *Eating Out* on page 296). Pets by advance arrangement. Inquire about rock-climbing packages. $ early and late season; $$–$$$.

**The Summit Lodge** (802-422-3535; summitlodgevermont.com), 200 Summit Road, Killington. Sited on a knoll just off Killington Road, it's open year-round except for mud and stick seasons. Amenities include a large indoor hot tub, saunas, an outdoor heated pool, a game room, and massage therapy. In summer there are also red clay tennis courts, racquetball, bocce, and horseshoes. O'Dwyer's Public House and the Poolside Bar provide meals and relaxing atmospheres. The 45 guest rooms vary, though all have private bath, cable TV, and king and queen beds (the family rooms sleep up to six). $–$$$.

♂ **Mountain Meadows Lodge** (802-775-1010; mountainmeadowslodge .com), 285 Thundering Brook Road,

Killington. The main building is an 1856 barn, now a classic lodge with an informal dining room, a game room, and a spacious sunken living room with a lake view. Anne and Bill Mercier cater to people who like the outdoors in both winter and summer. Great for weddings, family reunions, and retreats, the lodge fills on weekends in warm weather. It has 17 guest rooms and two suites, many great for families, all with private bath. There's a sauna and outdoor Jacuzzi. Kent Lake abuts the property and is good for fishing, canoeing, and swimming. In winter, there's a ski-touring center. Continental breakfast included on weekdays, full breakfast on weekends. Lunch can be arranged, and dinner is served in high season. Includes a full breakfast. $–$$$.

**Killington Mountain Lodge** (802-432-4302), 2617 Killington Road, Killington. This 103-room, four-story, Adirondack-style hotel has gabled ceilings, skylights, balconies, and a two-story lobby with a fieldstone fireplace. Also, a spa with lap pool, Jacuzzis, and exercise room. The Pub serves light fare seasonally. Free breakfast buffet daily with room. $–$$.

**The Trailside Inn** (802-422-8800; trailsideinnvt.com), 115 Coffee House Road, Killington. A longtime Killington-area lodge, now owned by Joe De Sena of Spartan Race fame. It features wide-plank pine floors, a comfortable great room, family room, and pool. You have a choice of standard rooms, suites, bunkrooms, and self-contained spaces in the two-story Barn and Loft, sleeping 10. $–$$.

CAMPGROUNDS See *Green Space* on page 288 for information on camping in **Calvin Coolidge** and **Gifford Woods State Parks**.

IN RUTLAND AND BEYOND

SUMMER RESORT **Lake Bomoseen Lodge** (802-468-5251; lakebomoseen lodge.com), 2551 VT 30, Bomoseen. Lake Bomoseen was a celebrity playground in the big band era of Benny Goodman and Glenn Miller. This resort includes the more than 150-year-old inn, completely renovated by new owners, as well as a chalet, condo apartments, cottages, and lakeside efficiencies. $$.

INNS AND BED & BREAKFASTS

IN RUTLAND

**Antique Mansion Bed & Breakfast** (802-855-8372; antiquemansionbb.com), 85 Field Avenue, located across the street from the Rutland Country Club (see *Golf* on page 286). The 1867 Proctor-Clement House includes three suites and one downstairs room, all with private bath. Rates include breakfast, and informal afternoon tea. $.

IN SHREWSBURY, UP IN THE HILLS 10 MILES SOUTHEAST OF RUTLAND

**Smith Maple Crest Farm** (802-492-2151; smithmaplecrestfarm.com), 2450 Lincoln Hill Road. This handsome white-brick farmhouse sits high on a ridge in the old hilltop center of Shrewsbury. It was built in 1808 as Gleason's Tavern and is still in the same family—taking in guests off and on for more than 150 years. The family also raises beef cattle and produces maple syrup (see *Farms* on page 300). Some rooms share a bath. Rates include full breakfast. $.

**Crisanver House** (802-492-3589; crisanver.com), 1434 Crown Point Road. Set on 120 acres of woods and meadows, this is a find—but it's frequently booked weekends for weddings. The 1802 portion of the house offers four guest rooms and two suites, all with down comforters and pillows, exposed beams and original art. There are also three cottages. The living room, with a fireplace and grand piano, adjoins a sunny conservatory maximizing the panoramic view. A barn accommodates 120 people for weddings and parties. In summer there's a heated pool and an all-weather tennis court. Dinner can be pre-arranged. Rates include a full served breakfast. $$.

**The Buckmaster Inn** (802-492-3720; buckmasterinn.com), 20 Lottery Road. Built as the three-story Buckmaster Tavern beside the Shrewsbury church in 1801, the house includes four guest rooms, each with a private bath. There is a spacious living room, a library with fireplace and TV/DVD player, and a long, screened-in porch for summer and fall. Stay includes full breakfast. Deposit by check required with reservation. No credit cards. $.

## MOTELS

### IN RUTLAND

**Mendon Mountain Orchards** (802-775-5477; mendonorchards.com), 1894 US 4, Mendon, less a motel than a series of pleasant, very reasonably priced (under $100 per night) old-fashioned cabins, surrounded by orchards, with a pool and a shop for homemade goodies, apples in-season, cider, and flowers. Pet-friendly. $.

CAMPGROUNDS See *Green Space* on page 294 for information on campgrounds in **Lake Bomoseen State Park**, **Half Moon Pond State Park**, and **Lake St. Catherine State Park**.

## ✳ Where to Eat

### DINING OUT

### IN THE KILLINGTON AREA

**Red Clover Inn Restaurant & Tavern** (802-775-2290; redcloverinn.com),

7 Woodward Road, Mendon. Open for dinner Thurs.–Mon., reservations appreciated. Destination dining for foodies. Save room for desserts such as almond chocolate galette. Inquire about monthly wine dinners and the chef's tasting menu. $$$.

**The Countryman's Pleasure** (802-773-7141; countrymanspleasure.com), 3 Town Line Road, Mendon. Open Wed.–Sat. Austrian chef-owner Hans Entinger is known for his Austrian-German specialties: veal schnitzel, Bavarian sauerbraten, veal à la Holstein, and classics like roast half duckling and rack of lamb. Vegetarian fare is available. There's a long wine list, and international beers as well as international coffees and non-alcoholic wines and beers are served. The atmosphere is cozy and informal, with an open fireplace, in this 1824 farmhouse. $$.

**The Vermont Inn** (802-775-0708; vermontinn.com), 78 Cream Hill Road, Mendon; just off US 4 in Killington. Open for dinner Tues.–Sat. Dining room huge fieldstone fireplace features a large pub-area patio with a view of the mountains. Menu is varied, with salads, appetizers, and desserts. $–$$.

**Choices Restaurant & Rotisserie** (802-422-4030; choicesrestaurant killington.com), Glazebrook Center, 2820 Killington Road, Killington. Open for dinner nightly in winter, Wed.–Sun. in summer. Chef Claude Blais has an enthusiastic following at this combination bistro/brasserie/pub. The menu offers appetizers, salads, soups, raw bar, sandwiches, and pastas, not to mention entrées ranging from curried vegetables with couscous to filet mignon, plus a children's menu. $$.

**Mountain Top Dining Room at the Mountain Top Inn and Resort** (802-483-2311; mountaintopinn.com), 195 Mountain Top Road, Chittenden. Open daily for breakfast, lunch, and dinner; reservations expected. The lower-level dining room is large and formal with a big stone fireplace and views of the lake and mountains. The menu changes seasonally. $$$.

The adjacent, casual **Mountain Top Tavern** is open daily for lunch and dinner. The menu features wraps, salads, grilled sandwiches, burgers, and a full bar.

**Peppino's Ristorante Italiano** (802-422-3293; peppinosvt.com), 1 mile up Killington Road, Killington. Open nightly for dinner in summer and ski season. A traditional and reliable Italian restaurant with dining-out decor, a large choice of pastas and all the classics, from linguine with clams to sirloin pizzaiola, as well as staple house specialties. $$–$$$.

**The Garlic** (802-422-5055; thegarlicvermont.net), 1724 Killington Road, Killington. Open nightly, with a broad range of tapas at the bar. A cozy, informal setting for hearty Italian fare, with a choice of pasta dishes and entrées featuring the namesake ingredient. Reservations not taken, but the place is popular, so prepare to wait; full bar. $$.

### IN RUTLAND

**Little Harry's** (802-747-4848; littleharrys.com), 121 West Street. Open daily 5–10 p.m. This offspring of the popular Harry's Cafe in Mount Holly is romantically lit and decorated. The menu is varied, with pad Thai, Jamaican jerk scallops, and cioppino, to name a few. $$–$$$.

**The Palms** (802-773-2367; palmsvermont.com), 36 Strongs Avenue. Open Mon.–Sat. for dinner. The Palms, serving Italian fare, opened its doors on Palm Sunday, 1933, and in 1948 it served the first pizza in Vermont. Now operated by the fifth generation of the Sabataso family, it's a family-geared place that tastes like history. Neapolitan-style pizza remains a specialty, along with the comfort food you'd expect. $$.

**Table 24** (802-775-2424; table24.net), 24 Wales Street. Open Mon.–Sat. for lunch and dinner. Chef-owner Stephen Sawyer provides contemporary decor as well as local ingredients and flavors. A wood-fired rotisserie slow-roasts

chicken. Prime rib, macaroni and cheese, and meatloaf are all on the menu, as are burgers and sandwiches. $$–$$$.

### ELSEWHERE

**Lakehouse Pub & Grill** (802-273-3000; lakehousepubandgrille.com), 3569 VT 30, Bomoseen on Lake Bomoseen. Open daily for lunch and dinner, closed for winter season. This popular waterfront spot features a wooden hillside stairway leading down to umbrella-shaded waterside tables, or spectacular sunset views from the air-conditioned indoor dining room, and a menu of seafood specials, and pork, chicken, and steak. $$.

**The Victorian Inn at Wallingford** (802-446-2099), 55 North Main Street, US 7, Wallingford, serves dinner Tues.–Sat., brunch on Sundays. Swiss-born chef Konstantin Schonbachler, formerly executive chef at the Kennedy Center in Washington, DC, brought his European culinary talents when he bought this French Second Empire home in the center of Wallingford. Guests now eat in one of three downstairs rooms in a casually elegant ambience. Inquire about a wide variety of cooking classes. $$$$.

### EATING OUT

### IN THE KILLINGTON AREA

**McGrath's Irish Pub** at the Inn at Long Trail (802-775-7181; innatlongtrail.com), 709 US 4, Killington. Open nightly for dinner and drinks. The 22-foot-long bar is made from a single log, and a protruding boulder from outside can be seen in both the pub and the dining room. The first place to serve Guinness on tap in Vermont, the pub boasts the state's largest selection of Irish whiskey and features Irish country and folk music on weekends. The house specialties are Guinness stew and shepherd's pie. There's serious fare in the adjoining dining room, but it's the pub that's truly special.

**Charity's 1887 Saloon and Restaurant** (802-422-3800; charitystavern.com), 2194 Killington Road, Killington. A favorite local gathering place since 1971, serving steaks, seafood, and pasta, along with craft beers.

**Back Behind Restaurant & BBQ Smokehouse** (802-422-9907; backbehind.com), 8492 US 4, Killington, at the junction of US 4 and VT 100 south. Open Thurs.–Mon. for dinner year-round, lunch on weekends in summer, Thurs.–Mon. weekdays in winter. A zany museum-like atmosphere (look for the red caboose and antique Mobil gas pump), barnboard, stained glass, a big hearth. Specialties such as venison and saloon roast duck augment a full barbecue menu; generous portions and children's menu.

**The Foundry at Summit Pond** (802-422-5335; foundrykillington.com), 63 Summit Path, Killington. Open for lunch and dinner daily, Sunday brunch. Formerly named The Gristmill and designed to look like one, it's sited on the pond in front of Summit Lodge and features a vintage waterwheel. The interior is airy and pleasing, dominated by a huge stone hearth. Varied menu.

**Swiss Farm Market** (802-746-9939; swissfarmmarket.com), 3932 VT 100, Pittsfield Village. The town's genuine general store, formerly the Pitt-Stop, is under the same ownership as Swiss Farm Inn, legendary for its breakfasts. The deli here is a standout, judging from the Harvest Chicken Salad—homemade, with apple and cranberry mayo on a fresh ciabatta roll.

BREAKFAST **Maple Sugar & Vermont Spice** (802-773-7832; vtsugarandspice.com), 43 US 4, Mendon. Open daily 7–2 with breakfast all day. A pancake restaurant housed in a large replica of a classic sugarhouse surrounded by a 50-acre sugarbush. Besides dining on a variety of pancake, egg, and omelet dishes, along with soups and sandwiches, you can watch both maple candy and cheese being made several days a week. Gift shop.

**Swiss Farm Inn** (802-746-8341; swissfarminn.com), 4441 VT 100, Pittsfield. The inn offers the "world's best breakfast" of blueberry buttermilk pancakes, raspberry-rhubarb-stuffed French toast, eggs any style, home-fried potatoes, country smoked bacon, and home-baked muffins Thurs.–Sun. This is a local hot spot. Family-friendly lodging is also available.

**Sunup Bakery** (802-422-3865; sunupbakery.com), 2250 Killington Road, Killington. Open daily in winter; Fri.–Sun., May–June; Thurs.–Mon., July–October. Located in an adorable A-frame chalet, breakfast is served all day. The menu is varied with several innovative vegetarian options (sometimes hard to find in the area). Local and organic as much as possible, no processed food. Excellent lunch sandwiches.

PIZZA **Outback Pizza & Nightclub** (802-422-9885; outbackpizzakillington.com), 2841 Killington Access Road, Killington. Open evenings until midnight Sun.–Thurs.; to 2 a.m., Fri. and Sat. Features wood-fired brick-oven pizza with outdoor patio seating and live music.

**iPIE Pizzeria & Lounge** (802-422-4111; ipiepizzeria.com), 1307 Killington Road. Open daily at 11. Pleasant atmosphere and options including grilled chicken salad and specialty panini as well as a variety of fairly exotic specialty pizzas.

**Picarello's Pizza** (802-746-8331), 55 Lower Michigan Road, Pittsfield. Just off VT 100, on the southern edge of the village. Open from 5 p.m., Thurs. and Fri. nights. A long-established insider's spot with limited eat-in space and a signature eggplant Parmesan as well as a variety of great pizzas.

BREWS **Long Trail Brewing Company** (802-672-5011; longtrail.com), 5520 US 4, Bridgewater Corners (near VT 100A), produces Long Trail Ale as well as Blackberry Wheat, IPA, Pale Ale, and Double

Bag, plus seasonals and Brewmaster Limited Editions. Pub fare daily 11–6 with riverside seating (in summer); gift shop, taproom, and tours.

**Liquid Art Coffeehouse & Gallery** (802-422-2787; liquidartvt.com), 37 Miller Brook Road, Killington. Open daily. Look for the blue A-frame on the rocks, 2 miles up Killington Access Road on the right. The gallery features local artists, the brews are espresso with variations such as macchiato and rolo latte; also chai and loose teas. "Morning Nibbles" include housemade crepes; all-day "Light Bites" could be an herb-roasted chicken sandwich or sweet Italian sausage polenta lasagna. Inquire about monthly wine dinners.

APRÈS-SKI **The Wobbly Barn Steakhouse** (802-422-6171), 2229 Killington Road, Killington. A steakhouse offering national music and comedy acts, themed parties, dancing, blues, rock and roll. Ski season only.

**McGrath's Irish Pub at the Inn at Long Trail** (802-775-7181; innatlongtrail .com), 709 US 4, Killington. Live Irish music on weekends to go with the Gaelic atmosphere and Guinness on tap. See *Eating Out* on page 296.

**Pickle Barrel Nightclub** (802-422-3035; picklebarrelnightclub.com), 1741 Killington Road, Killington. Regional and national live music acts, best nightclub in Vermont next to Higher Ground in South Burlington. Purchase tickets online.

**Jax Food and Games** (802-422-5334; jaxfoodandgames.com), 1667 Killington Road, Killington. A popular local hangout and night spot with deck dining in warm weather; jazzy interior, sports bar with "food and games." Boasting Killington's biggest burger and reasonably priced lobsters.

**Lookout Tavern** (802-422-5665; lookoutvt.com), 2901 Killington Road, Killington. Free shuttle service offered to and from lodging properties. A lively venue with a wide selection of reasonably priced food and drink.

*Note:* In our opinion, the best après-ski happens right at the mountain, with ski boots still on.

IN RUTLAND

**The Yellow Deli** (802-775-9800; yellowdeli.com/rutland), 23 Center Street. One of a dozen establishments around the country, the Rutland Yellow Deli is operated by the Twelve Tribes, imaginatively decorated with wood slab tables and intimate booths, and a sidewalk café in summer. The stress is on wholesome food: sandwiches on homemade bread, salads, soups, a smoothie bar plus coffees, herbal teas, and maté.

**Roots the Restaurant** (802-747-7414; rootsrutland.com), 51 Wales Street. Serving lunch and dinner daily, closed Mon. A friendly local eatery featuring hearty local food and traditional specials like fish-and-chips as well as more innovative dinners, often made with local emu. Chef Donald Billings also owns The Bakery (122 West Street, 802-775-3220), where sandwiches on homemade bread include meats from North Country Smokehouse alongside veggie fillings such as eggplant or pea-and-ricotta.

**Gill's Delicatessen** (802-773-7414; gillsdeli.com), 68 Strongs Avenue. Open daily except Sun. Gill's is short for "Gilligan's," and Kathy Gilligan Phillips is the second generation to run the oldest bakery/deli in Rutland. There are 10 tables, but most people take their sandwiches on hefty homemade rolls to go.

**Seward Family Restaurant** (802-773-2738), 224 North Main Street, Rutland. Open daily for breakfast, lunch, and dinner; Sunday brunch. This diner and dairy bar has been in the Seward family since 1947. After downing a burger or fried chicken with "Freedom Fries," dig into the "Pig's Dinner," an extra-large banana split served in a trough.

## ELSEWHERE

**Birdseye Diner** (802-468-5817; birdseyediner.com), 590 Main Street, Castleton. This restored 1940s Silk City diner, open all day, is a popular spot for college students and local residents alike.

**Perry's Main Street Eatery** (802-287-5188) 253 Main Street, Poultney. Open daily for three meals, this family-run diner is renowned for its fluffy pancakes and big breakfasts. At dinner, comfort food reigns, including ribs and mac-and-cheese.

**Wheel Inn Restaurant** (802-537-2755), 730 Lake Road, Benson. Open for three meals daily. The Wednesday–night chicken-and-biscuits is famous for miles, and there's liver and onions every day. This wagon-wheel-covered dining room is a delightful throwback.

## ✳ Entertainment

Also see *Après-Ski* on page 298.

**Paramount Theatre** (802-775-0903; paramountvt.org), 30 Center Street, Rutland. This theater is still vital at more than 100 years old. In fact, it's one of Vermont's best entertainment venues with international and national tours featuring music, dance, and theater. There are local dramatic groups and musicians, too, as well as a classic film series. Check website for tickets and schedules of events.

**Merchant's Hall** (802-855-8081; merchantshall.com), 42 Merchants Row, Rutland. A multipurpose event space. There are art installations and lectures here, but the raison d'être is theater and music.

**Flagship Premium Cinemas** (802-786-8004; flagshipcinemas.com), 143 Merchants Row, Rutland, shows first-run flicks.

**Peak Races** (peakraces.com) puts on hard-core adventure races year-round. Key events include a snowshoe challenge, ultramarathon, bike challenges, and the infamous summer and winter Death Races. For those fainter of heart (perhaps literally), the wild events are a spectacle to behold. Based at **Amee Farm** (see *Farms* on page 300) in Pittsfield.

**Killington Music Festival** (802-773-4003; killingtonmusicfestival.com), a series of mostly chamber music concerts in Ramshead Lodge at Killington Ski Resort and at a scattering of other local sites; weekends in July and August; also a series of Young Artist Concerts in July.

**Cooler in the Mountains** (killington .com), a free, family-friendly, outdoor concert series during July and August held at the Killington Resort Base Lodge featuring regional and national touring acts.

## ✳ Selective Shopping

ART GALLERIES & CRAFTS STUDIOS **Handmade in Vermont** (802-446-2400; handmadeinvermont.com), 205 South Main Street, Wallingford. Open Mon.–Sat. Housed in America's first pitchfork factory (built 1791), this marble structure is now owned by White Rocks Land Trust and operated by a consortium of artists and craftspeople. Ironwork, especially lighting fixtures, is featured, along with Danforth Pewter and a wide selection of Vermont-crafted glass, pottery, furniture, and jewelry.

**Peter Huntoon Studio** (802-235-2328; peterhuntoon.com), 17 Studio Lane, Middletown Springs. Open by appointment. Huntoon is one of Vermont's premier watercolorists, who also teaches and conducts workshops at his studio. His work is available for viewing and for sale online.

*Note:* See **Open Studio Weekend** under *Special Events* on page 301 and vermontcrafts.com.

Also see **Liquid Art Coffeehouse & Gallery** under *Brews* on page 298.

*Note:* See Open Studio Weekend under *Special Events* on page 301 and vermontcrafts.com.

BOOKSTORES **The Book Shed** (802-537-2190; thebookshed.com), 3225 Lake Road, Benson. Hours by appointment. Housed in what used to be the town clerk's office, this used- and antiquarian-book store with 15,000 volumes is one of the biggest things going in this tiny town.

FARMS **Amee Farm** (802-746-8196; ameefarm.com), 4275 VT 100, Pittsfield. Produce and livestock are raised, for a seasonal farm stand, but primarily for the lodging extension of Pittsfield's most distinguished wedding venue, Riverside Farm (riversidefarmweddings.com). The farm can also be rented as a retreat—bed & breakfast rooms are available in off-seasons, worth an inquiry.

**Smith Maple Crest Farm** (802-492-2151; smithmaplecrestfarm.com), 2450 Lincoln Hill Road, Shrewsbury. Award-winning maple syrup and all-natural Vermont beef are the specialties on this working Vermont farm, which also offers an excellent-value bed & breakfast (see *Lodging* on page 294). Visit the sugarhouse or order online.

**Hathaway Farm & Corn Maze** (802-775-2624; hathawayfarm.com), 741 Prospect Hill Road, Rutland. The largest corn maze in Vermont, covering 12 acres, is cut in a different thematic shape each year. It operates July–October daily (except Tues.) and some weekends during other seasons. A Saturday-evening "Moonlight Madness" includes glow sticks and a marshmallow roast. The farm offers wagon rides and an interactive livestock barn. The farm also raises grass-fed beef and produces maple syrup, both available in the seasonal farm shop.

FARMERS' MARKETS The region is rich in farmers' markets, with four in Rutland alone, including one that is year-round based at the Rutland Area Good Co-op (rutlandcoop.com). Additional farmers' markets can be found in Castleton, Fair Haven, Mount Holly, and Poultney.

SPECIAL SHOPS **Greenbrier Gift Shop** (802-775-1575; greenbriervt.com), 2057 US 4, Killington. You can't miss this massive 7,000-square-foot barn gift shop stuffed full with Vermont products, clothing, baby items, home decor, and wedding gifts.

**Base Camp Outfitters** (802-775-0166; basecampvt.com), 2363 US 4, Killington. In winter this is the area's best source of "free heel"—cross-country, snowshoes, telemark, et cetera—gear and clothing. Owner Mike Miller and his wife, Diane, also operate the Mountain Meadows Ski Touring Center. In summer hiking and disc golf have become hugely popular on the property.

**Norman Rockwell Museum** (802-773-6095; normanrockwellvt.com), 654 US 4 east, Rutland. Open daily, more of a store than a museum, but for Rockwell buffs it offers thousands of Rockwell's magazine covers, ads, posters, portraits, and other published illustrations, displayed chronologically with small, almost unreadable typed captions. The gift shop, with its many Rockwell prints and cards, is large and portrays an interesting profile of the artist (1898–1978) and a documentary of changing American culture and graphic styles.

GENERAL STORES **W. E. Pierce Store & Shrewsbury Co-op** (802-492-3326; piercesstore.com), 2658 Northam Road, Shrewsbury. This traditional country store nestled up in the mountains is run as a community-managed cooperative. Besides the basics, there's a local artisan section, local wine and beer, chef-prepared food, and everything from community workshops to sing-alongs.

**East Poultney General Store** (802-287-4042), 11 On the Green, East Poultney. An old-fashioned general store. The baked goods have a better-than-average reputation, as does the savory food, which might include chicken wings, lobster bisque, or crabcakes.

Also see Pittsfield's two general stores under *Eating Out* on page 297.

WINERY **Whaleback Vineyard** (802-287-0730; whalebackvineyard.com), 202 Old Lake Road, Poultney. Over 4,000 grapevines on 7 acres cover this old-farm-turned-vineyard between Lake St. Catherine and the Green Mountains. Wine tastings Wed.–Sun. Tours available on request.

## ✱ Special Events

Also see *Entertainment* on page 299.

*January–March:* Frequent **alpine ski and snowboard events** at Killington Resort and Pico Mountain (killington .com).

*Memorial Day weekend:* **Open Studio Weekend** (vermontcrafts.com) for artisan and crafts studios throughout the region.

*June–August:* Sunday- and Wednesday-evening **Concerts in the Park**, Rutland, (rutlandrec.com), and Tuesday **Castleton University's Concerts on the Green**, Castleton (castleton.edu).

*Late June–August:* **Friday Night Live**, 6–10. Downtown Rutland streets become a stage for live entertainment, open-air shopping, and dining (rutlanddowntown .com). **Killington Music Festival** (killingtonmusicfestival.org), Saturdays at 7 at Ramshead Lodge at Killington Ski Resort—a series of classical music concerts.

*July 4:* **Rutland Fireworks Extravaganza**, Vermont State Fairgrounds, Rutland (rutlandvermont.com); **Poultney Fourth of July Parade** and fireworks (poultneyvt.com); **Killington Independence Day Parade** (killingtontown.com).

*Mid-July:* **Annual Killington Wine Festival** (killingtonchamber.com).

*Early August:* **Art in the Park Fine Art & Craft Festival**, Rutland, sponsored by the Chaffee Center (chaffeeartcenter .org), in Main Street Park. Also held Columbus Day weekend.

*Mid-August:* **Vermont State Fair** (vermontstatefair.org)—midway, exhibits, races, demolition derby, and tractor pulls animate the old fairgrounds on US 7 south, Rutland.

*First weekend of October:* **Killington Brewfest** (killington.com).

*Columbus Day weekend:* **Art in the Park Fine Art & Craft Festival**, Rutland, (chaffeeartcenter.org).

*Last Saturday in October:* Rutland City's **Halloween Parade**, one of the oldest and best (rutlandrec.com/halloween).

*Early December:* **Vermont Holiday Festival** at Killington's Grand Resort Hotel—over 100 decorated trees, sleigh rides, workshops, and more (killingtonpico.org).

# CHAMPLAIN VALLEY

■

## CHAMPLAIN VALLEY

## LOWER CHAMPLAIN VALLEY

Including Middlebury, Vergennes, Brandon,
and Bristol

## BURLINGTON REGION

## THE NORTHWEST CORNER

Including the Champlain Islands,
St. Albans, Swanton, and Enosburgh

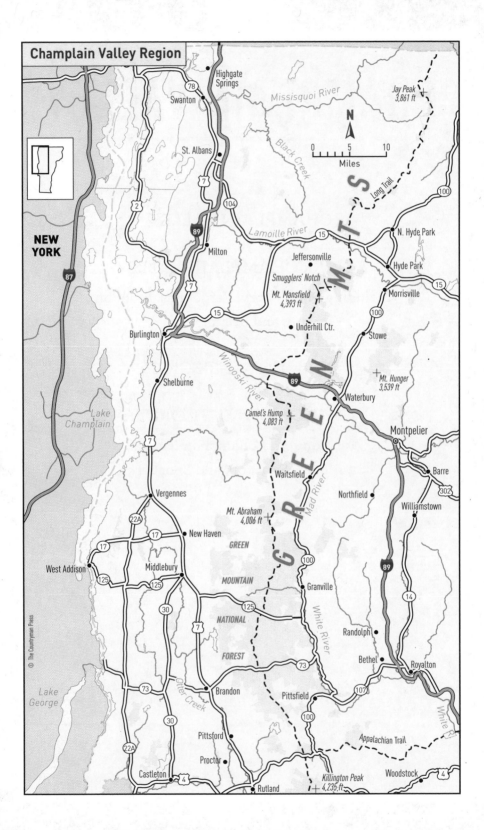

# Champlain Valley Region

NEW YORK

Highgate Springs

Swanton

78

St. Albans

7

2

104

89

Milton

7

15

Burlington

Shelburne

Lake Champlain

7

Vergennes

22A

17

17

New Haven

17

West Addison

125

Middlebury

125

125

30

GREEN

MOUNTAIN

NATIONAL

FOREST

7

Lake George

73

30

22A

Brandon

Otter Creek

Pittsford

Proctor

Castleton

4

Rutland

Missisquoi River

Black Creek

Jay Peak 3,861 ft

N

0    5    10
Miles

Long Trail

100

Lamoille River

15

N. Hyde Park

Jeffersonville

Hyde Park

15

Smugglers' Notch

Morrisville

Mt. Mansfield 4,393 ft

100

Underhill Ctr.

Stowe

Winooski River

89

Mt. Hunger 3,539 ft

Waterbury

Camel's Hump 4,083 ft

Montpelier

Waitsfield

Mad River

Barre

302

Northfield

Williamstown

Mt. Abraham 4,006 ft

89

14

100

Granville

White River

125

Randolph

73

Bethel

Royalton

Pittsfield

107

100

White

Appalachian Trail

Woodstock

4

Killington Peak 4,235 ft

87

© The Countryman Press

GREEN MTS

# CHAMPLAIN VALLEY

L ake Champlain begins in New York and flows north to Canada. For much of its 110 miles, the New York–Vermont border runs down its center. Still, the country's sixth largest lake belongs to Vermont in all the important ways, beginning 20,000 years ago. That's when the glacial waters receded, revealing islands and a wide valley on its eastern shores as opposed to rocky hills rising to mountains—the Adirondacks—on the west.

Traces of human habitation in this fertile valley date back 7,500 years. Archaeological finds of pottery and trading beads suggest both domestic life and distant travel for valley residents by 1000 BC. But it's not the indigenous people who gave the lake its modern name. That honor went to Samuel de Champlain, the first European to set foot in present-day Vermont in 1609.

In the eighteenth and early nineteenth centuries, Lake Champlain served as a strategic military corridor. Ethan Allen and the Green Mountain Boys captured Fort Ticonderoga on the New York shore from the British in 1775. During the following winter the fort's heavy cannons were dragged on sleds through thick snow and forest to Boston, where they were mounted above the harbor, ultimately forcing the British to evacuate the city.

Early in the nineteenth century, Burlington grew into a metropolis as a lumber shipping port. It remains by far Vermont's largest and most dynamic city, one squarely facing Lake Champlain and offering access points for sailing, paddling, and swimming. Burlington is also home to several colleges, including the University of Vermont. In the Lower Valley, Middlebury—home to its own prestigious liberal arts school—is another cultural, dining, and lodging center.

Lake Champlain, which forms Vermont's west coast, is 12 miles wide at its widest, less than a mile at its narrows. It is 400 feet deep in places, deep enough to harbor the mythical lake creature Champ (mascot of Burlington's minor-league baseball team, the Vermont Lake Monsters).

# LOWER CHAMPLAIN VALLEY

*Including Middlebury, Vergennes, Brandon, and Bristol*

Addison County packs as much contrasting scenery within its borders as any region in the country. Look east for a view of the high, western wall of the Green Mountains, laced with hiking trails and pierced by four of the state's highest, most dramatic "gaps" (passes). The mountains drop abruptly through widely scattered hill towns—Lincoln, Ripton, and Goshen—into a 30-mile-wide, farm-filled valley, a former ocean floor that now contains Vermont's largest concentration of dairy farms and orchards. Lake Champlain is far narrower here than around Burlington, and the Adirondacks in New York seem close enough to touch, gracing the cows, barns, and apple trees with a spectacular backdrop.

Middlebury, the hub of Addison County, is home to a prestigious private college, several museums, a world-class opera company, and many restaurants. Brandon, a visitor-friendly community 15 miles south of Middlebury, is the southern gateway to the Lower Champlain Valley.

Throughout the Valley, the Lake Champlain shoreline is notched at regular intervals with quiet and accessible bays, from Mount Independence to Chimney Point north to Basin Harbor and Button Bay State Park. Thanks to widely scattered lodging, it's possible to stay in the heart of farm (Addison and Bridport) and orchard (Shoreham) country, in historic towns such as Bristol and Vergennes (the country's smallest city), and in the Green Mountain towns of Ripton and Goshen, close to wooded walking/ biking and ski trails, with occasional, but spectacular, lake and valley views.

GUIDANCE **Addison County Chamber of Commerce** (802-388-7951; addisoncounty .com), 93 Court Street, Middlebury, is open Mon.–Fri. The staff at this walk-in information center offer help finding lodging, even in foliage season, when accommodations may be difficult to find. The chamber also maintains an unstaffed information booth on the common in Vergennes.

**Brandon Area Chamber of Commerce** (802-247-6401; brandon.org), 4 Grove Street, Brandon. The visitor center, open daily year-round, is housed in the historic Stephen A. Douglas birthplace, which also hosts the **Brandon Museum**, open mid-May–mid-October. The center is well stocked with brochures, including an informative walking tour guide to the town's rich architectural heritage and 10 *Gateways to Adventure* guides, also available for download at gatewaystobrandon.com.

GETTING THERE *By car:* The major north–south highway is US 7, but if arriving from Boston, approach through the Middlebury or Brandon Gap (see *Scenic Drives* on page 318). From the west, take the Champlain Bridge in Crown Point, NY, or the seasonal ferries described below.

*By ferry:* **Lake Champlain Transportation Company** (802-864-9804; ferries.com) operates a ferry from Essex, NY, to Charlotte, VT, year-round, weather permitting.

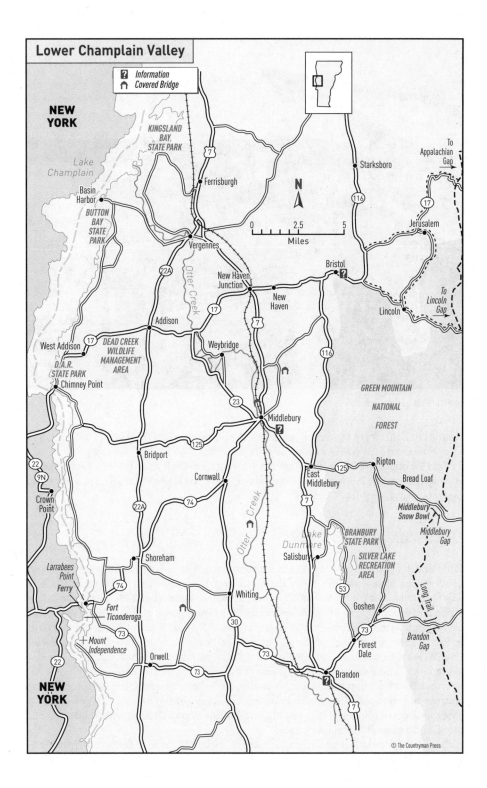

# Lower Champlain Valley

**?** Information
**⌂** Covered Bridge

**NEW YORK**

*Lake Champlain*

*KINGSLAND BAY STATE PARK*

Ferrisburgh

7

Starksboro

To Appalachian Gap

116

Basin Harbor

*BUTTON BAY STATE PARK*

**N**

0    2.5    5
**Miles**

Jerusalem

17

Vergennes

22A

*Otter Creek*

New Haven Junction

New Haven

Bristol **?**

To Lincoln Gap

Addison

17

7

Lincoln

West Addison

17

*DEAD CREEK WILDLIFE MANAGEMENT AREA*

Weybridge

116

**GREEN MOUNTAIN**

*D.A.R. STATE PARK*

Chimney Point

23

⌂

Middlebury ⌂
**?**

**NATIONAL**

**FOREST**

Bridport

125

Cornwall

East Middlebury

125

Ripton

Bread Loaf

22

9N

22A

74

*Otter Creek*

7

*Middlebury Snow Bowl*

*Middlebury Gap*

Crown Point

Shoreham

*Lake Dunmore*

*BRANBURY STATE PARK*

Salisbury

*SILVER LAKE RECREATION AREA*

*Larrabees Point Ferry*

74

Whiting

53

Goshen

*Long Trail*

Fort Ticonderoga

30

73

Forest Dale

*Brandon Gap*

Mount Independence

73

Orwell

73

73

Brandon **?**

22

**NEW YORK**

7

© The Countryman Press

FORT TI FERRY  LISA HALVORSEN

Operating hours vary by season, so check the website or call for times. The trip takes 25 minutes and puts you in just above Ferrisburgh.

**Fort Ticonderoga Ferry** (802-897-7999; forttiferry.com). The cable car-ferry travels between Larrabees Point and Fort Ticonderoga, NY, making the crossing in 7 minutes. Operates early May–late October.

# ✳ Towns and Villages

**Middlebury** (population 8,496) is the county seat, the hub of Addison County, and home to one of the nation's most sought-after private colleges. Middlebury College was founded in 1800 by Gamaliel Painter, a surveyor who settled here before the Revolution and accompanied Ethan Allen on the Fort Ticonderoga raid. Another benefactor was Joseph Battell (see sidebar on page 311), wealthy proprietor of the Bread Loaf Inn in Ripton, now the nucleus of the summer Bread Loaf School of English and the Bread Loaf Writers' Conference. Emma Hart Willard, a pioneer for the education of women, was another Middlebury luminary. Some of the town's most distinctive buildings—the courthouse, Middlebury Inn, Battell House, and the white-steepled Congregational church—are grouped, along with compact business blocks, around the green. It's a short walk down Main Street to the historic Marble Works District with shops, restaurants, and a view of Middlebury Falls.

**Brandon** (population 3,966; brandon.org) is rich in historic architecture, from Federal style to Queen Anne. Its entire center, comprising around 240 buildings, is on the National Register of Historic Places. Several of these historic mansions are open

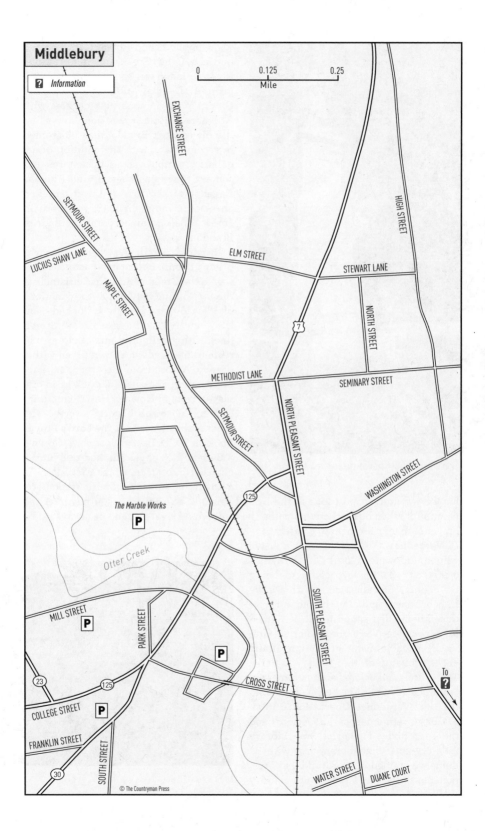

BRANDON CIVIL WAR MONUMENT LISA HALVORSEN

to the public as bed & breakfasts. Located between Otter Creek and the Neshobe River, Brandon was the birthplace of Stephen A. Douglas (1813–61), the "Little Giant" of the famous 1858 debates with Abraham Lincoln, when Douglas was an Illinois senator. Brandon has blossomed in recent years, with the addition of art galleries, antiques shops, bookstores, and some of the region's best dining. Thomas Davenport, who invented and patented an electric motor in 1838, was born in Forest Dale, an unincorporated village of Brandon.

**Bristol** (population 3,788; discover bristolvt.com). Billing itself as the "Gateway to the Green Mountains," Bristol is at the foot of Lincoln Gap, at the junctions of VT 116 (less heavily trafficked than US 7) and VT 17. Its broad Main Street, lined with a delightful mix of stores and restaurants, leads to a town green with a gazebo. Across from the green, an elaborate hand-painted stagecoach is on display in front of Howden Hall Community Center, the town's historical society. Its other main attraction is the **Lord's Prayer Rock** on VT 17. In 1891 Joseph C. Greene, a Buffalo, NY, physician, had this prayer chiseled into an immense rock slab. As a boy living in nearby South Starksboro, his job was to transport logs to the Bristol sawmill, a treacherous journey over the mountain. When he reached this point, the route would level out, and he always said a prayer of thanks for making it safely.

**Vergennes** (population 2,588; vergennesdowntown.org), Vermont's oldest city (1788), lays claim to being the country's smallest city. With a large francophone population, it's no surprise that Ethan Allen suggested it be named for Comte de Vergennes Charles Gravier, French minister of foreign affairs and negotiator of the Treaty of Paris. The stately mansions and commercial buildings along Main Street, including the 1897 **Vergennes Opera House** (802-877-6737; vergennesoperahouse.org) and the 1912 **Bixby Memorial Free Library** (802-877-2211; bixbylibrary.org) with its immense stained-glass rotunda, are testaments to the city's nineteenth-century

LORD'S PRAYER ROCK LISA HALVORSEN

# JOSEPH BATTELL AND MIDDLEBURY

The distinctive stone bridge that Colonel Joseph Battell built in downtown Middlebury is but one element of an enormous and enduring legacy that this eccentric bachelor left to the state of Vermont and to Middlebury College in particular.

Battell was born in 1839 to a wealthy and influential Vermont family. He attended Middlebury College, but ill health kept him from finishing his degree. Instead, he traveled the world, and upon his return, he bought land in Ripton, where he ran an inn, mainly for his friends. Today that land and those buildings house two of the college's most highly regarded summer programs: the Bread Loaf School of English and the Bread Loaf Writers' Conference. In addition to being publisher of the *Middlebury Register*, a local newspaper, Battell was an author. One of his oddest efforts was *Ellen, or, The Whisperings of an Old Pine*, a dense tome that is seldom read but much wondered about.

Battell loved mountains and woods and hated cars, so much so that he refused to allow cars on the road to his Ripton inn. Yet it was because of Battell that the stone bridge carrying traffic across Otter Creek in downtown Middlebury exists.

The original bridge was made of wood, erected in 1787, and replaced multiple times with more wooden bridges, until 1891, when the last wooden bridge burned. Middlebury's town fathers, in a fit of economy, decided to build an iron bridge on the site. Battell was opposed to the move, arguing that a stone bridge would last significantly longer than an iron one. So determined was he that he said that if the town put up $12,000 of the $17,000 estimated cost, he and his father Philip would split any additional expenses out of their own pockets. The bridge was completed in 1893 for $31,247.

A pioneering conservationist, Battell often sent his hired man into the woods, armed with blank deeds and instructions to buy as much acreage as he could from any farmer or logger he met. Over time he acquired about 35,000 acres, including Camel's Hump, which he donated to the state of Vermont for use as a state park. His landholdings reached over Bread Loaf Mountain from East Middlebury to Hancock, Granville, and Rochester along VT 100 and followed the spine of the Green Mountains from Mount Ellen south to Brandon Gap. He died in 1915, bequeathing most of his land to Middlebury College, which sold off much of it over the years, keeping only a few hundred acres.

Battell began breeding Morgans on his Weybridge farm in the late 1800s, an interest that would prove instrumental in saving one of America's earliest horse breeds from extinction. He hired architect Clinton Smith to build the beautiful white farm buildings that still stand. With his typical intensity, he spent years tracing the pedigrees, which he published in his first volume of the *Morgan Horse Register* in 1894. Then in 1907 he gave his farm and his horses to the US government, which bred Morgans for cavalry mounts until 1951, when the farm was turned over to the University of Vermont. It remains a working horse farm to this day, dedicated to preserving and improving the breed. Guided tours are offered from May–October (see *Cultural Attractions* on page 315).

prosperity. The library has an impressive collection of Vermont materials and a small museum with Native American artifacts and local memorabilia.

**Shoreham** (population 1,265) is known for its orchards and farms. Shoreham Village is a beauty, with a classic Congregational church (1846), a Masonic temple (built in 1852 as the Universalist church), and the graceful St. Genevieve Catholic Church (1873). VT 74 takes you to Larrabees Point, the site of the small, car-carrying "Fort Ti" cable ferry. It has held the franchise from the Vermont and New York legislatures since 1799, but records indicate the service was initiated by Lord Jeffery Amherst in 1757 for use by his soldiers in the campaigns against the French. Next door is Teachout's

Lakehouse Store & Wharf, built in 1836. Continue south on VT 73 to the turnoff for the Mount Independence State Historic Site (see *Historical Attractions* on page 317).

Orwell (population 1,250). Orwell, a small farming community southwest of Middlebury, is best known for Mount Independence, a well-preserved Revolutionary War site. It has a pretty village green with a brick Congregational church (1843) on a rise by the white-clapboard town hall (built in 1810 as the Baptist church). The **First National Bank of Orwell** (founded as the Farmer's Bank of Orwell) was chartered in 1863, and today the interior looks much the same, with many original features, including three stand-up desks with ledger racks. The painted vault door was installed in the 1880s. It is the oldest national bank in New England and among the oldest in the country, and it serves as a de facto community center, with notices of upcoming events tacked to tellers' cages. Another village gathering place is **Buxton's General Store**, the genuine article.

## ✳ Must See

**The Champlain Bridge** connects **Chimney Point State Historic Site** in Addison (VT 17) to the **Crown Point State Historic Site** in Crown Point, NY, (NY 185), over Lake Champlain. Due to deterioration over time, the original 1929 toll bridge had to be demolished in 2009. Local architect Ted Zoli designed the new bridge, which opened in November 2011 and has pedestrian and bicycle lanes on both sides. During its construction, archaeological digs unearthed artifacts revealing human habitation since glacial waters receded 9,000 years ago. Evidence was discovered of a 1731 French fort, as was 1790s redware by Vermont potter Moses Bradley, which you can view at **Chimney Point**. Additional historic sites, **Mount Independence** and **Fort Ticonderoga**, make for a pleasant loop tour. See details under *Historical Attractions* on page 317.

CHAMPLAIN BRIDGE LISA HALVORSEN

♦ ⟐ **Lake Champlain Maritime Museum** (802-475-2022; lcmm.org), 4472 Basin Harbor Road, Vergennes. Open late-May–mid-October, daily. Admission. The museum's 14 buildings, spread over 4 acres, contain Native American and Revolutionary War artifacts, a working blacksmith shop, and dozens of small craft built around the lake over a 150-year period. Exhibits reveal the lake's dramatic role in history, colorful characters, and the stories of hundreds of shipwrecks still beneath the surface. Learn about Lake Champlain's Underwater Historic Preserves and how nautical archaeologists in the conservation lab preserve artifacts. Working replicas of Benedict Arnold's 1776 gunboat *Philadelphia II* and the Colonial-era bateau *Perseverance* are open to visitors. The museum also is a port-of-call for the full-size replica 1862 canal schooner *Lois McClure*. View the ship's itinerary and log on to the museum's website. Inquire about shipwreck tours, special lectures, and boatbuilding and blacksmithing courses.

🌺 **Lemon Fair Sculpture Park** (lemonfairsculpturepark.com), 4547 VT 73 East, Shoreham. Open weekends, May–November 1. Free. Art lovers Frank and Elaine Ittleman have created an outdoor sculpture park on their Shoreham property, which includes a 1-mile walking trail through a meadow with more than 30 sculptures, many by Vermont artists. Some are for sale, and all are described on the provided information sheet about the artists and their pieces.

⟐ **Shoreham Bell Museum** (802-897-2780; shorehambellmuseum.com), 127 Smith Street, Shoreham. Open by chance—look for the OPEN sign—or by appointment most afternoons. Free but donations accepted. Judith Blake and her late husband Charles collected more than 5,500 bells—cow bells, town crier bells, Tibetan prayer bells, and many more—so many that she decided to open a museum. Her eclectic collection includes numerous antiques and bells with interesting backstories.

## ✳ To Do

BICYCLING It's no coincidence that the country's first bicycle touring company was founded in this area. **VBT Bicycling and Vacations** (855-445-5501; vbt.com) was started in Bristol in 1971 and now has its headquarters in Williston. The Champlain Valley, with its relatively flat terrain and mountain views, has an abundance of back roads leading through covered bridges, connecting historic sites and comfortable inns with swimming holes, ice cream stands, and antiquing stops en route. Exercise caution on narrow roads that have heavy truck traffic, such as VT 22A and VT 30. The area's bicycling info clearinghouse is champlainbikeways.org. A number of bike shops in the area offer rentals, sales, and service, among them Frog Hollow Bikes (802-388-6666; froghollowbikes.com), 74 Main Street, Middlebury, and Little City Cycles (802-877-3000; littlecitycycles.com), 10 North Main Street, Vergennes.

**Country Inns Along the Trail** (800-838-3301; inntoinn.com), 52 Park Street, Brandon. Customized road and mountain bike tours begin and end in Brandon, visiting a number of inns along the way. Walking/hiking and cross-country skiing tours also are available.

MOUNTAIN BIKING **Blueberry Hill Outdoor Center** (802-247-6735; blueberryhilltrails.com), 1245 Goshen-Ripton Road, Goshen. The center maintains 50 km of trails, suitable for mountain biking, within the Moosalamoo National Recreation Area. **Green Mountain Bikes** (802-767-4464; greenmountainbikes.com), 105 North Main Street, Rochester, offers drop-off and pickup service.

BIRDING **Little Otter Creek Wildlife Management Area**, Vergennes, and the **Dead Creek Wildlife Management Area**, Addison (off VT 17), are particularly rich in bird life, especially during spring and fall migration seasons; Dead Creek attracts up to 20,000 snow geese. The Chimney Point area and **Whitney/Hospital Creek Wildlife Management Area** (including the McCuen Slang Fishing Access) provide great lake access for viewing waterfowl and shorebirds. **Button Bay State Park** (vtstateparks.com) is another birding hotspot. The Otter Creek Audubon Society's website (ottercreek.wordpress .com) provides local birding information, or download the **Lake Champlain Birding Trail** brochure at lakechamplainregion.com/outdoors/birding. Also see *Green Space* on page 319.

BOATING **Waterhouses Marina** (802-352-4433; waterhouses.com), 937 West Shore Road, Salisbury (Lake Dunmore), rents paddleboats, canoes, and motorboats; also sells fishing supplies and fuel.

**Champlain Houseboat Charters** (802-558-4574; champlainhouseboatcharters .com), located at **Chipman Point Marina**, 68 Chipmans Point Road, Orwell, rents house-boats that can accommodate eight.

✎ **Button Bay State Park** (802-475-2377), 5 Button Bay State Park Road, Ferrisburgh, has canoe, kayak, rowboat, and pedal-boat rentals. **Branbury State Park** (802-247-5925), 3570 Lake Dunmore Road, Salisbury, offers similar rentals on Lake Dunmore. **D.A.R. State Park** (802-759-2354), 6750 VT 17 West, Addison, has a boat launching area for Lake Champlain (vtstateparks.com).

COVERED BRIDGES *Note:* These bridges are marked on the Lower Champlain Valley map.

The **Pulp Mill Bridge** between Middlebury and Weybridge, spanning Otter Creek near the UVM Morgan Horse Farm, is a rare double-barreled (two-lane) bridge. Built circa 1820, it is Vermont's oldest covered bridge.

**Halpin Bridge** (1824), Middlebury, 2 miles east of US 7, off Halpin Road, spans a natural waterfall on the New Haven River and is the highest bridge above the streambed in the state.

**Station (or Salisbury) Bridge**, a 136-foot Town lattice bridge built in 1865, crosses Otter Creek in Cornwall, 2 miles east of VT 30 on Swamp Road.

**Shoreham Covered Railroad Bridge**, East Shoreham off the Whiting–Shoreham Road (turn south onto Shoreham Depot Road). A 108-foot Howe Truss bridge built in 1897 by the Rutland Railroad is one of the few remaining railroad covered bridges left in Vermont. It's a designated state historic site.

CULTURAL ATTRACTIONS **Middlebury College Museum of Art** (802-443-5007; museum.middlebury.edu), 72 Porter Field Road, Middlebury, at the Kevin P. Mahaney Center for the Arts. Open Tues.–Sun., closed during college holiday periods. Free. The college's distinguished permanent collection ranges from the

PULP MILL BRIDGE   LISA HALVORSEN

decorative arts through modern painting, with emphases on photography, nineteenth-century European and American sculpture, and contemporary prints. Permanent and changing exhibits are displayed in galleries within the multitiered arts center, which also includes a café and several performance areas.

**Vermont Folklife Center** (802-388-4964; vermontfolklifecenter.org), 88 Main Street. Open Mon.–Sat. This renowned folk-life education organization, founded in 1984, collects and preserves the traditional arts and heritage of Vermont, primarily through taped interviews; its archive contains more than 5,000 audio and video recordings plus 20,000 photographs. The center mounts changing exhibits in its gallery and maintains an excellent on-site gift shop.

KEVIN P. MAHANEY CENTER FOR THE ARTS  LISA HALVORSEN

⚓ **The UVM Morgan Horse Farm** (802-388-2011; uvm.edu/morgan), 74 Battell Drive, Weybridge. Open daily May 1–October 31; admission charged. Colonel Joseph Battell began breeding Morgans on this farm in the 1870s and is credited with saving the breed (America's first developed breed of horse) from extinction. The farm is now a breeding and training center operated by the University of Vermont. Guided tours of the stables and paddocks are available, along with an audiovisual presentation about the Morgan horse and the farm.

⚓ ♿ **National Museum of the Morgan Horse** (802-388-1639; morganmuseum.org), 34 Main Street, Middlebury. Open Wed.–Sat. Admission by donation. Chronological displays describe the history of the Morgan horse in America. Changing exhibits include original works of art to historical materials.

DISC GOLF The **Vergennes School Community Disc Golf Course** (gmdgc.org/courses) includes 18 holes at Vergennes High School and the adjacent Vergennes Elementary School, and it is open to the public after school, weekends, and in the summer.

FISHING **Otter Creek** is a warm-water stream good for smallmouth bass and northern pike. The cooler **Neshobe River**, especially the section through Forest Dale, is better for trout, and rainbows can be found in the **Middlebury River** just below Ripton. The **New Haven River** between Lincoln and Bristol and south of New Haven Mills also offers good trout fishing. The Vermont Outdoor Guide Association (voga.org) and the Vermont Fish and Wildlife Department (vtfishandwildlife.com) are both good sources for information.

**Stream & Brook Fly-Fishing** (802-989-0398; streamandbrook.com) offers beginners' programs and full- and half-day guided trips.

FITNESS CENTERS AND SPAS **Vermont Sun** (vermontsun.com) sports and fitness center has locations in Middlebury (802-388-6888) and Vergennes (802-877-2030) with group fitness classes, training equipment, an Olympic-size pool, and racquetball courts. **Middlebury Fitness** (802-388-3744; middleburyfitness.com) in Middlebury features a wide variety of fitness and wellness classes. **Village Spa**

(802-465-8255; brandonvillagespa.com), Brandon, and **Waterfalls Day Spa** (802-388-0311; middleburyspa.com), Middlebury, offer a full menu of spa services.

GOLF **Ralph Myhre Golf Course** (802-443-5125; ralphmyhregolfcourse.com), 317 Golf Course Road (VT 30), just south of the Middlebury campus, an 18-hole public course is owned and operated by the college. Open mid-April–November.

    **The Basin Harbor Club** (802-475-2311; basinharbor.com), 4800 Basin Harbor Road, Vergennes. Vermont's first Audubon Cooperative Sanctuary Golf Course is an 18-hole course overlooking Lake Champlain. It was designed by world-renowned architect Geoffrey Cornish. Open early May–mid-October. The Basin Harbor Club offers several dining options.

    **Neshobe Golf Club** (802-247-3611; neshobe.com), 224 Town Farm Road, Brandon (just off VT 73). Open April–October. Eighteen holes and a full-service club with restaurant, pro shop, and driving range.

HIKING **The Green Mountain National Forest District Office** (802-747-6700; fs.usda .gov), 231 North Main Street, Rutland, has information on area day hikes. For **Country Inns Along the Trail** (802-247-3300; inntoinn.com), a dozen inns collaborate to provide lodging along an 80-mile stretch of the Long Trail and some of its side trails, including back roads through the Green Mountain National Forest and trails through Moosalamoo National Recreation Area for multiday self-guided and guided treks.

    **Trail Around Middlebury** (802-388-1007; maltvt.org). The Middlebury Area Land Trust has created an 18-mile loop that circles the town and strings together two parks and a half-dozen woodland paths. The most scenic segment is the Otter Creek Gorge Trail, running along the river and traversing meadows, forests, and wilderness areas. The Land Trust publishes The Trail Around Middlebury (TAM), a free map/guide (see website), and organizes hikes and treks throughout the year.

    **Snake Mountain**, Addison. From VT 22A, take VT 17 east; turn right after a mile onto Mountain Road Park for about 2 miles. The trail, often muddy at the start, gets a bit steeper and rockier as you reach the summit, which has lovely lake and Adirondack views and vestiges of the aptly named Grand View Hotel, which closed in 1925. Descend via the Red Rock Pond trail, which passes a pretty pond. The trails follow an old carriage route, and wildflowers abound in spring.

    **Mount Abraham**, Lincoln. The 360-degree panorama at the summit of Vermont's fifth highest peak, elevation 4,006 feet, is magnificent, although be forewarned, the two access trails are strenuous. The 5.8-mile Battell Trail up the western flank takes about four hours round-trip. To reach the trailhead, turn north on Quaker Street in Lincoln Village, then right on Elder Hill Road. The parking area is 2 miles ahead. Another option is to take the Long Trail. It crosses Lincoln Gap Road near the top of the gap. Plan on three-and-a-half hours round-trip. Keep in mind that the road is not plowed in winter.

    **Moosalamoo National Recreation Area** (802-779-1731; moosalamoo.org), an Abenaki word meaning "he trails the moose" or "the moose departs," is a 15,857-acre tract within the Green Mountain National Forest that is prime moose habitat. It's crisscrossed with hiking trails and a 10-mile spur of the Long Trail. A popular hike is the trek to Mount Horrid Cliffs, a rocky outcropping with memorable Adirondack views. The trailhead is at the parking area just before the top of Brandon Gap on VT 73. Follow the Long Trail north for 0.4 mile to a blue-blazed spur trail with steps cut into the rock. Although steep, it's short (0.1 mile stretch), but worth it for the views. Note: The cliff trail may be closed March–August to protect nesting peregrine falcons. Area will be posted. You can continue on the Long Trail, which ends at a parking area on VT 125.

HISTORICAL ATTRACTIONS ✈ ♿ **Chimney Point State Historic Site** (802-759-2412; historicsites.vermont.gov), 8149 VT 17 West, Addison, at the Champlain Bridge. Open Memorial Day–mid-October, Wed.–Sun., Mon. holidays. The museum exhibits, housed in a 1785 tavern, explore the history of the Native Americans and the first European settlers; the Barnes family, who owned the property for over a century; and lake transportation, including the ferries and original bridge at this location. The Chimney Point Trail, a short outdoor walking trail with interpretive signs, tells about the history and engineering of the bridge.

✈ ♿ **Crown Point State Historic Site** (518-597-4666; parks.ny.gov/historic-sites), 21 Grandview Drive, Crown Point, NY. Grounds open year-round, free. Admission for museum, open early May–mid-October. Just across the Lake Champlain Bridge from Chimney Point, VT. The original fort was Fort St. Frederic, built by the French in the 1730s. The British captured it in 1759 and built their own fort, known as His Majesty's Fort of Crown Point. In 1775 American colonists overtook it and hauled its cannons and heavy ordnance to Boston to fight the British. The complex includes eighteenth-century ruins (see website for downloadable map), walking trails, and a museum with artifacts found on the site. *Note:* The historic Crown Point Pier, Champlain Memorial Lighthouse, and toll-keeper's house, all close by, are worth visiting

✈ **Fort Ticonderoga** (518-585-2821; fortticonderoga.org), 30 Fort Ti Road, Ticonderoga, NY. Open mid-May–late October, daily. Admission. Accessible via the Fort Ticonderoga Ferry from Larrabees Point, Shoreham (see *Getting There* on page 307). Built by the French (who named it Fort Carillon), it was captured and held by the British until 1775, when Ethan Allen and his Green Mountain Boys took the fort by surprise, capturing the guns that eventually helped free Boston. Daily programs, demonstrations, and guided tours of the historic King's Garden; behind-the-scenes tours; and special events, including reenactments, tell the story of the fort and its soldiers. The restored eighteenth-century stone fort's museum displays weapons, uniforms, and artifacts. Board the *Carillon*, a replica 1920s touring boat, for a narrated 90-minute tour of the lake and area history (Tues.–Sun).

**Henry Sheldon Museum of Vermont History** (802-388-2117; henrysheldonmuseum .org), 1 Park Street, Middlebury. Open Tues.–Sat. Admission. The research center is open Thurs.–Fri. afternoons and by appointment. One of America's oldest history museums is located in an 1829 Federal-style brick building, originally home to two wealthy marble quarry owners. Sheldon was an obsessive collector of nineteenth- and early-twentieth-century furniture, paintings, newspapers, apparel, toys, and other everyday items, many once belonging to Addison County residents.

**John Strong D.A.R. Mansion** (802-759-2309; johnstrongmansion.org), 6656 VT 17 West, Addison. Open Memorial Day–Labor Day, weekends. Admission. General John Strong, an early settler and a Revolutionary War patriot, built his residence here in 1796 with brick from his own clay pits on the "Salt Lick," where he first hunted deer. Furnishings reflect five generations of the family. The house was purchased by the Daughters of the American Revolution in 1934 to tell Strong's story and to preserve this outstanding example of early domestic architecture.

✈ ♿ **Mount Independence State Historic Site** (802-948-2000; historicsites.vermont .gov), 497 Mount Independence Road, Orwell. Grounds open year-round; museum open Memorial Day weekend–Columbus Day, daily. Admission. This National Historic Landmark is one of America's best-preserved Revolutionary War sites. A state-of-the-art visitor center tells the story of the 12,000 men who built a massive fort here in 1776 to fend off the British army, many of them freezing to death the following winter. An exhibit displays the military trappings, clothing, and even food they left behind. Six miles of marked hiking trails, including one that is handicapped-accessible, start at the visitor center, weaving past the remains of the hospital, batteries, blockhouses, and barracks of this once-bustling fort.

SWIMMING **Middlebury Gorge**, East Middlebury, off VT 125 just above the Waybury Inn, where the road suddenly steepens beyond the bridge. Paths lead down to the river.

**Dog Team Tavern Hole**, 3.1 miles north of Middlebury, off Dog Team Tavern Road. Park near the site of the former restaurant and walk along the riverbank until you find an appealing spot in the bends of the New Haven River. There's a small beach area with a gentle current.

**Lake Pleiad**, behind the Middlebury College Snow Bowl about 8 miles from Middlebury east on VT 125. Park in the lot past the snow bowl entrance at the intersection of the Long Trail. Follow the trail for half a mile, turning right onto Lake Pleiad Trail and following it to the lake. A truly idyllic setting, this is the perfect spot to swim and picnic. Take in the pristine surroundings from the large rocks on the western end.

**Bartlett Falls**, Bristol. Near the beginning of Lincoln Gap Road (off VT 116 in Rocky Dale), look for the pull-off for this popular swimming hole with its 14-foot cliffs. A bronze plaque explains that the land is a gift from Irving Wesley Sr., in memory of his son who died at 19 fighting a 1943 forest fire in British Columbia. It's a beautiful spot by a stream with shallow falls dropping into pools, although it gets crowded on hot summer days. Swimming shoes are a good idea.

**Lake Dunmore** (see *Green Space* on page 320), a scenic lake with a firm, sandy bottom and an extensive sandy beach; ideal for recreation and picnics.

**Vermont State Parks** (vtstateparks.com). **Button Bay State Park** is the only state park with a swimming pool, **D.A.R. State Park** has a swimming beach on Lake Champlain, and **Branbury State Park** has beach access on Lake Dunmore. See also *Green Space* on page 320.

SCENIC DRIVES **Middlebury Gap.** This is a popular approach to Addison County from the southeast. This stretch of VT 125 is more dramatic driving east to west. Begin in Hancock and stop at Texas Falls (see the map in "The White River Valleys" on page 227). The road quickly crests at its junction with the Long Trail, near the Middlebury Snow Bowl. Then it's all downhill through the woods until the Bread Loaf Inn (now part of Middlebury College) improbably appears. The Robert Frost Wayside Picnic Area and the Interpretive Trail are a short distance beyond. Adjacent to the picnic area is an unmarked dirt road to the Homer Noble Farm, where the poet spent his summers from 1940 to his death in 1963. The picturesque hill town of Ripton is just below, and as the road continues to plunge into the valley, watch for glimpses of the Adirondacks in the distance.

**Brandon Gap.** VT 73 is a high road over Goshen Mountain and through Brandon Gap, which is a Long Trail crossing. Several wooded hiking trails and a rest area where you can stop for views of Mount Horrid's Great Cliff are at the height-of-the-land. The road then rushes downhill along Brandon Brook, joining VT 100 and the White River below Rochester.

*Note:* A well-surfaced dirt road (Goshen-Ripton Road) off VT 125, just south of Ripton, will take you through the **Moosalamoo National Recreation Area**, and past Blueberry Hill Inn (see *Lodging* on page 322), to VT 73 near Forest Dale in the Brandon Gap.

**Appalachian Gap.** East from Bristol, VT 17 climbs steadily for 4 miles (past the Jerusalem Corners Country Store), eases off for a couple of miles, and then zigzags steeply to crest at more than 3,000 feet, yielding some stunning views before dropping into the Mad River Valley. It's even more spectacular heading west.

**Lincoln/Appalachian Gap Loop.** From Bristol, follow VT 17/116 to the turnoff for Lincoln 2 miles east of Bristol, past Bartlett Falls (be sure to stop) to Lincoln and out Downingsville Road to Jerusalem, back down on VT 116 to VT 17.

**Lincoln Gap.** Follow VT 17/116 east from Bristol, as above, but from Lincoln continue on the narrow Gap Road, unpaved in sections. Again you have beautiful views, and you are quickly down in Warren. *Note:* Unsuitable for trailers and RVs. Closed in winter.

## ✳ Winter Sports

CROSS-COUNTRY SKIING **Rikert Nordic Center** at the Bread Loaf Campus of Middlebury College (802-443-2744; rikertnordic.com), 106 College Cross Road, Ripton. This college-owned land has 50 km of groomed trails, including near the Homer Noble Farm once owned by Robert Frost and the Middlebury College Ski Bowl. Elevations range from 975 to 1,500 feet. Rentals, accessories, lessons, and repairs.

⌒ **Blueberry Hill Outdoor Center** (802-247-6735; blueberryhilltrails.com), 1245 Goshen–Ripton Road, Goshen, has 70 km of trails within 22,000 acres of the Green Mountain National Forest and Moosalamoo National Recreation Area, reaching backcountry elevations of 1,400–3,100 feet, ensuring snow even in marginal seasons. The center has ski and snowshoe rental equipment, waxing, and repairs; trail-use fee gets you free soup noon–2.

DOWNHILL SKIING AND SNOWBOARDING ⌒ **Middlebury College Snow Bowl** (802-443-7669; middleburysnowbowl.com), 6886 VT 125, Hancock. A throwback to a less commercial era of skiing, this college-owned ski area has three chairlifts—two triples, one double, and a carpet lift—that access 17 trails and six glades on 110 acres, 40 percent covered by snowmaking. It offers a ski school, shop, rentals, and a cafeteria offering some of the most affordable food for a ski area. From Christmas Eve through March, Addison County Transit Resources (802-388-2287; actr-vt.org) runs a regular shuttle service with several stops starting at Middlebury College. Full fare is $1.

## ✳ Green Space

Also see *Birding, Hiking, Swimming, Scenic Drives* on pages 314–18.

### ON OR NEAR LAKE CHAMPLAIN

✪ ⌒ **Dead Creek Wildlife Management Area** (802-759-2398; vtfishandwildlife .com), Addison. Located 1 mile west of VT 22A on VT 17, this 2,858-acre refuge is

DEAD CREEK WILDLIFE MANAGEMENT AREA VISITOR CENTER LISA HALVORSEN

popular with paddlers and birders. More than 200 bird species have been sighted here including bald eagles, snowy owls, and waterfowl. During spring and fall migrations, flocks of snow and Canada geese numbering in the thousands can be observed at the viewing area, which has signage about the geese and other avian species. Stop at the visitor center to watch a video about the area and learn about waterfowl management, local wildlife and birds, the role of game wardens, and other relevant topics through the interactive exhibits.

✦ **Button Bay State Park** (802-475-2377; vtstateparks.com), 5 Button Bay State Park Road, Ferrisburgh. Open Memorial Day–Columbus Day weekends. Named for the unusual, clay "buttons" found in years past along its shore, this 253-acre area overlooks the lake and Adirondacks; 53 RV/tent sites, 13 lean-tos, four cabins, picnic areas, swimming (in state park pool only), fishing, boat rentals, nature museum, and trails.

🐾 ✦ **D.A.R. State Park** (802-759-2354; vtstateparks.com), 6750 VT 17 West, Addison, is a 95-acre park on Lake Champlain with 71 campsites, including 24 lean-tos, boat access to the lake, and a smooth shale beach for swimming. Remnants of the area's first Colonial homestead, owned by Revolutionary War patriot John Strong, can be seen near the picnic pavilion.

## IN OR NEAR THE GREEN MOUNTAIN NATIONAL FOREST

🐾 ✦ **Lake Dunmore** on VT 53 (off US 7) in Salisbury is a 1,000-acre lake lined with summer cottages at the foot of Mount Moosalamoo. On its east shore is 🐾 ✦ **Branbury State Park** (802-247-5925; vtstateparks.com), a favorite with campers for its natural sandy beach, boating, and hikes to **Ethan Allen's Cave** (from the campground) and **Falls of Lana**, just south of the park entrance. It's a half-mile trek to the falls and picnic area, and another 1.6 miles to secluded Silver Lake, which has 15 primitive no-fee campsites and a picnic area. Swimming and dogs permitted. Religious camp meetings were held here in the 1880s, and later, a large hotel (constructed as a seminary) until 1942 when fire destroyed it. A 2.5-mile trail loops around the lake. The area can also be accessed on foot or by mountain bike via the 0.6-mile Goshen Trail on Green Mountain National Forest Road 27 (Silver Lake Road), off Goshen Road.

**Moosalamoo National Recreation Area** (802-779-1731; moosalamoo.org), stretching from the western slopes of the Green Mountains to Lake Dunmore, has more than 70 miles of well-maintained trails on all terrains for four-season outdoor recreation. Visit the website for a downloadable map and information on activities and camping.

🍁 **Robert Frost Country** In 1983 then-governor Richard Snelling designated part of the Green Mountain National Forest as Robert Frost Country. A 16-mile stretch of VT 125 that winds through the forest from East Middlebury to Hancock was named the **Robert Frost Memorial Drive**. The **Robert Frost Interpretive Trail**, a relatively flat 1.2-mile path through meadows and woods, has a number of trailside plaques with Frost's scenery-inspired poems. This trail is popular with cross-country skiers and snowshoers, and, in summer, blueberry pickers. A portion is handicapped-accessible. Just beyond the trail's parking area is the **Robert Frost Wayside Area**. A dirt road adjacent to this picnic area leads to the Homer Noble Farm, which the poet purchased in 1940. Park in the lot and walk past the white wood-frame farmhouse to the rustic cabin (not open to the public), where he preferred to sleep and write. Now a National Historic Landmark, the property is owned by Middlebury College, which also owns the adjacent Bread Loaf campus. Frost was a regular participant at the Bread Loaf Writers' Conference held each summer since the 1920s.

# ✳ Lodging

## INNS

### IN THE MIDDLEBURY AREA

♂ 🐾 ✎ ♿ **The Middlebury Inn** (802-388-4961; middleburyinn.com), 14 Court Square, Middlebury, has been welcoming travelers since 1827. The spacious lobby, with its formal check-in desk and portraits of the Battell family and Robert Frost, is a firm reminder of the renovated inn's heritage. The 71 guest rooms are divided among four adjoining buildings. The 1825 Porter Mansion, with a luxury suite, eight rooms, curved staircase, and other handsome architectural details, was renovated with wedding parties in mind. Pets are welcome in the Courtyard Annex motel units for a daily fee. The **Waterfalls Day Spa** (see *Fitness Centers and Spas* on page 316) and **Morgan's Tavern** (see *Dining Out*) on page 325 are located at the inn. Room rates include complimentary afternoon tea. $-$$$.

♂ 🐾 ♿ **Swift House Inn** (802-388-9925; swifthouseinn.com), 25 Stewart Lane, Middlebury. The former family estate of the legendary philanthropist Jessica Stewart Swift, the Swift House is now under the ownership of Dan and Michele Brown. Antiques, elaborately carved marble fireplaces, formal gardens, and extravagant wallpaper and upholstery add to the charm of this 1814 mansion. (Ask to see the vintage elevator.) Nine guest rooms are in the main house, five are in the Victorian gatehouse, and six contemporary-styled ones with fireplace and whirlpool tub are in the renovated 1886 carriage house. **Jessica's Restaurant** serves upscale meals (see *Dining Out* on page 325). Pets are welcome in the Carriage House for an extra fee. $-$$$.

♂ 🐾 ✎ ♿ **Waybury Inn** (802-388-4015; wayburyinn.com), 457 East Main

**HISTORIC LAKE RESORT**

## HISTORIC LAKE RESORT

**B**asin Harbor Club (802-475-2311; basinharbor.com), 4800 Basin Harbor Road, Vergennes. Open mid-May–mid-October. Vermont's premier lakeside resort is located on 700 acres and offers accommodations in the main lodge, three guesthouses, and 74 cottages scattered along the shore. Since 1886, when they first began taking in summer boarders, members of the Beach family have assiduously kept up with the times. Over the years a heated outdoor swimming pool, an 18-hole golf course, a wellness center, tennis courts, a private boat club, and even an airstrip have been added. Ardelia's, the main dining room, expects guests to dress for dinner, while the poolside **Ranger Room**, **Red Mill Restaurant** (802-475-2317), and outdoor venues offer casual dining. Ask about special packages. $$$-$$$$. ♂ 🐾 ✎

Street, East Middlebury. Robert Frost was a frequent guest at the inn, a former stagecoach stop, although it was the 1980s TV show, *Newhart*, that put it on the map. Ask innkeepers Tracey and Joe Sutton to see show memorabilia as you relax at this quiet country inn in one of the 13 imaginatively furnished rooms. Two-night minimum stay required on peak weekends and holidays. Cooked-to-order breakfast included. The dining room is open to the public. (See *Dining Out* on page 325.)

### IN BRANDON

♂ 🐾 ♿ **Lilac Inn** (802-247-5463; lilacinn.com), 53 Park Street. A Brandon-born financier built this romantic old mansion with an imposing five-arched façade in 1909, which Doug and Shelly Sawyer now run as an inn. Nine antiques-filled guest rooms with luxurious bathrooms with deep, clawfoot tubs; a glassed-in ballroom with a crystal chandelier; and a wide entrance hallway with a grand staircase at the front keep the grand historic feeling alive. Rates include a three-course breakfast served in the sun-filled garden room. The inn is open to the public for breakfast; reservations a must. $$–$$$.

♂ ☗ ✧ ⚅ **The Brandon Inn** (802-247-5766; historicbrandoninn.com), 20 Park Street. A large brick landmark opposite the village green, this inn dates from 1786 and is on the National Register of Historic Places. Sarah and Louis Pattis, innkeepers since 1988, offer 39 rooms, two of them suites. The inn's 5 landscaped acres include a swimming pool (with Jacuzzi) and a stretch of the Neshobe River, good for trout fishing. An 18-hole golf course is nearby. Complimentary country breakfast, May–December. $$.

## ELSEWHERE

✿ ♂ ☗ ✧ **Blueberry Hill Inn** (802-247-6735; blueberryhillinn.com), 1245 Goshen–Ripton Road, Goshen. Over the past four decades Tony Clark has turned this blue farmhouse on a back country road in the Moosalamoo National Recreation Area into one of New England's most famous country inns. The inn has 11 rooms, four original to the 1813 home, and offers gourmet cuisine, peace and quiet, and four-season outdoor recreation. Breakfast (included) is a hearty affair, and chef Tony gets creative in the kitchen when it comes to the four-course prix fixe dinners (extra), often using produce straight from the garden. There's a bottomless cookie jar, with cookies also available by mail-order. The property includes a swimming pond, gardens, and blueberries for picking. The inn's **Blueberry Hill Outdoor Center** maintains more than 70 km of trails for year-round use, including cross-country skiing, and it serves free hot soup at lunch in winter. $$–$$$.

♂ ✧ **The Inn at Baldwin Creek** (802-453-2432; baldwincreek.net), 1868 North 116 Road, Bristol. A classic 1797 Vermont farmhouse inn set on 25 acres, including a perennial garden and paths to the creek for wading and fishing. The five guest rooms, including two suites—one with queen sleigh bed, gas fireplace, and Jacuzzi tub—come with a farm-fresh breakfast. Longtime innkeepers Linda Harmon and Doug Mack also run **Mary's Restaurant at Baldwin Creek** (see *Dining Out* on page 326), a favorite regional dining spot, renowned as a farm-to-table innovator. Chef Doug hosts special farmhouse dinners featuring local farmers, cooking classes, and overseas culinary tours. $–$$.

☗ ⚅ **The Shoreham Inn** (802-897-5081; shorehaminn.com), 51 Inn Road, Shoreham. Andrew and Elizabeth Done, who bought the inn in 2017, welcome guests to their 1790 inn with its 10 beautifully decorated guest rooms, including three two-story, loft-style suites in a vintage timber-frame sheep barn. The inn is at the center of a quaint village, surrounded by apple country, not far from Lake Champlain and Middlebury. A full breakfast is included, and guests can make reservations to eat at the inn's gastropub, also open to the public. (See *Dining Out* on page 327). $$–$$$.

## BED & BREAKFASTS

### IN AND AROUND MIDDLEBURY

✧ ⚅ **The Inn on the Green** (802-388-7512; innonthegreen.com), 71 South Pleasant Street, Middlebury. This inviting 1803 Federal townhouse, overlooking the village green, has two suites that each sleep four in the main house, plus nine spacious rooms in the renovated carriage house, all named for local towns. Complimentary breakfast-in-bed baskets are delivered to your door, but afternoon tea service requires that you emerge from under the covers. Although you may not want to leave once you settle in, should you decide to go exploring, innkeepers Bruce and Brenda Grove are happy to provide suggestions. $–$$.

♂ ♿ **Cornwall Orchards
Bed & Breakfast** (802-462-2272;
cornwallorchards.com), 1364 VT
30, Cornwall. Miles Peterle and Lise
Anderson, the new owners of this 1783
farmhouse B&B with four guest rooms,
encourage guests to explore the 13-acre
property, including the gardens, woods,
and heritage apple orchard, one of the
last remaining stands of a commercial
orchard, planted in 1910. The outdoor
deck has views of the orchard and an
English perennial garden. A hot breakfast, using fresh organic or local Vermont ingredients, is served in the airy
dining room. $–$$.

☕ ♪ **Chipman Inn** (802-388-2390;
chipmaninn.com), 3062 VT 125, Ripton.
Innkeeper Joan Bullock first bought this
1828 inn in 1978 and ran it with the help
of her children until 1985, when she sold
it. The hospitality business was in her
blood, and in 2012 she bought back the
inn, which she now runs with her son
Christopher. The nine-room inn is close
to Bread Loaf and the **Rikert Nordic
Center** (see *Winter Sports* on page 319),
Robert Frost's farmhouse and cabin, and
the Robert Frost Interpretive Trail. It has
a Tap Room—those are Frost's snowshoes
above the hearth—where guests and
the public can enjoy a cocktail, a glass
of wine, or a local brew. A full breakfast
is included, and a four-course dinner is
served every evening for an additional
charge. $$.

## SOUTH AND WEST OF
## MIDDLEBURY

☕ ♪ **Buckswood Bed & Breakfast** (802-
948-2054; buckswoodbandb.com), 633
VT 73, Orwell. Linda and Bob Martin
offer two guest rooms (private baths)
and ample common space in their 1814
home, located in a pleasant country
setting just east of Orwell Village.
Breakfast is included. Dinner by reser-
vation. Well-behaved pets allowed, as
Bob and Linda's Airedale, Abby, enjoys
company. $.

## IN BRANDON

**Inn at Neshobe River** (802-247-8002;
innatneshoberiver.com), 79 Stone Mill
Dam Road. This attractive 1786 farm-
house set on 5 acres above the Neshobe
River adjoins the 18-hole Neshobe Golf
Club. Innkeepers Bob and Rhonda Foley
offer four comfortable, tastefully fur-
nished guest rooms, breakfast included.
Guests can lounge in the two art-filled
living rooms, take a swim in the river, or
visit the on-site **Neshobe River Winery**
(see *Wineries*) and **Foley Brothers Brew-
ing,** famous for its Fair Maiden double
IPA. Wine or beer tasting is compli-
mentary for guests. $–$$.

♠ ☕ **The Inn on Park Street** (802-247-
3843; theinnonparkstreet.com), 69 Park
Street. Park Street is Brandon's Park Avenue, lined with the town's finest homes,
most of them on the National Register
of Historic Places. Judy Bunde, a professional pastry chef, offers six guest rooms
in this delightful Queen Anne Victorian.
In winter months a fire crackles in the
tastefully furnished living room with its
baby grand piano; in summer you can
eat on the spacious porch. Breakfast and
evening dessert and coffee, both featuring Bunde's delicious baked goods, are
complimentary. The "Cooking with Chefs"
program is wildly popular, as are girl-
friend weekends—definitely inquire. Dinner for groups by prior arrangement. $–$$.

**Rosebelle's Victorian Inn** (802-247-
0098; rosebelles.com), 31 Franklin Street.
Open April–October. This restored,
1830s mansard-roofed house has four
elegantly decorated guest rooms, a
high-ceilinged living room with a fireplace, and a large dining room—the setting for afternoon tea and full breakfasts.
Hostess Ginette Milot speaks French.
Two-night minimum stays are required
for weekend reservations during fall foliage season and special holidays. $–$$.

## IN VERGENNES

♠ ♪ **Emerson Guest House** (802-877-
3293; emersonhouse.com), 82 Main

Street. This 1850 French Second Empire mansion, once owned by a prominent local judge, has five high-ceilinged guest rooms (four with shared bath) and a suite with private bath. Your hosts, the Carmichaels—Susan, an artist, and Bill, a musical theater pro with Broadway credits including *Les Misérables*—serve scrumptious home-cooked breakfasts (included in rates) in a downstairs nook. The house is on 4 acres, with walking trails, gardens, and apple trees, and it is a short walk from the center of town. Common space includes a library and a living room with a vintage 1927 Steinway. $–$$.

♂ ☀ ⅙ **Strong House Inn** (802-877-3337; stronghouseinn.com), 94 West Main Street. Built in 1834 by Samuel Paddock Strong in the graceful Federal style, this roomy old house features fine detailing, such as curly maple railings on the freestanding main staircase. The 15 guest rooms are located in the main house and in Rabbit Ridge Country House, a newer annex in back, and include full breakfast and afternoon refreshments. Several suites are available, ideal for romantic getaways, including the often-requested Adirondack Room with its floor-to-ceiling stone fireplace, king-size canopied four-poster bed, double Jacuzzi, wet bar, and French doors opening to a private deck and gardens. Inquire about quilting, crafting, and other special weekends. $–$$$$.

### IN BRISTOL

♂ ♪ **Dreamhouse Country Inn** (802-453-2805; dreamhousecountryinn.com), 382 Hewitt Road. This classic Gothic Revival cottage, built in 1852, is set on 6 acres with three lovely guest rooms, one a bridal suite with jetted tub. Innkeepers Sue and Steve Alario go out of their way to make your stay memorable from the three-course gourmet breakfasts to free use of bicycles and snowshoes, and extras, such as an en-suite breakfast, massage, or cake to celebrate a special occasion. Ask about their cooking classes and Friday and Saturday night full-course dinners. $–$$.

**The Lawrence House Victorian Bed & Breakfast** (802-453-5709; thelawrencehousebnb.com), 48 North Street. This stunning three-story Queen Anne-style Victorian home was built in 1897 by William Abbott Lawrence, a wealthy horse speculator, for his new bride. Owners Kathleen and Martin Clark have preserved the home's historic character, furnishing the three guest rooms and common areas with period furnishings. Rates include a hearty country breakfast. $–$$.

OTHER LODGING The Addison County Chamber of Commerce (802-388-7951; addisoncounty.com) lists rental cottages on both Lake Dunmore and Lake Champlain.

CAMPGROUNDS D.A.R. State Park, Addison, and Branbury State Park, Salisbury, are popular options within the Vermont State Park system (vtstateparks .com). See *Green Space* on page 325.

🐾 ♪ **Lake Dunmore Kampersville** (802-352-4501; kampersville.com), 1457 Lake Dunmore Road, Salisbury. The campground, located on Lake Dunmore, is open early May–late October with tent and RV sites with full hookups. Campground amenities include two pools, a recreational hall, mini-golf, playing fields, and boat rentals with convenient access to Lake Dunmore for swimming, boating, and fishing. Weekly cabin rentals.

## ✳ Where to Eat

DINING OUT

### IN THE MIDDLEBURY AREA

♂ ♪ ⅙ **Fire & Ice Restaurant** (802-388-7166; fireandicerestaurant.com), 26 Seymour Street, Middlebury. Open for dinner daily, lunch served Fri.–Sun.

This is not so much a restaurant as a dine-in museum, with seating in cleverly themed rooms with eclectic decor including a 1921 Hacker-Craft motorboat. The salad bar, reputedly the largest in Vermont, has more than 55 items. The restaurant has been a local favorite since 1974, specializing in slow-roasted prime rib, hand cut to order. Entrées come with a self-serve bread and cheese board. The **Big Moose Pub** serves more casual fare, with daily drink specials. $–$$$$.

&#9855; **Jessica's Restaurant** at the Swift House Inn (802-388-9925; jessicasvermont.com), 25 Stewart Lane, Middlebury. Dinner is served Thurs.–Sun. year-round, also Wed., June–December. Chef Rob Fenn, a Middlebury native, changes the menu with the seasons, but there's always a range of entrées that span Europe, Asia, and New England. The bar has received the *Wine Spectator* Award of Excellence every year for the past decade for its wine list, and has a selection of local beers on tap, including Otter Creek brews. Ask to be seated in the book-filled library with its fireplace or, for intimate dining, the porch. $$–$$$.

&#9883; &#9855; **The Lobby** (802-989-7463; lobbyrestaurantvt.com), 7 Bakery Lane, Middlebury. Open daily for lunch and dinner; brunch is served Sat.–Sun. Preferred seating at this hip eatery is on the covered outside deck or by the bank of windows overlooking Otter Creek. Walls are covered with chalkboards with quotes from culinary luminaries; patrons are welcome to add their own. At lunch, try the Brie grilled cheese with house-made merguez (lamb sausage), raspberries, and balsamic vinaigrette. Creative burgers, including a black bean quinoa burger with herb goat cheese, are served all day. $$–$$$.

**Morgan's Tavern at the Middlebury Inn** (802-388-4961; middleburyinn.com), 14 Court Square, Middlebury. Breakfast and afternoon tea daily, lunch weekdays, dinner Wed.–Sun., Tavern menu Tues. Local ingredients are combined to create homey favorites such as Angus sirloin steak and chicken Cordon Bleu, but also more eclectic offerings including Faroe Island blackened salmon. $–$$$.

**Rough Cut** (802-458-8972; roughcutbbq.com), 51 Main Street, Middlebury. Dinner, Wed.–Sun.; lunch, Fri.–Sun. One of Middlebury's newest restaurants offers food with soul, a creative take on classic barbecue and southern regional food. "Rough Cuts"—entrées such as pulled pork, spare ribs, and brisket—come with two sides. Full bar with 12 beers on tap specializing in bourbon drinks. Patrons are invited to ride the mechanical bull. Owner Ben Wells also owns the **Marquis Theatre** (802-388-4841; middleburymarquis.com), a few doors down, which includes the **Southwest Café**, serving Mexican food to moviegoers and the public.

&#9883; &#9855; **Tourterelle Restaurant** (802-453-6309; tourterellevt.com), 3629 Ethan Allen Highway, New Haven. Open for dinner Wed.–Sat. Reservations recommended. On a stretch of US 7 dominated by farms and fields, this grand, cupola-topped stagecoach inn, which also has three well-appointed guest rooms, is an oasis of civility. New York chef Bill Snell and his French wife Christine have transformed the former Roland's Place into an elegant French country estate. The menu features French country cuisine, made with the freshest Vermont products. Weddings and events are a specialty. $$–$$$.

&#9855; **Waybury Inn** (802-388-4015; wayburyinn.com), 457 East Main Street (VT 125), East Middlebury. Open daily for dinner, Fri.–Sat. for lunch; Sunday for brunch. This inn's claim to fame is its stand-in role as the Stratford Inn on Bob Newhart's eponymous 1980s TV show. Larry, Darryl, and Darryl would likely be fixtures at the pub ($–$$). For a more elegant experience, dine in the Pine Room for local venison or mushroom Wellington. $$–$$$.

## IN BRANDON

✪ **Café Provence** (802-247-9997; cafeprovencevt.com), 11 Center Street. Open daily for lunch and dinner. On Sunday, brunch replaces lunch. Closed Mon. in winter. Chef-owner Robert Barral, a former New England Culinary Institute instructor, has a near-monopoly on Brandon dining, with this upscale-casual restaurant, **Center Street Bar** (802-465-8347, open daily) downstairs, and **Gourmet Provence Bakery & Wine Shop** down the street (802-247-3002; 37 Center Street). The fare at Café Provence changes regularly but always includes such crave-worthy seafood as the chef's signature stew, a lobster-tarragon broth filled with shellfish and served over saffron risotto. Enjoy the outdoor terrace in summer. Inquire about special events and Barral's famous cooking classes. $–$$$.

## IN VERGENNES

🌿 ⚓ ♿ **Ardelia's at Basin Harbor Club** (802-475-2311; basinharbor.com), 4800 Basin Harbor Road. Open mid-May–mid-October. Dinner at Ardelia's, named for a first-generation Beach family owner and innkeeper, is a dress up affair—jackets are expected for gentlemen over 12. That's just one of many throwbacks at this lakeside resort, which has changed little since it opened in 1886. The single exception is the creative cuisine of the formal, multi-course dinners prepared by executive chef Philippe Ducro. A buffet breakfast is served in this dining room daily. For casual fare, head to **Red Mill Restaurant** (802-475-2317), also on-site. $$$–$$$$.

✪ **Black Sheep Bistro** (802-877-9991; blacksheepbistrovt.com), 253 Main Street. Open nightly for dinner, this intimate bistro has been wildly popular since its debut in 2002. The innovative French-inspired menu will make you feel as if you're on a side street in Paris; the service is first-rate. Start with the signature duck cigar rolls with apricot-tarragon dipping sauce, followed by pork scaloppini or the bacon-and-Brie-stuffed chicken in balsamic cream. All entrées are accompanied by a creamy garlic mash and crisp, salty frites with addictive dipping sauces. Terrace seating in summer. Reservations essential. $$.

((ᵖ)) ♿ **Vergennes Laundry by CK** (802-870-7157; vergenneslaundry.net) 247 Main Street. Open Wed.–Sat. for dinner, Wed.–Sun. for brunch. A change in ownership of this wood-fired bakery inside a former laundromat in fall 2017 has meant a new menu, with a focus on brunch and prix-fixe, three-course dinners. The new chef-owner Christian Kruse, a New England Culinary Institute graduate, also serves breads, pastries, and coffees in keeping with the tradition of the former owners. $$–$$$$.

## IN BRISTOL

**The Bobcat Café & Brewery** (802-453-3311; thebobcatcafe.com), 5 Main Street. Open daily for dinner. This eatery began as a community effort, and in 2008, came under the same ownership as the **Black Sheep Bistro** in Vergennes. A reclaimed wood bar sets the mood for dining on contemporary comfort food and handcrafted beers. Hearty pub fare changes with the seasons, but flavorful vegetarian options and the signature venison-chorizo meatloaf are always on the menu. $$.

♿ **Mary's Restaurant at Baldwin Creek** (802-453-2432; baldwincreek.net), 1868 North 116 Road, Bristol (junction of VT 116 and VT 17). Open for dinner Wed.–Sat., Sunday brunch year-round; Sun. for dinner, May–October. A founding member of the Vermont Fresh Network, chef Doug Mack has been using local ingredients at Mary's and the **Inn at Baldwin Creek** since 1983. Much of the restaurant's produce comes from gardens and greenhouses on the property. There's a choice of three dining rooms, but when it comes to starters, there's nothing to debate. Just order a cup or bowl of the deservedly famous creamy garlic soup. The menu changes seasonally, with entrées ranging from lobster poutine to a simple pasta in ricotta-mint pesto. The website lists culinary events, cooking classes, and culinary tours. Reservations required. $$–$$$$.

## ELSEWHERE BUT WORTH THE DRIVE

**Gastropub at The Shoreham Inn** (802-897-5081; shorehaminn.com), 51 Inn Road (VT 74), Shoreham. Dinner is served Thurs.–Mon. in the downstairs pub at this British-style gastropub in a late eighteenth-century inn. Note the beautiful copper-topped bar and mantel mirror from Greenwich, England. The restaurant serves pub food, including traditional Irish pork pies, but it also has a number of hearty meat and fish entrées. $–$$.

## EATING OUT

### IN THE MIDDLEBURY AREA

✍ ♿ **A & W Drive-in** (802-388-2876), 1557 US 7 South, a few miles from Middlebury. Vermont's (and possibly New England's) last surviving drive-in with carhop service, open in summer months. The 1960s roadside spot still dispenses its root beer the old-fashioned way, in frosted glass mugs. A hard-core bacon cheeseburger is the obvious choice, but save room for the fried cheese curds, too.

🍴 ✍ ♿ **American Flatbread Middlebury Hearth** (802-388-3300; americanflatbread.com), 137 Maple Street at the Marble Works. Open Tues.–Sat. for dinner, with outdoor seating when possible. This company started in the Mad River Valley and remains the Middlebury area's only true craft pizzeria. The all-natural pies are made with organic flour and toppings and baked in a wood-fired oven.

✪ 🍴 ♿ **Costello's Market** (802-388-3385; costellosmarket.com), 2 Maple Street at the Marble Works. Open Tues.–Sat. The freshest fish around and a slew of Italy's best meats and cheeses fill the case here. But the real attraction is the prepared food. If you're lucky, chef John Hamilton will be slow-roasting his heavenly porchetta for fennel-scented sandwiches. If not, check out the ample sandwich and Po' Boy options, fish tacos, and inexpensive plated meals such as risotto or beef braciole. No indoor seating, so you will need to take it to go.

**The Diner** (802-388-3297; thedinervt.com), 66 Commerce Street. A Middlebury landmark since the mid-1930s, this cozy eatery, open daily, serves breakfast and lunch all day. The menu includes classic comfort foods from pancakes to patty melts, but also the unexpected, including a South African chicken curry and Cajun-style blackened haddock fillet on a baguette.

♿ 🛜 **Otter Creek Bakery** (802-388-3371; ottercreekbakery.com), 14 College Street. Open daily. Hugely popular at lunchtime for soups, salads, and deli sandwiches ranging from homemade hummus with veggies in a pita pocket to fresh crabmeat salad. Breads are the specialty, baked from scratch with no preservatives, in a dozen varieties,

A & W DRIVE-IN, MIDDLEBURY  ERICA HOUSKEEPER

TWO BROTHERS TAVERN LISA HALVORSEN

including wheat berry and onion Asiago. There are fresh, flaky croissants, too, plus dozens of cookies, tarts, and cakes.

⚓ **Rosie's Restaurant** (802-388-7052; rosiesrestaurantvt.com), 886 US 7 South, Middlebury, 1 mile south of downtown. Open daily. This popular family restaurant has been serving meatloaf with mashed potatoes and gravy, chicken 'n biscuits, and other comfort foods like "Mom used to make it" for more than 30 years. Kids' menu and daily specials.

((•)) **Two Brothers Tavern** (802-388-0002; twobrotherstavern.com), 86 Main Street, Middlebury. Open daily for lunch, dinner, and late night. Local hangout serving upscale comfort food with several Vermont microbrews on tap. Open mic, karaoke, live music, and trivia nights keep things lively in the downstairs lounge.

## IN BRANDON

((•)) **Cattails** (802-247-9300; cattailsvt .com), 2146 Grove Street. (US 7, just north of Brandon). Lunch, Tues.–Sun.; dinner daily; breakfast Sundays. Head

chefs Lance Chicoine and Stephanie Kellogg run this family eatery that serves up large portions of home-style American fare with occasional touches of Asia, the American South, and the Southwest. Children's menu. Early-bird dinner specials.

## IN VERGENNES

🍴 ⚓ ♿ **3 Squares Café** (802-877-2772; threesquarescafe.com), 141 Main Street. Open for three square meals daily. Chef-owner Matt Birong's restaurant is a Golden Barn member of the Vermont Fresh Network, but not all of his food is grown in the Green Mountains. As a proud investor in a Dominican Republic cacao farm, he handpicks pods that become chocolaty treats back home in Vergennes. Besides sipping chocolate (a dessert option), cacao drinks, and housemade truffles, Birong uses cacao in his mole sauce, chilis, and other dishes. The exotic ingredient is just a small part of what makes 3 Squares beloved by locals. Breakfast is served until 3 each day, while lunch and dinner bring a roster of perfectly balanced panini, salads, and daily specials.

**Bar Antidote** (802-877-2555; barantidote.com) 35 Green Street. Open Tues.–Sat. for dinner. How locally focused is this bar and restaurant? Chef-owner Ian Huizenga's menu is inspired by ingredients from his own farm and other area producers. His triple pork meatloaf is stuffed with pork tenderloin and wrapped in bacon. There are grilled enchiladas, flatbreads, and charcuterie, too, to be enjoyed with a local craft beer from **Hired Hand Brewing Company**, located above the restaurant, another of Huizenga's endeavors.

### IN BRISTOL

((y)) **Bristol Bakery & Café** (802-453-3280; bristolbakery.com), 16 Main Street. Open daily; Sunday brunch. This landmark restaurant, in business for three decades, is filled with the aroma of coffee and bread, hung with local art, and furnished with comfortable chairs. Enjoy a muffin as you browse the Internet or read your morning paper. Stop by at lunch for soups, specialty salads, or sandwiches. Breads are baked fresh each morning. A second location is open in Hinesburg.

### ELSEWHERE

🍴 ✏ ♿ **The Bridge** (802-759-2152; thebridgerestaurantvt.com), 8013 VT 17, West Addison. Open daily, except Tues., for breakfast, lunch, dinner. Home-cooked food with quick and friendly service. Portions are generous, and the low prices reflect the throwback nature of the rib-sticking comfort food, including maple cream pie. Kids' menu. Take-out window in summer for food and ice cream.

✏ ((y)) **lu•lu** (802-777-3933; luluvt.com), 185 Main Street, Vergennes. Open daily. Sisters Laura and Martha Mack opened their artisan ice cream shop in 2012. Ice cream is made in small batches. Flavors change daily and are all made from fresh local cream and eggs with creative add-ins such as lemon poppy seed cake or whiskey-soaked cherries.

COFFEEHOUSE ((y)) **Carol's Hungry Mind Café** (802-388-0101; carolshungrymindcafe.com), 24 Merchants Row, Middlebury. Open daily. This riverside coffeehouse offers soft music, art, pastries, sandwiches, and plenty of spots to settle in with a book or a group of friends. Check the website for upcoming events.

## ✳ Entertainment

**Mahaney Center for the Arts** (802-443-3168; middlebury.edu/arts/mcfa), 72 Porter Field Road, Middlebury College, Middlebury. The 370-seat concert hall in this dramatic building on the southern edge of campus offers a full series of concerts, recitals, plays, dance performances, and films.

♂ **Town Hall Theater** (802-382-9222; townhalltheater.org), 68 South Pleasant Street, Middlebury. This community theater in a restored 1884 town hall on the green stages music, dramatic performances, and children's events throughout the year. It's home to the nationally acclaimed, professional **Opera Company of Middlebury** (802-382-9222; ocmvermont.org), **Middlebury Actors Workshop** (middleburyactors.org), **Middlebury Community Players** (middleburycommunityplayers.org), and the occasional **After Dark Music Series** (afterdarkmusicseries.com). It's also a fun location for weddings and events.

**Compass Music & Arts Center** (802-247-4295; cmacvt.org), 333 Jones Drive, Brandon. This venue, located on the former Brandon Training School campus, celebrates music and the creative arts through performances, workshops, and changing exhibits. Regular exhibits include a collection of historic phonographs, radios, TVs, and movie projectors. Local and emerging artists are represented in changing shows. The

MIDDLEBURY'S TOWN HALL THEATER ADDISON COUNTY CHAMBER OF COMMERCE

Compass Center also houses a handful of artisan studios, specialty shops, and the **SoundBite Café**.

**Vergennes Opera House** (802-877-6737; vergennesoperahouse.org), 120 Main Street, Vergennes. A renovated, century-old theater that once rang with the sounds of vaudeville now offers occasional music and theater. Check the website for an events schedule.

**Brandon Town Hall** (802-247-5420; brandontownhall.org), 49 Center Street. This beautiful 1861 hall is open for movies, music, and community activities. Home to the **Brandon Town Players** (802-247-6720; brandontownplayers.org), a community theater group.

See also *Special Events* on page 335.

## ✳ Selective Shopping

ANTIQUES **Branford House Antiques** (802-483-2971; branfordhouseantiques .com), 6691 US 7, Brandon. A large, handsome 1850s farmhouse and barn filled with a variety of antiques, specializing in furniture.

**Broughton Auctions** (802-758-2494; tombroughtonauctions.com), 2550 VT 22A, Bridport. Throughout the summer, auctions are held under the blue-and-white tents (Broughton also rents tents for events) at the Auction Barn, once the home of the Bridport Cheese Factory and later a milk plant for H. P. Hood. Check the website for on-site auctions. Even if you aren't looking to buy anything, it's worth coming just to hear Tom Broughton hold forth.

**Middlebury Antique Center** (802-388-6229; middantiques.com), 3255 US 7, East Middlebury. Open daily year-round. Furniture and furnishings representing 50 dealers at the same location for 25 years. Storewide sale the second Tuesday of every month with discounts up to 30 percent.

**Stone Block Antiques** (802-877-3359), 219 Main Street, Vergennes. Owner Greg Hamilton has been buying and selling antiques since the 1980s. The store, located not far from the village green,

VERGENNES OPERA HOUSE LISA HALVORSEN

has a number of great finds, including eighteenth- to early twentieth-century furniture and American and European decorative arts. It's worth a call if you plan to be in the area any day but Friday, the only day the store is officially open.

*Note*: A number of smaller antiques dealers in the Lower Champlain Valley are open by appointment only. You can find a list and contact information through the Vermont Antiques Dealers' Association (vermontantiquesdealers.com)

## ART GALLERIES AND CRAFTS STUDIOS

### IN MIDDLEBURY

**Danforth Pewter** (802-388-8666; danforthpewter.com), 52 Seymour Street. Open daily. Middlebury's iconic artisan brand has a workshop and store that permits visitors to view craftspeople spinning "holloware" and shaping pewter plates, jewelry, and ornaments; visitors can then purchase the handcrafted items.

**Edgewater Gallery at Middlebury Falls** (802-458-0098; edgewatergallery -vt.com), 1 Mill Street. Open daily year-round. Located in the former space for the Vermont State Craft Fair at Frog Hollow, Edgewater continues the tradition of showcasing Vermont-based artists and artisans with a varied collection of arts and fine crafts in many price ranges. It also has a second Middlebury venue, **Edgewater Gallery on the Green**, at 6 Merchants Row (802-989-7419).

**Sweet Cecily** (802-388-3353; sweetcecily.com), 42 Main Street. Open daily, June–December, closed Sunday, January–May. Nancie Dunn bills her shop as "a country store for today" with a fun selection of crafts, gift items, and Vermont products. The shop's screened-in back porch offers a great view of Middlebury Falls.

**Vermont Folklife Center Heritage Shop** (802-388-4964; vermontfolklife center.org), 88 Main Street. Open Tues.–Sat. One-of-a-kind, handmade traditional art and a wide variety of visual art from Vermont creators, plus books and recordings.

### IN BRANDON

**Brandon Artists Guild** (802-247-4956; brandonartistsguild.org), 7 Center Street. Open daily year-round. This standout nonprofit gallery represents more than 50 local artists and artisans.

**Warren Kimble Gallery & Studio** (802-247-4280; warrenkimble.com), 10 Park Street. Open by appointment for serious inquiries about purchasing original paintings by "America's best-known living folk artist."

### IN BRISTOL

**Art on Main** (802-453-4032; artonmain .net), 25 Main Street. Schedule varies by season; check website for hours. This exceptional nonprofit community artists' cooperative gallery displays a changing selection of art, crafts, textiles, and jewelry from nearly 100 local craftspeople for sale.

**Robert Compton Pottery** (802-453-3778; robertcomptonpottery.com), 2662 North VT 116, just north of Bristol. Showroom open daily, but best to call ahead. A complex of kilns, studios, and gallery space has evolved out of a former farmhouse and now contains the work space of this seasoned potter, who uses salt glazes and Japanese wood-firing techniques to produce everything from water fountains and crockery to sinks and cremation urns.

### WORTH A DETOUR

**Lincoln Pottery** (802-453-2073; judithbryantpottery.com), 220 West River Road, Lincoln. Judith Bryant creates wheel-thrown stoneware. Her studio and showroom are located in a renovated dairy barn. Visitors are welcome, but call ahead.

## MADE IN MIDDLEBURY: FACTORY TOURS AND SHOPPING

Downtown Middlebury offers plenty of shopping and browsing, but a number of local ventures have outgrown their downtown digs, migrating to the northern fringe of town on and around Exchange Street (see the map on page 309), where they remain visitor-friendly. Here **Otter Creek Brewing** (802-388-0727; ottercreekbrewing.com), 793 Exchange Street, is the big draw, open daily for free guided tours, free samples, and sales of its craft beers. Otter Creek opened in 1991, in the plant presently occupied by **Vermont Soap** (802-388-4302; vermontsoap.com), 616 Exchange Street, open Tues.–Sat. You can view the soap museum, with its vintage equipment, products, and advertising, and buy natural soap by the pound. The factory outlet also sells bath and body and green home cleaning products. **Woodchuck Cider House** (802-388-0700; woodchuck.com), 1321 Exchange Street, has a self-guided tour and a Cider House and Tap Room with 20 ciders on tap. Open Wed.–Sun. At the **Vermont Coffee Company** (802-398-2776; vermontcoffeecompany.com), a local coffee roaster at 1197 Exchange Street, observe the coffee-roasting process through a viewing window as you enjoy a fresh brew or espresso drink.

At **Maple Landmark Woodcraft** (802-388-0627; maplelandmark .com), 1297 Exchange Street, one of the country's largest wooden toy manufacturers—known for "Name Trains" and "Montgomery Schoolhouse" lines—watch the toymakers through plate-glass windows or call ahead to arrange a factory tour. Open Mon.–Sat. year-round, Sundays. seasonally. Around the corner is **Beau Ties Ltd.** (802-388-0108; beautiesltd.com), 69 Industrial Avenue. While mainly a catalog business, someone is always on hand in the store to knot ties for novices. Choices include seemingly every fabric imaginable;

**VERMONT SOAP** LISA HALVORSEN

✎ **Norton's Gallery** (802-948-2552; nortonsgallery.com), 51 VT 73, Shoreham, 1 mile south of the car ferry to Fort Ticonderoga. The small red gallery overlooking Lake Champlain houses a whimsical menagerie of dogs, cats, rabbits, birds, fish, flowers, and vegetables—all sculpted from wood by Norton Latourelle, a full-time woodcarver since 1975. Sculpted dog portraits are a specialty. Call in advance to make sure the gallery is open.

*Note*: Visit vermontcrafts.com for complete listings of area artisans and details on Vermont Open Studio Weekends, held each year in the spring and fall.

### BOOKSTORES

#### IN MIDDLEBURY

✎ **Monroe Street Books** (802-398-2200; monroestreetbooks.com), 1485 US 7 (2 miles north of downtown). Open daily. Dick and Flanzy Chodkowski stock more than 80,000 volumes at Vermont's largest bookstore selling used and out-of-print books. Specialties include children's books (many inscribed or signed

MAPLE LANDMARK WOODCRAFT LISA HALVORSEN

also ascots, scarves, and accessories. Open weekdays; tours by appointment. Newcomers to the area include two distilleries. **Stonecutter Spirits** (802-388-3000; stonecutterspirits.com), 1197 Exchange Street, uses barreling techniques from around the world to age their gin and whiskey. Open Thurs.–Sun. **Appalachian Gap Distillery** (802-989-7362; appalachiangap.com), 88 Mainelli Road, handcrafts spirits in its solar-powered distillery. Open daily. Both offer tastings. The breweries and distilleries are part of the **Middlebury Tasting Trail** (middtastingtrail .com), which also includes **Lincoln Peak Vineyard** (see *Wineries*); **Whistle Pig Whiskey** (802-897-7700; whistlepigwhiskey.com), 52 Seymour Street, open Thurs.–Sun.; **Drop-In Brewing Company** (802-989-7414; dropinbrewing.com), 610 US 7 South, open daily; and **Windfall Orchard** (802-462-3158; windfallorchardvt.com) 1491 VT 30, Cornwall; call for hours.

by the author), graphic novels, and Vermontiana.

**Otter Creek Used Books** (802-388-3241; ottercreekusedbooks.com), 99 Maple Street. Open Mon.–Sat., Sundays by chance. Don't know what you want? Owner Barbara Harding will help you find the perfect read, among the 25,000 titles that overflow the shelves of her shop in the historic Marble Works.

**The Vermont Book Shop** (802-388-2061; vermontbookshop.com), 38 Main Street. Open daily. The longtime bookstore, popular with generations

of families, was established in 1947 by Robert Dike Blair, one of New England's best-known booksellers. Robert Frost was a frequent customer for more than two decades, and the shop has sold many autographed Frost poetry collections. Chris and Becky Dayton have owned the full-service independent bookstore since 2007.

✎ **Ollie's Other Place** (802-382-8558; vermontbookshop.com/ollies) at 13 Washington Street is an offshoot of the Vermont Book Shop and sells children's books, gifts, and toys. It hosts Pajama

Storytime, Friday evenings in summer, for its youngest readers. Open Tues.–Sat.

## BEYOND MIDDLEBURY

& **Book & Leaf** (802-465-8424; bookandleaf.com), 10 Park Street, Brandon. Open Tues.–Sat. Patrons of this charming independent bookstore can enjoy a cup of coffee or tea with homemade pastries before browsing the diverse selection of new and used books, including many pulp fiction titles (owner Steve Errick is the primary collector) and books on the outdoors and New England history. Special events include talks by Vermont authors, entertainment by local musicians, and a Saturday morning French club.

& **Bulwagga Books & Gallery** (802-623-6800; middlebury.net/bulwagga), 3 South Main Street, Whiting, at the Whiting Post Office. Open Tues.–Sat. This used and rare book seller has more than 10,000 titles plus an art gallery and a reading room with mountain views, where patrons can enjoy coffee, tea, and scones. Vermont products and crafts also are for sale.

FARMERS' MARKETS Seasonal farmers' markets are held throughout the Lower Champlain Valley, including Middlebury, Brandon, and Vergennes. The Middlebury Farmers' Market is held year-round. Additional markets take place in smaller villages depending on harvest—check details for all at vermontagriculture.com.

FARMS ⁊ **Champlain Orchards** (802-897-2777; champlainorchardscidery.com), 3597 VT 74 West, Shoreham. Seasonally, you can pick apples, berries, cherries, peaches, and other fruits at this century-old, family-run orchard overlooking Lake Champlain. The orchard has a year-round farm market that sells both fresh and hard ciders during harvest season.

⁊ **Douglas Orchard & Cider Mill** (802-897-5043), 1050 VT 74, Shoreham. This family-run orchard offers pick-your-own strawberries, raspberries, and apples in season. The small retail store also sells hand-knit felt hats.

**Golden Russet Farm & Greenhouses** (802-897-7031; goldenrussetfarm.com), 1329 Lapham Bay Road, Shoreham. A certified-organic farm raising a variety of flowers, vegetables, and herbs, which they sell to area stores and restaurants and also offer for sale at their seasonal farm stand and greenhouse. Open daily in spring–late June. Call ahead the rest of the year.

⁊ **Maple View Farm** (802-247-5412; mapleviewfarmalpacas.com), 185 Adams Road, Brandon. Deb and Ed Bratton breed alpacas on their 100-acre farm. Visitors are welcome, although it's best to make an appointment. The on-site **Vermont Fiber Mill and Studio** (802-236-9158; vermontfibermill.com), open Thurs.–Sun., supplies the farm store with clothing, blankets, and rugs, all made from alpaca fiber. The mill also offers custom fiber processing and hosts fiber-related workshops.

**Monument Farms Dairy** (802-545-2119), 2107 James Road, Weybridge. One of Vermont's few surviving milk producer-handlers, the farm is open for tours by appointment only, although you can buy milk and dairy products, weekdays, at the store. Try the chocolate milk.

**Wood's Market Garden** (802-247-6630; woodsmarketgarden.com), 93 Wood Lane (US 7), Brandon, just south of downtown. Open daily in-season. The farm grows 50 kinds of vegetables and fruits on 60 acres, in addition to bedding plants and ornamentals in its seven greenhouses.

SPECIAL SHOPS **Daily Chocolate** (802-877-0087; dailychocolate.net), 7 Green Street, Vergennes. Open Tues.–Sat. At this boutique chocolatier, GMO-free, organic handmade chocolates made from locally produced cream, butter, and maple syrup fill the cases. Customer favorites include the black rum caramels, peppermint patties, and lemon lavender white chocolate bark.

**Vermont HoneyLights** (802-453-3952; vermonthoneylights.com), 9 Main Street, Bristol. Open daily. An assortment of hand-poured and rolled 100 percent beeswax candles are produced in this cute shop and workshop.

WINERIES **Autumn Mountain Winery** (802-247-6644; autumnmountainwinery .com), 1246 Franklin Street (US 7), Brandon. Otter Valley Winery, started in 2011 by Stephen and Ursula Zahn, changed hands, reopening in 2017 as Autumn Mountain Winery. New owners Jonathan and Jennifer Lutkus produce wines from Marquette, St. Croix, La Crescent, and Frontenac grapes in their five-acre (and growing) vineyard. Tasting room and gift shop open Fri.–Sun., March–December. The couple also have renovated and reopened the seasonal, pet-friendly cabins on the property.

🐾 ♿ **Lincoln Peak Vineyard** (802-388-7368; lincolnpeakvineyard.com), 142 River Road, New Haven. Open daily Memorial Day–mid-October, less frequently in winter. This vineyard grows all its own grapes on 12 acres on this rocky New Haven hilltop. The Marquette, which won Best In Show Red at the 2015 International Cold Climate Wine Competition, is a local favorite. Tasting room and porch overlooking pond.

**Neshobe River Winery** (802-247-8002; neshoberiverwinery.com), 79 Stone Mill Dam Road, Brandon. Located at the Inn at Neshobe River on the edge of the Neshobe Golf Club, this small family-run winery is open for tastings May–October, Wed.–Sun., as is **Foley Brothers Brewing** (802-465-8413; foleybrothersbrewing .com), which shares the barn. The brewery, started by Patrick and Daniel Foley in 2012, typically has several IPAs on tap. Wood-fired pizza is sometimes available; call ahead to ask.

CIDERIES **Shacksbury** (802-458-0530; shacksbury.com) 11 Main Street,

Vergennes. Open Wed.–Sun. The cidery makes limited-release, old world-style ciders from foraged fruit, traveling Vermont's backroads in search of "forgotten" apple trees—wild heritage varieties, decades or centuries old. Co-founders Colin Davis and David Dolginow have selected several to propagate, both to preserve these apples and to expand their source for making cider.

## ✳ Special Events

*Note:* For current happenings check the *Addison Independent* (addison independent.com) or *Seven Days* (seven daysvt.com) calendars of events.

*Late February:* **Middlebury College Winter Carnival** (middlebury.edu), Middlebury College. The country's oldest student-run winter carnival, featuring an ice show, concerts, snow sculpture contest, and ski races.

*Mid-March:* **Vermont Chili Festival**, Middlebury. Vermont Chamber of Commerce Top Ten Winter Event. The downtown overflows with restaurants and caterers from around the state competing for prizes and the thousands of folks who come to watch and taste.

*Late April/early May:* **Middlebury Maple Run** (middleburymaplerun.com), Middlebury. In addition to the main event, a half marathon and two-person relay, there's a 3-mile fun run, followed by a post-race party.

*July 4:* **Bristol** hosts a colorful **Independence Day Parade** (bristol4th.com) with its hilarious Great Bristol Outhouse Race, live music, crafts and food vendors, and a parade. The celebration starts the night before, with music, food, and fireworks. **Brandon** (brandon.org) has a parade, family games, a pie-eating contest, and fireworks.

*Early July:* The free, weeklong **Festival on the Green** (festivalonthegreen .com), Middlebury, features individual performers and groups such as the Bread & Puppet Theater and a potpourri of music from folk to jazz to exotic international talent.

*Mid-July:* **Basin Bluegrass Festival** (basinbluegrassfestival.com), Brandon—a weekend of food, crafts, music, and pickin'. **Moosalamoo Goshen Gallop** (goshengallop.com) is billed as "the toughest 10k in New England." The race course includes rural roads and wilderness trails in the Moosalamoo National Recreation Area. Runners have the option of competing in a 5k instead.

*Early August:* **Addison County Field Days** (addisoncountyfielddays.com), New Haven—Vermont's largest agricultural fair.

*Late August:* Vergennes Day (vergennesdowntown.org), Vergennes. Highlights are a street fair, rubber duckie race, arts walk, road races, music, and street dance.

*Fourth Saturday in September:* **Bristol Harvest Festival** (discoverbristolvt.com). This annual event on the Bristol Town Green includes music, crafts, 5k race, pie-eating contest, and car show.

*Late September/early October:* **Annual Ladies Road Rally** (vergennes operahouse.org), Vergennes, is a popular fundraiser for the Vergennes Opera House. Vintage cars with lady drivers only. Rally ends at the town green at the **Eat on the Green Festival** (vergennesdowntown.org).

*First Saturday in October:* **Dead Creek Wildlife Day** (802-759-2398)—wildlife-related exhibits and activities, bird banding, nature walks, and music.

*Late October:* **Spooktacular** (experiencemiddlebury.com), Middlebury—family-friendly Halloween event with music, games, costumes, and trick-or-treat sidewalk parade. **Pumpkins in the Park** (vergennesdowntown.org), Vergennes—all are invited to bring their carved pumpkins for judging and evening lighted pumpkin displays.

*Early December:* **Magic on Main Street** (vergennesdowntown.org), Vergennes—merry evening of holiday shopping, food, and drinks. Month-long holiday celebrations include Bristol's **Cool Yule** (discoverbristol .com) and **Very Merry Middlebury** (experiencemiddlebury.com)

# BURLINGTON REGION

F ew American cities the size of Burlington offer as lively a social and economic scene, with its busy downtown, its vibrant business community, its interesting shops and excellent restaurants, or its easy access to boats, bike paths, and ski trails. Sited on a steep slope, the city overlooks the widest portion of Lake Champlain, with magnificent views of the Adirondacks beyond. It is Vermont's financial, educational, medical, and cultural center. While its fringes continue to spread over recent farmland (the core population hovers near 43,000), the metro count has climbed to more than 150,000 in towns that were once farming communities but now branch out into broader recreational and economic pursuits.

The community was chartered in 1763, four years after the French were evicted from the Champlain Valley. The lake at the heart of so much that goes on in this region, Champlain, is named for Samuel De Champlain, the French explorer. Later, Ethan Allen, his three brothers, and a cousin were awarded large grants of choice land along the Onion River (now the Winooski). In 1791 Ira Allen secured a legislative charter for the University of Vermont (UVM), from which the first class, of four, was graduated in 1804. UVM now presides over the city from its perch atop the hill, enrolling more than 11,000 students annually, considerably larger than the private Champlain College, which is also in town.

Ethan and Ira would likely find their way around the city today, with main streets running much as they did in the 1780s—from the waterfront, uphill past shops and neighborhoods, to the school Ira founded, then over to Winooski Falls, site of Ira's own grist- and sawmills. The ravine that divided the city in Ira's time is gone, but the shape of things remains.

Along the waterfront, Federal-style commercial buildings house shops, businesses, and restaurants. The ferry terminal and neighboring Union Station (now a part of Main Street Landing), built during the city's late-nineteenth-century boom period as a lumber shipping port—when the lakeside trains connected with myriad steamers and barges—are now the summer venues for excursion trains, ferries, and cruise boats. The neo-Victorian Burlington Community Boathouse is everyone's window on Lake Champlain, to sit sipping a morning coffee or sunset aperitif, or to lunch or dine beside the water. The adjacent Waterfront Park and promenade are linked by bike paths to a series of other lakeside parks (bike and in-line skate rentals abound), which include swimmable beaches. Just north of Waterfront Park is the Lake Champlain Community Sailing Center where you can rent a sailboat, paddleboard, canoe, or kayak.

Halfway up the hill, the graceful Unitarian Church, designed in 1815 by Peter Banner, stands at the head of Church Street—a bricked, traffic-free marketplace for four long blocks, a promenade that's become a twenty-first-century-style common, the place everyone comes to graze. Changes are in the works here, too, with expansion of the commercial and residential sectors, new shops and housing to accommodate the growing population and carry the city into the future.

Today the waterfront includes several parks, including Oakledge (formerly a General Electric property) just south of downtown, North Beach (with an urban campground), and Leddy (site of a former rendering plant) in the North End. The waterside green space is linked by a 12-mile recreational path that includes the Burlington Bike

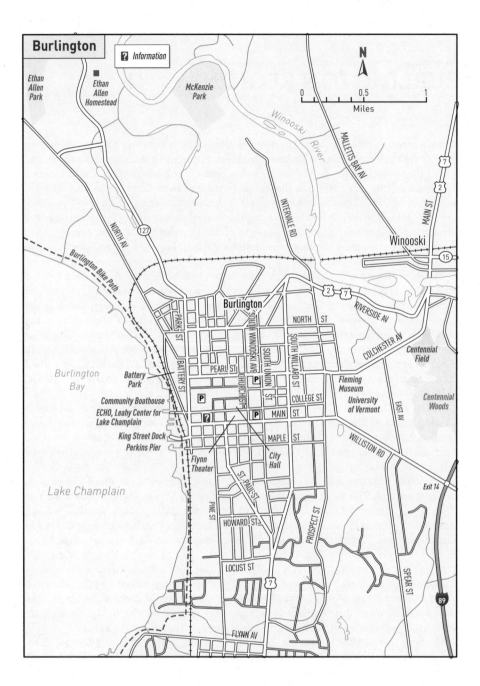

Path, extending across the Winooski River into Colchester and across Lake Champlain to the Champlain Islands, merging with the Missisquoi Valley Rail Trail (see "The Northwest Corner" on page 369).

Burlington is a walkable destination. Downtown high-rise hotels and several pleasant B&Bs are within walking distance of sights, entertainment, dining, shopping, and water excursions. Of course, it's also appealing to bed down in the Vermont countryside that's still within a quick drive of the city, so we have included B&Bs in nearby Jericho, Williston, Richmond, and Shelburne.

The Shelburne Museum, 6 miles south of the city, draws visitors like a magnet, with treasures ranging from a vintage Lake Champlain steam paddlewheeler and lighthouse to world-class paintings and folk art. Neighboring Shelburne Farms is quite simply New England's most fabulous estate, with prize-winning cows (and cheese), miles of lakeside walks, and a mansion in which you should dine, sleep, or at least breakfast.

GUIDANCE **The Lake Champlain Regional Chamber of Commerce** (802-863-3489; 877-686-5253; vermont.org), 60 Main Street, Burlington. Open weekdays year-round, this welcome center is housed in the former motor vehicles building, halfway between Church Street and the waterfront. This site is augmented by a staffed information booth at the airport that is open daily.

**The Burlington Parks & Recreation Department** (802-864-0123; enjoyburlington .com) maintains much of the waterfront, bike path, parks, and activities, as well as a useful website.

**The Lake Champlain Byway** connects Grand Isle County (see "The Northwest Corner" on page 369) and Addison County (see "Lower Champlain Valley" on page 306) directly through the Burlington region (also known as Chittenden County) via Lake Champlain. All associated activities and routes can be found at lakechamplain byway.com.

GETTING THERE *Note:* Burlington is Vermont's singlemost car-free destination, accessible by bus from Boston and Montreal and by train from New York City and Montreal, blessed with good local public transport and little need to use it.

*By air:* **Burlington International Airport** (802-863-1889; burlingtonintlairport.com) is in South Burlington, just 3 miles from Burlington's downtown, served by American Airlines, United, Delta, and JetBlue. Nine car rental agencies are on-site or close-by available, as is taxi and bus service.

*By train:* **Amtrak** (800-USA-RAIL; amtrak.com). The Vermonter (Washington, DC, to St. Albans via New York City and Springfield, MA) stops at Essex Junction, 5 miles north of Burlington. (The station is served by taxis and Burlington CCTA buses.) Faster, more scenic service from New York City is available via the Adirondack to Port Kent, NY, which connects with the ferry to Burlington.

*By bus:* **Greyhound** (800-231-2222; greyhound.com) offers service to Albany, Boston, New York City, Montreal, Portland, and many points in between. Buses depart from Burlington International Airport and the city.

*By car:* I-89, US 7, and US 2.

*By ferry:* **The Lake Champlain Transportation Company** (802-864-9804; ferries .com), King Street Dock, Burlington. Descended from the world's oldest steamboat company, LCTC offers three local car-ferry services. Between June and October, the car ferries make the 75-minute crossing between Burlington and Port Kent, NY. Year-round, depending on ice, they also ply between Charlotte, just south of Burlington, and Essex, NY. Year-round service is offered on the 15-minute run between Grand Isle (see "The Northwest Corner" on page 369) and Plattsburgh, NY.

GETTING AROUND *By bus:* **Chittenden County Transportation Authority** (802-864-2282, CCTAride.org). CCTA bus routes radiate from the Downtown Transit Center, located between Cherry and Pearl streets, serving all Chittenden County towns and outward to St. Albans, Middlebury, and Montpelier, with 19 bus routes seven days a week (Sunday is limited). The fleet of buses is now low-emission, clean diesel—a landmark environmental move for Burlington.

## ✳ Towns and Villages

**Jericho** (jerichovt.gov). Northeast of Burlington, Jericho is best known for the **Old Red Mill** (jerichohistoricalsociety.org; 802-899-3225), on VT 15 at Jericho Corners (open daily, except January–March, when it's open only Wed.–Sun.). This nineteenth-century red mill set above a small gorge is one of the most photographed buildings in Vermont and appropriately houses prints and mementos relating to one of the state's most famous photographers, Wilson A. "Snowflake" Bentley. The Jericho farmer was the first person in the world to photograph individual snowflakes. He collected more than 5,000 microphotos. A basement museum also tells the story of the many mills that once lined six sets of falls nearby. Sales from the craft and gift shop benefit the preservation of the building, which is owned by the Jericho Historical Society. A 20-acre park behind the mill, along the river, offers picnic tables and hiking trails. Head to nearby Jericho Center off VT 15 on the River Road to Brown's Trace Road, whose oval village common sits across from the **Jericho Center Country Store** (802-899-3313; jerichocountrystore.com), a busy, genuine, old-fashioned market that's been operating since 1807. The popular market trades in local products and produce as well as a fine selection of country store staples, with a busy deli counter for hot and cold takeout. A friendly ghost is said to help keep stock.

THE OLD ROUND CHURCH IN RICHMOND  RACHEL CARTER

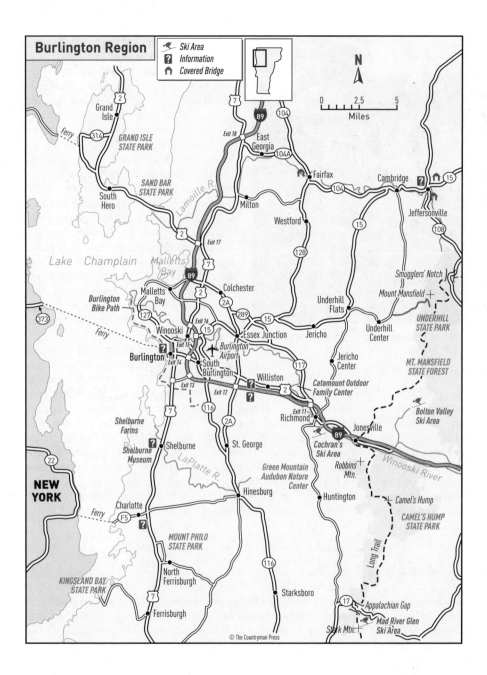

## Burlington Region

**Ski Area**
**Information**
**Covered Bridge**

N

0   2.5   5
Miles

Grand Isle

GRAND ISLE STATE PARK

Ferry

SAND BAR STATE PARK

South Hero

East Georgia

Exit 18

Fairfax

Cambridge

Jeffersonville

Milton

Westford

Lake Champlain

Malletts Bay

Burlington Bike Path

Ferry

Malletts Bay

Colchester

Smugglers' Notch

Mount Mansfield

UNDERHILL STATE PARK

Underhill Flats

Winooski

Exit 16

Essex Junction

Jericho

Underhill Center

MT. MANSFIELD STATE FOREST

Burlington

Exit 15

Exit 14

Burlington Airport

South Burlington

Jericho Center

Williston

Exit 13

Exit 12

Catamount Outdoor Family Center

Exit 11

Richmond

Jonesville

Bolton Valley Ski Area

Winooski River

Shelburne Farms

Shelburne Museum

Shelburne

St. George

Cochran's Ski Area

Robbins Mtn.

NEW YORK

Green Mountain Audubon Nature Center

Hinesburg

Huntington

Camel's Hump

CAMEL'S HUMP STATE PARK

Charlotte

MOUNT PHILO STATE PARK

Long Trail

Ferry

KINGSLAND BAY STATE PARK

North Ferrisburgh

Starksboro

Appalachian Gap

Ferrisburgh

Stark Mtn.

Mad River Glen Ski Area

© The Countryman Press

**Richmond** (richmondvt.com). East of Burlington on US 2 (I-89, Exit 11) and the Winooski River, Richmond was badly damaged in the flood of 1927 and then again during Hurricane Irene in 2011, but the architecturally interesting downtown remains, as does the library (a former church). Across the Winooski River lies the **Old Round Church** (oldroundchurch.com). This 16-sided building, one of the most unusual in the state, was constructed in 1812–13 as a community meetinghouse to serve five denominations; in winter its illuminated windows are a vision of Christmas past.

THE MILL AND WATERWHEEL AT SHELBURNE MUSEUM PAT GOUDEY O'BRIEN

**Shelburne** (shelburnevt.org). Beyond the commercial sprawl of Shelburne Road (US 7 south from Burlington) lie two of Vermont's greatest treasures, both the legacy of nineteenth-century railroad heirs William Seward and Lila Vanderbilt Webb. In the 1880s the couple hired Frederick Law Olmsted to landscape their 4,000-acre lakeside model farm, and in 1946 their daughter-in-law, Electra Havermeyer Webb, founded a major museum of Americana. Today 1,400 acres of the estate—**Shelburne Farms**—survive as a combination inn, demonstration, and working farm, complementing the exhibits in no fewer than 39 buildings in the nearby **Shelburne Museum**. Inevitably shops and attractions continue to multiply along US 7, including the **Vermont Teddy Bear Company**.

**Winooski** (onioncity.com) is just across the 32-foot Winooski Falls from Burlington. Ira Allen was the first to harness the water that subsequently powered several mammoth brick nineteenth-century mills, attracting workers from Ireland, Canada, and Eastern Europe who settled in the cottages that line the village streets. The falls, with an art deco bridge, and the common, framed by the vintage 1867 Winooski Block and the handsome Champlain Mill (now an office complex that's home to MyWebGrocer), still form the center of town, which gained a controversial and complicated roundabout in 2005 and a continuing sprawl of luxury condos overlooking the falls. St. Michael's College, with its summer-stock Playhouse (presenting a variety of professional theater performances—see *Entertainment* on page 362), is just up Allen Street (VT 15) in Colchester.

## ✳ Must See

**Shelburne Museum** (802-985-3346; shelburnemuseum.org), 6000 Shelburne Road, is open daily 10–5. Admission charged, family day pass available. This fascinating "collection of collections" features American folk art and memorabilia, but it also includes paintings by Rembrandt, Degas, Monet, and Manet. Each of more than three dozen buildings—many of them transplants from around New England—houses a different collection of historic interest. The 45 landscaped acres include flower and herb gardens, an apple orchard, and more than 90 varieties of lilacs.

An adequate description of the collections (more than 150,000 objects) would fill a separate chapter. Highlights include a 1915 steam locomotive and a vintage 1890 private Palace Car; the side-wheeler *Ticonderoga*, in her landlocked spot near the Colchester Reef Lighthouse; folk art; and paintings. Children will glory at the operational carousel and miniature circus.

Acquisitions continue, but this is still substantially the collection of one woman, gathered at a time when few people were interested in Americana. Electra Havemeyer was 18 in 1910 when she bought her first cigar-store figure. Three years later she married James Watson Webb of Shelburne (son of the wealthy couple who had built Shelburne Farms; see below). Over the next 30 years she raised five children, traveled widely, and managed homes on Long Island, in Manhattan, and at a 50,000-acre "camp" in the Adirondacks, as well as the Shelburne estate. Gradually she filled all her holdings (even her indoor tennis court) with her treasures, founding the museum in 1947. She died in 1960, but her vision for the museum was fulfilled by their son, the late J. Watson Webb Jr. Inquire about gallery talks and special events.

**Shelburne Farms** (802-985-8686; shelburnefarms.org), at 1611 Harbor Road, Shelburne, just west of US 7. The Farm Store and Visitor Center (802-985-8442), with an exceptional introductory film, is open daily year-round, 9–5:30 (10–5 in the off-season). Mid-May–mid-October, general admission for the walking trails, children's farmyard, and cheese-making operation on the 1,400-acre lakeside property; full one-and-a-half-hour open wagon tours are offered four times daily mid-May–mid-October. Guided tours available. There is no charge to use the extensive walking trails the rest of the year (leashed pets are welcome on the grounds November–April). Inquire about house and garden tea tours, Breeding Barn tours, and special events. This grand 1880s lakeside estate is now a nonprofit environmental education center and working farm whose mission is to cultivate a conservation ethic. Founded by railroad magnate William Seward Webb and his wife, Lila Vanderbilt Webb, it initially comprised 3,800 acres. Its magnificent setting was landscaped by Frederick Law Olmsted (who also designed New York's Central Park) with the help of America's pioneer forester Gifford Pinchot. Manhattan architect Robert Henderson Robertson designed the magnificent Norman-style barns and the 100-room summer "cottage," known then as Shelburne House, on a bluff overlooking Lake Champlain.

The mansion is now the **Inn at Shelburne Farms** (open mid-May–mid-October; see *Lodging* on page 355 and *Dining Out* on page 357). The immense, five-story, 416-foot **Farm Barn**, where livestock were kept, is now a place for children to collect eggs, learn to milk a cow, or enjoy a tractor-drawn wagon ride. It also houses the cheesemaking facility, education center, and **O Bread Bakery**. The **Coach Barn**, once the family stable, now hosts weddings, special events, art exhibits, and workshops. The massive **Breeding Barn**, where Dr. Webb's English Hackneys were bred, is now used for large-scale events; guided tours are given Monday afternoons. The farm's prize-winning cheddar cheese, made from the milk of its own herd of Brown Swiss cows, is sold, along with other Vermont products, in the Farm Store. More than 10 miles of walking trails wind from the Visitor Center, networking the farm and providing sweeping views of Lake Champlain and the Adirondacks. Inquire about naturalist-led bird walks and special events.

*Tip:* **Inn at Shelburne Farms** is open to the public by reservation for breakfast as well as dinner. Enjoy the most elegant breakfast in New England, or dine on local delicacies as you watch the sun set over the lake. Before you go, get a glimpse of the spectacular library and stroll the lakeside perennial, herb, and rose gardens.

**Burlington Waterfront** (enjoyburlington.com). As noted in the chapter introduction, Burlington's revived waterfront affords dramatic views and is accessible to the public. The handsome (vintage 1915) train station and nearby buildings make up **Main Street Landing** at the base of Main Street, home to businesses and a performing arts theater. The King Street Dock remains home to the **Lake Champlain Transportation Company** (LCTC), established in 1826. At the base of College Street at the College Street Pier, the (1991) **Community Boathouse** echoes the design of the Lake Champlain

Yacht Club, a prestigious gentlemen's domain built on this site in 1889. **The ECHO Lake Aquarium and Science Center**, operated by the Champlain Basin Science Program, doubles as a research facility and science museum. ECHO, which stands for "ecology, culture, history, and opportunity," is becoming a world-class museum irresistible to kids (see *For Families* on page 347). The **Burlington Bike Path** links these sites with the nearby **Waterfront Park** to the north (which includes a stroller-friendly fishing pier and a boardwalk promenade with swings) and with **Perkin's Pier** (parking, boat launch, picnic area, canal boat exhibit, and waterfront benches) just to the south. Farther south is **Oakledge Park**, with two picnic shelters, a beach, and a wheelchair-accessible tree house. Several more beaches and parks stretch in both directions. Not surprisingly, shops and restaurants have proliferated along neighboring Battery Street; **Battery Park**, on a high bluff overlooking the lake, is the visually majestic setting for free summer concerts and frequent special events.

# ✳ To Do

AIR RIDES **Above Reality Hot Air Balloon Rides** (802-899-4007; balloonvermont .com) offers balloon rides at launch locations near the base of Mount Mansfield, near the company base in Jericho. **Mansfield Heliflight** (802-893-1003; mansfieldheliflight .com), 159 Catamount Drive, Milton. Hour-long flight tours are offered.

BICYCLING The **Burlington Bike Path** (802-864-0123; enjoyburlington.com) runs for 7.6 miles along the waterfront, connecting six different parks, beginning with Oakledge Park in the south and continuing into the Champlain Bikeway, making for a 12-mile trail. A bike bridge spans the Winooski River, continuing the path through Colchester to a bike ferry that links it with the Champlain Islands. Fun side trips include **Ethan Allen Park**, with its stone lookout tower, the **Ethan Allen Homestead**, Intervale Community Farms, and the Salmon Hole Fishing Area near the Winooski bridge. **Rental bikes** (including tandems, trailers, and trail-a-bikes) are available from **Local Motion's Trailside Center** (802-652-2453; localmotion.org), on the Burlington waterfront stretch of the Bike Path at College Street, as are maps and bike lockers. The path is used for walking, running, and in-line skating, as well as biking. Note that CCTA buses have bicycle racks. For serious bicyclists, we recommend the Greater Burlington Hiking and Biking Map, published by Map Adventures (mapadventures .com), which details several Burlington-area loops and longer tours on both sides of Lake Champlain, using ferries. You can also download a free Burlington biking map at localmotion.org.

Mountain bikers should check out the 500-acre **Catamount Outdoor Family Center** (802-879-6001; catamountoutdoor.com), 592 Governor Chittenden Road, Williston, for a variety of mountain bike events, workshops, and camps. **Sleepy Hollow Inn, Ski & Bike Center** (802-434-2283; skisleepyhollow.com), 427 Ski Lodge Drive, Huntington, features over 10 miles of single-track plus another 20 miles of converted ski trails, linking to the Catamount Outdoor Family Center Mountain Bike Trail. Trail fees.

There is also the **Essex Transportation Trail**, a 3-mile rail-trail from the Essex Police Station to VT 15 (Lang Farm); the **Shelburne Recreation Trail**, from Bay Road through Shelburne Bay Park to Harbor Road; and the unpaved **Intervale Bikepath**, from Gardener's Supply on Intervale Avenue to the Ethan Allen Homestead. For bike parts and repairs as well as an interesting historic bike experience, visit **Old Spokes Home** (802-863-4475; oldspokeshome.com), 322 North Winooski Avenue, Burlington.

LAKE CHAMPLAIN AS SEEN FROM OAKLEDGE PARK  RACHEL CARTER

BIRDING **The Birds of Vermont Museum** (802-434-2167; birdsofvermont.org), just down the road from the **Green Mountain Audubon Nature Center** (see *Green Space* on page 352) at 900 Sherman Hollow Road, Huntington. Open May–October, daily 10–4; by appointment in winter. Admission charged. Amazingly life-like carvings of more than 200 species of birds by the late Robert Spear Jr.; also nature trails, recorded birdsongs.

BOATING Boats of all sizes abound in the Burlington Bay Harbor, which extends north to Malletts Bay and south to Shelburne Bay. Most towns in the area also sport their own lake or pond, and the **Winooski River** offers several access points for kayaking and even tubing.

Canoes and kayaks can be rented at **North Beach** in Burlington (enjoyburlington .com) from Canoe Imports (802-651-8760). **Lake Champlain Community Sailing Center** (802-864-2499; communitysailingcenter.org), located along the Burlington Bike Path, is a nonprofit, public-access sailing center with a host of learn-to-sail and learn-to-canoe programs for kids, adults, and families, as well as watercraft rentals. At **True North Kayak Tours** (802-238-7695; vermontkayak.com) mother-and-son team Jane and Dovid Yagoda offer instruction and guided tours from a variety of locations on Lake Champlain. Inquire about multiday paddles through the Champlain Islands with B&B lodging. The popular and classic sloop *Friend Ship* located near the Burlington Community Boathouse offers daily cruises July–September (802-825-7245; whistlingman.com).

*Spirit of Ethan Allen III* (802-862-8300; soea.com). Seasonal, daily scenic cruises as well as themed dinner cruises aboard a triple-deck, 500-passenger excursion boat, departing from the Burlington Community Boathouse mid-May–mid-October. Narrated sightseeing, plus sunset cruises; dinner, lunch, and brunch cruises, murder mystery cruises, live music cruises, and specialty food cruises. Check website for a complete list and pricing.

CULTURAL ATTRACTIONS **Shelburne Craft School** (802-985-3648; shelburnecraft school.org), 64 Harbor Road, Shelburne. This nonprofit complex has been holding classes for children and adults for over 65 years. It offers year-round workshops of varying lengths in pottery, woodworking, fiber, metal, stained glass, and all the fine arts, and shows local work in the on-site gallery, a former library. Summer camp programs for children.

**Robert Hull Fleming Museum** (802-656-0750; uvm.edu/~fleming), 61 Colchester Avenue, on the University of Vermont campus. Open daily (closed Mon.) year-round, hours vary winter to summer. Limited parking. Admission charged, family rates. Varied collections of early to postmodern art, natural history, archaeology, and geology. Holdings include ancient primitive art from several cultures and continents, a collection of American portraits and landscapes (from the eighteenth century to contemporary works), a Native American collection, and frequent special exhibits showcasing everything from Picasso to the history of shoes. Gift shop and café. The building was designed by the renowned firm of McKim, Mead & White, which also designed UVM's Ira Allen Chapel (1927) and Burlington's City Hall.

**Burlington City Arts** (802-865-7166; burlingtoncityarts.org), 135 Church Street, Burlington, next to City Hall. Open Tues.–Fri. 9–5, Sat. noon–5. Free to view exhibits. A nonprofit community space that began as a fine arts gallery showcasing innovative Vermont artists has blossomed into a multiuse contemporary art center featuring local and regional exhibitions, classes and programs, and special events including music, film, and performance.

**South End Arts & Business Association** (802-859-9222; seaba.com), 404 Pine Street, Burlington. Located in Burlington's industrial-turned-artistic South End, this group (known locally as SEABA) puts on the Annual Art Hop in September (see *Special Events* on page 366) and First Friday Art Walks year-round, showcasing South End businesses and the growing number of art galleries, crafts spaces, and interesting forms of artistic expression in the neighborhood. SEABA also operates its own art gallery, open Mon.–Fri. 9–5, no charge.

DIVING **Lake Champlain Historic Underwater Preserves** (lakechamplainregion .com). The Vermont Division for Historic Preservation (through the Agency of Commerce and Community Development; accd.vermont.gov/historic-preservation) maintains seven shipwrecks, identified by yellow Coast Guard–approved buoys, at various points on Lake Champlain; all are open to scuba divers. The Horse Ferry, the Coal Barge, the O. J. Walker canal boat, and the General Butler are off Burlington. The Phoenix and the Diamond Island Stone Boat are in Colchester and Vergennes, respectively, and the *Champlain II*, a passenger ship, lies on the New York side across from Basin Harbor. Register at the **Waterfront Diving Center** (802-865-2771; waterfrontdiving .com), 214 Battery Street, Burlington, which provides equipment rentals and repair; instruction in snorkeling, underwater archaeology, photography, and scuba; and charters to historic preserved shipwrecks.

FISHING **Schirmer's Fly Shop** (802-863-6105, schirmersflyshop.com), 34 Mills Avenue, South Burlington, specializing in Ed Schirmer's own flies, tackle, accessories, guided trips, and instruction.

For fishing guides, contact the Vermont Outdoor Guide Association (voga.org), and for licensing, visit vtfishandwildlife.com. The **Salmon Hole fishing area** off Riverside

Avenue, just west of the Winooski bridge, is a popular local spot, as is the **Fishing Pier** on the Burlington waterfront behind the Water Department Building next to the Coast Guard station.

FOR FAMILIES *Note:* The best family resource in the area and probably all of northern Vermont is maintained at findandgoseek.net. For a print guide, look for *Kids VT*, a free monthly newspaper available around the state.

✪ **ECHO Lake Champlain Aquarium** (802-864-1848; echovermont.org), 1 College Street, Burlington, open daily year-round, 10–5. Closed Thanksgiving, Christmas Eve, and Christmas Day. Admission charged (ask about annual passes and group rates). This is the place to see (and handle) what's swimming in the lake (not only the fish, but a display on "Champ," the local Loch Ness monster) as well as what shouldn't be in the lake. Changing exhibits range from plastinated human remains to bloodsucking fauna; lots of hands-on programming. An environmental-themed café offers lunch, and the gift shop teems with science-minded toys and collectibles.

**Vermont Teddy Bear Company Factory and Museum** (802-985-3001; vermontteddybear.com), 6655 Shelburne Road (US 7) at the south end of Shelburne Village. Open daily 9–5; later in summer. A phenomenon in its own right, the huge, fanciful birthplace of well over 100,000 teddy bears a year includes a museum depicting teddy bear history and an entertaining 30-minute tour (free for children under 12). There is, of course, a huge teddy bear store; be prepared to make a purchase.

**The Vermont Lake Monsters** (802-655-4200; vermontlakemonsters.com). Minor-league baseball team plays at Centennial Field in Burlington (off Colchester Avenue) all summer. There is free parking at the Trinity Campus parking lot at the northern end of East Avenue. The field is a few minutes' walk away. The season is mid-June–September 1, tickets are cheap, the park is lovely, the concession food is pretty good, and there's a giant Day-Glo dancing Champ mascot for the kids. All in all, a great time—and the baseball isn't bad.

**Ben & Jerry's** (802-862-9620; benjerrys.com), 36 Church Street, Burlington. This scoop shop isn't the original location, but the world's legendary ice cream makers did get their start a few blocks away (on the southwest corner of St. Paul and College streets). Factory tours are at the Waterbury location (see "Stowe and Waterbury" on page 395).

**Catamount Outdoor Family Center** (802-879-6001; catamountoutdoor.com), 592 Governor Chittenden Road, Williston, offers a growing number of camps and events geared toward youth.

GOLF **Vermont National Country Club** (802-864-7770; vnccgolf.com), 1227 Dorset Street, South Burlington, an 18-hole, Jack Nicklaus–designed championship course; **Rocky Ridge Golf Club** (802-482-2191; rockyridge.com), St. George (5 miles south on VT 2A from Exit 12 off I-89), 18 holes; **Kwiniaska** (802-985-3672; kwiniaska.com), 5531 Spear Street, Shelburne, 18 holes, Vermont's longest course; **Williston Golf Club** (802-878-3747; willistongolfclub.com), 424 Golf Course Road, Williston, 18 holes; **Essex Country Club** (802-879-3232; essexccvt.com), 332 Old Stage Road, Essex Junction, 18 holes; **Cedar Knoll Country Club** (802-482-3186; cedarknollgolf.com), 13020 VT 116, Hinesburg, 27 holes; **Links at the Lang Farm** (802-878-0298; linksatlangfarm.com), 39 Essex Way, Essex, 18 holes; **West Bolton Golf Club** (802-434-4321; westboltongolfclub.com), 5161 Stage Road, West Bolton, 18 holes; **Catamount Country Club** (802-878-7227; catamountcountryclub.com), 1400 Mountain View Road, Williston, 9 holes; **Arrowhead Golf Course** (802-893-0234; arrowheadvt.com), 350 Murray Avenue, Milton, 9 holes.

HIKING See hiking options under *Green Space* including area state parks (vtstateparks .com) on page 349. The Green Mountain Club (greenmountainclub.org) publishes *A Day Hiker's Guide to Vermont*, which offers numerous hikes in the area.

HISTORICAL ATTRACTIONS **The Ethan Allen Homestead** (802-865-4556; ethanallen homestead.org), off VT 127 just north of the downtown Burlington waterfront (take the North Avenue Beaches exit off VT 127, the Northern Connector). Open May–October, Thurs.–Mon. 10–4, closed Tues. and Wed. Vermont's godfather is memorialized here in the timber farmhouse in which he lived out the last years of his turbulent life; he died in 1789. The visitor center offers a film, interesting descriptive and multimedia exhibits, and a gift shop. The setting is a working garden and an extensive park with some 4 miles of walking trails along the Winooski River and wetlands. Admission charged.

ROCK CLIMBING **Petra Cliffs** (802-657-3872; petracliffs.com), 105 Briggs Street, Burlington. Indoor climbing center with mountaineering guide tours. Petra Cliffs operates the programming at the Bolton Adventure Center.

    **Northern Lights Climbing** (802-316-3300; northernlightsvt.com), 14 Freeman Woods Road, Essex Junction. Directly connected to The Essex (see *Resorts* on page 354), Northern Lights provides "the outback" experience of the area's premier resort and operates as a stand-alone with outdoor rock and ice climbing walls, zipline tours, geocaching, and a variety of team development programs, camps, and events.

SWIMMING **North Beach** (802-862-0942; enjoyburlington.com), off North Avenue at 60 Institute Road, Burlington (turn at Burlington High School), is the city's longest (and most crowded), providing tent and trailer sites, picnic tables, playground, a snack bar and change room, and swimming from a long, sandy beach, late May–mid-September; vehicle charge, pedestrians and bicyclists free. A growing number of lakeside and music events take place throughout the season. **Leddy Park** (802-865-5399; enjoyburlington .com), a more secluded, tree-lined beach with picnic areas, grills, and tables (farther north off North Avenue from North Beach, turn left before the shopping mall onto Leddy Park Road and drive to the end). **Oakledge Park** (802-865-7247; enjoyburlington .com) is at the other end of town, a cozy beach with a rocky spit, sheltered picnic area, and open-air picnic tables with grills, three tennis courts, two softball fields, volleyball courts, and walking trails. It's at the southern end of the bike path off US 7, at the end of Flynn Avenue. Fee for parking; pedestrians and bicyclists free. A trail leads to an extravagant tree house; handicapped accessible. **Red Rocks Park** (802-864-4108; sburlrecdept.com), Central Avenue. South Burlington's small but serviceable public beach is valued mostly for its forested hiking trails, with a few picnic tables overlooking the lake. Fee for all users. **Sand Bar State Park** (802-983-2825; vtstateparks.com), in Milton as US 2 heads into the Champlain Islands, offers broad sandy beach access for swimming and picnics, especially good for little kids; fee for all users. **Lake Iroquois** (town.williston.vt.us), south from Williston off US 2 on Pond Road in St. George, offers a surprisingly pristine lake with family-friendly beach for swimming, fee for all users.

# ❄ Winter Sports

CROSS-COUNTRY SKIING **Northern Vermont Nordic Skiing and Snowshoe**, a weatherproofed map detailing cross-country and snowshoeing trails throughout the region, is available at local outlets and from Map Adventures (mapadventures.com). Also see: the Bolton Valley sidebar on page 350.

**Catamount Outdoor Family Center** (802-879-6001; catamountoutdoor.com), 592 Governor Chittenden Road, Williston. The 35 km of groomed trails at this 500-acre recreation area include a 3-km loop that's lit 5–8:30 for night skiing on select evenings, weather depending. All of it radiates over rolling terrain, both wooded and open. Geared to families. Guided tours, rentals, instruction, sledding hill, snowshoe trails, and warming hut. Trail fee.

**Sleepy Hollow Inn, Ski & Bike Center** (802-434-2283; skisleepyhollow.com), 427 Ski Lodge Drive, Huntington. An 870-acre tract offers 35 km of well-groomed cross-country ski trails that weave up to the elevated Butternut Cabin (which can be rented all year) with its gorgeous views of Camel's Hump. Another 20 km are good for snowshoeing, and there are rentals, lessons, and a warm-up lodge with accommodations (see *Lodging* on page 355). Popular with the locals, Sleepy Hollow also offers night skating on its pond and skiing on a 2 km loop each Mon., Wed., and Fri.

*Note:* See *Green Space* below for more about local parks with trails that lend themselves to cross-country skiing.

**Cochran Ski Area** (802-434-2479; cochranskiarea.com), 910 Cochran Road, Richmond. When Mickey and Ginny Cochran bought this hillside farm in 1961, little did they know that in 1998 it would become the nation's first nonprofit ski area and the incubator of Olympic champions. Two generations of Cochrans have joined the US Ski Team; two have won top trophies. What started as a single backyard slope with a 400-foot rope tow has stretched into a good-size racing mountain with six trails and three lifts, including a rope tow, a T-bar, and a handle lift. This is the state's best children's and instructional spot. Olympic gold medalist Barbara Ann Cochran runs "Ski Tots," teaching parents to instruct their own 3- to 5-year-olds. The lodge serves hot snacks and rents equipment, there's a ski school, and free Lollipop races are held each Sunday; winners receive lollipops. Open Tues. and Thurs. 2:30–5 p.m., Fri. 2–8 p.m.; weekends and school vacation weeks 9–4 (check ahead, as all school vacation weeks are not the same).

*Note:* See also Smugglers' Notch Resort in "North of the Notch," "Stowe and Waterbury," and "Sugarbush/Mad River Valley." Five major alpine areas are within easy striking distance of Burlington.

ICE SKATING **Gordon H. Paquette Arena at Leddy Park** (802-862-8869; enjoyburlington.com), off North Avenue, Burlington, offers an Olympic-sized rink with public skating as well as hockey and figure-skating instruction. Snack bar, rentals, and skate sales. Check the website or call for the schedule.

**C. Douglas Cairns Arena** (802-658-5577; cairnsarena.com), 600 Swift Street, South Burlington, offers public skating, rentals, skate sharpening, and a snack bar.

SLEIGH RIDES **Shelburne Farms** (802-985-8442; shelburnefarm.org) offers rides in 12-passenger sleighs through a nineteenth-century landscape of sculpted forests and snow-covered fields, with visions of opulent barns in the distance. Daily late December–January 1 (except Christmas), then weekends through February. Fee charged.

## ✳ Green Space

**Burlington Parks and Recreation** (802-864-0123; enjoyburlington.com). Burlington's lakeside parks are superb. **Oakledge Park** (take Flynn Avenue off Pine Street or US 7) offers swimming and picnicking, and sports a wheelchair-accessible tree house (parking fee, but you can bike or walk in). **Red Rocks Park** just south, occupying the

# BOLTON VALLEY

Bolton Valley Resort (802-434-3444; 877-926-5866; boltonvalley.com), Bolton, within easy reach of the Burlington area, is a small gem worth discovering. It has several standout points, beginning with the base elevation at 2,100 feet, the highest of any Vermont ski resort, with an annual average of 300 inches of natural snow. The base village is cozy and Alpine-like, keeping everything within walking distance, ski-in, ski-out hotel, a wood-fired pizzeria, the Village Café, and both fitness and wellness centers. There's something for everyone: snowshoeing, an extensive Nordic trail system, and three terrain parks with jumps and rails. Bolton is the largest of the few night skiing destinations in the state, with sunset views over Lake Champlain and the Adirondack Mountains from lift-served westward-facing slopes. Three lighted Terrain Parks also provide nighttime fun for riders. Set atop a winding, 4-mile scenic road, the resort is a 15-minute drive from the Burlington airport. After a hiatus, the resort is once more owned by a group led by one of the resort's original founders, Ralph Deslauriers, who lives on-site, along with several of his five children. The family is expanding activities, which include an indoor winter farmers' market.

NIGHT SKIING AT BOLTON VALLEY RESORT MIKE WOOD

**DOWNHILL SKIING AND SNOWBOARDING** *Vertical drop:* 1,704 feet.

*Trails:* 71; 6 lifts—2 quads, 3 double chairs, 1 surface. Seventy-one trails cover 300 skiable acres, roughly a third of them geared toward intermediate-level skiers, a third to beginners, and a third to experts.

*Night Skiing:* 10 trails and terrain served by 4 lifts.

*Base elevation:* 2,100 feet.

*Skiing and Riding Schools:* Children's programs include lessons for children from ages 4 and up, snowboard lessons for ages 6 and up, and include supervised activities throughout the day with dedicated instructors.

*Snowmaking:* 60 percent.

*Rates:* Full-season, half-day, night-skiing, and package ticket options. Lift tickets are considerably lower than in southern Vermont, with plenty of enticements: Saturday-night and early-season ticket deals, plus ski packages that include overnights and breakfast at the resort's Village Café.

**CROSS-COUNTRY SKIING** Ranging in elevation from 1,600 to 3,200 feet, this 100-km network is Vermont's highest cross-country system, with snow that usually lasts well into April. About 15 km are machine groomed. Additional expansive backcountry terrain beyond the resort stretches over some 1,200+ acres of rolling country, with classes and new guided tours to help visitors get into it. There is a wide and gently sloping 1-mile Broadway and a few short trails for beginners, but most of the terrain is backwoods, much of it splendidly high wilderness country. The upper backcountry is easily accessible via the Wilderness Lift; from there you take the Heavenly Highway and you're in the thick of it for miles. There's a ski school, rentals are available in the cross-country center, and experienced skiers are welcome to stay in the area's high hut, the Bryant cabin, by reservation. Telemarking is a specialty here. Trail fee.

The legendary 12-mile **Bolton-to-Trapp** trail originates here (this is by far the preferred direction to ski it), but it requires spotting a car at the other end or on Moscow Road.

## SUMMER/FALL

In summer the resort offers day camps for hotel guests and local kids. The trails fill with hikers and mountain bikers. The Ponds has become a popular spot for scenic mountaintop weddings and other special events. The resort sits within 8,000 acres of unspoiled natural area teeming with wildlife and terrific alpine views. With its steep access road veering off a lonely stretch of US 2 between Montpelier and Burlington, this is a genuinely self-contained resort whose atmosphere is guaranteed to make you want to stay put for a while,

**LODGING** A five-floor, 60-room hotel, with standard and deluxe rooms, also suites. Some rooms come with fireplace and kitchenette; most have kings or multiple doubles and balconies with mountain views. Condominium rentals on-site and off. ($–$$ includes a breakfast coupon.) The tavern has a pub menu; Fireside Flatbread offers wood-fired pizza; the sports center includes a poolside lounge, wellness center, workout facility, jacuzzi, a rec area for tennis, pickle ball, game room, and snack bar. The Ponds wedding facility has water and mountainside views. Stay-and-ski packages available. Also some off-site condominiums available for rental. Inquire at the inn.

peninsula that divides Burlington from South Burlington (take Queen City Park Road off US 7), offers walking and cross-country ski trails as well as a beach. **Ethan Allen Park** (North Avenue, past the high school) is a 67-acre preserve, once part of Ethan's farm (near the Homestead) and webbed with trails that climb to the Pinnacle and to a Norman-style stone tower built on Indian Rock in 1905; both high points offer panoramic views of Lake Champlain.

**Winooski Valley Park District** (802-863-5744; wvpd.org) consists of 13 parks, one a wetlands, one landlocked, and most maintained as nature preserves. A few contain canoe launches and bike paths. **The Intervale** (entrance on the corner of Riverside Avenue and N. Prospect Street), along the Winooski River, offers walking as well as bike trails; it includes the Intervale Community Farm (intervalecommunityfarm.com) and Gardener's Supply (a retail and catalog outlet—gardeners.com). Also along the Winooski: a children's discovery garden, a museum in the 67-acre park around the Ethan Allen Homestead (ethanallenhomestead.org), and walking trails at **Macrae Farm Park**. **Delta Park**, at the mouth of the Winooski River, has an elevated bike and recreation path that connects via bike bridge with Burlington's Mayes Landing. **Centennial Woods** offers nature trails; access is from East Avenue.

**Bayside Park** (colchestervt.gov), off Blakely Road in Colchester. The site of a 1920s resort, this 22-acre park now offers a playground, beach, shuffleboard and tennis courts, sports facilities, and walking trails. In winter this is also a popular spot for ice fishing, sailboarding, and ice skating.

**Sand Bar State Park** (802-893-2825; vtstateparks.com) is part of the 1,000-acre Sand Bar Wildlife Refuge, a result of tens of thousands of years of sediment washing down from what is now the Lamoille. It is most notably known for its sandy beach and water access that without the sandbar would be over 150 feet deep. Swimming and boat rentals.

## TO THE EAST

**Underhill State Park** (802-899-3022, vtstateparks.com), on the western edge of 4,393-foot Mount Mansfield, the state's highest peak, lies within the 44,444-acre Mount Mansfield State Forest. Camping mid-May–mid-October, a Civilian Conservation Corps log picnic pavilion, and four trails to the summit ridge of Mount Mansfield. It's accessed by taking Pleasant Valley Road to Mountain Road west of Underhill Center.

**The Green Mountain Audubon Nature Center** (802-434-3068; vt.audubon.org), 255 Sherman Hollow Road, Huntington. (Turn right at Round Church in Richmond; go 5 miles south to Sherman Hollow Road.) Trails wind through 230 acres of representative habitats (beaver ponds, orchards, and woodlands). Interpretive classes offered. Groups are welcome to watch and help with the sugaring each year. Open all year, but call ahead to confirm.

**Camel's Hump State Park** provides access to Vermont's most distinctive and third highest mountain (4,083 feet). It's best accessed from Huntington via East Street, then East Street to Camel's Hump Road. Request a free map and permission for primitive camping (at lower elevations) from the Vermont State Parks office in Waterbury (802-241-3655; vtstateparks.com). The **Green Mountain Club** (802-244-7037; greenmountainclub.org) at 4711 Waterbury Stowe Road (VT 100) in Waterbury Center also has maps for maintained shelters, lodging, and the Hump Brook Tenting Area. The name "Camel's Rump" was used on Ira Allen's map in 1798, but by 1830 it was known as "Camel's Hump." *Note:* All trails and roads within the park are closed during mud season in spring.

## TO THE SOUTH

**LaPlatte River Marsh Natural Area,** Shelburne; parking on Bay Road. Managed by The Nature Conservancy of Vermont, this 211-acre preserve at the mouth of the LaPlatte River is rich in bird life. It is traversed by an easy trail (45 minutes round-trip).

**Shelburne Bay Park** (shelburnevt.org), Shelburne. The Shelburne Recreation Department maintains trails along the bay through mixed woods.

**Shelburne Farms.** More than 10 miles of easy trails on 1,400 acres landscaped by Frederick Law Olmsted, who designed New York's Central Park. Check in at the visitor center—see *Must See* on page 343.

**H. Laurence Achilles Natural Area** (nature.org), Shelburne, access off Pond Road. A short hiking trail leads to Shelburne Pond.

**Mount Philo State Park** (802-425-2390; vtstateparks.com), 5425 Mount Philo Road, Charlotte. Founded in 1924, Vermont's oldest state park has a small, intimate, mountaintop picnic area and campground, with spectacular views of the valley, lake, and Adirondacks. A short but steep ascent off US 7 (not recommended for trailers or large RVs); 10 campsites; admission fee.

## ✳ Lodging

### IN BURLINGTON

HOTELS **Hotel Vermont** (802-651-0080; hotelvt.com), 41 Cherry Street. Burlington's first boutique hotel is resolutely a product of its home state. The modern lobby is crafted from Vermont granite, slate, and reclaimed wood. The 120 rooms and five suites keep up the Green Mountain vibe with flannel robes and Johnson Woolen Mill blankets; local, high-end toiletries; and Vermont books by the bed. Conference rooms available. Bikes are provided free of charge for two hours at a time. Yoga, massages, and regular cultural events, including concerts and trivia, are offered available on-site. At standout restaurant **Juniper**, chef Douglas Paine serves breakfast, lunch, and dinner, all with local ingredients. A spinoff of Waterbury's landmark **Hen of the Wood** restaurant is accessible through a separate entry off the hotel's lobby. Reservations should be made well in advance, but there's often room at the bar if you want creative cocktails, oysters, or high-end ham. $$ hotel; $–$$ dining.

### BED & BREAKFASTS

### IN BURLINGTON

**Willard Street Inn** (802-651-8710; willardstreetinn.com), 349 South Willard Street. Burlington's most elegant "green" inn, this 1881 brick mansion built grandly in the upscale hill section (a few blocks from Champlain College) offers 14 guest rooms, all with private bath. Guests enter an elaborate cherry-paneled foyer and are drawn to the many-windowed, palm-filled solarium with its checkered marble floor and baby grand piano. The living room has a hearth, a tiny gift shop, and vintage portraits. Mornings start with coffee in the dining room, followed by a chef-prepared breakfast served in the solarium. Guest rooms range in size and detailing from spacious master bedrooms and suites to smaller rooms on the third floor. $$–$$$ includes a full breakfast. Ask about off-season specials. Children 12 and over.

**Lang House on Main Street** (802-652-2500; langhouse.com), 360 Main Street. Nine rooms with private bath in this lovely Victorian home are done in period and modern furnishings, antiques, and lush fabrics. Common areas include the living room, sunroom, and breakfast area with historic images of Burlington. City attractions are within walking distance. Well-behaved children of all ages welcome, but Willoughby and Biba prefer to be the only pups in-house. $$ includes breakfast,

**Howard Street Guest House** (802-864-4668; howardstreetguesthouse .com), 153 Howard Street. Two bright, spacious suites in a detached carriage barn surrounded by a patio and flowerbeds. The one downstairs is colorful and contemporary with kitchenette, a queen, and a twin. The upstairs is similar, with skylights. Besides the queen bed, it has a pullout sofa and a "secret" closet cot for Harry Potter fans. No breakfast, though guests can help themselves to coffee, tea, cereal, and juice. The house is a 15-minute walk from the waterfront and Church Street shopping. Two-night minimum. $$.

**Sunset House** (802-864-3790, sunsethousebb.com), 78 Main Street. Paul and Nancy Boileau are your hosts at this 1854 Queen Anne–style home, a former boardinghouse, just two blocks from the waterfront. The four air-conditioned guest rooms share two baths and are decorated with family antiques; there's a kitchen nook and a living room for visitors' use. $$ includes continental breakfast.

**One of a Kind** (802-862-5576; oneof akindbnb.com), 53 Lakeview Terrace. The flower garden of Maggie Sherman's modest 1910 house looks out over a stunning lake panorama. Her second-floor suite has a queen-size bed, a private bath, and a sunny sitting room with a pantry that is stocked with local, organic foods she provides so you can take breakfast at your leisure. The Carpe Diem Cottage has one bed, a fully equipped kitchen stocked with breakfast foods, and a private bath. Rates are the same for either the suite or the cottage. Children over 12. Two-night minimum; single-night and off-season rates upon request. $$.

**254 South Union Street Guesthouse** (802-862-7843; 254southunion .com), 254 South Union Street. An 1887 gabled Queen Anne in an architecturally picturesque neighborhood about four blocks from Church Street with a tastefully furnished guest room and a suite, both with private entrance and bath. The suite, with its queen-size bed and full-size pull-out sofa, has a fully equipped kitchen, dining area, and sitting room. The smaller room, which sleeps two in a queen, has a gas fireplace. No breakfast, but owner Cindy Secondi provides snacks and fresh coffee each morning. $$.

## BEYOND BURLINGTON

RESORTS **The Essex, Vermont's Culinary Resort & Spa** (802-878-1100; essex resortspa.com), 70 Essex Way, Essex. Set on 18 acres in a suburban area 10 miles northeast of downtown Burlington, this contemporary, neo-colonial complex has grown into the largest resort and spa this side of Stowe, and the only one with such a dedicated commitment to the culinary experience. A former partner with the New England Culinary Institute, the resort now operates as its own entity with multiple cooking classes and a program at the Cook Academy. Restaurants include a tavern and the sophisticated Junction, a contemporary restaurant with an open kitchen and a creative prix fixe menu. Accommodations in the 120 rooms include spa or deluxe suites and fireplace rooms. A $15 resort fee covers shuttles, unlimited coffee/tea in the lobby, multiple newspapers, spa access, and parking. Children of all ages are welcome, as are pets (additional fee).

Besides the first-rate food and lodging, the complex boasts conference and wedding facilities, a 22,000-square-foot, full-service spa with a salon, 10 treatment rooms, an indoor pool, saunas, steam rooms, an outdoor hot tub, lounges, and a fitness center. The grounds include an 18-hole golf course, an outdoor heated pool, hiking trails, bicycle rentals, snowshoeing, gardens, and hot-air balloon rides. Fly-fishing enthusiasts will appreciate its on-site casting pond with guides and instruction. Rock and ice climbing as well as ziplines can be found at Northern Lights Rock & Ice (see *Rock Climbing* on page 348). The resort also offers Vermont Tennis Vacations with accommodation packages. Additional amenities include a game room, a gift shop, and a library. The extensive Essex Shoppes & Cinema is right around the corner. Inquire about activity packages. $$–$$$.

**Bolton Valley Resort** (802-434-3444; boltonvalley.com), Bolton. A high mountain valley with a cluster of shops, condominiums, and an indoor sports center. In winter it's snow-minded, with slope-side lodging and night skiing; in summer the focus is on hiking. Facilities include a five-floor, 60-room hotel, 20 suites, and condominium rentals. Some rooms come with a fireplace and kitchenette; most have kings or multiple doubles and balconies with mountain views. The sports center houses an exercise room, a pool, tennis courts, a game room, and a snack bar. The Ponds wedding facility overlooks the water as promised, as well as the Green Mountains. $$–$$$; condos higher, depending on size.

INNS **Inn at Shelburne Farms** (802-985-8498; shelburnefarms.org), Shelburne. Open mid-May–mid-October. Guests are treated to a peerless taste of Edwardian grandeur in this 100-room, Queen Anne–style mansion built by William Seward Webb and Lila Vanderbilt Webb on a spectacular bluff overlooking Lake Champlain. Completed in 1899, the house is the centerpiece of a 1,400-acre estate. Turn-of-the-twentieth-century furnishings predominate. Play billiards in the richly paneled game room, leaf through one of the 6,000 leather-bound books, or play the piano in the library. There's also an elegant tearoom (ask about the inn's special Tea Tours); the

Marble Dining Room has long windows overlooking the formal gardens and lake. Don't miss the third-floor playroom with its dollhouses.

Guest rooms vary in size and elegance—from the second-floor master bedroom to servants' quarters to the two secluded cottages and three-bedroom house—which means room prices also vary. Guests have access to tennis, boating, sumptuous gardens, and miles of splendid walking trails. There is a two-night minimum stay on weekends. Breakfast and dinner are extra and memorable. $$–$$$.

**Sleepy Hollow Inn, Ski & Bike Center** (802-434-2283; skisleepyhollow.com), 427 Ski Lodge Drive, Huntington. This family-owned lodge is the eco-friendly choice: it's heated with solar energy. The house is built on 870 private acres deep in the forest off a dirt road between Richmond and Hinesburg. Six of the eight guest rooms have a private bath, and most have a queen-size bed; two are equipped with two twins, one with four. There is a two-room suite and a wheelchair-accessible unit with a wide shower, a full-size Murphy bed, two twins, and a working fireplace. Common areas include two spacious living rooms with woodstoves, one upstairs, one down, and the fresh, hot breakfasts are served family style featuring family-made maple syrup. A 17-sided event center and attached pavilion, built in 2006 to resemble Richmond's picturesque Old Round Church, can be rented for weddings. A wood-fired sauna hut sits at the edge of a garden pond that ices over for skating in winter. Biking and ski trails lead through meadows and woods to views of Camel's Hump. Trek the mile uphill to the Butternut Cabin, a woodstove-heated cabin with mountain views that sleeps eight (no electricity or running water). $50 per night in summer, $100 in winter (for four), includes firewood and trail passes. Lodge rooms run $135–155, including breakfast.

**BED & BREAKFASTS  Barnhouse B&B** (802-985-3258; urpampered.com), 9 McDonald Farm Road, Shelburne. This 100-year-old dairy barn (on what was old McDonald's farm!) is now a light-filled haven of exposed beams, gardens, and in- and outdoor sitting areas. The wheelchair-accessible Water Garden Room has a queen bed and opens onto a private water-fountain garden that used to be the silo. A circular stairway leads to the Balcony Hayloft Suite (good for families) with a queen on one end, two twins on the other, a private bath, and an open balcony with a hanging chair under a skylight. Both rooms contain air filters, magnetic mattress pads, filtered water, and a free magnetic (hands-free) back massage. A hot homemade breakfast is included. $$.

**Homeplace B&B** (802-899-4694, homeplacebandb.com), 90 Old Pump Road, Essex. This intriguing, H-shape house is secluded in a 100-acre wood at the end of a half-mile driveway. There's a big, secluded swimming pond in the rear, a duck pond in the front, a screened-in terrace with bucolic views, and a bevy of animals: chickens, horses, sheep, dogs, a donkey, and a cat. There are six guest rooms, four with private bath. Innkeeper Mariot Huessy serves up eggs from the hens for breakfast, served in the hexagonal barn. Children and pets welcome; $25 for extra person and per pet, by prearrangement. $ double, including breakfast.

**Hidden Gardens B&B** (802-482-2118; thehiddengardens.com), 693 Lewis Creek Road, Hinesburg. This post-and-beam house is surrounded by 250 acres of land trust forest and bordered with gardens that cascade down the side of a hill to a trout-stocked pond and continue the length of a small field. A sunken garden by the house is filled with water lilies, orchids, and large, exotic blossoms, and the grounds are laced with waterfalls, trails, and Japanese-like microgardens. The two guest rooms, one a double and one a king, feature elegant linens and share a bath. The common rooms are spacious and sunny with vaulted ceilings, fine art, a granite-countered kitchen, and a bevy of Labrador retrievers. Guests can build a bonfire by the pond, fish, swim, stay in the rustic pondside cabin, or hike wooded trails. Children over 8 welcome. $ with breakfast.

**Heart of the Village Inn** (802-985-9060; heartofthevillage.com), 5347 Shelburne Road, Shelburne. A handsome 1886 home that's truly in the heart of town. All nine guest rooms have a private bath and a new flat-screen TV. The most deluxe are in the carriage house: the two-room honeymoon or Webb Suite, for example, has two skylights, sofas, and a two-person whirlpool bath. The Barstow Room has wheelchair access. $$, with breakfast and afternoon refreshments included.

**Sinclair Inn Bed & Breakfast** (802-899-2234; sinclairinnbb.com), 389 VT 15, Jericho. This fully restored 1890 Queen Anne "painted lady" is located in a village setting within easy driving distance of Richmond and Burlington. Six guest rooms each have a private bath, and one is fully handicapped accessible. The lawns overflow with perennials and water lilies. $, double, includes a full breakfast, complimentary beverages, and afternoon treats.

**The Richmond Victorian Inn** (802-434-4410; richmondvictorianinn.com), 191 East Main Street, Richmond. This classy house has five comfortable guest rooms, all with private bath, individually decorated with antiques, and equipped with down comforters, bathrobes, and good reading lights. $, for a double, includes a full gourmet breakfast (invite friends to join you at $15 per person additional).

**Elliot House** (802-985-2727; elliot house.com), 5779 Dorset Street, Shelburne. This updated 1865 Greek Revival farmhouse adjoins 400 acres of Nature Conservancy land with hiking and cross-country ski trails and mountain views both east and west. All three graciously furnished guest rooms have a private bath. Common areas include a library and sitting room with piano. Swimming pool. Rates, with homemade breakfast, $.

**Inn at Charlotte** (802-425-2934; innatcharlotte.com), 32 State Park Road, Charlotte. This contemporary home on the US 7 turnoff to Mount Philo has four rooms, all with bath, private entrance, and TV. Two have king-size beds and cathedral ceilings and open out onto an oval pool. There are tennis courts, a basketball net, and leather-sofa-filled common areas; breakfast is served family style. $, includes full breakfast.

**Windekind Farm** (802-434-4455; windekindfarms.com), 1425 Bert White Road, Huntington. Hidden away in a 160-acre upland valley that's seen little development since it was last farmed around 1935, this expansive spot offers sweeping views and total quiet, save the gurgling of a brook. Camel's Hump State Park spreads for miles, providing space for an extensive network of upland trails. Mark Smith and his Dutch-born wife, Marijke, live in a restored farmhouse and accommodate guests in a flock of contemporary cottages. The Studio is an upstairs apartment with mountain views, and the Breidaclick Cottage is a converted post-and-beam blacksmith shop. Outside are numerous gardens and ponds, plus ducks, heifers, friendly dogs, endless acres for hiking and cross-country skiing. The grounds are ideal for weddings and tented receptions. Children and pets welcome. $–$$.

ADDITIONAL LODGING Numerous non-chain hotels, motor inns, and extended-stay suites are sprinkled throughout the area.

CAMPING **North Beach Campground** (802-862-0942; enjoyburlington.com), 60 Institute Road, Burlington, has 137 shaded campsites for tents or RVs within 45 wooded acres a few minutes' walk from Burlington's largest sandy beach, with its snack bar, changing rooms, and grill-equipped picnic tables. Open May 1–Columbus Day.

*Note:* See **Underhill State Park, Camel's Hump State Park**, and **Mount Philo State Park** at vtstateparks.com. Also **Maple Wind Farm** (maplewindfarm.com) for yurt rentals in Huntington.

## ✳ Where to Eat

*Note:* Burlington has the best restaurant scene between Boston and Montreal, though many of the choicest tables are out of the downtown area. Reservations are essential everywhere when dining in downtown Burlington. If reservations are not accepted, we suggest going early or after 8 p.m.

DINING OUT **Inn at Shelburne Farms** (802-985-8498; shelburnefarms.org), Shelburne. Open for daily breakfast and dinner, as well as Sunday brunch by reservation mid-May–late October. This turn-of-the-twentieth-century manor offers imaginative cuisine using ingredients grown at Shelburne Farms. Brunch is also an event and requires a reservation weeks in advance. Inquire about prix fixe Sunday suppers. $$.

**The Kitchen Table Bistro** (802-434-8686; thekitchentablebistro.com), 1840 West Main Street, Richmond. Dinner Tues.–Sat. Steve and Lara Atkins operate this superlative bistro in a brick-walled home that once belonged to Vermont's first governor. They've been nominated for several James Beard Foundation awards, both together and separately. Steve's pastas are always worth the carb splurge, though meat dishes, such as mustard-crusted pork, are not to be missed. Lara's open-faced coffee-chocolate sundae with candied almonds is a signature dessert, but look for her seasonal fruit ice creams and sorbets.

**Leunig's Bistro** (802-863-3759; leunigsbistro.com), 115 Church Street,

Burlington. A favorite in Burlington, it's open weekdays for lunch and dinner nightly, brunch on weekends. In classic French bistro style, Leunig's has dark wood, gleaming coffee machines, romantic lighting, a full bar, and streetside tables for people-watching, all of which makes it Church Street's most popular establishment. Entrées feature Vermont twists on Gallic fare. Not in the mood for a full meal? Head to the art deco upstairs lounge. Frequent live entertainment. $$.

**A Single Pebble** (802-865-5200; asinglepebble.com), 133 Bank Street, Burlington. Open nightly for dinner, weekdays for lunch; also dim sum Sundays. No fried rice, egg rolls, or MSG here. Instead you get Chop Your Head Off Soup, for example, a savory blend of ground pork, shredded cabbage, and rice cakes; or Ants Climbing a Tree, a smoky-tasting blend of cellophane noodles, ground pork, black mushrooms, scallions, and tree ear fungus. All is served on china and placed on a lazy Susan to encourage sharing. There are numerous small dishes to choose from, like dumplings and mock eel. Reservations essential. $$.

**Trattoria Delia** (802-864-5253; trattoriadelia.com), 152 St. Paul Street, Burlington. Open nightly 5–10, reservations essential. Exposed wooden beams, a roaring fire, and Italian pottery make this one of Burlington's most romantic restaurants. Designer Karl Lagerfeld is a fan of the beef tenderloin in Barbera wine and white truffle butter. An excellent selection of digestivi and dolce to follow. $$–$$$.

EATING OUT *Note:* Thanks to Burlington's huge student population and insatiable hunger for novel cuisine, the restaurant scene is a highly varied, ever-expanding thing. Stroll up and down Church Street or check out the restaurant listings on Burlington-based alternative weekly *Seven Days*' website (sevendaysvt.com).

IN BURLINGTON

**The Farmhouse Tap & Grill** (802-859-0888; farmhousetg.com), 160 Bank Street. The only trace of a McDonald's downtown is this temple to homegrown burgers and numerous brews—located on the former site of the Golden Arches. Besides the main dining room and bar, there's a basement lounge and outdoor bier-garten. Any of which is fitting for a charcuterie plate, a house-dry-aged burger or a cult beer from near or far. The same owners keep the farm-to-table aesthetic at the forefront just down the street at **El Cortijo Taqueria Y Cantina** (802-497-1668; cortijovt.com; 189 Bank Street), in a shiny metal diner car. Go early for both—first come, first served, as reservations are not accepted.

**Duino Duende** (802-660-9346; duinoduende.com), 10 North Winooski Avenue. Between its sister properties, Radio Bean (see *Coffeehouses* on page 361) and Light Club Lamp Shop, this bohemian eatery blends the eclectic sounds of Radio Bean with the smells of international street food. Dishes globe hop from Belgium to Nepal, El Salvador to Korea, but the best dish is the all-American fried-chicken-and-waffles. Lunch and dinner served daily. Open late.

**American Flatbread, Burlington Hearth** (802-861-2999; americanflatbread.com), 115 St. Paul Street. Open daily for dinner; Mon.–Fri. lunch; Sat.–Sun. brunch. In the dead of winter, the wood-fired oven radiates heat. The mostly organic pizzas are made to order and ideal for pairing with the in-house brews on tap. The weekend brunch eggs Benedict pizza is deservedly legendary. No reservations, so plan to wait or go early.

**August First Bakery & Café** (802-540-0060; augustfirstvt.com), 149 South Champlain Street. Open Mon.–Sat. for breakfast and lunch. Touring Burlington, you may see a youth delivering slow-leavened artisan bread on a bike.

This spacious bakery is the source. For baked goods, head into the Main Street entrance for quick service. In the mood for a panini, soup, or salad made from local ingredients? Relax at the South Champlain café space next door without your computer. August First's screen-free policy has gotten it international press.

**Bluebird Barbecue** (802-448-3070; bluebirdbbq.com), 317 Riverside Avenue. Open daily for dinner. The massive trays of regional barbecue served here are worth a trip off the beaten path to this road that connects Burlington to Winooski. You could settle for a plate of smoked tacos or ribs, but we recommend trying a little bit of everything with a family-style combo.

**Pascolo Ristorante** (802-862-9010; pascolovt.com), 83 Church Street. Open for lunch and dinner daily. People-watch on the pedestrian mall or descend to the brick-and-cork-bedecked basement for Italian classics handmade from Vermont ingredients. Watch a chef create the pasta from scratch before slurping up your pappardelle con funghi or tagliatelle Bolognese. Pizzas are wood-fired and topped with local takes on Italian meats and cheeses.

**Pizzeria Verita** (802-489-5644; liveatnectars.com), 1156 St. Paul Street. Diners at Burlington's only destination for authentic Neapolitan pizza sit among piles of split logs that power the 900-degree pizza oven. What emerges is chewy, soft, and covered in homemade mozzarella. From there, choose toppings such as fire-roasted corn and speck or fig and Gorgonzola. The salads and creative cocktails are as winning as the pies, but save room for ricotta-and-Nutella-filled dessert pizza, too.

**The Vermont Pub & Brewery** (802-865-0500; vermontbrewery.com), 144 College Street. Open daily for lunch, dinner, and late night. Despite the modern building, there's an old beer-hall feel at this pub specializing in ales and lagers brewed on the premises. The menu isn't gourmet, but it includes American bar standards as well as British favorites such as toad in the hole and bangers and mash.

**Penny Cluse Cafe** (802-651-8834; pennycluse.com), 169 Cherry Street. Open daily for breakfast and lunch. This breakfast spot is known as much for its long lines as for its southwestern-tinged food. The flavorful Vermont ingredients make even an egg-and-cheese sandwich an event here, though picante egg dishes including huevos rancheros are the hallmark. Can't wait? Try sister restaurant **Lucky Next Door** (802-399-2121), which serves pressed sandwiches and salads for three meals daily.

**Mirabelles** (802-658-3074; mirabelles cafe.com), 198 Main Street. A delightful bakery that serves eclectic, international breakfast, and lunch daily. The mouth-watering Euro-style pastries are pricey but worth every indulgent penny.

## ON THE WATERFRONT

**Shanty on the Shore** (802-864-0238; shantyontheshore.com), 181 Battery Street. Open daily for lunch and dinner for seafood that's handy to the ferry. The building was once the home and general store of Isaac Nye, the nineteenth-century "Hermit of Burlington." Children's menu.

**The Skinny Pancake** (802-540-0188; skinnypancake.com), 60 Lake Street, at College Street. Known as much for being a music venue as for being a casual creperie, this restaurant also has locations in Montpelier and the Burlington airport. Sweet and savory crepes are on the menu as well as burgers and salads. Fondue in winter.

## IN WINOOSKI

**Sneakers Bistro & Café** (802-655-9081; sneakersbistro.com), 28 Main Street. Open daily 7–3. Big, heavy breakfasts such as a range of Benedicts and Kahlúa-dipped French toast have attracted lines down the block for decades.

**Misery Loves Co.** (802-497-3989; miserylovescovt.com), 46 Main Street. Open Tues.–Sat. for lunch and dinner; Sunday brunch. This former food truck made its name with its nap-inducingly heavy sandwiches and burgers. They're still served at lunchtime, but dinner is seriously innovative, with groundbreaking platings of seafood and local veggies that earned the co-chefs James Beard Foundation award recognition. Their bakery, across the street at 25 Winooski Falls Way (802-497-1337), serves Stumptown Coffee Roasters brews and creative pastry daily. Try a loaf of levain, made from spent grain used in the beer at nearby Four Quarters Brewing.

**Mule Bar** (802-399-2020; mulebarvt .com), 36 Main Street. Open daily 3 p.m.–1 a.m. This craft beer and comfort food establishment is almost always busy, but it's worth braving the crowds. Sit at a high table or outside for charcuterie and cheese, homemade pasta, or a burger. The funky 16-tap list changes constantly, but it is always packed with surprises from Vermont and farther afield.

**Our House Bistro** (802-497-1884; ourhousebistro.com), 28 Main Street. Open daily for dinner. Weekday lunch is replaced by a popular brunch on the weekend. The stuffed Dutch pancakes here give Sneakers' brunch a run for its money. At dinner, signature "twisted comfort food" includes an eclectic mac-and-cheese menu. (Surf-and-turf mac! Peanut-butter-and-jelly mac!) Meatloaf and fries are served in miniature fryer baskets.

**Dharshan Namaste Asian Deli** (802-654-8000), 212 Main Street. Open daily for lunch and dinner. A Nepalese and Vietnamese couple fuse their native cuisines at this homey little restaurant.

## ALONG WILLISTON ROAD (US 2)

**Al's French Frys** (802-862-9203; alsfrenchfrys.com), 1251 Williston Road, South Burlington. Open daily for lunch, dinner, and late night. This incredibly popular vintage 1944 house of grease boasts an America's Classics award from the James Beard Foundation. In-season, try the black raspberry or mint creemees. Cash only.

**The Bagel Place** (802-497-2050; thebagelplacevt.com), 1166 Williston Road, South Burlington. The bagel sandwiches here are served in a café surrounded by reclaimed wood from vintage Vermont barns. Try the perfectly balanced Italian sandwich, or a Caprese, filled with fresh mozzarella, tomato, basil, and prosciutto. For dessert, try the marzipan bagel.

**Parkway Diner** (802-652-1155), 1696 Williston Road, South Burlington. Open daily for breakfast and lunch. The Worcester Lunch Car might be of a 1950s vintage, but the food here isn't. Barbecue seitan and quirky specials such as fried pork on a cheddar biscuit with chipotle Hollandaise share menu space with an open-faced hot turkey sandwich, made from a freshly roasted bird each day.

## IN ESSEX

**Firebird Café** (802-316-4265; thefirebirdcafe.com), 163 Pearl Street. Open daily for breakfast and lunch. California boy Jake Tran imports the burritos and breakfast he enjoyed as a kid to Vermont. Breakfast and lunch are both served all day, so you can order a smoked salmon eggs Benedict with poblano cream sauce alongside a kicking pork carnitas burrito in tangy salsa verde.

## IN RICHMOND

**One Radish Eatery** (802-434-7770; oneradishvt.com), 39 Esplanade, Richmond. Breakfast, lunch, dinner in casual comfort. Locally sourced and well prepared, salads, pizza, savory soups. Live music on Thursday nights.

## IN HINESBURG

**Bristol Bakery** (802-482-6050; bristolbakery.com), 16 Main Street. Open daily for breakfast and lunch. Dinner every day but Sun. Bagels, croissants, and other baked goods are this spot's raison d'être, but savory specialties include fresh, local salads; tacos; and huevos rancheros.

**Hinesburgh Public House** (802-482-5500; hinesburghpublichouse.com), 10516 US 116. That's not a typo: The extra *h* in this restaurant's moniker is a reminder of a time in history when the town did indeed spell its name that way. But the only thing old-fashioned about this community-supported eatery is its menu of foods sourced from the town's own farms. Chicken-corn chowder uses Vermont Smoke & Cure bacon produced out back, while burgers are served from buns produced by a tiny local bakery.

## IN SHELBURNE

**Rustic Roots** (802-985-9511; rusticrootsvt.com), 195 Falls Road. Breakfast and lunch Wed.–Sat., dinner Fri. and Sat. Everything is made from scratch here, including breads, condiments, and cured meats. The French-inflected menu changes with the seasons, but the Rustic Breakfast—two eggs, coffee-maple sausage, fennel-rubbed Canadian bacon, and a buttery popover—is a staple worth many a return visit.

**Barkeaters** (802-985-2830; barkeatersrestaurant.com), 97 Falls Road. Lunch and dinner, after hours tavern. Tues.–Sat., 11:30–2:30 lunch: bar menu 2:30–4:30; dinner 4:30–9; Sunday brunch, 10–2. Closed Monday.

A rustic, Adirondack-inspired restaurant and tavern close to the heart of Shelburne. Varied menu, attentive service.

## IN WILLISTON

**Chef's Corner Café Bakery** (802-878-5524; chefscornervt.com), 300 Cornerstone Drive. Gourmet chef-inspired salads and sandwiches as well as breakfast seven days a week. The South African chef-owner knows his way around European-style pastries. There's also a location in Burlington's South End (802-660-7111, 208 Flynn Avenue).

**Sakura Sushi and Kitchen** (802-288-8052), 19 Taft Corners. Open daily for lunch and dinner; Sunday is dinner only. This homestyle Japanese hole-in-the-wall replaces a fancy atmosphere with Japanese game shows on TV. Service is super fast, so you'll get your pork katsu curry, udon beef soup, or sushi dinner in mere minutes. There are Japanese groceries, too, should you need to scratch your Pocky itch.

TEAROOMS **Dobra Tea** (802-951-2424; dobratea.com), 80 Church Street (entrance on Bank Street), Burlington. Open 11–11 daily. The first North American branch of what started as a Czech teahouse chain, this temple to tea connoisseurs offers more than 100 varieties from around the globe, all served as they would be in their homeland. Each pot is freshly brewed at the precise temperature and time required. In the back you can shed your shoes and lounge on pillows, the way a tea drinker would in Uzbekistan.

COFFEEHOUSES **Muddy Waters** (802-658-0466), 184 Main Street, just up from Church Street, Burlington, open every day, all day. Excellent coffee, homemade desserts, vegan specials, smoothies, beer, and wine by the glass in a dimly lit, brick-walled den with sofas, lots of reading material, and earnest conversation. Bring a book or project—this is the spot for the artistic crowd. Sometimes there is live jazz.

**Uncommon Grounds** (802-865-6227; ugvermont.com), 42 Church Street, Burlington. They roast their own here, offering a large selection, along with teas and Italian-syrup-based drinks. Down a piece of chocolate cake while perusing the day's papers, laid out on wooden holders. Outdoor seating in summer.

**Maglianero Café** (802-861-3155; maglianero.com), 47 Maple Street, Burlington. The direct-sourced coffees and teas attract professionals and hipsters alike. So do the excellent pastries and ice creams available at the counter. In summer, food trucks park out front, making Maglianero a one-stop shop for lunch, dessert, and a dose of caffeine.

**Speeder and Earl's** (speederandearls .com). A zany shop at 412 Pine Street (802-658-6016), open daily. The roastery's fun, flavored beans include Black Forest chocolate and maple French roast varieties.

**Radio Bean** (802-660-9346; radiobean.com), 8 North Winooski Avenue, Burlington. This Bohemian coffeehouse doubles as the best place for unplugged music acts, including frequent stops by Burlington's better-known musicians. Multiple shows each day mean cocktails replace coffee well into the night. Head two stores over to Light Club Lamp Shop for dessert and yet more tunes.

## ✳ Entertainment

*Note:* For current arts and entertainment in Burlington, check the websites of **Burlington City Arts** (burlingtoncityarts .org) and *Seven Days* (sevendaysvt.com), the latter of which is the alternative newsweekly available free at most area businesses. Also see *Special Events* at the end of this chapter.

MUSIC **Vermont Symphony Orchestra** (802-864-5741; vso.org), based in Burlington. One of the country's first statewide philharmonics presents a concert series at venues including the Flynn Center for the Performing Arts (see *Theater*) and Shelburne Farms, as well as children's music series, outreach programs, residencies, and choral and chamber concerts throughout the year.

**Burlington Choral Society** (802-878-5919; bcsvermont.org). This volunteer, 100-voice choir presents several concerts a year.

**The Burlington Discover Jazz Festival** (802-863-7992; discoverjazz.com), Burlington, 10 days in early June, a jazz extravaganza that fills city parks, clubs, restaurants, and ferries. Ticketed shows and free open-air events.

THEATER **Flynn Center for the Performing Arts** (802-86-FLYNN; flynn center.org), 153 Main Street, Burlington. The city's prime stage for music and live performance is a refurbished art deco movie house, now home to regional, national, and international plays, musical comedies, concerts, dance troupe performances, and lectures. Constantly evolving, it houses the Amy Tarrant Art Gallery and is the home of Burlington's **Lyric Theatre Company** (lyrictheatrevt .org). Next door and down the stairs, the FlynnSpace black box hosts professional **Vermont Stage Company** (vtstage.org)—known for contemporary and original works—as well as the excellent **Flynn Arts Summer Youth Theater**, which performs two shows each summer.

**Royall Tyler Theatre** (802-656-2094; uvmtheatre.org), 116 University Place, on the University of Vermont campus, Burlington, stages a seasonal repertory of classic and contemporary plays.

**Main Street Landing Performing Arts Center** (802-864-7999; mainstreetlanding.com), 60 Lake Street, Burlington. A nonprofit, independently run complex that acts as a forum for local production groups. The neo-Victorian brick complex facing the waterfront houses a 130-seat theater and a film presentation room; a creperie, **The Skinny Pancake** (see *Eating Out* on page 359), operates downstairs.

**Saint Michael's Playhouse** (802-654-2281; saintmichaelsplayhouse.org), at St. Michael's College, Colchester, presents four Equity theater performances each summer. The college theater department also puts on a show each spring and fall (smcvt.edu).

**Lane Series** (802-656-4455; uvm.edu/laneseries) sponsors major musical and theatrical performances around Burlington fall through spring.

DRIVE-IN **Sunset Drive-In** (802-862-1800; sunsetdrivein.com), 155 Porter's Point Road, Colchester. In summer, the four screens show nightly double features, after the "Let's All Go to the Lobby" short, of course. There's also a snack bar and a playground.

LIVE MUSIC VENUES For jazz, blues, rock, and dance clubs, check out these nightspots, in Burlington: **Nectar's** (802-658-4771; liveatnectars.com), 188 Main Street, where Phish got their start, and above it **Club Metronome** (802-865-4563; clubmetronome.com), for live bands and DJs. **Red Square** (802-859-8909; redsquarevt.com) and **RiRa Irish Pub** (802-860-9401; rira.com) both have live music most nights. **Drink** (802-860-9463) specializes in comedy and jazz, while **Radio Bean** (see *Coffeehouses*) and **The Skinny Pancake** (see *Eating Out*) are also sure bets for live music. **Higher Ground** (802-652-0777; highergroundmusic.com), 14 Williston Road, South Burlington, is the state's best place for live music and events such as the Winter Is a Drag Ball, with a ballroom and smaller Showcase Lounge. Bands and music publications alike describe it as New England's best live music venue. **The Old Lantern** (802-425-2120, oldlantern.com) in Charlotte boasts the largest maple dance floor in the state in a restored 1800s barn.

## ✱ Selective Shopping

DOWNTOWN Burlington boasts the Church Street Marketplace (see the sidebar on page 365 and churchstreetmarketplace.com). Burlington's South End (seaba.com), clustered around the Pine

Street area, brings to light some of the area's artsy and industrial-style shops.

If you head outside Burlington on Williston Road/US 2, you'll reach the Dorset Street area, with the University Mall (umallvt.com). Farther down US 2 is the Taft Corners shopping area of Williston, which includes Maple Tree Place and the Majestic 10 movie theater (shopmtp.com). VT 15 from Burlington to Essex via I-289 leads to the Essex Shoppes & Cinema (essexshoppes.com).

ANTIQUES **Architectural Salvage Warehouse** (802-879-4221; greatsalvage.com), 11 Maple Street, Essex Junction. The place to explore vintage artifacts salvaged from old houses, such as crystal doorknobs, clawfoot tubs, marble sinks, and stained-glass windows.

**Champlain Valley Antiques Center** (802-985-8116; vermontantiquecenter.com), 4067 Shelburne Road, Shelburne. Tom Cross has an ever-changing collection of Vermont furniture, folk art, crocks and jugs, and historical items.

ART GALLERIES AND CRAFTS STUDIOS *Note:* See also *Cultural Attractions* on page 346 and vermontcrafts.com for a full list of studios and info on Open House Weekend, held every Memorial Day weekend.

**Montstream Studio & Art Gallery** (802-862-8752; kmmstudio.com), 129 St. Paul Street, Burlington. Open daily except Sundays. Native-born watercolorist and oil painter Katharine Montstream depicts the lake and mountain landscapes of the Burlington waterfront and downtown area in greeting cards, prints, and paintings.

**Lawrence Ribbecke** (802-658-3425; ribbeckeglass.com), 377 Pine Street, Burlington, features over 500 types of glass, including stained-glass masterpieces depicting the local landscape.

**Dug Nap** (802-860-1386; dugnap.com), whose animals and locals evoke a dark humor reminiscent of Gary Larson's *The Far Side,* shows his work by appointment at his studio, which is only a block south of City Hall at 184 Church Street, Burlington.

**Frog Hollow on the Marketplace** (802-863-6458; froghollow.org), 86 Church Street, Burlington. The Vermont State Craft Center showcases everything from furniture and art glass to handwoven scarves and jewelry of every sort.

**Bennington Potters North** (802-863-2221; benningtonpotters.com), 127 College Street, Burlington, sells kitchenware, home furnishings, glass, woodenware, and the ever-enduring Bennington Pottery. A good selection of seconds in the basement.

**Furchgott Sourdiffe Gallery** (802-985-3848; fsgallery.com), 86 Falls Road, Shelburne, has rotating shows and does restoration and framing.

**The Vermont Gift Barn** (802-658-7684; vermontgiftbarn.com), 1087 Williston Road, South Burlington. An assortment of Vermont-made products, from specialty foods and weavings to jewelry, pottery, furniture, fine art prints, and glass.

BOOKSTORES **The Crow Bookshop** (802-862-0848; crowbooks.com), 14 Church Street, Burlington. Well-stocked shelves of new, used, and remainder books in two rooms with creaky floors and great prices.

**Flying Pig Children's Books** (802-985-3999; flyingpigbooks.com), 5247 Shelburne Road, Shelburne. Former teachers Josie Leavitt and Elizabeth Bluemle have created an award-winning bookstore with close to 40,000 titles for kids and adults. Bluemle herself is an award-winning children's book author.

**Phoenix Books** (802-448-3350; 802-872-7111; phoenixbooks.biz), 191 Bank Street, Burlington; 21 Essex Way, #407, Essex. This independent chain of four shops has a fine selection of local books and popular (and kids') titles. The Essex location boasts a café that serves coffee and wine along with its snacks. The shop has also opened locations in Rutland and Chester and owns the Yankee Bookshop in Woodstock.

FARMS & WINERIES **Charlotte Village Winery** (802-425-4599; charlottevillage winery.com), 3968 Greenbush Road, Charlotte. A winemaking operation with a viewing deck overlooking acres of pick-your-own blueberry fields. Free wine tastings daily Memorial Day–December.

**Shelburne Vineyard** (802-985-8222; shelburnevineyard.com), 6308 Shelburne Road, Shelburne. Open daily year-round. Taste nine wine varieties for a $7 fee that includes the glass. Tours explain the winemaking process; tables and chairs overlook undulating vines with the lake in the distance. The on-site shop includes Vermont edibles and novelties such as wine racks made from antlers.

**Lang Farm** (802-316-1210; langbarn .com), 51 Upper Main Street (VT 15), Essex Junction. Antiques center, nursery, and garden shop open daily year-round. Links at Lang Farm operates here, and the barn is most notably known as a wedding and event venue. In fall, there's a corn maze.

**Sam Mazza's Farm** (802-655-3440; sammazzafarms.com), 277 Lavigne Road, Colchester. Open daily year-round. The farm's market clearly labels what was grown on-site and uses those ingredients in its outstanding country-style baked goods. A petting zoo, pick-your-own berries, and an autumn corn maze attract families.

**Shelburne Orchards** (802-985-2753; shelburneorchards.com), 216 Orchard Road, Shelburne. Over 80 acres of apple trees dot this delightful local place for apple picking and some of the area's best local food-related events. Open daily, with a farm store; picnickers always welcome. Special deals for seniors.

**Adams Apple Orchard & Farm Market** (802-879-5226; adamsfarmmarket .com), 986 Old Stage Road, Williston. Pick-your-own apples and large farm market selling Vermont

The city's shopping and dining hub, Church Street Marketplace (churchstmarketplace .com) extends four car-free blocks, from the graceful Unitarian Church, designed in 1815 by Peter Banner, to City Hall at the corner of Main Street. Outdoor concerts often take place at its head, and the bricked promenade is spotted with benches and boulders from different parts of the state. The marketplace buildings themselves, a mix of nineteenth-century and art deco styles, house more than 100 shops and an ever-growing roster of restaurants. Stop at a café to watch the colorful parade of Burlingtonians and pups as they walk by. Chances are, at least one street musician will serenade you. Unlike Boston's Quincy Market, Church Street is a public thoroughfare, open daily and geared as much to residents as to tourists. With new downtown development recently approved, side streets off the marketplace will soon see new shops, restaurants, and residences adding to the lively mix.

products and tasty doughnuts; open daily mid-April–December.

FARMERS' MARKETS The **Burlington Farmers' Market** held Saturdays in City Hall Park (winter in Memorial Auditorium) is a fun place to stroll with the kiddies past artful pies, plants, fruits, cheeses, breads, and veggies, along with African samosas, honey meads, and Tibetan take-out. At the back are crafts, jewelry, clothes, and art. It can get crowded.

The area has the most concentrated location of farmers' markets in the state. Essex Junction, Hinesburg, Jericho, Milton, Richmond, Shelburne, South Burlington, Westford, Williston, and Winooski all have weekly markets in-season, some monthly in winter. For all locations, times, and details, see vermontagriculture.com.

FOOD AND DRINK **Lake Champlain Chocolates** (802-864-1807; lakechamplainchocolates.com), 750 Pine Street, Burlington. Vermont's premier chocolate company offers free tours (and samples) at its Burlington factory, plus a delectable souvenir selection, including seconds. A café serves flavored coffees, hot chocolate drinks, chocolate ice creams, and more. A store and scoop shop is also located at 65 Church Street.

**Snowflake Chocolates** (802-899-3373; snowflakechocolate.com), 81 VT 15, Jericho Corners. Bob and Martha Pollak have handcrafted chocolates at this store since 1986. Try the sea-salted caramels.

**The Great Harvest Bread Company** (802-660-2733; greatharvestburlington .com), 382 Pine Street, Burlington, also provides a sandwich-ordering and eating area for its varied loaves and fruit-filled pastries. The cinnamon swirl and apple-cheddar breads are our favorites.

**Magic Hat Brewing Company** (802-658-BREW; magichat.net), 5 Bartlett Bay Road, South Burlington (turn off US 7 at the Jiffy Lube). A continuously expanding microbrewery offering tours, samples, and retail shop; navigate the complex and interactive website for hours, events, and giveaways.

See other breweries in the sidebar on page 368.

**Chef Contos Kitchen & Store** (802-497-3942; chefcontos.com), 65 Falls Road. The Charlie Trotter protégée, whose family owned the famous Chez Paul in Chicago, sells hard-to-find, cult gourmet goods and cookware at her elegant store. Check the website for the not-to-be-missed classes.

SPECIAL SHOPS **Peace and Justice Store** (802-863-8326; pjcvt.org), 60 Lake Street, Burlington, run by the city's active Peace and Justice Center, a source of alternative publications and fair-trade crafted items—jewelry, cards, clothing—all purchased from wholesalers committed to nonexploitation and social justice. Check the events bulletin board.

**Gardener's Supply** (802-660-3505; gardeners.com), 128 Intervale Road, Burlington. One of the largest catalog seed and garden suppliers in New England, with a retail store and nursery adjacent to demonstration gardens along the Winooski River in Burlington's Intervale.

**Old Gold** (802-864-7786; oldgoldvt .com), 180 Main Street, Burlington. A well-cultivated collection of vintage clothing is the main draw here, but colorful new clothes and accessories meet the aesthetic, too. Looking for a costume? This is the place.

**Horsford's Nursery** (802-425-2811; horsfordnursery.com), 2111 Greenbush Road, Charlotte. It's worth visiting this 100-year-old farm just to roam the bounty of blooming flowers, perennials, and the two antique glass greenhouses.

**Harrington's** (802-985-2000; harringtonham.com), 5597 Shelburne Road, Shelburne, sells the corn-cob-smoked meats and other goodies prepared at its headquarters on US 2 in Richmond. Across the street from the Shelburne Museum, buy a variety of prepared foods or get a sandwich made to order. **The Shelburne Country Store** (802-985-3657; shelburnecountrystore .com), 29 Falls Road (just off US 7), Shelburne, encloses several gift galleries under the same roof—a sweets shop, cards, foods, housewares, lampshades, and more.

## ✳ Special Events

*Early January:* **Vermont Cat Show** (catshows.us/vermontff). Vermont Fancy Felines pose for ribbons and rest between rounds in lavish travel homes on display at the Sheraton Burlington. The people-watching is even more interesting than the cats.

*Late January:* **Vermont Farm Show** (vtfarmshow.com), this long-running show, held at the Champlain Valley Exposition in Essex Junction, is interesting even to non-agrarian types. Consumer Night features a Buy Local Market with multiple vendors and the Capital Cook-Off.

*Early February:* **Burlington Winter Festival/Penguin Plunge**, Waterfront Park—snow and ice sculptures, vending (enjoyburlington.com),and the annual icy dip into Lake Champlain to benefit Special Olympics Vermont (penguinplunge.org).

*Saturday before Lent:* **Magic Hat Mardi Gras** (magichat.net)—Burlington hums with a packed crowd for this parade and block party on the Church Street Marketplace.

*March:* In odd years the **Vermont Flower Show** (greenworksvt.org) is held at the Champlain Valley Exposition—three days of color and fragrance to mark the end of winter. Sugarhouses everywhere open their doors for **Maple Open House Weekend** (vermontmaple.org) in late March.

*Memorial Day weekend:* **Key Bank Vermont City Marathon & Relay** (vermontcitymarathon.org)—hundreds participate, thousands spectate; activities all over Burlington. **Vermont Open Studio Weekend** (vermontcrafts.com)—art galleries and crafts studios across the state open their doors for demos and sales.

*June:* **Art's Alive Festival of Fine Art** (seaba.com/arts-alive) is a month-long celebration of the arts in Burlington. **Burlington Discover Jazz Festival** (discoverjazz.com)—for 10 days the entire city of Burlington becomes a stage for more than 200 musicians. **Lake Champlain International Father's Day Fishing Derby** (mychamplain.net)—held annually on Father's Day weekend.

*Late June:* **Burlington Food & Wine Festival** (burlingtonfoodandwinefestival

# BURLINGTON'S ARTISTIC SOUTH END

Though Church Street may be Burlington's sunny heart, bohemian Pine Street is its artistic soul. Businesses located between Main Street and Flynn Avenue are a highly concentrated mix of galleries, studios, and eclectic restaurants. For lunch, there's old standard **Myer's Bagel Bakery** (802-863-5013), *the* place for Montreal-style bagels, smoked sandwiches, and excellent baked goods. Just across the street, **Four Corners of the Earth** (802-657-3869) serves up the world between two slices of bread in the form of sandwiches with flavors including Jamaican Avocado and Iraqi Turkey. **Feldman's Bagels** (802-540-0474) handles the New York side of things with local cream cheese schmears and matzah ball soup.

On the artistic side, the **S.P.A.C.E. Gallery** (802-578-2512) hosts monthly group shows of the artists whose studios are located in the building, known as the Soda Plant for its previous factory tenant. **ArtsRiot** (802-540-0406) is not just a gallery, but a multipurpose event space hosting concerts, movie screenings, and even yoga. Its restaurant features locally inspired, chef-driven takes on fast food, but the kitchen also opens up to pop-up meals including a popular Ethiopian night. **SEABA Center** (802-859-9222) hosts regular shows featuring members of the South End Arts and Business Association and offers frequent classes. It also puts on one of Burlington's biggest events of the year, the South End Art Hop (see *Special Events* on page 366). Don't miss the world's tallest filing cabinet on your right as you head toward 208 Flynn Avenue and its **Flynndog Gallery**. The space is actually just a long hallway filled with revolving local works, but there's lots to see, and **Chef's Corner South End** (802-660-7111) serves its European pastries and exquisite soups right in the building.

.com) at Waterfront Park, Burlington—tastings and pairings from Burlington's best chefs and their favorite wines. **Vermont Quilt Festival** (vqf.org), New England's oldest and largest quilting event, at the Champlain Valley Exposition in Essex Junction.

*July 3:* **Burlington Independence Day Celebration** (enjoyburlington.com) on the Burlington waterfront and in the harbor—the state's most intense fireworks display, over the lake, with live bands, children's entertainment, a parade of boats, and lots of vendors.

*Mid-July:* **Vermont Brewer's Festival** (vtbrewfest.com)—local microbreweries ply their stuff under tents at Waterfront Park.

*August:* **Lake Champlain Maritime Festival** (lcmfestival.com), Burlington waterfront—a historic boat festival held in conjunction with the Lake Champlain Maritime Museum by day and well-staged concerts at night. **Champlain Valley Fair**, at the Champlain Valley Exposition in Essex Junction (cvexpo.org), late August—a traditional country fair with livestock and produce exhibits, pig races, rides, and an embarrassment of rich food.

*September:* **Burlington Book Festival** (burlingtonbookfestival.com), three days of readings, lectures, workshops, book signings, and events. **Shelburne Farms Harvest Festival** (shelburnefarms.org)—an annual festival held at this working and educational farm on the shores of Lake Champlain. At the **Small Farms Food Festival** at Shelburne Orchards (shelburneorchards.com), local farms offer tasting menus, live bluegrass, apple picking, sweet cider, and doughnuts. **South End Art Hop** (seaba.com)—a tour of some 400 art studios in Burlington's South End with a fashion show, music, food, workshops, and demonstrations.

*October:* **Vermont International Film Festival** (vtiff.org), a week's worth of independent, documentary, and outsider films, at area cinemas. **East Charlotte Tractor Parade** (tractorparade.com), held in front of Spear's Corner Store in East Charlotte—tractors of all sizes with

## BEER, HERE!

**V**ermont boasts more cheesemakers and brewers per capita than any other state. But while the curds require lots of rural space to keep cows, beer makers seem to mushroom daily in the old warehouse spaces of the Burlington area. The late Greg Noonan, founder of **The Vermont Pub & Brewery** (see *Eating Out* on page 359), is widely considered to be the father of Vermont's craft brewing scene. Just down St. Paul Street from his old stomping grounds, **American Flatbread Burlington Hearth** (see *Eating Out* on page 358) is home to **Zero Gravity Craft Brewery** (802-497-0054), whose constant rotation ranges from IPAs to a harvest gruit ale containing carrots, chervil, and blackberries. On Pine Street, **Citizen Cider** (802-448-3278) provides a pubby alternative to beer drinking, with its range of local apple libations served alongside corn dogs and poutine. **Magic Hat Brewing Company** (802-658-2739) and **Switchback Brewing Co.** (802-651-4114) are the biggest producers on the scene, and both offer regular tours at their factories in South Burlington and Burlington, respectively. Down Shelburne Road, **Fiddlehead Brewing Company** (802-399-2994) fills growlers perfect for enjoying over wood-fired pies from **Folino's Pizza** (802-881-8822) just across the hall in the same Shelburne building. **Four Quarters Brewing** (802-391-9120), in Winooski invites guests to its tasting room on weekends and hosts frequent events. Many other breweries are too small as of this writing to host regular visitors, but check the **Vermont Brewers Association** website (vermontbrewers.com) to see them all. And don't forget to get your tickets early for the **July Vermont Brewers' Festival** (vtbrewfest.com). Tickets to the bacchanal are known to sell out in hours.

drivers of all ages parade through the tiny center of one of the Burlington area's most thriving agricultural communities. **Essex Fall Craft Show**, Champlain Valley Exposition, Essex Junction, could be the state's largest crafts fair (vtcrafts .com). **Vermont Tech Jam** (techjamvt .com) is an annual expo of tech companies producing cutting-edge technology in the Green Mountains. **Nightmare**

**Vermont** (nightmarevermont.org) is an adult-geared indoor haunted event held in the Burlington area in late October. **Spookyville Vermont**, a less-scary event, is offered for children.

*Early December:* **Vermont International Festival** (vermontinternational festival.com)—food, crafts, dance, and music from around the world, at the Champlain Valley Exposition.

# THE NORTHWEST CORNER

*Including the Champlain Islands, St. Albans,*
*Swanton, and Enosburgh*

I-89 is the quickest but not the most rewarding route from Burlington to the Canadian border. At the very least, motorists should detour for a meal in St. Albans and a drive through the farm country around Swanton or Enosburgh. Or allow a few extra hours—or days—to meander up US 2 through the Champlain Islands on the Lake Champlain Byway.

## THE ISLANDS

The cows, silos, and mountain views couldn't be more Vermont. But what about those beaches and sailboats? They're part of the picture, too, in this island chain stretching south from Quebec comprising the Alburgh peninsula and three main islands—South Hero, North Hero, and Isle La Motte—connected by bridges and causeways.

This is Grand Isle County, Vermont's smallest county. It was homesteaded by Ebenezer Allen in 1783 and has been a quiet summer retreat since the 1870s, when visitors began arriving by lake steamer to stay at farms. Around the turn of the twentieth century, the coming of the railway spawned several hotels, and with the advent of automobiles and Prohibition, US 2—the main road down the spine of the islands—became one of the most popular routes to Montreal, a status it maintained until I-89 opened in the 1960s.

Happily, in the decades since, time, like the interstate, seems to have passed these islands by.

A summer destination first, this also is a great place to visit in September and October, when its many apple orchards are being harvested and bicycling is at its best. Ice fishing fills inns in winter, as this area of Lake Champlain offers some of the state's finest angling opportunities. Just leave driving a truck onto the ice to the locals.

Each island has its own character. South Hero is renowned for its apple orchards and Snow Farm Vineyard, which hosts a popular summer music concert series. The South Hero Land Trust has preserved the Round Pond Natural Area and Landon Community Trail, both great options for walks. Round Pond also allows horseback riding. North Hero has a legendary general store, but its state parks make it popular with travelers.

Isle La Motte is the smallest and quietest of the islands, a favorite destination for bicyclists. It's the site of the first European settlement in Vermont and is the place where Samuel de Champlain first set foot on shore. St. Anne's Shrine, near the northern tip, marks the spot. It's also home to the world's oldest coral reef and Fisk Farm, which has an intriguing tie to Theodore Roosevelt.

## ST. ALBANS AND SWANTON

**St. Albans** (population 6,918, surrounded by St. Albans town, 5,999) The community secured a place in the history books on October 19, 1864, when 22 armed Confederate soldiers held up three banks, stole horses, and escaped back to Canada with $208,000,

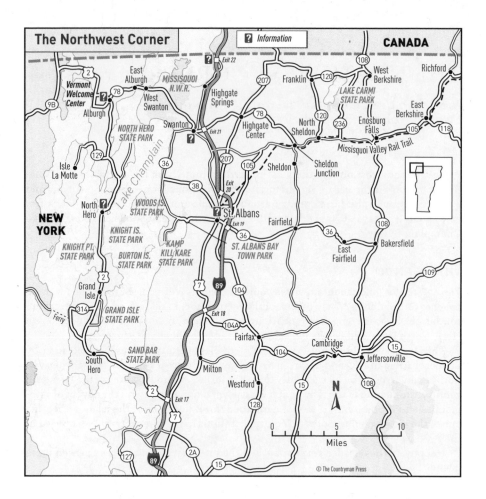

making this the northernmost engagement of the Civil War. One of the raiders was wounded and eventually died, as did Elinus J. Morrison, a visiting builder. The surviving Confederates were arrested in Montreal, tried, but never extradited. Their leader, Lieutenant Bennett H. Young, rose to the rank of general. When he visited Montreal again in 1911, a group of St. Albans dignitaries paid him a courtesy call at the Ritz-Carlton.

After the Civil War, St. Albans boomed as headquarters for the Central Vermont Railroad, once the largest railway in New England, employing more than 1,700 people just in St. Albans. This and the story of the St. Albans Raid are dramatized in the **St. Albans Museum.**

**Swanton** (population 6,427) Archaeological digs have unearthed evidence that Algonquin tribes lived here as far back as 8,000 BC. The French settled the area in the 1740s, naming it 15 years later for Thomas Swanton, a British officer in the French and Indian Wars. Due to its proximity to the Canadian border (only 6 miles north), Swanton witnessed a fair bit of smuggling in the nineteenth century and during Prohibition.

During World War I the long-abandoned Robin Hood–Remington Arms plant produced millions of rounds of ammunition for the Allied armies. Today a sizable chunk of the population is of Abenaki origin, and the Abenaki Tribal Council and museum are based here. The idyllic Village Green Park is home to a pair of swans, a tradition since 1963, when Queen Elizabeth II sent the town two swans for its bicentennial, erroneously believing that its name had something to do with swans.

GUIDANCE **Franklin County Regional Chamber of Commerce** (802-524-2444; frccvt.com), 2 North Main Street, Suite 101, St. Albans. Open weekdays. Facing Taylor Park, with plenty of easy parking, this is a friendly office stocked with brochures.

**Lake Champlain Islands Chamber of Commerce** (802-372-8400; 800-262-5226; champlainislands.com), 3501 US 2, North Hero. Next door to the Hero's Welcome General Store, this office is open year-round and publishes a list of accommodations, restaurants, and marinas.

**Swanton Chamber of Commerce** (802-868-7200; swantonchamber.com), 34 Merchants Row, Swanton, located at the northern end of Village Green Park.

DOWNTOWN ST. ALBANS  LISA HALVORSEN

**Lake Champlain Byway** extends from Addison County through the islands. Check the website for information (lakechamplainbyway.com).

GETTING THERE *By car*: From I-89, take Exit 17, then US 2 to reach the Champlain Islands. Exits for St. Albans and Swanton are Exits 19 and 21, respectively. If entering from New York State, hop on US 2 at Rouses Point.

*By ferry*: **Lake Champlain Transportation Company** (802-864-9804; ferries.com) offers 14-minute ferry crossings between Gordon's Landing, Grand Isle, and Cumberland Head, NY, year-round, around the clock.

*By train*: **Amtrak** (800-USA-RAIL; amtrak.com). The Vermonter, which has carry-on bike service, runs from St. Albans to Washington, DC. The ticket office is located at 40 Federal Street, St. Albans. Local taxi service is available from the station.

## ✳ Must See

✐ ⟐ **St. Albans Museum** (802-527-7933; stamuseum.com), 9 Church Street (top end of Taylor Park), St. Albans. Open June–October, Wed.–Sat. Admission. This impressive historical society museum, housed in the former Franklin County Grammar School built in 1861, explores the history of St. Albans and the region. Exhibits focus on Abenaki archeology; military history, including the famous St. Albans Raid; rural medicine; period fashion; and notable Franklin County residents. The Railroad Room,

SWANTON'S SWANS LISA HALVORSEN

set up like a century-old waiting room with ticket office and telegraph equipment, tells the story of St. Albans' heyday as a Central Vermont Railroad hub.

*✿* **Hyde Log Cabin** (802-372-5440), US 2, Grand Isle. Open Memorial Day–mid-October, Fri.–Sun. Admission. Built by pioneer and Revolutionary War veteran Jedediah Hyde Jr. in 1783 when this was a wilderness area, accessible only by water, the one-room home is believed to be the oldest original log cabin in New England, and possibly in the United States. The Grand Isle Historical Society has furnished it with eighteenth-century artifacts: furniture, kitchenware, toys, tools, and clothing. Adjacent to the cabin is the **Block Schoolhouse** (originally the District # 4 Schoolhouse). Although built in 1814 as a schoolhouse, it also served as a church and community gathering place.

*✿* ♿ **President Chester A. Arthur State Historic Site** (802-933-8362; historicsites.vermont.gov), 4588 Chester Arthur Road, Fairfield. Open July–mid-October, weekends and Monday holidays. Free but donations appreciated. A 1950s reconstruction of the parsonage where the 21st president lived as an infant contains pictorial exhibits about his life and political career, including the controversy over his birthplace—the US or Canada—which impacted the question of his eligibility for the presidency. The site also has a nature trail and monument marking the location of the cottage where Arthur was born in 1829. Farther down this road is the North Fairfield Church, built in 1840 on the site of

ST. ALBANS MUSEUM LISA HALVORSEN

# A NORTHERN PILGRIMAGE

St. Anne's Shrine (802-928-3362; saintannesshrine.org), 92 St. Anne's Road, Isle La Motte. Open mid-May–mid-October, free admission. Daily outdoor Masses and Sunday services are held here in summer in an open-sided Victorian chapel set on 13 lakeside acres. A gold statue devoted to Our Lady of Lourdes that once stood in the Burlington Cathedral dominates the property, a gift in 1991 from the Burlington Diocese. The shrine has a public beach and picnic area in a large pine grove, presumably descended from what explorer Samuel de Champlain described as "the most beautiful pines I have ever seen" when he stepped ashore in 1609 on this spot. Champlain is honored here with a massive granite statue, which was carved in Vermont's Pavilion at Montreal's Expo 67. This is the site of Vermont's first settlement, a French fort built in 1666. The visitor center has a bookstore, a gift shop, and the History Room, where you can learn about the shrine's heritage and view artifacts and information about the Chazy Fossil Reef. Spiritual retreats are held here, and camping is offered seasonally for those making a pilgrimage. ♂ ⚹

ST. ANNE'S SHRINE  LISA HALVORSEN

the original church where the Reverend William Arthur, his father, preached. The Fairfield Town Hall (802-827-3261) at 25 North Street has a small museum dedicated to Arthur, open weekdays during business hours.

**Cold Hollow Sculpture Park** (512-333-2119; coldhollowsculpturepark.com), 4280 Boston Post Road, Enosburg Falls. Open Thurs.–Sun., late June–early October. Free. Hayfields and meadows serve as a backdrop for more than 50 sculptures created by metal sculptor David Stromeyer. Pick up a map at the information booth for a self-guided walk through the 35-acre

HYDE LOG CABIN  LISA HALVORSEN

park. Or join one of the artist's "walking conversations" where he shares insight into his artistic vision for selected works.

## ✳ To Do

🐾 ✦ **Missisquoi National Wildlife Refuge** (802-868-4781; fws.gov/refuge/missisquoi) includes 6,729 acres on Lake Champlain's eastern shore in Swanton north to Alburgh, including most of the Missisquoi River Delta where it flows into Missisquoi Bay. The refuge began in 1943 under the authority of the Migratory Bird Conservation Act. Predominantly wetlands, it's a mix of habitats, including riverine, floodplain forests, open fields, and hardwood forests, making it attractive to a number of bird, mammal, amphibian, and reptile species. Open from dawn to dusk year-round. The visitor center is open mid-May–mid-October. See *Green Space* on page 379.

BICYCLING With their flat roads, splendid views, and light traffic on back roads, the islands are popular for biking. Stop by the Chamber of Commerce (see *Guidance* on page 371) for a free Champlain Islands Bikeways map/guide, which details five themed loops, or download it at champlainbikeways.org. Isle La Motte is especially well suited to bicycling. The 12.5-mile "Island Line" crosses Lake Champlain from Colchester to South Hero along the rail bed of the old Rutland Railroad. Lake views don't get any better than this, and it's flat to boot. **Local Motion's Island Line bike ferry** (802-861-2700; localmotion.org) transports passengers and bikes across the 200-foot "cut" where a swing bridge once operated to enable trains to cross the lake. The bike ferry operates May–October. Season and day passes are available. A 26.4-mile section of the former Central Vermont Railroad line was converted to the Missisquoi Valley Rail Trail, another popular trail for bicyclists; see sidebar on page 377.
    *Rental bikes:* **Allenholm Bicycle Rental Shop** (802-372-5566; allenholm.com), South Hero; **Hero's Welcome General Store** (802-372-4161; heroswelcome.com), North Hero. For repairs: **Ken's Island Peddler** (802-372-4809), Grand Isle; **White's Bikes and Outfitters** (802-524-4496), Georgia.

BIRDING Located on the Atlantic Flyway, the islands are particularly rich in bird life. Herons, eagles, ospreys, and cormorants, among others, migrate through the area. Prime birding sites include the South Hero Swamp; Mud Creek Wildlife Management Area, Alburgh; and the Sand Bar Wildlife Refuge across from Sand Bar State Park. See also Knight Island and Alburgh Dunes State Parks (Vermont's only sand dunes) under *Swimming* on page 378. Just east of Alburgh, the Missisquoi National Wildlife Refuge (see sidebar on page 377) is the region's prime birding area and protects Shad Island, the largest blue heron rookery in Vermont. Download the **Lake Champlain Birding Trail** brochure at lakechamplainregion.com/outdoors/birding. For wildlife viewing, visit North Hero (protected turtle nesting beach) and Lake Carmi (140-acre peat bog) State Parks (vtstateparks.com).

BOAT EXCURSIONS Captain Holly Poulin of **Driftwood Tours** (802-373-0022), North Hero, operates day tours, sunset and moonlight cruises, and fishing trips on her 23-foot pontoon boat and runs dinner cruises in conjunction with the North Hero House (see *Lodging* on page 380). All trips leave from the **North Hero House Marina**. Ferry service for campers and their gear to Knight Island and Woods Island State Parks and private tours can be arranged.

# THE WORLD'S OLDEST CORAL REEF

Around 480 million years ago, Chazy Reef, which underlies the southern third of Isle La Motte, was a biologically diverse community of some of the earth's earliest invertebrates, including squiggly-mouthed cephalopods, snail-like gastropods, and moss animals known as bryozoa. It's the oldest fossilized coral reef in the world and has been preserved through the efforts of Linda Fitch, owner of the Fisk Farm; the Isle La Motte Preservation Trust; and the Lake Champlain Land Trust. You can search for fossils in the outcroppings at two locations: the Fisk Quarry Preserve and the Goodsell Ridge Preserve (802-862-4150; lclt.org/goodsell-and-fisk-quarry-preserves). The latter also has an interpretive center (open seasonally) where you can explore the reef's history and geology before taking the 1-mile Walk Through Time trail. Descriptive panels in the meadows and cedar forests lay out a timeline of the earth's evolution, explaining the changes that occurred. Each foot of the exhibit represents approximately a million years of the earth's natural history.

The Fisk Marble Quarries on West Shore Road, the oldest in the state, were used by the French in 1664 to make a kiln for Fort St. Anne, Vermont's first colonial settlement. The Fisk family acquired them in the 1780s and worked them for more than four generations. In 1884 the quarries passed to Nelson W. Fisk, who recognized their potential for high-end construction material. When polished, this black marble was magnificent, a coveted medium for façades such as New York's Radio City Music Hall, the US Capitol building, and the Vermont Statehouse. In 1897, as lieutenant governor, he hosted President William McKinley at the family mansion, now the site of Fisk Farm. It was while Vice President Teddy Roosevelt was visiting in 1901 that McKinley was fatally shot, and it fell on Fisk to break the news to the next president.

Among the exhibits at the nearby Isle La Motte Historical Society (802-928-3422), 24 Quarry Road, Isle La Motte, is a piece of local stone, partially polished to marble, graphically illustrating its value as building material. The museum, comprising an 1840s stone schoolhouse, a slab-log cabin, and a blacksmith shop, also displays the cane chair used by McKinley and Roosevelt during their stays at the Fisk mansion and the industrial looms of weaving entrepreneur Elizabeth Fisk, who, with her prominent husband, were their hosts. Open Sat. afternoons, July–August, and by appointment. Admission.

FOSSILS AT GOODSELL RIDGE PRESERVE LISA HALVORSEN

FERRIES Instead of a tour, take the Grand Isle-Cumberland Head Ferry (802-864-9804; ferries.com) to get out on Lake Champlain. It operates daily, year-round, around the clock. A one-way trip lasts 14 minutes, and only cash is accepted, although there's an ATM at the dock. Or take the seasonal ferry to **Burton Island State Park** (802-524-6021; vtstateparks.com) from **Kamp Kill Kare State Park** in St. Albans.

BOATING Rental boats are available in North Hero from **New England Power Boat Service** (802-372-5131; nepbvt.com) and **North Hero Marina** (802-372-5953; northheromarina.com). **Hero's Welcome General Store** (802-372-4161; heroswelcome .com) and the **North Hero House Marina** (802-372-4732; northherohouse.com) rent kayaks and canoes only. In South Hero, **Apple Island Resort Marina** (802-372-3922; appleislandresort.com) offers powerboats, kayaks, canoes, rowboats, and pontoon boats. **Ladd's Landing Marina** (802-372-5320; laddslandingmarina.com), at the bridge in Grand Isle, rents sailboats, small motorboats, canoes, kayaks, rowboats, and boat slips. Canoe, kayak, rowboat, and pedal-boat rentals also are available at several Vermont State Parks (888-409-7579; vtstateparks.com), including **Alburgh Dunes**, **Burton Island**, **Grand Isle**, **Kill Kare**, **Knight Point**, and **Lake Carmi**.

FISHING Lake Champlain is considered one of the finest freshwater lakes for fishing in the country. With the right bait and a little luck, you can catch trout, salmon, walleye, bass, pike, and several other species. **The Missisquoi National Wildlife Refuge** (see sidebar on page 378 and *Birding* on page 374) is a source of walleye, northern pike, largemouth bass, bullhead, white perch, and yellow perch.

**Bronzeback Guide Service** (802-868-4459; bronzebackguideservice.com), 2934 US 7, Highgate Springs, is a fully equipped charter offering guided fishing tours, bait and tackle, ice fishing trips, and shanty rentals.

LAKE CARMI STATE PARK  LISA HALVORSEN

# RAILS-TO-TRAILS RECREATION

**M**ississquoi Valley Rail Trail (802-524-5958; mvrailtrail.com). The 26.4-mile recreational path, once the route of the Central Vermont Railroad, runs from St. Albans to Sheldon Junction, then winds along the Missisquoi River (and VT 105) to Enosburg Falls and up to Richford at the Canadian border. It's open for cross-country skiing, biking, walking, snowmobiling, and leisurely strolling—but not for ATVs, off-road vehicles, or dirt bikes. Most people do the trail in segments, given the length and round-trip factor. A trail guide and map with details on access points, parking, and other handy information is available by request or online from the Northwest Regional Planning Commission (802-524-5958; mvrailtrail.org). See *Bicycling* on page 374 for rental and repair shops.

Fishing is popular at many of the state parks (vtstateparks.com). Vermont fishing licenses are required for anyone 15 or older; info at vtfishandwildlife.com.

GOLF ⚙ **Alburg Golf Links** (802-796-3586; alburggolflinks.com), 230 VT 129, Alburgh, 3 miles west of South Alburgh; 18-hole course on the shores of Lake Champlain with gentle, shady terrain and mountain views. **Links on the Lake Restaurant and Bar** serves lunch and dinner, Mon.–Sat., and brunch on Sunday, 10–2, during golf season.

**Apple Island Resort** (802-372-9600; appleislandresort.com), 71 US 2, South Hero. A nine-hole, par-3 golf course. Pro shop, rental carts, and clubs.

**Bakersfield Country Club** (802-933-5100), 7595 Old Boston Post Road, Bakersfield. An 18-hole course with stunning views, including from the hilltop clubhouse.

**Champlain Country Club** (802-527-1187; champlaincountryclub.com), 581 St. Albans Road (US 7), Swanton, 3 miles north of St. Albans. A challenging 18-hole course, built in 1915, with a play time of around four hours. Pro shop and clubhouse restaurant.

**Enosburg Falls Country Club** (802-933-2296; efccvt.com), 53 Elm Street, Enosburg Falls. A reasonably priced 18-hole course with friendly staff and good views from the restaurant.

**Richford Country Club** (802-848-3527), 249 Golf Course Road, Richford. A hilly, scenic nine holes, just a half-mile from the Canadian border. Established in 1929.

HISTORICAL ATTRACTIONS ✐ **Abenaki Tribal Museum and Cultural Center** (802-868-2559), 100 Grand Avenue, Swanton. Usually open Mon.–Fri. 9–4 (call ahead to confirm). The headquarters for the Abenaki Tribal Council houses a small museum, with clothing, tools, and crafts. The stars of this exhibit are the ceremonial headdresses, canoes, and the intricate handwoven baskets. A mile north of Swanton on Monument Road is the former site of an Abenaki Christian mission, marked by a historical marker and totem pole.

✐ ♿ **The Swanton Historical Society Railroad Depot Museum** (802-868-5436; swantonhistoricalsociety.org), 58 South River Street, Swanton. Open Tues.–Sat., in summer; by appointment the rest of the year. The museum is housed in a restored 1890s train depot, relocated to this site to save it from the wrecking ball. Note the separate waiting rooms for ladies and men and the scores of historical photos and artifacts that tell the story of the railroad's impact on the area. A 1937 Missisquoi Bay Bridge tollhouse, 1910 Central Vermont Railway caboose, and the foundation of a roundhouse can be viewed on the grounds. Opposite the museum, a restored 1902 Pennsylvania truss bridge marks the start of a 1-mile walking path, the first section of the 93-mile **Lamoille**

# WHERE THE BIRDS ARE

**T**he Missisquoi National Wildlife Refuge (802-868-4781; fws.gov/refuge/missisquoi), 29 Tabor Road, 6 miles northwest of Swanton, off VT 78. The visitor center is open May–October, Mon.–Sat.; call to confirm hours. Grounds are open dawn–dusk, year-round. This 6,729-acre wildlife and waterfowl refuge provides habitat for more than 200 species of birds. Raptors, marsh birds, songbirds, and great blue herons are frequent visitors, and migratory birds stop over on their voyage from northern breeding areas to wintering areas farther south. Most of the refuge is accessible only by boat (see *Boating* on page 376) although there are a number of trails for hiking. The Black Creek and Maquam Creek Trails wind through meadow, woods, and marsh for about 1.5 miles (a two-hour ramble), with interpretive markers for flora and fauna. The walking trails convert to cross-country ski use in winter. Ask for a trail map at the visitor center, which also has exhibits on local geology, history of human habitation, and bird and animal life. In July and August, you can pick blueberries in the bog off Tabor Road, not far from the center.

**Valley Rail Trail** (802-229-0005; friendslvrt.org), which will extend from Swanton to St. Johnsbury when completed.

✎ **Vermont State Parks** (888-409-7579; vtstateparks.com). Vermont's Northwest Corner has eight state parks—nine if you count Sand Bar State Park in Milton at the southern gateway to the Champlain Islands—all with water access for swimming, some with access for boating; and many with nature centers, trails, and special activities such as evening music concerts. Structures in some can be linked to the Civilian Conservation Corps, created during the Great Depression to provide employment for young men.

SWIMMING ✎ **Alburgh Dunes State Park** (802-796-4170; vtstateparks.com), 151 Coon Point Road, Alburgh. Popular with locals, this park features the longest sandy beach on Lake Champlain. Its shallow, protected waters make it an excellent swimming spot for young ones. It's also a standout for its rare flora and fauna. Call for directions or ask locally.

✎ **Knight Point State Park** (802-372-8389; vtstateparks.com), 44 Knight Point Road, North Hero. This 54-acre park, located on the southern tip of North Hero, has a quiet

SWANTON HISTORICAL SOCIETY RAILROAD DEPOT MUSEUM   LISA HALVORSEN

sandy beach and a nature trail that loops around the point. From the beach you can watch boats pass through the drawbridge between the islands. Canoes and rowboats are available for rent, and there are picnic tables with grills.

✎ **Sand Bar State Park** (802-893-2825; vtstateparks.com), 1215 US 2, Milton, fills to capacity on sunny weekends in summer, but during the week it's a quiet oasis, with its shallow, sandy beach and adjacent 1,000-acre wildlife refuge. The park has picnic tables, cooking grills, and a play area for children. Canoes, kayaks, and stand-up paddleboards are available for rent.

❦ **Lake Carmi State Park** (802-933-8393; vtstateparks.com) near Enosburg Falls is the largest state park campground with two beaches for campers (see *Green Space* below). It has a day-use swimming area with a nature center and boat rentals.

Grand Isle, Kamp Kill Kare, and Burton Island State Parks also have beaches, leaving the region with no shortage of places to take a dip.

## ✳ Winter Sports

CROSS-COUNTRY SKIING/SNOWSHOEING ❦ **Hard'ack Recreation Area** (802-370-2380; stalbansvt.myrec.com), 179 Congress Street, St. Albans, offers a free, local outdoor space for families with groomed cross-country ski trails, snowshoe trails, ice skating, sledding, and even downhill skiing and snowboarding with a 700-foot rope tow; bring your own equipment.

**Hero's Welcome General Store** (802-372-4161; heroswelcome.com) in North Hero rents cross-country skis and snowshoes.

ICE FISHING By mid-January the season is in high gear, typically lasting until March, depending on "ice-out." Missisquoi Bay and the numerous smaller bays and access points of the Champlain Islands from Alburgh Passage west to the broad lake or east to the inland sea are popular fishing spots. Information on licenses, fees, maps, and safety protocol can be found at vtfishandwildlife.com.

ICE SKATING ❦ **Collins Perley Sports & Fitness Center** (802-527-1202; maplerun .org/o/cpsc), 890 Fairfax Road, St. Albans, has a public skating rink with rentals.

❦ **Hard'ack Rec Area** operates a free public rink; equipment rentals are not available.

❦ Ice skating on **Lake Champlain** when North Hero Bay is frozen is quintessential Vermont winter fun. A variety of skate rentals can be found across the street at **Hero's Welcome General Store** (802-372-4191; heroswelcome.com).

## ✳ Green Space

❦ ♿ **Ed Weed Fish Culture Station** (802-372-3171; vtfishandwildlife.com), 14 Fish Hatchery Road, Grand Isle (2 miles from US 2 on VT 314; turn right at the hatchery sign), open daily. Free. Fish are brought to the facility as freshly spawned eggs (up to 2.2 million eggs at any one time), incubated, and then transferred to a series of tanks. Interactive exhibits, video, and freshwater aquariums introduce visitors to Lake Champlain's fish species. The retention pond has a wildlife blind for observing waterfowl.

**Mud Creek Wildlife Management Area** (vtfishandwildlife.com) on VT 78, Alburgh, has nature trails and is an excellent spot for viewing ducks and other birds.

Also see the **Missisquoi National Wildlife Refuge** (see sidebar on page 378). This is the area's largest nature preserve and includes a major interpretive center, worth a stop even if you lack the time to walk, fish, or boat here.

❦ **Fisk Quarry Preserve** and **Goodsell Ridge** on Isle La Motte are described in the sidebar, *The World's Oldest Coral Reef* on page 375.

❦ **St. Albans Bay Park** (802-524-7589; stalbanstown.com), 4 miles west on VT 36, is ideal for family picnics, with several tables and grills along the waterfront, but the water is too shallow and weedy for decent swimming.

⚓ **Kamp Kill Kare State Park** (802-524-6021; vtstateparks.com), 2714 Hathaway Point Road (off VT 36), St. Albans Bay. Once the site of a fashionable summer hotel and then, for years, a boys' summer camp, the 17-acre property was purchased by the Vermont State Parks system in 1967. Although many of the buildings were demolished, the original hotel building was not, and today it houses a small museum with exhibits on the site's history. Surrounded on three sides by the lake, the park affords beautiful views and can be crowded on weekends, but it's usually blissfully quiet other days; swimming beach, playgrounds, boat launch, rowboat rentals, and shuttle (fee) to Burton Island.

**Burton Island State Park** (802-524-6353; vtstateparks.com), a lovely, 253-acre island, is reached from Kill Kare by park boat or on your own. Facilities include 14 tent sites, 26 lean-tos, three cabins, four remote tent sites, and a 100-slip marina with electrical hookups and 15 moorings. Campers' gear is transported to campsites by park vehicle. Fishing off this beautiful haven is usually excellent. Nature center, museum, swimming beach, hiking trails, and boat rentals. **Burton Island Bistro** (802-524-2212) serves breakfast and lunch on weekdays. Day-use is permitted.

🐾 ⚓ **Lake Carmi State Park** (802-933-8383; vtstateparks.com), 460 Marsh Farm Road, Enosburg Falls. Set in rolling farmlands, the 482-acre park has 138 tent/RV sites, the largest camping area in the state. Facilities include two cabins and 35 lean-tos, some on the beach of this sizable lake; nature trails, nature center, boat ramp, and boat rentals. Lake Carmi is the state's fourth-largest state park.

# ❋ Lodging

## ISLANDS

*Note:* See *Guidance* on page 371. The chamber of commerce lists numerous vacation rentals and lakeside cottages.

RESORTS ♂ ⚓ ♿ **North Hero House** (802-372-4732; northherohouse.com), 3643 US 2, North Hero. This century-old summer hotel has a lakeside-resort feel and stunning views. Owner Walter Blasberg has made substantial improvements over the past two decades to the inn, which includes 26 guest rooms and suites, many with private porch, located in the main inn and in three buildings clustered at the water's edge. Guests can enjoy the glass-enclosed greenhouse sitting area and dining at Oscar's Oasis pub, the Main Dining Room (see *Dining Out* on page 385), and the waterside Steamship Pier Bar & Grill (open seasonally). The North Hero House Marina features a long, grassy dock at which Champlain steamers once docked; boat and slip rentals are available. Try paddle surfing, fishing, or a sunset cruise. Check the website for special events, including their Murder Mystery Dinners, and packages. $–$$.

♂ 🐾 ⚓ **Shore Acres Inn & Restaurant** (802-372-8722; shoreacres.com), 237 Shore Acres Drive, North Hero. Open April–December. Set in sweeping, peaceful, beautifully groomed grounds, 23 comfortable rooms face the lake and the Green Mountains. Four of the guest rooms are in the garden house, a longer walk. The rooms are decorated with locally handcrafted furniture. Breakfast is included, and dinner can be enjoyed in the Lake Champlain Room (see *Dining Out* on page 384). Amenities include lawn chairs, two clay tennis courts, a driving range, lawn games, game room, waterfront dockings and moorings, and a 1.5-mile private shore for swimming. $–$$.

## INNS AND BED & BREAKFASTS

### IN ALBURGH

♂ **The Ransom Bay Inn** (802-796-3399; ransombayinn.com), 4 Center Bay Road, Alburgh. Open May–December. Originally a stagecoach stop, this beautiful stone house built circa 1795 is set back from US 2 and is within walking distance of a small beach. Innkeepers Richard and Lorraine Walker speak English and French and have maintained the inn to be worthy of its Vermont State Register of Historic Places designation. The four guest rooms are nicely furnished with period antiques. Rates include a full breakfast with their specialty, homemade croissant French toast. Seasonal dining is available seven days a week in summer; reservations recommended. (See *Dining Out* on page 385.) $.

✎ **Thomas Mott Homestead B&B** (802-796-4402; thomas-mott-bb.com), 63 Blue Rock Road, Alburgh. Open May–October. This 1830s lakeside farmhouse is splendidly sited on a quiet back road along Alburgh's eastern shore, handy to the Missisquoi National Wildlife Refuge and located on the Lake Champlain Bikeways route. Hosts Susan and Bob Cogley are longtime residents delighted to help plan your stay in the area. The four Victorian-style guest rooms all have lake views. Guests are welcome to swim, fish, and play horseshoes or croquet. Rates include a hearty breakfast that might include homemade yogurt and treats made from local produce. Dinner available upon request. Children over 12 welcome. $–$$.

### IN GRAND ISLE

✎ **Adams Landing** (802-372-4830; adamslandingvt.com), 1 Adams Landing Road Extension, Grand Isle. Open year-round; closed Mon.–Tues. In this lovely big, rambling, secluded house on the west shore, Sally Coppersmith and Jack Sartore offer two rooms with shared bath and a suite with private bath, a fridge, and library. Rates include breakfast and afternoon refreshments. Children 11 and older welcome. Inquire about Kelsey House, a fully equipped two-bedroom house with a lovely wraparound porch overlooking Lake Champlain adjacent to the inn. $–$$.

♂ ✎ **Ferry Watch Inn** (802-372-3935; ferrywatchinn.com), 121 West Shore Road, Grand Isle. Open May–November. This wonderfully restored home, built in 1800, overlooks the broad lake with spectacular views of the Adirondacks and ferry crossings. Janet and Troy Wert offer three guest rooms (two with shared bath) with antique double beds. A historic barn is available for weddings and events. $.

### IN SOUTH HERO

✎ **Allenholm Orchards Bed & Breakfast** (802-372-5566; allenholm.com), 150 South Street, South Hero. Open year-round. Pam and Ray Allen offer the Island Orchard Suite—a bedroom furnished in family antiques, including a queen-size canopy bed, a large living room with an additional bed, and a full-size pool table, as well as a full private bath and patio. The suite is on the lower level of the Allens' modern home, adjacent to their orchard, Vermont's oldest commercial orchard. A country breakfast featuring homegrown apples is served upstairs in the dining room or, if you prefer, on your patio. $–$$.

✪ **Crescent Bay Farm** (802-324-5563; crescentbaybb.com), 153 West Shore Road, South Hero. Open May–October; off-season by prior arrangement. This restored 1820s farmhouse is a working farm near **Snow Farm Vineyard** (802-372-9463; snowfarm.com), also owned by the innkeepers Dave and Julie Lane. The four comfortable guest rooms, three with en suite bathrooms, are furnished with country antiques. The Lanes operate this working homestead, raising llamas for wool and home-spun yarn; you'll also find pigs, a maple sugaring operation, cats and dogs, flower gardens, lake views, and one of the many miniature stone castles scattered around the Champlain Islands. Full breakfast included. $$.

ELSEWHERE

⚓ **Ruthcliffe Lodge & Restaurant** (802-928-3200; ruthcliffe.com), 1002 Quarry Road, Isle La Motte. Open mid-May–mid-October. This lakeside compound at the end of Quarry Road includes a small motel and lodge with a total of six rooms, many with lakeside panoramas. Mark and Kathy Infante include a full country breakfast with the stay. Multicourse Italian-American dinners are served nightly in-season. There's a 40-foot, water's-edge patio for dining, as well as the cozy knotty-pine dining room in the lodge. Swimming and fishing are right outside the front door; rental boats and bikes are available. Inquire about the Meadow House cottage rental and different packages. $–$$.

HOUSEKEEPING COTTAGES ⚓ 🏊 ♿

**Fisk Farm** (802-928-3364; fiskfarm .com), 3849 West Shore Road, Isle La Motte. Open May–October. Owner Linda Fitch offers two lovely guest cottages for weekly rentals (shorter periods considered in early and late season) on the site of the former Fisk family estate, which was where Vice President Theodore Roosevelt first heard the news that President William McKinley had been shot in 1901. The three-bedroom Hemond House in the village center also is available to rent. In summer Fisk Farm hosts Sunday-afternoon teas with live music and showcases the work of local artists in a renovated horse barn. See *Entertainment* on page 387. $–$$.

CAMPGROUNDS See Kamp Kill Kare, Burton Island, and Lake Carmi State Parks under *Green Space* on page 379. The complete rundown on state parks is at vtstateparks.com. For a list of private campgrounds and RV parks, visit the

PLAQUE AT FISK FARM  LISA HALVORSEN

Vermont Campground Association's website (campvermont.com).

🐾 🏊 **Apple Island Resort** (802-372-3800; appleislandresort.com), 71 US 2, South Hero. Open May–October. Lakefront camping and an RV campground that includes RV site rentals with hookups and campsite, cottage, and cabin rentals. A fully operational resort with a marina (see *Boating*), golf course (see *Golf*), and store. The **Arnold Zlotoff Tool Museum**, open Saturdays in-season, is located on the grounds of the resort.

🐾 🏊 **Grand Isle State Park** (802-372-4300; vtstateparks.com), 36 East Shore Road South, Grand Isle. Open mid-May–mid-October. Vermont's second-largest (and most visited) state campground has 117 tent/trailer campsites, 36 lean-tos (no hookups), and four cabins on 226 acres, with a beach, playground, nature trail, nature center, and recreation building. This family-friendly campground is perfect for smaller children and a family's first camping trip. Campers also have free entry to **Knight Point State Park** and **Alburgh Dunes State Park**.

🏊 **Homestead Campground** (802-524-2356; homesteadcampground.net), 864 Ethan Allen Highway (US 7), Georgia, (I-89, Exit 18) offers 160 shaded campsites with water and electric hookups, laundry facilities, hot showers, cabin and camper rentals, a playground, and two swimming pools. Seasonal RV rentals; late April–mid-October.

**Knight Island State Park** by way of **Burton Island State Park** (802-524-6353). The *Island Runner* (802-524-6353), a ferry operating between Memorial Day and Labor Day by the state, crosses the water to Knight Island on weekends from Kamp Kill Kare State Park and Burton Island every few hours, weekdays only from Burton Island. There's also an optional gear delivery service. The seven campsites at Knight Island are primitive—even clothing is optional! To maximize privacy, campsites are hidden from public view.

**Woods Island State Park** (802-524-6353), 2 miles north of Burton Island. Primitive camping is available on this 125-acre island. Five widely spaced campsites with no facilities are linked by a trail. The island is unstaffed, although there are daily ranger patrols; reservations for campsites must be made through Burton Island State Park (see above). No public transportation to the island; the best boat access is from Kamp Kill Kare State Park.

## ST. ALBANS AND BEYOND

RESORT ✥ ♿ **Tyler Place Family Resort** (802-868-4000; tylerplace.com), 175 Tyler Place, Highgate Springs. Open late May–mid-September. All-inclusive stays are usually Sat.–Sat. One of the country's oldest family resorts, founded in 1933, the 165-acre resort has many guests who return year after year to enjoy the heated indoor and outdoor swimming and wading pools, tennis courts, kayaking, fishing, sailboarding, and more. Yoga, massage, and a variety of workshops are offered for adults with age-appropriate activities for younger guests. Accommodations include 70 cottages and two-bedroom family suites in a contemporary inn, more than 40 with a fireplace. The inn has a spacious dining room with good food and a big lounge with a bar.

Reduced-rate packages are available in early and late season. $.

BED & BREAKFASTS ♂ ☀ **Tabor House Inn** (802-868-7575; taborhouseinn.com), 58 Homestead Street, West Swanton. This 1890s mansion on the shores of Maquam Bay borders the **Missisquoi National Wildlife Refuge**. Innkeeper Jennifer Neville Bright attended an auction held by the previous owners, never intending to buy the place. The five guest rooms include the spacious Lake Shore Suite with a private balcony and Jacuzzi, upstairs above the well-named "Great Room." A 60-foot, screened-in porch overlooks the lawn and lake. A full breakfast is included, and dinner can be arranged—not a bad idea, because you probably won't want to stir once you are here. Bright also owns the **1906 House** in Enosburg Falls. $–$$.

♂ ☀ ✥ **Back Inn Time** (802-527-5116; backinntimevt.com), 68 Fairfield Street, St. Albans. Built by a wealthy merchant named Victor Atwood in 1858, the inn, now owned by Ron and KarenMarie Peltier, is an easy walk from the center of town. The living room, chandeliered dining room, and library of this handsome Victorian look much as they would have in the 1860s, but the five guest rooms, including two with fireplace, are all modern luxury. Bedding and toiletries are of optimal quality, a hint of the relaxation to come with an on-site massage, concert, or cooking class. Breakfast is included, although dinner is by reservation only. There's also a self-catering apartment. $–$$

🐾 ☀ ✥ ♿ **Buck Hollow Farm** (802-849-2400; buckhollow.com), 2150 Buck Hollow Road, Fairfax. Open year-round. Each of the four rooms in the beautifully renovated 1790s carriage house includes antiques—a passion of innkeepers Brad and Jacquie Schwartz—and a queen-size four-poster bed. Guests are encouraged to use the outdoor hot tub and the heated pool or to browse the antiques shop. In winter there's cross-country skiing on the 400-acre property. A full country breakfast is included. A number of special discounts and special weekends are offered, especially November–April. $–$$.

♂ **The 1906 House** (802-933-3030; the1906house.com); 527 Main Street, Enosburg Falls. This colonial revival house with *porte cochere* was originally built for Moses Perley, a prominent dry goods store owner. Jennifer Neville Bright bought the property in 2014, turning the century-old home into a stunning six-room inn and events venue, preserving the hardwood floors and other original features as much as possible. The rooms are all named after local towns; three have shared baths. Full breakfast included. Note to skiers: The inn is nicely situated between Jay Peak and Stowe Mountain Resort. Jennifer also owns the **Tabor House Inn** (802-868-7575) in West Swanton. $–$$.

## ✳ Where to Eat

### THE ISLANDS

DINING OUT ⅙ **Blue Paddle Bistro** (802-372-4814; bluepaddlebistro.com) 316 US 2, South Hero. Open year-round for dinner. Days and hours vary by season. This colorful gathering place showcases local art in the upstairs dining room. To get it off the ground, owners Mandy Hotchkiss and Phoebe Bright gave paddles to investors. Now the paddles cover the walls, and the unpretentious café hums with activity year-round as guests enjoy entrées such as crab-stuffed ravioli, coffee-crusted pork tenderloin, or the half-pound paddle burger, a house favorite. Outdoor deck in summer. $$–$$$.

⅙ **Lake Champlain Room at Shore Acres Inn & Restaurant** (802-372-8722; shoreacres.com), 237 Shore Acres Drive, North Hero. Open April–December,

**BLUE PADDLE BISTRO** LISA HALVORSEN

hours and days vary by season. It's dining with a view here; the dining room's large windows command a sweeping vista of the lake, with Mount Mansfield and its flanking peaks in the distance. Chef Dan Rainville incorporates local produce and meats in his menu, catering to the needs of both picky eaters and more adventurous palates. For smaller appetites, the restaurant offers bistro plates. Reservations for dinner, especially in summer and fall foliage season, are recommended. $$–$$$.

✪ **North Hero House Main Dining Room** (802-372-4732; northherohouse .com), 3643 US 2, North Hero. Open year-round, weekends only in the off-season, daily in busier seasons; call ahead. Reservations recommended. Dine on the glassed-in, lake-view veranda of the historic old inn, at one of the umbrella-covered tables on the lawn and outdoor patio, or in the glass-covered greenhouse (also used for private parties). Produce is grown in on-premise gardens. **The Steamship Pier Bar & Grill** is open July and August on the waterfront at the North Hero House Marina—a sought-after spot in summer. $–$$$.

((ŋ)) **Ransom Bay Inn** (802-796-3399; ransombayinn-vt.com), 4 Center Bay Road, Alburgh. Open for dinner daily in summer, some weekends in other seasons; call ahead. Longtime innkeepers Richard and Lorraine Walker, both culinary school graduates, have created an attractive dining space downstairs in their historic stone inn. In summer, tables are set on a deck overlooking the garden. In fall, there's fireside dining. $–$$$.

EATING OUT 🍴 **Cook Sisters Café and Catering** (802-372-0101); 308 US 2, South Hero. Open year-round, Tues.–Sat. Brunch served on Saturdays. The menu at this cozy 18-seat farmhouse restaurant, named for chef-owner Christine Mack's mother and aunts, changes with the season, but patrons can expect reasonably priced options featuring local

foods. Gluten-free and other dietary requests accommodated. Eat-in or take-out.

**Hero's Welcome General Store** (802-372-4161; heroswelcome.com), 3537 US 2, North Hero. Open daily year-round. An upscale general store and island institution that serves deli sandwiches, many named for Vermont historical figures; baked goods and coffee with waterside seating.

**No Name Tiki Bar & Grill at North Hero Marina** (802-372-3900; northheromarina.com), 2253 Pelot's Point Road, North Hero. Open May–September. It's not gourmet, but there's a full bar with six beers on tap and unbeatable views at this tiny lakeside restaurant. Boaters should call ahead to make sure dock space is available.

✪ **Papa Pete's Snack Bar** (no phone), 35 Bridge Road, North Hero. Days spent lolling in nature call for barbecue, and this is the only place on the islands to get it. Pulled pork and ribs emerge from a pig-shaped smoker at this seasonal stand located at the junction of North Hero and Alburgh. Or you can try the Reuben balls or poutine, hand-cut fries smothered in gravy and topped with real Canadian cheese curds.

**South End Café at Hall's Orchard** (802-928-3091), 4445 Main Street, Isle La Motte. Located in a renovated carriage barn attached to the main stone house, the café is open May–October (days vary, call ahead) for breakfast and light luncheon fare, mainly homemade pastries and sandwiches. The real draw is the stock of sweet-but-potent ice ciders pressed on the premises.

ST. ALBANS & SWANTON

DINING OUT ✪ 🍴 **One Federal Restaurant & Lounge** (802-524-0330; onefederalrestaurant.com), 1 Federal Street, St. Albans. Open daily for lunch and dinner. Chef Marcus Hamblett uses produce from Vermont farms to supply this classic American restaurant, which he and his wife Erica opened in the historic St. Albans Foundry and Implement Co. building in 2009. The food is prepared with exceptional flavor and polish. Start with poutine or frickles, uber-thin pickle slices deep fried in batter and served with zesty ranch dipping sauce—which are the house specialty. For a true taste of terroir, try the Vermonter burger, a local beef patty stacked with Cabot cheddar, crispy bacon, and grilled apples, then drizzled with maple syrup. Outdoor seating and concert series in summer. $$–$$$.

&. **Mill River Brewery BBQ & Smokehouse** (802-582-4182; millriverbrewing .com), 10 Beauregard Drive, St. Albans. Open Wed.–Sun. Co-owner and brew master Dan Fitzgerald's passion for making beer and gathering friends together to sample the latest with a home-cooked meal fostered the idea of a family-run restaurant and brew house. Mainstays on the menu are barbecue platters, including a sampler of three meats and two sides, with all meats smoked in-house. There are also burgers, sandwiches, wraps, and entrées ranging from shepherd's pie to pan-seared salmon. Pints and flights of their brews are available, including their award-winning Pour George Pilsner. $–$$$.

EATING OUT ✔ &. ((ŋ)) **Bayside Pavilion** (802-524-0909), 15 Georgia Shore Road, St. Albans. Open daily. From Taylor Park follow Lake Street for 4 miles until it dead ends at Lake Champlain. The eatery, which opened as Barker's Restaurant in 1921, has a strong local following. It offers a full bar, kids' menu, live music on weekends, and ample portions for moderate prices. In summer, ask to be seated on the dock overlooking St. Albans Bay.

🦞 ✔ &. **Maple City Diner** (802-528-8400), 17 Swanton Road, St. Albans. Open daily for breakfast, lunch, and dinner. Maple is indeed the theme at this diner owned by the couple behind One Federal. Sap buckets, antique taps,

and other maple-themed paraphernalia decorate the walls, and bacon waffles drenched in maple butter are a local favorite. Don't have time for a meal? Grab a maple sticky bun or giant cupcake.

✔ ((ŋ)) **Mimmo's Pizzeria Restaurant** (802-524-2244; mimmositalian.com) 22 South Main Street, St. Albans. Domenico (Mimmo) Spano grew up in Italy and continues to emphasize Euro hospitality at his casual pizzeria. New York-style pizza, pasta, calzones, and sandwiches make up most of the menu, but leave room for a big plate of fried-to-order zeppoli. Mimmo's has a second location at 4 Carmichael Street, Essex Junction (802-288-9494).

((ŋ)) **Thai House** (802-524-0999), 339 Swanton Road, St. Albans. Open for lunch and dinner except Sunday. There's a wide selection of well-prepared Thai favorites here, but also some showstoppers, including whole fried fish and soufflé-like Thai custard with sticky rice.

✔ ((ŋ)) **Twiggs Gastropub** (802-524-1405; twiggsvt.com), 24 North Main Street, St. Albans. This inviting Main Street eatery offers reasonably priced food and a good selection of Vermont craft beers, boutique wines, and signature cocktails in a cozy setting. Hand-formed Angus beef burgers, gourmet mac 'n cheese with house-made beer cheese sauce, flatbreads, and sandwiches make up the bulk of the upscale-pub menu, but there are also soups, salads, and other dinner options, including beer-battered fish and chips and baked haddock. Kids' menu.

COFFEE SHOPS For coffee and light fare in St. Albans, stop by the **Catalyst Coffee Bar** (802-393-9808; catalyst coffeebar.com), 22 North Main Street, for syphon-brewed coffee and sweet and savory bites; **The Traveled Cup** (802-524-2037), 94 North Main Street, for home-made soups and sandwiches; or **The Grind Café** (802-393-8205; roastedvt

.cafe), 34 South Main Street, which roasts its own coffees in-house.

## ✳ Entertainment

❂ ♂ ♪ **Music at Snow Farm Vineyard** (802-372-9463; snowfarm.com), 190 West Shore Road, South Hero. Join the locals for the Thursday-evening summer music series on the vineyard's lawn. The music ranges, over the course of the season, from classical to jazz to classic rock. It's free. Just bring a picnic and a chair (bug spray is a good idea, too). You can buy wine, craft beer, and dinner, including wood-fired pizza. Picnicking begins at 5 with music at 6:30. The winery hosts its **Winter Wine Down Music Series** Friday evenings, November–March, featuring wine tastings, local musicians, and food. Dinner can be ordered on-site.

❂ ♂ **The Arts at Fisk Farm** (802-928-3364; fiskfarm.com), 3849 West Shore Road, Isle La Motte. A music series in the Fisk Farm Tea Gardens runs Sunday afternoons, June–September, with arts and crafts shows in the Horse & Carriage Barn. Free except for refreshments. Admission is charged for the Pro-Series Concerts in the Barn—music by professional chamber groups on select Saturdays in June, July, and August. Both are sponsored by the Isle La Motte Preservation Trust. See also *Lodging*.

♂ **The Islands Center for Arts and Recreation** (802-372-4174) schedules events at **Knight Point State Park** (802-372-8389) in North Hero, including Music in the Park and performances of the world-famous Herrmann's Royal Lipizzan Stallions each summer. Information is available on the event calendars at vtstateparks.com or champlainislands .com.

♂ ♿ **Enosburg Falls Opera House** (802-933-6171; enosburgoperahouse.org), 123 Depot Street, Enosburg Falls. This 1892 structure fell into decades of disuse until the community rallied to raise the necessary funds to restore it. The intimate stage is the site for year-round events, including Vermont Symphony Orchestra concerts, plays, musicals, and a variety of live-music events. Tickets and schedules online.

♂ **Grand Isle Lake House** (802-372-5024; grandislelakehouse.com), 34 East Shore Road, Grand Isle. Built on Robinson's Point as the Island Villa Hotel in 1903, this is a classic mansard-roofed 25-room summer hotel with a wrap-around porch, set on 55 acres of lawn with lake views. From 1957 until 1993 it was a girls' summer camp run by the Sisters of Mercy. Since 1997 it has been owned by the Preservation Trust of Vermont and plays host to a variety of public concerts, including the Vermont Symphony Orchestra; it is available for large weddings and retreats.

## ✳ Selective Shopping

ANTIQUES The usual count is a half-dozen shops, but they are all seasonal and tend to close as one thing, open as another. Standbys include the **Back Chamber Antiques Store** (802-372-4347) 3585 US 2, North Hero; and **Tinkers Barn** (802-372-4754), 479 US 2, South Hero.

ART GALLERIES AND CRAFTS STUDIOS **McGuire Family Furniture Makers & Vermont Clock Company** (802-928-4190; vermontclock.com), 239 Main Street, Isle La Motte. Open year-round, but call first. Two generations of this talented family are involved in the day-to-day production of antique reproduction furniture in spare, heirloom, Shaker, and eighteenth-century designs: pegleg tables, grandfather clocks, dressers—anything you want designed, some of it surprisingly affordable. The McGuires also handcraft replica Shaker and early American clocks.

(ᵞₚᵞ) **Grand Isle Art Works** (802-378-4591; grandisleartworks.com), 259 US 2, Grand Isle. Open Wed.–Sun.; hours vary by season. Check the website for

TINKERS BARN  LISA HALVORSEN

updates. Housed in a quirky 1797 farm-house, this gallery displays and sells art from a wide selection of Vermont artists, both well known and obscure. **The Café at the Gallery** serves edible art of its own, using locally sourced ingredients.

**GreenTARA Space** (802-355-2150; greentaraspace.com), 3275 US 2, North Hero. The gallery, named for the Tibetan goddess of enlightened activity, houses art exhibits and a coffee and tea bar inside a renovated nineteenth-century church. It offers art and environmental workshops, bird walks, and music programs for the public. Studio space is available for working artists and researchers.

**Island Craft Shop** (802-372-3945), an artists' cooperative located at 6 South Street in South Hero, features the work of local and area artisans. Open daily mid-May–late October.

## FARMS AND FARMERS' MARKETS
One of Vermont's strongest agricultural regions, the Northwest Corner abounds in farmers' markets. Vendors sell farm-fresh and local food, products, and gifts at markets in Grand Isle, South Hero, Enosburgh, Richford, and St. Albans in the summer months. See vermontagriculture.com for dates and times.

*❧* **Boston Post Dairy** (802-933-2749; bostonpostdairy.com), 2061 Sampson-ville Road (VT 105), Enosburg Falls. Closed Sunday. The farm, named after the Old Boston Post Stagecoach road that once ran through the property, is owned and operated by Robert and Gisele Gervais and their four daughters. They make and sell goat and cow milk cheeses on the premises, including the multi-award-winning Eleven Brothers goat cheese (named for Robert and Gisele's 11 sons). The retail store also sells goat's milk soap, maple products, and baked goods. Visit the goats or observe the cheesemaking process through the viewing window.

*🐾 ❧* **Carman Brook Maple & Dairy Farm** (802-868-2347; cbmaplefarm .com), 1275 Fortin Road, Swanton. Fifth-generation farmers Daniel and Karen Fortin welcome visitors to their century-old farm to learn about maple sugaring and stock up on maple syrup, maple candy, and other maple products.

In spring you can visit the sugarhouse to watch them make syrup. On-site gift shop.

ORCHARDS ✈ **Allenholm Farm** (802-372-5566; allenholm.com), 111 South Street, South Hero. Open late May–December. This seventh-generation orchard, one of Vermont's oldest, offers pick-your-own apples in the fall with a farmstead selling apple products, Vermont cheese, honey, maple syrup, jams and jellies, maple creemees, and Papa Ray's famous homemade pies. There's also a petting paddock filled with friendly farm animals seeking a snack, along with a seasonal café featuring farm-fresh products from local farms. See also *Biking* and *Lodging*.

✈ **Hackett's Orchard** (802-372-4848; hackettsorchard.com), 86 South Street, South Hero. Open May–December. Maple syrup, fruits, berries, and freshly picked vegetables are available at this family-run business in summer; apples, cider, and pumpkins in fall. Fresh cider doughnuts are a specialty, as are the

GOATS AT BOSTON POST DAIRY  LISA HALVORSEN

homemade fruit pies. Apple picking typically begins after Labor Day. The farm has a family picnic play area and wagon rides.

((•)) **Hall's Apple Orchard** (802-928-3091; hallhomeplace.com), 4445 Main Street, Isle La Motte. This apple and pear orchard produces fruit for a range of ice ciders produced by Hall Home

CHAMPLAIN ISLANDS FARMERS' MARKET  LISA HALVORSEN

Place, the cidery run by Steve and Carol Hall Stata on a property that's been in the family since the late 1700s. The South End Café (see *Eating Out*) is attached to the 1820s house, built with stone quarried on the island.

✎ **West Swanton Orchards and Cider Mill** (802-868-9100), 9 Fourth Street (VT 78), West Swanton. Open June–November. A family-owned orchard with a cider mill and gift shop featuring Vermont products and homemade baked goods. Take a walk on the nature trail that winds through the 62 acres of trees or stop by in the fall to pick apples or pumpkins.

WINERIES AND BREWERIES **14th Star Brewing Company** (802-528-5988; 14thstarbrewing.com), 133 North Main Street, St. Albans, is a Vermont veteran-owned craft brewery. Founder Steve Gagner came up with the idea while serving in Afghanistan, started the brewery in 2011, and moved it to its current location, a former bowling alley, in 2014. Its

taproom has several of its own beers on tap and guest beers, ciders, and meads. Half pours, full pours, and four-beer samplers are offered. Closed Mon.

**Due North Winery** (802-285-2053), 206 Skunks Misery Road, Franklin. Erich Marn is owner-vintner of this small winery, which sold its first wines in 2012. He typically opens the tasting room on Sunday afternoons for free tastings of his Highland White, Red Sundress, and other wines. Other days, call ahead to ask if the winery is open or stop by their booth at the St. Albans Farmers' Market, Saturdays in summer at Taylor Park.

**Hell's Gate Distillery** (802-922-4047; hellsgatedistillery.com), 6293 Ethan Allen Highway, Georgia. Siblings and co-owners Judi and Joe St. Hilaire established the distillery in 2015 as another avenue for using the black currants grown on the family farm. The distilled spirits—they produce a 65-proof brandy and a 40-proof liqueur—complement their line of black currant products, including teas, jams, and simple syrups,

DUE NORTH WINERY LISA HALVORSEN

**SNOW FARM VINEYARD** LISA HALVORSEN

marketed under the trade name Vermont Currant. The distillery's name is a nod to Georgia's history, when the town was dubbed Hell's Gate by smugglers because its support of the Canadian trade embargo during the War of 1812 effectively blocked any smuggling activity. The tasting room is open Sunday afternoons, year-round.

♂ ♿ **Snow Farm Vineyard** (802-372-9463; snowfarm.com), 190 West Shore Road, South Hero. Open year-round. The Lane family, who started the winery in 1996, initially processed and bottled wine from grapes grown in New York's Finger Lakes, gradually replacing these with grapes grown on the farm's 14 acres. Vineyard tours are offered in summer and early fall with wine tastings daily. The winery displays the work of various artists and features live music in summer and winter concert series. (Also see *Entertainment*.)

SPECIAL STORES

ST. ALBANS

**Artist in Residence** (802-528-5222; artistinresidencecoop.com), 10 South Main Street. Open Tues.–Sat. This cooperative gallery showcases the work of more than 40 area painters, jewelry designers, weavers, sculptors, and other artisans. Featured artist receptions are held the first Thursday of the month.

♬ **The Eloquent Page** (802-527-7243; theeloquentpage.com), 70 North Main Street, St. Albans. Donna Howard stocks more than 35,000 used and collectible books, with a big section on Vermont and a wide variety of doll, dollhouse, and children's titles.

BEYOND

((ૢ)) **Hero's Welcome General Store** (802-372-4161; heroswelcome.com), 3537 US 2, North Hero. This nineteenth-century landmark stocks a bit of everything, from Vermont gourmet food products, wine, and bulk candy to toys, sporting goods, books, and kitchenware. Sandwiches and salads can be purchased at the deli (see *Eating Out*) with seating inside and dockside, making this a popular community gathering spot. Canoes, kayaks, bikes, ice skates, cross-country skis, and snowshoes available for rent.

*⚬* **Maple City Candy** (802-868-5400; maplecandyvt.com), 6 Brooklyn Street, Swanton. Open Mon.–Sat. All of its maple products—maple sugar candy, fudge, maple cream, maple cotton candy, chocolate maple bark, and more—are made on-site using pure maple syrup purchased from area farms. The shop also sells Vermont novelties and operates a seasonal creemee stand.

## ✱ Special Events

Also see *Entertainment*.

*☀ ⚬ Mid-February:* **Great Ice!** (great icevt.org). The weekend festival centers around Lake Champlain's City Bay in North Hero Village; Christmas tree bonfire; chili cook-off; pancake breakfast; ice hockey; kids' ice fishing derby; ice golf; dogsled rides; skating; Over 'n Back Trek to Knight Island by skate, ski, or foot.

*⚬ Late April:* **Vermont Maple Festival** (vtmaplefestival.org), St. Albans. For three days the town turns into a nearly nonstop "sugarin' off" party, courtesy of the local maple producers, augmented by a parade, live music, crafts and antiques shows, culinary competitions, maple products contests, a pancake breakfast, and other events.

*⚬ First weekend in June:* **Vermont Dairy Festival** (vermontdairyfestival

.com), Enosburg Falls. The annual festival features a parade, a youth milking contest, a pageant, a crafts fair, a cow plop contest, midway rides, a dairy baking competition, and more.

*Early July:* **Great Race Triathlon/ Duathlon** (stalbanschamber.com). This legendary run-bike-paddle event in St. Albans Bay is held over the July 4th holiday weekend in conjunction with **Bay Day**, a beach day for families, with volleyball and horseshoe tournaments, music, and fireworks at dusk.

*⚬ Early August:* **Franklin County Field Days** (franklincountyfielddays .org), Airport Road, Highgate Center. Classic old-time country fair with musical entertainment; midway games and rides; horse shows; cattle judging; tractor, horse, and oxen pulls; and 4-H events.

*⚬ Late November–early December:* **Festival of the Trees** (vtfestivaloftrees .com), St. Albans. This annual week-long event kicks off the holiday season with several holiday-themed events for families including a tree-lighting ceremony, breakfast with Santa, a holiday tree showcase, a stroll down Main Street, an evening gala, a holiday tractor parade, and **Running of the Bells**, a 1-mile fun run/walk where participants don festive holiday costumes.

# STOWE AREA AND NORTH OF THE NOTCH

■

## STOWE AND WATERBURY

## NORTH OF THE NOTCH AND THE LAMOILLE REGION

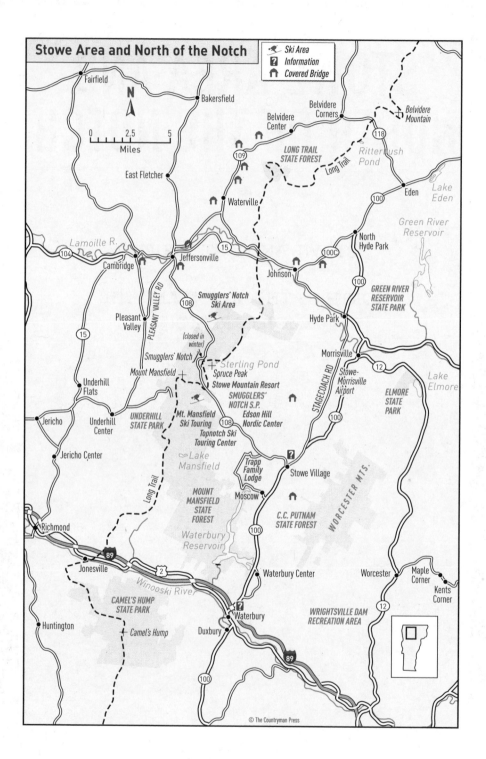

**Stowe Area and North of the Notch**

⛷ Ski Area
❓ Information
🏠 Covered Bridge

N

0   2.5   5
Miles

Fairfield
Bakersfield
Belvidere Center
Belvidere Corners
Belvidere Mountain
118
LONG TRAIL STATE FOREST
Long Trail
Ritterbush Pond
East Fletcher
109
Eden
Lake Eden
Waterville
Green River Reservoir
100
Lamoille R.
104
Cambridge
Jeffersonville
15
Johnson
100C
North Hyde Park
100
GREEN RIVER RESERVOIR STATE PARK
Pleasant Valley
108
Smugglers' Notch Ski Area
Hyde Park
15
(closed in winter)
Morrisville
12
Stowe-Morrisville Airport
Lake Elmore
Smugglers' Notch
Mount Mansfield
Sterling Pond
Spruce Peak
Stowe Mountain Resort
SMUGGLERS' NOTCH S.P.
ELMORE STATE PARK
PLEASANT VALLEY RD
Underhill Flats
Jericho
Underhill Center
UNDERHILL STATE PARK
Mt. Mansfield Ski Touring
108
Edson Hill Nordic Center
STAGECOACH RD
100
Jericho Center
Topnotch Ski Touring Center
Lake Mansfield
Trapp Family Lodge
Stowe Village
Long Trail
MOUNT MANSFIELD STATE FOREST
Moscow
100
C.C. PUTNAM STATE FOREST
WORCESTER MTS.
Richmond
89
Waterbury Reservoir
CAMEL'S HUMP STATE PARK
Jonesville
2
Winooski River
Waterbury Center
Worcester
Maple Corner
Kents Corner
Huntington
Camel's Hump
Duxbury
Waterbury
WRIGHTSVILLE DAM RECREATION AREA
12
89
100

© The Countryman Press

# STOWE AND WATERBURY

Stowe is best known for scoring Vermont a spot on the map as the "ski capital of the East." But the mountain town is also a year-round vacation destination and the state's premier spa locale. The 200-year-old village on VT 100 looks just like a Vermont village is supposed to look, and it's set against the massive backdrop of Mount Mansfield.

Stowe Mountain Resort established its ski area in 1938 and remains a major national ski destination, but, truth be told, Stowe attracts more visitors in summer and fall than in winter. From June through mid-October, it offers golf, tennis, theater, hiking, fishing, and mountain biking on an extensive backcountry trail system. The view from the summit of Vermont's highest mountain, accessible by both gondola and the vintage Toll Road, is truly spectacular, and low-key natural beauty can be found along the 5.5-mile Stowe Recreation Path that begins in the village and parallels the Mountain Road, meandering through meadows and raspberry patches.

The 10 miles of VT 100 connecting Stowe and Waterbury is lined with outlets for Vermont products and includes the Ben & Jerry's Factory. Waterbury itself is the region's gateway (I-89, Exit 10) with a small but thriving downtown, a destination in its own right for food and drink. Grab an artisanal pizza, a plate of smoked meat, or a hard-to-find beer. Waterbury Reservoir, accessible from Waterbury Center, is the obvious place in this area to swim and paddle a canoe or kayak.

GUIDANCE **The Stowe Area Association** (802-253-7321; 1-800-GOSTOWE; gostowe .com), 51 Main Street, Stowe. The SAA publishes seasonal guides, makes lodging reservations, and maintains an expansive, professionally staffed welcome center, open daily 9–5, Sun. 11–5.

The **Revitalizing Waterbury** organization maintains two websites, revitalizing waterbury.com and discoverwaterbury.com. Extensive information is provided at the **Green Mountain Coffee Café and Visitor Center** in the historic Waterbury Train Station on Rotarian Place in Waterbury (across from Rusty Parker Park).

GETTING THERE *By plane:* The **Stowe-Morrisville Airport**, 7 miles north, provides private plane services and charters. Or fly into **Burlington International Airport**, 27 miles from Waterbury, 34 miles from Stowe, which is served by major carriers (see "Burlington Region").

*By train:* **Amtrak** (800-USA-RAIL; amtrak.com) comes from Washington, DC, via New York City and Springfield, MA, and stops in Waterbury.

*By bus:* **Greyhound** (800-231-2222) stops in Montpelier with connections from Boston, New York City, and points south.

*By car:* From most points, I-89, Exit 10, and 15 minutes north on VT 100.

GETTING AROUND During winter season and select peak weekends in summer and fall, **Stowe Mountain Road Shuttle** (802-223-7BUS; ridegmt.org) circles the 7 miles between the village and the mountain for free. Pick up a schedule at the SAA welcome center (see *Guidance*). For taxi service, try **Peg's Pickup/Stowe Taxi** (800-370-9490). More at gostowe.com.

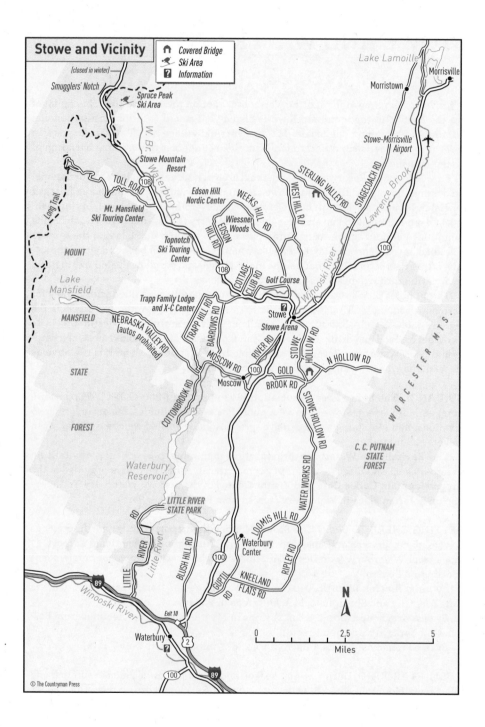

**Stowe and Vicinity**

*(closed in winter)* —

Covered Bridge
Ski Area
Information

Lake Lamoille

Morrisville

Morristown

Smugglers' Notch

Spruce Peak
Ski Area

Stowe-Morrisville
Airport

W. Br. Waterbury R.

Long Trail

Stowe Mountain
Resort

TOLL ROAD

108

Edson Hill
Nordic Center

WEEKS HILL RD

STERLING VALLEY RD

WEST HILL RD

STAGECOACH RD

Lawrence Brook

Mt. Mansfield
Ski Touring Center

Wiessner
Woods

MOUNT

Topnotch
Ski Touring
Center

EDSON HILL RD

108

COTTAGE CLUB RD

Golf Course

Winooski River

100

Lake
Mansfield

Trapp Family Lodge
and X-C Center

MANSFIELD

NEBRASKA VALLEY RD
(autos prohibited)

TRAPP HILL RD

BARROWS RD

MOSCOW RD

RIVER RD

Stowe

Stowe Arena

STOWE HOLLOW RD

N HOLLOW RD

W  O  R  C  E  S  T  E  R      M  T  S .

STATE

COTTONBROOK RD

100

Moscow

GOLD
BROOK RD

STOWE HOLLOW RD

FOREST

Waterbury
Reservoir

WATER WORKS RD

C. C. PUTNAM
STATE
FOREST

LITTLE RIVER
STATE PARK

RIVER RD

Little River

LOOMIS HILL RD

RIPLEY RD

BLUSH HILL RD

100

Waterbury
Center

GUPTIL RD

KNEELAND
FLATS RD

89

Winooski River

LITTLE

Exit 10

N

Waterbury

2

0          2.5          5

Miles

100

89

© The Countryman Press

# ✳ Must See

**Mount Mansfield** (802-253-3500; stowe.com), the highest point in Vermont—4,393 feet at the Chin—yields a truly spectacular view, accessible primarily in summer, unless you can clamber up to the summit from the Cliff House restaurant at the top of the gondola over ice and snow. In summer, take the Toll Road or an eight-passenger gondola. **The Mount Mansfield Auto Toll Road** (802-253-3000) begins 7 miles up VT 108 from the village of Stowe; look for the sign on your left before the Inn at the Mountain. Open late May–mid-October, 9–4, weather permitting. Motorcycles and bikes not permitted. The steep mid-nineteenth-century road, a ski trail in winter, once led to a hotel first built in the 1840s that served guests until 1957. The road now leads to the Mount Mansfield Summit Station, just below the Nose (4,062 feet). A half-mile Tundra Trail follows the Long Trail (red-and-white blazes on the rocks) north to Drift Rock (a 20-minute trek); another mile and you reach the summit of Mount Mansfield (4,393 feet). The round-trip takes two hours. A naturalist is on hand May–November. The **Gondola Skyride** (see *Stowe Mountain Resort*) will get you within hiking distance of the Chin. However you get there, the view from the summit (the Chin) is spectacular on a clear day: west across 20 miles of farmland to Lake Champlain; east to the Worcester Range across the Stowe Valley; north to Jay Peak (35 miles distant) across the Lamoille Valley; and south, back along the Green Mountains, to Camel's Hump. Mount Washington is visible to the east, Whiteface to the west.

**Smugglers' Notch** (elevation 2,162 feet) is reached by an extremely winding and narrow stretch of VT 108 just north of Mount Mansfield, with 1,000-foot cliffs towering

MOUNT MANSFIELD SEEN FROM BRYCE HILL ROAD IN CAMBRIDGE AND JEFFERSONVILLE  PAT GOUDEY O'BRIEN

**STOWE RECREATION PATH** STOWE AREA ASSOCIATION

on either side at the top. The first carriage road through this pass wasn't opened until 1894, but the name reflects its use as a route to smuggle cattle down from Canada during the War of 1812, not to mention hooch during the Prohibition era. One of two formally designated State Scenic Roads in Vermont, Smugglers' Notch is known for its colorfully named rock formations: Smugglers' Head, Elephant Head, the Hunter and His Dog, the Big Spring, Smugglers' Cave, and the Natural Refrigerator. The Long Trail North, clearly marked, provides a mile-plus hike to Sterling Pond, beautiful at 3,000 feet, and stocked with fish. Elephant Head can be reached from the state picnic area on VT 108; a 2-mile trail leads to this landmark—from which you can continue to Sterling Pond and out to VT 108 again a couple of miles above the picnic area. No one should drive through Smugglers' Notch without stopping to see the Smugglers' Cave and clamber around on the rocks. The Notch is closed in winter, inviting cross-country skiing and snowshoeing.

**Stowe Recreation Path** is a 5.3-mile paved path that begins in Stowe Village behind the Community Church, winds up through fields, wildflowers, and raspberry patches, and parallels Mountain Road (but at a more forgiving pitch). It's open year-round to walkers, joggers, bicyclists, in-line skaters, and (winter) cross-country skiers. There are spots for swimming and fishing, landmark bridges, and points of access to local shops and restaurants. Note that the **Quiet Path** along the West Branch River, a mile loop off the main path (it begins across from the Golden Eagle), is reserved for walkers (no mountain bikers or in-line skaters).

**Vermont Ski & Snowboard Museum** (802-253-9911; vtssm.com), Old Town Hall, 1 South Main Street, Stowe. Open Wed.–Sun. See the actual lifts that carried the first skiers up the Vermont mountains and the ski equipment they used to come down. Discover how dozens of tiny ski areas grew into the handful of mega-resorts that dominate the industry today. Watch old ski movies and vintage ski footage on a giant plasma screen. More than 10,000 items chronicle winter sports in Vermont. The museum shop sells ski-related gifts.

*Note:* For **Ben & Jerry's Ice Cream Factory Tours** see *To Do—For Families.*

## ✳ To Do

AIR RIDES For **hot-air ballooning**, inquire at Stoweflake Mountain Resort & Spa (802-253-7355; stoweflake.com). Whitcomb Aviation's **Stowe Soaring**, based at

Stowe-Morrisville State Airport (802-888-7845; stowesoaring.com), offers **glider rides**, instruction, and rentals. Also see the Gondola Skyride on Mount Mansfield in *Stowe Mountain Resort*.

BIKING Mountain biking is to spring, summer, and fall in Stowe what skiing is to winter. Diverse trail systems at destinations like Trapp Family Lodge have beefed up Stowe's appeal to mountain bikers. **Trapp Family Lodge** (802-253-5755, trappfamily .com) offers trail passes and rentals. Rent also at **AJ's Ski & Sports** (802-253-4593; ajssportinggoods.com), **Pinnacle Ski & Sports** (802-253-7222; pinnacleskisports.com), **MountainOps** (802-253-4531; mountainopsvt.com) in Stowe. Neophytes head for the 5.5-mile **Stowe Recreation Path** (see *Must See*); next there's a 10-mile loop through part of the **Mount Mansfield State Forest** and into the **Cottonbrook Basin**.

BOATING **Umiak Outfitters** (802-253-2317; umiak.com), Stowe, rents canoes and kayaks. They also offer lessons and guided trips on the Winooski and Lamoille rivers, on Lake Champlain, and throughout the state. **Bert's Boats** (802-644-8189; bertsboats .com), Jeffersonville, also offers a variety of group tours.

CARRIAGE RIDES **Gentle Giants Sleigh & Carriage Rides** (802-253-2216; gentlegiantsrides.com) in Stowe offers sleigh and carriage rides. **Trapp Family Lodge** (802-353-5813; trappfamily.com) offers wagon and carriage rides, while draft horses pull guests in sleighs at **Stowehof Inn & Resort**.

COVERED BRIDGES The **Gold Brook Bridge** in Stowe Hollow, also known as Emily's Bridge because Emily is said to haunt it after hanging herself from it (due, the story goes, to unrequited love). It's the most famous "haunted structure" in the state (take School Street about 8 miles to Covered Bridge Road). There is another picturesque bridge spanning Sterling Brook off Stagecoach Road, north of the village.

DISC GOLF The **Center Chains Disc Golf Course** and **Harwood Union Disc Golf Course** are both in Waterbury. More info at gmdgc.org.

FISHING The Little River in Stowe is a favorite for brook trout, along with Sterling Pond on top of Spruce Peak and Sterling Brook. **Catamount Fishing Adventures** (802-253-8500; catamountfishing.com), run by Willy Dietrich, is located in Stowe. It offers year-round guide service, including ice fishing. The **Fly Rod Shop** (802-253-7346; flyrodshop.com) in Stowe carries a full line of gear and offers full- and half-day guided tours.

FITNESS **The Swimming Hole** (802-253-9229; theswimmingholestowe.com) has an Olympic-size pool, a toddler swimming area, a waterslide, a fitness center with group-size rooms, aqua aerobics, personal training, and swimming instruction.

FOR FAMILIES **Ben & Jerry's Ice Cream Factory Tours** (802-882-1240; benjerry.com), located on VT 100 in Waterbury, just north of Exit 10. No American ice cream has a story to match that of the Vermont-made sweet and creamy stuff concocted by high school buddies Ben Cohen and Jerry Greenfield, whose personalities linger though Unilever has purchased the company. More than two decades ago, they began churning out Dastardly Mash and Heath Bar Crunch in a Burlington garage; the plant they built in Waterbury is Vermont's number one attraction. Ice cream is made Mon.–Thurs., but a half-hour tour of the plant is offered daily 10–6 (9–8 in July and August), except

MOUNTAIN BIKING NEAR TRAPP FAMILY LODGE  TRAPP
FAMILY LODGE

Thanksgiving, Christmas, and New Year's Day. The tour includes a free sample of one of the many "euphoric flavors." The grounds include picnic facilities and some sample black-and-white cows. Nominal admission fee.

*More ice cream:* Ice cream is popular in Stowe; you can get it at **Depot Street Malt Shop** (802-253-4269); dripping with eclectic flavors at **Stowe Ice Cream** (802-253-0995); and at **Lake Champlain Chocolates**, located among the shops at "A Special Place" (802-241-4150) on VT 100 in Waterbury—a one-stop shopping spot for Vermont products.

**Apple Tree Learning Centers** (802-253-4321; appletreelc.com) offers a year-round series of "discovery camps" for kids visiting the Stowe area, ranging from bouldering and climbing to biking and nature exploration.

**Kid's Summer Mountain Adventure Camps** (802-253-3685), based at Stowe Mountain Resort, offer activities for kids 4–12, ranging from outdoor excursions to ropes courses and sports. The camps also "take the kids to mountain attractions so you don't have to" (see *Alpine Slide*).

**Stowe Golfpark** (802-253-9951) at the Sun & Ski Inn, Mountain Road, offers 18 holes of miniature golf (May–October 10–9:30).

GOLF **Stowe Country Club & Vermont Golf Academy** (802-253-4893; stowe.com) is an 18-hole course with a 40-acre driving range, a putting green, a restaurant, a bar, a pro shop, and a school. The Stowe Mountain Club offers an additional 18-hole course for members and resort guests named among *Golf Magazine*'s "top 10 new places to play." **Stoweflake Mountain Resort & Spa** (802-253-7355; stoweflake.com) has a nine-hole, executive course adjacent to the Stowe Country Club, offering golf packages. **Ryder Brook Golf Club** (802-888-3525; ryderbrookgc.com), VT 100, 6 miles north of Stowe in Morrisville, offers nine holes, a driving range, a putting green, rentals, and a snack bar. **Blush Hill Country Club** (802-244-8974; bhccvt.com) is a picturesque nine-hole course in Waterbury, with a restaurant and pro shop.

HIKING AND WALKING See Stowe Recreation Path, Mount Mansfield, and Smugglers' Notch in *Must See*.

**Green Mountain Club (GMC)** (802-244-7037; greenmountainclub.org), south of Stowe Village on VT 100 in Waterbury Center, maintains a Hiker's Center stocked with maps, guides (like the popular *Long Trail Guide* and *Day Hiker's Guide to Vermont*), and gear. Inquire about workshops and special events. Information available at the **Stowe Area Association** (802-253-7321; gostowe.com).

Popular local hikes include **Stowe Pinnacle**, a 2.8-mile climb; and **Mount Hunger** (4 miles), the highest peak in the Worcester Range. **Taft Lodge** (3.4 miles) is steep but takes you to the oldest lodge on the Long Trail. **Belvidere Mountain** in Eden is a three-and-a-half-hour trek, yielding good views in all directions. **Ritterbush Pond** and **Devil's Gulch**, also in Eden, are about two-and-a-half hours round-trip, and **Elmore Mountain** in **Elmore State Park** is a two- to three-hour hike with spectacular views.

**Camel's Hump**, from Waterbury. See "Burlington Region" for details. This trail is also detailed in *50 Hikes in Vermont* (Backcountry Publications). One trail starts from Crouching Lion Farm in Duxbury; it's a six-and-a-half hours round-trip to the summit of Vermont's third highest mountain. Pick up a map at the **GMC Hiker's Center** (see above) and sign in at the trailheads.

**Little River Trail System**, Mount Mansfield State Forest, Waterbury. There are seven beautiful trails through the Ricker Basin and Cotton Brook area, once a settlement for 50 families who left behind cellar holes, stone fences, cemeteries, lilacs, and apple trees. Accessible from both Stowe and Waterbury. See also *Barre/Montpelier Area* for hiking in the Worcester Range.

*Note: Northern Vermont—Hiking Trails*, published by Map Adventures of Portland, ME (207-879-4777; mapadventures.com), is worth picking up. Again, sign in at the trailheads if you can.

HORSEBACK RIDING **Edson Hill Manor Stables** (802-253-7371; edsonhill.com), Stowe, offers guided trail rides (also pony rides) through upland wilds and fields, geared to various levels, as well as lessons.

**Topnotch Stables** (802-253-6433; topnotchresort.com), Mountain Road, also offers trail rides and lessons.

ROCK CLIMBING Check with **Umiak Outfitters** (802-253-2317; umiak.com) in Stowe for instruction and ropes course. Warm up on the **Climbing Wall** at Stowe Mountain Resort (802-253-3500; stowe.com).

SPAS The **Spa at Topnotch** (802-253-8585; topnotchresort.com) and the **Spa at Stoweflake** (802-253-7355; stoweflake.com) both offer over-the-top service. At Stoweflake, facilities include 30 treatment rooms, a Hungarian mineral soaking pool, an aqua solarium, and a 102-degree massaging waterfall. The 120 treatments include a maple sugar body polish, for a local touch. Topnotch has had a major face-lift; the crown jewel is the "Pathways to Wellness" program, which tailors each experience to the individual guest.

**The Spa at Stowe Mountain Lodge** (802-760-4782; stowemountainlodge.com) is no less indulgent. Perhaps it could be seen as the thinking man's (or woman's) R&R destination, what with offerings including craniosacral massage and chakra balancing along with the usual rubs and scrubs.

**Green Mountain Inn** (802-253-7301; greenmountaininn.com) in Stowe Village offers an updated health club, including an outdoor pool and a partnership with Stowe Village Massage, also a yoga facility. **Golden Eagle Resort** (802-253-4811; goldeneagleresort .com) offers massage, aromatherapy, and Reiki with fewer bells and whistles.

SWIMMING **Waterbury Reservoir**, the best local beach, is accessible from **Little River State Park** and from **Waterbury Center State Park** (see *Green Space* and *Campgrounds*). **Sterling Falls Gorge, Moss Glen Falls**, and the swimming holes in **Ranch Valley** are all worth checking; ask locally for directions. The nonprofit community pool is **The Swimming Hole** (802-253-9229; theswimmingholestowe.com), featuring a competition-size pool in a barn with a toddler and child swimming area and waterslide. Many lodging places also have their own pools that nonguests may use for a fee.

TENNIS **The Topnotch Tennis Center** (802-253-9649; topnotchresort.com), Stowe. Highly acclaimed with four indoor and six outdoor courts, pro shop, instruction, ball machines, round-robins, and over 30 programs; open daily (hours vary).

**Inn at the Mountain Tennis Club** (802-253-3656; stowe.com). Six well-maintained clay courts adjacent to Inn at the Mountain, open daily (hours vary).

Free public courts can be found at the town recreation area off School Street. A number of inns have courts available to the public; inquire at the Stowe Area Association (802-253-7321; gostowe.com).

# ❄ Winter Sports

CROSS-COUNTRY SKIING A 150-km network of trails connecting ski centers in this area offers some of the best ski touring in New England. Given the high elevation of much of this terrain, the trails tend to have snow when few other areas do, and on windy, icy days, cross-country can be better in Stowe than downhill. All four touring centers (in Stowe) honor the others' trail tickets (if you ski, not drive, from one to the next).

**Trapp Family Lodge Cross-Country Ski Center** (802-253-5755; trappfamily.com). Located on Trapp Hill Road, this is one of the oldest and most beautiful commercial trail systems—40 km of set trails and a total of 85 km of trails at elevations of 1,100–3,000 feet. The basic route here is up and up to the resort's cabin in the woods, a source of homemade soups and chili. Start early enough in the day and you can continue along ridge trails or connect with the Mount Mansfield system. Lessons, equipment rental and sales, and a refreshment lounge, as well as guided and backcountry tours.

**Edson Hill Nordic Center** (802-253-7371; edsonhill.com), 1500 Edson Hill Road. Relatively uncrowded on the uplands north of Mountain Road, the area offers 30 miles of set trails, 25 more on outlying trails at elevations between 1,200 and 2,150 feet; instruction, rental, sales, full lunches, and guided tours available.

**Topnotch Ski Touring** (802-253-6433; topnotchresort.com), 4500 Mountain Road, Stowe. Novice to expert, a total of 20 km of groomed trails on 120 private acres; instruction, equipment rental at MountainOps; trails through Topnotch Resort.

Remember: Backcountry skiing is best done with a guide if you don't know the area. **Umiak Outfitters** (802-253-2317; umiak.com) offers backcountry tours as well as a moonlit dinner tour special.

ICE SKATING Ice skating is available at the Olympic-size **Stowe Arena** (802-253-6148) in the village. Call for public skating times. The town of Waterbury has a large skating arena with rentals called the **Ice Center of Washington West** (802-244-4040; icecenter.org).

SLEIGH RIDES See *Carriage Rides*.

SNOWMOBILING **Snowmobile Vermont** (802-253-6221; snowmobilevermont.com) offers rentals and tours and information about the sport statewide.

SNOWSHOEING **Umiak Outdoor Outfitters** (802-253-2317; umiak.com) offers guided moonlit snowshoe tours, fondue and gourmet dinner tours and even a package tour at Ben & Jerry's Factory in Waterbury so you can snowshoe before you eat the ice cream. **Trapp Family Lodge Cross-Country Ski Center** has designated more than 15 km of its trails as snowshoe-only. The **Stowe Mountain Resort Cross-Country Center** has cut 5 km of dedicated trails and permits snowshoers on all 80 km of its cross-country trails. **Topnotch Resort** has also designated some snowshoe-recommended routes and permits snowshoes on all 20 km of its trails.

The obvious place to go is, of course, up the unplowed stretch of VT 108 into Smugglers' Notch, and the more adventurous can also access more than 40 miles of hiking terrain on and around Mount Mansfield, but it's best to check with the **Green Mountain Club** (see *Hiking and Walking*), which also sponsors a February Snowshoe Festival. Local rental sources are plentiful, and many inns offer snowshoes for guests to use. Pick up a copy of *Northern Vermont Adventure Skiing*, a weatherproofed map/guide detailing trails throughout the region. It's available at Umiak and other local stores in Stowe.

## ✳ Green Space

For fees and reservation rules, see *Campgrounds* in "What's Where." Note that state parks are staffed seasonally but can be accessed year-round. All state parks on lakes have boat rentals during the open season.

**Mount Mansfield State Forest** is the largest state forest in Vermont, comprising 27,436 acres, many of which lie on the western flank of the mountain (Stowe is east). The 10-mile Cottonbrook Trail starts at Cottonbrook Road off Nebraska Valley Road in Stowe. Follow the blazes.

RUSTY PARKER PARK IN WATERBURY  PAT GOUDEY O'BRIEN

## STILL VERMONT'S PREMIER RESORT

**S**towe Mountain Resort (800-253-4SKI; stowe.com for information, snow reports, and slope-side lodging). While rope tows at New England's other pioneer ski areas were powered by Ford engines, at Stowe the engine was a Cadillac. Stowe continues to maintain its status as New England's most upscale ski resort. Spruce Camp Base Lodge is now the resort's central base, with restaurants, shops, rentals, and indoor and outdoor hearths. It adjoins a pedestrian plaza with more shops and restaurants and the six-story Spruce Mountain Lodge and Spa, plus "mountain cabins" (posh condos) and private homes. New England's first fully automated snowmaking system keeps the slopes dusted top-to-bottom. Across the road and connected by the skis-on Over-Easy transfer gondola is the original Mansfield Lodge and the trail system that includes the legendary Front Four, plunging almost vertically down; tree-shaded glades and some of the longest trails in the East; and intermediate trails that snake down at more forgiving angles. It's an easy traverse from this side of the mountain to the trails served by the eight-person, high-speed gondola to the summit Cliff House, from which long, ego-building runs like Perry Merrill sweep to the valley floor. Freestyle terrain parks (small, medium, and large) and half-pipe can be accessed from anywhere on Mount Mansfield.

*Lifts:* 8-passenger gondola, intermountain transfer gondola, 3 high-speed quad chairlifts, 4 double and 2 triple chairlifts, 2 surface.

*Trails:* 116, also glade skiing; 25 percent expert, 59 percent intermediate, 16 percent beginner.

*Vertical drop:* 2,360 feet on Mount Mansfield, 1,550 feet on Spruce Peak.

*Snowmaking:* Covers 80 percent of the terrain trails served by all of the 12 lifts.

*Facilities:* 3 base lodges each offer food and services with rentals and ski shops at Mansfield and Spruce; restaurants include Cliff House (see *Eating Out*) atop the busiest lift, Octagon Café, The Great Room, The Cottage, and the award-winning Solstice (see *Dining Out*).

*Ski school:* 200 instructors; a lift especially designed for beginners at Spruce Peak, where novices learn to make the transition from easy to intermediate trails; advanced ski school program at Mount Mansfield.

*Night skiing:* More than 20 acres on Mount Mansfield are lighted Thurs.–Sat. nights 5–9.

*For children:* Day care from 6 weeks to 6 years in Cubs Infant Daycare. The Children's Learning Center offers day care or a combo of care and lessons at Spruce Peak.

*Rates:* See stowe.com for current ticket prices.

Stowe Mountain Resort Cross-Country Ski Center (802-253-3688), Mountain Road. Located near Inn at the Mountain, this center offers 35 km of set trails, plus 45 km of backcountry trails, at elevations of 1,200–2,800 feet. It's possible to take the Toll House lift partway up the Toll Road and ski down (a good place to practice telemarking). You can also take the quad close enough to the summit to enable you to climb to the very top (via the Toll Road) for a spectacular view out across Lake Champlain; the descent via the Toll Road is relatively easy. Connecting trails link this system with the Trapp Family Lodge trails along some of Stowe's oldest ski trails, such as Ranch Camp and Steeple, dating to the 1920s, as well as new backcountry trails (and tours) winding along the curved inner face of the mountain.

**Smugglers' Notch State Park** (802-253-4014; vtstateparks.com), Stowe; 10 miles up Mountain Road (VT 108) from Stowe Village, a small and quaint park with camping available.

✪ **Elmore State Park** (802-888-2982; vtstateparks.com), Lake Elmore. Drive 14 miles north of Stowe on VT 100, then east to Morrisville, south 5 miles on VT 12; 709 acres with a beach, bathhouse, concession stand, rental boats, camping, CCC community center, and hiking trail up Elmore Mountain with fire tower.

## SUMMER/FALL

**Mount Mansfield**, the highest point in Vermont—4,395 feet at the Chin—yields a truly spectacular view, accessible primarily in summer, unless you can clamber up to the summit from the Cliff House restaurant at the top of the gondola over ice and snow. In summer there are two easy ways up: the Toll Road and an eight-passenger gondola. **The Mount Mansfield Auto Toll Road** (802-253-3000) begins 7 miles up VT 108 from the village of Stowe; look for the sign on your left just before Inn at the Mountain. Open late May–mid-October, 9–4, weather permitting. Motorcycles and bikes not permitted. First laid in the mid-nineteenth century, this steep, winding road led to a now-demolished hotel that served the public until 1957. The road also serves as a ski trail in winter. It climbs to the Mount Mansfield Summit Station, just below the Nose (4,062 feet). A half-mile Tundra Trail follows the Long Trail (red-and-white blazes on the rocks) north to Drift Rock (the trek should take 20 minutes); another mile along the trail brings you to the summit of Mount Mansfield (4,395 feet). The round-trip takes two hours. A naturalist is on hand May–November. The **Gondola Skyride** (802-253-3000;) operates mid-June–mid-October at Mount Mansfield, weather permitting, 10–4:30 p.m. The eight-passenger gondola runs from Midway Lodge to the Cliff House; half an hour's trek brings you up to the Chin. However you get there, the view from the summit (the Chin) is spectacular on a clear day: west across 20 miles of farmland to Lake Champlain; east to the Worcester Range across the Stowe Valley; north to Jay Peak (35 miles distant) across the Lamoille Valley; and south, back along the Green Mountains, to Camel's Hump. Mount Washington is visible to the east, Whiteface to the west.

## YEAR-ROUND

**Stowe Mountain Lodge** (802-253-3560; stowemountainlodge.com), 7412 Mountain Road. This resort indeed has a lodge theme, but it's a Disney version, all soaring ceilings, marble floors, and stone walls lined with birch trees. Guests of this centerpiece of the $400 million Spruce Peak alpine village enjoy 312 guest rooms, a spa and wellness center, ski-in/ski-out access, privileges at Stowe Mountain Club (the resort's private 18-hole golf course), and a heated outdoor pool. **Solstice** restaurant (see *Dining Out*) features farm-to-table cuisine; **Hourglass Bar** serves more relaxed versions of the same.

**Solstice** at Stowe Mountain Lodge is open for breakfast, lunch, and dinner during ski, summer, and fall seasons; limited hours in off-season. A soaring space with an open kitchen and unsurpassed views of Spruce Peak Mountain any time of day. With furniture hand carved by Vermont-based artistic woodworkers Parker Nicholls and Charles Shackleton, and custom pottery pieces designed by Miranda Thomas, Solstice offers a feast for all the senses. The menu, at once refined and casual, changes with the seasons, but it always includes the signature truffled pot roast. Dinner reservations requested. Entrées $$. **Hourglass Lounge** has more casual dining, including flatbreads and build-your-own burgers and grilled cheese.

**Waterbury Center State Park** (802-244-1226; vtstateparks.com), Waterbury Center. A very popular swimming beach with spectacular views and fun boating activities.

**Little River State Park** (802-244-7103; vtstateparks.com), Waterbury, on Waterbury Reservoir with miles of historic hiking trails. See *Hiking and Walking*.

**Wiessner Woods** (802-253-7221; stowelandtrust.org). An 80-acre preserve with nature trails maintained by the Stowe Land Trust. The entrance is on Edson Hill Road, the next right after the entrance to Stowehof Inn.

# ✳ Lodging

## STOWE

Most accommodations are found either in Stowe Village or along—or just off—the 7.2-mile Mountain Road (VT 108), which connects the village with the ski slopes.

RESORTS **Trapp Family Lodge** (802-253-8511; trappfamily.com), 700 Trapp Hill Road, is a mountain resort modeled on the Austrian schloss once owned by the family of *Sound of Music* fame. Johannes von Trapp and son Sam von Trapp live nearby and remain involved in the property's operations, including Austrian-inspired lagers at the new Trapp Family Brewery. The 96-room lodge includes a 12-suite luxury wing with a charming greenhouse sitting room; three common rooms with fireplaces, and a library, cocktail lounge, large dining room, and conference facilities. Over 100 time-share guesthouses and 21 "fractionally owned" villas (inquire about vacancies) are arranged in tiers on the slope below, commanding sweeping views of the Worcester Range. The inn's 2,500 acres are webbed with cross-country ski and mountain biking trails, also good for splendid walks. There are tennis courts and a spring-fed pool, and the Fitness Center has an indoor pool, a sauna, and a workout room. A sugarhouse operates in early spring, live music plays in summer, and a two- or three-day minimum is mandatory in peak periods like foliage and Christmas. $$$.

**Edson Hill Manor** (802-253-7371; edsonhill.com), 1500 Edson Hill Road. A former Colorado mining prospector's country estate set on 38 acres on a high slope, most of the living room beams were originally hewn for Ira and Ethan Allen's barn, which stood in North Burlington for more than a century. The nine Manor guest rooms and 15 Carriage House units are each different, most with wood-burning fireplaces. The Vermont aesthetic reaches to the dining room, as well, where chef Chad Hanley prepares dishes such as pork belly with arugula salad and a maple-poached egg. Facilities include stables, outdoor pool, multiple ponds, and 4.4 km of cross-country trails. $$$.

**Green Mountain Inn** (802-253-7301; greenmountaininn.com), 18 South Main Street. Lowell Thomas, President Chester Arthur, and President Gerald Ford were guests in this brick-and-clapboard landmark, which dates back to 1833, when it was built as a private home. According to legend, a deceased horseman by the name of Boots Berry has tap-danced above Room 302 since his untimely end in 1902. Most rooms have no ghosts, but they do have a fireside double Jacuzzi, a DVD player with surround sound, a marble bath, and original artwork. The reasonably priced downstairs Whip Bar & Grill serves comfort food; afternoon tea and cookies are served in the living room. Guests enjoy complimentary use of Athletic Club facilities located on the other side of the year-round outdoor heated pool. Kids can enjoy a substantial game room, while parents mingle at wine and cheese parties. $$$–$$$$.

⊘ **Stowehof Inn** (802-253-9722; thestowehof.com), half a mile off VT 108 on the road to Edson Hill. This Swiss-chalet-style structure was built in 1949 and remains a retro fantasy world—part hobbit hole, part Swiss chalet. Forty-six guest rooms include suites and fireplaced demi-suites with optional kitchenettes. All with private bath and balcony with superlative views. Windows everywhere let in the view. The film *Four Seasons* was filmed here and the ambience remains solid, while the amenities and comforts stay with the trends. Facilities include the lower-level Fritz Bar and game room, the Mansfield Room for breakfast and panoramic views, tennis courts, a triangular pool with mountain views, an indoor pool, a sauna, a fitness room, a Jacuzzi, tennis courts, and cross-country ski trails connecting with the larger network. All lodging packages include breakfast. $$.

✪ **Topnotch Resort and Spa** (802-253-8585; topnotchresort.com), 4000 Mountain Road. Everything from standard hotel accommodations to sumptuous resort homes place guests in the lap of luxury. The spa (see *Fitness*) provides showers, whirlpools, steam rooms, saunas, and leather-chaired fireplace lounges, as well as a 60-foot-long indoor pool with skylights and a waterfall. The Ledges, recently added family units, come with two or three bedrooms and many other bells and whistles. The red MountainOps across Mountain Road serves as a cross-country ski center in winter (50 km of groomed trails connect with other trail systems in Stowe) and a riding stable. For meals, there's the hip-but-relaxed **Roost** or the stately, glass-sided **Flannel** (see *Dining Out*). $$–$$$.

**Stoweflake Mountain Resort & Spa** (802-253-7355; stoweflake.com), 1746 Mountain Road. Opened more than 30 years ago as a small ski lodge, Stoweflake has mushroomed into a spa and 120-room resort, including 9 luxury suites and 60 townhouses. Comfortable inn-style rooms are in the original lodge and nicely furnished motel rooms are in the garden wing (besides its own motel wing, the resort includes the former Nordic Motor Inn). **The Stoweflake Spa** (see *Fitness*) includes a Cybex circuit, a racquetball/squash court, an indoor pool, Jacuzzis, saunas, 30 treatment rooms, and a glass-roofed Aqua Solarium containing a Hungarian mineral pool and a heated jet-filled "pond" with a 15-foot waterfall. Tennis courts, badminton, volleyball, croquet, horseshoes, a putting green, and a nine-hole executive par-3 golf course sidle up to the **Stowe Country Club** right next door. Charlie B's Pub serves three meals a day. Dining, spa, and getaway packages. $$–$$$$.

**Commodores Inn** (802-253-7131; commodoresinn.com), 823 South Main Street, VT 100 south. All 72 rooms have a private bath; those in the back have a view of the lake. Living room with fireplace, sports lounge, quiet rooms, and a game room; also, there are three Jacuzzis with saunas and an indoor and outdoor pool. The **Stowe Yacht Club Dining Room** overlooks a 3-acre lake where model sailboat races are held, not to mention canoeing, kayaking, and fishing. Children 6 and under stay and eat free. $$.

## INNS AND BED & BREAKFASTS

**The Stowe Inn** (802-253-4030; stoweinn.com), 123 Mountain Road. Listed on the National Register of Historic Places, this rambling old inn is set just above Stowe Village at the base of Mountain Road. The inn has 16 rooms with private baths and 20 "country lodge rooms" in the Carriage House (motel/lodge style), most of which allow pets. Guests share common areas with fireplaces, a game room with billiards, a Jacuzzi in the main building, an outdoor pool, and the River House Restaurant. Children under 12 stay free, and continental breakfast is included. $–$$$.

✎ ❦ **Fiddler's Green Inn** (802-253-8124; fiddlersgreeninn.com), 4859 Mountain Road, 5 miles from the village toward the mountain. Less than a mile from the lifts, this yellow 1820s farmhouse can sleep no more than 18 guests (making it great for small groups) in seven small but comfortable guest rooms. $.

**Brass Lantern Inn** (802-253-2229; brasslanterninn.com), 717 Maple Street (VT 100), is a welcoming B&B at the northern edge of the village. Since 2009, George and Mary Anne Lewis have made constant upgrades to this renovated 1800s building with planked floors and comfortable common rooms. Nine guest rooms are furnished with antiques and country quilts; all have private bath, and six have a whirlpool tub and a gas-burning fireplace. Seven have HD TVs with digital cable. There's an outdoor hot tub and classic game room. A three-course farm breakfast using local ingredients, afternoon tea, and cookies are included in the rates. Children over 8 are welcome. $–$$.

**Mountain Road Resort** (802-253-4566; mountainroadresort.com), 1007 Mountain Road. A one-of-a-kind art collection separates this ultramodern ski lodge from the pack. The inn comprises two buildings with 31 guest rooms, several smaller buildings, and 16 acres of woods. Owner Eben Burr believes the inn houses the largest non-museum collection of emerging and midcareer artists in the United States, and all of the art is for sale, with all proceeds going directly to the artists. Rooms include private patios and porches and 32-inch flat-screen TVs. Guests are welcome to enjoy the pools, a hot tub, and a sauna or a massage. Freshly baked goods are served with apple cider, lemonade, and tea each afternoon, along with drinks at the bar. $–$$.

ELSEWHERE

CONDOS/RENTALS **Butler House** (802-253-7422; butlerhousestowe.com), 128 Main Street. Six modern apartments in this 1830 home in the center of downtown each have a kitchen or kitchenette. Some rooms have gas fireplaces and all retain their original pine floors. Inquire about weekly rates. $.

**Stowe Country Homes** (800-639-1990; stowecountryrentals.com) handles condos and houses. **Stowe Mountain Resort** operates magnificent mountainside condo and rental villages—one of the leading features of the multiyear expansions. Among them are the **Townhouse and Lodge Condominiums at Inn at the Mountain** and the **Stowe Mountain Lodge Condominiums and Townhouses** at Spruce Peak. All info at stowe.com. If you're hoping more for a village feeling than a slope-side feeling, **The Green Mountain Inn** has options in Stowe Village— greenmountaininn.com.

**The Village Green at Stowe** (802-253-9705; vgasstowe.com), 1003 Cape Cod Road, Stowe. Seven nicely designed buildings set on 40 acres (surrounded by the Stowe Country Club links) contain 73 two- and three-bedroom townhouses, all brightly furnished. A recreation building has a heated indoor pool, Jacuzzi, sauna, and a swell game room, as well as an outdoor pool and two tennis courts.

**Mountainside Resort at Stowe** (802-253-8610; mountainsideresort.com), 171 Cottage Club Road. Halfway between the mountain and town, these one- to four-bedroom condos offer a resort feel with complete indoor fitness and pool center, nice yard space with grills, tennis and basketball courts, and game room; all services. $$–$$$.

**Stowe Cabins** (802-244-8533; stowecabins.com), VT 100, Waterbury Center. Tucked into a pine forest whose logging roads become cross-country ski and snowshoeing trails in winter. Completely furnished one- and two-bedroom units with kitchen, Wi-Fi, and TV. Standard and deluxe rooms (gas fireplaces); $–$$.

CAMPGROUNDS
See *Green Space* and vtstateparks.com for state parks.

WATERBURY

CAMPGROUNDS **Little River Camping Areas** (802-244-7103; off-season reservations), 3444 Little River Road, Waterbury. Six miles north of Waterbury on the 830-acre Waterbury Reservoir: 81 tent and trailer campsites, including 20 lean-tos, plus swimming beaches, playgrounds, boat launch, boat rentals, ball field, nature museum, hiking, and snowmobile trails in **Little River State Park**.

See also *Green Space* and vtstateparks.com for state parks.

INNS AND BED & BREAKFASTS **The Old Stagecoach Inn** (802-244-5056; oldstagecoach.com), 18 North Main

Street, downtown Waterbury. A classic stagecoach inn built in 1826 with a tri-ple-tiered porch but substantially altered in the 1880s, with oak woodwork, ornate fireplaces, and stained glass. Eight guest rooms and three efficiency suites—from a queen-bedded suite with a sitting area, a fireplace, and a private bath to small rooms with shared bath. Two efficiency suites are studios; the other suite has two bedrooms and a sitting area. Many rooms are large enough to accommodate families. Living room adjoining the library, fully licensed bar. A full break-fast, including a selection of hot dishes, is included. Pets allowed in suites. $–$$.

**Moose Meadow Lodge** (802-244-5378; moosemeadowlodge.com), 607 Cros-sett Hill, Waterbury. Greg Trulson and Willie Docto have created a mountain sanctuary with Adirondack touches in this cedar log inn. Mounted trophies, exposed wood walls, a wraparound deck with mountain views, a large stone fireplace, and exotica (trophies include a water buffalo from Uganda and a 155-pound black bear). The guest rooms are rustically luxurious with private bath; two have a two-person steam bath, and the basement hot tub seats five. The tree house next door is a two-story "glamping" spot on stilts, overlooking a pristine pond. The 86 acres are blissfully secluded. Snowshoes are available at no charge. You may choose to tackle the 25-minute uphill hike to the Sky Loft, a glass-enclosed mountaintop gazebo with 360-degree views. Rates include an imaginative gourmet breakfast. $$.

## ✳ Where to Eat

### IN STOWE

DINING OUT ✪ **Flannel at Topnotch Resort & Spa** (802-253-8585), 4000 Mountain Road. Open daily for break-fast, lunch, and dinner. Chef Cortney Quinn adds eye-appeal to the dishes like beet pappardelle and dayboat scallops

with sweet pea risotto. A special menu of flatbreads and sandwiches is served poolside. **The Roost**, with its central shuf-fleboard table/dining bar, serves up small plates, simple suppers, and cheese and charcuterie plates until late.

**Harrison's Restaurant & Bar** (802-253-7773; harrisonsstowe.com), 25 Main Street. Open nightly for dinner beginning at 4:30. A basement restaurant comfy as a hobbit hole, where seafood and steaks are a specialty. Crabcakes, or chicken with caramelized apples and cheddar cream sauce, are prepared with flair. $$–$$$.

**Plate** (802-253-2691; platestowe.com), 91 Main Street. Dinner Wed.–Sun. The winner of *Seven Days* newspaper's best new Vermont restaurant outside Chitten-den County. Paneled with dark wood and artfully hung with nests of bare light-bulbs, this petite restaurant has style to spare. From burgers to steaks, chicken, fish, pork. Entrées $–$$.

**Trapp Family Dining Room** (800-826-7000, ext. 5733; trappfamily.com), 700 Trapp Hill Road. Open daily for break-fast and dinner; reservations required. A dress code is in effect, and cell phone use is prohibited. Produce originates in the gardens and greenhouse, maple syrup in the on-premise sugarhouse, and beer in the Trapp Family Brewery. $$$.

EATING OUT **Whip Bar & Grill** (802-253-4400; thewhip.com), 18 Main Street at The Green Mountain Inn. Open daily; lunch begins at 11:30, dinner at 5:30; Sunday brunch is a specialty. This old tavern, decorated with antique buggy whips, a brass dumbwaiter, and vintage photos, boasts Stowe's first liquor license, from 1833. In summer there's patio dining; in winter the focus is on a roaring hearth. Light fare such as burg-ers and lobster rolls, in addition to stir-fries and turkey dinner.

**Piecasso Pizzeria & Lounge** (802-253-4411; piecasso.com), 1899 Mountain Road. Lunch and dinner daily. There's a growing nightlife scene at this modern take on the New York–style pizzeria, but families are just as welcome as the cool kids. Besides the locally focused pizzas, you may be treated to an organic green salad topped with lobster or fettuccine with wild mushrooms. Don't forget to pair your meal with a Vermont beer or cider.

**Depot Street Malt Shop** (802-253-4269), 57 Depot Street. Open daily for lunch and dinner. A fun, 1950s decor with a reasonably priced diner-style menu to match, including 1950s-style fountain treats like malted frappes, egg creams, and banana splits.

**Sushi Yoshi** (802-253-4135, sushistowe.com), 1128 Mountain Road. Open daily for lunch and dinner. Birch trees line the dining room of this chic eatery specializing in well-prepared, Americanized Japanese cuisine. Seating areas include hibachi tables, a sushi bar, and a martini bar, as well as traditional tables. Bento boxes offer a great way to try a little bit of everything.

**The Bench** (802-253-5101; benchvt .com) 492 Mountain Road. Daily dinner. Nearly every dish at this wood-covered restaurant and pub touches fire before hitting the plate. Start with wood-roasted mussels, then tear into a wood-fired pizza topped with duck confit, local Brie, and pears.

BREAKFAST ✪ **Dutch Pancake Cafe at the Grey Fox Inn** (802-253-5330), 990 Mountain Road. Open daily for breakfast only. There are flat, American-style pancakes available here, but ignore those. Instead, go for the puffy, buttery Dutch ones, served in 80-plus different varieties. We recommend the apple-and-bacon version, soaked to your liking in sweet stroop.

BREAKFAST AND LUNCH ✪ **Trapp Family Lodge DeliBakery** (802-253-5705; trappfamily.com), 700 Trapp Hill Road. Watch Trapp Lager being brewed while you wait for your Austrian-style pastry or bratwurst with sauerkraut. There's afternoon tea across the parking lot in the **Lounge**.

APRÈS-SKI There are reputedly 50 bars in Stowe. Along Mountain Road, destinations include the **Matterhorn Restaurant** (802-253-8198; 4969 Mountain Road), which serves up food and live music. **The Pub at Grey Fox** (802-253-5330; 990 Mountain Road) has a groovy selection of concert DVDs and big screens on which to show them. **Burt's Irish Pub** (802-253-6071; 135 Luce Hill Road) is a friendly townie bar with excellent Colombian food. **Sunset Grille & Tap Room** (802-253-9281; 140 Cottage Club Road) serves barbecue and pub grub until midnight.

## IN WATERBURY

DINING OUT **Hen of the Wood** (802-244-7300; henofthewood.com), 92 Stowe Street. Open for dinner Tues.–Sat. Reservations a definite must—at least a week in advance or even more. In 2008 *Food & Wine* magazine named chef Eric Warnstedt (co-owner with William McNeil) one of "the best new chefs in America." Now he's one of the godfathers of the Vermont locavore movement, with numerous James Beard Foundation nominations under his locally crafted belt. The Waterbury location is just a quarter mile from the I-89 exit in a vintage 1835 gristmill overlooking a waterfall. McNeil's award-winning wine list is extensive. Inquire about special wine-tasting events. $$–$$$.

**Michael's on the Hill** (802-244-7476; michaelsonthehill.com), 4182 Waterbury Stowe Road (VT 100), Waterbury Center. Dinner Wed.–Mon. Swiss chef-owner Michael Kloeti describes his cuisine as "locally driven innovative European." The ambience is elegant yet relaxed and the food is reliably delicious. The menu changes to make use of what's best in the season, but there's always a stellar gnocchi dish and chocolate fondue. $$$–$$$$.

EATING OUT **The Reservoir Restaurant & Tap Room** (802-244-7827;

waterburyreservoir.com), 1 S. Main Street. Daily dinner, weekend lunch. Warm wood and ambient lighting set the tone in this pub known for its assiduously researched 38-tap list. Comfort food made from Vermont ingredients includes fried chicken, a wide variety of burgers, and fish tacos. $$.

✪ **Prohibition Pig** (802-244-4120; prohibitionpig.com), 23 S. Main Street. Daily dinner, lunch Fri.–Mon. Beers here include suds brewed in-house. Still, old-fashioned, "medicinal" cocktails inspire this restaurant's name and its exceptional bar. A smoker also turns out the restaurant's eponymous "pig" and other barbecue, but the burgers are local favorites, too. Don't miss the panko-fried pimiento cheese, a classic on the southern-fried menu.

## ✳ Entertainment

**Spruce Peak Performing Arts Center** (802-760-4634; sprucepeakarts.org) is a technically advanced 420-seat theater created to be the cultural soul of Stowe Mountain Resort's Spruce Peak community. Professional musicians from a variety of genres, dance, theater, and other staged artistic expressions dominate the schedule.

**Stowe Theatre Guild** (802-253-3961; stowetheatre.com), staged upstairs at the Akeley Memorial Building in Stowe Village, offers a series of four or more musicals, including classics and newer works, each summer.

**Stowe Performing Arts** (802-253-7792; stoweperformingarts.com) presents a series of spring and summer concerts in village locations, as well as concerts by distinguished orchestras and performers staged in summer in the natural amphitheater of Trapp Meadow. Patrons are invited to bring a preconcert picnic. The setting is spectacular, with the sun sinking over Nebraska Notch.

**Stowe Cinema 3 Plex & Lounge** (802-253-4678), at the Stowe Center, VT 108.

Standard seats as well as a bar viewing area for first-run films.

## ✳ Selective Shopping

ART GALLERIES AND CRAFTS STUDIOS **Helen Day Art Center** (802-253-8358; helenday.com), the former wooden high school in Stowe Village, attached to the library, open in summer daily noon–5 except Mon., closed Sundays too in winter. The changing art exhibits are well worth checking out. The Stowe Historical Society operates the mid-nineteenth-century Bloody Brook Schoolhouse museum located next door and is open on request in summer months.

**Stowe Craft Gallery & Design Center** (802-253-4693; stowecraft.com), 55 Mountain Road, Stowe. Open 10–6 daily. Outstanding crafts from throughout the country, including contemporary glass, furniture, jewelry, and ceramics. The interior design showroom on Main Street features lighting, rugs, hardware, and furniture.

**Ziemke Glass Blowing Studio** (802-244-6126; zglassblowing.com), 3033 VT 100, Waterbury Center. Open every day but Thanksgiving and Christmas. Artist Glenn Ziemke crafts his classically inspired glassware and art on-site and sells it exclusively here.

**West Branch Gallery & Sculpture Park** (802-253-8943; westbranchgallery .com), 17 Towne Farm Lane, Stowe, 1 mile up Mountain Road, behind the Rusty Nail. Open Tues.–Sun. 11–5. Indoor/outdoor space promoting emerging and midcareer artists of contemporary sculpture and exhibitions in glass, oil, steel, stone, and mixed media.

**Where the Bears Are** (802-241-2100), 6572 Waterbury Stowe Road), VT 100. On-site carvers create one-of-a-kind wooden sculptures, primarily with chainsaws. A variety of lifelike and whimsical bears and other woodland creatures grace the lawns outside. Inside, a small array of gifts are available, but the shop focuses on the artists and carvers. Carvings by order also available.

FARMERS' MARKETS The Waterbury, Stowe, and Stowe Mountain Resort Farmers' Markets are held seasonally. Details at vermontagriculture.org.

FLEA MARKETS **The Waterbury Flea Market** (802-244-5916), the biggest in northern Vermont, rolls out its tables every weekend May–October, 7–7 (weather permitting), on a grassy, dedicated spot on US 2 north of the village (Exit 10W off I-89).

FOOD AND DRINK **Cabot Annex** Store (802-244-6334), 2653 Waterbury Stowe Road (VT 100), Waterbury, 1.4 miles north of Ben & Jerry's, open year-round. A collection of shops, including the Cabot Annex, plus more specializing in Vermont products: Lake Champlain Chocolates, The Kitchen Store at J. K. Adams, Danforth Pewter, Rocking R Vermont T-Shirts & Gifts, Green Mountain Camera, Ziemke Glass Blowing Studio.

**Cold Hollow Cider Mill** (800-3-APPLES; coldhollow.com), 3600 Waterbury Stowe Road (VT 100), Waterbury, is one of New England's largest producers of fresh apple cider; visitors can watch it being pressed and sample the varieties. The cider doughnuts emerge hot from the fryer, ready to melt in your mouth. The retail store in this big red barn complex stocks every conceivable apple product, plus plenty of Vermont swag and gifts. There's lunch, including hearty locavore sandwiches at the **Apple Core Luncheonette**. Open year-round, daily 8–6.

(((•))) **Green Mountain Coffee Café and Visitor Center** (877-TRY-BEAN; waterburystation.com), housed in the renovated 1867 working Amtrak station, Park Row, Waterbury. Open daily 7–6. Displays tell the story of Green Mountain Coffees from around the world, available for a nominal donation along with pastries, light lunches, and Wi-Fi.

**Harvest Market** (802-253-3800; harvestatstowe.com), 1031 Mountain Road, Stowe. A high-end take-out spot featuring freshly baked country breads and other baked goods as well as housemade granola, an espresso bar, Vermont cheeses, gourmet items, and prepared foods.

**Trapp Family Brewery** (802-826-7000; trappfamily.com), Trapp Hill Road, Stowe. This microbrewery is located on the lower level of the DeliBakery (see *Eating Out*) at the Trapp Family Lodge, drawing its spring water on location. Three lagers—Golden Helles, Vienna Amber, and Dunkel Lager—are on tap at the Trapp Brewery in addition to rotating seasonal brews.

**The Alchemist** Brewery & Visitor Center (802-244-7744; alchemistbeer.com), 100 Cottage Club Road, Stowe. Open Tues.–Sat. 11–7. Relocated from downtown Waterbury to new facilities in Stowe, where the public can visit, taste, and buy all the favorites, including Heady Topper.

SPECIAL STORES **Bear Pond Books** (802-253-8236), 38 Main Street, Stowe Village. Open daily. A family-owned independent bookstore with an entire section devoted to Vermont books.

SHAW'S GENERAL STORE, SINCE 1895 IN STOWE PAT GOUDEY O'BRIEN

**Shaw's General Store** (802-253-4040, heshaw.com), 54 Main Street, Stowe Village. Established in 1895 and still a family business, a source of shoelaces and cheap socks as well as expensive ski togs and Vermont souvenirs.

**Stowe Mercantile** (802-253-4554; stowemercantile.com), 38 Main Street, Stowe. A diverse country store with a large, eclectic selection of clothing and gifts.

**Nebraska Knoll Sugar Farm** (802-253-4655; nebraskaknoll.com), 256 Falls Brook Lane, Stowe. Lewis and Audrey Coty's sugarhouse is open March–October, selling maple products at "sugarhouse prices." Sited up beyond Trapp Meadow, it's a lovely little drive.

**Stowe Street Emporium** (802-244-5321; stowestreetemporium.com), 23 Stowe Street, Waterbury. A nineteenth-century storefront in downtown Waterbury with treasures from near and far, open year-round.

## ✳ Special Events

*Mid-January:* **Stowe Winter Carnival** (stowewintercarnival.com) is one of the oldest in the country, showcasing nationally sanctioned ice sculptures.

*Last weekend of February:* **Stowe Derby** (stowe.com), one of North America's oldest downhill/cross-country ski races, this 10-mile race from the summit of Mount Mansfield to Stowe Village attracts about 900 entrants.

*Late June:* **Stowe Wine & Food Classic** (802-253-0399; gostowe.com). Three days of wine tastings, pairings, live auction, gala dinner, seminars, and the Grand Tasting Event, offering small bites from an impressive roster of Vermont's best chefs.

*Summer-long:* **Exposed! Outdoor Sculpture Exhibition** (helenday.com), Helen Day Art Center, Stowe, tours with the sculptors. Maps available.

*July 4:* **Stowe Independence Day Celebration** starting at 11 a.m. in

CHAINSAW SCULPTING AT WHERE THE BEARS ARE ON VT 100 IN WATERBURY CENTER  PAT GOUDEY O'BRIEN

midtown—parade, food, games, performers, and fireworks. Separate festivities in the village of Moscow with a parade that moves to the music of radios.

*Mid-July:* **Stoweflake Hot Air Balloon Festival** (stoweflake.com)—annual balloon launch and tethers with live music, food, a beer garden, and a kids' activity corner.

*Mid-August:* **Vermont Antique and Classic Car Meet** (vtauto.org). Over 800 models on display in Waterbury, three days, 8–5. Parade, car auction, fashion-judging contest, auto-related flea market, plus a Saturday-night Oldies Street Dance and Block Party.

*Mid-September:* **Annual British Invasion** (britishinvasion.com). North America's largest all-British sports car show—contests, food, and displays in Stowe.

*Pre-Halloween:* **Lantern Tours** (stowelanterntours.com), mid-September–October 31. Carry an antique lantern on a "ghost walk" through Stowe, hearing tales of the village's resident ghosts. Walks begin at the visitor center on Main Street.

*Second weekend of October:* **Stowe Foliage Arts Festival**. Three days of juried art and fine crafts from over 150 exhibitors, wine tasting, music, and demonstrations of traditional crafts.

# NORTH OF THE NOTCH AND THE LAMOILLE REGION

**V**ermont's most dramatic road winds up and up from Stowe through narrow, 2,162-foot-high Smugglers' Notch, then down and around cliffs and boulders into villages in the Lamoille region. In the early 1800s, the region earned its name when smugglers established a route through the notch to bring embargoed and illegal goods into the US from Canada during hostilities with Britain. In the Prohibition Era, bootleggers hauled their wares through the mountain pass, using caves to hide whiskey away from government revenue agents. Today, the notch is a favorite destination in warm weather for visitors seeking hiking, rock climbing, and nature lore. The route, VT 108, is at its best in autumn, just before falling leaves give way to the snow. It's closed in winter when snow flies, but a popular route in summer. On the way down into Cambridge, just as it seems the forested twists and turns will never end, an entire condominium town rises like an apparition above the trees. This is **Smugglers' Notch Resort**, a family-geared destination clustered at the bottom of ski trails on 3,640-foot-high Madonna Mountain. In summer "Smuggs" features reasonably priced condo lodging with children's programs, hiking, biking, and swimming.

As VT 108 finally levels into Jeffersonville on the valley floor, it's clear that this is a different place from the tourist-trod turf south of the Notch. This is the Lamoille Region, what people who live there call "a Vermonter's Vermont," with real downtowns and true working landscapes.

Jeffersonville has been a gathering place for artists since the 1930s, and Johnson, 9 miles west along VT 15, is home to the Studio Center, nurturing writers as well as artists. It's easy to see why artists like this luminous landscape, with its open, gently rolling farm country. The Lamoille River itself is beloved by fishermen and canoeists, and bicyclists enthuse about the little-trafficked roads.

While Smugglers' Notch is a memorable approach route, the prime access to the Lamoille Region is VT 100, the main road north from Stowe, which joins VT 15 (the major east–west road) at Morrisville, a commercial center for north-central Vermont. Just west on VT 15 is Hyde Park, the picturesque county seat, famed for its summer theater.

North of the Lamoille Region is the even less-trafficked Missisquoi River Valley, and between the two lies some highly unspoiled country.

**GUIDANCE Lamoille Region Chamber of Commerce** (802-888-7607; 800-849-9985; lamoillechamber.com), 34 Pleasant Street, Morrisville, covers the area with an office that's open year-round. An information booth at the junction of VT 15 and VT 100 at the Morrisville Mobil station is open May–October. **Smugglers' Notch Chamber of Commerce** (smugnotch.com) operates a useful website and information booth at the Mobil station in Jeffersonville at another junction of VT 100 and VT 15.

**GETTING THERE** *By air:* See "Burlington Region." Given 48 hours' notice, Smugglers' Notch Resort arranges transfers for guests.

*By train:* **Amtrak** stops at Essex Junction (800-USA-RAIL; amtrak.com), farther south on VT 15.

*By car:* When the Notch is closed in winter, the route from Stowe via Morrisville is 26 miles, but in summer via VT 108 it's 18 miles from Stowe Village. From Burlington, it's 30 miles east on VT 15 to the intersection with VT 108 in Jeffersonville. If you're coming from the Northeast Kingdom, access is on VT 15, 109, and 108.

## ✳ To Do

**Smugglers' Notch.** During the War of 1812, Vermonters hid cattle and other supplies in the Notch prior to smuggling them into Canada to feed the enemy—the British army. A path through the high pass existed centuries before European settlement, but it wasn't until 1910 that the present road was built, which, with its 18 percent grade, is as steep as many ski trails and more winding than most. Be advised that the path from Jefferson-ville is steep and winding, but large trucks are prohibited, as they cannot traverse the narrow roadway on the far side of the Notch. Realizing that drivers are too engrossed with the challenge of the road to admire the wild and wonderful scenery, the state's Department of Forests and Parks has thoughtfully provided a turnoff just beyond the height-of-land. An information booth here is staffed in warm-weather months; this is a restful spot by a mountain brook where you can picnic, even grill hot dogs. The Big Spring is here, and prior to your climb, you can ask about hiking distances to other colorfully named landmarks: the Elephant Head, King Rock, the Hunter and His Dog (an outstanding rock formation), Singing Bird, the Smugglers' Cave, and Smugglers' Face. See the "Stowe and Waterbury" chapter for details about the trails to Sterling Pond and Elephant Head.

○ **ArborTrek Canopy Adventures** (802-644-9300; arbortrek.com). Thrill seekers and nature lovers alike will be inspired as they soar through the backcountry forest of Smugglers' Notch Resort suspended in the air on 4,500 feet of ziplines. Following an extensive review and practice session, guides lead you on a nature walk and then up into your first tree. Safely hooked into a complete harness, you soar through the tree canopy and over mountain brooks, with views of the mountains in special clearings. The tour lasts two-and-a-half to three hours, and reservations are a must. Minimum age is 8; participants 16 and under must be accompanied by an adult. There are also weight, health, and basic mobility requirements.

BICYCLING *Rentals:* Mountain bikes for adults and children can be rented from **3 Mountain Outfitters** (802-332-6854; smuggs.com) at Smugglers' Notch Resort in full- or half-day increments. Child carriers are also available to rent.

The broad spectrum of back roads in this region make for excellent mountain bik-ing. Our best advice is to pick up the Lamoille County Road Map, published by a partnership of the Smugglers' Notch and Lamoille regions chambers and the Stowe Area Association. There are several sections of rail trails along the Lamoille River that make for great biking. Some are developed recreation paths such as the **Cambridge Greenway**, running 1.5 miles from Cambridge to the **Poland Covered Bridge** in Jeffersonville. Other parts of the former railroad trail are less developed . . . for now. Exciting news: The **Lamoille Valley Rail Trail** is currently in development to pick up the end of the **Missisquoi Valley Rail Trail** (see "The Northwest Corner" on page 369) and extend a continuous rec path to St. Johnsbury. Be sure to check with the chambers for updates.

CANOEING AND KAYAKING  The **Lamoille River** from Jeffersonville to Cambridge is considered good for novices in spring and early summer, with two small sets of rapids. More challenging rapids can be found in sections from **Lake Lamoille** to Johnson.

**Bert's Boats** (802-644-8189; bertsboats.com), at 73 Smugglers View Road in Jeffersonville, rents canoes and kayaks and offers shuttle service, tours, and instruction. Customized paddles can include a tour to Peterson Gorge or Boyden Valley Winery and Spirits in Cambridge (with camping).

**Vermont Canoe & Kayaks** (802-644-8336) 4805 VT 15, Jeffersonville, affiliated with Sterling Ridge Log Cabin Resort in Jeffersonville, offers guided canoe and kayaking trips, as well as instruction and rentals.

**Umiak Outfitters** (802-253-2317; umiak.com) operates rentals and rapids instruction at the junctions of VT 15 and 108 in Jeffersonville from Memorial Day to Labor Day.

COVERED BRIDGES  *In and around Jeffersonville:* Look for the **Scott Bridge** on Canyon Road across the Brewster River near the old mill; the 84-foot-long bridge is 0.8 mile south on VT 108 from VT 15. To find the **Poland Bridge** (built in 1887, for walking only) from the junction of 108 and 15, drive east on 15 and take your first left on Cambridge Junction Road. Heading west on VT 15 toward Cambridge Village, look for Lower Valley Road; the **Gates Farm Bridge** (1897) is a few hundred feet from the spot where the present road crosses the river.

*In Waterville and Belvidere:* Back on VT 109, continue north to Waterville and, at Waterville Town Hall (on your right), turn left; the **Church Street Bridge** (1877) is in 0.1 mile. Back on VT 109, continue north; the **Montgomery Bridge** (1887) is east of the highway, 1.2 miles north of the town hall. Go another 0.5 mile north on VT 109 and turn right; the **Kissin' Bridge** (1877) is in 0.1 mile. Continue north on VT 109, and 1.5 miles from the Waterville Elementary School (just after the bridge over the North Branch), turn left and go 0.5 mile to the **Mill Bridge** (1895) in Belvidere. Back on VT 109, continue north 0.9 mile, then turn left to find the **Morgan Bridge** (1887). See "Jay Peak and Newport Area" on page 469 for a description of six more covered bridges another dozen miles north in Montgomery.

*In Johnson:* Take VT 100C north from its junction with VT 15 for 2.6 miles and turn right; the **Scribner Bridge** (around 1919) is 0.3 mile on your right.

*Note:* For detailed descriptions of all these sites, see *Covered Bridges of Vermont* by Ed Barna (The Countryman Press).

DISC GOLF  Two courses can be found: The Woods at Smugglers' Notch and the Johnson State Disc Golf Course—info at gmdgc.org.

FISHING  The stretch of the Lamoille River between Cambridge and Morrisville reputedly offers great fly- and spin fishing for brown trout. Lake Eden and Lake Elmore offer diverse shorelines for good bass fishing. Fishing licenses at vtfishandwildlife.com.

GOLF  **Copley Golf Club** (802-888-3013; copleygolfclub.com), 377 Country Club Road, Morrisville, is a nine-hole course open April–October.

**Bakersfield Country Club** (802-933-7595; bakersfieldcountryclub.com), 7595 Boston Post Road, Bakersfield, is a nice drive north on VT 108 for an 18-hole course open from when it's warm enough to when it's too cold.

HIKING  **Prospect Rock**, Johnson. An easy hike yields an exceptional view of the Lamoille River Valley and the high mountains to the south. Look for a steel bridge to the

Ithiel Falls Camp Meeting Ground. Hike north on the white-blazed Long Trail 0.7 mile to the summit.

**Belvidere Mountain–Ritterbush Pond** and **Devil's Gulch.** These are basically two stretches of the Long Trail; one heads north (three-and-a-half hours round-trip) to the summit of Belvidere Mountain, the other south (two-and-a-half hours round-trip) to a gulch filled with rocks and ferns. Both are described in the Green Mountain Club's *Long Trail Guide.*

**Sterling Pond**, Jeffersonville. This is one our favorite hikes, accessible from the top of the Notch parking area, beginning across the road from the information booth. Look for the LONG TRAIL sign and register. Follow the white blazes to a T-intersection (about 35 to 45 minutes up). Turn left at the sign for Sterling Pond Shelter. It's a short walk to the "the highest trout pond in the state." For views, follow the trail around the end of the pond, through the woods, and turn left off the Long Trail, up a short rise to a clearing at the top of Sterling Lift. Return by the same route.

**Elmore Mountain**, Elmore. A surprisingly steep hike for 2,600 feet, Elmore Mountain showcases particularly beautiful hardwood forests once you reach the summit, with a fire tower on top and sweeping views of the agricultural and rugged landscape below (vtstateparks.com).

HISTORIC ATTRACTIONS **The Noyes House Museum, Morristown Historical Society** (802-888-7617; noyeshousemuseum.com), 122 Lower Main Street (VT 100), Morrisville. Open Fri.–Sat., June–August, Sat. only September–October; guided tours. Admission by donation. Carlos Noyes was a nineteenth-century banker who spent much of his fortune expanding this 1820 Federal-style homestead. Its 18 rooms and carriage barn contain one of the state's best collections of Vermont memorabilia, including an 1,800-piece Cheney pitcher and Toby jug collection. The staff regularly curates new exhibits showcasing specific aspects of historical day-to-day life, including Victorian etiquette and funerary practices during the Civil War.

HORSEBACK RIDING **LaJoie Stables** (802-644-5347; lajoiestables.com), 992 Pollander Road, Jeffersonville. Horseback riding offered all year, including trail rides, pony rides, and overnight treks. Also sleigh and wagon rides.

LLAMA TREKS **Northern Vermont Llama Co.** (802-644-2257; northernvermontllama co.com), 766 Lapland Road, Waterville. Treks depart from the Smugglers' Notch Resort and head into the backcountry. Geoff and Lindsay Chandler offer half-day treks in summer and by appointment in fall. Snacks are provided, and llamas will carry additional snacks you bring. Call for rates and to reserve. Back at the farm, purchase stuffed animals made from the wool shorn from your new friends. The farm is also home to mini donkeys and Christmas trees.

**Applecheek Farm** (802-888-4482; applecheekfarm.com), 567 McFarlane Road, Hyde Park. Trek on "wilderness trails." While you're there, take a tour, pick up organic meats, produce, and bread at the farm store, and inquire about special events.

PICNICKING There are several outstanding roadside picnic areas: on VT 108, 0.2 mile north of the junction with VT 15 at Jeffersonville, four picnic tables (one covered) on the bank of the Lamoille; on VT 108 south of Jeffersonville Village on the east side of the highway; on VT 108 in Smugglers' Notch itself (see page 415); on VT 15, just 1.5 miles east of the Cambridge–Johnson line.

SCENIC DRIVES Four loop routes are especially appealing from Jeffersonville:

# SKIING AT "SMUGGS"

**S**mugglers' Notch Resort. (802-332-3654; smuggs.com) 4323 VT108 South, Smugglers' Notch. While "Smuggs" remains a serious ski resort throughout the winter season, year-round it's geared to families and groups: self-contained, family-focused, and reasonably priced.

## IN WINTER

**DOWNHILL SKIING & SNOWBOARDING** The resort is a major ski and riding destination, with a top elevation of 3,640 feet and 78 trails connecting three mountains: Morse, Madonna, and Sterling. It includes terrain to serve or challenge all levels of ability, from small children on gentle slopes to accomplished skiers and snowboarders looking for Black Diamond trails. Cross-country and snowshoeing trails crisscross the terrain and dip into the forested landscape all around.

The village base area offers a base lodge, ski shop, restaurants and café, a pub, and rentals, with ski and boarding lessons available.

*Lifts:* 6 double chairlifts, 2 surface.

*Trails:* 78, including two 3.5-mile trails; 25 percent expert, 56 percent intermediate, 19 percent beginner; 300 acres marked on three connected mountains; 700 acres unmarked; 3,000 acres of terrain.

*Vertical drop:* 2,610 feet

*Snowmaking:* 61 percent

*Ski school:* Children's ski and snowboard camp, group and private lessons for all ages and abilities. Beginners enjoy Morse Mountain while intermediate and advanced skiers and riders take on Madonna and Sterling mountains.

**SKIING AT SMUGGLERS' NOTCH RESORT** SMUGGLERS' NOTCH RESORT

**Stowe/Hyde Park** (44-mile loop). Take VT 108 south through Smugglers' Notch to Stowe Village, drive up the old Stagecoach Road to Hyde Park (be sure to see the old Opera House), and head back through Johnson.

**Belvidere/Eden** (40-mile loop). From Jeffersonville, VT 109 follows the North Branch of the Lamoille River north to Belvidere Corners; here take VT 118, which soon crosses the Long Trail and continues to the village of Eden. Lake Eden, 1 mile north on VT 100, is good for swimming and boating; return on VT 100, 100C, and 15 via Johnson.

**Jericho/Cambridge** (38-mile loop). From Jeffersonville, drive southwest on Upper Pleasant Valley Road, a magnificent drive with the Green Mountains rising abruptly on your left. Turn right at Smugglers' Notch Inn on Church Street in Jeffersonville—toward

*For children:* Day care for kids 6 weeks–3 years; Discovery Dynamos Ski Camp for 3- to 5-year-olds; Adventure Rangers Ski and Snowboard Camps for 6- to 10-year-olds; The Notch Squad is for kids 11–15; Mountain Explorers Ski Program for 16- to 17-year-olds; lesson and evening activities; 2 teen centers.

## WARM WEATHER

Family-friendly activities abound on the more than 3,000 acres of Vermont mountain and forest land. Onsite are summer day camps; a water park joins natural ponds and water ways for swimming, boating, and fishing. A 26,000-square-foot Fun Zone 2.0, including indoor slot-car races, a climbing tower, obstacle course, laser tag, and food, is adjacent to SmuggsCentral heated pools and hot tubs, and the tennis courts. Throughout the summer season, "Smuggs" maintains an exceptionally well-organized day program with fishing, movies, nature hikes, tennis, music and dance, arts and crafts, disc golf, and more. Parents can do their own thing and shared activities include evening bonfires and fireworks.

**LODGING** Includes more than 650 condominium units in a variety of shapes accommodating a total of 3,200 people. Condos are grouped into "neighborhoods," each with its own central facilities. All offer full kitchen facilities, TV, phones, Internet access, and in-building access to laundry facilities. Units are all privately owned and vary widely from studios to five-bedroom suites. Some are wheelchair accessible.

**DINING Hearth & Candle** (802-644-1260; smuggs.com). Open daily. Reservations recommended. If you have kids, there's a room for you. Want a kid-free zone? Another area will keep you from the madding crowd. Or if you're just in it to wash away your sorrows, there's room at the bar. All this segregation means you're in for precisely the experience that you want from the Notch's only fine-dining establishment. Conservative diners will find classics such as potpie, but wild boar with ricotta gnocchi and salads filled with homemade bacon keep foodies satisfied. Entrées $$–$$$.

**Green Mountain Deli** (802-644-1141). Open daily. Lcated in the Village Lodge, it offers deli fare and lunches, with vegetarian options and daily specials, and baked goodies for dessert. $.

**Bootleggers Lounge** (802-644-5017). Open nightly from 7. for après-ski, lounge, music, and dancing. Adults only after 9 p.m.

**Ben & Jerry's Scoop Shop** Open daily in the Village Lodge. Ice cream, low-fat frozen yogurt, and sorbets in cones, sundaes, or shakes.

Underhill, take a right onto Bryce Hill Road—dirt—and come out onto Lower Pleasant Valley Road. Turning left on Lower Pleasant Valley Road, you arrive at VT 15 in Cambridge Village. Turn left to return to Jeffersonville.

**Jeffersonville/Johnson** (18-mile loop). From the junction of VT 15 and 108, head north on VT 108, but turn onto VT 109 (note the Poland Covered Bridge on your right). Take your first right, Hogback Road, which shadows the north bank of the Lamoille River most of the way into Johnson. Stop at the VT 15 and 100C junction for water from the Johnson Spring; return via VT 15.

SWIMMING **Brewster River Gorge**, accessible from VT 108 south of Jeffersonville (turn off at the covered bridge).

**Lake Eden** in the Eden Recreation Area (802-635-7725), on VT 100 north from Morrisville, is a large lake with a popular swimming recreation area open Memorial Day–Labor Day.

**Cady's Falls** in Morristown is a waterfall swimming area located above Lake Lamoille. Parking area on Stagecoach Road.

WALKING The **Cambridge Greenway** (see *Bicycling* on page 415) recreation path runs 1.5 miles along the Lamoille River from Jeffersonville east.

**Lamoille County Nature Center** (802-888-9218; lcnrcd.com), 1586 Cole Hill Road, Morrisville. Two nature trails offer easy walking and the chance to see deer, bear, a variety of birds—or at least tracks—and lady's slippers in early summer. Inquire about programs offered in the outdoor amphitheater.

## ❋ Winter Sports

*See* sidebar for **Smugglers' Notch Resort** on page 418.

SLEIGH RIDES **Applecheek Farm** (802-888-4482; applecheekfarm.com), 567 McFarlane Road, Hyde Park. John and Judy Clark's gentle Belgians, Sparky and Sam, take you through the woods by day or night. Hot beverage and farm tour included. Bring your voices and instruments! Wagon rides offered in the warmer months.

**LaJoie Stables** (802-644-5347; lajoiestables.com), 992 Pollander Road, Jeffersonville. Hour-long sleigh rides are offered all winter. In summer, they're replaced by pony rides.

SNOWMOBILING **Green Mountain Snowmobile Adventures** (802-644-1438; greenmtnsnowmobile.com), 29 Sand Hill Drive, Jeffersonville. Day and evening tours leave from Smugglers' Notch Resort.

## ❋ Lodging

RESORTS *See* sidebar for **Smugglers' Notch Resort** on page 418.

**Sterling Ridge Resort** (802-644-8265; sterlingridgeresort.com), 155 Sterling Ridge Drive, Jeffersonville. Sterling Ridge is a secluded log cabin village with a variety of attractively furnished accommodations. Scott and Sue Peterson have built 18 one- and two-bedroom log cabins, each with a fireplace, cathedral ceiling, fully equipped kitchen, and outdoor grill. For more spacious accommodations, try the two- to three-bedroom Field & Stream, built exclusively for the magazine. Or book the three-bedroom Wilderness Cabin, the four-bedroom Pond House, or the seven-bedroom Mansfield House. The inn's 360 acres are webbed with 20 km of trails; facilities include a hot tub and outdoor pool. Mountain bikes, boats, and snowshoes are available. Pets in some cabins. $$–$$$.

INNS AND BED & BREAKFASTS **Nye's Green Valley Farm Bed & Breakfast** (802-644-1984; nyesgreenvalleyfarm .com), 8976 VT 15 West, Jeffersonville. Marsha Nye Lane and her husband, David, preside over this 1810 brick colonial, a former stagecoach tavern. Her great-grandfather purchased the property in 1867, it changed hands many times, and then she scooped it up. Today it accommodates guests in four air-conditioned rooms, two with private bath. Common rooms are furnished with rare antiques, including a collection of handblown inkwells. Breakfast draws from the farm and gardens; there's also a pond and a year-round campfire pit. $.

**Smugglers' Notch Inn** (802-644-6607, smuggsinn.com), 55 Church Street, Jeffersonville. Originally built in 1790, the inn remains historic and full of character. Each of the 11 rooms has a private bath. A restaurant, tavern, and bakery keep guests fed, while a hot tub and in-room massage help with sore après-ski muscles. $

**Fitch Hill Inn** (802-888-3834; fitchhillinn.com), 258 Fitch Hill Road, Hyde Park. Handy to areas in the North Country, this eighteenth-century hill-top house has six air-conditioned guest rooms, each with private bath. Most are named for a state. Each is equipped with ceiling fans. Two are able to accommodate more than two people. Two rooms, New Hampshire and Green Mountain, come with a small kitchen, two-person whirlpool tub, and fireplace. Stay includes a full breakfast and afternoon snack. Children over 8 are welcome in the Green Mountain Suite. $–$$

**The Governor's House in Hyde Park** (802-888-6888; onehundredmain .com), 100 Main Street, Hyde Park. This is the place for a taste of *Downton Abbey*. Suzanne Boden has completely restored this sumptuous mansion to reflect the styles of 1893—when the house was erected—and of 1759 when the Longfellow House, after which it was designed, was built in Cambridge, MA. Eight guest rooms, six with private bath. Boden serves an elegant afternoon tea in the library on Thursdays and Sundays and al fresco suppers when there is a production at Hyde Park Opera House across the street. Guests are invited to arrive early for lemonade and croquet on the expansive lawns, or simply to sit on the back portico and enjoy hors d'oeuvres (BYOB) as the sun sets behind the mountains. Stay includes a three-course breakfast and tea. Inquire about the Elope to Vermont package or the renowned Jane Austen weekends. $$.

**Maple House Inn** (802-888-6565; maplehouseinnofvt.com), 103 Maple Street, Morrisville. This former religious retreat is now a four-suite bed & breakfast: all suites have a private bath and kitchenette. An indoor pool, wet bar, hot tub, and waterfall rock wall help guests have a good time (children of all ages are welcome, and there are toys and snacks just for the kids). The Galaxy of Stars 45-seat home theater boasts an old-fashioned popcorn machine and plays films per guests' requests; also available for retreats and weddings. Rates include breakfast. $–$$.

MOTEL **Sunset Motor Inn** (802-888-4956; sunsetmotorinn.com), 160 VT 15 West, Morrisville. Fifty-five units, some with whirlpool bath and refrigerator, and three fully equipped three-bedroom houses with easy access to Smugglers' Notch and an outdoor pool. The family-friendly **Charlmont Restaurant** is right next door. Kids 12 and under stay free. Pets allowed in some rooms. $–$$.

CAMPGROUNDS **Brewster River Campground** (802-644-6582; brewsterrivercampground.com), 289 Campground Drive, Jeffersonville. Open mid-May–mid-October. Twenty tent sites, group camping pavilion, three small trailer sites (not suitable for vehicles with indoor plumbing), and a tepee, lean-to, cabin, and apartment on 20 secluded acres with a 40-foot waterfall and a river where you can pan for gold. There's a fire pit, picnic tables, and a modern bathhouse (free hot showers); no pets (but there's a local kennel). Tent sites are $25 per night; hookups $30; $43 for the lean-to or tepee; cabin is $54.

**Mountain View Campground** (802-888-2178; mountainviewcamping.com), 3154 VT 15 East, Morrisville. RV, tent sites, and cabins on the Lamoille River. Swimming pools, playground, multiple outdoor game areas.

Both **Elmore State Park** and **Smugglers' Notch State Park** offer camping;

remote camping accessible only by canoe at **Green River State Park**. Info at vtstateparks.com.

## ✳ Where to Eat

**DINING OUT  158 Main** (802-644-8100; 158main.com), 158 Main Street, Jeffersonville. Serving breakfast, lunch, and dinner daily except Mon. and closing Sun. at 2. This menu, chock-full of "innovative traditionalism," features organic vegetables from local farms; big, fresh salads; and the usual steaks, sandwiches, and flatbreads. The high-ceilinged, hardwood-floored dining room, formerly a dry goods store, shares space with a bakery selling fudge-covered brownies, cookies, Italian- and French-style baguettes, and whole wheat loaves fresh from the oven. **Jeffersonville Pizza Department** is located upstairs. Fully licensed bar with good wine and a few local beers on tap. $–$$.

*Also see* **Smugglers' Notch Resort** on page 418.

### EATING OUT

### IN JEFFERSONVILLE

**Cupboard Deli** (802-644-2069; thecupboarddeli.com), 4837 VT 15, at the junction of VT 15 and 108. The deli has a giant selection of homemade and ready-made sandwiches. It's nearly impossible to leave without a few selections from the exhaustive collection of home-baked goods. The s'mores bar is not to be missed.

**The Family Table** (802-644-8920; familytablevt.com), 4807 VT 15, at the junction of VT 15 and VT 108. Open for all three meals, Thurs., Fri., and Mon., lunch and dinner 11–9; Sat., Sun., breakfast, lunch, dinner 8 a.m.–9 p.m. Home cookin', if your dad happened to have two degrees from Johnson & Wales. The family-friendly, large menu has all the staples, prepared better than you're used to.

**Brewster River Pub & Brewery** (802-644-6366; brewsterriverpubnbrewery .com), 4087 VT 108. Open Mon.–Sun. At this chef-owned pub, order duck wings and wild mushroom risotto to go with your house-brewed Saison, Porter, or IPA.

✪ **Burger Barn** (802-730-3441), 4968 VT 15. Open daily in-season. You may see a Burger Barn food truck elsewhere in the region, but this green-and-cow-spotted trailer spawned the mobile business. Using beef from Boyden Farm just down the road as a canvas, chefs make glorious burger art in this unexpected setting. Try the Ethan Allen burger, with Cabot sharp cheddar, grilled apples, and homemade cranberry-garlic mayo.

### IN JOHNSON

**The Dream Cafe** (802-635-7423), 38 Lower Main Street. Breakfast, lunch, and afternoon snacks seven days a week. Laid-back student hangout with art on the walls and freshly brewed java, teas, and smoothies; also panini and sandwiches. You order in the kitchen of this nineteenth-century house and sit down in the mango-color living room or in the former dining room.

**Downtown Pizzeria & Pub** (802-635-7626; downtownpizzeriavt.com), 21 Lower Main Street. Open Tues.–Sun. for dinner and late night; frequent live music and karaoke. It's often difficult to find real, New York-style pizza in the Green Mountains. Here, it's the real deal, served with Vermont beers.

### IN MORRISVILLE

**10 Railroad Street** (802-888-2277; 10railroadstreet.com), 10 Railroad Street. Open daily. The railroad setting inside this historical train station includes human-size tracks to chug from table to bathroom. The upscale comfort food consists of classics such as a BLT and mac-and-cheese, both stuffed with lobster.

✿ **Lost Nation Brewing** (802-851-8041; lostnationbrewing.com), 87 Old Creamery Road. Taproom open 11:30–9, Wed.–Sun. This house belongs to some of Vermont's favorite craft brews (see *Wine and Beer* on page 425), including salted, coriander-flavored Gose. But the guests of honor are meals handcrafted as carefully as the suds. The dry-rubbed, smoked pork shoulder is served on focaccia from nearby Elmore Mountain Bread. It can all be enjoyed inside or in the outdoor biergarten.

APRÈS-SKI  For a bit of local flair, head to **Brewster River Pub & Grill** (802-644-6366; brewsterriver pubnbrewery.com), formerly the raucous Brewski. As you head back to Jeffersonville, you can still stop at **The Family Table** (802-644-8920; familytablevt.com—see *Eating Out* on page 422), which will tempt you into a full dinner, or head into the historic **Village Tavern** (vttavern.com) at Smugglers' Notch Inn (see page 419).

## ✳ Entertainment

**Lamoille County Players** (802-888-4507; lcplayers.com) at the Hyde Park Opera House, 85 Main Street, Hyde Park. A community theater that stages four productions a year, including at least two musicals. The opera house is the proud owner of one of Vermont's legendary painted curtains, completed in 1911 by Charles Hardin Andrus.

**Cambridge Arts Council** (cambridge artsvt.org) stages concerts, coffeehouses, and contra dances in Jeffersonville and Cambridge; check the website. It also puts on the Cambridge Music Festival—see *Special Events* on page 425.

**Dibden Center for the Arts** (802-635-1476; jsc.edu), Johnson State College, Johnson. A 500-seat theater plays host to music, theater, dance, and comedy performed by students and local residents

as well as regional and national professional acts.

**Bijoux Cineplex 4** (802-888-3293; bijou4.com), 4 Portland Street (VT 100), Morrisville. Traditional downtown movie house; $6 for bargain matinees on weekends.

## ✳ Selective Shopping

ANTIQUES  *Note:* VT 15 from Cambridge to Morrisville is a great drive for antiquing. Shops and outlets may vary, including:

**Smugglers' Notch Antiques** (802-644-2100; smugglersnotchantiques .com), 906 VT 108 S., Jeffersonville. This dairy-barn-turned-antiques-center contains 10,000 square feet of antiques, specializing in custom-made and antique furniture.

**The Buggy Man Antiques Shop** (802-635-2110), 853 VT 15 West, Johnson. Open Fri.–Sun. 10–5, more in summer. A big old barn and eighteenth-century farmhouse filled with antiques and estate sale items.

ART GALLERIES AND CRAFTS STUDIOS  *Note:* For full artisan listings, visit vermontcrafts.com and make note of **Vermont Open Studio Weekend** every Memorial Day weekend (see *Special Events* on page 425).

**Visions of Vermont Gallery** (802-644-8183; visionsofvermont.com), 94 Main Street, Jeffersonville. Open Tues.–Sun. After getting its start showcasing the landscape paintings of Eric Tobin, Visions of Vermont has expanded to include three galleries and dozens of Vermont artists.

**River Arts** (802-888-1261; riverartsvt .org), 74 Pleasant Street, Morrisville. Offers classes, exhibitions, and events throughout the year. Check website for schedule.

**Bryan Memorial Art Gallery** (802-644-5100; bryangallery.org), 180 Main

Street, Jeffersonville. Open 11–4, daily in summer, Thurs.–Sun. in spring and fall; by appointment in winter. Built by Alden Bryan in memory of his wife and fellow artist, Mary, this mini museum features a dynamic collection representing more than 200 New England landscape painters in revolving exhibits.

**Vermont Studio Center** (802-635-2727; vermontstudiocenter.org), 80 Pearl Street, Johnson. Since 1984, this nonprofit center has absorbed more than two dozen buildings in the village of Johnson. The lecture hall is a former meetinghouse, and the gallery, exhibiting the work of artists in residence, is in a former grain mill one street back from Main, down by the river. As host to 600 international writers and artists annually, this unique program stages frequent gallery shows, readings, and lectures open to the public.

FARMERS' MARKETS Johnson and Morrisville both hold seasonal farmers' markets. A year-round Farmers' Artisan Market is held at the River Arts Center in Morrisville the second Saturday of the month. More info at vermontagriculture .com.

FARMS **Applecheek Farm** (802-888-4482; applecheekfarm.com), 567 McFarlane Road, Hyde Park. A real Vermont farm success story, this multigenerational family farm grew from a dairy and maple sugaring operation to one of the most revered grass-fed poultry and meat producers in the Northeast. Eggs, raw milk, emu oil, and maple syrup are all available. Animals include cows, chickens, pigs, guinea fowl, emus, ducks, and turkeys. Tours, special events, wagon rides; catering for weddings and events occurs in the banquet hall. See also *Llama Treks* on page 417 and *Sleigh Rides* on page 420.

**Boyden Farm** (802-644-5974; boydenbeef.com), 44 VT 104,

INSIDE THE FARM STORE IN JEFFERSONVILLE PAT GOUDEY O'BRIEN

Cambridge. This splendid former dairy farm bordering the Lamoille River—in the family for four generations—is now known for its beef and wine. Boyden beef can be found in restaurants throughout this book. Over 100 acres of maple trees also supply the farm's maple syrup operation; farther pastures are covered with grapes. See *Canoeing* on page 416 for a guided paddle to the farm with camping. Seasonal attractions include a summer concert series that includes the Cambridge Music Festival (see *Special Events* on page 426), hayrides, and a corn maze. The Barn is also host to some of Vermont's most elaborate farm weddings.

WINE AND BEER **Boyden Valley Winery and Spirits** (802-644-8151; boydenvalley.com), 64 VT 104, Cambridge. An impressive collection of Vermont wines is crafted on this farm. More than 8,000 grapevines and local Lamoille Valley fruit make up Boyden Valley red, white, fruit, and dessert wines as well as the innovative Vermont Ice Cider brand. Stop in for a tasting in the restored 1875 carriage barn. Check the website for info on tours, tastings, and special events.

**Rock Art Brewery** (802-888-9400; rockartbrewery.com), 632 Laporte Road, Morrisville. Open Mon.–Sat. 9–6. Stop in for a tasting and tour at this established brewery, known for a growing collection of 20-some varieties. Grab some growlers on-site to take home.

**Lost Nation Brewing** (802-851-8041; lostnationbrewing.com), 87 Creamery Road. This 7,000-barrel brewery takes its cures from rare European beer styles. Kegs and growlers are available to take home, or you can choose a seat in the taproom to try several varieties.

SPECIAL STORES **Johnson Woolen Mills** (802-635-2271; johnsonwoolenmills.com), 51 Lower Main Street, Johnson. Open year-round, Mon.–Sat. 9–5, Sun. 10–4. Although wool is no longer loomed in this picturesque mill, clothing is still made on the premises, as it has been since 1842. This mill's label can still be found in shops throughout the country, and its famous, heavy green wool work pants and checked jackets are a uniform for Vermont farmers. Although there are few discounts at the factory store, the selection of wool jackets and pants—for men, women, and children—is exceptional.

**Marvin's Country Store** (802-635-7483; butternutmountainfarm.com), 31 Lower Main Street, Johnson. Open Mon.–Sat. 9–5:30, Sun. 11–4. This is the retail outlet for the Marvin family's Butternut Mountain Farm maple products, plus a variety of Vermont specialty foods and gifts.

**Ebenezer Books** (802-635-7472), 2 Lower Main Street West, Johnson. Open Mon.–Sat. 10–6. An inviting independent bookstore specializing in new and used children's books, fiction, and local authors as well as toys, CDs, and art.

**Vermont Maple Outlet** (802-644-5482; vermontmapleoutlet.com), 3929 VT 15, Jeffersonville. A nice selection of cheese, syrup, handmade jams, gift boxes, and numerous maple products. Open daily 9–5.

## ✳ Special Events

Also see *Entertainment* on page 423.

*Last weekend of January:* **Winterfest**—annual area event featuring outdoor recreation, entertainment, Pie for Breakfast event, lasagna dinner, and fireworks.

*Mid-February:* **Northern Vermont Snowshoe Race & Smugglers' Notch Snowshoe Festival** (smuggs.com)—a day of snowshoe treks, walks, and races for all ages held at Smugglers' Notch Resort.

*Memorial Day weekend:* **Open Studio Weekend** throughout Vermont (vermontcrafts.com), where artisans open their studios for tours and shopping.

*July 4:* **Fourth of July Celebration**, Jeffersonville and Smugglers' Notch

Resort (smuggs.com)—an outstanding small-town parade and celebration with carnival fun, games, crafts, cow plop bingo, and a frog-jumping contest on the green behind the elementary school. Evening brings food, live music, and fireworks at Smugglers' Notch Resort.

*Late July:* **Lamoille County Field Days** (lamoillefielddays.com), VT 100C, Johnson—a classic small-town agricultural fair with family-friendly entertainment.

*Labor Day:* **Cambridge Area Rotary Fun Run & Walk** (rotarycambridge .org)—a 5K footrace (or walk) for all ages and ability levels on some fine Vermont back roads; town celebration with race awards, barbecue on the green, and flea market to follow.

*Early September:* **Cambridge Music Festival** (cambridgemusicfestival.com)—a daylong showcase of Vermont musical acts.

*First Saturday of December:* **Festival of Lights** (lamoillechamber.com)—a winter holiday jubilee in downtown Morrisville with horse and wagon rides, caroling, cookie walk, tree lighting, and Santa.

# THE NORTHEAST KINGDOM

■

# THE NORTHEAST KINGDOM

*You know, this is such beautiful country up here it should to be called the Northeast Kingdom of Vermont.*

It was in 1949 that Senator George Aiken made this remark to a group in Lyndonville. The name he coined has since stuck to Vermont's three northeastern counties: Orleans, Caledonia, and Essex.

This is the state's most rural and lake-spotted corner, encompassing more than 2,000 square miles, including 37,575 acres of public lakes and ponds and 3,540 miles of rivers. Aside from a few dramatic elevations, such as Jay Peak and Burke Mountain, this is a predominantly high, open, glacially carved plateau of humped hills and rolling farmland, with some lonely timber country along the northern reaches of the Connecticut River.

For many decades neither Burke Mountain nor Jay Peak had much impact on surrounding communities in summer and fall. That has changed. Patrons from both sides of the border are drawn to Jay Peak's 18-hole golf course and year-round facilities and to Kingdom Trails—more than 100 miles of biking, hiking, and skiing trails that web the high country surrounding the village of East Burke as well as the ski mountain itself.

In the era of trains and steamboats, large hotels clustered in Newport on Lake Memphremagog, and around dramatic and fjordlike Lake Willoughby; both Newport and Island Pond were busy rail junctions. Current focal points have shifted from the lakes to the ski areas, given their lodging base and dual-season appeal, but the quieter corners of this magnificent region continue to attract creative spirits, and family farms survive in this locavore era. There are also widely scattered opportunities for horseback riding as well as hiking, biking, and boating. Winter sports include ice fishing, snowshoeing, snowmobiling, and cross-country skiing. This entire area is a fly-fishing mecca, drawing serious anglers to wilderness brooks and ponds as well as to rivers and lakes.

The key to this Kingdom is following farm roads and—in the process of finding an isolated craftsperson, a maple producer, or a swimming hole—stumbling on breathtaking views and memorable people. Frequently you come across the region's oldest thoroughfare, the **Bayley-Hazen Military Road**, now hard-topped in some places, dirt, or a biking/hiking trail in others (see sidebar on page 429).

BORDER CROSSINGS AND REQUIREMENTS  **Derby Line, Vermont/Stanstead, Quebec** is a major border crossing; I-91 continues north as Highway 55, linking to the major east–west highway between Montreal and Quebec City. Less busy crossings include **North Troy** (VT 243), **Norton** (VT 114 to Canadian Route 147), and **Beecher Falls** (VT 253). Passports or equivalent documents such as a NEXUS enhanced driver's license or US Passport Card are required for US citizens reentering by car.

The US requires Canadians to have a passport or an enhanced driver's license.

# THE BAYLEY-HAZEN MILITARY ROAD

The Bayley-Hazen Military Road was conceived as an invasion route from the Connecticut River to Canada, and in 1772 George Washington ordered construction to begin. Given military reversals, its progress was sporadic, but more than 50 miles were eventually completed before it became obvious that the road could as easily serve as an invasion route just as easily *from* as *to* Canada. A flop as a military effort, the Bayley-Haven served significantly as a settler's route after the Revolution, and today it remains a popular mountain-biking route.

BAYLEY HAZEN ROAD CHRISTINA TREE

GUIDANCE **The Northeast Kingdom Travel and Tourism Association** (travelthe kingdom.com) offers links to local chambers and an overview of things to do. Also check Guidance in each subchapter.

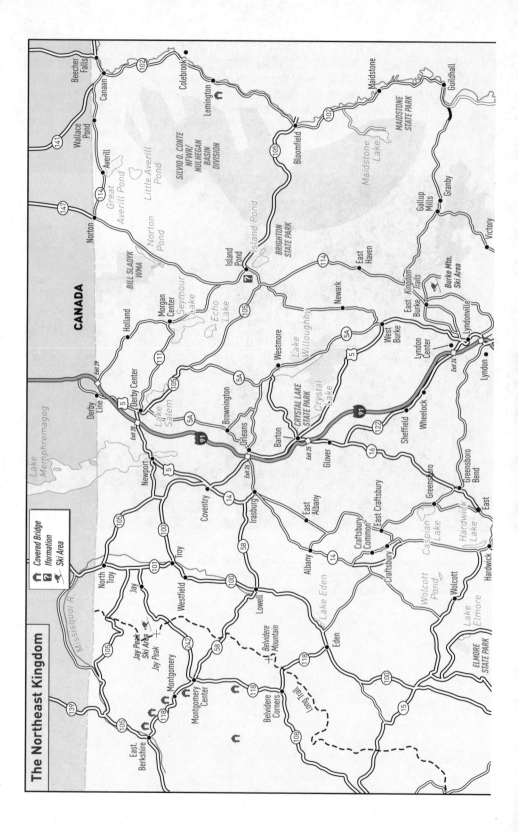

# The Northeast Kingdom

**Covered Bridge**
**Iformation**
**Ski Area**

CANADA

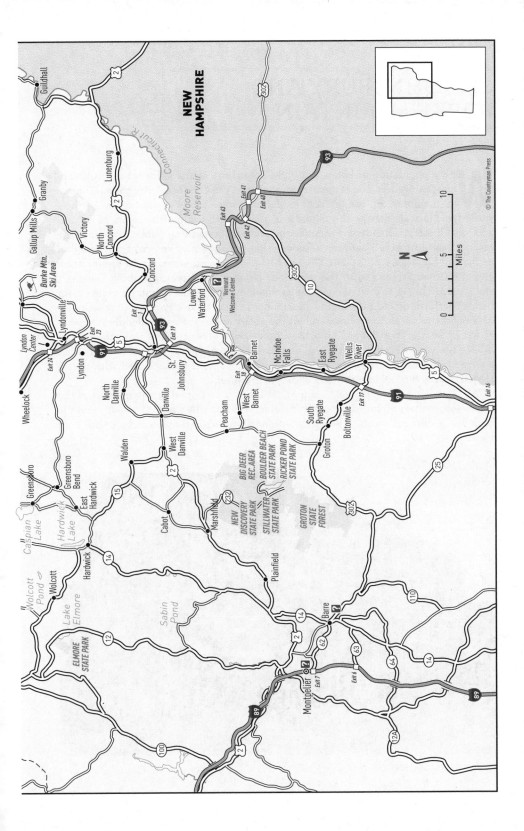

# ST. JOHNSBURY AND BURKE MOUNTAIN

With a population of about 7,600, St. Johnsbury is the shire town of Caledonia County and the largest community in the Northeast Kingdom. Thanks to members of the Fairbanks family, who began manufacturing their world-famous scale here in the 1830s, it is graced with a superb museum of natural and local history, a handsome athenaeum, and an outstanding public academy. The general late-nineteenth-century affluence that St. J (as it is known) enjoyed as an active rail junction and industrial center has been commemorated in ornate brick along Railroad Street and in the mansions along Main Street, set above commercial blocks. This is a spirited community, boasting one of the country's oldest town bands (performing Monday nights all summer in Courthouse Park); a busy calendar of concerts, lectures, and plays; and all the shops and services needed by residents of widely scattered villages along the Connecticut River to the south, the rolling hills to the southwest and northwest, and the lonely woodlands to the east. Less than a dozen miles north, the wide main street of Lyndonville is also lined with useful shops. Nearby Burke Mountain draws skiers in winter.

As US 2 climbs steeply west from St. Johnsbury to Danville, a panorama of the White Mountains unfolds to the east. The village of Danville itself is a beauty, and the back roads running south to Peacham and north to Walden follow ridges with long views.

MAIN STREET, ST. JOHNSBURY CHRISTINA TREE

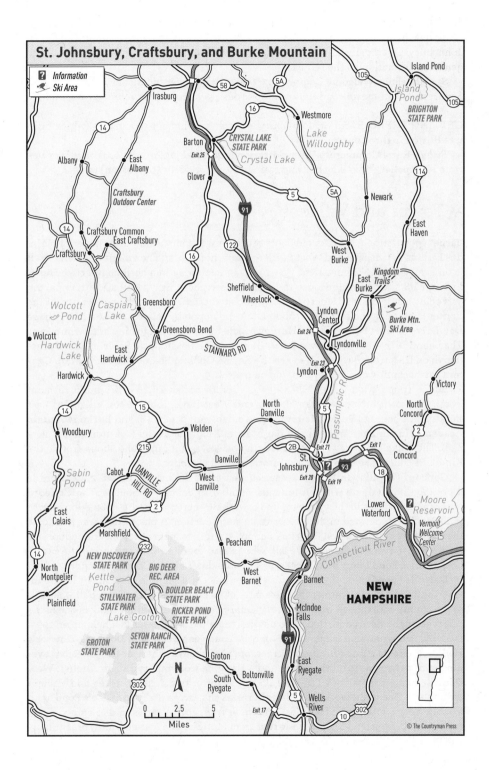

# St. Johnsbury, Craftsbury, and Burke Mountain

**?** Information
**⛷** Ski Area

Island Pond

*Island Pond*

105

105

BRIGHTON STATE PARK

Irasburg

58

5A

Westmore

16

*Lake Willoughby*

14

Barton
*Exit 25*

CRYSTAL LAKE STATE PARK

*Crystal Lake*

Albany

East Albany

Glover

*Craftsbury Outdoor Center*

5

5A

Newark

114

East Haven

14

Craftsbury Common
East Craftsbury

91

122

West Burke

*Kingdom Trails*

East Burke

Craftsbury

16

*Wolcott Pond*

*Caspian Lake*

Greensboro

Sheffield

Wheelock

Lyndon Center

*Burke Mtn. Ski Area*

Wolcott

*Hardwick Lake*

Greensboro Bend

East Hardwick

STANNARD RD

*Exit 24*

Lyndonville

Hardwick

15

North Danville

*Exit 23*

Lyndon

5

*Passumpsic R.*

Victory

North Concord

2

Woodbury

14

Walden

215

Danville

2B

*Exit 21*

St. Johnsbury

*Exit 1*

Concord

Cabot

DANVILLE HILL RD

West Danville

*Exit 20*

**?**
93

*Exit 19*

18

*Sabin Pond*

2

East Calais

Marshfield

Peacham

Lower Waterford

**?**
*Moore Reservoir*

232

West Barnet

*Connecticut River*

*Vermont Welcome Center*

North Montpelier

14

NEW DISCOVERY STATE PARK

*Kettle Pond*

BIG DEER REC. AREA

Barnet

Plainfield

STILLWATER STATE PARK

BOULDER BEACH STATE PARK

RICKER POND STATE PARK

McIndoe Falls

**NEW HAMPSHIRE**

*Lake Groton*

GROTON STATE PARK

SEYON RANCH STATE PARK

**N**

302

Groton

South Ryegate

Boltonville

East Ryegate

0   2.5   5
Miles

*Exit 17*

5

Wells River

10

302

© The Countryman Press

GUIDANCE **Northeast Kingdom Chamber of Commerce** (802-748-3678; 800-639-6379; **nekchamber.com**), 2000 Memorial Drive, Suite 11 (Green Mountain Mall), St. Johnsbury. Open daily 8:30 a.m.–9 p.m. with walk-in info about lodging, dining, and general information on the region.

**St. Johnsbury Welcome Center** (802-748-7121; discoverstjohnsbury.com), 51 Depot Square in its vintage railroad station, is open daily year-round but volunteer-dependent.

GETTING THERE *By car* St. Johnsbury is at the junction of I-91 and I-93 (which links it to Boston in three hours).

*By bus:* **Rural Community Transportation** (802-748-8170; riderct.org) offers service from **Montpelier** (linked by bus and train to New York City and Boston) to St. J.

## ❋ Towns and Villages

**Barnet** (population 1,700). An old Scots settlement encompassing the villages of McIndoe Falls as well as East and West Barnet and Barnet Center. The village of Barnet itself is on a curve of the Connecticut River, almost lost today in a curious intertwining of I-91 and US 5. **Goodwillie House** in Barnet Center, built in 1790 by a Scottish pastor, served as a stop on the Underground Railroad and now houses the collections of the Barnet Historical Society; unfortunately it's only open by request and on Fall Foliage Day. Drive to West Barnet to find **Harvey's Lake** (good for both fishing and swimming). The beautiful, round, red **Moore Barn** sits above the Passumpsic River in East Barnet (north on US 5 from Barnet). Also see the **Karmê Chöling Shambhala Meditation Center** (karmecholing.org) under *Lodging* on page 445.

**Burke** (population 1,750; Chamber of Commerce 802-626-4124; burkevermont .com). The town includes Burke Hollow and West Burke, but it's the village of East Burke that's home to **Burke Mountain** (see sidebar on page 442) and **Burke Mountain Academy**. In summer and fall the big draw is **Kingdom Trails** (see sidebar on page 438). The village is a busy cluster of lodging places, restaurants, and shops around the Kingdom Trails base area; a general store; and a gas station.

**Concord** (population 1,200). Six miles east of St. Johnsbury on US 2, Concord is a proudly built village with an unusual number of columned houses. The **Concord Museum** is upstairs in the tower-topped town hall; there's a picture of St. Johnsbury's Railroad Street, painted in the 1940s, on its stage curtain. A plaque declares this to be the site of the country's first "Normal School" to train teachers in 1823. The school was founded by Reverend Samuel R. Hall, who is also credited with inventing the blackboard. **Miles Pond** offers boat access, as does **Shadow Lake** in Concord Center.

**Danville** (population 2,334; danvillevt.com) is set high on a plateau, with a bandstand and Civil War monument in the center of its large green. The town hall was built as the county courthouse, and the small, square Passumpsic Savings Bank is one of the safest strongholds around, thanks to devices installed after it was last held up, in 1935. Danville is the national headquarters for the **American Society of Dowsers**. **Dowser's Hall** (802-684-3417), 184 Brainerd Street, open weekdays. There are Wednesday evening summer concerts on the green and a Danville Community Fair in August. **West Danville** is a crossroads (VT 15 and US 2) cluster of two general stores and a major crafts shop. One of the world's smallest libraries sits across the road at **Joe's Pond**, with a public beach with picnic facilities. The water from Joe's Pond is said to empty, eventually, into Long Island Sound, while that from Molly's Pond (a mile south) presumably winds up in the Gulf of St. Lawrence.

# MUST SEE

Fairbanks Museum & Planetarium (802-748-2372; fairbanksmuseum.org), 1302 Main Street, St. Johnsbury. Mon.–Sun., closed Mon., November–March; admission $ (planetarium shows on weekends). Franklin Fairbanks wished for this museum "to be the people's school." The Fairbanks family's wealth came from manufacturing their world-famous scale and they traveled the world, collecting much of what's displayed in this wonderfully Victorian-style "Cabinet of Curiosities." Opened in 1891, this is said to be the country's oldest science education museum, and it is the state's only public planetarium. Far more than a period piece, this remains a stimulating natural science museum with interactive displays and a seasonal butterfly house, bee tree, and weather station, and it's heated with solar panels and recycled fuel.

**DRAWING IN THE GALLERY** FAIRBANKS MUSEUM

The main hall is capped by a 30-foot-high, barrel-vaulted ceiling, its floor lined with Victorian-style cabinets displaying thousands of stuffed animals: from mice to a vintage 1898 moose, from bats to bears (including a superb polar bear), birds galore (from hummingbirds to passenger pigeons), reptiles, fish, and insect nests. Franklin Fairbanks was passionate about nature, and the collection represents most native species of mammals and birds, a total of 3,000 specimens. An extensive and varied geologic collection, started by Franklin, is also displayed, along with a living exhibit of local wildflowers in bloom. The balcony, which circles the entire hall level, is lined with historical displays depicting local nineteenth-century life (including the Civil War) and exhibits drawn from a 5,000-piece collection representing most of the world's far corners—Malaysia, the Orient, the Middle East, and Africa—by the Fairbanks family and their friends. An interactive Exploration Station invites hands-on discovery. The planetarium presents the current night sky as it appears in the Northeast Kingdom. The museum is also a US weather observation station, and its daily *Eye on the Sky* forecasts are a fixture of Vermont Public Radio (VPR).

St. Johnsbury Athenaeum and Art Gallery (802-748-8291), 1171 Main Street, is open Mon.–Sat., Wed., Fri. 10–5:30; Tue.–Thur. 2–7 p.m.,; Sat. 9:30–3; closed Sun. ($ admission charge for the art gallery.) In the 1870s Horace Fairbanks personally selected the original 9,000 leather-bound books for the library and the gallery paintings by Hudson River School artists, including Albert Bierstadt, whose large, newly restored rendition of the *Domes of the Yosemite* is the centerpiece. Natural light through an arched skylight enhances the effect of looking into the Yosemite Valley.

Lyndon (population 6,000). An up-and-down roll of land encompasses the villages of Lyndonville, Lyndon Center, Lyndon Corner, Red Village, and East Lyndon, and the neighborhoods of Vail Hill, Pudding Hill, Darling Hill, and Squabble Hollow. Lyndon isn't a tourist town, but it offers real, down-home hospitality and **five covered bridges**. The village of Lyndonville sprang into existence with the 1860s arrival of the railroad and remained an important railyard for the B&M until the twentieth century. Besides a handsome (long-gone) station and a number of brick rail shops, the company laid out broad streets, planted elm trees, and landscaped Bandstand Park. **Northern Vermont University-Lyndon** is on Vail Hill (T. N. Vail was the first president of AT&T; he came here to buy a horse and ended up buying a farm, which eventually turned into 20 farms, much of the land of which is now occupied by the campus). Lyndonville's famous product, **Bag Balm**, has been manufactured since 1899. Band concerts are held Wednesday evenings during summer months in Bandstand Park, also in Lyndonville. The **Lyndon Area Chamber of Commerce** (lyndonvermont.com) maintains a seasonal information kiosk. The **Caledonia County Fair** runs for five days at the fairgrounds in early August.

Peacham (population 730). High on a ridge overlooking the White Mountains, this is a small but aristocratic village, settled soon after the revolution. All three Peachams (South, East, and Center) are worth exploring, as are the roads between. **Peacham Library** (802-592-3216) at the center of the village offers restrooms and a gallery; across the way is the new, community-owned **Peacham Café** (peachamcafe .org). During Foliage Festival the village stages "Ghost Walks," with current residents impersonating long-deceased counterparts, in hilltop **Peacham Cemetery**—which tells its own story and offers one of the best views in the Kingdom any day.

## ✳ Must See

**Stephen Huneck's Dog Mountain, Gallery, and Dog Chapel** (800-449-2580; dogmt .com), 143 Parks Road, St. Johnsbury, marked from US 2. Gift shop open May–October Mon.–Sat. Chapel and grounds are open at all times. The full-scale wooden chapel "welcomes all creeds and breeds. No dogma allowed." Visitors are welcome to bring (or email) photos of their beloved animals to grace the chapel walls. The gallery showcases the late artist's stylish, carved wooden animals and bold, fanciful furniture, panels, and jewelry, as well as his children's books, featuring his black Lab Sally. A total of 150 acres are webbed with snowshoeing and hiking trails. Dogs are welcome everywhere on Dog Mountain, inside and out.

**St. Johnsbury History and Heritage Center** (802-424-1090; stjhistory.org), 421 Summer Street, St. Johnsbury. Open June–September Mon.–Sat. 10–4; reduced days off-season. The town's rich historical collection, ranging from archival photos and Fairbanks scales to vintage vehicles, is well worth a stop.

**Maple Grove Farms of Vermont** (802-748-5141; maplegrove.com), 1052 Portland Street (US 2 East), St. Johnsbury. Open year-round. Billed as "the world's oldest and largest maple candy factory"—in business since 1915—this is an old-fashioned factory in which maple candy is made from molds. A film in the adjacent museum depicts maple production and displays tools of the trade. The gift store stocks many things besides maple.

**The American Society of Dowsers** (802-684-2565; dowsers.org) is headquartered in Dowser's Hall (open weekdays 9–5), 184 Brainerd Street, just off the common in Danville; the bookstore sells books, tapes, and dowsing equipment. Check out the labyrinth in the rear of the building. The ancient art of dowsing is the art of finding water

CHAPEL AT STEPHEN HUNECK'S DOG MOUNTAIN  CHRISTINA TREE

through the use of a forked stick, a pair of angle rods, or a pendulum. The society has thousands of members throughout the world.

COVERED BRIDGES  Five are within the town of **Lyndon**—one 120-foot, 1865 bridge across the Passumpsic, 3 miles north of town off VT 114; one as you enter town, a genuine 1869 bridge moved from its original site; two in Lyndon Corner (one dating from 1879, the other from 1881, both west off US 5); the fifth in Lyndon Center on VT 122. Pick up a map at the **Freight House** in Lyndonville. See *Scenic Drives* below for directions to the recently restored **Greenbank's Hollow Bridge** in South Danville.

 **The Great Vermont Corn Maze** (802-748-1399; vermontcornmaze.com), Patterson Farm, 1404 Wheelock Road, North Danville. Open August–mid-October. It takes from 40 minutes to two hours to thread the miles of pathways between walls of corn. "Cheater Poles" along the way permit a quick exit. A barnyard nature center, gardens, and "Miney's Korny Kid Korn Maze" are geared toward younger children. Call first if the weather is questionable. Everyone we've talked to who has found this place has been enthusiastic, but we've also spoken to people who never did find it. Begin at the blinking light on US 2 in Danville and head north; it's best to download the map on the website.

SCENIC DRIVES  **US 2 west from St. Johnsbury to Danville**. As the road climbs steadily, the White Mountains rise like a white wall in the distance. This actually looks even better if you are driving east from Danville. Either way, be sure to pull off (there's an eastbound pullout) to appreciate the panorama.

 **Danville Hill Road**. Continue west on US 2 from West Danville to East Cabot; after Molly's Pond, take the right-hand turn—Danville Hill Road, marked for Cabot. This is a

# A HUB FOR BIKERS

**K**ingdom Trails Association (kingdomtrails.org). This nonprofit conservation organization has created access to a network of 100 miles of trails for non-motorized use. In warm weather it maintains trails for mountain biking (all abilities), and in snow season it grooms separate segments for fat tire biking, snowshoeing, and skiing. The trails are a composite of several systems on both private and public land, radiating from the village of East Burke. They thread pastures and woods and vary from narrow single-track and double-diamond downhill trails on Burke Mountain itself to wide, old logging and fire roads.

April through October, pick up a pass at **The Kingdom Trails Welcome Center** (802-626-0737), 478 VT 114, in the middle of the village, back behind the Northeast Kingdom Country Store with ample parking and changing rooms. In winter the welcome center moves to Darling Hill (between East Burke Village and Lyndonville), where 20+ miles are groomed for fat bikes and 20 km for skate and classic skiing, accessing backcountry and snowshoeing trails.

**The Kingdom Trails Nordic Adventure Center** (802-626-6005) beside The Wildflower Inn (see *Lodging* on page 443). Year-round equipment sales, rentals, and repairs are available at **East Burke Sports** (802-626-3215; eastburkesports.com) and at **Village Sport Shop Trailside** (802-626-8448), housed in a barn at The Wildflower Inn. This cluster of services on Darling Hill Road has become known as The Junction on Kingdom Trails. It includes food options (see *Eating Out* on page 448) and a base for **Kingdom Experiences** (802-427-3154; kingdomexperiences .com), offering instruction and guided tours. Check kingdomtrails.org for more sources of clinics, camps, and tours, also for year-round updates on trail conditions. See the sidebar on Burke Mountain on page 442 for details about seasonal, lift-accessed **Burke Bike Park** trails.

**BURKE BIKERS** ADAM LUKOWSKI FOR BURKE MOUNTAIN

high road with long mountain views; note the **Cabot Creamery Visitor Center** in *Heart of the Kingdom*.

**Darling Hill Road** from VT 114 in East Burke, 5 miles south to VT 114 in Lyndonville, follows a ridge past a magnificent former estate that once encompassed many old homesteads and still offers great views.

**Danville to Peacham via Greenbank's Hollow.** At the Danville Green, two roads head south for Peacham. Follow the road posted for Dowser's Hall, rather than Peacham Road. This runs right through the covered bridge in Greenbank's Hollow, with picnic benches and a historic plaque describing this "forgotten village." In 1849 Benjamin Greenbank converted an existing mill into a five-story wooden textile factory, the centerpiece of a village destroyed by fire in 1885. Only the stone foundations of the mill, the rushing stream, and the bridge survive.

**Lyndon to Greensboro Bend.** An old ridge road with splendid views, 17-mile **Stannard Mountain Road** is unpaved but usually well graveled most of the way, best traveled in summer and fall. Check locally, though, because there are occasional washouts. The views are best driving west.

# ✳ To Do

BIKING, YEAR-ROUND  *See* **Kingdom Trails Association** on page 438.

FISHING is huge here. The Kingdom is pocked with glacial lakes and laced with streams. For regulations, check under Fish & Game at nekchamber.com. Check out **Harvey's Lake** in West Barnet, the **Moore Reservoir**, **Shadow Lake**, and **Miles Pond** in Concord, **Ricker** and **Levi ponds** in Groton State Forest, as well as the **Lamoille, Passumpsic, Moose,** and **Connecticut rivers.** Local lakes are also good for salmon, lake and rainbow trout, and perch. There are trout in the streams, too. Look for the ♿ fishing platform in **Passumpsic Village** on the Passumpsic River.

At **Seyon Ranch** in Groton State Park (see *Lodging* on page 446) there is squaretail trout fishing, with flies only, from boats rented at the site.

GOLF  **St. Johnsbury Country Club** (802-748-9894; golfstjcc.com), 4357 Memorial Drive, St. Johnsbury, off US 5 north, open daily mid-May–October. This is an outstanding PGA-rated, 18-hole course, truly one of the Kingdom's gems. The original nine holes were designed in 1923; nine more were added by Geoffrey Cornish. Amenities include cart rentals and **Greenside Restaurant.**

**Kirby Country Club** (802-748-9200), 487 US 2, Concord, 5 miles east of St. Johnsbury. Open daily April–November. A challenging nine-hole course and clubhouse offer great views; reasonably priced.

HIKING AND WALKING TRAILS  See *Green Space* on page 440, as well as **Kingdom Trails Association** on page 438. Download a copy of *Hiking in the Northeast Kingdom* (travelthekingdom.com).

HORSEBACK RIDING  **D-N-D Stables** (802-626-8237) in East Burke. Seasonal guided rides for all abilities on trails that extend from the farm to local snowmobile and cross-country trails, as well as the Kingdom Trails system. Younger children are welcome to ride in the ring. Rides are tailored to the rider (maximum of four) and can be as long as desired.

PADDLING East of St. Johnsbury, the Moore and Comerford reservoirs, created by dams, are good for canoeing (there are two boat launches in Lower Waterford)—as we found out one evening, listening to birdcalls and watching a baby beaver swim steadily toward a beaver lodge beneath the pines. Below the Comerford Dam, the stretch of the Connecticut River south to McIndoe Falls (now the McIndoe Dam) is excellent, and the portage around the dam isn't difficult. Other rivers that invite canoeing are the Passumpsic and Moose, which join the Sleeper at St. Johnsbury. A boat launch on the Moose River can be accessed from Concord Avenue in St. J, and look for a boat launch on the Passumpsic in Passumpsic Village, 5 miles south of St. Johnsbury. Canoe and kayak rentals are available from **Village Sport Shop** (802-626-8448), 511 Broad Street, Lyndonville. This area is pocked with lakes, and launches are shown on the state map.

SWIMMING There are public beaches on **Harvey's Lake** in West Barnet; **Joe's Pond** in West Danville; **Molly's Pond** in Marshfield; **Miles Pond** in Concord; and within **Groton State Forest**, notably at **Boulder Beach State Park** (802-584-3823; vtstateparks.com). If you can find it, also check out **Ticklenaked Pond** in Ryegate (off US 302 west of Wells River).

## ❋ Winter Sports

CROSS-COUNTRY SKIING, SNOWSHOEING, AND FAT TIRE BIKING *See* **Kingdom Trails Assocation** on page 438.
   **Seyon Ranch State Park** (802-584-3829; vtstateparks.com). This isolated 1890s hunting/fishing lodge deep in Groton State Forest has been winterized and caters to cross-country skiers, with 5 miles of groomed trails.

SLEIGH RIDES **Allen Farms** (802-467-3453), 2929 US 5, West Burke, offers horse-drawn sleigh rides on lovely trails, winding up with hot chocolate.

SNOWMOBILING Given the extent of the trail system, accessibility to the trails from local lodging places, and dependable snow cover, this area is becoming as well known among snowmobilers as it is to cross-country skiers. The trail systems, however, seldom cross. Contact the **Northeast Kingdom Chamber of Commerce** (802-748-3678; 800-639-6379; nekchamber.com) for a list of the local clubs from which you must purchase a VAST membership in order to use the trails. Rentals are available from **All Around Rental Store** (802-748-7841), St. Johnsbury.

## ❋ Green Space

**Groton State Forest** (802-584-3829; vtstateparks.com), off VT 232 (which runs north–south, connecting US 2 and US 302. This 25,600-plus-acre forest is a scenic and rugged place, home to seven state parks, eight lakes, and several ponds. There's an extensive year-round trail system. The area was intensively logged, beginning in 1873 with the opening of the Montpelier & Wells Railroad that ran through the forest, ending in the 1920s, when most of the timber had been cut. Subsequent fires further altered the landscape from evergreens to mostly maple and birch. The naturalist-staffed **Groton Nature Center** (802-584-3823) in **Boulder Beach State Park** (a day-use area featuring a swim beach on Lake Groton), marked from VT 232, is open June–early September and serves as the information source for the forest and the trailhead for the 2.5-mile trail to Peacham Bog. **Seyon Lodge State Park** (see *Lodging* on page 446) is on Noyes Pond in another part of the forest, catering to groups, fishermen, and cross-country skiers. Favorite hikes in the **Groton State Forest Trail System** include the **Peacham Bog Natural Area** and two trails to the summit of **Owls Head Mountain** (there's a summer road as well as a trail), where a handsome old CCC wood-and-stone watchtower commands spectacular views.

**Victory Basin**, alias Victory Bog. This 4,970-acre preserve administered by the Vermont Fish and Wildlife Department includes a 25-acre boreal bog with rare plant life, 1,800 acres of wetlands, 1,084 acres of hardwoods, and 71 acres of clearings and old fields. There's camping in its five separate campgrounds: **Discovery State Park** (802-584-3042) has a total of 47 campsites, 14 of which are lean-tos; beach privileges and hiking trails; primitive camping. Phone 802-584-3822 for **Stillwater State Park**, on the west side of Lake Groton (63 tent sites, 16 lean-tos; campers' beach, rental boats, and boat launch) and for **Big Deer State Park** (28 tent/trailer sites but no hookups) near Boulder Beach and the Groton Nature Center. **Ricker Pond State Park** (802-584-3821) has a total of 33 campsites, 22 of them lean-tos, on the south side of Ricker Pond; campers' beach, rental boats, nature trail, and dump station. **Kettle Pond State Park** (802-426-3042), on the south side of the pond, has walk-in fishing, group camping, hiking, and snowmobiling. Make reservations at parks@vt.gov; 888-409-7559.

**Fred Mold Park**, near the confluence of the Passumpsic and Moose rivers, is a great picnic spot by a waterfall and old mill. **The Arlington Preserve**, accessible from Waterman Circle, is a 33-acre nature preserve with woods, meadows, and rock outcroppings.

# ✳ Lodging

## INNS AND BED & BREAKFASTS

### IN THE ST. JOHNSBURY AREA

♿ **Rabbit Hill Inn** (802-748-5168; rabbithillinn.com), 48 Lower Waterford Road (off VT 18), Lower Waterford. All 19 rooms and suites in this pillared landmark and suites are romantic confections, 15 with working fireplace, many with canopy bed (no twins), in-room Jacuzzi for two, and "indulging" bathrooms. They are divided between the main house and the neighboring 1795 Tavern House. All are themed so they vary widely in look and feel; check choices on the website. There's a capacious living room, a full-service bar in the Snooty Fox Pub, and a cozy game room/library. Children should be older than 14—really, this place is all about couples stealing time together. Summer golf privileges, winter cross-country skiing, and snowshoeing. The inn is set in a classic village. $$–$$$ includes breakfast and tea. Dinner is served.

**Estabrook House B&B** (802-751-8261; estabrookhouse.com), 1596 Main Street, St. Johnsbury. A vintage 1856 painted lady on the quiet, residential end of Main Street and within walking distance of the Fairbanks Museum and St. Johnsbury

RABBIT HILL INN, LOWER WATERFORD CHRISTINA TREE

# BURKE MOUNTAIN

**DOWNHILL SKIING AND SNOWBOARDING** Burke Mountain (866-966-4820 BURKE-VT; skiburke .com), East Burke. "The Vermonter's Mountain" is a big peak with a respectable vertical, known for excellent terrain and reasonable prices. It's a sister property to Jay Peak, with a dual-season pass option. The mountain is also the home of Burke Mountain Academy, a prep school for aspiring racers, known for the number of graduates who become Olympic contenders (over 50 Olympians).

*Lifts:* 2 quad chairlifts (1 detachable), 2 surface lifts

*Trails and slopes:* 50 trails, 110 acres of glades

*Elevation:* 3,267 feet

*Vertical drop:* 2,011 feet

*Snowmaking:* 70 percent

*Snowboarding:* 3 terrain parks, season-long freestyle program

*Programs:* Kids' programs during weekends and holiday periods; ski school, rentals

*Tip:* Best intermediate trail is East Bowl, a 2-mile, old-style trail that winds with natural contours, offering breathtaking views of the Presidential Range.

*Facilities:* Burke Mountain Hotel and Conference Center sits slope-side, just below Mid Burke, featuring 116 suites, an outdoor heated pool and hot tub, View Pub, Willoughby's Restaurant, Edmund's Coffee Shop, a retail store, and Day Lodge Cafeteria; **Sherburne Base Lodge** includes the glass-walled Tamarack Grill as well as a cafeteria; a midslope lodge, with its **Bear Den Lounge**, serves the upper mountain.

*Other:* See **Kingdom Trails Association** sidebar on page 438 for Nordic skiing, snowshoeing, and fat tire biking.

## SUMMER /FALL

**Mountain Road** A 2.5-mile toll road leads to the summit of Burke Mountain (3,500 feet). Beware of the strain on your brakes when you're coming down! It's amazing how many bicyclists make the climb. The view, just steps from the summit parking lot, is through trees to the White Mountains and points east. To the west the view encompasses Lake Willoughby and the Green Mountains. Now **Darling State Park**, this preserve is part of a larger tract donated to the state in 1933; the toll road was constructed by the Civilian Conservation Corps. It's open, along with a primitive campground, May–late October.

**Burke Bike Park** offers lift-assisted mountain bike trails from the Sherburne Express Chairlift located at the Sherburne base lodge. The park offers 19 trails, 3 of which are accessed

Athenaeum. The house is spacious, comfortable, and uncluttered. Most of the second-floor, antiques-furnished guest rooms share a bath; one is private. The feel is that of staying in a friend's house. There is ample common space, including a "media room/library." $–$$ rates include a full breakfast.

🍽 **Emergo Farm B&B** (802-684-2215; emergofarm.com), 261 Webster Hill, Danville. Just north of the village, this strikingly handsome, prizewinning working dairy farm has been in the same family for six generations and Lori Webster is a hospitable host. The upstairs front room, tastefully furnished with family antiques, has a private bath and view of the White Mountains. There is also a one-bedroom apartment with full kitchen and sitting room. The farm's 230 acres include a hilltop with panoramic views. Farm tours are offered (there are 250 head of Holstein cattle). Rooms from $ includes a full breakfast.

BURKE MOUNTAIN HOTEL  ADAM LUKOWSKI FOR BURKE MOUNTAIN

from the summit. A combination of excavated jump trails, single-track, and even a dual slalom course will keep the entire family entertained. Tickets are required.

**Year-round lodging: Trailside lodging: Burke Mountain Hotel and Conference Center** (802-626-7400; 866-966-4820), 2559 Mountain Road, East Burke. New in 2016, this five-floor, two-wing, 116-room ski lodge is sited almost midway up the mountain, commanding a distant view of Willoughby Gap. The studio, one-, two-, and three-bedroom units all include kitchens and eating areas, most with balconies and a full kitchen option. Amenities include an outdoor heated pool and hot tub, pub, restaurant, fitness center, two conference areas/ballrooms, a retail shop, day lockers for ski and snowboards, and an indoor mountain bike storage area. $$ rates spike and fall, depending on the day and season. Visit skiburke.com for current rates and to book.

## IN THE BURKE MOUNTAIN AREA

✪ ✎ 🐾 **The Wildflower Inn** (802-626-8310; wildflowerinn.com), 2059 Darling Hill Road, Lyndonville. The O'Reilly family's genuinely hospitable retreat clusters around a nineteenth-century farmhouse, high on a ridge with sweeping views. It's set in its own 300 acres, with extensive flower gardens and trails maintained by **Kingdom Trails** (see page 438); its winter office is next door. The neighboring

**Village Sports Shop Trailside** offers bike, ski, and snowshoe rentals; lessons and guided tours are also available next door. There's a landscaped pool (also one for toddlers), as well as play spaces for young children and a playing field for older youngsters. Breakfast and dinner are at **Juniper's** (see *Dining Out* on page 448) with its view and seasonal patio, and the view is shared by the Spokeasy Lounge. Rooms and suites are divided between the main house and annexes.

EMERGO FARM B&B, DANVILLE CHRISTINA TREE

There's also a two-bedroom retreat, sleeping eight with two baths. Rates from $–$$$, depending on room and season; also biking and cross-country skiing/snowshoeing packages.

♂ ☀ ♿ **The Inn at Mountain View Farm** (802-626-9924; innmtnview.com), 3383 Darling Hill Road, East Burke. Open May–October. Like The Wildflower Inn, this is part of a one-time 9,000-acre hilltop estate owned by Elmer Darling, a Burke native who built the brick creamery in 1890 to supply dairy products to his Fifth Avenue hotel. The inn includes the neighboring "Farm House" and the magnificent red barns and other outbuildings. Marilyn Pastore has tastefully decorated the 14 guest rooms (private baths), which are divided between the Creamery and the Farm House (three luxury suites). The Creamery houses the inn's sitting room and a dining room serving breakfast to guests. The inn is a favorite weekend venue for weddings and reunions, and for bicyclists midweek. $–$$$.

✪ ✿ ♂ ☀ **The Village Inn of East Burke** (802-626-3161; villageinnofeastburke.com), 606 VT 114, East Burke. Chris and Karri Willy's comfortable, affordable B&B offers genuine hospitality and many rarely found amenities, like a fully equipped guest kitchen; an inviting living room with a fireplace, books, games, and a satellite TV; an indoor sauna, laundry facilities, extensive gardens, a streamside picnic/lounging area, a locked storage space for skis and bikes plus air, and tools for bicyclists, who are also welcome to shower after rides even if they've checked out. There are seven comfortable rooms with private bath, each different and varying in size; also there is a studio and a three-bedroom apartment with kitchen facilities and private entrances. $–$$. Rates include a full-choice breakfast next door in the attractive dining room (with patio) that's a base for Chris Willy's catering business. $–$$.

**Willoburke Inn and Lodge** (802-427-3333; willoburke.com), 638 VT 114, East Burke. This lodge on 5 brookside acres has a contemporary feel with spacious exposed-raftered sitting area and fireplace. The eight guest rooms (with private bath) are fitted with locally crafted furniture; try for one of the four back rooms (two up/two down) overlooking the brook; a two-bedroom apartment in the neighboring Greek Revival home sleeps six and includes a full kitchen and living room. Facilities include locked area for bicycles and skis. European-style buffet breakfast and afternoon snack included in rates: $–$$. The inn's

WILDFLOWER INN, LYNDONVILLE CHRISTINA TREE

INN AT MOUNTAIN VIEW, EAST BURKE   CHRISTINA TREE

**Nordic Spa** (open to non-guests) is sited on the brook. Three barrel-shape saunas (available year-round); patrons first steam, then plunge into a cold tub or the brook before immersing themselves in a hot tub.

### ELSEWHERE

MOTOR LODGES **Fairbanks Inn** (802-748-5666; stjay.com), 401 Western Avenue (US 2 east), St. Johnsbury. This attractive three-story, 45-unit motel on the outskirts of town has central air-conditioning, cable, dataports, an outdoor heated pool, and fitness center privileges.

    **Comfort Inn & Suites** (802-748-1500; comfortinn.com), off I-91, Exit 20, US 5 South, St. Johnsbury. A 107-unit high-rise motel with an indoor heated pool, a fitness center, a video arcade, cable, dataports, direct VAST trail access.

OTHER **Karmê Chöling Shambhala Meditation Center** (802-633-2384; karmecholing.org), 369 Patneaude Lane, Barnet. The oldest (founded in 1970) of New England's Buddhist meditation centers, Karmê Chöling follows the Tibetan Buddhist path of understanding one's own mind through meditation. What began as a small center in an old farmhouse now includes 540

THE VILLAGE INN OF EAST BURKE   CHRISTINA TREE

wooded, path-webbed acres, six meditation halls, a practice pavilion, an azuchi (Zen archery range), a large organic garden, private guest rooms, and dining facilities. The centerpiece remains the original, now expanded farmhouse with its beautiful main shrine room. Visitors are welcome (call beforehand), but this is all about one- to seven-day retreats (many are geared to weekends) on a variety of themes but with the practice of "mindfulness meditation" at their heart.

**Seyon Lodge State Park** (802-584-3829; vtstateparks.com) in Groton State Forest. This 1890s hunting/fishing lodge on Noyes Pond—Vermont's only public fly-fishing pond—is deep in Groton State Forest, staffed and open year-round except for stick and mud seasons. In winter it caters to fishermen, cross-country skiers, snowshoers, and snowmobilers. There are double and queen beds, and bunk rooms with shared baths, accommodating a total of 16, serving up to 30 for meals. It's also popular with small groups, which take advantage of the conference space with a hearth. $.

## ✳ Where to Eat

DINING OUT **Rabbit Hill Inn** (802-748-5168; rabbithillinn.com), 48 Lower Waterford Road (VT 18), Lower Waterford. Dinner (except Wednesday) open to outside guests by reservation. The attractive dining room holds just 15 tables, and both food and atmosphere are carefully orchestrated. There's candlelight, and music many nights, to complement an à la carte menu that might include Vermont-raised pork loin, roast saddle of lamb, and honey-lacquered duck. Gorgeous desserts. $$–$$$.

**Bailiwicks on Mill** (802-424-1215; bailiwicksfinerestaurant.com), 98 Mill Street, St. Johnsbury. Open Mon.–Thurs. from 5 p.m., Fri.–Sun. 11:30–9. A pleasant ambience in a nineteenth-century mill. Reservations advised on weekends.

You have St. J's wonderful "dining out" option but there's also a wine and martini bar inside with an imaginative pub menu. Seasonal balcony seating. Mixed reviews.

**Creamery Restaurant** (802-684-3616), 46 Hill Street. Danville. Open Tues.–Sat. A former creamery with a blackboard menu featuring homemade soups and curries, along with salads, pies, and a choice of meat and seafood dishes. Breads and soups are homemade, and salad comes with all dinners; also a pub menu. $$.

EATING OUT

IN AND AROUND ST. JOHNSBURY

♿ **Kingdom Taproom** (802-424-1355; kingdomtaproom.com), 397 Railroad Street. Open Mon.–Thurs. 4–10 p.m., Fri., Sat. until 2 a.m., Sun. noon–8. A great addition to St. J dinner choices. The ambiance is casual and hip, the focus is on specialty and local beers, and the food is more creative than typical pub food, from freshly baked sourdough bread with garlic oil and the charcuterie board to a barbecue brisket. You go down some steps to enter, but there is elevator access in the rear.

**The Wine Gate** (802-748-3288), 25 Depot Square, St. Johnsbury. Open daily except Sunday. Housed in a former rail warehouse beside the handsome station that's now a welcome center, this is an attractive space with a lunch menu featuring a wide choice of cold and hot panini and salads. There are also reasonably priced entrées and a tapas menu.

**Cantina di Gerardo** (802-748-0598; cantinadigerardo.com), 378 Railroad Street, St. Johnsbury. Open Fri.–Sun. for lunch and dinner. A family run restaurant with authentically southern Italian fare: pizzas, hot and cold sandwiches, classic red-sauce dishes, daily specials, wine, and beer.

**Pica Pica** (802-424-1585; pica-pica.us), 1214 Main Street. Open Wed.–Sat. Vermont's first and only Filipino restaurant is a hit. "Pica Pica" refers to small or shared plates, rice, meat and veggie dishes, soups, and stews that are distinctive and delicious.

(((•))) **Bread & Butter** (802-424-1590), 139 Eastern Avenue. Open Mon.–Sat. Housed in a vintage brick former post office building owned by the singer Neko Case. New in 2017, it fills the bright space (formerly Dylan's) hung with local art and offers a limited menu but gets raves for its house-made bagels and quiche.

&. ✪ **Anthony's Diner** (802-748-3613), 321 Railroad Street, St. Johnsbury. Open 6:30 a.m.–8 p.m. Tues.–Sat.; closing at 4 p.m. Sun.–Mon. Anthony and Judy Proia have run this cheerful family-geared diner since 1979. Regulars gather around the counter, and there are plenty of booths. Breakfast includes corned beef hash and specialty omelets. There are "specials" at all three meals. The fries (try the sweet potato) and onion rings are made fresh, along with the soups; the pies are a point of pride.

✪ **Good Fellas Tavern & Restaurant** (802-748-4249; goodfellasvt.com), 59 Parker Road, just off US 2, east of Danville Village. Open Tues.–Sat. 4–9 p.m., Sat. noon–9. Known for homemade soups, seafood, steaks, and pasta, this is a reliable country restaurant with a sports bar, a separate dining area, and a seasonal deck that's great for families.

**Kham Thai Cuisine** (802-751-8424; khamsthai.com), 1112 Memorial Drive (US 5 north), St. Johnsbury. Open daily 11–9, Sun. noon–8. A great addition to local dining options, known for fresh ingredients and spices, reasonably priced, reliable.

## IN LYNDONVILLE

✪ **Café Sweet Basil** (802-626-9713; cafesweetbasil.com), 32 Depot Street. Open for lunch Wed.–Fri. 11:30–2, for dinner Wed.–Sat. 5:30–8:30. A spacious storefront with a warm ambiance, mismatched tables and chairs, art antiques, and an open kitchen. Freshly made soups and salads with plenty of vegetarian options at lunch and a reasonably priced dinner menu featuring Tex-Mex, also daily specials. Owner Delise Robarts is well known for her fresh ingredients and imaginative fare. Don't pass up a skillfully concocted cocktail or dessert.

**Miss Lyndonville Diner** (802-626-9890), 686 Broad Street (US 5). Open 6 a.m. until supper. An expanded vintage railroad car diner, famed for breakfast, from strawberry pancakes with whipped cream and blueberry pancake rollups to corned beef hash and country-fried steak; there are also plenty of lunch and dinner choices.

(((•))) **Grindstone Café** (802-626-0742), 102 Depot Street. Open daily. Best espressos in town and an inviting place to linger with a Danish or gluten-free doughnut.

(((•))) **The Lyndonville Freight House** (802-626-1174; thelyndonfreight house.com), 1000 Broad Street. Open daily 7–5:30. Owned by a family of organic farmers, this informal eatery is housed in a former freight station (1868), one of two buildings left from the 22 built here by the Boston & Maine. We have raved about the food and ice cream in the past but were disappointed by a recent breakfast: the oatmeal was instant and they charged 89 cents per person for maple syrup. Railroad memorabilia is much reduced, but there is still a wide choice of ice cream, an upstairs crafts corner, and occasionally a real freight train, rumbling by.

## IN EAST BURKE

✪ **Foggy Goggle Osteria** (802-417-3500), 66 Belden Hill Road, East Burke. Open Thu.–Mon. The white farmhouse is hidden back behind the village and apart from the larger parking area. An "osteria," co-owner Sara Miles explains, is a simple, roadside Italian restaurant; fare runs from burgers and pizza to pollo al rustica plus pad Thai and beef tenderloin. We can vouch for the quality, ambience, and pollo rustica. $–$$.

JUNIPER'S AT THE WILDFLOWER INN  CHRISTINA TREE

🍃 **Juniper's at The Wildflower Inn**
(802-626-8310; wildflowerinn.com),
between Lyndonville and East Burke, 2059
Darling Hill Road. Open (except November and April) Mon.–Sat. 5:30–9 p.m.
Reservations advised if you want a table
on the sunporch, overlooking a spread of
hills and valleys, or on the seasonal patio.
The beef—from burgers to rib-eye—is from
grass fed belted Galloway cattle raised
here on Darling Hill. The reasonably
priced menu includes braised lamb shank
and pork schnitzel, as well as vegetarian
options. There's also a good kid's menu.

**Mike's Tiki Bar** (mikestikibar.com) and
**The Vermont Food Truck** (802-626-1177),
open daily 11–9 during biking season at the
base area for Kingdom Trails single-track
mountain bike network, East Burke. In
the middle of the village, but tucked back
beside the Kingdom Trails parking lot and
its shower house, the thatched bar and truck
together supply reasonably priced food and
drink (30 mostly local beers on tap).

**Burke Publick House** (802-626-1188;
burkepub.com), 482 VT 114, in the village out back of the Northeast Kingdom
Country Store. Open daily 5–9 p.m., later
Fri. and Sat. This former cow barn is a
cheerful pub, known for great burgers
but with a full menu and full bar.

(((•))) **Café Lotti** (802-427-3633;
cafelottivt.com), 603 VT 114. Open
Mon.–Thurs. 7–6, Fri.–Sun. until 8 p.m.;
closing earlier in winter. A great middle-
of-the-village gathering spot with great
coffee. This welcoming space was built
in 1838 as a Methodist church with
long windows, revamped with a central
hearth as the area's best restaurant, then
vacant for a stretch until Johnny (long
obssessed with creating the perfect cup
of coffee) and Linda (a serious biker)
Lotti reopened it as a café.

**Tamarack Pub & Grill** (802-626-7390),
Sherburne Base Lodge, 223 Sherburne
Lodge Road, East Burke. Open seasonally. Pub feel and food, comfortably worn
and welcoming.

**East Burke Market** (802-626-5010;
eastburkemarketvt.com), 461 VT 114, the
village's genuine general store, with a
solid deli as well as burgers and homemade baked goods. We recommend the
freshly made chicken salad on whole
wheat for a picnic.

## ELSEWHERE

**Bentley's Bakery & Café** (802-684-
3385; bentleysbakeryvt.com), 20 Hill
Street (just off US 2), Danville. Open

April–December, Wed.–Fri. 6:30–3, weekends 7:30–1:30. Tarah Fontaine specializes in artisanal cakes and has created a special café with outstanding stuffed croissants and pastries for breakfast, quiche, and panini, as well as soups and salads for lunch.

**Three Ponds** (802-727-3300), 12 VT 15 (junction of US 2 & VT 15), West Danville. Open 7–3 except Tues., Wed. A handy and delightful spot for breakfast or lunch, new at this writing but already known for the house corned beef hash, sweet potato fries, and (surprise!) great falafels.

**Mooselook Restaurant** (802-695-2950; mooselookrestaurant.com), 1058 Main Street (US 2), Concord. Open from 6 a.m. daily for all three meals. Basic comfort food. For visitors the bonus is what's on the walls: dozens of vintage photos of what this area was all about more than a century ago.

**Upper Valley Grill** (802-584-3101), 2967 Scott Highway, Groton, junction of US 302 and VT 232. Open 6 a.m.–8 p.m.; until 9 Fri.–Sat. Handy to Groton State Forest, this is a welcoming oasis at the junction of two lonely roads.

**Peacham Café** (802-357-4040; peachamcafe.org), 643 Bayley-Hazen Road, Peacham. Housed in the former fire station beside the general store in the middle of Peacham Village. Generally open 6–2, but check. This community-owned café with its limited menu hits the spot in this scenic but otherwise totally rural area.

## ✻ Entertainment

**Catamount Arts** (802-748-2600; catamountarts.org), 115 Eastern Avenue, St. Johnsbury. The former Masonic Temple is a venue for this long-established, nonprofit arts center featuring nightly screenings in two theaters: the larger Cinema 1, screening popular films, and the smaller Cinema 2 with regional premieres, mini series, and programs devoted to Vermont filmmakers. There's an extensive video library and a gallery showcasing local artists; also live performances, periodic coffeehouses, and special events.

**Star Theatre** (802-748-9511; stjay theatre.com), 18 Eastern Avenue, St. Johnsbury. Cinemas 1-2-3; first-run movies.

**Vermont Children's Theater** (summer only: 802-626-5358), 2283 Darling Hill Road, Lyndonville. Sited next to The Wildflower Inn, this seasonal theater is staged in a former hay barn. Local youngsters (some 120 are usually involved) perform amazingly well.

*Band concerts:* **St. Johnsbury Town Band concerts**, weekly all summer at the bandstand in Town Hall Park, Mon. 8 p.m. **Lyndonville Town Band concerts**, every Wed. in summer at 8; **Danville concerts** on the green, Sun. at 7 in July and August.

## ✻ Selective Shopping

ANTIQUES SHOPS **Route 5 Collectibles Plus** (802-626-5430), US 5, 277 Main

CAFÉ LOTTI IN EAST BURKE CHRISTINA TREE

Street, Lyndonville. Open daily, except Tues., 10–5. A multidealer and consignment shop.

**Antiques & Emporium** (802-626-3500; antiquesandemporium.com), 182 South Wheelock Road, Lyndonville. Open daily 10–5, except Tues. Housed in a former grade school, a multigroup shop with everything from rugs and clocks to furniture, pottery, and prints.

BOOKSTORES ✪ **Green Mountain Books & Prints** (802-626-5051; greenmtnbooks.com), 1055 Broad Street, Lyndonville. Open Mon.–Sat. This is a long-established destination for book lovers. With 37,000 or so volumes (80 percent used, 20 percent new) on a wide range of topics, it's a treasure trove that can keep you happily digging for hours. On the other hand, owner Kim Crady-Smith is adept at finding just what you are looking for, including rare out-of-print titles. There's comfy seating, a great children's room, and an extensive selection of books on Vermont.

**Boxcar & Caboose Bookshop** (802-748-3551; boxcarandcaboosee.com), 394 Railroad Street, St. Johnsbury. A well-stocked downtown store, with a large children's section and café.

## CRAFTS SHOPS AND ART GALLERIES

### IN THE ST. JOHNSBURY AREA

✪ **Northeast Kingdom Artisans Guild** (802-748-0158; nekartisansguild.com), 430 Railroad Street, St. Johnsbury. Open Mon.–Sat.; closed Mon. off-season. This magnificent cooperative shop showcases work by more than 100 Vermont artists in many media.

✪ **Joe's Pond Craft Shop** (802-684-2192; joespondcrafts.com), 2748 US 2 West, West Danville, adjoining Hastings Store at the junction with VT 15. Open May–December, Tues.–Sun. Deborah Stresing can usually be found at her loom behind the counter in the barn she has filled with well-chosen quilts, baskets, block prints, woodworking, floorcloths

GREEN MOUNTAIN BOOKS, LYNDONVILLE  CHRISTINA TREE

and rag rugs (her own), cards, felted bags—the work of close to 40 craftspeople in all.

FARMS & FARM STANDS **Brigid's Farm** (802-592-3062), 123 Slack Street, Peacham. Call ahead. A small farm with sheep, angora goats, and dairy goats with a weaving studio and mittens, handspun yarns, spinning wheels, natural dye extracts, and supplies for sale.

**Snowshoe Farm** (802-592-3153; snowshoefarm.com), 520 The Great Road, Peacham. Open year-round, but call first. Ron and Terry Miller breed alpacas and process their fiber, selling it along with hand-knit or woven alpaca products.

COUNTRY STORES ✪ **Hastings Store** (802-684-3398), 2748 US 2, West Danville. Jane Hastings Larabee represents the third generation of her family to manage the store and post office serving "64 people in the village and the 300 cottages on the lake." Garey Larrabee is known locally for his homemade sausage, as well as for the doughnuts and blueberry cake he makes fresh each morning. Built as a nineteenth-century stagecoach stop, the rambling, double-porched store is positioned across US 2 from Joe's Pond.

SPECIAL SHOPS **Caplan's Army Store Work & Sportswear** (802-748-3236), 457 Railroad Street, St. Johnsbury. At a time when it's getting harder and harder to find a decent army-navy store, this is the genuine article. Established in 1922 and still run by the same family, a serious source of quilted jackets, skiwear, Woolrich sweaters, hunting boots, and such; good value and friendly service.

**Moose River Lake and Lodge Store** (802-748-2423), 370 Railroad Street, St. Johnsbury. Open except Sundays. Antiques, rustic furniture, and accessories for the home, camp, or cabin: taxidermy specialties, deer antlers and skulls, prints, pack baskets, fishing creels and snowshoes, folk art, an extensive wine collection, and more.

*⌀* **Artesano Mead** (802-584-9000; artesanomead.com), 1334 Scott Highway, Groton. Check the website for varieties (including sparkling and spiced meads), tours, and special events. Open seasonally Wed.–Sun.; call ahead to check. Housed in Groton's former general store, Mark Simakaski and Nichole Wolfgang produce a rich golden wine made from honey using their own and other Vermont bees. For kids (and adults) there is also great house-made ice cream and bees to watch at work behind glass.

**Samadhi Store and Workshop** (802-633-4440; samadhitore.com), 30 Church Street, Barnet. Open Mon.–Fri. 9–4:30, Sat. 11–3:30. A nonprofit offshoot of nearby Karmê Chöling, selling meditation cushions and yoga mats made on-site, as well as singing bowls and gongs, robes, teas, Vermont-made raku incense bowls, meditation benches, and tables.

SUGARHOUSES **Rowell Sugarhouse** (802-563-2756), 4962 VT 15, Walden. Visitors are welcome year-round, 9–5. Maple

HASTINGS STORE, WEST DANVILLE  CHRISTINA TREE

cream and candy as well as sugar; also Vermont honey, sheepskins, crafts, and paintings.

**Goodrich's Sugarhouse** (802-563-9917; goodrichmaplefarm.com), just off US 2 by Molly's Pond in East Cabot. Open every day except Sundays/holidays. A family tradition for seven generations, open to visitors March–December with a full line of award-winning maple products.

**Goss's Sugar House** (802-633-4743), 101 Maple Lane, Barnet. Gordon and Pat Goss won a blue ribbon in the past for their syrup at the Caledonia County Fair. They welcome visitors, sell year-round, and will ship.

**High Meadow Farm** (802-467-3621), East Burke. The sugarhouse is open in-season. Call for directions.

## ✳ Special Events

*February:* **Snowflake Festival**, Lyndonville–Burke. Events include a crafts show, snow sculptures, ski races for all ages and abilities, sleigh rides, music, and art.

*March:* **Maple Open House Weekend** (vermontmaple.org). **WinterBike** at Kingdom Trails (kingdomtrails.org), East Burke. **Cultural Festival**, midmonth, at Lyndon State College, Lyndonville (lyndonstate.edu).

*Late April:* **World Maple Festival** (worldmaplefestival.org), St. Johnsbury.

*Memorial Day weekend:* **Vermont Open Studio Weekend** (vermontcrafts.com).

*June:* **Tour de Kingdom** (tourdekingdom.com), first weekend, a competitive and recreational century ride through the Lake Region.

*June–October:* **Farmers' markets**, in downtown St. Johnsbury, Craftsbury, and Hardwick.

*July:* **Peacham Independence Day festivities** include a ghost walk in the cemetery, with past residents impersonated by present ones. **Burklyn Arts Council Summer Craft Fair** (burklyn-arts.org)

Saturday closest to July 4, in Bandstand Park, Lyndonville. **Stars and Stripes Festival**, last weekend, Lyndonville—big auction, parade featuring Bread and Puppet, Uncle Sam, barbecue.

*August:* **Danville Fair** (danvillevtchamber.org) on the green features a parade with floats, more than 75 years of tradition. **Caledonia County Fair** (caledoniacountyfair.com) third week, Mountain View Park, Lyndonville—horse, pony, and ox pulls; livestock shows; midway, rides, demolition derby, and music. **Burke Bike 'n Brew** (skiburke.com), an annual festival featuring music, food, crafts, mountain bike races, and beer.

*September:* **Burke Mountain Bike Race**, first weekend after Labor Day, up the Toll Road. **Burke Fall Foliage Festival**, last Saturday.

*September–October:* **Colors of the Kingdom**, held in mid-September, pairs the St. Johnsbury autumn festival with a Fairbanks Museum fall event: crafts fair, farmers' market, planetarium show, parade, trains rides, and more. **Northeast Kingdom Fall Foliage Festival**, the last week in September or first one in October. Seven towns take turns hosting visitors, feeding them breakfast, lunch, and dinner; and guiding them to beauty spots and points of interest within their borders. In Walden, the specialty is Christmas wreath-making; in Plainfield, farm tours; in Peacham, a ghost walk and crafts fair; in Barnet, the historical society house is open, and guided tours of backroads are outstanding. The day in Groton includes a parade, lumberjack's breakfast, and chicken pie supper. For details, contact the The Northeast Kingdom Travel and Tourism Association (see *Guidance* on page 438).

*October:* **Autumn on the Green** in Danville.

*First weekend of December:* **Burklyn Christmas Crafts Market**—a major gathering of North Country craftspeople and artists in the Lyndon Town School. **North Pole Polar Express** (Lyndon).

# HEART OF THE KINGDOM

In this high, open farm country, fields roll away to distant mountains and woods are spotted with small lakes and large ponds. Get lost along the well-maintained dirt farm roads that web this area. Find your way to Craftsbury Common, with its white homes, academy, and church; to the beach on Caspian Lake in Greensboro; to the Stone House Museum in Brownington; and the Bread and Puppet Museum in Glover.

Barton boomed in the late nineteenth century, when six passenger trains a day stopped in summer, bringing guests to fill the town's long-gone hotels and the gingerbread-style "camps" (still there) on Crystal Lake. Lake Willoughby, with its dramatic, fjordlike "Gap," was a far better-known destination more than a century ago than it is now.

What this area offers, besides beauty, is a sense of discovery. So much is here, but quietly. On the hottest of days there's plenty of space on its beach at the foot of Lake Willoughby. On the best snow day of the season, you may ski alone on a Craftsbury Outdoor Center trail.

**GUIDANCE** **Heart of Vermont Chamber of Commerce** (802-472-5906; heartofvt.com) serves surrounding towns, including Walden, Craftsbury, Greensboro, Cabot, and Woodbury.

**Barton Area Chamber of Commerce** (centerofthekingdom.com) serves the lakes-rich area that includes Orleans and Lake Willoughby. Both websites are worth checking.

## ✳ Towns and Villages

**Barton** The hotels are gone, but Crystal Lake remains beautiful, with a cliff-like promontory on one side and **Crystal Lake State Beach** (see *Swimming* on page 460) on its northern shore. Barton also offers golf and a number of services for surrounding towns. The **Crystal Lake Falls Historical Association** maintains the Pierce House Museum (802-525-3084), 97 Water Street, open June–August, Sun. 1–5 p.m.) with a short hiking path behind, spanning a waterfall.

**Brownington Historic District** is a crossroads village full of outstanding, early-nineteenth-century buildings, the core of a once proud hill town long since eclipsed by such valley centers as Barton, Orleans, and Newport. The centerpiece is the **Old Stone House Museum** (see sidebar on page 456); don't miss the panorama from the Prospect Hill Observatory, up behind the restored Orleans County Grammar School.

**Cabot** (population 2,000). Known during the War of 1812 for its distilleries, this distinctly upcountry village is now famed for its cheese. **Cabot Farmers Co-op Creamery** is Vermont's major cheese producer, and its visitor center is a popular attraction. Cabot is called the mother of the Winooski because the river rises in four of its ponds. Technically the town is in Washington County, but it's tightly bound into the network of Kingdom roads and farms.

**Craftsbury** (population 1,162; townofcraftsbury.com). Few places convey such a sense of tranquility and order as the village of **Craftsbury Common**. In summer, petunias bloom in window boxes, and the green of the grass contrasts crisply with the white fences. In winter, the general whitewash of this scene contrasts with the blue of the sky. Throughout the year there are nearby places to stay and books to check out at the desk in the new **Craftsbury Public Library** (802-586-9683), with its rockers on the porch, comfortable reading corners, Wi-Fi, and imposing portraits of Ebenezer Crafts and his son Samuel. Due to debt, Ebenezer was forced to sell his tavern in Sturbridge, MA (the still-popular Publick House). He made his way here over the Bayley-Hazen Military Road, eventually bringing his family and 150 of his Sturbridge neighbors this way on sleds. Ebenezer was quick to establish a school. Samuel, a Harvard graduate who served three terms as governor, founded Craftsbury Academy, which still functions as the high school for the town. The **Sterling College** campus adds to the mix. In East Craftsbury the **John Woodruff Memorial Library** (802-586-9692) preserves the look of the general store (vintage 1840s) while offering its stock of 20,000 books, including many children's titles, to visitors as well as to residents. Many farmers welcome visitors to their sugarhouses during sugaring season in late March and early April and sell syrup from their farmhouses year-round. **Craftsbury Outdoor Center** (*see* sidebar on page 458) offers one of the most extensive and dependable cross-country ski networks in New England; its summer sculling program is also nationally recognized. An extensive web of well-surfaced dirt farm roads meanders in all directions, beloved by bicyclists and runners. In 1930 Craftsbury had close to 100 farms, each with an average of 10 cows. In 2010 there were still 1,760 cows, and many farms had diversified.

**Greensboro** (population 770). Greensboro's year-round population (770) triples in summer thanks to a tightly knit, high-brow, low-key summer cottage colony founded in the 1890s on Caspian Lake. The year-round **Highland Center for the Arts** (*Entertainment*) is a gift from a member. The lake isn't visible from the middle of the village, but its public beach is right there around the corner, within walking distance of **Willey's Store**. Greensboro has been home to **Circus Smirkus** (see *Entertainment* on page 466). The **Greensboro Historical Society** (802-533-2457), 29 Breezy Avenue, is worth a visit, open most days in summer.

**Hardwick**. The village's Victorian architecture is a reminder of the town's heyday as one of the world's major granite processors. The granite was actually in Woodbury, where it arrived by rail. Thousands of skilled European craftsmen moved to town beginning in the 1870s and continuing into the 1920s; a number of French Canadians remain. The Lamoille River runs through town, good for fly-fishing, beneath the swinging (pedestrian) bridge linking Main Street with parking. East Hardwick is also worth finding. The **Hardwick Town House** (see *Entertainment* on page 465) is noted for its hand-painted stage curtains and frequent concerts, live productions, and lectures.

## ✳ Must See

**Cabot Creamery Visitor Center** (802-563-3393; cabotcheese.com), 2878 Main Street, Cabot Village (no way can you miss it). Open year-round. This is home base for Cabot, Vermont's foremost cheesemaker, cooperatively owned by dairy farmers since 1919. The center showcases its products and dramatizes its cheesemaking process, but it no longer offers tours.

LAKES **Lake Willoughby**, Westmore. Vermont's most dramatic lake, nearly 5 miles long and more than 300 feet deep, shaped like a stocking with a foot toward the north and Mount Pisgah and Mount Hor rising to more than 2,500 feet on opposite sides at the southern end.

DOWNTOWN HARDWICK, FROM THE VILLAGE RESTAURANT  CHRISTINA TREE

**Crystal Lake**, Barton. Roughly 3 miles long and about 1 mile wide, in places more than 100 feet deep, this glacial lake is beautifully sited between roughly hewn mountains. **Crystal Lake State Park** (see *Swimming* on page 460) is justly popular; summer rental cottages can be found through the Barton Area Chamber of Commerce. Also see *Fishing* below.

The town of Glover also harbors three small, fish-stocked lakes: **Daniels Pond**, **Shadow Lake**, and **Lake Parker**.

## ✳ To Do

BIKING  This pristine area offers hundreds of miles of dirt and logging roads. Request the excellent bike map of the Kingdom from the **Northeast Kingdom Travel and Tourism Association** (travelthekingdom.com) or download it from **centerofthekingdom .com**. For bike rentals, see the sidebar on **Craftsbury Outdoors Center** on page 458 and, in the previous chapter, on **Kingdom Trails** on page 438.

BIRDING  The most famous birds in the Kingdom are the peregrine falcons that nest on Mount Pisgah on Lake Willoughby. Falcons return in spring, nest during summer, and leave by August. Early morning and late afternoon are the best times to see them from the north end of the west-facing cliff. Over 100 species of birds have been spotted around Lake Willoughby alone.

BOATING  See **Craftsbury Outdoor Center** sidebar on page 458.
**White Caps Campgrounds** (802-467-3345) at the southern end of Lake Willoughby rents canoes and kayaks.

FISHING  Also see the introduction to "The Northeast Kingdom" on page 428.

The Old Stone House Museum (802-754-2022; oldstonehousemuseum.org), 109 Old Stone House Road off VT 58 east of Orleans in Brownington. Open May 15–October 15, Wed.– Sun. 11–5 for guided tours from the visitor center at the Alexander Twilight House; last tour at 4. Admission. The "Old Stone House" is a striking, four-story, granite building, completed in 1836 as a 30-room dormitory for the Orleans County Grammar School. It's the

THE OLD STONE MUSEUM COURTESY OF THE OLD STONE MUSEUM

Lake Eligo and Caspian Lake in Greensboro, and Little and Great Hosmer ponds in Craftsbury. The Lamoille River in Hardwick is good for trout and perch.

GOLF Mountain View Country Club (802-533-7477; mvccvt.com), 112 Country Club Road, Greensboro, nine holes. Established 1898; open to nonmembers midweek only. Use of carts permitted only for health reasons.

Orleans Country Club (802-754-2333), 316 Country Club Lane, Orleans (VT 58), near Lake Willoughby. April–November; 18 holes, rentals, instruction. Lake Willoughby Golf (802-723-4783; lakewilloughbygolf.com), 25 Coles Mountain Lane,

centerpiece of the **Brownington Historic District**, the remnants of a once much larger crossroads village, and it was built by Alexander Twilight (1795–1875), the first African American to attend an American college (Middlebury, 1823) or to serve in a state legislature (Vermont House of Representatives, 1836). Twilight arrived in 1829 to assume his duties as a Congregational minister and schoolmaster at the newly opened school, which enrolled students from throughout Orleans County and needed lodging. He proposed a dormitory but failed to gain the support of school trustees, and it's still a mystery how he managed it. The Stone House now houses Orleans County historical collections and includes dozens of murals by Rufus Porter, one of the era's premier

BREAD AND PUPPET THEATER MUSEUM CHRISTINA TREE

itinerant artists. The museum encompasses several surrounding buildings, including the restored Grammar School/Grange Hall, a working blacksmith shop, and a perennial garden. **Old Stone House Day** (second Sunday in August) is one of the Kingdom's biggest annual events, but it's on quiet days that we find this hilltop cluster most appealing. Any day, pick up the walking tour guide and don't miss the view from the observatory tower on Prospect Hill. Check the website for year-round special events and workshops. ✪

   **Bread and Puppet Theater Museum** (802-525-3031; breadandpuppet.org), 753 Heights Road (VT 122), Glover. Open mid-June–October, 10–6. The internationally known Bread and Puppet Theater tours in winter, but much of the year the weathered, vintage 1863 dairy barn is open to anyone who stops (free, but donations welcome). It houses one of the biggest collections and some of the biggest puppets in the world: huge and haunting puppet dwarfs, giants, devils, and other fantastic figures of good and evil, the artistic expressions of German-born Peter Schumann, who founded the Bread and Puppet Theater in 1962 and moved it to Glover in 1974. You can inquire about tours, but usually visitors wander and wonder. Publications, postcards, and "Cheap Art" are sold in the shop. Sat. and Sun. in July and August, and performances are staged in the outdoor arena in the neighboring field and in the timber-frame theater. Also see *Entertainment* on page 465.

Westmore. This hilltop, nine-hole, family-friendly course is well worth finding. Check the website for directions.

   **Barton Golf Course** (802-525-1126), Telfer Hill Road, Barton. April–September, 18 holes, cart rentals, and low fees. **Grandad's Invitational** (467-3739), Newark. This nine-hole course is a local legend.

HIKING AND WALKING  **Mount Pisgah** and **Mount Hor**, Lake Willoughby. Named respectively for the place where the Lord sent Moses to view the Promised Land and for the place Moses's brother Aaron died after the Lord commanded him to

# CRAFTSBURY OUTDOOR CENTER

Craftsbury Outdoor Center (802-586-7767; craftsbury.com), 535 Lost Nation Road, Craftsbury Common. Begun in 1976 as a cross-country ski and sculling center, this is now an 800-acre multi-seasonal outdoor recreation destination. Facilities are sited on Great Hosmer Pond and trails traverse rolling fields, woods, and maple and evergreen groves, set against the distant Green Mountains.

## SUMMER/FALL

**SCULLING** This nationally recognized program offers three-, four-, six-, and seven-day May–September sessions, open to ages 12 and up at all skill levels.

**RUNNING** Five, six-, and seven-day camps are offered late June–August, some fall weekends. Different sessions focus on training for triathlons, marathons, road racing, Masters running, and just plain fun and fitness. Open to all ages 12 and up, all abilities.

RUNNING AT THE CRAFTSBURY OUTDOOR CENTER

go there, these twin mountains, separated by a narrow stretch of lake, form Willoughby Gap. Both are within the 7,000-acre Willoughby State Forest and offer well-maintained hiking trails. Mount Pisgah (2,751 feet), on the east side of the lake (access marked from VT 5A), has fairly short climbs yielding spectacular views of the White Mountains; trails up Mount Hor (2,648 feet) begin on the Civilian Conservation Corps road, 1.8 miles west of its junction with VT 5A, and also offer panoramic views of the Green Mountains to the west. For details, consult *50 Hikes in Vermont* (Backcountry Guides) and *Day Hiker's Guide to Vermont* (Green Mountain Club).

**Wheeler Mountain.** The trail begins on Wheeler Mountain Road, which leaves the north side of US 5, 8.3 miles north of West Burke and 5 miles south of Barton Village. From the highway, the unpaved road climbs 1.9 miles to the trailhead.

CRAFTSBURY CENTER IS ONE OF NEW ENGLAND'S PRIME DESTINATIONS FOR CROSS-COUNTRY SKIERS  JOHN LAZENBY

**MOUNTAIN BIKING** Rent or BYO a fat tire bike. There are countless miles of surrounding roads through glorious farm country; also 20 km of single-track trails on the property.

## WINTER

**CROSS-COUNTRY SKIING** The 105 km of well-marked trails are groomed for skating and for diagonal stride. Thanks to their elevation and grooming, trails are usually skiable into April. Geared to top athletes but also to skiers of every ability. The center also maintains the Highland Lodge trail network, accessible via a connecting trail and shuttle on weekends. The Activity Center offers rentals and instruction. There are also snowshoe and fat tire bike rentals and dedicated trails. The **Craftsbury X-C Ski Marathon**, 25 and 50 km races for the true competitors, 10 km for ordinary skiers, is held the last weekend of January.

**LODGING** for 90 guests starts at two rustic lodges and goes up to trailside cabins, with many choices in between. Facilities include a fitness room and sauna, swimming, and access to boating on Great Hosmer Pond. Rates include three plentiful meals served buffet-style in the dining hall. Check the website for rates, which vary with the type of accommodation and season; kids under 6 are free. Pets are allowed in one cottage (cleaning fee). $$.

**Bald Mountain.** There are excellent views from the newly restored fire tower at the summit of this, the tallest peak in the Willoughby Lake area. Trails ascend to the summit from both the north (Lookout's Trail, 2.8 miles) and the south (Long Pond Trail, 2.1 miles). From the north side of Bald Mountain, you can hike on trails and wilderness roads all the way to the summit of Mount Hor; Haystack Mountain (a side trip) has excellent views and two trails. Details can be found in *Day Hiker's Guide to Vermont* (see *Hiking and Walking* in "What's Where" on page 38).

SCENIC DRIVES **West Burke to Westmore.** The stretch of VT 5A along Lake Willoughby is one of the most breathtaking drives anywhere in the state.

    **Lake Willoughby to Island Pond shortcut.** An easy route to navigate from Westmore on Lake Willoughby: Turn north in the middle of the village on Hinton Ridge Road

STILLMEADOW FARM CHRISTINA TREE

and follow it through high, rolling farmland and forest (never mind the name changes) until it reaches a T intersection. Turn right and right again onto VT 105 into Island Pond. The reverse direction is even more beautiful but too tricky.

**Greensboro Village to East Hardwick.** The road passes through Hardwick Street (that's the name of the hamlet) and a fine collection of Federal and Greek Revival houses; from Greensboro Village to Hardwick, it makes a beeline through high and open farm country; and from Craftsbury Common north to VT 14 through Albany and Irasburg, it follows the rich farmland of the Black River Valley.

SWIMMING **Crystal Lake State Beach** (802-525-6205), 90 Bellwater Avenue, Barton (just east of the village off VT 16), is open daily late May–September, with a lifeguard, a bathhouse (built of stones quarried on the lake and built in the late 1930s by the CCC), and picnic facilities; and **Pageant Park**, a mile farther east on VT 16, is a town-owned park open daily until 10 p.m., with a bathhouse and camping (primarily tenting). **May Pond**, also along VT 16 in Barton, is a great spot for swimming, canoeing, and kayaking. **Lake Willoughby** has small public beaches at both its northern and southern tips.

BEACH AT THE NORTHERN END OF LAKE WILLOUGHBY CHRISTINA TREE

**Caspian Lake**, Beach Road, Greensboro Village. This is a great spot for small children, with gradually deepening clear water. There's a large, free parking lot and space to spread blankets.

**Shadow Lake Beach** in Glover is marked from VT 16. The most accessible of Glover's three lakes, with free parking; also good for small children.

## ❄ Winter Sports

See sidebar: **Craftsbury Outdoor Center** on page 458.

SNOWMOBILING Northeast Kingdom Snowmobile Map is free from the **Northeast Kingdom Chamber of Commerce** (800-639-6379). Also see "Island Pond and Beyond" on page 484. Tours.

## ❄ Green Space

**Barr Hill Nature Preserve**, Greensboro. Turn right at the town hall and go about half a mile to Barr Hill Road (another left). The trails at Barr Hill, managed by The Vermont Nature Conservancy, overlook Caspian Lake. Don't miss the view from the top. In winter, ski and snowshoe trails are maintained by Craftsbury Outdoor Center.

**Hardwick Trails**, Hazen Union School, Hardwick. Six miles of nonmotorized nature and recreational trails wind through the woods behind the high school in the middle of the village.

## ❄ Lodging

✦ ✪ ♂ **Highland Lodge** (802-322-4456; highlandlodge.com), 1608 Craftsbury Road, Greensboro. This rambling B&B, with its ten rooms and ten cabins, is a beloved local icon, set on 136 acres on Barr Hill, overlooking Caspian Lake, with a private beach and lake access. The "Lodge" is really an 1860s farmhouse, converted to an inn in the 1920s—since then it's acquired a loyal following, and its comfortable look and feel has survived to the present. New owner Heidi Lauren Duke is a singer and opera director, tuned to Greensboro's burgeoning arts scene. The House Bar serves dinner and is open to the public on weekends year-round, plus special events and weddings. The snow season connects their well-maintained cross-country ski and snowshoe trails to Craftsbury Outdoor Center. Rates: $160 for lodge rooms, $$ for cabins.

♿ **Willoughvale Inn and Cottages** (802-525-4123; willoughvale.com), 793 VT 5A, Westmore. The contemporary inn and cottages are sited on Vermont's most dramatic lake. Guests can swim or paddle from the dock. Windows maximize the view. Ten guest rooms in the inn itself include two "luxury suites." Across

HIGHLAND LAKE HOUSE CHRISTINA TREE

the road, three housekeeping cottages with fireplaces are right on the lake; there are four more two-bedroom "lake view" cottages up behind and above the inn. A taproom and light dinners (*Dining Out*) are available. May–October. Standard rooms with queen beds in the main inn are $–$$ with continental breakfast; cottages run $$–$$$.

✪ **Rodgers Country Inn** (802-525-6677; rogerscountryinn.com), 582 Rodgers Road, West Glover. Not far from Shadow Lake and handy to Craftsbury Outdoor Center, this proud old farmhouse has been in Jim Rodgers's family since the 1800s. Far from any traffic, it's surrounded by its 400 acres, beckoning guests out for a walk down to the beaver pond or a bike ride along miles of hard-packed farm roads; Nancy Rodgers delights in tuning in guests to the best of what's out there. Shadow Lake is good for swimming, boating, and fishing. There's plenty of common space—an enclosed porch, living rooms (flat-screen TV and DVD), and a game room with Ping-Pong

table. A full breakfast, included in reasonable rates, is served in the bright dining room off the open kitchen. The food is farm fresh and delicious, and there's good conversation. Inquire about winterized cabins.

✪ 🐾 **The Kimball House** (802-472-6228; kimballhouse.com), 173 Glenside Avenue, Hardwick. This is a capacious, handsome, 1890s painted lady set high above downtown Hardwick. Sue and Todd Holmes began hosting guests after their four children moved on. All three guest rooms are upstairs (one has twin iron beds) and share two full baths, one upstairs and one down. Sue is a hospitable host and delighted to help guests explore. There's plenty of common space, plus a big wraparound porch and backyard. A light dinner is offered with advance notice. A full breakfast is included in rates. $.

✎ ✪ **Mountain View Dairy Bed & Breakfast** (802-754-8494; mountainviewdairybedandbreakfast .com), 725 Poutre Drive, Irasburg. Off the

RODGERS COUNTRY INN

VIEW FROM THE KIMBALL HOUSE, HARDWICK CHRISTINA TREE

options. A large country breakfast is included in rates. $.

**Mountain Lake Cottages** (802-525-3072; vermontmountainlakecottages .com), 52 Old 5A Road, Westmore. Open April 15–October 15. A line of 10 exceptional log cottages all facing directly on Lake Willoughby above a sloping lawn, a total of more than 4 acres with an expanse of waterfront. This prime location was understandably the site of one of the lake's major nineteenth-century hotels. The two-room cottages each have a stone fireplace in the sitting/dining area, along with full kitchen, heat, and a front porch. Owner Renee Leveille is a hospitable host, inviting guests to swim off the dock and venture out onto the lake in a rowboat or kayak. Amenities include a rec hall, a tennis court, and a little take-a-book/leave-a-book library. Mid-June–August, $$–$$$.

Also see **Craftsbury Outdoor Center** sidebar on page 458.

beaten track, this is a third-generation, 221-acre dairy farm with a spectacular view east across rolling hills. Denis and Carol Poutre are up at 4 every morning milking the cows that spend most of the day decoratively distributed over the hill behind this tidy farmhouse. The three comfortable guest rooms are upstairs, sharing a large, immaculate bathroom. No one else was there the night we stayed. This is a great find for families, as guests are invited into the barn to help with the milking and other chores, haying, and sugaring in-season; there are walking/snowshoeing trails. Denis has an easy laugh, and Carol, a grandmother who looks ridiculously young and energetic, both enjoy their guests. Although this seems miles from anywhere, especially the first time you try to find it (don't use your GPS or you never will), it's not far from lunch and dining

## ✻ Where to Eat

**The Parker Pie Co.** (802-525-3366; parkerpie.com), 161 County Road in the back of the Lake Parker Country Store, West Glover Village. Open except Mon., 11–9; until 10 Fri.–Sat. Check the website for special menus and live music. A renowned foodie destination in the back of the village store, featuring thin-crust New York–style pizza, cooked on stone, with locally sourced toppings that include veggies and cheeses as well as smoked sausage and bacon, a dazzling choice of specialty pies., also local greens and pub food. A dozen revolving beers on tap and wine by the glass.

⌇ **Parson's Corner** (802-525-4500; parsonscorner.com), 14 Glover Road (VT 16 on the southern edge of Barton). Open except Tues. 5 a.m.–2:30 p.m. This cheerful, family-owned eatery serves breakfast all day and daily specials. Soups, slaw, ice cream, and a lot more made from scratch. Children's menu.

HARDWICK STREET CAFÉ  CHRISTINA TREE

♿ **Hardwick Street Café** (802-433-9399) at **Highland Center for the Arts** (802-533-2000; highlandartsvt.org), 2875 Hardwick Street, Greensboro; Open year-round, Tues.–Sat. for lunch and dinner, Sunday brunch; snacks only in mid-afternoon. It's advisable to reserve during performances (see *Entertainment* on page 465). This glass-walled café is an unexpected find just south of the village, tucked into this major performance center/art gallery. At lunch, crepes—savory and sweet—are the specialty, along with soups, salads and sandwiches; the dinner menu is limited but appealing.

**Positive Pie** (802-472-7126; positivepie.com), 87 South Main Street, Hardwick. Open daily 11:30–9:30, bar until 10:30 or 11 p.m. Despite the bar and big screen, this place appeals to families. There's a long list of specialty pizzas, some gluten-free and vegan, as well as salads, poutine, and serious entrées like honey-glazed pork loin.

♻ **The Village Restaurant** (802-472-5701), 19 Main Street, Hardwick. Open Wed.–Sun. 6–3. Sited at the junction of VT 14 and VT 15, this landmark little diner can fill the bill. Recently totally renovated, and under new ownership, it's cleaner and cozier, with better views of the Lamoille River than before. A good stop in Hardwick for families. Particularly good for breakfast, especially if you like hash browns, this is the spot that has locals raving.

**Connie's Kitchen Bakery & Deli** (802-472-6607; conskitchen.com), 4 South Main Street, Hardwick. Mon.–Fri. 6:30–3, Sat. 7–2. From-scratch buttermilk doughnuts, breads, cream pies, cookies, and brownies (gluten-free options). You'll also find daily soups (maybe butternut squash or black and white Mexican bean), lunch deli sandwiches on a choice of house-made breads, salads, and daily specials.

**Craftsbury General Store** (802-586-2440; craftsburygeneralstore.com), 118 South Craftsbury Road. A happening place since Emily McLure took over. A well-stocked store featuring local products, a choice of pizzas, salads, and build-your-own as well as signature sandwiches like chèvre caprese and Craftsbury cheese steak, kids' menu, and everything as local as possible.

**Gills Bar & Grill at WilloughVale Inn and Cottages** (802-525-4123; willoughvale.com), 793 VT 5A, Westmore. Open for dinner late May–October, Tues.–Sun. Tables overlook Lake Willoughby. The atmosphere is casual. Entrées range from fish-and-chips to New York strip sirloin.

**Carriage House & Grill** (802-754-1010), 27 Water Street, Orleans. Open daily for breakfast/lunch; dinner Thurs.–Sat. Minutes from I-91 but off Main Street (VT 58). A great breakfast/lunch spot; go with the specials for dinner.

BREWS  **Hill Farmstead Brewery** (802-533-7450; hillfarmstead.com), 403 Hill Road, Greensboro. Open Wed.–Sat. This back-road farm is a mecca for beer lovers who come to sample growlers and tote home as many bottles as they can manage, given that this is the only place you can buy the bottles and the selection of ales—all brewed in Shaun Hill's family barn. Available on draft mostly in local places.

TEA ○ **Perennial Pleasures Nursery and Tea Garden** (802-472-5104; perennialpleasures.net), East Hardwick (posted from VT 16); Open Memorial Day–Labor Day noon–4 except Mon. Rachel Kane is known for her traditional English Cream Tea, served with scones, cakes, savories, and fresh cream. The brick Federal-era house is set in an outstanding three-acre nursery of perennial plants and flowers (open May–mid-September, 10–5). A destination for serious gardeners. A shop features summer hats and gardening tools.

## ✳ Entertainment

**Highland Center for the Arts** (802-533-2000; highlandartsvt.org), open year-round. Despite a façade partly patterned on Shakespeare's Globe Theater, the center fits unobtrusively into its site south of the village. It includes an art gallery, a 250-seat state-of-the-art theater, and smaller performance spaces (films are shown Wednesday evenings); see *Where to Eat* on page 464 for the center's glass-walled **Hardwick Street Café** (802-433-9399); open Tues.–Sat. for lunch and dinner, Sunday brunch.

**Bread and Puppet Theater Museum** (802-525-3031; breadandpuppet.org), VT 122, Glover. These huge and haunting puppet dwarfs, giants, and devils perform in July and August Friday evenings (7:30 p.m.) in the timber-frame theater and Sunday afternoons (3 p.m.) in the natural outdoor amphitheater.

**Craftsbury Chamber Players** (800-639-3443; craftsburychamberplayers .org) has brought chamber music to northern Vermont for 40 years. The series runs mid-July–late August. Check the current schedule for performances at Hardwick Town House, the Presbyterian church in East Craftsbury, and the Fellowship Hall in Greensboro. Performers are faculty members at The Juilliard School of Music.

**Hardwick Town House** (802-472-8800; hardwicktownhouse.org), 127 Church Street, Hardwick. This 1860 schoolhouse is the venue for a variety of

CRAFTSBURY GENERAL STORE   CHRISTINA TREE

programs: film, drama, music, lectures, and other live performances. The stage features a vintage hand-painted curtain.

**Summer Music from Greensboro** (summermusicfromgreensboro.net). Late July–August, a series of chamber and other music concerts.

**Circus Smirkus** (802-533-7443; smirkus.org), 1 Circus Road, Greensboro. June–mid-August. For more than 30 years, Greensboro has been home to this nationally recognized program cultivating acrobatic and other circus skills for children, now with two campuses and dual roles as a summer camp geared to all ages and abilities, and a highly professional touring troupe with summer performances here and throughout New England.

**The Music Box** (802-586-7533; the musicboxvt.org), 147 Creek Road, Craftsbury. Built as a piano-tuning studio and offering exceptional acoustics, this is a frequent venue for concerts and performances.

**Craftsbury band concerts** at the band shell on the common, Sunday at 7 p.m. in July and August. In **Greensboro**, concerts on the dock at Caspian Lake, summer Sundays at 7:30 p.m.

## ✳ Selective Shopping

**ART AND CRAFT ✪ Miller's Thumb Gallery** (802-533-2045; millersthumb gallery.com), 14 Breezy Avenue, Greensboro Village. Open May 15–October 15, daily from 11. Art and quality craftsmanship in many media, including wearable art and furnishings, housed in an old gristmill with its raceway still visible through a window in the floor.

**✪ Mill Village Pottery** (802-586-9971), 6 Mill Village Road (on the way to Craftsbury Outdoor Center), Craftsbury Common. Open summer and fall, usually off-season, too, but call ahead. Potter Lynn Flory makes a variety of glazed, one-of-a-kind vessels and specializes in the "Yunan steamer," a lidded ceramic

pot with a conical chimney in its center, designed to retain vitamins and minerals.

**Greensboro Barn** (802-533-9281; greensborobarn.com), 491 Country Club Road, Greensboro. You will find Jennifer Ranz here at her pottery wheel in this standout, vintage 1886 barn most days in summer and fall. The high-fired glazed stoneware is dishwasher safe. There are also limited-edition watercolor reproductions of Vermont landscapes.

**BOOKS Galaxy Bookshop** (802-472-5533; galaxybookshop.com), 41 South Main Street, Hardwick. Open daily. Sandy Scott and Andrea Jones preside over this mid-village, full-service bookstore, a delight to step into. A mural of Hardwick with a night sky rendition of the "galaxy" runs across one wall, above shelves full of books. Many Vermont writers and unusual titles are featured, along with a strong children's section. An armchair invites lingering, and the frequent author readings and special events attract a far-flung community.

**GENERAL STORES Willey's Store** (802-533-2621), 7 Breezy Avenue, Greensboro Village. Open 6:30–6, Sun. 8–1. One of the biggest and best general stores in the state, in business for over a century; an

UPSTAIRS IN WILLEY'S STORE, GREENSBORO CHRISTINA TREE

extensive grocery, produce, and, a large hardware wing. The dairy case is a prime outlet for locally made, nationally distributed Jasper Hill Cheese clothing. Upstairs the extensive footwear department now has a wine-tasting corner, a clue to the village's rising profile.

**Currier's Quality Market** (802-525-8822), 2984 Glover Street, Glover. Open year-round daily. The Currier family's general store is a must-stop, if just to see the 948-pound stuffed moose and a variety of formerly live animals lurking in the aisles and festooned from the rafters of this old-style emporium. In addition to staples and a good deli counter with hot specials, this is a major sporting goods store, selling fishing and hunting licenses and stocking extensive gear.

**Craftsbury General Store** (802-586-2440; craftsburygeneralstore.com), 118 South Craftsbury Road. Currently a source of handmade specialty pizzas and picnic fare, as well as toys, local eggs, wine, and staples. Grab a paper and coffee and sit by the woodstove. See *Eating Out* on page 464.

**Evansville Trading Post** (802-754-6305; evansvilletradingpost.com), 645 Evansville Road (VT 58), Brownington. Open daily, year-round. A genuine old general store selling gas, groceries, coffee, and doughnuts, as well as pottery and crafted gifts, including jewelry and moccasins from the local Abenaki clan. Inquire about the annual powwow held here.

FARMS AND FARM STANDS **Pete's Greens** (petesgreens.com), 266 South Craftsbury Road. Open late May–October south of Craftsbury Village. Look for the colorful signs and roof planted in flowers and veggies. Pete Johnson's certified-organic vegetable farm supplies restaurants and stores through much of Vermont. Founder of Hardwick's Center for Agricultural Economy, he has pioneered year-round organic farming in this area. The farm stand carries local meats and cheese along with as many as

CURRIER'S QUALITY MARKET CHRISTINA TREE

100 varieties of vegetables in high season; he also offers locally produced staples such as grains, honey, and syrup. Still, it's not a big place, and it's not staffed. Pay on the honor system.

✪ **Stillmeadow Farm** (802-755-6713), 158 Urie Road, South Albany. Open May–July. Call before coming. The dairy cows are gone but the greenhouses at this handsome farm, one that's been in the same family since the 1830s, are worth a visit. Betty Urie sells a variety of vegetable plants and flowers; hanging baskets and planters are specialties.

**Willoughby Gap Farmstand** (802-467-3921), Off VT 5A, just south of Lake Willoughby. Open June–last signs of foliage, Tues.–Sun. 11–6. MORE THAN A FARMSTAND, the sign proclaims, and this is true. There are farm-grown veggies, pickles, maple popcorn, plus handmade quilts and other crafted items, picnic tables, farm animals, and special events.

**Agape Hill Farm** (802-472-3711; agapehillfarm.com), 618 Houston Hill Road, Hardwick. Open May–October. Llama trail walks and farm tours that include feeding the farm animals.

MAPLE SYRUP **Gebbie's Maplehurst Farm** (802-533-2984), 2183 Gebbie Road, Greensboro. Peter and Sandra Gebbie are major local maple producers,

**RED SKY TRADING POST** CHRISTINA TREE

perpetuating a business that's been welcoming visitors for generations. **Sugarmill Farm** (802-525-3701), VT 16 south of Barton Village. Mid-March–mid-November The Auger family sells its own syrup; sugar-on-snow in-season.

OTHER **Red Sky Trading** (802-525-4736; redskytrading.com), 2894 Glover Street (VT 16), Glover. Closed Tues. Doug and Cheri Safford's red barn store is an irresistible mix of good things to nibble on, local produce and products, garden art, antiques, and kitsch.

## ✳ Special Events

*Last weekend of January:* **Craftsbury X-C Ski Marathon** (craftsbury.com)—a great classic technique event open to skiers of all skills; 25 and 50 km races for the true competitors, 10 for ordinary skiers.

*Late March:* **Maple Open House Weekend** (vermontmaple.org).

*May:* **Vermont Open Studio Weekend** (vermontcrafts.com) on Memorial Day weekend. **Hardwick Spring Festival**, last weekend, includes a parade, a crafts fair, and a chicken barbecue.

*June–October:* **Farmers' markets**, in Craftsbury Sat. 10–1; in Hardwick Fri. 3–6.

*June:* **Antique Gas/Steam Engine Show** at the Old Stone House Museum in Brownington (oldstonehousemuseum .org).

*July:* The **July 4 parade** in Cabot is the best around. **Antiques and Uniques Fair** in Craftsbury Common.

*August:* **Circus Smirkus** (smirkus .org), Greensboro. A children's circus camp that stages frequent performances. **Craftsbury Old Home Day**, Craftsbury Common—parade, games, and crafts. **Orleans County Fair** (orleanscountyfair .net) last week, in Barton, an old-fashioned event at the extensive fairground— horse, pony, and ox pulls, harness racing, stage shows, demo derby, tractor pull, arts, crafts, and agricultural exhibits. **Kingdom Farm & Food Days** (kingdomfarmandfood.org). **Old Stone House Day** (oldstonehousemuseum.org) open house, many events in Brownington Village.

# JAY PEAK AND NEWPORT AREA

Memphremagog is Vermont's second largest lake, stretching from Newport 32 miles north to Magog, Quebec. Once a busy rail junction and destination in its own right, Newport is reclaiming its lakefront. There's an attractive boathouse, a departure point for daily lake cruises and for a lakeside walkway/bike path that runs along the lake to the Canadian border at Derby Line.

Jay Peak Resort, 18 miles west of Newport, is now the area's big destination and economic engine, a major year-round destination with a championship 18-hole golf course, the Northeast's largest weatherproofed water park, a professional hockey arena, and a large bed base.

Newport is far quieter than in the days when the 400-room Memphremagog House stood beside the railroad station, Newport House was across the street, and the New City Hotel was nearby. Guests came by train from Boston and Philadelphia. Lindbergh came with his *Spirit of St. Louis*, and there was a racetrack and a paddle-wheeler.

The waters of Quebec and Vermont mingle in Lake Memphremagog, and the international line runs right through the Haskell Opera House in Derby Line—the audience in America attends concerts performed in Canada. Even the major border crossing (passports or equivalent documents required) at Derby Line isn't especially busy. There are four more rural crossings along this border, which divides two very different cultures. "Vive la difference!"

East of Newport you are quickly in little-trafficked lake country: Lakes Derby, Salem, Seymour, and Echo all have good fishing, and dozens of smaller ponds have boat launches. West of Jay Peak, VT 242 plunges down in to sleepy Montgomery, where the prime attraction is still its six covered bridges.

GUIDANCE **Vermont's North Country Chamber of Commerce** (802-334-7782; vtnorth country.org) maintains a walk-in visitor center, 246 the Causeway in Newport. Days/ hours vary with season.

**Top of Vermont** (802-988-4120; topofvt.com), Jay Peak–centered website with local listing.

**Vermont Welcome Center** (802-873-3311) on I-91 south in Derby Line, half a mile south of the border. Daily 7–7, with restrooms, Green Mountain coffee, live attendant, information.

## ✳ Towns and Villages

**Newport.** With a population of 4,589, smaller than neighboring Derby, this is the seat of Orleans County. There are restrooms and ample parking at the **Gateway Center** (84 Fyfe Drive) by the marina, also seasonal take-out and tables both inside and out. There's also access here to a six-mile walking/running/biking path along the waterfront. The city's past splendor is recalled in archival photos mounted by the **Memphremagog Historical Society** of Newport in the State Office Building. Step into the vintage 1868 **Goodrich Memorial Library** for a sense of the era. **Newport Parks & Recreation**

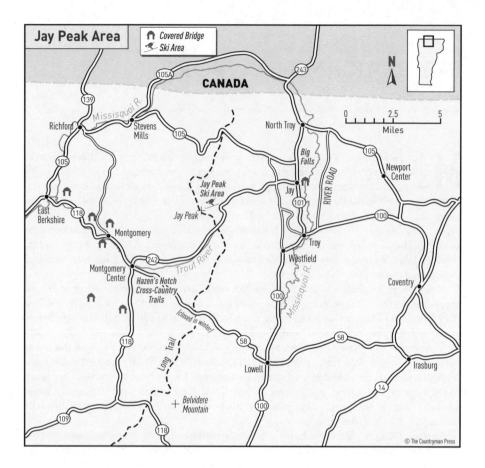

(newportrecreation.org) also maintains **Gardner Memorial Park**, with extensive playing fields and a picnic area by the Clyde River (across the footbridge from Vermont's **North Country Chamber Visitor Center**), and maintains a 36-acre park with camping at **Prouty Beach**. (See *Swimming* on page 474.) Check their website for seasonal information about rental kayaks, canoes, and skateboards.

**Montgomery** (population 1,201) is known for its six covered bridges (see *Must See* on page 471.). It began as a lumbering center and was for a long time one of the world's major producers of timothy grass seed. The Montgomery Historical Society's collection is housed in an 1835 wooden church, open June–September at stated hours; the society also sponsors Saturday-evening concerts on the common in July and August. Lunch and shopping can be found two miles east in **Montgomery Center**, the crossroads of VT 242 (to Jay Peak) and VT 118 (north to Richford and south to Stowe). It's also the terminus for VT 58, which angles back through **Hazen's Notch** over a high forest pass and down through fields into Lowell. An inviting drive in summer, it's open only for the first four miles in winter, just far enough to access the dependably snowy trails at **Hazen's Notch Cross-Country Ski and Snowshoeing Center**.

**Derby Line/Sanstead, Quebec.** Unfortunately the post-9/11 security at this border has created a wall between two communities that have been historically knit. The international line famously runs between the stage and audience of Derby Line's **Haskell Opera House** (see *Entertainment* on page 482).

NEWPORT GATEWAY CENTER  CHRISTINA TREE

## ✳ Must See

LAKES **Lake Memphremagog**, Newport. Vermont's second largest lake stretches 32 miles north to Magog, Quebec. Only five miles of the lake are within the United States. The name is said to be Abenaki for "Beautiful Waters." On the western shore look for Owls Head, a distinctive monadnock that's also a ski area, and for the monastery of **St. Benoit du Lac** (see below). Also check listings under *Boating*, *Fishing*, and *Swimming*.

**Seymour Lake.** There is a public beach in the tiny village of Morgan Center, also the spot to rent boats for fishing for landlocked salmon. In winter this lake is peppered with fishing shanties, and there is a system of ungroomed cross-country trails.

**Echo Lake.** Much smaller than Seymour Lake and adjoining it on the south, this lake is circled by a dirt road and gently rolling hills. There is also public boat access. Good fishing for trout and landlocked salmon.

**Jay Peak summit.** The spectacular view from the top is accessible via the 60-person tram at Jay Peak Resort. See the sidebar on page 475.

**Montgomery's covered bridges.** There are six Town lattice covered bridges: one right in Montgomery Village over Black Falls Creek; one south on VT 118; another nearby but three miles off VT 118 on West Hill on an abandoned side road over a waterfall; another northwest on VT 118 over the Trout River; and two in Montgomery Center, both a mile west of VT 118 over the Trout River (see our map of the area on page 470). Montgomery Village itself is picturesque.

**Abbaye de St. Benoit du Lac** (819-843-4080; st-benoit-du-lac.com), 1 Rue Prinicipale, Austin, Quebec. Open daily. This French Benedictine monastery, founded in 1912, is sited on the west shore of Lake Memphremagog. It's an imposing building with a landmark tower. The resident monks welcome visitors for daily Mass and daily Eucharist (11 a.m.) and vespers (5 p.m.), at which time Gregorian chant is sung. The big, popular shop sells monastery products such as cheese and hard cider, as well as books and recordings of Gregorian chants, vestments, and religious articles. In autumn the

## LOCALLY SOURCED

**N**ortheast Kingdom Tasting Center (802-334-1790; nektastingcenter.com), 150 Main Street, Newport. This former hardware store is a bright, open market with high ceilings and a contemporary, industrial feel, a place to sample local syrup and spirits, meat and cheese. In a back corner **Jocelyn and Cinta's Bake Shop** is an open kitchen filled with busy bakers and the aroma of breads, cakes, and pies—made with all-natural local ingredients, no preservatives. The **Vermont Eden Ice Cider Company** (edenicecider.com), based in nearby West Charleston, has fermenting tanks in the basement (tours offered). It's featured at **The Tasting Bar**, a central attraction in the center that also offers samplings of Vermont-brewed spirits like Dunc's Mill elderflower rum from St. Johnsbury and Bar Hill Gin from Caledonia Spirits in Hardwick. You'll also find a film on maple syrup production and a selection of products from **Butternut Mountain Farm**. Locally sourced pub and comfort food, as well as Vermont spirits and beers, are featured here at the Newport Ciderhouse Bar & Grill (802-354-1791), open daily for lunch through dinner.

orchards are open for PYO. The easiest route from Newport is via the North Troy border crossing, then through Mansonville, South Bolton, and Austin. The shop is open Mon.–Sat. 9–10:45 a.m. and 11:45 a.m.–5 p.m.; Sun. noon–5 in summer, closed Sundays in winter. Retreats are offered for men in a guesthouse on the grounds and for women in a neighboring convent.

## ✳ To Do

BIKING **Newport–Derby Line Bike Path** takes you from downtown Newport up along the eastern shore of Lake Memphremagog on the old railbed to the Canadian border and beyond. You will need to stop and have your passport checked at the border. See **vtnorthcountry.org** for a detailed list of area bike routes. Bike rentals from **The Great Outdoors** (117 Waterfront Plaza, Newport).

    **Missisquoi Valley Rail Trail** (see "The Northwest Corner" on page 369) begins in Richford and runs 26.4 miles west to St. Albans. A time-honored and tested 22.6- or 33.7-mile ride in the Jay area begins at the Black Lantern Inn (see *Lodging* on page 478) in Montgomery Village, passes two covered bridges along VT 118 north, and takes you to East Berkshire; you can continue to Enosburg Falls, where **Lake Carmi** offers camping and swimming, or turn onto Richford Road, looping back to Montgomery or up into Canada.

BOATING **Newport Marine** (802-334-5911) at Farrants Point on Lake Memphremagog rents aluminum boats with small motors, also pontoons.

    **Montgomery Adventures** (802-370-2103; montgomeryadventures.com), 262 Deep Gibou Road, Montgomery Center. Canoe and kayak rentals, tours, and shuttle service for paddling on the Missisquoi River.

FISHING **Montgomery Adventure**s (see above) offers guided fishing/camping tours, also ice fshing.

GOLF The **Jay Peak Championship Golf Course** at Jay Peak Resort (jaypeakresort .com); see the sidebar on page 475. **Newport Country Club** (802-334-2391), off Mount

NEWPORT MARINA CHRISTINA TREE

Vernon Street, overlooking the lake. Eighteen holes, rentals, instruction, and restaurant; April–November.

HIKING  The **Long Trail** terminates its 262-mile route at the Canadian border, 10 miles north of Jay Peak, but the trek up Jay itself is what most hikers look for here. The most popular ascent is from VT 242, 1.2 miles west of the entrance to the ski area; the round-trip hike takes three hours. For details on this and the section of the trail between Hazen's Notch and VT 242, as well as the final, fairly flat leg to the border, see the *Long Trail Guide*, published by the Green Mountain Club, which maintains the trail and four shelters in this area.

   **Hazen's Notch Association** (802-326-4799; hazensnotch.org), 1423 Hazen's Notch Road (VT 58), Montgomery Center. Open May 15–November 15. No trail fee, but contributions appreciated. Twenty miles of this network are maintained for hiking, winding through 2,500 acres of privately owned woods and meadows; it's 15 minutes to Bear Paw Pond. The 2-mile-long Burnt Mountain Trail ascends to the 2,700-foot summit of Burnt Mountain, an open summit with 360-degree views that include Hazen's Notch, the Jay Mountains, Mount Mansfield, and Lake Champlain. Stop by the welcome center on VT 58. Dogs must be leashed. Check the website for details about ecology day camps for children 6–9, Adventure Day and Overnight Camps for those 10–15, also about frequent nature walks and special events.

SCENIC DRIVES  **Big Falls of the Missisquoi**. River Road hugs the river, paralleling VT 101 between Troy and North Troy. You can access the falls from either town or from Vielleux Road off VT 101 at its junction with VT 105. This last is the prettiest route, through farmland and through the covered bridge south of the falls. Look for the unmarked pulloff in a grove of pine trees. The falls, thundering through a deep gorge, are awe-inspiring.

**Hazen's Notch.** From Montgomery Center, an unpromising narrow road, VT 58, climbs steeply east, quickly changing to dirt. In winter, it's open only for the first 4 miles and is a popular ski-touring spot. In summer, it's a beautiful road, dappled with sunlight through the thick foliage. Look for a picnic spot near the height-of-land, close to a clear roadside spring. A historic site plaque says the road through the high pass was built by General Moses Hazen in 1778–79, commissioned by George Washington himself. The road was begun in 1776, 48 miles to the southeast at the town of Wells River on the Connecticut River, and was intended to reach St. John, Quebec. It was abandoned on this spot in April 1779 when the news that British patrols might use it as an invasion route (it was meant to work the other way) reached the camp at Hazen's Notch.

SWIMMING In Newport, **Prouty Beach** (802-334-7951; newportrecreation.org/prouty-beach), 266 Prouty Beach Road, is a 35-acre lakeside park with a camping and disc-golf area as well as a swim beach on Lake Memphremagog. On Seymour Lake, there is a public beach in **Morgan Center**.

## ✳ Winter Sports

See **Jay Peak Resort** sidebar on page 475 for downhill skiing/snowboarding.

CROSS-COUNTRY SKIING ✪ **Hazen's Notch Association** (802-326-4799; hazens notch.org), welcome center at 1423 Hazen's Notch Road (VT 58), Montgomery Center. Hazen's Notch is a road through a high pass that—like the more famous Smugglers' Notch north of Stowe—is closed in winter. The original road dates from 1779, commissioned by George Washington. This is one of the first nonprofit ski centers in Vermont, still maintained by founder Rolf Anderson. It offers reliably snowy, well-marked trails for people of all abilities, looping through woods and open meadows on 2,500 acres of private land, meticulously tracked for cross-country and snowshoeing (also see *Hiking* on page 473). You can ski up to 25 km without returning to the **Welcome Center**—but please check in and pay the trail fee. Trails offer fine views of Jay Peak and the Cold Hollow Mountains. Early and late in the season, this tends to be one of a half-dozen cross-country networks in New England that have snow (elevation 900–2,800 feet). We last spent a beautiful morning skiing here on a March day that was too windy to ski at Jay Peak. Ten miles of dedicated snowshoe trails include the path up Burnt Mountain. Lessons and rentals, also full-moon snowshoe tours. No dogs or walking please.

**Montgomery Adventures** (see *Boating* on page 472) offers guided snowshoe tours.

## ✳ Lodging

RESORT See the sidebar for **Jay Peak Resort** on page 475.

INNS AND BED & BREAKFASTS

IN THE NEWPORT/DERBY LINE AREA

✪ **Little Gnesta B&B** (802-334-3438; littlegnesta.com), 115 Prospect Street, Newport. On a quiet block a short walk from Main Street shops and restaurants, this house has been thoroughly restored as a B&B. Ruth Sproull was inspired by a trip to Sweden to create an uncluttered, restful atmosphere. White is the dominant color, and guests are asked to remove their shoes upon entering. The four guest rooms are simply furnished, bright, and comfortable—two on the first floor and two on the second, all with private bath. Rates include a Swedish-style

# SKI AND SPLASH AT JAY PEAK

**J**ay Peak Resort (802-988-2611; 800-451-4449; snow conditions 802-988-9601; jaypeakresort.com), 4850 VT 242, Jay. In winter, storms sweep down from Canada or roll in from Lake Champlain, showering Jay Peak with dependable quantities of snow. The original trails here are in an area called Stateside, on a shoulder of Jay Peak. Still considered some of the toughest runs in Vermont, they were carved 60 years ago by local residents. An enterprising Kiwanis group (it included the parish priest) convinced the Vermont Legislature to reroute existing roads up over the high ridge from which Jay's access road rises, thus linking it to northwestern Vermont as well as to the Northeast Kingdom. They imported an Austrian skimeister to create a true trail system and ski school. In the early 1960s Weyerhaeuser Corporation acquired the ski area and installed a Swiss-built tramway to Jay's Peak, which it topped with a Sky Haus tram station, a building that emphasizes the crest of the summit and gives it a distinctly Matterhorn-like cap. Jay Peak is just an hour's drive from Montreal, and for many years its owners were Montreal-based Peak. However, under its present ownership, it has morphed from a great ski area into one of the East's premier self-contained resorts.

Jay's glitziest attraction, the **Pump House**, is a 50,000-square-foot, glass-enclosed water park that makes waves year-round, and next door is the **Ice Haus**, a National Hockey League–size ice arena. More than 300 condo-style rooms in three slope-side lodges complement a base area forest of condominiums. Down the road a clubhouse, with the attractive Clubhouse Grille, serves the 18-hole championship golf course and doubles as a Nordic ski center in winter.

Much of this transformation has been financed by the EB5 federal program that encourages foreign investment by expediting the procurement of green cards by immigrants in exchange for a $500,000 investment in a project that provides jobs in high-unemployment areas. The resort continues to evolve.

**SKIING/BOARDING** While there's an easy-intermediate trail (Northway) off the summit, Jay Peak regulars duck into glades right off the top. Jay's 20 glades and extreme chutes are what draw many of its regulars, who like to strike out into 150 acres of backcountry terrain. Unlike regular runs, wooded trails ("glades") cannot be covered by man-made snow and so require a lot of the natural stuff, which is what Jay Peak has in spades: an average of 375 inches annually. That's twice the snow many New England areas receive. Admittedly, given its exposed position, Jay can be windy and frigid in January and February (we try to visit in March), which is the reason—along with spectacular snowfall—why regulars are

BACKCOUNTRY SKIING AT JAY JAY PEAK RESORT

drawn by "off-piste" skiing through glades and into the backcountry beyond. In nearby Hazen's Notch, cross-country skiers also find some of the most dependably snowy and beautiful trails in New England.

*Lifts:* 60-passenger aerial tramway; 4 quad chairs, 1 triple, 1 double; 2 moving carpet.

*Vertical drop:* 2,153 feet.

*Trails and slopes:* 79 trails, glades, and chutes totaling more than 50 miles of skiing, spread over two peaks, connected by a ridgeline; 100-plus acres of gladed terrain.

*Off-piste skiing:* 100-plus acres.

*Snowboarding:* Three terrain parks; board demo center, rentals, and instruction.

THE PUMP HOUSE  JAY PEAK RESORT

*Snowmaking:* 80 percent of the total 385 acres.

*Snowshoeing:* Weekly snowshoeing walks led by a naturalist.

*Facilities:* Austria Haus, Tram Haus, and Stateside base lodge with cafeteria, pub, and ski and rental shop. The Tower Bar. Alice's Table Restaurant. The Foundry Pub and Grille. Mountain Dick's Pizza. Howie's Restaurant. The Bullwheel Pub. Buddy's Mug. Clips and Reels. The Clubhouse Grille. Taiga Spa. And the Aroma Café. Four-hundred-person conference center. The Drink pub. The Warming Shelter snack bar. Nursery and day care facilities. Rentals. Van service is from Burlington International Airport (80 miles away) and from the Amtrak station in St. Albans (a 45-minute drive).

*Ski school:* US- and Canadian-certified instructors, adult and junior racing clinics, and American Teaching Method (ATM). Telemarking instruction and rentals offered.

*For children:* Mountain Explorers for both skiing and snowboarding for 6- to 10-year-olds, Mountain Adventurers for ages 10–17, kinderski for ages 3–5. Day care for ages 2–7.

*Rates:* check out multidays and with lodging packages, also student and zone rates.

**Jay Peak Ski Touring Center** (800-451-4449), 4850 VT 242, Jay. The resort maintains 12 km of groomed cross-country trails emanating from the golf course; rentals and lessons.

**Ice Haus** (802-802-988-2710; open year-round). A professional-size hockey rink designed primarily for tournaments but with time scheduled for public skating. Nominal admission, rental skates, also helmets, hockey sticks, and skate sharpening.

**Pump House Indoor Waterpark** (802-988-2710), open year-round. Glass-walled with a retractable glass roof and kept at 86 degrees every day, this roughly 50,000-square-foot phenomenon features "La Chute," described as a black-diamond waterslide with a 45-mph descent through twists, turns, and flips, part of "the only aqualoop on the continent." It also boasts the largest indoor activity river in the country and offers a kids' play area. There's also a **Mountain Kids Adventure Center** and **Clips and Reels**, an entertainment center complete with a Clip 'n Climb facility, state-of-the-art arcade, and a 142-seat movie theater, located across from the Stateside Hotel.

**GOLF The Jay Peak Championship Golf Course** (802-327-2184). Designed by Graham Cooke, this highly rated 18-hole course emphasizes natural features and offers some memorable views. Lessons and lodging at the clubhouse.

**AERIAL TRAM to Jay Peak summit.** The 60-person aerial tram hoists visitors to the 3,861-foot summit. The view sweeps from Mount Washington to Montreal, back across the lake, down the spine of the Green Mountains, and southwest across Lake Champlain to the Adirondacks. It operates daily during ski season and from the last weekend in June through Labor Day, then in foliage season mid-September–Columbus Day.

A DESTINATION 18-HOLE GOLF COURSE  JAY PEAK RESORT

**LODGING** At this writing the resort can accommodate more than 4,000 people in three condo-hotels and 500 condominiums clustered around the two base areas and the golf course. There is a 24-hour shuttle bus service. Slope-side condo-style lodging options include the 57-room **Tram Haus** and 172-room **Hotel Jay**, both located at the main base area and handy to the Pump House and many year-round facilities. The 84-room **Stateside Hotel** is part of the Stateside base area.

**DINING Tram Haus: Alice's Table** (802-327-2323). Open for lunch and dinner, locally sourced menu, tables from an old barn. **Tower Bar** (802-327-2324), lunch and dinner (sports bar, music, and pub menu). **Clubhouse Grille** (802-988-2770). Open for three meals.

TRAM HAUS LODGE  JAY PEAK RESORT

breakfast of breads, cheese, meat, and yogurt. Inquire about longer stays. $.

✿ ⚲ ☗ **Cliff Haven Farm Bed & Breakfast** (802-334-2401; cliffhavenfarmbedandbreakfast.com), 5463 Lake Road, Newport Center. Mim LeBlanc's nineteenth-century post-and-beam farmhouse is a real gem. Set on 300 acres, it overlooks Lake Memphremagog from a rise—which continues to rise, through meadows to a swim pond near the height of their land. Our ground-floor guest room was really a spacious suite, tastefully and comfortably decorated. All four guest rooms have a private bath with a whirlpool tub; they're also fitted with a gas fireplace, antiques, TV/DVD, microwave, and a small fridge. Rates include a full breakfast and afternoon tea, less if you stay three nights. Children under 12 are free. Well-behaved pets accepted but cannot be left alone. $–$$.

**Derby Line Village Inn** (802-873-5071; derbylinevillageinn.com), 440 Main Street, Derby Line. One of the town's proudest mansions (vintage 1909), this is now a hospitable inn, best known for its restaurant (see *Dining Out* on page 480)—but that's on a different side of the house than you access as a guest. There are five guest rooms, each with private bath, A/C, and a fireplace (electrified). Full breakfast included in rates; $.

**Lake Salem Inn** (802-766-5560; lakesaleminn.com), 1273 VT 105, Derby. This attractive inn with its columned porch is set on 7 acres overlooking Lake Salem. Joe and Mo Profera offer four guest rooms, all with private bath. The spacious first-floor library room has a queen-size sleigh bed and a sitting area, the Zen Room is airy and tranquil, and both the Wyoming Room and the Hideaway have lake views and a deck. There's an attractive common space, a back deck, and a boat dock with kayaks and canoes. Rates include a full breakfast. Dinner available on weekends for guests and the public. $–$$.

**Water's Edge B&B** (802-334-7726), 324 Wishing Well Avenue, Newport. Several miles north of downtown Newport, Pat Bryan's contemporary house sits right on the edge of Lake Memphremagog. The common space is tasteful and includes a deck. The three guest rooms include a queen room with a lake view, a corner queen with two windows on the lake ($120), and a suite with a sitting area and gas stove ($150). All rooms have a private bath and TV. In summer guests have use of the canoe, rowboat, and dock; in winter there's snowmobile and ice-fishing access right out the front door. Bird-watching year-round. Rates include a full breakfast. Residents include two gentle Saint Bernards.

**A Place in Time** (802-334-6950; aplaceintimebedandbreakfast.com), 235 Vance Hill Road, Newport Center. Vincent and Trish Buttice have nicely restored this nineteenth-century farmhouse and welcome guests to a first-floor suite with private bath. $.

**Newport City Inn & Suites** (802-334-6558; newportcitymotel.net), 444 East Main Street, Newport. This two-story, 82-room motel has units that vary in size; facilities include an indoor pool. $–$$.

IN THE JAY PEAK AREA

✪ **Black Lantern Inn** (802-326-3269; blacklanterninn.com), 2057 North Main Street (VT 118), Montgomery. A white-pillared brick inn built in 1803 as the Montgomery Village stage stop, 10 miles west of Jay Peak, this is an appealing place to stay. Fifteen rooms are divided between the main inn and neighboring Burdette House, all nicely decorated and varying from standard size to a two-bedroom suite. Adirondack chairs are also positioned behind the inn, with a view of Hazen's Notch. Some rooms have a fireplace or wood-burning stove and a steam shower or whirlpool bath. There is a low-beamed, charming dining room (see *Dining Out* on page

481) and a cozy brewpub featuring the house handcrafted brew. Beyond the porch is the village with its six covered bridges, and from the back there is a hot tub under the gazebo with a view of Hazen's Notch, a venue for small weddings. Summer is low season: $–$$; $$$ for a three-bedroom unit. Rates include full breakfast.

♂ 🐾 **Phineas Swann Bed & Breakfast Inn** (802-326-4306; phineasswann.com), 195 Main Street, Montgomery Center. Darren and Lynne Drevik have the right touch. Accommodations are divided among upstairs rooms in the main house, luxurious suites in the Carriage House, and fully equipped, dog-friendly apartments in River House. Common rooms are elegantly comfortable. In summer the deck and gardens invite you outside and down to the Trout River. Amenities include many bells and whistles, including long-distance, toll-free phones and an outdoor hot tub. $–$$ for rooms, $$–$$$ for one- and two-bedroom suites (less off-season), includes a full

breakfast and all-day snacks. Inquire about romance packages and periodic farm-to-table dinners.

🐾 ✐ **The INN** (802-326-4391; theinn .us), 241 Main Street, Montgomery Center. New York transplants Nick Barletta and Scott Pasfield have created a special place with the feel of a quirky boutique hotel, unfussily stylish, with accommodations ranging from a spacious honeymoon suite to economical family rooms and bunkrooms. Pasfield, a renowned photographer, is the eye behind objects ranging from a wax bust of Elvis to a couch stenciled with images of automatic weapons that make the shared spaces feel like a secret museum. Comfortable, carefully decorated guest rooms are divided between the Victorian house and a family-geared cottage by the Trout River ($–$$). Rates include full breakfast; food is taken seriously here. See *Dining Out* on page 481.

✐ **Jay Village Inn** (802-988-2306; stayatjay.com), 1078 VT 242, Jay. Three miles downhill from Jay Peak in Jay

BLACK LANTERN INN, MONTGOMERY  CHRISTINA TREE

Four Corners, this classic log ski lodge is best known as a convivial restaurant and pub—but the rooms upstairs have been tastefully refurbished, all with private bath. There are seven double rooms, varying in size and shape, and four family suites (sleeping four to five). The quietest rooms are on the third floor and include our favorite, with a fireplace and sleigh bed. In summer there's a heated pool, and the outside hot tub gets year-round use. Three meals are served; see *Dining Out* on page 481. $.

**Couture's Maple Shop and Bed & Breakfast** (802-744-2733; maplesyrup vermont.com), 560 VT 100, Westfield Pauline and Jacques Couture raised six children in this 1892 farmhouse while also maintaining a dairy farm and a sizable maple syrup business. Three guest rooms with queen-size bed and pullout couch share a bath; a family room (private bath) sleeps four. The cow barn is out the back door, and the sugarhouse is just up the hill. Rates include a full breakfast served in the renovated farm kitchen. $–$$.

## ✻ Where to Eat

### DINING OUT

#### IN THE NEWPORT AND LAKES AREA

✪ ✐ **Derby Line Village Inn** (802-873-5071; derbylinevillageinn.com), 440 Main Street, Derby Line. Open Wed.–Sun. 4:30 p.m.–close, also 2:30 p.m. for Sunday brunch. Chef-owner Fritz Halbedl, a veteran of 14 years as an executive chef with Royal Caribbean Cruises, has created a bright, informally inviting dining room overlooking the garden in one of the town's grandest mansions. The Austrian-accented menu includes potato pancakes, bratwurst or knackwurst, and vegetarian strudel as well as schnitzels and (local) venison stew with mushrooms, served over red cabbage and spaetzle. Patrons are welcome to dine on a mix of starters and entrées. There's a carefully chosen selection of draft beers. Entrées $$.

**Newport Ciderhouse Bar & Grill** (802-334-1791; newportciderhouse.com) 150 Main Street, Newport. Open Mon.–Sat. Tucked into a bright, streetside corner of the Northeast Kingdom Tasting Center. There is a cheery, open feel to the space, a popular downtown place for lunch and dinner. Local ingredients include meats from the adjacent butcher shop and local brews and ciders on tap. Dinner entrées $–$$.

**Le Belvedere** (802-487-9147; lebelve dererestaurant.com), 100 Main Street. Open Wed.–Sun. for dinner. With windows and seasonal patio dining overlooking the lake, this casually elegant place styles itself as "upscale dining" and has a prime downtown lakeside location, and a large bar. Entrées $$–$$$.

✐ ✐ ✪ **The Eastside Restaurant and Pub** (802-334-2340; eastsiderestaurant .net), 47 Landing Street, Newport. Open for lunch and dinner weekdays, breakfast too on weekends; the Sunday breakfast buffet is big. A large old landmark with the best lake view of any restaurant in town, also a seasonal outdoor deck and dock. The reasonably priced lunch menu might include lamb stew and biscuits or grilled chicken salad. The salad bar can be a meal in itself. Many locals come just for dessert (try the pecan ribbon). Dinner entrées $–$$. Children's menu. Weddings are a specialty.

**Derby Cow Palace** (802-766-4724; derbycowpalace.com), Main Street (US 5), Derby. Open Tues.–Sun. 11 a.m.–close, Mon. from 3 p.m. Owner Doug Nelson also owns the largest local dairy operation and Cow Town Elk Ranch. This large log-hewn restaurant, festooned with elk horns, specializes in meat, from burgers to prime rib and elk sirloin. Fully licensed, with a bar menu. Dinner entrées $–$$.

**Lago Trattoria** (802-334-8222; lago trattoria.com), 95 Main Street, Newport. Open nightly from 5 p.m. The decor is modern Italian, and chef-owner Frank Richardi claims not to fry anything except calamari. The menu includes pastas and staples like chicken Marsala and cacciatore. From pizzas and from Frank's homemade lasagna to fish and steak at market prices. $–$$.

## IN THE JAY PEAK AREA

**The Belfry** (802-326-4400), 14 Amidon Road (VT 242), between Montgomery Center and the Jay Peak access road. Open nightly 4–9, later on weekends. No reservations, and during ski season you'd better get here early (or late) if you want a booth. Built in 1902 as a schoolhouse, this is the area's most popular pub, and the food is good. The soup is homemade, and the blackboard lists daily specials, like pan-blackened fish and grilled lamb chops. The menu features "Belfry Steak" ("price depends on the chef's mood"), salads, burgers, and deep-fried mushrooms. Inquire about music. If you've been here a day or two, chances are you will recognize someone in the crowd around the mirrored oak-and-marble back bar.

**Black Lantern Inn** (802-326-3269; theblacklanterninn.com), 2057 North Main Street (VT 118), Montgomery Village. Open nightly 4–9. With its original name (for some years this was the Montgomery House) and new, local owners, this delightful, low-beamed old dining room is once more a popular place to dine. The inviting brewpub offers a large selection of beers on tap, including the house handcrafted brew and the reasonably priced menu; entrées $–$$.

**The INN** (802-326-4391; theinn.us), 241 Main Street, Montgomery Center. Open for dinner Thurs.–Sun. The old upcountry inn dining room with a hearth and adjacent lounge is warmly lit and welcoming, and the menu is varied, from burgers to Asian noodles to honey mustard grilled pork chops and pan-seared ribeye, also house cocktails and local beers on draft. Service on the outdoor deck in summer. $–$$$.

**Jay Village Inn** (802-988-2306; jay villageinn.com), 1078 VT 242, Jay. Open daily for three meals. A lively dining scene in a warm, informal lodge atmosphere with a big stone fireplace at the center of the dining room and the pub tucked into its own space. $–$$ with nightly specials, frequent music.

**Hidden Country Restaurant** (802-744-6149; hiddencountryrestaurant.com), off VT 100, Lowell. Call ahead, but posted hours in summer are Wed.–Sat. 4:30–9 p.m., Sun. 9 a.m.–7:30 p.m. Open weekends in winter. Begun in 1988 by Joe St. Onge, this restaurant offers atmosphere that must be experienced to be appreciated. The specialty is the prime rib. Big portions come with soup and salad bar. Rolls and desserts are housemade, and the specialty cocktails and Friday fish fry are famous. There's a trout pond for paid fishing and an eight-hole, chip-and-putt golf course. No credit cards.

COW PALACE, DERBY CHRISTINA TREE

## EATING OUT

### IN THE NEWPORT AREA

**The Brown Cow** (802-334-7887), 350 East Main Street, Newport, open daily 5 a.m.–1 p.m., Sun. 6 a.m.–1 p.m. This is a great spot to linger over breakfast. Chef salads, steak dinners, and homemade ice cream and pie.

((•)) **Newport Natural Market and Café** (802-334-2626; newportnatural.com), 194 Main Street, Newport. Open Mon.–Sat. 8–8, Sun. 10–6. This attractive café offers a choice of a regular menu as well as vegan and vegetarian, a variety of espressos, fruit smoothies and herbal teas, panini, soups and wraps, smoked tempeh, a good salad bar, and wholesome baked goods.

✪ **Brenda's Homestyle Cookin' Restaurant** (802-334-3050; brendas homestylecookin.com), 125 Main Street, Newport. Open daily 6:30–2 for breakfast and lunch, breakfast only on Sunday. A down-home coffee shop that's surviving in the new Newport.

### IN THE JAY AREA

**Bernie's Restaurant** (802-326-4682), 72 South Main Street, Montgomery Center. Open 6:30 a.m.–10 p.m. Bigger than it looks from its greenhouse-style front, this is a genuine gathering spot for the area. Breakfast options include bagels and eggs, any style, and the breads are baked daily, for sale separately as well as to be used for sandwiches. Soups are a luncheon specialty, and at dinner the menu ranges from sautéed scampi to pasta. Fully licensed pub in back, nightly specials. Chef-owner John Boucher frequently presides behind the counter.

### ELSEWHERE

**Morgan Country Store** (802-895-2726; themorgancountrystore.com), VT 111, Morgan Center. Open 6 a.m.–7 p.m., Sun. 8–5. A genuine general store with a post office, live bait, and an extensive breakfast, lunch (burgers, sandwiches, and salads), and pizza menu.

**Martha's Diner** (802-754-6800), 585 US 5/VT 14, Coventry. Open Mon.–Fri. 5 a.m.–2 p.m., Sat. 5:30–2, Sun. 6–2. A classic 1950s chrome diner operated by the same family for more than 30 years, serving local diner fare with flair, poutine, hash browns, fried chicken with buttermilk waffles, pea soup, and much more.

## ✳ Entertainment

**Haskell Opera House** (802-873-3022; in Canada 819-876-2471; haskellopera.org), Derby Line. This splendid vintage 1904 theater has perfect acoustics, three antique stage sets, a rare roll-up curtain depicting scenes of Venice, and a rococo interior. Its season runs May–mid-October and includes performances by a resident theater company, opera, dance, and a variety of outstanding concerts.

**City Cinema** (802-334-8610; city cinemanewport.com), 137 Waterfront Plaza, Newport. First-run films on three screens.

## ✳ Selective Shopping

### IN AND AROUND NEWPORT

✪ **The Pick & Shovel** (802-334-8370; thepicknshovel.com), 54 Coventry Street. Don't miss Newport's family-owned mega general store, just off Main Street, a vast complex selling everything from home hardware (miles of it) to clothing to pets (42 tanks of fish), plus sugaring supplies, grain, and much, much more. The antithesis of big box stores, although it's bigger than most of them. There's a sense of adventure, and staff is plentiful. Worth a visit just for the fun of it, and don't pass on **Tim & Doug's Ice Cream.**

✪ **MAC Center for the Arts** (802-334-1966; memphremagogartscollaborative .com), 158 Main Street, Suite 2, Newport. Open daily in summer; closed Tues. in winter. This impressive shop showcases the varied work of more than 50 local artisans. Check the website for workshops and special events.

**The Great Outdoors** (802-334-2831; greatoutdoorsvermont.com), 117 Waterfront Plaza, Newport. In summer the store features an extensive array of fishing gear and sells fishing licenses; four-season sporting goods. Rental bikes, kayaks, and canoes, also rental in-line skates, snowshoes, cross-country skis, and snowboards.

**Country Thyme** (802-766-2852; countrythymevermont.com), 60 VT 111, Derby (near the junction of VT 111 and US 5). Every inch of the ground floor in Kay Courson's house is crammed with gifts, toys, specialty foods, Christmas decorations, and more.

**Kingdom Brewing** (802-334-7096; kingdombrewingvt.com), 1876 VT 105, Newport Center. Tasting room generally open Thurs.–Sat.; call for hours. Using a geothermal type of fermentation, American grains, and locally produced ingredients such as maple sap, spruce tips, and apples, Brian and Jenn Cook create a variety of light to robust beers. They dispose of the spent grains from the process by feeding them to the Black Angus cattle on their farm.

**Louis Garneau USA Factory Outlet** (802-334-1036; louisgarneau.us), 3916 US 5, Derby. Open daily 9–5. Cyclists know this Canadian brand name well, and the outlet at their big new distribution center is a definite stop for those interested in gear.

IN THE JAY AREA

**Jay Country Store** (802-988-4040), 1077 VT 242, Jay. Open daily. The center of Jay Village, selling papers, gas, food, and wine basics, also a deli, plus an interesting assortment of gift items and cards.

**Mountain Fiber Folk** (802-326-2092; mtfibefolk.com), 188 Main Street, Montgomery Center. Open Thurs.–Mon. This is a cooperative selling hand-spun yarn as well as knitwear, art dolls, wall hangings, and knitting supplies.

**Couture's Maple Shop** (802-744-2733; maplesyrupvermont.com), 560 VT 100, Westfield. Open year-round, Mon.–Sat. 8–6. A long-established maple producer: maple candy, cream, granulated sugar, pancake mix, and salad dressing, as well as syrup; will ship anywhere.

**Jed's Maple Products** (802-744-2095; jedsmaple.com), 475 Carter Road, Westfield. Syrup, candy, and frosted nuts. Inquire about the annual Mud Season Sugar on Snow Party.

**Berry Creek Farm** (802-744-2406; berrycreekfarmvt.com), 1342 VT 100, Westfield. An organic strawberry and vegetable farm selling plants and local produce as well as their own.

## ✳ Special Events

*February:* **Newport Winter Festival. Winter Festival. Mountain Mardi Gras** at Jay in late season.

*March:* **Sugaring** throughout the region.

*June:* **Tour de Kingdom** (tourdekingdom.org), five days of riding. Check the website for fall events.

# ISLAND POND AND BEYOND

The crossroads of Vermont's lonely, northeasternmost corner, the village of Island Pond has the look and feel of an outpost. A historic marker in front of the city-size depot reads: "Pioneer railroad planner John A. Poor's dream of an international railroad connecting Montreal, Canada, with the ice-free harbor of Portland, ME, became a reality on July 18, 1854, when the first through trains met at this great half-way point on the Grand Trunk railway." During the late nineteenth century and into the twentieth, Island Pond hummed with the business of servicing frequent passenger trains and freight trains transporting logs and wood pulp. No longer. Today Island Pond is a quiet village on a pond with an island in its center. Brighton State Park east of town offers a sandy beach, and there's a pleasant pondside park in the village itself. The religious community Twelve Tribes (known locally as "The Tribe") has restored several Victorian houses and operates The Tannery, a destination clothing and shoe store. In winter Island Pond is the region's snowmobiling capital.

The lake-spotted woodland east and south of Island Pond is now largely publicly owned, much of it by the Silvio O. Conte National Fish and Wildlife Refuge and teeming with moose, black bear, and other wildlife. There's great fishing in the waters in and around Quimby Country, the region's oldest and one of Vermont's most appealing resorts (see sidebar on page 490). Continuing east you hardly notice the short bridge across the Connecticut River (here a trout stream) as you cross from Canaan, VT, to Stewartstown, NH.

ISLAND POND COVERED STEPS CHRISTINA TREE

BORDER CROSSINGS are staffed 24 hours in Norton (VT 147), Canaan (VT 141), and Beecher Falls (VT 253). Passports required.

GUIDANCE **Island Pond Welcome Center** (802-723-9889; islandpond.com); VT 105/114 at the south end of Main Street. Open daily during summer, foliage, and snowmobiling seasons, but volunteer-dependent. A beautiful welcome center with restrooms as well as historical and crafts displays.

**North Country Chamber of Commerce** (northcountrychamber.org), based in Colebrook, NH, also this section of Vermont.

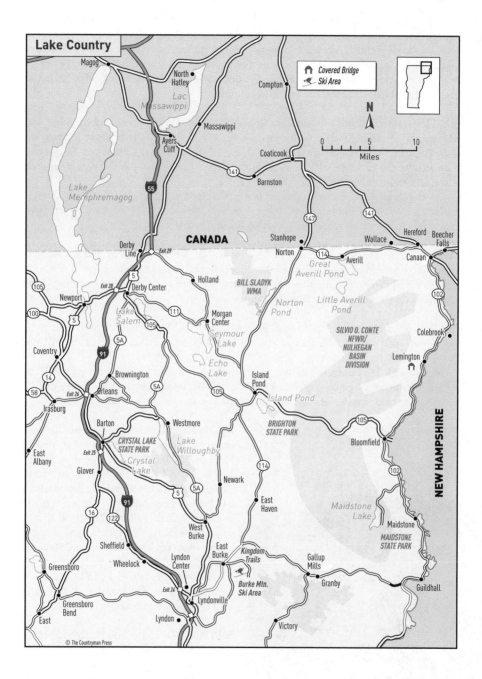

Lake Country

Magog

North Hatley

Lac Massawippi

Massawippi

Ayers Cliff

Compton

Coaticook

Barnston

Covered Bridge
Ski Area

N

0        5        10
Miles

55

Lake Memphremagog

Derby Line

Exit 29

Holland

Stanhope

Norton

141

147

114

Wallace

Hereford

Beecher Falls

Canaan

CANADA

Great Averill Pond

Averill

BILL SLADYK WMA

105

Newport

Exit 28

Derby Center

5

11

Morgan Center

Norton Pond

Little Averill Pond

102

100

5

Lake Salem

105

Seymour Lake

SILVIO O. CONTE NFWR/ NULHEGAN BASIN DIVISION

Colebrook

Coventry

91

5A

Echo Lake

Island Pond

Lemington

Brownington

14

58

Orleans

Exit 26

5A

105

Island Pond

Irasburg

Barton

Westmore

BRIGHTON STATE PARK

105

Bloomfield

East Albany

CRYSTAL LAKE STATE PARK

Exit 25

Lake Willoughby

114

102

Glover

Crystal Lake

5

5A

Newark

NEW HAMPSHIRE

East Haven

Maidstone Lake

Maidstone

16

91

122

West Burke

Maidstone State Park

Sheffield

Wheelock

Lyndon Center

East Burke

Kingdom Trails

Gallup Mills

Guildhall

Greensboro

Exit 24

Burke Mtn. Ski Area

Granby

Lyndonville

Greensboro Bend

Lyndon

Victory

East

© The Countryman Press

# ✳ To Do

*Note:* **NorthWoods Stewardship Center** (802-723-6551; northwoodscenter.org), 10 Mile Square Road, East Charleston (5 miles west of Island Pond), is a 1,700-acre preserve with 40 km of walking/skiing and snowshoeing trails. Aside from its formal nature hikes, guided canoeing, and frequent outreach programs, the center also serves as an informal clearinghouse for local canoe, fishing, tracking, and nature guides, 35 km of groomed skiing and snowshoeing trails. Rentals.

**BOATING** **NorthWoods Stewardship Center** (see *Note* above) offers rental canoes and kayaks and offers guided expeditions on a variety of waters. **Clyde River Recreation** (802-895-4333; clyderiverrecreation.com), 2355 VT 105, West Charleston (a quarter mile east of the junction of VT 5A and 105) offers canoe and kayak rentals, guided tours, and shuttles for the Clyde River.

On the **Connecticut River**, Canaan is a good place to put in, but there are several rapids at the start. Canoeing is also good below Colebrook, NH, for 3 miles but then rather fast for an equal distance. (See also *Fishing* below.)

**FISHING** Biologist Ken Hastings of Colebrook, NH, with his **Osprey Fishing Adventures** (603-922-3800; ospreyfishingadventures.com), is the fishing guru for this stretch of the river, offering one- and three-day fly-fishing trips on his driftboat. Also see *Green Space* and **Quimby Country** under *Lodging*.

**HIKING** **Bluff Mountain** (2,380 feet) looms over Island Pond to the north. It's a popular climb with spectacular views. The trail starts from VT 114, north of the village. Inquire locally for directions.

**Monadnock Mountain** (elevation 3,140 feet), in Lemington, towers over the Connecticut River and Colebrook, NH. A trail runs west, beginning as a driveway off VT 102 near the bridge to Colebrook. An abandoned fire tower crowns the summit.

THERE IS AN ISLAND IN THE POND  CHRISTINA TREE

**SNOWMOBILING** The website **snowmobile.islandpond.com** has all you need to know. Island Pond is the snowmobiling capital of the Kingdom, from which groomed VAST (**Vermont Association of Snow Travelers**; vtvast.org) trails radiate in all directions. The local Brighton Snowmobile Club maintains a snow phone: 802-723-4316. **Kingdom Cat Corp.** (802-723-9702; kingdomcat.com) on Cross Street in Island Pond is the main snowmobile rental operation in the area, and offers guided tours.

**SWIMMING** There are state facilities at **Brighton State Park** (802-723-9702; vtstateparks.com) in Island Pond, a large beach that is sandy and shallow for quite a way out, great for children.

ESSEX COUNTY COURTHOUSE, GUILDHALL CHRISTINA TREE

SCENIC DRIVES **Island Pond Loop**. This 66-mile loop circles the northeastern corner of Vermont, beginning in Island Pond and heading north on VT 114. The Canadian National Railway's Grand Trunk line from Montreal to Portland, ME, hugs the highway the full 16 miles to Norton. This railway was once Montreal's winter lifeline to Europe, as goods could not be shipped in to or out of the frozen port of Montreal during the coldest months. About halfway to Norton, near the south end of long and slender Norton Pond (there's a boat launch on VT 114), a gravel road to the left leads into the **Bill Sladyk Wildlife Management Area**, frequented by hunters, fishermen, and loggers. Just before you reach the tiny village of Norton (opposite slightly larger Stanhope, Quebec), the forest thins out and farmland reappears. Norton was the site of the notorious Earth People's Park, a 1960s-style, loosely governed hippie commune that once numbered hundreds of residents but is now state owned; no one is allowed to live there. The road passes several farms, a school, and the **Norton Country Store** (open daily), then swings abruptly eastward to avoid the imposing Canadian port-of-entry.

**Eastern Townships detour** (easterntownships.org). Some 15 minutes north on VT 147 brings you to Coaticook with "the world's largest pedestrian suspension bridge" (lit at night) spanning Coaticook Gorge. Compton is another 10 minutes' drive north. From Coaticook return on scenic VT 141 along Lake Wallace and into Canaan. If you head eastward along the US side of the border, VT 114 reenters the forest, passing a series of lakes, most of which are dotted with hunting and fishing camps. In Averill Gore (population 9) stop for bait and directions to the boat launch on Great Averill Pond at the **Lakeview Store** (open daily.) East of the store, Forest Road leads to **Quimby Country**, one of Vermont's oldest and most appealing resorts (see page 490). Shortly after passing Big Averill, you leave the St. Lawrence watershed and begin a rapid descent into the Connecticut River Valley. Halfway from Averill to Canaan, the road skirts the south shore of sizable Wallace Pond, almost entirely within the province of Quebec.

**Canaan**, 14 miles east of Norton. In the far corner of Fletcher Park (at the junction of VT 114 and VT 141), the handsome 1846 Greek Revival building houses the Canaan Historical Society's changing exhibits upstairs. You barely notice the Connecticut

River, here just a fledgling stream spanned by a brief bridge into West Stewartstown, NH. These far corners of Vermont and New Hampshire form a North Country region of their own. Check out northcountrychamber.org for details. NH 3 runs north to **Pittsburg** and the series of four lakes strung along the 22 semi-wilderness miles north of town. This stretch of NH 3 is known as "Moose Alley" for reasons scarily easy to grasp if you drive it on a summer evening. Die-hard Connecticut River buffs may want to hike in to its source, a small pond accessible via a path beside the NH 3 border station (restrooms).

From Canaan our loop turns south on VT 102, through lush river-bottom farmland, to **Lemington**, and past the impressively long **Columbia covered bridge**. This stretch of the river valley alternately narrows and widens, and the road tunnels through forest, broken occasionally by farms, fields, and glimpses of impressive mountains. In **Bloomfield** the Grand Trunk railroad line angles east across the road, heading for Portland. Here our route turns west on VT 105 (it's 16 miles back to Island Pond).

For another rewarding detour, however, continue at least the mile down VT 102 to the wooded path (on the left) into **Brunswick Springs**, once the site of a mineral springs resort. At this sacred Abenaki site, the resort's buildings repeatedly burned; only their foundations and an eerie cement stairway leading down to the riverbank remain. Please be respectful of the property, now owned by a local Abenaki group. Water from the sulfur springs still runs from spigots. Park next to the white wooden former schoolhouse (on your left, heading south). The road in is usually chained off. It's a pleasant 15-minute walk to the river. Another 4 miles south on VT 102 (and 5 miles in on a dirt road) brings you to **Maidstone State Park**, offering camping and swimming as well as fishing. The Connecticut River widens noticeably the farther south you drive on VT 102, and views of the White Mountains are increasingly dramatic. If you continue another 7 miles south to Guildhall, you are informed by a billboard-size sign that the town was "discovered" in 1754, chartered in 1761, and settled in 1764, making it the oldest town in northeastern Vermont (by contrast, Norton was not settled until 1860). An attractive, square green is flanked by historically interesting buildings: a tiny Essex Country courthouse, church, town hall (the Guild Hall, 1798), and an ornate 1909 classical revival library with stained-glass windows. An unassuming white-clapboard house serves as a county lockup.

Two miles downriver from Guildhall, a town road marked GRANBY runs west off VT 102, beginning as a paved road but becoming gravel well before reaching the tiny hamlets of Granby and Gallup Mills, about 8 miles from VT 102. This is wild, wooded, and boggy country, good for spotting moose and bear. Lumber camps and sawmills once peppered this area, and there was even a steam railway. The road finally descends about 8 miles west of Granby to reach VT 114, joining it a couple of miles north of East Burke. Take VT 114 some 12 miles north through rolling, mixed farm- and forestland to its junction with VT 105, 2 miles west of Island Pond.

## ❋ Green Space

**Brighton State Park** (802-723-4360; vtstateparks.com), Island Pond, 2 miles east on VT 105 to State Park Road. Open mid-May–mid-October. Campsites are nestled in a stand of white birch trees on Spectacle Pond: 63 tent/trailer sites, 21 lean-tos, and a rental cabin. The park includes frontage on the south shore of Island Pond, where there's a day-use area that features a sandy beach (check to make sure it's open), a bathhouse with restrooms, and rental boats. Hiking trails include a leisurely trek to Indian Point and wildlife. Watch for moose and loons.

**Maidstone State Park** (802-676-3930; vtstateparks.com), Brunswick. Open Memorial Day–Labor Day. Five miles south of Bloomfield on VT 102, then 5 miles on dirt road, this is the most remote Vermont state park and retains much of its wilderness forest of maple, beech, and hemlock. The park's camping and day-use facilities are on pristine **Maidstone Lake**, home to lake, rainbow, and brook trout. Moose sightings and the call of the loon (this is a nesting area) are common. There's a beach, picnic area, picnic shelter, hiking trails, 45 tent/trailer sites, and 37 lean-tos. This Nulhegan Basin is an important breeding habitat for migratory birds and nesting thrushes and warblers. Boreal forests in the basin support rare species such as spruce grouse, gray jay, Wilson's warbler, olive-sided flycatcher, rusty blackbird, black-backed woodpecker, and the three-toed woodpecker.

**Bill Sladyk Wildlife Management Area**, off VT 114, south of Norton Pond: 9,500 forested acres, also accessible via a gravel road past Holland Pond from Holland Village, 11 miles east of Derby. A detailed map is available from the **Fish and Wildlife Department** in Waterbury (802-241-3700).

**Silvio O. Conte National Fish and Wildlife Refuge, Nulhegan Basin Division** (802-962-5240; nulhegan.com). In 1999 when the Champion International Corporation announced plans to sell its holdings in Essex County, the US Fish and Wildlife Service purchased this 26,000-acre tract (roughly 10 miles in diameter) that's home to rare animals and migratory birds. The Vermont Agency of Natural Resources acquired some 22,000 adjoining acres; another 84,000 acres surrounding these preserves continue to be logged but with easements to protect their development. Over 100 species of birds nest in the Nulhegan Basin, which is home to moose, black bear, beaver, fisher, white-tailed deer, and coyote. The Nulhegan River and its tributaries harbor brook trout, bullhead, chain pickerel, chub, and more. The refuge is open to hunting, fishing, trapping, bird-watching, and hiking. It includes 40 miles of gravel roads, 17 miles of wooded pathways, and the Mollie Beattie Bog interpretive boardwalk (handicapped accessible). No biking. Request a map.

# ✳ Lodging

**Jackson's Lodge and Log Cabins** (802-266-3360; jacksonslodgevt.net), 213 Jackson Lodge Road, off VT 114, Canaan. This is a find for families looking for a reasonably priced lakeside vacation. Gloria Jackson is the second generation of her family to maintain this appealing lineup of 15 log cabins along Lake Wallace. Open late spring–fall. Two-bedroom cabins sleeping four are $185 per night, $875 per week. Three-bedroom cabins sleep six. Less in shoulder seasons. Ask about Wayfarer's Rooms (with bath and private deck). Café open weekends to the public for breakfast. The rustic central lodge is also a venue for events and weddings. Lake Wallace itself extends into Canada. $.

**The Lakefront Inn & Motel** (802-723-6507; thelakefrontinnislandpond.com),

127 Cross Street, Island Pond. Robert and Sharon Dexter's two-story motel in the center of the village overlooks the lake. The 20 units include standard rooms, efficiencies for two or four and suites for six with full kitchens and living rooms with a gas fireplace ($–$$$), cheaper in summer and fall. A floating dock is reserved for motel guests only during summer months and a heated multibay garage is available for guests to work on servicing their snowmobiles in winter.

CAMPGROUNDS See Brighton State Park and Maidstone State Park in *Green Space* on page 488.

# ✳ Where to Eat

🍴 **Essex House and Tavern** (802-723-9888; essexhouseandtavern.com),

# RUSTIC RESORT

**Q**uimby Country (802-822-5533; quimbycountry.com), Averill. This is the hidden gem of the Kingdom, one of Vermont's most historic and family-friendly resorts. Less than 3 miles from Canada and resembling a Maine North Woods sporting camp more than any other lodging in Vermont. It's set in literally thousands of acres of woodland, facing Forest Lake and a short walk in the woods from 1,200-acre Great Averill Pond. Each of the well-spaced 19 cottages (1 to 4 bedrooms) is different, but all have woodstoves or fireplaces in their living rooms and are named for a fishing fly. In the mellow clapboard lodge, a big stone hearth is the focal point of the book-lined common room. Many of the Adirondack-style furnishings

"THE ROCK" AT GREAT AVERILL POND  CHRISTINA TREE

QUIMBY COUNTRY'S LODGE OVERLOOKS FOREST LAKE  CHRISTINA TREE

date back to the 1890s, as do the polished wooden tables in the spacious, old-fashioned dining room and the rockers lining the porch, overlooking Forest Lake.

Quimby's opened in 1894 as a fishing lodge and under the management of Hortense Quimby, daughter of the founder, it evolved into a family-oriented resort, attracting an elite following so fiercely loyal that on Miss Quimby's death in the 1960s, a group of regulars formed a corporation to buy it and to perpetuate the special ambience. From early July–mid-August, rates include a children's program of hikes and swims, rainy-day activities, and family-inclusive picnics on a remote beach as well as a Friday sunset lobster feast at "The Rock" on Big Averill.

Amenities include kayaks, canoes, rowboats with trolling motors and sailboats, a tennis court, playground, and rec hall. Rates are per person (less for kids, free under age 3), and per person rates include all meals. From mid-June–July 4th weekend (the focus is on fishing; guides available) and mid-August–October, meals are limited to a breakfast buffet and cottage $ per couple per night. A great place for birders and naturalists (ask about the peat bog) as well as for fishermen, walkers, weddings, and reunions. ✐ ✪ 🐾

138 Cross Street, Island Pond. This nineteenth-century village inn has been recently renovated, and the tavern is a popular place for lunch and dinner. Local beers on tap and a full bar. Lunch choices are burgers, sandwiches, and specials. We can vouch for the vegetarian rice bowl. The dinner might include fish & chips, maple salmon, and steak tips ($$).

**K.T. Ray's on the Pond** (802-723-4590), 69 Cross Street, Island Pond. Open for all three meals daily except Mondays. Nice atmosphere, generous portions from the big breakfast menu through sandwiches and wraps, burgers and pasta, vegetarian options, and a "55+" menu. $.

**Spa Restaurant & Outback Pub** (603-246-3039; spa-outbackpub.com), 869 Washington Street, West Stewartstown, NH, just across the bridge from VT 114, Canaan, VT. Open daily for all three meals, from 4 most mornings. A cheerful diner that opens onto a more formal dining room for dinner as well as a pub on the lower level. $$.

**Hobo's Restaurant** (802-723-4601), 18 Cross Street, Island Pond. Features barbecue, from breakfast brisket hash to pulled pork platters, served with corn and maple corn at supper. $.

**Quimby Country** (802-822-5533; quimbycountry.com), 1127 Forest Lake Road, Averill. During the summer season the resort's old-style dining room overlooking Forest Lake is open to the public for dinner. Call to check the set menu, which varies in cost as well as in content with the night. On Friday a full-blast lobster feast is held in a beautiful spot on Big Averill Pond. $$–$$$.

**Jackson's Cafe** (802-266-3360) at Jackson Lodge (see *Lodging* on page 489) is a lovely dining room, open Memorial Day–Columbus Day, Fri. and Sat. 8–11 a.m. and Sun. 8–noon. Specials, known for crepes. The room is also available for wedding receptions and such. $.

**Café at April's Maple** (802-266-9624; aprilsmaple.com) under *Selective Shopping*. A cheery, tasty spot for lunch except Tues.

## ✳ Selective Shopping

**Simon the Tanner** (802-723-4452; simonthetanner.com), 2 Main Street, Island Pond. Open daily except Sat., closing at 3 p.m. on Fri., otherwise 9–5, until 8 on Thurs. This is an unlikely spot for a huge shoe store, but here it is, selling a wide variety of name-brand shoes at below-usual prices. There is also a nice selection of men's, women's, and children's clothing, a bargain basement, and a line of natural soaps and body care products made by the Twelve Tribes. The store is run by members of this international sect, which came to Island Pond decades ago, restoring houses and winning the respect of the community.

**April's Maple** (802-266-9624; aprilsmaple.com), 6507 VT 114, Canaan. Open Wed.–Mon. April Lemay is the energetic young entrepreneur who left for a corporate job, came home, and has established a major sugaring operation with nearly 15,000 taps on her grandparents' 800 acres. The gleaming Vermont-made evaporator is state-of-the-art, and shelves are filled with pure Vermont maple syrup plus other maple products, pancake mix, and other specialty foods. The sugarhouse has trails for hiking and snowshoeing, is handy to snowmobile trails, and has homemade chili and soup on tap. Inquire about complimentary tours—and be sure to try the irresistible Maple Cream Truffles when you stop in.

## ✳ Special Events

*July 4 weekend:* Parade, fireworks, boat parade, and duck race, Island Pond.

*Late June–August:* **Friday Night Live**, music, vendors, and food, Island Pond.

*Last week in August:* **North Country Moose Festival** (chamberofthenorthcountry.com) an annual festival with music, craft vendors, classic car show, and moose calling contest.

# INDEX